IN AID OF THE
HON'BLE
JUDGMENTS OF A MOOT COURT

VOL - I

Answers to questions that matter
A constitutional framework for governance in Pakistan
An in-depth legal analysis of the elephants in the room
A fresh look into human resource and public financial management

Muhammad Akhtar
PFM Specialist

DISCLAIMER: The author, printer and publisher are not liable for any consequences incurred or loss or damage suffered by a person as a result of his reliance on the information contained in this book and, to the maximum extent permitted by law, exclude all liability including negligence. This book is not a substitute of professional advice of a qualified lawyer. The views expressed in the book are personal thoughts of the author which may be taken as fiction.

KDP ISBN:
ISBN: 9798672295053

The ebook has been published by the Amazon.

Link to read and download:
https://www.amazon.com/dp/B08F7WQ7WS/

Dedication

to

Mr. Salman Siddique

A man par excellence,

A professional administrator

&

A matchless expert in public financial management

I pray for his happiness, health and wealth

Preface

It was March, 2018. I was watching a talk show on television in which efforts of the then Hon'ble Chief Justice of the Supreme Court of Pakistan for public welfare were being praised. Videos showing the Hon'ble Chief Justice visiting schools, hospitals and making appeals for donations for construction of dams were being aired and the anchorperson was claiming that poor performance of the legislature and the executive was a sufficient reason to legitimize actions of the Hon'ble Chief Justice. The experts invited in the talk show not only endorsed this variety of judicial activism, they also painted a rosy picture of a bright future emerging from it.

An environment scan at that time had caused me to think of what to do next as the job in hand was likely to be completed within a few weeks and the employer had no need to retain my services. While thinking over what lied behind and ahead and from where to start a new journey, I clinched the idea of doing something in aid of the Hon'ble as a quid pro quo for his extra efforts.

I talked to a friend and discussed the idea of working in aid of the Hon'ble in a safe and trouble-free manner. He suggested me to study legality of matters of my interest and of public importance relating to personnel and financial management in the public sector in Pakistan. He informed that moot courts are a regular feature of law colleges all over the world. He advised me to write moot court judgments. I accepted his wise counsel and selected the following subjects for in-depth legal study:

i. Legal justification of holding of posts in connection with affairs of the Provinces by federal employees. The Civil Service of Pakistan (Composition and Cadre) Rules, 1954, the Police Service of Pakistan (Composition, Cadre and Seniority) Rules, 1985 and inter-governmental deputations were shortlisted for ascertainment of their constitutionality;

ii. Discrimination against citizens on the ground only of religion, sex, residence, place of birth or disability in the matter of appointments in the service of Pakistan. Law and practice in the Khyber Pakhtunkhwa on the subject and the provincial quotas in federal services and posts in connection with affairs of the Federation were taken into consideration for the subject study;

iii. Relaxation of all rules and procedures for initial recruitment in the Service of Pakistan. A hypothetical example was conceived to study the subject;

iv. Dispute between the federation and federating units over jurisdiction to perform treasury and accounting functions of the Provinces by the Federation through the Controller General of Accounts. A decade-long legal battle in the courts of law on the issue has not been conclusive and the dispute still remains unresolved; and

v. Determination of remuneration of persons in the Service of Pakistan by the Hon'ble Superior Courts. In this respect, the case regarding restoration of commuted value of pension of the retired civil servants was chosen for study. Subsequently, the case regarding entitlement of the Hon'ble judges having less than five years of service as judges of the Hon'ble High Court to pension as retired judges of the Hon'ble High Court was added to the study.

I do not claim infallibility or perfection. There is absolutely no assertion that others lack capacity or will to resolve the above questions of law. This book is an expression of my sincere desire to understand the selected subjects, backed by full devotion and hard work of two years and experience of more than twenty-four years.

Subject-matter of moot court judgments in this book is informed by numerous sources including https://indiankanoon.org, www.pakistanlawsite.com, www.gao.gov and the Google.

I have said what I wanted to say on the selected subjects. Explaining what is written violates the principle that judges must lock their jaws and must never speak except through their written judgments.

As the book contains moot court judgments, therefore, any effort to find any policy preference in it would be futile as policy is a forbidden fruit for a judge.

None in this universe has more respect for the institution of judiciary than I do have. Despite my firm belief in unquestioned respect for the judiciary, I do hereby tender my unconditional apology to all who may not be comfortable with what has been expressed in this book. This written unconditional apology is being preferred to save my precious time and the public-paid time of others.

I have used the word 'Hon'ble' whenever and wherever I have referred to any court or a judge in these judgments. Use of this word shows my heart-felt respect for the institution of judiciary and the chosen individuals who decide cases in accordance with law. It may not be construed that the respect usually meant to be expressed through use of the word 'Hon'ble' is the respect I have no option to withhold.

Use of the noun 'We' in the judgments does not indicate a sense of superiority or judicial arrogance. It has been used as the judgments express views of more than one judges of the moot court.

During research for and drafting of this book, I have found that nothing should be taken for granted and every legal proposition must be subjected to a critical examination. Moreover, how things have always been does not furnish justification for their continuation or prohibits a challenge to their legal wisdom and desirability. One may endeavour to approach things and analyse theories with an open mind and with a courage to know the truth.

I apprehend that the legal views expressed in this book may face hostile reception as these may hit the status quo which suits a few who matter. George Orwell once said that the further a society drifts from truth, the more it will hate those who speak it. But I do believe that you cannot heal in the same environment that made you sick. I do not expect an overnight change due to what has been said in the book but I do hope that the book will have effect on human resource management and public administration in Pakistan. It needs, however, not to be said that when a bird sings, it does not sing for the advancement of music; it sings because it can't resist the song and wants to die empty.

The hard work required for completion of this book was a labour of love. It was a hobby for me and spending time on it was a pleasing experience.

The experience of writing of this book also compels me to submit two humble proposals for kind consideration of the legal fraternity:

(1) Selection of judges of the Hon'ble superior judiciary must be made on the basis of merit alone to be determined through competitive process open to all eligible and willing citizens; and

(2) Rule of law is not possible if the law does not offer best solutions which are practicable and comprehensively cover all aspects and minimize discretion to the extent possible. Emphasis on enforcement of impracticable and outdated law is sure to disrupt normal functioning, cause chaos and dysfunctionalize the whole system. Any reform effort must premise on developing a comprehensive, workable and the best possible legal framework. Best brains of the society need to be involved in a broad-based consultative process to review and reform the legal infrastructure.

Efforts to reform may not produce intended results if we do not know what exactly is the legal dispensation governing us right now, how it has evolved in its present form and where it is intended to lead us. When we think of reforms, we ascertain our objectives, understand the organizational capability built to achieve the objectives, identify weaknesses in this machinery, find solutions to make it more efficient, effective and economical or, if need be, experiment with new ideas to substitute existing systems and institutions. In-depth understanding of the existing system is, thus, a prerequisite for any successful reform. Moot court judgments in this book are efforts to understand the law as it is. A judgment can do no more than to identify the facts and law as they actually are and then to apply the law on the proven facts and to find a judicial resolution of the dispute under adjudication. Inquisitorial spirit to correctly understand the relevant facts and applicable law is sometimes mistaken as a distasteful criticism. It may, however, become necessary in the facts and circumstances of a case to raise apparently harsh questions to precisely understand a matter.

After publication of this book, I intend to write Volume-II of the "In Aid of the Hon'ble" containing draft legislative instruments including:

1. The Punjab Elementary and Secondary Education Bill;
2. The Punjab Financial Management Bill;
3. The Punjab Title to Immovable Property Bill; and
4. The Judicial and Legal Services Bill.

Volume-II of the "In Aid of the Hon'ble" will endeavour to demonstrate need and effectiveness of the policy interventions introducible through legislative instruments. The 'Hon'ble', for the purpose of the Volume-II of this book, is the legislature.

Suggestions for improvement in the book are welcomed.

May Allah Almighty continue to help, guide and bless all of us.

(Muhammad Akhtar)
Taj Mehal Park, Salamatpura, Lahore, Pakistan
daofsd@yahoo.com

Table of Contents

Chapter 1

Chapter 2

Chapter 3

Chapter 4

Chapter 5

Chapter 1

Fragile steel frame

"If you take that steel frame out of the fabric, it would collapse. There is one institution we will not cripple, there is one institution we will not deprive of its functions or of its privileges; and that is the institution which built up the British Raj – the British Civil Service of India."

(David Lloyd George, British Prime Minister from 1916 to 1922)

This Chapter attempts to study legal justification of holding of posts in connection with affairs of the Provinces by the federal employees. The Civil Service of Pakistan (Composition and Cadre) Rules, 1954, the Police Service of Pakistan (Composition, Cadre and Seniority) Rules, 1985 and inter-governmental deputations are the specific subjects which have been studied in this Chapter with sole focus on ascertainment of their constitutionality. The conclusions drawn require serious consideration for designing and putting in place a lawful steel frame for administration of the federation and the federating units. Since this question is a question of policy, therefore, it has not been addressed in the judgment.

IAH 2019 MOOT COURT JUDGMENTS 1

Present: Mr. Jamal Mustafa Kundan
                 Mr. Saleem Anwar Taya
                 Mr. Rasheed Ahmad

Azhar Hussain and others

------Petitioners

Versus

Federation of Pakistan and others

-----Respondents

Petitioners	Mr. Muhammad Faizan Akhtar, Senior Advocate, Supreme Court of Pakistan
Respondents	Mr. Sallar Khan, Attorney General for Pakistan for the Federation of Pakistan
	Mr. Saqib Sultan, Advocate General, Punjab for the Province of the Punjab
	Mr. Abdul Hameed Bhutta, Senior Advocate, Supreme Court of Pakistan for the Pakistan Administrative Service Welfare Association
	Mr. Allah Rakha Anjum, Senior Advocate, Supreme Court of Pakistan for the Police Service of Pakistan
Dates of hearing	01.08.2019, 16.08.2019, 19.08.2019 to 23.08.2019, 26.08.2019 to 30.08.2019, 02.09.2019 to 06.09.2019, 23.09.2019 to 27.09.2019 and 02.10.2019

JUDGMENT

MR. JAMAL MUSTAFA KUNDAN.- The petitioners have approached this Court under Article 184(3) of the Constitution of the Islamic Republic of Pakistan, 1973 (hereinafter referred to as the Constitution) for enforcement of some of their fundamental rights which also involve a number of questions of public importance with regard to constitutionality of the Civil Service of Pakistan (Composition and Cadre) Rules, 1954, to the extent of reservation, thereunder, of certain posts in connection with affairs of the Provinces for members of a Service of the Federation. During the course of proceedings in this case, questions were also raised about constitutionality of the Police Service of Pakistan (Composition, Cadre and Seniority) Rules, 1985 and the inter-governmental deputations. We have attended to all the questions in this single judgment as the questions of law in these cases are almost identical.

Facts regarding the Pakistan Administrative Service

2.   For proper understanding of the issues involved in the instant petition, it may be of material help to arrange relevant facts and circumstances in an intelligible form. Relevant facts in respect of the Pakistan Administrative Service, gleaned from the petition, submissions of the rival counsels and other sources, are summarized as follows:

    i.   The East India Company was, inter alia, empowered through Queen Elizabeth's Charter of 1600 to trade with India. The Company was subsequently empowered to govern and control territories under its possession in India.

    ii.   The said Company, initially in order to manage its trade and subsequently to transact governmental business, employed persons and created services to effectively deal with civil and military matters. "The term 'Civil Service' was first used to designate those servants of the East India Company who were engaged in mercantile work in order to distinguish them from those whose duties were of a naval or military nature." (Role of Higher Civil Servants in Pakistan by Dr. Ali Ahmed, 1968, page 3). Admission to the Civil Service was based upon the system of patronage under which the Directors of the said Company and the Board of Control used to nominate candidates for the civil service.

iii. The business of the Company in India was, initially, under the government of three Presidencies, one at Bombay, another at Madras, and a third at Calcutta. {Mill, J, The History of British India (London, 1817), p.10}. Each Presidency was independent within its own limits and responsible only to the Company in England. However, the Regulating Act of 1773 (13 Geo. III, C 63) provided for the appointment of a Governor-General and a Council for the Presidency of Bengal with powers of control over the Presidencies of Madras and Bombay. {Mill, J, The History of British India (London, 1817), p.11}. The Presidencies were, thus, united and the Services brought under the control of the Governor-General, which were previously under the control of the respective Governors, came to be known as All-India Services.

iv. The Government of India Act, 1853 substituted the system of nomination of candidates for entry into the civil service by the Directors of the Company and the Board of Control with a system based on selection on merit determined through an open competitive examination, inter alia, vide Section XLI of the Act ibid.

v. The British Parliament enacted the Government of India Act, 1858, which, inter alia, provided that India shall be governed by and in the name of Her Majesty. The powers of the Crown were to be exercised by the Secretary of State for India, assisted by the India Office and the Council of India. Section XXXII of the Act ibid, reproduced hereinbelow, authorized the Secretary of State in Council to make regulations for admission of candidates to the Civil Service of India:

> "**XXXII. Secretary of State in Council to make regulations for the admission of candidates to the Civil Service of India.-** With all convenient speed after the passing of this Act, regulations shall be made by the Secretary of State in Council, with the advice and assistance of the Commissioners for the time being acting in execution of Her Majesty's Order in Council of twenty-first May one thousand eight hundred and fifty-five for regulating admission of persons to the Civil Service of the Crown, for admitting all persons being natural-born subjects of Her Majesty (and of such age and qualification as may be prescribed in this behalf) who may be desirous of becoming candidates for appointment to the Civil Service of India to be examined as candidates accordingly, and for prescribing the branches of knowledge in which such candidates shall be examined, and generally for regulating and conducting such examinations under the superintendence of the said last-mentioned Commissioners, or of the persons for the time being entrusted with the carrying out of such regulations as may be from time to time established by Her Majesty for examinations, certificates, or other test of fitness in relation to appointments to junior situations in the Civil Service of the Crown, and the candidates who may be certified by the said Commissioners or other persons as aforesaid to be entitled under such regulations shall be recommended for appointment according to the order of their proficiency as shown by such examinations, and such persons only as shall have been so certified as aforesaid shall be appointed or admitted to the Civil Service of India by the Secretary of State in Council: Provided always, that all regulations to be made by the said Secretary of State in Council under this Act shall be laid before Parliament within fourteen days after the making thereof, if Parliament be sitting, and, if Parliament be not sitting, then within fourteen days after next meeting thereof."

vi. The Government of India Act, 1915 was a consolidating measure, repealing and re-enacting the numerous Parliamentary Statutes relating to the administration of British India which had been passed between the year 1770 and 1912. This Act was amended in certain minor respects by the Government of India Amendment Act, 1916 which also contained certain substantive provisions not incorporated in the principal Act. In 1919, the Act again underwent amendments by the passing of the Government of India Act, 1919. Section 45 of the Act of 1919 provides that the amendments made by that Act and the Act of 1916 shall be incorporated in the text of the Government of India Act, 1915, and that the Act, as so amended, shall be known as the Government of India Act. The "Government of India Act" is, thus, not a separate Parliamentary enactment but a properly certified version of the Act of 1915 as subsequently amended. Subsection (2) of section 2 of the Government of India Act provided as under:

> "In particular, the Secretary of State may, subject to the provisions of this Act, superintend, direct and control all acts, operations and concerns which relate to the government or revenues of India, and all grants of salaries, gratuities and allowances, and all other payments and charges, out of or on the revenues of India."

vii. Whereas the Secretary of State in Council was empowered to frame rules for the Indian Civil Service vide Section 97 the Government of India Act, certain posts in the Central and Provincial Governments, as specified in the Third Schedule to the Act, were reserved for the Indian Civil Service vide Section 98 of the said Act. Sections 97 to 100 of the Act are reproduced hereunder to serve as ready reference:

"Rules for admission to the Indian Civil Service
97. -
- (1) The Secretary of State in Council may, with the advice and assistance of the Civil Service Commissioners, make rules for the examination, under the superintendence of those Commissioners, of British subjects desirous of becoming candidates for appointment to the Indian Civil Service.
- (2) The rules shall prescribe the age and qualifications of the candidates, and the subjects of examination.
- (3) All rules made in pursuance of this section be laid before Parliament within fourteen days after the making thereof, or, if Parliament is not then sitting, then within fourteen days after the next meeting of the Parliament.
- (4) The candidates certified to be entitled under the rules shall be recommended for appointment according to the order of their proficiency as shown by their examination.
- (5) Such persons only as are so certified may be appointed or admitted to the Indian Civil Service by the Secretary of State in Council.

Offices reserved to the Indian Civil Service
98. Subject to the provisions of this Act, all vacancies happening in any of the offices specified or referred to in the Third Schedule to this Act, and all such offices which may be created hereafter, shall be filled from amongst the members of the Indian Civil Service.

Powers to appoint certain persons to reserved offices
99.-
- (1) The authorities in India, by whom appointments are made to offices in the Indian Civil Service, may appoint to any such

office any person of proven merit and ability domiciled in British India and born in British India of parents habitually resident in India and not established there for temporary purposes only, although the person so appointed has not been admitted to that service in accordance with the foregoing provisions of this Act.

(2) Every such appointment shall be made subject to such rules as may be prescribed by the Governor-General in Council and sanctioned by the Secretary of State in Council with the concurrence of a majority of votes at a meeting of the Council of India.

(3) The Governor-General in Council may, by resolution, define and limit the qualification of persons who may be appointed under this section, but every resolution made for that purpose shall be subject to sanction of the Secretary of State in Council, and shall not have force until it has been laid for thirty days before both Houses of Parliament.

Power to make provisional appointments in certain cases
100.-

(1) Where it appears to the authority in India by whom an appointment is to be made to any office reserved to members of the Indian Civil Service, that a person not being member of that service ought, under the special circumstances of the case, to be appointed thereto, the authority may appoint thereto any person who has resided for at least seven years in India and who has, before the appointment, fulfilled all the tests (if any) which would be imposed in the like case on a member of that service.

(2) Every such appointment shall be provisional only, and shall forthwith be reported to the Secretary of State, with the special reasons for making it; and unless the Secretary of State in Council approves the appointment, with the concurrence of a majority of votes at a meeting of the Council of India, and within twelve months from the date of the appointment intimates such approval to the authority by whom the appointment was made, the appointment shall be cancelled.

THIRD SCHEDULE
(Section 98)

OFFICES RESERVED TO THE INDIAN CIVIL SERVICE

Part 1.-General

1. Secretaries, joint secretaries, deputy secretaries and under secretaries to the several Governments in India, except the secretaries, joint secretaries, deputy secretaries and under secretaries in the Army, Marine and Public Works Departments.
2. Accountant-general.
3. Members of the Board of Revenue, in the presidencies of Bengal and Madras, the United Provinces of Agra and Oudh and the Provinces of Bihar and Orissa.
4. Secretaries to those Boards of Revenue.
5. Commissioners of customs, salt, excise and opium.
6. Opium agent.

Part-II.-Offices in the provinces which were known in the year 1861 as "Regulation Provinces".

7. District and sessions judges.

8. Additional district or sessions judges and assistant sessions judges.
9. District magistrates.
10. Joint magistrates.
11. Assistant Magistrates.
12. Commissioners of revenue.
13. Collectors of revenue, or chief revenue officers of districts.
14. Assistant collectors."

viii. Section 96B was inserted in the Government of India Act, 1915 through the Government of India Act, 1919 (9 % 10 Geo. 5, Ch. 101) which, inter alia, provided that the Secretary of State in Council may make rules regulating the classification of the civil services in India, the methods of their recruitment, their conditions of service, pay and allowances, and discipline and conduct. It was further provided that such rules may, to the extent and in respect of such matters as may be prescribed, delegate the power of making rules to the Governor-General in Council or to local governments, or authorize the Indian legislature or local legislature to make laws regulating the public services.

ix. The rules framed under Section 96B of the Government of India Act defined that the All India Services shall consist of:

"All officers serving under local (provincial) governments who are members of any of the following services:
a. The Indian Civil Service;
b. The Indian Police Service;
c. The Indian Forest Service;
d. The Indian Education Service;
e. The Indian Agriculture Service;
f. The Indian Service of Engineers;
g. The imperial branch of the Civil Veterinary Department;
h. Officers of the Indian Medical Service in civil employ; and any other service declared by the Secretary of State-in-Council to be All India Services;
i. Military officers and other officers holding posts borne on the provincial cadres of the above services."

(Problems and issues in Administrative Federalism by Shraram Maheshwari, 1992 (page No. 8, 9).

x. The All-India Services were the principal focus of enquiry by the Royal Commission on the Superior Services in India appointed by the British Government in 1923 under the chairmanship of Lee of Fareham. At the time when the Lee Commission was sitting the position with regard to the All-India Services was as follows:

Name	Sanctioned strength	Actual numbers
Indian Civil Service	1350	1290
Indian Police Service	732	739
Indian Forest Service	399	348
Indian Education Service	421	345
Indian Agriculture Service	157	109
Indian Veterinary Service	54	38

Indian Forest Engineering Service	18	17
Indian Medical Service (Civil)	420	373
Indian Service of Engineers	728	716
Total	**4279**	**3975**

xi.   The above-said Royal Commission on the Superior Services in India presented a profile of the services in the following words:

"The superior services are themselves divided into two classes, according as they administer subjects which are under the direct management of the central government in India or subjects which are primarily controlled by the Provincial Governments. The former class consists of the central services, which deal, inter alia, with the Indian states and frontier affairs, the administration of the state railways, with posts and telegraphs, customs, audit and accounts, and with scientific and technical departments such as Survey of India, the Geological Survey and the Archaeological Department. The other class which works primarily under the provincial governments comprises the All India Services. The term may at first sight appear inappropriate to services which are essentially concerned with administration in the provinces. It marks the fact, however, that these services are recruited by the Secretary of State, for work in any part of India, and that each, though scattered through the provinces, forms one service with one basis of remuneration. Though an officer of an All India Service is assigned to and as a rule remains in one province throughout his career, he may be transferred to another province, while a certain number of officers are taken by the Government of India from the provinces to assist in the discharge of its central functions. Services of this nature differ essentially from the provincial services which are recruited in a province solely for provincial work, and it is to mark this distinction that these services have been given the title of All India. As the main part of the actual administration of India is carried out by the provincial governments, it follows that the All India Services are the main executive agents of the administration throughout the country." (Report of the Royal Commission on the Superior Civil Services in India; 1922-24, pp.3-4).

xii.   Essential characteristics of the All-India Services were:

(a)   The Secretary of State for India was the competent authority for appointing a person to the Services;

(b)   No authority could dismiss a member of the Services except the Secretary of the State for India;

(c)   Conditions of recruitment and of service of the members of the Services were to be determined by the Secretary of State for India;

(d)   Posts were reserved in the Central and Provincial Governments for the Services; and

(e)   A member of the Services was allocated to a particular Province where he was required to serve throughout his life-long career with possibility of deputation to the Central Government.

xiii.   The cold logic of the constitutional changes under the Government of India Act, 1919 demanded disbandment of All India Services operating in the transferred fields. The Royal Commission on the Superior Services under the chairmanship of

Lee of Fareham recognized the apparent anomaly and recommended the stopping of recruitment to the Indian Education Service, the Indian Agriculture Service, the Indian Veterinary Service, the Indian Forest Service (in some provinces) and the Indian Service of Engineers (Roads and Buildings Branch). It was recommended that the personnel required for these branches of administration should, in future, be recruited and appointed by the provincial governments. The Commission also recommended that the provinces should take immediate steps to pass public service legislation regulating the provincial public services. Recruitment by the Secretary of State to the Buildings and Roads Branch of the Service of Engineers, the Education Service, the Agriculture Service and the Veterinary Service, ceased in 1924 on the recommendation of the Lee Commission.

xiv. The Report of the Joint Committee on Indian Constitutional Reform [Session 1933-34] Volume 1 (Part 1) made a comprehensive analysis of the public services in India at paragraphs 274 to 321 of the said Report. It observed that the Civil Services in India were classified in three main divisions: (i) the All-India Services; (ii) the Provincial Services; and (iii) the Central Services.

xv. The Joint Committee on Indian Constitutional Reform [Session 1933-34] recommended that the Secretary of State should continue to make appointments to the Indian Civil Service and the Indian Police, determine their conditions of service and posts in Central and Provincial Government should be reserved exclusively for these services. The Governor-General and the concerned Governor were recommended to be the heads of the Central Services and Provincial Services respectively.

xvi. Section 241 of the Government of India Act, 1935 provided that appointments to the services of the Federation and posts in connection with affairs of the Federation shall be made by the Governor-General or such person as he may direct and conditions of service of persons so appointed shall be determined through rules to be made by the Governor-General or by some person or persons authorized by him in this behalf. Similar role was assigned to the Governors in the Provinces in respect of services of the Provinces and posts in connection with affairs of the Provinces. Section 244 of the Act ibid provided that appointments to the civil services known as the Indian Civil Service, the Indian Medical Service (Civil), and the Indian Police Service (which last mentioned service shall thereafter be known as "the Indian Police") shall, until Parliament otherwise determines, be made by the Secretary of State. It was further provided that the respective strengths of the said services shall be such as the Secretary of State may from time to time prescribe, and the Secretary of State shall in each year cause to be laid before each House of Parliament a statement of the appointments made thereto and the vacancies therein. Section 246 provides for reservation of posts, through rules to be made by the Secretary of State, to be filled by persons appointed by the Secretary of State to a civil service of, or a civil post under the Crown in India. Section 247 of the Act ibid empowered the Secretary of State for India to determine conditions of service of persons appointed by him to a civil service or a civil post in India. As provided vide Section 250 of the Act ibid, Section 247 thereof was also applicable to persons appointed by the Secretary of State in Council.

xvii. Section 263 of the Government of India Act, 1935 provided that if an agreement is made between the Federation and one or more Provinces, or between two or more Provinces, for the maintenance or creation of a service common to the Federation and one or more Provinces, or common to two or more Provinces, or for the maintenance or creation of a post the functions whereof are not restricted to the affairs of the Federation or one Province, the agreement may make provision that the Governor-General or any Governor, or any Public Service Commission, shall do in relation to that service or post anything which would under the provisions of this chapter be done by the Governor or the Provincial Public Service Commission if the service or post was a service or post in connection with the affairs of one Province only.

xviii. The Government of India Act, 1935, provided for a Public Service Commission for the federation and a Public Service Commission for each province vide its Section 264 which also provided that two or more Provinces may agree-

    (a)   that there shall be one Public Service Commission for that group of Provinces; or

    (b)   that the Public Service Commission for one of the Provinces shall serve the needs of all the Provinces.

It further provided that Public Service Commission for the Federation, if requested so to do by the Governor of a Province, may, with the approval of the Governor-General, agree to serve all or any of the needs of the Province.

xix. Section 2 of the Civil Services (Conditions of Service) Ordinance, 1942 authorized the Central Government and the Provincial Governments to require a person serving in connection with affairs of that Government to serve in any place in India either itself or the Crown Representative or another Government in British India.

xx. Recruitment to the Indian Civil Service, the Indian Medical Service (Civil), and the Indian Police was discontinued in 1943 due to war emergency but after war the Secretary of State for India announced that no more recruitment will be made for these services in future.

xxi. His Majesty's Government announced on 20th of February, 1947, that power would be transferred to Indian hands by His Majesty's Government by June, 1948, in accordance with the Cabinet Mission Plan of May, 1946.

xxii. On 30th of April, 1947, the Viceroy of India made an announcement for "grant of compensation for premature termination of their service in India to members of Civil Services appointed by the Secretary of State and to regular officers and British Warrant Officers of the Indian Naval and Military Forces". Members of the Indian Civil Service were given an option to either accept compensation in consideration of their premature termination of service or to express their willingness to continue to serve one of the two Dominions (Pakistan and India) or their provincial governments.

xxiii. After the announcement of His Majesty's Government dated the 3rd of June, 1947, a circular letter was issued, by the Government of India, to the Chief Secretaries of all the Provincial Governments on the 18th of June, 1947, directing them to seek options from members of services of the Secretary of State, in terms of announcement of the Viceroy of India dated 30th of April, 1947. The Chief Secretaries were accordingly asked to make necessary arrangements for the purpose. In pursuance of these instructions, the individual letters to the officers concerned were sent and replies were obtained, and necessary orders were passed in respect of the officers whom the various Governments were not prepared to retain in service after the transfer of power.

xxiv. The Indian Independence Act, 1947, (10 & 1.1 Geo. 6, Ch. 30), passed by the British Parliament, became a law on 18th of July, 1947, the preamble thereto is as follows:

> "An Act to make provision for the setting up in India of two independent Dominions, to substitute other provisions for certain provisions of the Government of India Act, 1935, which apply outside those Dominions, and to provide for other matters consequential on or connected with the setting up of those Dominions".

By section I of the said Act, two independent Dominions to be known respectively, India and Pakistan, were to be set up in India as from the 15th day of August, 1947.

By section 7, it was specifically provided that as from the 15th of August, 1947, His Majesty's Government in the United Kingdom was to have no responsibility as respects the government of any of the territories which, immediately before that day, were included in British India. By section 8(2), the pre-existing Government of India Act, 1935, with modifications and adaptations to be made by the Governor-General and subject to any other provision or alteration to be made by the Constituent Assembly functioning as the interim Legislature, was to continue in force. By section 9 of the Act, the Governor-General was given powers to make provisions in order to bring the provisions of the Indian Independence Act into operation and for removing difficulties arising in connection with the transition of power from the British Government to the Dominions and to carry on the business of the Governor-General in Council in the interim period. It was specifically provided that the Governor-General's power in this behalf was to be retrospective as from the 3rd of June, 1947. Section 10 of the Act ibid made it clear that no provision of the Government of India Act, 1935 relating to appointments to the civil services of, and civil posts under, the Crown in India by the Secretary of State, or the provisions of that Act relating to the reservation of posts shall remain in force but rights of the civil servants appointed by the Secretary of State, or Secretary of State in Council with regard to remuneration, leave and pension, and disciplinary matters shall remain protected.

xxv. Ten Orders were made by the Governor-General under the Indian Independence Act, 1947 and were published in the Extraordinary Gazette on 14th of August, 1947. Two of them called the Indian (Provisional Constitution) Order and the Pakistan (Provisional Constitution) Order set out the omissions, additions and modifications to be made in the Government of India Act, 1935. A large number of sections of that Act, particularly those relating to the special responsibilities of the Governor-General and the Governors, their discretionary powers and individual judgment, the Secretary of State and the India office and the Secretary of State's services were omitted. Fifteenth day of August, 1947, was declared as the appointed day. Article 7(1) of the Pakistan (Provisional Constitution) Order, 1947 allowed, subject to any general or special orders or arrangements affecting his case, any person who immediately before the appointed day was holding any civil post under the Crown in connection with the affairs of the Province of Bengal (or Assam), the Punjab, the North-West Frontier Province or Sind shall, as from that day, be deemed to have been duly appointed to the corresponding post under the Crown in connection with the affairs of the Province of East Bengal, West Pakistan, the North-West Frontier Province or, as the case may be, Sind.

xxvi. Actions consequent to the letter of 18th of June, 1947 were taken. Of those who opted to continue to serve the new Dominions or Provinces thereof and whose options were accepted, 770 members of the Indian Civil Service joined India (Report on Indian and State Administrative Services and Problems of District Administration. New Delhi. 1962. p. 69 and 72). Pakistan received 82 Indian Civil Service officers only. (Constituent Assembly of Pakistan Debates. 1956. Vol. 1. P. 2104). In Pakistan, these officers were collectively termed Pakistan Administrative Service (PAS) officers. In 1950, PAS became Civil Service of Pakistan (CSP). Under Civil Servants Act of 1973, twelve groups were created out of which one was named District Management Group. With effect from 1st of June, 2012, the District Management Group was renamed as the Pakistan Administrative Service vide Establishment Division's O.M.No.6/3/2012-CP-II dated 21.05.2012.

xxvii. The Government of Pakistan published a resolution vide No.F.25/4/50-Ests (SEI) dated 8th of November, 1950 to notify its intention to create the Civil Service of Pakistan consisting of posts on the cadre of the former Indian Civil Service in the various Provinces and on the cadre of the former Indian Political Service and of most of the higher posts in the Central Secretariat. It was not spelt out in the said resolution that under what authority of law the Government had decided to constitute the Service. There was no mention in the aforesaid resolution of any agreement between the Provinces and the Federation for creation of the Service. It was also not clarified that how posts in connection with affairs of the Provinces could be reserved for such a Service in view of Section 10 of the Indian Independence Act, 1947, Article 7(1) of the Pakistan (Provisional Constitution) Order, 1947, read with announcement of the Viceroy of India made an 30th April, 1947 and letter of the Government of India dated 18th June, 1947 addressed to the Chief Secretaries of all the Provincial Governments, and deletion of all Sections from the Government of India Act, 1935 relating to the Indian Civil Service and reservation of posts therefor.

xxviii. The Government of Pakistan, through a Notification of the Establishment Division bearing No. F.25/12/51-SEI, dated 01.06.1954 issued the Civil Service of Pakistan (Composition and Cadre) Rules, 1954 to constitute a Service of the Federation to be known as the Civil Service of Pakistan, reservation of certain posts for the said Service both in connection with affairs of the Federation and of the Provinces, making the Governor-General the appointing authority for this Service, the members being liable to serve the Federal Government or any Provincial Government, the Governors to report to the Governor-General any reserved or cadre post remaining vacant for more than three months and the Governor-General was empowered to frame rules, subject to section 10 of the Indian Independence Act, 1947, regulating the remuneration and other conditions of service of members of the Service. He was also authorized, vide Rule 16 ibid to provide, through rules, for the conduct and discipline of officers of the Service, and it was provided that officers of the Service shall at all times obey such rules, and shall perform such duties as may be assigned to them. It was provided in these rules that if the Governor-General directs that a cadre post shall be filled, the Governor shall appoint a person to fill it in accordance with the provisions of these rules. Rule 7(1) of the Rules provided for reservation of cadre posts not exceeding 30% of the superior executive posts in any province to be filled by members of the Provincial Civil Services (Executive Branch). Rule 12 of the Rules ibid provided that no change shall be made in the duties of the holder of any reserved post if, in the opinion of the Governor-General, the character of that post would thereby be altered. Rule 13 (1) of the said Rules provided that the Governor-General may from time to time, and in the case of posts in connection with the affairs of a Province, after consultation with the Governor of that Province, remove any post from the Schedule or include any post therein. It was provided in Rule 15 of the said Rules that the transfer of an officer belonging to the Service from one Province to another or from the Centre to a Province or from a Province to the Centre shall be made by the Central Government in consultation with the Provincial Government or Governments concerned. Preamble of the said Rules cites an agreement between the Governor-General and the Governors of East Bengal, the Punjab, Sindh and the North-West Frontier Province and sub-sections (1) and (2) of section 241 of the Government of India Act, 1935 as legal authority allowing issuance of the said Rules.

xxix. On 3rd of October, 1955, the Establishment of the West Pakistan Act, 1955, was enacted through which the Governors' Provinces of the Punjab, the North West Frontier and Sind, the Chief Commissioner's Province of Baluchistan, the Capital of the Federation, the States of Bahawalpur and Khairpur, the Baluchistan States Union, the Tribal Areas of Baluchistan, the Punjab and the North-West Frontier, and the States of Amb, Chitral, Dir and Swat were incorporated into the Province of West Pakistan.

xxx. The Constituent Assembly of Pakistan approved the Constitution of Pakistan, 1956, on 29th of February, 1956, which was enforced on 23rd of March, 1956. Article 182 of the said Constitution provided that appointments to the services of the Federation or posts in connection with affairs of the Federation shall be made by the President or such person as he may direct. The President was also authorized to determine, through rules, conditions of service in respect of members of the federal services and posts in connection with affairs of the Federation. As regards services of a Province or posts in connection with affairs of a Province, exactly similar role was assigned to the concerned Governor. Article 183 dealt with the All-Pakistan Services and Article 221 repealed the Government of India Act, 1935 and the Indian Independence Act, 1947, together with all enactments amending or supplementing those Acts. Article 233 protected rights of persons appointed by the Secretary of State as regards salary, allowances, leave, pension and in disciplinary matters.

xxxi.   The Constitution of Pakistan, 1962, was promulgated on 1st of March, 1962 and came into effect on 8th of June, 1962. Article 174 of this Constitution provided that subject to the Constitution, the appointment of persons to, and the terms and conditions of service of persons in, the service of Pakistan may be regulated by law. Article 178 empowered the President or a person authorized by him to make appointments to an All-Pakistan Service or to a civil service of the Centre, or to a civil post in connection with the affairs of the Centre. The President or a person authorized by him was also empowered to determine, through rules, conditions of service of persons so appointed. Similar powers were vested in the concerned Governor in respect of civil services of the Province or posts in connection with affairs of the Province.

xxxii.   The Listed Posts (Substantive Appointments) Act, 1967, was an Act of the National Assembly which authorized the President, by rules, to prescribe a percentage of the superior posts in connection with the affairs of a Province borne on the cadre of the Civil Service of Pakistan which may be filled by persons who were not members of the Civil Service of Pakistan. A post so fiiled was referred to as the "listed post." Substantive appointment of a person, not being a member of the Civil Service of Pakistan, to a listed post was to be made by the President after consultation with the Provincial Government concerned and the Central Public Service Commission. The President was empowered to make rules to prescribe-

(a)   the percentage of the reserved superior posts as listed posts;
(b)   the remuneration and other terms and conditions of service of persons appointed to listed posts; and
(c)   such other matters as may be necessary for carrying out the purposes of this Act.

No rules have been claimed to be made under the aforementioned law.

xxxiii.   The Constitution of the Islamic Republic of Pakistan, 1973, was approved by the Parliament on 10th of April, 1973 and it came into force on 14th of August, 1973. Its Article 240 deals with the Service of Pakistan, as defined in Article 260. It specified that the appointments to and the conditions of service of persons in the service of Pakistan shall be determined by or under Act of the Parliament in case of the services of the Federation, posts in connection with the affairs of the Federation and All-Pakistan Services and by or under Act of the respective Provincial Assembly in the case of the services of a Province and posts in connection with affairs of a Province. "All-Pakistan Service" was defined as a service common to the Federation and the Provinces, which was in existence immediately before the commencing day or which may be created by Act of the Parliament.

xxxiv.   The Civil Servants Ordinance, 1973 (XIV of 1973) was promulgated to regulate conditions of appointment and of service of the civil servants of the federation.

xxxv.   The Parliament enacted the Civil Servants Act, 1973, to regulate, by law, the appointment of persons to, and the terms and conditions of service of persons in the service of Pakistan. The Act was applicable to all civil servants, wherever they may be and a civil servant was defined as a person who is a member of an All-Pakistan Service or of a civil service of the Federation, or who holds a civil post in connection with affairs of the Federation. Besides dealing with tenure of office of the civil servants, appointment, probation, confirmation, seniority, promotion, posting and transfer, termination of service, reversion to lower post, retirement, employment after retirement, conduct, efficiency and discipline, pay, leave, pension and gratuity, provident fund, benevolent fund, group insurance, right of appeal, it authorized the President to make rules to carry out purposes of the Act ibid. Any rules, orders or instructions in respect of any terms and conditions of service of civil servants duly made or issued by an authority competent to make them and in force immediately before the commencement of this Act were deemed to be rules made under the Act subject to their consistency with the Act.

xxxvi. The Federal Government, vide Secretary Establishment Division's D. O. Letter No.1/1/73-ARC, dated 21.08.1973 notified the following decisions of the Federal Government:

"(a) All the services and cadres would be merged into a single unified graded structure with equality of opportunity for all who enter the service at any stage based on the required professional and specialized competence necessary for each job.

(b) All 'classes' among Government servants would be abolished and replaced by a single unified graded structure, a Peon or equivalent at the bottom, a Secretary or Departmental Head at the top. The existing classification of dividing the services into Class I to Class IV would no longer operate. The road upwards to the very top to be open to all on merit and required educational and professional qualifications.

(c) The use of `service' labels would be discontinued forthwith.

(d) The Unified Structure would be designed to provide for entitlement to promotions to the higher posts throughout the range of public service; for horizontal movement from one cadre to another including the movement of technical personnel to the cadre of general management carrying posts of an executive nature; there would also be scope for out of turn promotion to the exceptionally meritorious officers.

(e) The correct grading of each post would be determined by job evaluation, job description, professionalism and specialization.

(f) With the merger of all classes and services into a single Unified Graded Structure, the various functional and professional services will become branches of a single service.

(g) There would be provision that Government may take talented officers from the private sector such as banking, insurance, industry and trade as well as from other professions for jobs at the appropriate levels in the Central and Provincial Secretariats and Departments as well as Government sponsored corporations, autonomous and semi-autonomous bodies."

xxxvii. The Federal Government created the following functional groups or services through various executive orders:

1. Accounts Group;
2. Commerce and Trade Group;
3. Customs and Excise Group;
4. District Management Group;
5. Foreign Service of Pakistan;

6.	Income Tax Group;
7.	Information Group;
8.	Military Lands and Cantonment Group;
9.	Office Management Group;
10.	Police Service of Pakistan;
11.	Postal Group; and
12.	Railways (Commercial and Transportation) Group.

The District Management Group was created by the Establishment Division through office memorandum No. 2/2/74 ARC dated 23.02.1974.

xxxviii. The following groups were declared All Pakistan Unified Grades (APUG):
1. District Management Group (DMG) (BPS-17 to 22)
2. Police Service of Pakistan (PSP) (BPS-17 to 22)
3. Secretariat Group (BPS-19 to 22)

xxxix. The Establishment Division's Notification No. S.R.O. 1307(1)/73, dated 14.09.1973 notified the Civil Servants (Change in Nomenclature) Rules, 1973 made by the President of Pakistan exercising his powers under section 25 of the Civil Servants Ordinance, 1973 (XIV of 1973), rule 3 thereof reads as follows:

"Notwithstanding anything contained in any rule, order, resolution or instruction, the names of the Civil Service of Pakistan and the Police Service of Pakistan are, with immediate effect, changed to All-Pakistan Unified Grades and all references to Civil Service of Pakistan and Police Service of Pakistan in any rule, order, resolution or instruction shall be construed as references to All-Pakistan Unified Grades."

xl. The President of Pakistan, in exercise of the powers said to be conferred by Rule 3 of the Civil Service of Pakistan (Composition and Cadre) Rules, 1954, made rules which were notified through Establishment Division's Notification No. S.R.O.1238 (I)/73, dated 21.08.1973, Rule 5(1) whereof reads as follows:

"Every Government Servant, not being a member of the Service, who is holding a Cadre post, at the commencement of these rules shall, subject to the approval of the President, become a member of the Service."

Through the above said Notification, Rule 7 of the Civil Service of Pakistan (Composition and Cadre) Rules, 1954 was omitted. The Schedule to the said Rules was also substituted through which number of reserved posts in the Punjab was increased from 58 to 115.

xli. The Establishment Division notified vide its Notification No. 1/1/73-ARC, dated 14.09.1973 that under Rule 5 (1) of rules promulgated vide S.R.O. 1238 (I)/73, dated the 21st August, 1973, that the President was pleased to approve the appointment of all Government servants who were holding a cadre post on the 21st August, 1973, to All-Pakistan Unified Grades.

xlii. The Punjab Civil Servants Act, 1974, and the rules framed thereunder regulate certain services of the Province and posts in connection with affairs of the Province. The posts purported to be reserved for a Service of the Federation under the Civil Service of Pakistan (Composition and Cadre) Rules, 1954 have been covered under the said Act and the rules framed thereunder.

xliii. An eleven-member Committee of the Provincial Assembly of the Punjab, after a thorough and broad-based consultative process including giving a patient hearing to officers of the District Management Group and the Provincial Civil Service and examining legal opinion of the Law and Parliamentary Affairs Department, submitted a detailed report to the Provincial Assembly which was unanimously approved by the Provincial Assembly through a resolution dated 23rd of December, 1986. Notwithstanding resolution of the Provincial Assembly, the recommendations of the said Committee, however, have not so far been implemented.

xliv. On 19.09.1993, a formula for reservation of posts in connection with affairs of the Provinces for the All Pakistan Unified Grades was presented by the Establishment Division in a meeting chaired by the then Caretaker Prime Minister and attended, among others, by the Governors and Chief Ministers of the four Provinces. It was decided in the meeting to approve the following formula for reservation of posts in connection with affairs of the Provinces for the All Pakistan Unified Grades:

	BPS-17	BPS-18	BPS-19	BPS-20	BPS-21
Punjab	25%	40%	50%	60%	65%
Sind	25%	40%	50%	60%	65%
NWFP	25%	40%	50%	60%	65%
Baluchistan	25%	40%	50%	60%	65%

Subsequently, the above formula was inserted in Rule 7 (1) of the Civil Service of Pakistan (Composition and Cadre) Rules, 1954 in 2014 vide S.R.O No. 88(I)/2014 dated 10-02-2014.

xlv. The Punjab Provincial Management Service Rules, 2004, regulate the Punjab Provincial Management Service. Rule 3 of the Rules ibid declares that the Service shall consist of the posts as specified in Schedule-II of the said Rules. Method of appointment to various posts encadred for the said Service has been given in these rules.

xlvi. The S.R.O No. 88(I)/2014 dated 10.02.2014 substituted reference to sub-section (1) and (2) of Section 241 of the Government of Indian Act, 1935, in the preamble of the Civil Service of Pakistan (Composition and Cadre) Rules, 1954 with Article 146 of the Constitution. The same S.R.O introduced some other amendments in the said Rules.

Arguments and prayer of the petitioners

3. In the background of the above facts and circumstances, the petitioners have advanced the following arguments in favour of their case:

(a) The Civil Service of Pakistan (Composition and Cadre) Rules, 1954, were based on Section 263 and 241 of the Government of India Act, 1935. Section 18 of the Indian Independence Act, 1947, partially saved the existing laws including the Government of India Act, 1935, subject to the express provisions of Section 10 of the Indian Independence Act, 1947. According to the said Section 10, provisions relating to the Secretary of State's services were not to continue. Section 244 of the Government of India Act, 1935 was omitted through the Indian Independence Act, 1947. The explicit effect of Section 10 was that Section 263 and 241 of the Government of India Act, 1935 ceased to exist with effect from August 15, 1947, the date on which the Indian Independence Act, 1947 came into force. The Civil Service of Pakistan (Composition and Cadre) Rules, 1954, notified on June 1, 1954, were, therefore, ultra vires at inception.

(b) Sections 241 and 263 of the Government of India Act, 1935 do not provide for an All-India or All-Pakistan Service; hence, constitution of an All-Pakistan Service through the Civil Service of Pakistan (Composition and Cadre) Rules, 1954, is without lawful authority and jurisdiction.

(c) The Civil Service of Pakistan (Composition and Cadre) Rules, 1954 are claimed to be based upon an agreement said to be concluded by the Governor-General of Pakistan and Governors of the federating units.

This agreement does not exist and is a fraud and the superstructures built upon this agreement cannot survive.

(d) The Civil Service of Pakistan (Composition and Cadre) Rules, 1954 expressly term the Civil Service of Pakistan a Service of the Federation which cannot be construed a service common to the Federation and the Provinces in terms of Section 263 of the Government of India Act, 1935, and provisions of the Constitution with particular reference to its Article 240. Officers of the Civil Service of Pakistan or the District Management Group or the Pakistan Administrative Service, when posted in the Provinces, perform provincial functions e.g. revenue administration, coordination. These functions are not common to the Federation and the Provinces.

(e) The Federation was not lawfully competent to assume powers vested in the Provinces vide Section 241 (1) (b) of the Government of India Act, 1935 through the Civil Service of Pakistan (Composition and Cadre) Rules, 1954.

(f) The posts specified in the schedule to the Civil Service of Pakistan (Composition and Cadre) Rules, 1954 are posts in connection with affairs of the Province of the Punjab and in accordance with clause (b) of Article 240 of the Constitution, appointments to and conditions of service in relation to the said posts could only be determined by or under an Act of the provincial legislature. The Civil Service of Pakistan (Composition and Cadre) Rules, 1954 are, thus, in clear violation of the said Article.

(g) The Civil Service of Pakistan (Composition and Cadre) Rules, 1954 were promulgated on 1st of June, 1954, when there were four provinces in Pakistan. On 3rd of October, 1955 with the promulgation of the Establishment of West Pakistan Act, 1955, the three provinces and certain states were incorporated into province of West Pakistan. Neither the Province of the Punjab existed as such on the said date, nor did the Governor of the Punjab existed on the basis of whose alleged consent the Civil Service of Pakistan (Composition and Cadre) Rules, 1954 were framed. Thus, the agreement which was the basis of the said Rules, stood frustrated and the Rules were rendered inoperative as a consequence thereof.

(h) First Constitution of Pakistan was promulgated on March 2, 1956. Article 224 of the 1956 Constitution saved the existing laws while Article 219 extended application of the General Clauses Act, 1897 for interpretation of the 1956 Constitution. The Civil Service of Pakistan (Composition and Cadre) Rules, 1954 were not an existing law within the contemplation of the said Article 224. In absence of any provision similar to Section 263 of the Government of India Act, 1935 in the Constitution of 1956, Article 224 of the Constitution of 1956 or Section 24 of the General Clauses Act, 1897 will not have the effect of saving the Civil Service of Pakistan (Composition and Cadre) Rules, 1954. Section 24 of the General Clauses Act, 1897 contemplates repeal and re-enactment of a statute. The expression "re-enactment" must necessarily contain a provision with which the Civil Service of Pakistan (Composition and Cadre) Rules, 1954, could be saved.

(i) The schedule to the Civil Service of Pakistan (Composition and Cadre) Rules, 1954 fixed 58 posts (by designation) to be the cadre posts. Vide SRO No. 1237(1)/73, dated 21.08.1973, the Federal Government substituted the said schedule by increasing the number of posts to

115. The said SRO, in fact, amounted to amendment of Civil Service of Pakistan (Composition and Cadre) Rules, 1954 which could not have been done except after compliance with Rule 13 of Civil Service of Pakistan (Composition and Cadre) Rules, 1954. The said SRO having been unilaterally issued by the Federal Government, without consultation with the Governor of the Province of Punjab, is wholly unsustainable.

(j) Deletion of Rule 7 of the Civil Service of Pakistan (Composition and Cadre) Rules, 1954, vide SRO No. 1237(1)/73 dated 21.08.1973, by the President is contrary to Article 240 of the Constitution, which had already come into force at the time the said SRO was notified. Under Article 240, only the National and Provincial Legislatures are competent to make or amend laws relating to the respective Civil Services. The President has no authority to amend any laws / rules except in accordance with law and the Constitution. Therefore, the deletion of Rule 7 (among other amendments) of the Civil Service of Pakistan (Composition and Cadre) Rules, 1954 vide SRO No. 1237(1)/73 dated 21.08.1973 is ultra vires and consequently PCS officers continue to have a 30% share in the cadre posts under the Civil Service of Pakistan (Composition and Cadre) Rules, 1954.

(k) Promotion of a civil servant in Punjab is governed by Section 8 of the Punjab Civil Servants Act, 1974 and Rule 12 of the Punjab Civil Servants (Appointment & Conditions of Service) Rules, 1974. The expression "qualification" referred to in Section 8 does not include training. Requirement of passing departmental examination could, however, be found in Rule 12 supra, but the requirement of mandatory training as a pre-condition for promotion does not have the backing either of Section 8 or Rule 12, as the case may be. Thus the Notification dated June 4, 2004 has the effect of modifying the substantive provisions of law as well as the Rules, which could not have been done by an executive order.

(l) The Caretaker Government was not lawfully competent to introduce a formula for reservation of posts in connection with affairs of the Provinces for a Service of the Federation. The formula of 1993 is, therefore, without lawful authority and jurisdiction.

(m) The Federal Government and the Government of the Punjab are acting in violation of Articles 2-A, 3, 4, 8, 9, 25, 27, 38, 97, 137, 141, 142, 227, 240 and 241 of the Constitution and are denying the petitioners their fundamental right to be treated in accordance with law. The petitioners have legitimate expectation to be treated justly, fairly, in accordance with law and without any adverse discrimination. Right to be considered for fair career progression is a fundamental right which is of great public importance. This right is being denied to the petitioners on grounds not admissible in law.

(n) Officers belonging to various federal services e.g. Postal Group, Commerce and Trade Group, Information Group, Pakistan Audit and Accounts Group have been posted in the Province without any lawful authority.

(o) The post of the Chief Secretary, Punjab, is a post in connection with affairs of the Province but no PCS officer has ever been posted as Chief Secretary.

(p) It was provided vide Notification No.1/1/73-RA, dated 14.09.1973 that the government servants who were holding cadre posts on 21.08.1973 stood appointed to the All Pakistan Unified Grades (APUG) but the benefit of this notification was not extended to the PCS officers.

4. The petitioners, in addition to prayer of grant of any other just and equitable relief, have prayed for the following:

(a) The Civil Service of Pakistan (Composition and Cadre) Rules, 1954 (as amended from time to time), the SRO. 1237(1)/73 dated August 21, 1973 and the 1993 Formula devised at the IPCC meeting dated 19.09.1993, SRO. 88, 2014 and such other illegal executive orders may kindly be declared illegal, ultra vires the Constitution, unsustainable and set aside accordingly.

(b) Directions may kindly be issued to the Respondent Governments that DMG/APUG officers appointed against provincial posts of BS-17 to BS-22 in the Province of the Punjab be withdrawn by the Federal Government forthwith and only PMS officers should serve on the posts of provinces being provincial civil servants.

(c) That all administrative posts under the Government of the Punjab, as specified in the Punjab Provincial Management Service Rules, 2004, may kindly be directed to be filed in only in accordance with the method provided therein, i.e., through promotion of the PCS officers to the said posts.

(d) Alternatively, in case the Civil Service of Pakistan (Composition and Cadre) Rules, 1954 (as amended from time to time) and the SRO. 1237(1)/73 dated August 21, 1973 are found to be valid, a declaration may kindly be passed that DMG/APUG officers may only be posted in the Province of Punjab against cadre posts specified under the 1954 Rules with PCS officers having 30% share in the said cadre posts.

(e) Any and all amendments in the 1954 Rules through the 1993 Formula and up to SRO 88, 2014 may kindly be declared as illegal, ultra vires the Constitution, unlawful, without lawful authority and of no legal effect.

(f) The Respondent Governments may kindly be directed to refrain from making illegal / irregular postings of junior officers to senior posts whereby senior PCS officers are forced to serve under junior DMG officers.

(g) The Notification dated 04.06.2004, whereby mandatory training for promotion up to grade 21 has been prescribed for PCS officers, may kindly be declared as illegal, unlawful, without legal authority and ultra vires the provisions of Section 8 of the Punjab Civil Servants Act, 1974 read with Rule 12 of the Punjab Civil Servants (Appointment and Conditions of Service) Rules, 1974, as the same has been issued mala fide, in order to block the promotion of PCS officers of Punjab.

(h) Allocation of posts in favour of the "All Pakistan Unified Groups' purporting to be in existence according to 2004 Rules, may, kindly, be declared as invalid due to non-existence of any such group under the law.

Arguments and prayers of the Federation

5. The Federation of Pakistan made, inter alia, the following submissions;

(a) The issues raised and the assertions made by the petitioners are neither "questions of law of public importance" nor any infringement or non-enforcement of "fundamental rights", as enshrined in Chapter 1 Part-II of the Constitution has occurred. Both conditions are essential for invocation of the Hon'ble Supreme Court's original jurisdiction under Article 184(3) of the Constitution.

(b)   The Civil Service of Pakistan (Composition and Cadre) Rules, 1954 had valid legislative imprimatur at the time of their creation and were saved, protected and granted continuity in all the later constitutions and legislations e.g. Establishment of West Pakistan Act, 1955, 1956 Constitution and 1973 Constitution. Therefore, both creation and continuity of 1954 Rules is consummately intra vires under all the Constitutions / legislations.

(c)   Contrary to the petitioner's contention, Section 241 and 263 of the Government of India Act, 1935 continued to be in force under Section 10 of the Indian Independence Act, 1947. The only provisions of the Government of India Act, 1935, which ceased to be in force under Section 10 of the Indian Independence Act, 1947 related to appointments by the Secretary of State and posts' reservations. Therefore, the agreement to create CSP was valid under Section 263 of the 1935 Act and the 1954 Rules themselves had the valid legal sanction under Section 241 of the 1935 Act (and all other sections which empowered the Governor-General in this behalf).

(d)   At present, sharing of posts between All Pakistan Service / APUG and PCS is done through a mutually agreed formula of 1993. Presently, there is deficiency / understaffing of APS / APUG officers posted in the provinces in every pay scale. Therefore, the assertion that the APUG officers have usurped the share of the PCS, determined under the 1993 formula, is absolutely baseless.

(e)   Federal Government merely places the services of an APS / APUG officer at the disposal of a provincial government as per their request and requirements. Once an APS / APUG officer is placed at the disposal of a provincial government, his further posting against a particular post becomes the sole and exclusive prerogative of that provincial government.

(f)   Under Section 10 of the Indian Independence Act, 1947, Secretary of State's powers for appointment to civil services and posts and reservation of posts ceased to be in force. These powers did not devolve i.e. in matters of appointments and posts' reservation, the underlying concept or mechanism was that of cessation of powers not devolution of powers. However, as far as the matters of remuneration, leave, pension and rights regarding disciplinary proceedings were concerned, the powers of the Secretary of State devolved to the appropriate level but only in case of persons who had been appointed before the commencing day.

(g)   Under Section 10 of the West Pakistan Establishment Act, 1955, all laws in force in the West Pakistan before the commencement of 1955 Act were continued to apply to the areas and persons to whom they would have applied as if 1955 Act would not have been passed. Section 10 (2) of the 1955 Act includes "Rules" and "Public notification" in the definition of the term "Law" used in Section 10(1) of 1955 Act.

(h)   An agreement is not required for creation of an All-Pakistan Service. On the other hand, 1973 Constitution does not prohibit entering into a consensual arrangement like the 1993 formula.

(i)   Through Resolution No. F.25/4/50-Ests (SEI) published in the official gazette on 08.11.1950, the Federal Government made its intention public to form a "Central Service" and reservation of certain posts under the Federal and the Provincial Governments for the said Service.

The Civil Service of Pakistan was created under the Civil Service of Pakistan (Composition and Cadre) Rules, 1954 and the officers of the Indian Civil Service and the Pakistan Administrative Service were appointed to it. The Resolution No. F.25/4/50-Ests (SEI) was translated into the Civil Service of Pakistan (Composition and Cadre) Rules, 1954 under statutory powers of the Governor-General under Section 241 of the Government of India Act, 1935 and all other enabling powers.

(j) The creation of the District Management Group through an office memorandum is not violative of Article 240 of the Constitution as the same was lawfully issued by the Federal Government and published in the Estacode, hence, it, being not in conflict with any provision of Civil Servants Act, 1973, has acquired the force of law on the strength of the language of sub-section (2) of Section 25 of the Act.

(k) DMG is not a Provincial Service but an All-Pakistan Service meaning thereby that it is common to the Federation and the Provinces within the contemplations of Article 240 of the Constitution. It is ingeminated that the DMG officers may be posted both in the Provinces and the Centre.

(l) The Civil Service of Pakistan (Composition and Cadre) Rules, 1954 do not prohibit posting of the DMG officers on non-cadre posts. Rule 14 of the Civil Service of Pakistan (Composition and Cadre) Rules, 1954 made it binding upon a CSP officer, posted in a Province, to submit himself to the orders of the Provincial Government under which he is serving and his whole time is at the disposal of the Provincial Government.

(m) The decisions regarding the posts-sharing formula of 1993 were taken in the Inter-Provincial Coordination Committee's meeting held on 19.09.1993; hence, these are valid both procedurally and substantively and have the force of law. Prior to this, the Provincial Cabinet of the Government of the Punjab, in its meeting held on 08.07.1992 recommended a formula for distribution of posts amongst Federal and Provincial Services. The recommendations of the Punjab Cabinet were forwarded to the Federal Government vide letter dated 07.10.1992 for final approval in terms of Article 240 of the Constitution and Section 5 of the Civil Servants Act, 1973, as the DMG belongs to All Pakistan Services and their matters can only be decided by the Federal Government. Accordingly, meeting of the Inter-Provincial Coordination Committee was convened on 19.09.1993 under the chairmanship of the then Prime Minister of Pakistan in terms of Rule 21 of the Rules of Business of the Government of Pakistan and the same was attended by the Governors, Chief Ministers and Chief Secretaries of the four Provinces wherein it was decided that the posts in the Provinces will be distributed between All Pakistan Services and the Provincial Services in accordance with the agreed ratio.

6. The Federation of Pakistan has asserted that the petition is not maintainable on facts and law and, therefore, the same may be dismissed with costs.

Arguments and prayer of the Province of the Punjab

7. The Province of the Punjab filed a written reply to the petition important points whereof are summarized hereinbelow:

(a) The Governor-General and the Governors of East Bengal, the Punjab, Sind and the North-West-Frontier Province made an agreement, as contemplated in Section 263 of the Government of India Act, 1935, for the constitution of a Service of the Federation to be known as the Civil Service of Pakistan and decided that certain posts in connection with affairs of the Provinces shall be filled by the members of the said Service. The Civil Service of Pakistan (Composition and Cadre) Rules, 1954 were competently framed under Section 241 of the Government of India Act, 1935.

(b)   The Civil Service of Pakistan (Composition and Cadre) Rules, 1954 fall within the definition of "existing law" and stand lawfully saved and protected in terms of Article 224 of the Constitution of the Islamic Republic of Pakistan, 1956, Article 225 of the Constitution of the Islamic Republic of Pakistan, 1962, Article 280(8) of the Interim Constitution of the Islamic Republic of Pakistan, 1972, Article 268 of the Constitution of the Islamic Republic of Pakistan, 1973, Section 25 of the Civil Servants Ordinance, 1973 and Section 25 (2) of the Civil Servants Act, 1973.

(c)   The apportionment of provincial posts amongst members of CSP and PCS was sanctified retroactively by Act XVI of 1967 which was an existing law on the commencing day of the 1973 Constitution.

(d)   The Civil Service of Pakistan (Composition and Cadre) Rules, 1954 were amended vide SRO. No. 1237 (1)/73 dated 21.08.1973 in exercise of powers conferred by Section 25 of the Civil Servants Ordinance, 1973. In principle, Statutory Regulatory Order, made in the exercise of delegated legislative power, has the force of law and its legality is not ordinarily called in question.

(e)   The concept of All Pakistan Service is integral to the Federal structure and the same has been recognized and protected under Article 146 and 240 of the Constitution. In fact, this concept is indispensable not only to ensure national integration but also to enable the policy makers at the Federal Government level to have sufficient exposure to the problems of the people at grass-root level so that they are not disconnected from the ground realities while making policies at the highest level. Therefore, existence of an All-Pakistan Service, which starts its career at the grass-root level and finally rises at the national level, is not only necessary for national integration but also in the interest of public at large.

(f)   As regards the 1993 formula of apportionment of provincial posts between the DMG and the PCS, the same was lawfully approved by the Inter-Provincial Coordination Committee on the recommendations of the Government of the Punjab.

(g)   Section 263 of the Government of India Act, 1935 did not cease to exist by virtue of Section 10 of the Indian Independence Act, 1947, rather the said Section 10 merely removed the powers of the Secretary of State for India to make appointments to the Civil Service in the newly independent dominions with the modification that the same were thereafter to be exercised by the Governors General of the new dominions.

(h)   The Civil Service of Pakistan (Composition and Cadre) Rules, 1954 derive their substantive sanction from Articles 146, 240, 241, 268 and 275 of the Constitution read with Act XVI of 1967.

(i)   The Civil Service of Pakistan (Composition and Cadre) Rules, 1954, cannot be held to be nullified as a result of promulgation of the Establishment of West Pakistan Act, 1955.

(j) Rule 13 of the Civil Service of Pakistan (Composition and Cadre) Rules, 1954 applies to inclusion or exclusion of the category of posts in the Schedule to the said Rules and not to increase or decrease of the number of posts against each category.

(k) Creation of the District Management Group through office memorandum No. 2/2/74 ARC dated 23.02.1974 does not tantamount to creation of an All Pakistan Service, rather it is one of the Groups created within the All Pakistan Service which was already in existence.

(l) Rule 11 of the Punjab Civil Servants (Appointment & Conditions of Service) Rules, 1974 clearly provides for appointment of persons holding posts in All Pakistan Unified Grades to a certain number of posts in the Province as may be determined from time to time.

(m) The imposition of the condition of training for promotion is neither discriminatory nor does it affect the career prospects of the Provincial Civil Servants.

(n) Services of officers belonging to the occupational groups other than the DMG are requisitioned by the Provincial Government and these officers are posted against posts reserved for the All Pakistan Service and have no material effect on promotion prospects of the PCS officers.

(o) Posting as Chief Secretary of the Province is made by the Federal Government in terms of the Civil Service of Pakistan (Composition and Cadre) Rules, 1954.

(p) The Hon'ble Supreme Court of Pakistan has held in the case of Province of West Pakistan Vs. S.I. Mahbub, I.S.E, Chief Engineer (PLD 1962 SC 433) that:

"Even under the Independence Act of 1947, the position, after the 15th of August, 1947 was that the members of the former Secretary of State's services were as regards punishment to have the same or similar rights of appeal as they had prior thereto, with only this modification that the powers of the Secretary of State-in-Council were thereafter to be exercised by the Governor-General of Pakistan."

(q) Every civil servant is liable to serve anywhere, within or outside Pakistan, in any equivalent or higher post, under the Federal Government or any Provincial Government within the contemplation of Section 10 of the Civil Servants Act, 1973.

8. The Province of the Punjab has prayed that the constitutional petition under consideration may be dismissed as being pre-mature, misconceived and contrary to the scheme of the Constitution.

Arguments and prayer of the Pakistan Administrative Service Officers Association

9. Pakistan Administrative Service Officers Association joined the proceedings to defend its cause and plead its case. A written statement was filed by the said Association for the purpose noteworthy points whereof are as follows:

(a) The concept of an All India Service common to the centre and the provinces in pre-partition India in the form of the Indian Civil Service was there since 1888. The Civil Service of Pakistan (CSP) was constituted as a service common to the Federation and the Provinces vide Resolution No. F.25/4/50-Ests (S.E.I) dated 08.11.1950 issued by the Establishment Branch of the Cabinet Secretariat. The said resolution was based on the recommendations made at the Inter-Provincial Conference attended by all Provincial Premiers held under the chairmanship of the Prime Minister on 26th and 27th December,

1949. In pursuance of the said agreement of 1949, as well as section 241 of the Government of India Act, 1935 and all other empowering provisions, the Governor-General was pleased to promulgate the Civil Service of Pakistan (Composition and Cadre) Rules, 1954. The said Rules were validly and lawfully promulgated and granted continuity by the successive constitutions of the country.

(b) The Civil Service of Pakistan (Composition and Cadre) Rules, 1954 were most recently amended by SRO. 88 (1)/2014 dated 10.02.2014 issued by the President of Pakistan pursuant to his powers under section 25(1) of the Civil Servants Act, 1973 and all other provisions empowering him in this behalf. Amongst other amendments made to the Civil Service of Pakistan (Composition and Cadre) Rules, 1954 vide the aforesaid SRO, nomenclature of the Civil Service of Pakistan was changed to Pakistan Administrative Service. This Service is an All Pakistan Service common to the federation and the federating units as contemplated in Article 240 of the Constitution. This Service is indispensable not only to promote and ensure national integration and harmony but also to enable the policy-makers at the federal level to have sufficient exposure and awareness of the issues confronted by the provinces as well as solutions that are best suited to the needs of each province.

(c) The petition is not maintainable as it neither raises a question of public importance nor the petitioners have a locus standi to file it.

(d) The petition raises several issues which are now past and closed in view of amendments in the Civil Service of Pakistan (Composition and Cadre) Rules, 1954 introduced through the SRO. 88 (1)/2014 dated 10.02.2014; hence, the petition is liable to be dismissed.

(e) The challenge to 1993 formula of sharing of posts in connection with affairs of the Provinces has become an academic question in view of the SRO. 88 (1)/2014 dated 10.02.2014 which made it part of the Civil Service of Pakistan (Composition and Cadre) Rules, 1954.

(f) The Civil Service of Pakistan (Composition and Cadre) Rules, 1954, are not in conflict with Section 10 of the Indian Independence Act, 1947. The said Section was directed against Section 244 to 246 of the Government of India Act, 1935 and not against Section 241 thereof.

(g) The Civil Service of Pakistan (Composition and Cadre) Rules, 1954 created an All Pakistan Service, common to the federation and the federating units, which is exactly what has been contemplated in Article 240 of the Constitution.

(h) The Establishment of West Pakistan Act, 1955 did not have the effect of nullifying the Civil Service of Pakistan (Composition and Cadre) Rules, 1954 as Section 10(1) of that Act provided that all laws in force in West Pakistan immediately before the appointed day shall continue to apply to the areas and the persons to whom they would have applied if this Act had not been passed. Sub-section 10(2) of the Act ibid further clarified that the term "law" shall include rules issued by a competent authority. In this view of the matter, the Civil Service of Pakistan (Composition and Cadre) Rules, 1954 were saved and protected by the Establishment of West Pakistan Act, 1955.

(i) By virtue of Section 25(2) of the Civil Servants Ordinance, 1973, all rules in respect of any terms and conditions of service of civil servants in force immediately before the commencement of the said Ordinance were deemed to be rules made under that Ordinance in so far as they were not inconsistent with the provisions of that Ordinance. The Civil Service of Pakistan (Composition and Cadre) Rules, 1954 were in force before commencement of the 1973 Ordinance; hence, these were the rules deemed to have been framed under Section 25(2) of the said Ordinance. Since the President of Pakistan was competent to frame the Civil Service of Pakistan (Composition and Cadre) Rules, 1954, therefore, amendments introduced in the Rules through SRO 1237(1) 73 dated 21.08.1973 by the President of Pakistan were lawful.

(j)   The assumption regarding non-existence of an agreement for creation of the Civil Service of Pakistan is incorrect as the said agreement has specifically been mentioned in the preamble of the Civil Service of Pakistan (Composition and Cadre) Rules, 1954; minutes of the meeting held on 26th and 27th of December, 1949, which was chaired by the Prime Minister of Pakistan and attended, among others, by the Chief Ministers of the Provinces further confirm existence of the said agreement; the agreement was the basis of the Resolution No. F.25/4/50-Ests (SEI) published in the official gazette on 08.11.1950; no province has called in question existence or validity of the said agreement.

(k)   The Establishment Division's Office Memorandum No. 2/2/74-ARC dated 23.02.1974 did not create an All Pakistan Service. It only created the District Management Group as an occupational group within an already existing All Pakistan Service. Other occupational groups within the APUG were also created through office memoranda. Article 240(a) of the Constitution provides that appointments to and the conditions of service of persons in the service of the Federation and All Pakistan Services shall be determined by or under Act of Parliament. The Civil Servants Act, 1973 was enacted by the Parliament pursuant to the aforesaid Article of the Constitution. The Establishment Division's Office Memorandum No. 2/2/74-ARC dated 23.02.1974 has statutory force and is covered under the Civil Servants Act, 1973.

(l)   The Pakistan Administrative Service is not a provincial service but is an All Pakistan Service as contemplated in Article 240 of the Constitution.

(m)   Officers of an All Pakistan Service can be posted against posts other than those mentioned in the Civil Service of Pakistan (Composition and Cadre) Rules, 1954.

(n)   The decisions taken in the meeting of the Inter-Provincial Committee held on 19.9.1993 were valid procedurally as well as substantively. The SRO. 88 (1)/2014 dated 10.02.2014 made the post-sharing formula part of the Civil Service of Pakistan (Composition and Cadre) Rules, 1954.

(o)   Rule 7(2) of the Civil Service of Pakistan (Composition and Cadre) Rules, 1954 provides that the officers of the Punjab Provincial Management Services / Provincial Civil Services, recruited directly in BS-17 through respective Provincial Public Service Commission and have held a Cadre Post in the Province for not less than five years, shall be eligible for appointment in the Pakistan Administrative Service, against Cadre Posts, not more than 30% of the superior posts, borne on the Federal sub-cadre in BPS-19 and above on the recommendations of the respective Provincial Government, by the Federal Public Service Commission, in a prescribed manner. The upward mobility of officers of the Punjab Provincial Management

Services / Provincial Civil Services has improved as a result of the said Rule 7(2).

(p)   Non-appointment of holders (belonging to the Provincial Civil Services) of the cadre posts on 21.08.1973 to the All Pakistan Unified Grades (APUG) is said to be a violation of Notification No.1/1/73-RA, dated 14.09.1973. This assumption is incorrect because the said notification was applicable only to the officers of the All Pakistan Services; it was nomenclature of the Civil Service of Pakistan and the Police Service of Pakistan that was changed to the All Pakistan Unified Grades (APUG). The All Pakistan Services (Change in Nomenclature) Rules, 1973 were later repealed through S.R.O. 89(1)/2014 dated 10.02.2014.

(q)   The Pakistan Administrative Service is not responsible for the alleged problems being faced by the PCS officers in respect of their trainings and promotions.

10.   The Pakistan Administrative Service Officers Association has prayed that the instant constitutional petition may be dismissed.

11.   Counsels of the rival parties heard. Record perused.

Questions requiring adjudication

12.   The questions requiring adjudication by this Court in the facts and circumstances of the instant petition and other questions arising out of these proceedings may be as follows:

1.   Whether the petition is maintainable under Article 184(3) of the Constitution or not?

2.   What was the effect of Section 10 of the Indian Independence Act, 1947, Article 7(1) of the Pakistan (Provisional Constitution) Order, 1947, announcement of the Viceroy of India made on 30th of April, 1947 and letter of the Government of India dated 18th of June, 1947 addressed to the Chief Secretaries of all the Provincial Governments, and deletion of all Sections from the Government of India Act, 1935 relating to the Indian Civil Service and reservation of posts therefor, on the Indian Civil Service on the appointed day i.e. 15th of August, 1947?

3.   Whether was there any lawful authority for allowing members of the Indian Civil Service, who opted to serve Pakistan, to serve as members of the Pakistan Administrative Service from 15th of August, 1947 till coming into force of the Civil Service of Pakistan (Composition and Cadre) Rules, 1954?

4.   Whether the Civil Service of Pakistan (Composition and Cadre) Rules, 1954 are intra vires Section 241 of the Government of India Act, 1935, to the extent these rules create a Service of the Federation and reserve certain posts in connection with affairs of the Federation therefor?

5.   Whether the Civil Service of Pakistan (Composition and Cadre) Rules, 1954 are intra vires Section 241 of the Government of India Act, 1935 to the extent these rules reserve certain posts in connection with affairs of the Provinces for a Service of the Federation i.e. the Civil Service of Pakistan?

6.   Whether the Civil Service of Pakistan (Composition and Cadre) Rules, 1954 were framed by the Governor-General as a delegate of the Provincial Governors to the extent of posts in connection with affairs of the Provinces?

7.   Whether the Civil Service of Pakistan (Composition and Cadre) Rules, 1954 stood saved and protected under Article 224 of the Constitution of Islamic Republic of Pakistan, 1956, Article 225 of the Constitution of the Islamic Republic of Pakistan, 1962, Article 180 of the interim Constitution of 1972 and Article 241, 268 of the Constitution of the Islamic Republic of

Pakistan, 1973 and Section 24 of the General Clauses Act, 1897 as "existing law" to the extent of reservation of posts in connection with affairs of the Provinces for members of a Service of the Federation?

8. Whether the posts specified in the Schedule to the Civil Service of Pakistan (Composition and Cadre) Rules, 1954 are posts common to the Federation and the Provinces or posts in connection with affairs of the Federation and of the Provinces reserved and encadred for a Service of the Federation?

9. Whether an All Pakistan Service was lawfully in existence when the Constitution of the Islamic Republic of Pakistan, 1956 came into operation or whether the Parliament has created an All Pakistan Service through a law or has declared a service to be deemed to be an All Pakistan Service till date?

10. Whether the Civil Service of Pakistan (Composition and Cadre) Rule, 1954 are in conflict with federal structure of the Constitution to the extent of reservation of posts in connection with affairs of the Provinces for members of a Service of the Federation?

11. Whether appointment by transfer and orders for posting / transfer are synonymous to each other and whether appointment by transfer can be made in absence of recommendation of the selection authority and without observing due competitive selection process?

12. Whether Article 146 of the Constitution allows reservation of posts in connection with affairs of the Provinces for a Service of the Federation?

13. Whether the Listed Posts (Substantive Appointments) Act, 1967 (Act XVI of 1967) validated reservation of posts in connection with affairs of the Provinces for a Service of the Federation or not?

14. Whether prescription of training as a condition-precedent for being eligible to be considered for promotion for officers of the Punjab Provincial Management Service is lawful or not?

15. Whether mere lapse of time has made the Civil Service of Pakistan (Composition and Cadre) Rules, 1954 valid to the extent of reservation of posts in connection with affairs of the Provinces and other matters falling within exclusive provincial domain? Whether mere lapse of time has made the Civil Service of Pakistan (Composition and Cadre) Rules, 1954 valid to the extent of reservation of posts in connection with affairs of the Provinces and other matters falling within exclusive provincial domain?

16. Whether officers of the Pakistan Administrative Service can be posted on posts other than those specified in the Schedule to the Civil Service of Pakistan (Composition and Cadre) Rules, 1954?

17. Whether amendments made from time to time in the Civil Service of Pakistan (Composition and Cadre) Rules, 1954 were lawful?

18. Whether the creation of the District Management Group through an executive order or office memorandum was lawful?

19. Whether non-extension of benefit of the Notification No.1/1/73-RA dated 14.09.1973 to the PCS officers was lawful?

20. Whether officers of a federal service can be promoted against posts in connection with affairs of a Province and these officers can be assigned charge of posts higher than their pay scales?

21. Whether reservation of posts in connection with affairs of the Provinces for the officers of the Police Service of Pakistan under the Police Service of Pakistan (Composition, Cadre and Seniority) Rules, 1985 is lawful or not?

22. Whether this court can restrain an executive entity to perform functions assigned to it on mere apprehension of some illegality or should the court direct it to do or not to do something on the basis of fears of the petitioners?

23. What should be the appropriate order in the facts and circumstances of this case?

Question # 1

Whether the petition is maintainable under Article 184(3) of the Constitution or not?

13.   The Federation of Pakistan has averred that the issues raised and the assertions made by the petitioners are neither questions of law of public importance nor any infringement or non-enforcement of fundamental rights, as enshrined in Chapter 1 Part-II of the Constitution, has occurred. It has been argued that both conditions are essential for invocation of the Hon'ble Supreme Court's original jurisdiction under Article 184(3) of the Constitution. The Pakistan Administrative Service Officers Association has also asserted that the petition is not maintainable as it neither raises a question of public importance nor the petitioners have a locus standi to file it. On the other hand, counsel for the petitioners claims that the petitioners have a fundamental right to have equal protection of law and the question of unconstitutional treatment being meted out to them presents a number of substantial questions of law of public importance. It is claimed that interests of the petitioners represent interests of the entire community of the civil servants of the Provinces; therefore, the questions raised in the instant petition are of public importance.

14.   The petitioners are members of the Punjab Provincial Management Service and are presently holding different posts in connection with affairs of the Province of the Punjab. They have been employed by the Government of the Punjab as members of the Punjab Provincial Management Service, previously known as the Provincial Civil Service. Appointments of the petitioners and their conditions of service have been determined mainly by or under the Punjab Civil Servants Act, 1974. The Punjab Civil Servants (Appointment and Conditions of Service) Rules, 1974 and the Punjab Provincial Management Service Rules, 2004 contain important conditions of recruitment and of service of the petitioners. As members of the Punjab Provincial Management Service, the petitioners have a right to be treated in accordance with law and not otherwise. To enjoy the protection of law is a fundamental right under Article 25 of the Constitution. Moreover, employment under the Government is a lawful profession. The right to trade and profession, guaranteed by Article 18 of the Constitution includes the right to compete for appointment to a post in the public sector in accordance with law as has been held by the Hon'ble Supreme Court of Pakistan in a case reported as Mushtaq Ahmad Mohal Vs. Hon'ble Lahore High Court, Lahore (1997 SCMR 1043). Once appointed, the appointee has a fundamental right to expect a fair career progression. Any impermissible hurdle in the way of fair career progression need to be removed as legitimate expectation of fair career progression relates to the right to life of a civil servant. The Hon'ble Supreme Court of Pakistan has laid down the dictum of law on the subject of entertainment of petitions of the civil servants under Article 183(3) of the Constitution by treating a legitimate expectation for a fair career progression and treatment in accordance with law as fundamental rights in Tariq Azizud-Din's case (2010 SCMR 1301) and Orya Maqbool Abbasi's case (2014 SCMR 817). We are, therefore, constrained to hold that legitimate expectation to be considered for promotion or fair career progression in accordance with law is a fundamental right.

15.   The question of legality of reservation of posts in connection with affairs of the Provinces for members of a Service of the Federation under the Civil Service of Pakistan (Composition and Cadre) Rules, 1954 is a question of public importance as it not only concerns public services of all the four Provinces but is a matter which has far-reaching implications for the executive machinery of the Federation and of the Provinces. The executive machinery of the Provinces plays an important role in general welfare of the

public and enforcement of the fundamental rights. Rule of law will have little chance to survive if the provincial services are not given an assurance, in practice and through actions as required by the Constitution and the laws framed thereunder, that they have right to be treated in accordance with the Constitution. Determination of the questions of legality of the Civil Service of Pakistan (Composition and Cadre) Rules, 1954, the Police Service of Pakistan (Composition, Cadre and Seniority) Rules, 1985 and inter-governmental deputations requires interpretation of the Constitution and laws and rules relating to civil servants of the Federation and of the Provinces. These matters have material effect on the public in more ways than one. Adjudication of the lis at hand is, therefore, a matter of public importance within the framework of Article 184 (3) of the Constitution.

16.   We hold that the instant petition is maintainable under Article 184(3) of the Constitution of the Islamic Republic of Pakistan, 1973 as it raises questions of public importance with reference to enforcement of fundamental rights.

Question # 2

What was the effect of Section 10 of the Indian Independence Act, 1947, Article 7(1) of the Pakistan (Provisional Constitution) Order, 1947, announcement of the Viceroy of India made on 30th of April, 1947 and letter of the Government of India dated 18th of June, 1947 addressed to the Chief Secretaries of all the Provincial Governments, and deletion of all Sections from the Government of India Act, 1935 relating to the Indian Civil Service and reservation of posts therefor, on the Indian Civil Service on the appointed day i.e. 15th of August, 1947?

17.   The Joint Committee on Indian Constitutional Reform [Session 1933-34], observed as follows:

"The Indian Civil Services.

276. The Civil Services in India are classified in three main divisions: (1) the All-India Services; (2) the Provincial Services; and (3) the Central Services. The All-India Services, though they work no less than the Provincial Services under the Provincial Governments, are all appointed by the Secretary of State, and he is the final authority for the maintenance of their rights. Each All-India Service is a single Service and its members are liable to serve anywhere in India; but, unless transferred to serve under the Central Government, the whole of their career lies ordinarily in the Province to which they are assigned on their first appointment.

The All India Services.

277. The All-India Services consist of the Indian Civil Service; the Police; the Forest Service; the Service of Engineers; the Medical Service (Civil); the Educational Service; the Agricultural Service; and the Veterinary Service. Recruitment, however, by the Secretary of State to the Buildings and Roads Branch of the Service of Engineers, to the Educational Service, the Agricultural Service and the Veterinary Service, ceased in 1924 on the recommendation of the Lee Commission. The composition and total strength of these Services on 1st January, 1933, were as follows:

1	2	3	4
	Europeans	**Indians**	**Total**
Civil Service	819	478	1,297
Police	505	152	665

Forest Service	203	96	299
Service of Engineers	304	292	596
Medical Service (Civil)	200	S8	298
Educational Service	96	79	175
Agricultural Service	46	30	76
Veterinary Service	20	2	22
	2,193	**1,227**	**3,428**

The Provincial Services.

278. The Provincial Services (in the sense in which the expression is ordinarily used, which excludes not only the members of All-India Services working in the Province, but also the numerous Subordinate Services) are, and always have been, almost entirely Indian in composition, and cover the whole field of provincial civil administration in the middle grades. Appointments to these Services are made by the Provincial Governments who, broadly speaking, control their conditions of service, and show an increasing tendency to restrict their recruitment to candidates from the Province. In many branches of the administration members of All-India and Provincial Services work side by side, though the higher posts are usually filled by the former.

The Central Services.

279. The Central Services are concerned with matters under the direct control of the Central Government. Apart from the Central Secretariat, the more important of these Services are the Railway Services, the Indian Posts and Telegraph Service, and the Imperial Customs Service. To some of these the Secretary of State makes appointments, but in the great majority of cases their members are appointed and controlled by the Government of India; and, if these Services are taken as a whole, Indians out-number Europeans even in the higher grades, while, with the exception of the railways, the middle and lower grades may be said to be wholly Indian. The Anglo-Indian community has always furnished a large number of recruits to the Central Services, especially the Railways, the Posts and Telegraphs and the Imperial Customs Service."

18.   Paragraphs 91 and 92 of the report of the Joint Committee on Indian Constitutional Reform [Session 1933-34] are also relevant to the question under consideration, and are, therefore, reproduced below:

"All-India, Central and Provincial Services are all Crown Services

291. It is natural that the process by which during recent years Provincial Service officers have been gradually substituted for All-India officers in the transferred departments and greater powers of control have been delegated to the Provincial Governments should have tended to create a false distinction between the status of the All-India Services and that of the Provincial Services. The tendency has almost inevitably been to regard the Provincial Services as having ceased to be Crown Services, and as having become Services of the Provincial

Governments. This tendency has been emphasized by the argument, frequently advanced and accepted in the past both by Indians and Englishmen, that provincial self-government necessarily entails control by the Provincial Government over the appointment of its servants. This argument has, no doubt, great logical force, but it runs the risk of distorting one of the accepted principles of the British Constitution, namely, that civil servants are the servants of the Crown, and that the Legislature should have no control over their appointment or promotion and only a very general control over their conditions of service. Indeed, even the British Cabinet has come to exercise only a very limited control over the Services, control being left very largely to the Prime Minister as, so to speak, the personal adviser of the Crown in regard to all service matters. The same principle applies, of course, equally to the Services recruited by the Secretary of State for India, though this fact has been sometimes obscured by inaccurate references to the control of Parliament over the All-India Services. But, whatever misunderstandings may have arisen in the past as to the real status of the Provincial Services, there ought to be no doubt as to their status under the new Constitution. We have already pointed out that, under that Constitution, all the powers of the Provincial Governments, including the power to recruit public servants and to regulate their conditions of service, will be derived no longer by devolution from the Government of India, but directly by delegation from the Crown, i.e., directly from the same source as that from which the Secretary of State derives his powers of recruitment. The Provincial Services, no less than the Central Services and the Secretary of State's Services will, therefore, be essentially Crown Services, and the efficiency and morale of those Services will largely depend in the future on the development in India of the same conventions as have grown up in England.

Governor-General and Governors should be under the Crown, recognized as heads of Central and Provincial Services respectively

292. But, if such conventions are to develop in India as in England, they must develop from the same starting-point, from a recognition that the Governor, as the personal representative of the Crown and the head of the Executive Government, has a special relation to all the Crown Services. He will, indeed, be generally bound to act in that relation on the advice of his Ministers, subject to his special responsibility for the rights and legitimate interests of the Services, but his Ministers will be no less bound to remember that advice on matters affecting the organisation of the permanent executive services is a very different thing from advice on matters of legislative policy, and that the difference may well affect both the circumstances and the form in which such advice is tendered. We think, therefore, that the Constitution should contain in its wording a definite recognition of the Governor-General and the Governors respectively as, under the Crown, the heads of the Central (as distinct from the All-India) and Provincial Services. Appointments to these Services would accordingly run in the name of the Governor-General and Governor respectively, and it would, therefore, follow that no public servant appointed by the Governor-General or Governor will be subject to dismissal, save by order of the Governor-General or Governor."

19.   Paragraph 153 of the report ibid reads as follows:

"It is clear that, in any new constitution in which autonomous provinces are to be united under the Crown, not only can the provinces no longer derive their powers and authority by devolution by the Central Government, but the Central Government cannot continue to be an agent of the Secretary of State. Both must derive their powers and authority from a direct grant by the Crown. The legal basis of a reconstituted Government of India must be, first, the resumption into the hands of the Crown of all rights, authority and jurisdiction in and over the territories of British India, whether they are at present vested in the Secretary of State, the Governor-General in Council or the Provincial Governments and Administrations; and second, their redistribution in such manner as the Act may prescribe between the Central Government on the one hand and the Provinces on the other. A Federation of which the British Indian Provinces are the constituent units will thereby be brought into existence."

20.   Under Section 241 of the Government of India Act, 1935 services of the Federation, and posts in connection with the affairs of the Federation were to be regulated by the Governor-General of India or such person as he may direct. Similar powers were vested in the Governors of the respective Provinces in case of services of a Province, and posts in connection with the affairs of a Province. As regards the Indian Civil Service, the Secretary of State for India was made the authority to appoint a person to the said Service with power to determine strength of the said Service. (Section 244 of the Government of India Act, 1935). He was also empowered to reserve posts to be exclusively filled by officers of the Indian Civil Service and powers to make appointments and postings against the reserved posts were vested, in the case of posts in connection with the affairs of the Federation, in the Governor-General, exercising his individual judgment, and in the respective Governors in respect of posts in connection with affairs of that Province. (Section 244 of the Government of India Act, 1935). Here, power to make appointment to the Indian Civil Service and the power to make appointment to a reserved post need to be distinguished. Last appointment to the Indian Civil Service was made by the Secretary of State in 1943.

21.   On 30th of April, 1947, the Viceroy of India made an announcement for **"grant of compensation for premature termination of their service in India to members of Civil Services appointed by the Secretary of State and to regular officers and British Warrant Officers of the Indian Naval and Military Forces"**. Members of the Indian Civil Service were given an option to either accept compensation in consideration of their premature termination of service or to express their willingness to continue to serve one of the two Dominions (Pakistan and India) or their provincial governments. The said announcement provided that:

"1.   His Majesty's Government have announced their intention that the British Government's authority in India will be finally transferred to Indian hands by June, 1948. It is the aim of His Majesty's Government that the transfer of power should be effected in an orderly and regulated manner so that the new authorities may assume their responsibilities in conditions conducive to the best interests of India and maintenance of good relations with Great Britain. His Majesty's Government are confident that during this period of transition the Services and all those who man them, whether British or Indian, will respond to this call.

2.   **To those serving under covenant or other form of agreement with the Secretary of State for India or who**

hold commissions from His Majesty the King, the transfer of power will mean premature termination on that date of a career under the ultimate authority of His Majesty's Government and the British Parliament; and for many there is added to the heavy call of present duty the burden of anxiety for their own future and that of those who depend on them.

3. The Government of India are naturally and rightly most anxious and His Majesty's Government share their anxiety that the administration shall not be weakened by the loss of experienced officers. To this end, Government of India undertake that those members of the Secretary of State's Services who continue to serve under the Government of India after the transfer of power shall do so on their present terms as to scales of pay, leave, pensionary rights, and safeguards in matters of discipline and that provisions to this effect should be made in the Treaty to deal with matters arising out of the transfer of power. The Government of India will now propose to Provincial Governments that they should give similar assurances to members of the Secretary of State's service who agree to join Provincial services.

4. The Government of India recognise that some Indian members of the Secretary of State's services may be genuinely anxious about their prospects under the Provincial administrations where they are at present employed, and every effort will be made to arrange suitable transfers in such cases.

5. The Government of India agree that compensation should be payable to such Indian Officers of these services as-

    (1) are not invited to continue to serve under the Government of India after transfer of power; or

    (2) can satisfy the Governor-General that their actions in the course of duty during their service prior to the transfer of power have damaged their prospects, or that the appointments offered to them are such as cannot be regarded as satisfactory in the altered circumstances; or

    (3) can show to the satisfaction of the Governor-General that they have legitimate cause for anxiety about their future in the Province where they are now serving, and that no suitable transfer can be arranged.

    But the Government of India feel that sentiments of patriotism will naturally impel Indian Officers to continue to serve their country and that, in the light of the undertaking that they have given, and the consideration that in fact Indian members of the Service will have improved prospects, there is no ground, save in these special cases, for payment of compensation to Indian officers on account of the transfer of power.

6. His Majesty's Government have been reviewing the whole position. They have noted the undertaking which the

Government of India have given in regard to officers whom they desire, should continue to serve under the Government of India. They recognise the force of the Government of India's arguments, and they agree that to Indian Officers compensation should not be admissible except in the cases which I have just mentioned. Many Indian members of the Secretary of State's services will, however, become members of provincial services and in their cases His Majesty's Government's agreement that they need not be compensated is conditional upon the Provincial Governments guaranteeing the existing terms of service. If they are not prepared to do so, His Majesty's Government reserve the right to reconsider the matter.

7.   With these reservations I am now authorised by His Majesty's Government to inform members of the Secretary of State's services that they accept the obligation to see that they are duly compensated for the termination of their careers consequent on the transfer of power.......

8.   In pursuance of their wish to give all possible help to the Government of India in building up the new services, His Majesty's Government agree that their obligation covers the claim to ultimate compensation of those British members of the Services who are asked to serve on in India and decide to do so."

22.   A nine-member bench of the Hon'ble Supreme Court of India, in a case reported as "State of Madras and another vs K.M. Rajagopalan (1955 AIR 817) observed that the announcement of the Viceroy dated 30th of April, 1947 was based on the assumptions clearly stated or indicated therein,

    (1)   that transfer of power brings about an automatic premature termination of the services;

    (2)   on such termination, it would be open to the servant concerned either to decline to continue in the service of the new Government or to offer to continue his services: and

    (3)   that in case the individual servant intimated his desire to continue in service, it was open to the Government either to accept the offer or not."

23.   His Majesty's Government decided to advance the date of transfer of power and made an announcement on 3rd of June, 1947 to the effect that they are willing to anticipate the date of June, 1948 for the handing over of power by the setting up of an independent Indian Government or Governments at an even earlier date. His Majesty's Government proposed to introduce legislation for the transfer of power this year on a Dominion Status basis to one or two successor authorities according to the decisions taken as a result of this announcement.

24.   After the announcement of His Majesty's Government dated the 3rd of June, 1947, a circular letter was issued, by the Government of India, to the Chief Secretaries of all the Provincial Governments on the 18th of June, 1947, directing them to seek options from members of services of the Secretary of State, in terms of announcement of the Viceroy of India dated 30th of April, 1947. The said letter, inter alia, stated as follows:

"That in view of the latest announcement of His Majesty's Government (dated the 3rd June, 1947), it is essential to ascertain with the least possible delay, the wishes of individual officers to whom His Excellency the Viceroy's announcement of the 30th April 1947 applies in regard to continuance in service after the transfer of power. This will enable Government to decide which officers they should continue to retain in service after the transfer of power and to make arrangements to replace officers who desire to quit service, of their own accord or whom Government may not wish to continue in service".

25.   The Chief Secretaries were accordingly asked to make arrangements

"to send immediately to every officer belonging to any service specified in the schedule, and serving under the Provincial Government, a copy of the enclosed letter from the Government of India to the officers concerned, whereby the officer was asked to communicate within ten days of the receipt of the letter whether he wishes to continue in the service of the Government or whether he desires to retire from service".

26.   In pursuance of these instructions, the individual letters to the officers concerned were sent and replies were obtained and necessary orders were passed in respect of the officers whom the various Governments were not prepared to retain in service after the transfer of power.

27.   The Indian Independence Act, 1947, (10 & 1.1 Geo. 6, Ch. 30), passed by the British Parliament, became a law on 18th of July, 1947, Section 7(1) whereof specifically provided that, as from the appointed day, His Majesty's Government in the United Kingdom shall have no responsibility as respects the government of any of the territories which, immediately before that day, were included in British India. This also implied terminal end of the Secretary of State for India and his Services.

28.   Section 9 of the Indian Independence Act, 1947, provided as follows:
"Orders for bringing this Act into force. –
(1)   The Governor-General shall by order make such provision as appears to him to be necessary or expedient-
   (a)   for bringing the provisions of this Act into effective operation;
   (b)   ---------;
   (c)   for making omissions from, additions to, and adaptations and modifications of, the Government of India Act, 1935, and the Orders in Council, rules and other instruments made thereunder, in their application to the separate new Dominions;
   (d)   for removing difficulties arising in connection with the transition to the provisions of this Act;
   (e)   ------------;
   (f)   for enabling agreements to be entered into, and other acts done, on behalf of either of the new Dominions before the appointed day;
   (g)   ------------;
   (h)   ------------; and
   (i)   ------------.
   (2)   ------------.
(3)   This section shall be deemed to have had effect as from the **third day of June**, nineteen hundred and forty-seven, and any order of the Governor-General or any Governor made on or after that date as to any matter shall have effect accordingly,

and any order made under this section may be made so as to be retrospective to any date not earlier than the said third day of June:

Provided that no person shall be deemed to be guilty of an offence by reason of so much of any such order as makes any provision thereof retrospective to any date before the making thereof."

29. Section 10 of the Indian Independence Act, 1947, reads as follows:

"Secretary of State's services, etc.

10. –

(1) The provisions of this Act keeping in force provisions of the Government of India Act, 1935, shall not continue in force the provisions of that Act relating to appointments to the civil services of, and civil posts under, the Crown in India by the Secretary of State, or the provisions of that Act relating to the reservation of posts.

(2) Every person who-

(a) having been appointed by the Secretary of State, or Secretary of State in Council, to a civil service of the Crown in India continues on and after the appointed day to serve under the Government of either of the new Dominions or of any Province or part thereof; or

(b) having been appointed by His Majesty before the appointed day to be a judge of the Federal Court or, of any court which is a High Court within the meaning of the Government of India Act, 1935, continues on and after the appointed day to serve as a judge in either of the new Dominions,

shall be entitled to receive from the Governments of the Dominions and Provinces or parts which he is from time to time serving or, as the case may be, which are served by the courts, in which he is from time to time a judge, the same conditions of service as respects remuneration, leave and pension, and the same rights as respects disciplinary matters or, as the case may be, as respects the tenure of his office, or rights as similar thereto as changed circumstances may permit, as that person was entitled to immediately before the appointed day.

(4) Nothing in this Act shall be construed as enabling the rights and liabilities of any person with respect to the family pension funds vested in Commissioners under section two hundred and seventy-three of the Government of India Act, 1935, to be governed otherwise than by Orders in Council made (whether before or after the passing of this Act or the appointed day) by His Majesty in Council and rules made (whether before or after the passing of this Act or the appointed day) by a Secretary of State or such other Minister of the Crown as may be designated in that behalf by Order in Council under the Ministers of the Crown (Transfer of Functions) Act, 1946."

30. Article 7(1) of the Pakistan (Provisional Constitution) Order, 1947 reads as under:

"Subject to any general or special orders or arrangments affecting his case, any person who immediately before the appointed day is holding any civil post under the Crown in connection with the affairs of the Province of Bengal (or Assam), the Punjab, the North-West Frontier

Province or Sind shall, as from that day, be deemed to have been duly apppointed to the corresponding post under the Crown in connection with the affairs of the Province of East Bengal, West Pakistan, the North-West Frontier Province or, as the case may be, Sind."

31. Vide Schedule to the Pakistan (Provisional Constitution) Order, 1947, Sections 248, 249, 250, 251 and 252 of the Government of India Act, 1935, were omitted.

32. Other sections of the Government of India Act, 1935, (244, 246, 248 and 249 and 278 to 284-A) assigning any role to the Secretary of State for India in respect of the civil services were made inoperative and were impliedly omitted through Section 10 of the Indian Independence Act, 1947. The Federation of Pakistan, in its written statement in the instant case, has admitted that the provisions of the Government of India Act, 1935 relating to the Secretary of State for India and the All India Services ceased to be in force under Section 10 of the Indian Independence Act, 1947. It has been held by the Hon'ble Supreme Court of India, in a case reported as "State of Madras and another vs K.M. Rajagopalan (1955 AIR 817) that the resultant position was clearly this:

(1) There was no further recruitment to a special covenanted service by the Secretary of State.

(2) There was to be no statutory reservation of posts to be made by the Secretary of State.

(3) The conditions of service as made by the Secretary of State no longer continued in operation.

(4) No right of appeal or approach to the Secretary of State for redress of any personal grievances relating to such servants, or right of compensation, etc. for any adverse action to be determined by the Secretary of State, continued to subsist.

33. The Indian Civil Service stood abolished and tenure of their members came to an end on the appointed day in terms of article 7(1) of the Pakistan (Provisional Constitution) Order, 1947 and section 10 of the Indian Independence Act, 1947. A combined reading of the above-said legal provisions, announcement by the Viceroy on 30th of April, 1947, circular letter of the Government of India to the Chief Secretaries of all the Provincial Governments dated 18th of June, 1947 and schedule to the Pakistan (Provisional Constitution) Order, 1947 produces the inescapable result of deletion of various sections relating to the Secretary of State and his services, i.e., sections 244, 246, 248 and 249 and 278 to 284-A from the Government of India Act, 1935. With deletion of Section 244 and 246 of the Government of India Act, 1935, the Indian Civil Service lost the legal basis for its continued existence as such service. Members of this service were, however, given the option either to accept compensation in lieu of premature termination of their tenure or to continue to serve one of the two independent countries or their Provincial Governments if their options to continue to serve were acceptable to concerned Governments.

34. A nine-member bench of the Hon'ble Supreme Court of India, in a case reported as "State of Madras and another vs K.M. Rajagopalan (1955 AIR 817) has observed that:

"It is clear that the continuance contemplated by section 10(2) (a) of the Indian Independence Act and by section 240(2) and section 247 of the Government of India Act, as adapted, is the continuance impliedly brought about by this deeming provision in article 7(1) of the India (Provisional Constitution) Order. But it has to be noted that this provision is specifically preceded by the qualifying phrase "subject to any general or special orders or arrangements affecting his case". Thus, all persons who were previously holding civil posts are deemed to have been appointed and, hence, to continue in service, excepting those whose case is governed by "general or special orders or arrangements affecting his case". Now, omitting "general orders" which has no application in this case, there can be no reasonable doubt that the special orders or arrangements contemplated herein, in so far as the members of the Secretary of State's services are concerned, are the special orders or arrangements which followed on the Viceroy's announcement dated the 30th April, 1947, in pursuance of which the individual civil servants had been circularized and their wishes ascertained, and the Governments concerned had finally intimated their option not to invite the continuance of the service of particular individuals as has happened in the case of the present plaintiff."

35.   The Hon'ble Supreme Court of India, in the aforementioned judgment, settled the issue in the aforesaid judgment in the following words:

"It is clear, therefore, from the above discussion that apart from the fact that **the Secretary of State and his services disappeared as from the 15th August 1947**, section 10(2) of the Indian Independence Act and article 7(1) of the India (Provisional Constitution) Order proceeded on a clear and unequivocal recognition of the validity of the various special orders and the individual arrangements made and amount to an implicit statutory recognition of the principle of automatic termination of the services brought about by the political change. In our opinion, therefore, the services of the plaintiff came to an automatic termination on the emergence of Indian Dominion. The special order and arrangement affecting his case that, as made in pursuance of the Viceroy's announcement resulted in his service not being continued from and after the 15th August, 1947, and the plaintiff is not entitled to the declaration prayed for."

36.   The Federation of Pakistan, in its written statement in the instant case, has not advanced any arguments against any of the conculsions drawn and dclarations made by the Hon'ble Supreme Court of India in the case of "State of Madras and another vs K.M. Rajagopalan (1955 AIR 817). On the other hand, its assertion to the following effect clearly endorses the ratio decidendi of the aforesaid judgment:

"Under Section 10 of the Indian Independence Act, 1947, Secretary of State's powers for appointment to civil services and posts and reservation of posts ceased to be in force. These powers did not devolve i.e. in matters of appointments and posts reservation, the underlying concept or mechanism was that of cessation of powers not devolution of powers. However, as far as the matters of remuneration, leave, pension and rights regarding disclipnary proceedings were concerned, the powers of the Secretary of State devolved to the appropriate level but only in case of persons who had been appointed before the commencing day."

37.   The Province of the Punjab has stated in its written reply that the Hon'ble Supreme Court of Pakistan has held in the case of Province of West Pakistan Vs. S.I. Mahbub, I.S.E, Chief Engineer (PLD 1962 SC 433) that:

"Even under the Independence Act of 1947, the position, after the 15th of August, 1947 was that the members of the former Secretary of State's services were, as regards punishment, to have the same or similar rights of appeal as they had prior thereto, with only this modification that the powers of the Secretary of State-in-Council were thereafter to be exercised by the Governor-General of Pakistan."

38.   There is no conflict or inconsistency between the dictum of law laid down by the Hon'ble Supreme Court of India in the case of "State of Madras and another vs K.M. Rajagopalan (1955 AIR 817), the declaration made by the Hon'ble Supreme Court of

Pakistan in the case of Province of West Pakistan Vs. S.I. Mahbub, I.S.E, Chief Engineer (PLD 1962 SC 433) and the written submissions of the Federation of Pakistan on the question of consitutuional existence of the Indian Civil Service on the appointed day and its disappearance, as a Service, as from that date.

39. It is clear from the above that the Indian Civil Service, one of the Secretary of State's Services, ceased to exist from the appointed day and that the services of its members stood automatically terminated on 15th of August, 1947. The protection regarding conditions of service with respect to remuneration, leave, pension, rights in case of disciplinary matters and tenure of office or similar rights given to members of the Indian Civil Service who continued to serve after the appointed day did not amount to continuation of their service as members of the Indian Civil Service. This protection was in fact implementation of the undertaking given vide paragraph 3 of the announcement of the Viceroy dated 30th of April, 1947. The Viceroy's announcement dated 30th of April, 1947, makes no mention of any All India or All Pakistan Service automatically replacing the Indian Civil Service immediately on the transfer of power though it specifically mentioned in para 8 of announcement of the Viceroy dated 30th of April, 1947 of giving all possible help in building up the new Services. The provisions of Article 7(1) of the Pakistan (Provisional Constitution) Order, 1947 also do not refer to the persons in the Secretary of State's Services to continue in service as members of any All Pakistan Service though it specifically deals with the appointment of such other employees of Government to the posts they had held on the day immediately preceding the appointed day. This Article refers to appointments to posts and not appointments to Services. There is nothing on the record to show that any new Service replaced the Indian Civil Service at the changeover.

40. No member of the Indian Civil Service is known to have joined a Provincial Civil Service in Pakistan despite the fact that paragraph 6 of the announcement of the Viceroy dated 30th of April, 1947 specifically mentions that many Indian members of the Secretary of State's services will become members of provincial services.

41. The above discussion leads us to conclude and hold that the Indian Civil Service disappeared as such Service on 15th of August, 1947 (the appointed day) and its members (whose option to join the new dominion of Pakistan was accepted) could continue to hold posts held by them immediately before the appointed day but could not, in absence of express constitutional provisions providing for reservation of posts in connection with affairs of the Provinces for a Federal or an All Pakistan Service, function in the Provinces as members of the Pakistan Administrative Service.

Question # 3

Whether was there any lawful authority for allowing members of the Indian Civil Service, who opted to serve Pakistan, to serve as members of the Pakistan Administrative Service from 15th of August, 1947 till coming into force of the Civil Service of Pakistan (Composition and Cadre) Rules, 1954?

42. Before the appointed day i.e. 15th of August, 1947, there were three main services and types of civil posts in India, namely:

(a) Services of the Federation and posts in connection with affairs of the Federation under the rule-making authority of the Governor-General;

(b) Services of a Province and posts in connection with affairs of a Province under the rule-making authority of the Governor of the respective Province; and

(c) Services of the Secretary of State for India and posts reserved therefor under the rule-making authority of the Secretary of State for India.

43. Under Section 7(1) of the the Indian Independence Act, 1947, as from the appointed day, His Majesty's Government in the United Kingdom ceased to have any responsibility

with regard to the governments of any of the new dominions. As a result, role of the Secretary of State for India and his Services, as such services, came to an end and tenure of members of the Indian Civil Service was prematurely terminated.

44.   In terms of announcement of the Viceroy of India dated 30th of April, 1947, members of the Indian Civil Service were given an option to continue to serve, after the appointed day, under either of the proposed dominions or Provincial Governments thereof. Paragraph 4 of the said announcement provided that Government of India recognised that some Indian members of the Secretary of State's services may be genuinely anxious about their prospects under the Provincial administrations where they were then employed, and promised to take every effort to arrange suitable transfers in such cases. Of those who opted to continue to serve the new Dominions or Provinces thereof and whose options were accepted, 770 members of the Indian Civil Service joined India (Report on Indian and State Administrative Services and Problems of District Administration. New Delhi. 1962. p. 69 and 72). Pakistan received 82 Indian Civil Service officers only. (Constituent Assembly of Pakistan Debates. 1956. Vol. 1. P. 2104). In Pakistan, these officers were collectively termed Pakistan Administrative Service (PAS) and were allowed to serve as a Service as before the appointed day. In 1950, PAS was renamed as the Civil Service of Pakistan (CSP).

45.   The Federation of Pakistan, the Province of the Punjab and the Pakistan Administrative Service Officers Association have not claimed any lawful authority for functioning of the Pakistan Administrative Service and the Civil Service of Pakistan prior to coming into force of the Civil Service of Pakistan (Composition and Cadre) Rules, 1954. No justification whatsoever was furnished by any of these parties for keeping the principle of reservation of posts in connection with affairs of the Provinces for a service of the federation alive despite deletion of enabling provisions from the Government of India Act, 1935 and absence of any other lawful provision therefor.

46.   The same situation prevailed in India. The constitutional deviations (retention of the Indian Civil Service with the nomenclature of the Indian Administrative Service, reservation of posts in connection with affairs of the Provinces for that Service in absence of any enabling provision in the Government of India Act, 1935 as adapted through the India (Provisional Constitution) Order, 1947) were of such a serious nature that only an express validation through by an Article of the Constitution was found to be essential to validate what had been done in India in respect of the Indian Civil Service from the appointed day till coming into force of the Constitution of India. Accordingly, Article 312 of the Constitution of India reads as follows:

"**312. All India Services**

"(1)   Notwithstanding anything in Chapter VI of Part VI or Part XI, if the Council of States has declared by resolution supported by not less than two thirds of the members present and voting that it is necessary or expedient in the national interest so to do, Parliament may by law provide for the creation of one or more all India services (including an all India judicial service) common to the Union and the States, and, subject to the other provisions of this Chapter, regulate the recruitment, and the conditions of service of persons appointed, to any such service.

(2)   The services known at the commencement of this Constitution as the Indian Administrative Service and the Indian Police Service shall be deemed to be services created by Parliament under this article."

47.   The subject of All-India Services was assigned to the Federation through entry appearing at serial number 70, reproduced below, of the Union List in Seventh Schedule of the Constitution of India:

"70. Union Public Service; All-India Services; Union Public Service Commission."

48.   Article 392 of the Constitution of India provided that "the President may, for the purpose of removing any difficulties, particularly in relation to the transition from the provisions of the Government of India Act, 1935, to the provisions of this Constitution, by order, direct that this Constitution shall, during such period as may be specified in the order, have effect subject to such adaptations, whether by way of modification, addition or omission, as he may deem to be necessary or expedient; provided that no such order shall be made after the first meeting of Parliament duly constituted under Chapter 11 of Part V ".

49. As there was only one House during the transitional period, there were bound to be difficulties in the application of the Constitution, which envisaged a bicameral legislature. Consequently, the President of India passed the Constitution (Removal of Difficulties) Order No. II on January 26, 1950, by which, among other adaptations, he made an adaptation in Article 312 also, to this effect: -

"In clause (1), omit 'if the Council of States has declared by resolution supported by not less than two-thirds of the members present and voting that it is necessary or expedient in the national interest so to do".

50.   After removal of the omitted words, Article 312 read as follows: -

"(1)   Notwithstanding anything in Part XI, Parliament may by law provide for the creation of one or more all-India services common to the Union and the States, and subject to the other provisions of this Chapter, regulate the recruitment, and the conditions of service of persons appointed to any such service."

51.   The All-India Services Act, 1951 (LXI of 1951) was enacted thereafter which defined the All-India Services as the Indian Administrative Service or the service known as the Indian Police. Section 3 of the Act authorized the Central Government, after consultation with the Governments of the States concerned to make rules for the regulation of recruitment, and the conditions of service of persons appointed to an All India Service. Section 4 of the Act ibid provided that:

"All rules in force immediately before the commencement of this Act and applicable to an all-India service shall continue to be in force and shall be deemed to be rules made under this Act."

52. Thus, unconstitutional acts in respect of the Indian Administrative Service from the appointed day to the promulgation of the Constitution of India were validated by the Constitution; foundation was provided for the Indian Administrative Service in the Constitution; difficulties faced in operationalization of that constitutional provision were removed through a Presidential Order and the Indian Administrative Service was provided backing and support of a statute through enactment of All-India Services Act, 1951 (LXI of 1951). We do not deem it necessary at this moment to examine the question that whether the concept of reservation of posts in connection with affairs of the Federation and of the Federating Units for an All India Service and the concept of an All India Service to man posts common to the Federation and of the Provinces are identical or not. We may address this question later in this judgment.

53.   Contrary to the actions taken in India to provide constitutional and statutory protection and validity to the Indian Administrative Service, similar constitutional and statutory validity and protection was not provided to the Pakistan Administrative Service or the Civil Service of Pakistan. Even before finalization of the Constitution for Pakistan, the Constituent Assembly could easily do so through appropriate amendments in the Government of India Act, 1935. The Constituent Assembly of Pakistan passed more than ten Acts to introduce various amendments in the Government of India Act, 1935 but no amendment was passed to provide legal protection and sanctity to the Pakistan

Administrative Service or the Civil Service of Pakistan. Record shows that the Constituent Assembly was fully aware of its lawful competence to validate actions requiring legislative sanction. Just to illustrate, statement of objects and reasons of the Validation of Laws Act, 1955 (passed by the Constituent Assembly of Pakistan) is reproduced hereinbelow:

> "During the period of its existence, the Constituent Assembly has in all passed 44 Acts, to none of which was the assent of the Governor-General sought although it was necessary to do so under sub-section (3) of section 6 of the Indian Independence Act, 1947. This defect was pointed out when Maulvi Tamizuddin Khan's Case was brought before the Federal Court. After careful examination of all the laws passed by the Constituent Assembly, it has been found necessary to accord assent to the Acts mentioned in the Schedule and assent was accorded to all of them after the pronouncement of the Federal Court.
>
> But each of the laws mentioned in the Schedule remained in operation from the date of its enactment and from each of them have been flowing numerous orders and rules and other administrative and executive actions all of which are, on account of this defect, illegal. In order to confer validity on all these orders, rules and other administrative and executive actions, it is necessary that retrospective operation should be conferred on the assent. It has been held by the Federal Court that the Constituent Assembly is competent to give retrospective effect to the assent. This Bill is being introduced in order to confer upon these Acts, retrospective operation from the date of their enactment irrespective of the date of assent.
>
> It is obvious that if the laws are not validated, the entire country would be thrown into a state of confusion and disorder. It is, therefore, hoped that the Assembly would pass this Bill into law and will save the country from confusion and disorder the limits of which are beyond conception."

The fact that the Constituent Assembly did not take any action to validate anything relating to the Pakistan Administrative Service or the Civil Service of Pakistan is meaningful and has consequences.

54. We are constrained to hold that the Pakistan Administrative Service or the Civil Service of Pakistan existed and functioned, from the appointed day till coming into force of the Civil Service of Pakistan (Composition and Cadre) Rules, 1954 in complete absence of any constitutional or statutory authority. These rules neither attempt nor are claimed to have filled the constitutional and statutory vacuum under which the Pakistan Administrative Service and the Civil Service of Pakistan worked during the aforesaid period. This conclusion drawn by us must not be misconstrued to mean that the requisite constitutional or statutory sanction was provided by the Civil Service of Pakistan (Composition and Cadre) Rules, 1954.

Question # 4

Whether the Civil Service of Pakistan (Composition and Cadre) Rules, 1954 are intra vires Section 241 of the Government of India Act, 1935, to the extent these rules create a Service of the Federation and reserve certain posts in connection with affairs of the Federation therefor?

55. Before undertaking an analysis of the rival contentions and offering views of this Court on the aforesaid question, it would be appropriate to first reproduce hereinbelow Resolution of the Government of Pakistan baring No. F.25/4/50-Ests (S.E.I) dated 08.11.1950 and the Civil Service of Pakistan (Composition and Cadre) Rules, 1954 (original as well as with up-to-date amendments):

Government of Pakistan

Cabinet Secretariat

(Establishment Branch)

Karachi, the 8ᵗʰ November, 1950

RESOLUTION

No.F.25/4/50-Ests (SEI). — Before the Partition, the premier administrative Service in India was the Indian Civil Service. This was a single service divided up into a number of cadres on a Provincial basis. Officers appointed to this Service were allotted to the various Provinces and they remained members of the Indian Civil Service cadre of their Provinces throughout their careers. **The Central Government met their own needs by the deputation of officers from the provinces.** There was also in undivided India the Indian Political Service, the two main sources of recruitment to which were the Indian Civil Service and the Indian Army.

2. The Government of Pakistan have decided to constitute their Civil Service as a centralized Service on an All-Pakistan basis. It will be called THE CIVIL SERVICE OF PAKISTAN. This decision has been taken in order to create a well-knit Civil Service for the whole of Pakistan, constituted and operated on a centralized basis, thereby increasing association between the various Provinces and developing homogeneity in administration. The members of this Service, who shall be liable to be posted to any of the Provinces of the Dominion, will be administratively more useful to the Central as well as the Provincial Governments than if they belonged to Provincial Cadres, because of the knowledge and experience they will acquire by serving in the Provinces of West Pakistan as well as in East Pakistan, and uniform standards of administration in all parts of the Dominion will also be achieved.

3. The Civil Service of Pakistan shall consist of a central cadre as distinct from the Provincial cadres of the former Indian Civil Service. All of the Service shall be liable to serve in any Province.

The Service shall consist of posts on the cadre of the former Indian Civil Service in the various Provinces and on the cadre of the former Indian Political Service and of most of the higher posts in the Central Secretariat. The posts which will form this centralized cadre are mentioned in the Annexure. Posts may in future be added to or removed from the cadre.

4. The principal decisions of Government with regard to the constitution of the Civil Service are given below: —

Initial Composition of the Service

Initially, the Civil Service of Pakistan shall be composed of the following: -

(a)   Officers of the former Indian Civil Service and the former Indian Political Service employed in Pakistan in continuation of service (other than those who might be transferred to the Pakistan Foreign Service);

(b)   Officers appointed to the Pakistan Administrative Service;

(c)   Officers to be recruited on an ad hoc basis from the Provincial Civil Services, in numbers not exceeding, for each PROVINCE, 10 percent of the duty posts reserved for the Civil Service of Pakistan in that Province.

The Central Government will lay down the procedure of making recruitment from the Provincial Civil Services.

Normal recruitment to the Service

In future, recruitment to the Service shall be made by selection on the basis of an open competitive examination to be held each year by the Federal Public Service Commission except in the case of officers of the Armed Forces, who may be appointed to the Service on the recommendations of the Commission arrived at through an interview and a scrutiny of service records.

Appointment and training

(1) Appointments to the Service shall be made by the Central Government.

(2) Candidates appointed direct to the Service will be appointed on probation and will be required to undergo training in the Civil Service Academy at Lahore.

(3) Rules regulating the conduct, discipline and training of probationers will be issued separately by the Central Government.

(4) A probationer on successful completion of his probation may be confirmed in the Service.

Initial postings and liability for transfer

(1) Transfers from one Province to another or from the Centre to a Province and *vice versa* shall be made by the Federal Government in consultation with the Provincial Governments concerned and shall be regulated in the interest of sound administration, prospects of promotion, suitability of officers for particular appointments and similar other considerations......................

(2) The units within which the centre will make transfers shall be—

(a) East Bengal,

(b) Punjab,

(c) Sind, and

(d) Frontier i.e. NWFP. Tribal Areas

Promotion and Leave

(1) Promotions from the junior scale to the senior scale on an officiating basis may be made by the Provincial Government concerned, but the Central Government shall be informed.

(2) Substantive appointments to the senior scale shall be made by the Federal Government on the recommendations of the Pakistan Public Service Commission, who will ascertain the views of the Provincial Government concerned and forward them to the Central Government with their own recommendations.

(3) Appointments at the Centre, including appointments of secretaries to Government, shall be treated as tenure appointments.

(4) The Provincial Governments may grant leave to officers of the Service for a period of 4 months or less. Leave in excess of 4 months shall be granted by the Central Government.

Listed Posts in Provinces

(1) Posts not exceeding 25 percent of the Superior posts allocated to the Provinces in the Annexure shall be treated as Listed appointments, which officers of the Provincial Civil Services will be eligible to hold. The position shall, however, be reviewed after 5 years.

(2) Promotion to Listed Posts shall be made in consultation with the Federal Public Service Commission, in accordance with the procedure which may be laid down by the Federal Government.

(3) Provincial Governments may make promotions to Listed Posts only on an officiating basis and in each case the Federal Government shall be informed. Confirmations in the Listed Posts shall be made by the Federal Government, on the recommendations of the Provincial Governments and in consultation with the Federal Public Service Commission.

(4) In the matter of disciplinary safeguards, permanent holders of Listed Posts shall have the same rights as members of the Service.

(5) Holders of Listed Posts shall not be liable to be transferred away from Provinces in which they are serving except to the Centre.

Appointments to Posts at the Centre

1. Not less than 2/3rd of posts of Deputy Secretary at the Centre shall be reserved for officers of the Service. For the remaining posts in these grades, officers of the Service as well as officers not belonging to the Service, i.e., officers of the Central Services Class I, the Secretariat Service, the General Administrative Reserve and the Provincial Services, shall be eligible.

This decision shall be reviewed at the end of 5 years.

2. Not less than 2/3rd of posts of Secretary and Joint Secretary at the Federal taken together shall be reserved for the Service but officers of the Service as well as officers not belonging to the service shall be eligible for appointment to the remaining posts in those grades.

Note: — The above decisions shall apply to posts other than the posts which may be included in the Pool of officers which is being constituted on the lines of the Pool of the Finance and Commerce Departments in undivided India.

5. **ORDERED** that this Resolution should be published in the official Gazette.

Civil Service of Pakistan (Composition and Cadre) Rules, 1954 (Original)

WHEREAS the Governor-General and the Governors of East Bengal, the Punjab, Sindh and the North-West Frontier Province have agreed that there shall be constituted a Service of the Federation to be known as the Civil Service of Pakistan and that certain posts in connection with the affairs of the Provinces shall be filled by members of that Service and specify, as far as need be, the conditions of service of its members, whether serving in posts in connection with the affairs of the Federation or of a Province:

NOW, THEREFORE, in pursuance of that agreement and in exercise of the powers conferred by sub-sections (1) and (2) of section 241 of the Government of India Act, 1935, and of all other provisions empowering him in this behalf, the Governor-General is pleased to make the following Rules: -

1. These Rules may be cited as the Civil Service of Pakistan (Composition and Cadre) Rules, 1954.

2. In these Rules, unless the context otherwise requires:
    (a) "Cadre post" means any duty post included in the Schedule;
    (b) "Commission" means the Pakistan Public Service Commission;
    (c) "Service" means the Civil Service of Pakistan.

3. Appointments to the Service shall be made by the Governor-General on the results of the open competitive examinations held by the Commission.

4. Persons appointed to the Service shall, unless the Governor-General otherwise directs, be appointed on probation and the Governor-General may make rules specifying the terms and incidents of such probation. In particular, he may provide for the removal from the Service during his term of probation of any person whose conduct and progress is unsatisfactory or for the withholding of increments from such persons.

5. The Cadre posts shall be filled either by members of the Service or by persons, not being members of the Service, in accordance with provisions of these Rules.

6. (1) Not more than 40% of the Cadre posts of Under-Secretary under the Central Government and not more than one-third of the Cadre posts of Deputy Secretary under the Central Government may be filled by officers not being members of the Service.

(2) Not more than one-third of the total of the Cadre posts of Secretary and Joint Secretary under the Central Government, taken together, may be filled by persons not being members of the Service.

Note:- The above shall apply only to posts other than those included in the Cadre of Finance & Commerce Pool.

7. (1) Cadre posts not exceeding 25% of the Superior Executive Posts in any Province may be filled by members of the Provincial Civil

Services (Executive Branch). Such appointments shall be made by the Governor-General on the recommendation of the Provincial Governments and in consultation with the Commission.

(2) Not more than one-third of the posts of District and Sessions Judge and equivalent Superior Judicial posts in Provinces shall be filled by recruitment from the Bar and not less than one-third from the Provincial Civil (Judicial) Services.

8. (1) The Governor-General, in the case of posts in connection with the affairs of the Federation, and the Governor in the case of posts in connection with the affairs of a Province, may, as the exigencies of the public service require, appoint a person not being a member of the Service to any Cadre post.

(2) Every such appointment made by a Governor shall be provisional and, if the person so appointed is intended to hold the appointment for a period exceeding 3 months, shall forthwith be reported to the Governor-General with the reasons for making it and if the Governor-General so directs the Governor shall thereupon cancel the appointment.

(3) Any person appointed to hold a Cadre post under this rule shall not be employed in the post for a period exceeding 12 months save with the previous sanction of the Governor-General.

9. (1) If a Governor proposes to keep any Cadre post in connection with the affairs of a Province vacant for a period exceeding 3 months, he shall forthwith make a report to the Governor-General of the reasons for the proposal, the period for which he proposes to keep the post vacant and whether it is proposed to make any and, if so, what arrangements for the performance of the duties of the post held in abeyance.

(2) If the Governor-General directs that the post shall be filled, the Governor shall appoint a person to fill it in accordance with the provisions of these rules.

10. The Governor-General may, by special or general order, temporarily dispense with the provisions of rules 8 and 9 requiring a Governor to report to the Governor-General any case in which a Cadre post is filled otherwise than under rule 7 by a person not being a member of the Service or in which a Cadre post is kept vacant for a period exceeding 3 months.

11. The Governor of a Province may direct that two Cadre posts in connection with the affairs of a Province shall be held jointly if he considers this necessary for the purpose of facilitating any leave arrangement or for a period not exceeding 3 months if he considers this necessary for any other purpose.

12. No change shall be made in the duties of the holder of any reserved post if, in the opinion of the Governor-General, the character of that post would thereby be altered:

Provided that this shall not apply to a temporary change consequential on leave arrangements or to a change not arising from leave arrangements which will not last more than three months.

13. The Governor-General may, from time to time, and in the case of posts in connection with the affairs of a Province, after consultation with the Governor of that Province, remove any post from the Schedule or include any post therein.

14. An officer belonging to Service shall be liable to serve anywhere

in Pakistan under the Central Government and may be deputed by that Government to serve under a Provincial Government. He shall submit himself to the orders of the Government under which he is serving for the time being and of all the officers and authorities under whom he may from time to time be placed by that Government. His whole time shall be at the disposal of the Government under which he is serving.

15. The transfer of an officer belonging to the Service from one Province to another or from the Centre to a Province or from a Province to the Centre shall be made by the Central Government in consultation with the Provincial Government or Governments concerned.

16.The Governor-General may, by rules, provide for the conduct and discipline of officers of the Service, and officers of the Service shall at all times obey such rules, and shall perform such duties as may be assigned to them.

17. Subject to the provisions of section 10 of the Indian Independence Act, 1947, the Governor-General may frame rules regulating the remuneration and other conditions of service of officers of the Service.

[Authority. --- **Estt. Division Notification No. F.25/12/51-SEI, dated 1-6-1954].**

SCHEDULE

CIVIL SERVICE OF PAKISTAN

CADRE STRENGTH

Superior Posts

CENTRE-

Secretaries in Ministries other than Ministries of Finance, Commerce, Economic Affairs and Foreign Affairs and Commonwealth Relations	8
Joint Secretaries in Ministries other than Ministries of Finance, Commerce, Economic Affairs and Foreign Affairs and Commonwealth Relations	12
Deputy Secretaries in Ministries other than Ministries of Finance, Commerce, Economic Affairs and Foreign Affairs and Commonwealth Relations	42
	--- 62

Posts under the Ministries of Finance, Commerce and Economic Affairs	18

EAST BENGAL

Chief Secretary	1
Member, Board of Revenue	1
Commissioners	3
Secretaries	8
Joint Secretaries	3
Deputy Secretaries	5

Provincial Transport Commissioner	1
District Magistrates	17
Additional District Magistrate	10
District Judges	15
Additional District Judges	8
Director of Land Records and Survey	1
Settlement Officer	1
Private Secretary to Governor	1
Secretary to Chief Minister	1
Commissioner of Excise and Taxation	1
Registrar of Co-operative Societies	1
Registrar, High Court	1
Judge, High Court	2
	81
Posts to be filled by promotion of Provincial Civil Service Officers at 25%	20
	61

PUNJAB

Financial Commissioner	1
Development Commissioner	1
Chief Secretary	1
Commissioners	3
Secretaries	4
Legal Rememberancer	1
Deputy Secretaries	4
Secretary to Governor	1
Secretary to Chief Minister	1
Deputy Commissioners	16
Colonization and Settlement Officers	4
Excise and Taxation Commissioner	1
Provincial Transport Controller	1
Director of Industries	1

Registrar of Co-operative Societies	1
Judges of High Court	2
Registrar, High Court	1
District and Sessions Judges	12
Additional District and Sessions Judges	2
	58

Posts to be filled by promotion of Provincial Civil Service Officers at 25%	14
	44

SIND

Chief Secretary	1
Secretaries	3
Secretary to Governor	1
Deputy Secretaries	2
Revenue Commissioners	1
Collectors	7
Deputy Commissioners, Upper Sind Frontier	1
Manager, Encumbered Estates	1
Revenue Officer, Lloyd Barrage	1
Anti-Corruption Officer	1
Judge, Chief Court	2
District and Sessions Judges	4
Rememberancer of Legal Affairs	1
	26
Posts to be filled by promotion of Provincial Civil Service Officers at 25%	6
	20

N.W.F.P

Revenue and Divisional Commissioner	1
Chief Secretary	1
Secretaries	6
Secretary to Governor	1

Political Agents, Kurram, Khyber, North Waziristan, Malakand and South Waziristan and Mohmands	6
Deputy Commissioners	6
Judicial Commissioner	1
District and Sessions Judges	3
Senior Sub-Judge, Peshawar	1
Additional District and Sessions Judges	2
Political Secretary to Governor	1
	29
Posts to be filled by promotion of Provincial Civil Service Officers at 25%	7
	22

BALUCHISTAN

Agent to the Governor-General	1
Revenue and Judicial Commissioner	1
Secretary to Agent to the Governor-General	1
District and Sessions Judge	1
Political Agent	5
	9
Posts to be filled by promotion of Provincial Civil Service Officers at 25%	2
	7

KARACHI

Chief Commissioner	1
Collector and District Magistrate	1
Additional District Magistrate	1
Secretaries to the Chief Commissioner	3
	6
Total	240
Posts to be filled by direct recruitment	0
Deputation Reserve at 15%	
Leave Reserve at 15%	
Training Reserve at 1%	4

Junior Posts
Centre

Posts of Under Secretaries in Ministries other than	50

Ministries of Finance, Commerce, Economic Affairs and Foreign Affairs and Commonwealth Relations	
Posts in Ministries of Finance, Commerce and Economic Affairs	14

EAST BENGAL	20
PUNJAB	10
SIND	11
N.W.F.P.	16
BALUCHISTAN	5
KARACHI	8
	134

Direct recruitment posts	470
Promotion posts	40
TOTAL AUTHORIZED STRENGTH	510

Civil Service of Pakistan (Composition and Cadre) Rules, 1954 (Amended upto date)

WHEREAS the Governor-General and the Governors of the Punjab, Sindh and the North-West Frontier Province have agreed that there shall be constituted a Service of the Federation to be known as the Pakistan Administrative Service and that certain posts in connection with the affairs of the Provinces shall be filled by members of that Service and specify, as far as need be, the conditions of service of its members, whether serving in posts in connection with the affairs of the Federation or of a Province:

NOW, THEREFORE, in pursuance of that agreement and in exercise of the powers conferred by Article 146 of the Constitution of Islamic Republic of Pakistan, 1973, and of all other provisions empowering him in this behalf, the President is pleased to make the following Rules: -

1. These Rules may be cited as the Civil Service of Pakistan (Composition and Cadre) Rules, 1954.

2. In these Rules, unless the context otherwise requires:

   (a) "Cadre post" means any duty post included in the Schedule;
   (b) "Commission" means the Pakistan Public Service Commission;
   (c) "Service" means the Civil Service of Pakistan.

3. Appointment to the service shall be made by the President on the basis of results of open competitive examination held by the Federal Public Service Commission, except in the case of officer of the Armed Forces, who may be appointed to the Service on the recommendation of the FPSC arrived at through an interview and a scrutiny of services record.

4. Persons appointed to the Service shall, unless the President otherwise directs, be appointed on probation and the President may make rules specifying the terms and incidents of such probation. In

particular, he may provide for the removal from the Service during his term of probation of any person whose conduct and progress is unsatisfactory or for the withholding of increments from such persons.

5. (1) The cadre posts shall be filled either by members of the Service or by persons not being members of the Service, appointed in accordance with the provisions of these Rules.

(2) The tenure of the member of the Service appointed to a Provincial sub-Cadre post other than a Chief Secretary appointed under Rule 15, shall be determined by the Provincial Government by Order.

(3) The tenure of the member of the Service appointed to a Federal sub-Cadre post shall be determined by the Federal Government by Order.

(4) A person who is not a member of the Service, temporarily appointed to a Provincial or Federal sub-Cadre post may not hold that post for a period exceeding one year, save with the approval of the Federal Government or the Provincial Government as the case may be.

6. (1) The posts described and borne on the "Schedule" of the Federal sub-Cadre appended herewith, excluding the posts in the Federal Secretariat specified below, shall be reserved for the officers of the Pakistan Administrative Service, namely: —

(i) 75% of the sanctioned posts of Deputy Secretary.

(ii) 65% of the sanctioned posts of Joint Secretary.

(iii) 100% posts of Senior Joint Secretary.

(iv) 35% of the sanctioned posts of Additional Secretary.

(v) 35% of the sanctioned posts of Federal Secretary.

(2) The Federal posts excluded under sub-rule (1) above, shall be reserved and apportioned amongst other services under the Federal responsibility, as may be specified by the Federal Government from time to time in public interest, keeping in view the deputation reserves of various services without further consultations with the federating units.

7.(1) The sanctioned posts in the respective Provincial sub-Cadre of the Schedule as specified below shall be reserved for the officers of the Pakistan Administrative Service as per agreed Posts-Sharing arrangement: —

BS-17	BS-18	BS-19	BS-20	BS-21
25%	40%	50%	60%	65%

(2) The officers of the Provincial Management Services/Provincial Civil Services, recruited directly in BS-17 through respective Provincial Public Service Commission and have held a Cadre Post in the Province for not less than five years, shall be eligible for appointment in the Pakistan Administrative Service, against Cadre Posts, not more than

30% of the superior posts, borne on the Federal sub-cadre in BPS-19 and above on the recommendations of the respective Provincial Government, by the Federal Public Service Commission, in a prescribed manner.

(3) An officer appointed under Rule 7(2) in the Service, shall not be liable to serve anywhere except the Province of his initial residence or under the Federal Government.

8. (1) The President, in the case of posts in connection with the affairs of the Federation, and the Governor in the case of posts in connection with the affairs of a Province, may, as the exigencies of the public service require, appoint a person not being a member of the Service to any Cadre post.

(2) Every such appointment made by a Governor shall be provisional and, if the person so appointed is intended to hold the appointment, for a period exceeding 3 months, shall forthwith be reported to the President with the reasons for making it and if the President so directs the Governor shall thereupon cancel the appointment.

(3) Any person appointed to hold a Cadre post under this rule shall not be employed in the post for a period exceeding 12 months save with the previous sanction of the President.

9. (1) If a Governor proposes to keep any Cadre post in connection with the affairs of a Province vacant for a period exceeding 3 months, he shall forthwith make a report to the President of the reasons for the proposal, the period for which he proposes to keep the post vacant and whether it is proposed to make any and, if so, what arrangements for the performance of the duties of the post held in abeyance.

(2) If the President directs that the post shall be filled, the Governor shall appoint a person to fill it in accordance with the provisions of these rules.

10. The President may by special or general order temporarily dispense with the provisions of rules 8 and 9 requiring a Governor to report to the President any case in which a Cadre post is filled otherwise than under rule 7 by a person not being a member of the Service or in which a Cadre post is kept vacant for a period exceeding 3 months.

11. The Governor of a Province may direct that two Cadre posts in connection with the affairs of a Province shall be held jointly if he considers this necessary for the purpose of facilitating any leave arrangement or for a period not exceeding 3 months if he considers this necessary for any other purpose.

12. No change shall be made in the duties of the holder of any reserved post if, in the opinion of the President, the character of that post would thereby be altered:

Provided that this shall not apply to a temporary change consequential on leave arrangements or to a change not arising from leave arrangements which will not last more than three months.

13. (1) The President may from time to time, and in the case of posts in connection with the affairs of a Province, after consultation with the Governor of that Province, remove any post from the Schedule or include any post therein.

(2) A Governor may, if the exigencies of the public service so require, create a cadre post in connection with the affairs of a Province below the rank of a Commissioner of a Division, for a period not exceeding three months. If subsequently the Governor proposes to retain that cadre post for a further period, he shall forthwith make a report to the President of the reasons for the proposal and the period for which he proposes to retain that post and shall act in accordance with such directions as the President may give.

14. An officer belonging to the Service shall be liable to serve anywhere in Pakistan under the Federal Government and may be deputed by that Government to serve under a Provincial Government. He shall submit himself to the orders of the Government under which he is serving for the time being and of all the officers and authorities under whom he may from time to time be placed by that Government. His whole time shall be at the disposal of the Government under which he is serving.

15. (i) The transfer of an officer belonging to the Service from the Province to another or from the Federation to a Province or from a Province to the Federation shall be made by Federal Government in consultation with the Provincial Government or Governments concerned.

(ii) A Provincial Government may post an officer belonging to the Service whose services have been placed at its disposal on any Cadre-post or equivalent in the public interest, under intimation to the Federal Government.

(iii) An officer so deputed to a Provincial Government shall not be posted in a higher post except with the approval of the Provincial Government and in accordance with the prescribed procedure.

(iv) A PAS officer shall be posted a Chief Secretary in a Province by the Federal Government in consultation with the Provincial Government concerned and due consideration will be given to the recommendations of the Provincial Governments:

Provided that consultation will mean the intimation of a name, or a panel of names of PAS officers to be conveyed to the Provincial Government concerned for such a posting, preferably in writing. If there is no response from a Provincial Government within 15 days, the Federal Government will proceed to make such an appointment of the named officer or any such officer named on the panel and it will be deemed to have the approval of the Provincial Government concerned:

Provided further that if urgency so warrants, the Federal Government may convey its proposal by telephone/fax or any other means and hold necessary consultation with the Provincial Government concerned. If there is no response upto 15 days, the Federal Government will proceed to pass appropriate orders. A written confirmation of the proceedings would be sent in each such case.

(v) The procedure of deputing to and withdrawal from any Province of a PAS officer will be the same as indicated above, except that Provincial Government may respond to the proposal within a period of one month.

16. (1) The President may by rules provide for the conduct and discipline of officers of the Service, and officers of the Service shall at all times obey such rules, and shall perform such duties as may be assigned to them.

(2) Notwithstanding anything contained in any other law, rule, contract or instructions to the contrary for the time being in force any person holding a Provincial or Federal sub-Cadre post may be directed by the appropriate government to report to another duty post, station, for training and proceed on leave, as per prescribed procedure.

17. The Cadre Schedule appended to the 1954 Agreement shall be amended from time to time, as per Rules 6 and 7 in consultation with Provinces.

[Authority. - Estt. Division's Notification No. F.25/12/51-SEI, dated 1-6-1954].

Schedule of Cadre strength of the Pakistan Administrative Service

FEDERAL GOVERNMENT

Superior posts

All posts of Deputy Secretary under the Federal Government and all posts of and above the rank of Joint Secretary under the Federal Government or borne on the strength of a Corporation set up or established by, or an organization or an establishment subordinate to, the Federal Government.

BALOCHISTAN

Superior posts of Commissioner's level and above	5
Chief Secretary	1
Member, Board of Revenue	1
Revenue Commissioner	1
Home Secretary	1
Commissioner, Planning and Development	1
Superior posts of senior scale level	7
Junior posts	3

SINDH

Superior posts of Commissioner's level and above	13
Chief Secretary	1
Member, Board of Revenue	1
Additional Member, Board of Revenue	2
Secretary	6
Revenue Commissioner	1
Land Commissioner	1
Commissioner, Social Security Institution	1
Superior posts of senior scale level	43
Junior posts	28

PUNJAB

Superior posts of Commissioner's level and above	24
Chief Secretary	1
Additional Chief Secretary	2
Additional Chief Land Commissioner	1
Member, Board of Revenue	4
Land Commissioner	2
Divisional Commissioner	5
Secretary	9
Superior posts of senior scale level	51
Junior posts	40

N.W.F.P

Superior posts of Commissioner's level and above	8
Chief Secretary	1
Development Commissioner	1
Divisional Commissioner	3
Member, Board of Revenue	1
Secretary	2
Superior posts of senior scale level	15
Junior posts	13

56. The preamble of the Civil Service of Pakistan (Composition and Cadre) Rules, 1954 provides that the Governor-General and the Governors of East Bengal, the Punjab, Sindh and the North-West Frontier Province had agreed that there shall be constituted a Service of the Federation to be known as the Civil Service of Pakistan and that certain posts in connection with affairs of the Provinces shall be filled by members of that Service and conditions of service of its members, whether serving in posts in connection with the affairs of the Federation or of a Province, shall be specified. It merits to be noted that no agreement between the Governor-General and the Governors was referred to in the Resolution of the Government of Pakistan, reproduced earlier in this judgment. Moreover, whereas in case of a company, a resolution is a conclusive determination of policy of the company by the vote of its board of directors, in case of legislative and executive bodies of the Government, it is a mere expression of something which do not have the effect of law and, therefore, is neither binding nor capable of conferring power and jurisdiction beyond what is sanctioned by or under the applicable law. It has not been indicated that which body approved the resolution. Irrespective of what body expressed itself in the form of this resolution, its legal sanctity has to be adjudged on the touchstone of the Constitution and the laws made thereunder and even if any legal effect is intended to be given to the expression of opinion contained in the resolution, the same shall be given by the competent authority in the prescribed manner through appropriate legal instrument.

57. Sub-sections (1) and (2) of section 241 of the Government of India Act, 1935 were cited as the enabling provisions for making of the original Civil Service of Pakistan (Composition and Cadre) Rules, 1954. Section 241 of the Government of India Act, 1935 reads as follows:

"(1) Except as expressly provided by this Act, appointments to the civil services of, and civil posts under, the Crown in India, shall, after the commencement of Part III of this Act, be made-

(a) in the case of services of the Federation, and posts in connection with the affairs of the Federation, by the Governor-General or such person as he may direct;

(b) in the case of services of a Province, and posts in connection with the affairs of a Province, by the Governor or such person as he may direct.

(2)   Except as expressly provided by this Act, the conditions of service of persons serving His Majesty in a civil capacity in India shall, subject to the provisions of this section, be such as may be prescribed---

    (a)   in the case of persons serving in connection with the affairs of the Federation, by rules made by the Governor-General or by some person or persons authorized by the Governor-General to make rules for the purpose;

    (b)   in the case of persons serving in connection with the affairs of a Province, by rules made by the Governor of the Province or by some person or persons authorized by the Governor to make rules for the purpose:

Provided that it shall not be necessary to make rules regulating the conditions of service of persons employed temporarily on the terms that their employment may be terminated on one month's notice or less, and nothing in this subsection shall be construed as requiring the rules regulating the conditions of service of any class of persons to extend to any matter which appears to the rule-making authority to be a matter not suitable for regulation by rule in the case of that class.

(3)   The said rules shall be so framed as to secure---

    (a)   that, in the case of a person who before the commencement of Part III of this Act was serving His Majesty in a civil capacity in India, no order which alters or interprets to his disadvantage any rule by which his conditions of service are regulated shall be made except by an authority which would have been competent to make such an order on the eighth day of March, nineteen hundred and twenty-six, or by some person empowered by the Secretary of State to give directions in that respect;

    (b)   that every such person as aforesaid shall have the same rights of appeal to the same authorities from any order which --

        (i)   punishes or formally censures him; or

        (ii)   alters or interprets to his disadvantage any rule by which his conditions of service are regulated; or

        (iii)   terminates his appointment otherwise than upon his reaching the age fixed for superannuation,

as he would have had immediately before the commencement of Part III of this Act, or such similar rights of appeal to such corresponding authorities as may be directed by the Secretary of State or by some person empowered by the Secretary of State to give directions in that respect;

    (c)   that every other person serving His Majesty in a civil capacity in India shall have at least one appeal against any such order as aforesaid, not being an order of the Governor-General or a Governor.

(4)   Notwithstanding anything in this section, but subject to any other provision of this Act, Acts of the appropriate

Legislature in India may regulate the conditions of service of persons serving His Majesty in a civil capacity in India, and any rules made under this section shall have effect subject to the provisions of any such Act:

Provided that nothing in any such Act shall have effect so as to deprive any person of any rights required to be given to him by the provisions of the last preceding subsection.

(5)   No rules made under this section and no Act of any Legislature in India shall be construed to limit or abridge the power of the Governor-General or a Governor to deal with the case of any person serving His Majesty in a civil capacity in India in such manner as may appear to him to be just and equitable:

Provided that, where any such rule or Act is applicable to the case of any person, the case shall not be dealt with in any manner less favourable to him than that provided by that rule or Act."

58.   Section 241 of the Government of India Act, 1935 grants exclusive rule-making jurisdiction to the Governor-General in respect of appointments to federal posts and services and determination of conditions of service of members of federal services or persons holding posts in connection with affairs of the federation. No party to this case has objected to the exclusive jurisdiction of the Governor-General with respect to the Services of the Federation and determination of conditions of recruitment and of service of their members or the posts in connection with affairs of the Federation by the Governor-General. Keeping this in view, the Civil Service of Pakistan (Composition and Cadre) Rules, 1954, to the extent these rules create a Service of the Federation to be known as the Civil Service of Pakistan and reserve certain posts in connection with affairs of the Federation for that Service cannot be declared ultra vires Section 241 of the Government of India Act, 1935. The power granted to the Federation under Section 241 of the Government of India Act, 1935 includes power to reserve posts in connection with affairs of the Federation for a Service of the Federation. The Federation also has lawful competence to provide for appointment of members of the Provincial Services to a Service of the Federation. The same position was maintained in the subsequent Constitutions of the Islamic Republic of Pakistan, relevant Articles whereof are reproduced hereinbelow to serve as ready reference:

Article 182 of the Constitution of the Islamic Republic of Pakistan, 1956

Recruitment and conditions of service

(1)   Except as expressly provided by the Constitution or an Act of the appropriate legislature, appointments to the civil services of, and civil posts in the service of, Pakistan shall be made-

(a)   in the case of services of the Federation and posts in connection with the affairs of the Federation, by the President or such person as he may direct;

(b)   in the case of services of a Province or posts in connection with the affairs of a Province, by the Governor, or such person as he may direct.

(2)   Except as expressly provided by the Constitution, or an Act of the appropriate legislature, the conditions of service of persons serving in a civil capacity shall, subject to the provisions of this Article, be such as may be prescribed-

(a)   in the case of persons serving in connection with the affairs of the Federation, by rules made by the President, or by some person authorized by the President to make rules for the purpose;

(b)   in the case of persons serving in connection with the affairs of a Province, by rules made by the Governor, or by some person authorized by the Governor to make rules for the purpose;

Provided that it shall not be necessary to make rules regulating the conditions of service of persons employed temporarily on the condition that their employment may be terminated on one month's notice or les; and nothing in this clause shall be construed as requiring the rules regulating the conditions of service of any class of persons to extend to any matter which appears to the rule-making authority to be a matter not suitable for regulation by rule in the case of that class:

Provided further that no such Act as is referred to in this clause shall contain anything inconsistent with the provisions of clause (3).

(3)   The rules under clause (2) shall be so framed as to secure-

(a)   that the tenure and conditions of service of any person to whom this Article applies shall not be varied to his disadvantage; and

(b)   that every such person shall have at least one appeal against any order which-

    (i)   punishes or formally censures him; or

    (ii)   alters or interpret to his disadvantage any rule affecting his conditions of service; or

    (iii)   terminates his employment otherwise than upon reaching the age fixed for superannuation:

Provided that when any such order of the President or of the Governor, the person affected shall have no right of appeal, but may apply for review of that order.

Article 178 of the Constitution of Islamic Republic of Pakistan, 1962

(1) Subject to this Constitution and law -

(a)   appointments to an All-Pakistan Service or to a civil service of the Centre, or to a civil post in connection with the affairs of the Centre, shall be made by the President or a person authorized by the President in that behalf; and

(b)   appointments to a civil service of a Province, or to a civil post in connection with the affairs of a Province, shall be made by the Governor of the Province or a person authorized by the Governor in that behalf.

(2)   Subject to this Constitution and law, the terms and conditions of service of persons serving in a civil capacity in the service of Pakistan (other than persons whose terms and conditions of service are specified in this Constitution) shall be as prescribed-

(a)   in the case of a person who is a member of an All-Pakistan Service or who is serving in connection with the affairs of the Centre- by rules made by the President or by a person authorized by the President in that behalf; and

(b)   in the case of a person (not being a member of an All-Pakistan Service) who is serving in connection with the affairs of a

Province- by rules made by the Governor of the Province or by a person authorized by the Governor in that behalf.

(3)   Rules made for the purposes of clause (2) of this Article shall be so framed as to ensure-

(a)   that the terms and conditions of service of a person (in so far those terms and conditions relate to remuneration or age fixed for superannuation) are not varied to his disadvantage; and

(b)   that where an order is made which-

(i)   punishes or formally censures a person;

(ii)   alters or interprets to the disadvantage of a person any rule affecting his terms or conditions of service; or

(iii)   terminates the employment of a person otherwise than upon his reaching the age fixed for superannuation,

he shall, except where the order is made by the President or a Governor, have at least one appeal against the order and, where the order is made by the President or a Governor, he shall have the right to apply to the "President or the Governor for a review of the order.

Article 217 of the interim Constitution of 1972
Subject to this Constitution, the appointment of persons to, and terms and conditions of service of persons in, the service of Pakistan may be regulated by law.

Article 221 of the interim Constitution of 1972
(1) Subject to this Constitution and law. -
(a) appointments to an All-Pakistan Service or to a civil service of the Federation, or to a civil post in connection with the affairs of the Federation, shall be made by the President or a person authorized by the President in that behalf; and
(b) appointments to a civil service of a Province, or to a civil post in connection with affairs of a Province, shall be made by the Governor of the Province or a person authorized by the Governor in that behalf.
(2) Subject to this Constitution and law, the terms and conditions of persons serving in a civil capacity in the Service of Pakistan (other than persons whose terms and conditions of service are prescribed in this Constitution) shall be as prescribed-
(a) In the case of a person who is a member of an All-Pakistan Service or who is serving in connection with affairs of the Federation, by rules made by the President or by a person authorized by the President in that behalf; and
(b) In the case of a person, not being a member of an All Pakistan Service, who is serving in connection with the affairs of the Province, by rules made by the Governor of the Province or by a person authorized by the Governor in that behalf.
(3)---.
(4)----.

Article 240 of the Constitution of the Islamic Republic of Pakistan, 1973

"Subject to the Constitution, the appointments to and the conditions of service of persons in the service of Pakistan shall be determined-

(a)   in the case of the services of the Federation, posts in connection with the affairs of the Federation and All- Pakistan Services, by or under Act of [Majlis- e- Shoora (Parliament)]; and

(b)   in the case of the services of a Province and posts in connection with the affairs of a Province, by or under Act of the Provincial Assembly.

Explanation. - In this Article, "All- Pakistan Service" means a service common to the Federation and the Provinces, which was in existence immediately before the commencing day or which may be created by Act of [Majlis- e- Shoora (Parliament)].

Article 260 of the Constitution of the Islamic Republic of Pakistan, 1973

"Service of Pakistan" means any service, post or office in connection with the affairs of the Federation or of a Province, and includes an All- Pakistan Service, service in the Armed Forces and any other service declared to be a service of Pakistan by or under Act of Majlis- e- Shoora (Parliament) or of a Provincial Assembly, but does not include service as Speaker, Deputy Speaker, Chairman, Deputy Chairman, Prime Minister, Federal Minister, Minister of State, Chief Minister, Provincial Minister, Attorney- General, Advocate- General, Parliamentary Secretary or Chairman or member of a Law Commission, Chairman or member of the Council of Islamic Ideology, Special Assistant to the Prime Minister, Adviser to the Prime Minister, Special Assistant to Chief Minister, Adviser to a Chief Minister or member of a House or a Provincial Assembly;"

59.   It is not the case of the petitioners before us that the Federation was not competent under the successive constitutions to create and regulate Services of the Federation and determine conditions of recruitment and of service of members of those Services. It has also not been disputed that posts in connection with affairs of the Federation can be encadred or reserved for a Service of the Federation through a suitable legislative instrument. The prayer of the petitioners to declare the Civil Service of Pakistan (Composition and Cadre) Rules, 1954, illegal, ultra vires the Constitution and unsustainable in their entirety, is, therefore, not legally tenable. This prayer is consequently turned down and it is declared that the Civil Service of Pakistan (Composition and Cadre) Rules, 1954, suffer from no constitutional or statutory infirmity in respect of the following matters:

(1)   Creation of the Civil Service of Pakistan as a Service of the Federation;

(2)   Reservation of certain posts in connection with affairs of the Federation for the Civil Service of Pakistan;

(3)   Provisions regarding appointments of persons belonging to the Provincial Services in the Civil Service of Pakistan as a Service of the Federation through appointment by transfer; and

(4)   Subject to the Constitution, determination of conditions of recruitment and of service of members of the Civil Service of Pakistan as a Service of the Federation to the extent as specified in the said Rules.

60.   In order to obviate chances of misunderstanding, it is clarified that the declarations made in the paragraph hereinabove are without prejudice to judicial determination of

legality of the Civil Service of Pakistan (Composition and Cadre) Rules, 1954 so far as these rules relate to the question of reservation of posts in connection with affairs of the Provinces and other allied questions which we intend to address later in this judgment.

Question # 5

Whether the Civil Service of Pakistan (Composition and Cadre) Rules, 1954 are intra vires Section 241 of the Government of India Act, 1935 to the extent these rules reserve certain posts in connection with affairs of the Provinces for a Service of the Federation i.e. the Civil Service of Pakistan?

61.   Section 241 of the Government of India Act, 1935 neither allowed reservation of posts in connection with affairs of the Provinces for a Service of the Federation nor envisaged surrender of authority of a Governor in respect of those posts or services of the Province, in part or full, to the Governor-General. There is no concept of All Pakistan Services in this Section. All the three Constitutions of Pakistan are silent on the question of reservation of posts in connection with affairs of the Provinces for a Service of the Federation. The dispensation of reservation of posts was introduced through Section 98 of the Government of India Act, 1915 in the following words:

> **"Offices reserved to the Indian Civil Service**
>
> Subject to the provisions of this Act, all vacancies happening in any of the offices specified or referred to in the Third Schedule to this Act, and all such offices which may be created hereafter, shall be filled from amongst the members of the Indian Civil Service."

62.   The same dispensation was continued through Section 246 of the Government of India Act, 1935, reproduced below:

> **"(1)**   The Secretary of State shall make rules specifying the number and character of the civil posts under the Crown (other than posts in connection with any functions of the Governor-General which the Governor-General is by or under this Act required to exercise in his discretion), which, subject to the provisions of this subsection, are to be filled by persons appointed by the Secretary of State to a civil service of, or a civil post under, the Crown in India, and except under such conditions as may be prescribed in the rules no such post shall, without the previous sanction of the Secretary of State-
>
> (a)   be kept vacant for more than three months; or
>
> (b)   be filled otherwise than by the appointment of such a person as aforesaid; or
>
> (c)   be held jointly with any other such post.
>
> **(2)**   Appointments and postings to the said posts (hereinafter in this Part of this Act referred to as "reserved posts") shall----
>
> (a)   in the case of posts in connection with the affairs of the Federation, be made by the Governor-General, exercising his individual judgment;
>
> (b)   in the case of posts in connection with the affairs of a Province, be made by the Governor of the Province, exercising his individual judgment.
>
> **(3)**   All rules made under this section shall, so soon as may be after they are made, be laid before each House of Parliament and, if either House of Parliament within the next subsequent twenty-eight days on which that House has sat after any such rule has been laid before it resolves that the rule shall be annulled, the rule shall thenceforth be void but without prejudice to the

validity of anything previously done thereunder or to the making of a new rule."

63.   The Government of India Act, 1935 was adapted as Provisional Constitution of Pakistan. Section 10 of the Indian Independence Act, 1947 and the Schedule to the Pakistan (Provisional Constitution) Order, 1947 deleted all provisions of the Government of India Act, 1935, which related to the Secretary of State for India, India Office, All India Services and reservation of posts in connection with affairs of a Province for an All India Service or a Service of the Federation. Sections 241 and 263 of the Government of India Act, 1935 are irrelevant to the concept of reservation of posts in connection with affairs of the Provinces for a Service of the Federation. The Constitution of Pakistan, 1956, 1962, interim Constitution of 1972 and Constitution of 1973 did not contain any provision similar to Section 98 of the Government of India Act, 1915 and Section 246 of the Government of India Act, 1935. In absence of any constitutional or statutory provision allowing reservation of posts in connection with affairs of a Province for a Service of the Federation, the Civil Service of Pakistan (Composition and Cadre) Rules, 1954 are in excess of lawful jurisdiction and, hence, are of no legal effect to this extent.

64.   It is a well settled principle of interpretation that:

> "Statutory rule cannot enlarge the scope of the section under which it is framed and if a rule goes beyond what the section contemplates, the rule must yield to the statute. The authority of executive to make rules and regulations, in order to effectuate the intention and policy of the Legislature, must be exercised within the limits of mandate given to the rule making authority and the rules framed under an enactment must be consistent with the provisions of said enactment. The rules framed under a statue, if are inconsistent with the provisions of the statute and defeat the intention of Legislature expressed in the main statue, same shall be invalid. The rule-making authority cannot clothe itself with power which is not given to it under the statute and thus the rules made under a statute, neither enlarge the scope of the Act nor can go beyond the Act and must not be in conflict with the provisions of statute or repugnant to any other law in force."

This principle of interpretation has been followed in the under mentioned cases: -

> Ahmad Hassan v. Govt. of Punjab 2005 SCMR 186, Institute of Patent Agents v. Lackwood (1894) AC 347, 359, 360, 364, 365; Harilal v. Deputy Director of Consolidation 1982 All LJ 223, Chief Inspector Mines v. K.C. Thapar AIR 1961 SC 838, 845, Narasimha Raju v. Brundavanasaha AIR 1943 Mad. 617, 621, Barisal Cooperative Central Bank v. Benoy Bhusan AIR 1934 Cal.537, Municipal Corporation v. Saw Willie AIR 1942 Rang. 70, 74, Hazrat Syed Shah Mustarshid Ali Al-Quadari v. Commissioner of Wakfs AIR 1954 Cal.436, Shankar Lal Laxmi Narayan Rathi v. Authority under Minimum Wages Act 1979 MPLJ 15, M.P. Kurmaraswami Raja AIR 1955 Mad. 326, K. Mathuvadivela v. RT Officer AIR 1956 Mad. 143, Kashi Prasad Saksena v.State of U.P. AIR 1967 All. 173, PLD 1975 Azad J&K 81, PLD 1966 Lah. 287, Shanta Prasad v. Collector, Nainital 1978 All. LJ 126, Dattatraya Narhar Pitale v. Vibhakar Dinka Gokhale 1975 Mah. LJ 701, Narayanan v. Food Inspector, Calicut Corporation 1979 Ker LT 469, Ganpat v. Lingappa AIR 1962 Bom. 104,105, Adarash Industrial Corporation v. Market Committee, Karnal AIR 1962 Punj. 426, 430, Shri Synthetics, Ltd, Ujjain v. Union of India 1982 Jab LJ 279, 1982 MPLJ 340, Central Bank of India v. Their Workmen AIR 1960 SC 12, Barisal Cooperative Central Bank v. Benoy Bhusan AIR 1934 Cal.537, 540, Rajam Chetti v. Seshayya ILR 18 Mad. 236, 245, Raghanallu

Naidu v. Corporation of Madras AIR 1930 Mad. 648, Pakistan v. Aryan Petro Chemical Industries (Pvt.) Ltd. 2003 SCMR 370, Ziauddin v. Punjab Local Government 1985 SCMR 365, Hirjina Salt Chemicals (Pak) Ltd. v. Union Council Gharo 1982 SCMR 522, Mehraj Flour Mills v. Provincial Government 2001 SCMR 1806, Collector of Sales Tax v. Superior Textile Mills Ltd. PLD 2001 SC 600.

65.   Since Section 241 and 263 of the Government of India Act, 1935 do not empower the Governor-General to encroach upon exclusive jurisdiction of the Governor in respect of services of the Province or posts in connection with affairs of the Province, therefore, he acted without lawful authority to the extent the Civil Service of Pakistan (Composition and Cadre) Rules, 1954 traveled beyond jurisdiction by dealing with posts in connection with affairs of a Province and reserving a certain number of those posts for the Civil Service of Pakistan. It has been held in Hoffmann-La Roche v. Secy. of State (1974)2 AII ER 1128, 1142 that a person acts unlawfully when he exceeds his powers or lacks powers.

66.   In view of, inter alia, the above discussion, we hold that reservation of posts in connection with affairs of the Provinces for the Civil Service of Pakistan under the Civil Service of Pakistan (Composition and Cadre) Rules, 1954 is, void ab initio, without lawful authority and jurisdiction and, therefore, of no legal effect.

Question # 6

Whether the Civil Service of Pakistan (Composition and Cadre) Rules, 1954 were framed by the Governor-General as a delegate of the Provincial Governors to the extent of posts in connection with affairs of the Provinces?

67.   The executive authority of the Federation and of the Provinces is co-extensive with the legislative powers of the Parliament and of the Provincial Assemblies, respectively. This executive authority includes subordinate legislation or rule-making where duly authorized by the concerned Legislature. Under the Government of India Act, 1935, Section 49, as adapted by the Pakistan (Provisional Constitution) Order, 1947, which served as the Constitution of Pakistan till the Constitution of 1956, the executive authority of a Province was to be exercised by the Governor, either directly or through officers subordinate to him. Section 59 (1) of the Act ibid provided that all executive actions of the Government of a Province shall be expressed to be taken in the name of the Governor. It was held in Sibnath Banerji case (AIR 1945 PC 156) that a Minister was an officer subordinate to the Governor-General. Following this analogy, it can safely be said that a Minister is the officer subordinate to the Governor in terms of Section 49 of the Government of India Act, 1935. In this view of the matter, powers conferred upon a Governor vide Section 241 of the Act ibid were available for exercise directly by the Governor himself or through a Provincial Minister. The Governor-General was not an officer subordinate to the Governor; hence, it was not permissible for him to exercise powers vested in the Governor with respect to services of the Province and posts in connection with affairs of the Province. A Governor was statutorily authorized to exercise his powers through officers subordinate to him and being subordinate to the Governor was a condition-precedent for being able to be a lawful delegate of the Governor. In the instant case, it cannot be said that the Governor-General was a lawful delegate of the Governor as he did not fall within the definition of an officer subordinate to the Governor. An agreement purporting to delegate powers of a Governor to a Governor-General in respect of services of the Province or posts in connection with affairs of the Province was ultra vires provisions of Section 241, 49 and 59 of the Government of India Act, 1935 and, hence, legally invalid. The superstructure of the Civil Service of Pakistan (Composition and Cadre) Rules, 1954, built upon an illegal instrument, is, therefore, without lawful authority and jurisdiction to the extent of posts in connection with affairs of the Provinces. It is trite law that to be treated in accordance with law not only means that the treatment should be lawful but also that only those lawfully competent should deal with the matter.

68.   Section 8(2) of the Indian Independence Act, 1947, provided that the new Dominions (Pakistan and India) shall be governed, till approval of their Constitutions, in accordance with the Government of India Act, 1935. Proviso (c) of Section 8(2) of the Indian Independence Act, 1947, specified that so much of the provisions of the Government of India Act, 1935, as requires the Governor-General or any Governor to act in his discretion or exercise his individual judgment as respects any matter shall cease to have effect as from the appointed day. The Pakistan (Provisional Constitution) Order, 1947, substituted Sections 9 and 50 of the Government of India Act, 1935, with the following:

> "**9.   Council of Ministers-**There shall be a Council of Ministers to aid and advise the Governor-General in the exercise of his functions."

> "**50.   Council of Ministers-**There shall be a Council of Ministers to aid and advise the Governor in the exercise of his functions."

69.   The above provisions made advice of the Prime Minister or, as the case may be, Chief Minister binding on the Governor-General and the Governor respectively. Such a provision is of material significance as held in a case reported as Muhammad Sharif Vs. Federation of Pakistan (PLD 1988 Lah. 725) that:

> "The significance of the provision requiring the President or the Governor to act in accordance with the advice of the Cabinet or the Prime Minister or as the case may be the Chief Minister is that if the President, or as the case may be, the Governor acts without such advice or against the advice so tendered or re-tendered, his action is unconstitutional and ultra vires.'

70.   In Shamsher Singh case from the Indian jurisdiction (AIR 1974 SC 2192), the petitioner was a provincial civil servant. He was removed from service without the advice of the Cabinet and the Governor's order was held to be ultra vires and was set aside. This view seems to have been noticed with approval in Al-Jehad Trust case (PLD 1997 SC 84).

71.   This Court passed a number of orders for filing of the agreement between the Governor-General and the Provincial Governors which is claimed to the basis of the Civil Service of Pakistan (Composition and Cadre) Rules, 1954. Despite repeated orders, a copy of the said agreement was not filed in the Court and it was admitted by the learned Attorney General that the said agreement was not in the shape of a formal document. This admission of the learned Attorney General amounts to accepting that no written and signed document exists which is claimed to be the basis of the Civil Service of Pakistan (Composition and Cadre) Rules, 1954.

72.   As the Governor-General and the Governors were bound to act strictly in accordance with advice of the Prime Minister and the concerned Chief Ministers respectively, it is but logical to assume that the said agreement would have been concluded as per the advice. The Governor-General and the Governors had no power to conclude the agreement in absence of lawful advice. Taking the argument to its logical end, the Governor-General was incompetent to frame the Civil Service of Pakistan (Composition and Cadre) Rules, 1954 without advice of the Prime Minister. Without prejudice to serious exceptions to the legality of the claimed agreement, issuance of advice by the Prime Minister was not legally possible without existence of the agreement upon which the Civil Service of Pakistan (Composition and Cadre) Rules, 1954 were primarily based.

73.   At the time of framing of the Civil Service of Pakistan (Composition and Cadre) Rules, 1954, there was no prohibition on disclosure of advice tendered to the Governor-General by the Prime Minister as Section 9 of the Government of India Act, 1935 was subsequently substituted by the following vide Section 2 of the Government of India (Fifth Amendment) Act which came into force on 21st September, 1954:

> "**9.   Council of Ministers. -**
> (1)   There shall be a Council of Ministers with the Prime Minister at the head to aid and advise the Governor-General in the

exercise of his functions. The Governor-General shall be bound by the advice of the Ministers.

(2) The question whether any, and if so, what advice was tendered by Ministers to the Governor-General shall not be inquired into in any court."

74. The Hon'ble Supreme Court of India has held in cases reported as (1997)3 SCC 591) and (1994) 3 SCC 1)} that "the material placed before the President by the Minister / Council of Ministers does not, thereby, become part of advice. Advice is what is based upon the said material. Material is not advice."

75. Al-Jehad Trust case (PLD 1997 SC 84) indicated that the Court can examine constitutionality of an advice tendered to the President. Examination of an advice is not possible without seeing the advice. Thus, both advice and material upon which advice is based, can be examined by this Court to determine constitutionality of the action taken in consequence thereof.

76. Nothing is on record to show that the agreement between the Governor-General and the Provincial Governors exists in the form of a formal written and signed document or the said agreement was concluded on the advice of the competent authority. In view of, inter alia, the above, the Civil Service of Pakistan (Composition and Cadre) Rules, 1954, to the extent these relate to posts in connection with affairs of the Provinces, cannot be claimed to have competently been made by a lawful delegate of the Provincial Governors.

77. Even if, for the purpose of arguments only, existence of the ministerial advice and the written and signed agreement made in consequence thereof is proved and use of the designations of the Governor-General and the Provincial Governors is attributed to the necessity of constitutional requirement of actions of the Governments to be expressed to be taken in their names, that advice and the agreement are incapable of conferring jurisdiction upon the Governor-General which was taken away through deletion of Section 246 of the Government of India Act, 1935. Silence or agreement of parties cannot grant jurisdiction which is denied by the Constitution or the statute governing the matter. In the instant case, the governing statute is the Government of India Act, 1935. As discussed earlier, Section 246 thereof stood deleted and Section 241 was irrelevant to the concept of reservation of posts in connection with affairs of the Provinces for a Service of the Federation.

78. The respondents in the instant case have referred to Section 263 of the Government of India Act, 1935, as a legitimate sanction of law for the purported agreement between the Governor-General and the Provincial Governors. To begin with, neither the Resolution of the Government of Pakistan nor the Civil Service of Pakistan (Composition and Cadre) Rules, 1954 refer to the said Section as a legal basis of the agreement. Moreover, the Services recruited by the Secretary of State for India have been dealt with in Section 244 of the Government of India Act, 1935. Section 263 of the Act ibid is neither relevant to the Secretary of State for India's services nor it relates to the posts in connection with affairs of a Province. All India or All Pakistan Services are not the subject matter of this Section.

79. It has been held in Himachal Road Tpt Corpn Vs. Sushila Devi (AIR 1980 SC 150) that reports of the committee which preceded the enactment of a legislation, report of joint parliamentary committee, report of a commission set up for collecting information leading to the enactment, are permissible external aids to construction of a statute.

80. Section 263 of the Government of India, 1935 becomes crystal clear when it is construed in the light of para 314 of the report of the Joint Committee on Indian Constitutional Reform [Session 1933-34], reproduced below:

Para 314 of the report of the Joint Committee on Indian Constitutional Reform [Session 1933-34]	Section 263 of the Government of India Act, 1935
"We regard it as essential that each Provincial Government should be able to	"If an agreement is made between the Federation and one or more Provinces, or

avail itself of the advice of a Public Service Commission. We recognise that it is not practicable to establish one Public Service Commission for all India, but we should view with some apprehension the setting up of some ten Provincial Public Service Commissions in addition to the Federal Public Service Commission. We hope, therefore, that advantage will freely be taken of the proposed provision, which we cordially endorse, whereby the same Provincial Commission would be enabled to serve two or more Provinces jointly, or alternatively that it should be open to a Province to make use of the services of the Federal Public Service Commission, subject to agreement with the federal authorities."	between two or more Provinces, for the maintenance or creation of a service common to the Federation and one or more Provinces, or common to two or more Provinces, or for the maintenance or creation of a post the functions whereof are not restricted to the affairs of the Federation or one Province, the agreement may make provision that the Governor-General or any Governor, or any Public Service Commission, shall do in relation to that service or post anything which would under the provisions of this chapter be done by the Governor or the Provincial Public Service Commission if the service or post was a service or post in connection with the affairs of one Province only."

81.   Main focus of Section 263 of the Government of India, 1935 is on performance of functions by the Federal Public Service Commission for the Federation and one or more Provinces or a Provincial Public Service Commission for more than one Provinces. This Section has nothing to do with reservation of posts in connection with affairs of a Province for Service of the Federation or creation or continuation of an All-India Service abolished in terms of Section 10 of the Indian Independence Act, 1947, Article 7 of the Pakistan (Provisional Constitution) Order, 1947 read with announcement of the Viceroy dated 30th of April, 1947. The said Section 263 has not been cited as a source of power allowing creation of the Civil Service of Pakistan. Subsequent reliance on this Section to justify legality of the Civil Service of Pakistan (Composition and Cadre) Rules, 1954 seems to be an after-thought. This Section is, therefore, not available to sanctify the Civil Service of Pakistan (Composition and Cadre) Rules, 1954 to the extent of reservation of posts in connection with affairs of a Province for a Service of the Federation. This Section has not been retained in the Constitution of Pakistan, 1956, 1962 and 1973. It is, therefore, not lawful now to rely upon this Section for the purpose of creation or continuation of an All Pakistan Service or reservation of posts in connection with affairs of a Province for a Service of the Federation. If the said Section 263 is interpreted to be allowing constitution or continuation of All India Services or All Pakistan Services after 15th of August, 1947, then Section 10 of the Indian Independence Act, 1947 comes in operation to delete it from the statute book.

82.   An analysis of para 314 of the report of the Joint Committee on Indian Constitutional Reform (Session 1933-34) and Section 263 of the Government of India Act, 1935 indicates that conclusion of agreement for entrustment of certain functions of more than one Governments to a public service commission would require posts the holders of which would perform those functions. To man these joint posts, a joint Service could also be created. The phrase "the maintenance or creation of a service common to the Federation and one or more Provinces, or common to two or more Provinces, or for the maintenance or creation of a post the functions whereof are not restricted to the affairs of the Federation or one Province" needs to be understood in this context and not as a substitute for the deleted Section 246 of the Government of India Act, 1935.

83.   In view of the above discussion, we hold that an agreement between the Federation and the Federating Units under Section 263 of the Government of India Act, 1935 could not lawfully make the Governor-General a valid delegate of the Provincial Governors for the purpose of exercise of their rule-making powers with respect to Provincial Services or posts in connection with affairs of the Provinces and powers of reservation of posts in connection

with affairs of the Provinces for a Service of the Federation or an All Pakistan Service were not available after deletion of Section 246 of the Government of India Act, 1935.

Question # 7

Whether the Civil Service of Pakistan (Composition and Cadre) Rules, 1954 stood saved and protected under Article 224 of the Constitution of Islamic Republic of Pakistan, 1956, Article 225 of the Constitution of the Islamic Republic of Pakistan, 1962, Article 180 of the interim Constitution of 1972 and Article 241, 268 of the Constitution of the Islamic Republic of Pakistan, 1973 and Section 24 of the General Clauses Act, 1897 as "existing law" to the extent of reservation of posts in connection with affairs of the Provinces for members of a Service of the Federation?

84.   The Federation of Pakistan maintains that the Civil Service of Pakistan (Composition and Cadre) Rules, 1954 were saved, protected and granted continuity in all the later constitutions and legislations e.g. Constitutions of Pakistan, 1956, 1962, 1972 and 1973 and the Establishment of West Pakistan Act, 1955. The Province of the Punjab avers that the Civil Service of Pakistan (Composition and Cadre) Rules, 1954 fall within the definition of "existing law" and stand lawfully saved and protected in terms of Article 224 of the Constitution of the Islamic Republic of Pakistan, 1956, Article 225 of the Constitution of the Islamic Republic of Pakistan, 1962, Article 280(8) of the Interim Constitution of the Islamic Republic of Pakistan, 1972, Article 241 and 268 of the Constitution of the Islamic Republic of Pakistan, 1973, Section 25 of the Civil Servants Ordinance, 1973 and Section 25 (2) of the Civil Servants Act, 1973. These submissions require examination in some detail.

85.   Section 292 of the Government of India Act, 1935 provided as follows:

Existing law of India to continue in force.

"Notwithstanding the repeal by this Act of the Government of India Act, but subject to the other provisions of this Act, all the law in force in British India immediately before the commencement of Part-III of this Act shall continue in force in British India until altered or repealed or amended by a competent

Legislature or other competent authority."

86.   Subsection (3) of Section 18 of the Indian Independence Act, 1947 reads as follows:

18.   Provisions as to the existing laws, etc.-

"(3)   Save as otherwise expressly provided in this Act, the law of British India and of several parts thereof existing immediately before the appointed day shall, so far as applicable and with the necessary adaptations, continue as the law of each of the new Dominions and several parts thereof until other provision is made by laws of the Legislature of the Dominion in question or by any other Legislature or other authority having power in that behalf."

87.   By virtue of Section 10 of the Indian Independence Act, 1947, Article 7 (1) of the Pakistan (Provisional Constitution) Order, 1947, read with announcement of the Viceroy dated 30th of April, 1947, the said Section 18(3) did not save any legal provision relating to the Indian Civil Service. Consequently, tenure of members of the Indian Civil Service came to an end and the Service disappeared on the appointed day.

88.   The Government of India Act, 1935, was adopted, with necessary amendments, as provisional Constitution of Pakistan through the Pakistan (Provisional Constitution) Order, 1947.

89.   The Government of India Act, 1935 and the Indian Independence Act, 1947 were repealed by Article 221 of the Constitution of Islamic Republic of Pakistan, 1956, reproduced below:

"The Government of India Act, 1935 and the Indian Independence Act, 1947, together with all enactments amending or supplementing those Acts, are hereby repealed:

Provided that repeal of the provisions of the Government of India Act, 1935, applicable for the purposes of Article 230 shall not take effect until the first day of April, 1957."

90.   Section 10 of the Establishment of the West Pakistan Act, 1955 provided as under:

"10. Continuation of laws. - (1) Except as otherwise provided in this Act, and subject to any order of the Governor-General under section 5 of this Act, and to the powers of any competent Legislature, all laws in force in West Pakistan immediately before the appointed day shall continue to apply to the areas and the persons to whom they would have applied if this Act had not been passed.

(2) For the purposes of this section "law" includes any Act of the Parliament of the United Kingdom, any law passed by a competent Legislature in India or Pakistan, and any Order-in-Council, Letters Patent, ordinance, order, regulation, rule, bye-law or public notification made or issued by a competent authority.

(3) For the purpose of bringing the provisions of the Government of India Act, 1935 into accord with the provisions of this Act, the Government of India Act, 1935, shall as from the appointed day be amended in accordance with the provisions of the First Schedule to this Act."

91.   Section 10 of the Establishment of the West Pakistan Act, 1955, reproduced hereinabove, saved and protected the Civil Service of Pakistan (Composition and Cadre) Rules, 1954, to the extent of creation of the Civil Service of Pakistan as a Service of the Federation, reservation of certain posts in connection with affairs of the Federation for that Service and matters connected therewith or ancillary thereto but it was incapable of saving these rules so far as reservation of posts in connection with affairs of the Provinces for the Civil Service of Pakistan and other matters falling within exclusive provincial jurisdiction were concerned.

92.   Article 224 of the Constitution of Islamic Republic of Pakistan, 1956 reads as under:

"Notwithstanding the repeal of the enactments mentioned in Article 221, and save as is otherwise expressly provided in the Constitution, all laws (other than those enactments) including Ordinances, Orders-in-Council, Orders, rules, bye-laws, regulations, notifications, and other legal instruments in force in Pakistan or in any part thereof, or having extra-territorial validity, immediately before the Constitution Day, shall, so far as applicable and with the necessary adaptations, continue in force until altered, repealed or amended by the appropriate legislature or other competent authority.

Explanation 1- The expression "laws" in this Article shall include Letters Patent constituting a High Court.

Explanation 2- In this Article "in force", in relation to any law, means having effect as law whether or not the law has been brought into operation."

93.   The protection purported to be given to the then existing laws was not extendable to the Civil Service of Pakistan (Composition and Cadre) Rules, 1954, to the extent it related to posts in connection with affairs of the Provinces, inter alia, for the following reasons:

I.   Principles applicable to Articles of the Constitution which attempt to validate acts done are also applicable in respect of the Articles of the Constitution which grant continuity to the existing laws. The

Supreme Court of Pakistan has held in State Vs. Zia-ur-Rehman (PLD 1973 SC 49) that the validity given to acts done or purported to be done in exercise of the powers given by the Martial Law Regulations or Orders "does not have the effect of validating acts done coram non judice or without jurisdiction or mala fide" and that the words "purported to be done or done in the purported exercise of powers" could not cover acts without jurisdiction etc." A constitutional provision allowing continued operation of existing laws is not a remedy to cure jurisdictional defects in an existing law. If a law has been made without jurisdiction or in excess of jurisdiction, it will remain invalid even if it is declared to be saved as an existing law. Its continuance as existing law only prohibits the possible objection on the ground that the law was made by a legislature or other authority to whom such power has been denied under the new Constitution and the same power has been vested in some other legislature or authority. Since the Civil Service of Pakistan (Composition and Cadre) Rules, 1954 have been framed by the Governor-General and these are in excess of jurisdiction to the extent these relate to posts in connection with affairs of the Provinces, therefore, Article 224 of the Constitution of Islamic Republic of Pakistan, 1956, does not save these rules to this extent.

II.   Continuity of an existing law is subject to its conformity to the Constitution which saves the existing law. There is no provision in the Constitution of the Islamic Republic of Pakistan, 1956 which allows reservation of posts in connection with affairs of a Province for a Service of the Federation. The Constitution of 1956 does not empower the President to determine appointments to and conditions of service of the persons holding posts in connection with affairs of a Province. There is no provision in the said Constitution comparable with Section 246 or 263 of the Government of India Act, 1935. The Civil Service of Pakistan (Composition and Cadre) Rules, 1954 are without jurisdiction so far as these rules attempt to reserve posts in connection with affairs of the Provinces for a Service of the Federation. It is trite law that every act of delegated authority contrary to the tenor of the commission under which it is exercised is void.

III.   When an Act is repealed, it must be considered except as to transactions past and closed, as if it had never existed. The effect of repeal is to dry up the source of power. In Watson Vs. Winch (1916) 1 KB 688), it was held that, where bye-laws have been made under powers conferred by a section of an Act, the repeal of the section abrogates the bye-laws unless they are preserved by the repealing Act by means of a saving clause..." (Page 1534 of N S Bindra's "Interpretation of Statutes" Tenth Edition). It has been held by the Hon'ble Supreme Court of India in a case reported as Air India Vs. Union of India (1995) 2 UJ 568 (SC) that:

> "If the subordinate legislation is to survive the repeal of its parent statute, the repealing statute must say so in so many words and by mentioning the title of the subordinate legislation."

Subordinate legislation said to be made under the Government of India Act, 1935 could survive its repeal only if it fell within four corners of the Constitution of 1956. Since this was not the case so far as the Civil Service of Pakistan (Composition and Cadre) Rules, 1954 (to the extent of reservation of posts in connection with affairs of the Provinces for a Service of the Federation) were concerned, therefore, these rules were not saved as existing law to the extent of their repugnancy with the Constitution of 1956.

IV. The Civil Service of Pakistan (Composition and Cadre) Rules, 1954 created a Service of the Federation. These rules do not term it an All-Pakistan Service. There is no other law and set of rules which may be said to have created an All Pakistan Service. Article 183 of the Constitution of the Islamic Republic of Pakistan, 1956, defines "All-Pakistan Services" as the services common to the Federation and the Provinces which were the All-Pakistan Services immediately before the Constitution Day. It has been seen that neither the Civil Service of Pakistan (Composition and Cadre) Rules, 1954 nor any other legal instrument created an All Pakistan Service; therefore, it is but logical to conclude that no All Pakistan Service was in existence on the Constitution Day. The Constituent Assembly had power to declare that the Civil Service of Pakistan created through the Civil Service of Pakistan (Composition and Cadre) Rules, 1954 shall be deemed to be an All Pakistan Service created under the Constitution in the same manner as was done by the Constituent Assembly of India vide Article 312 of the Constitution of India. The power to validate has been held to be ancillary and incidental to the power to legislate (AIR 1944 FC 1, 10). This power was not exercised by the Constituent Assembly of Pakistan to grant retrospective validity to the Civil Service of Pakistan or to declare the Civil Service of Pakistan as an All Pakistan Service. Since this was not done by the Constituent Assembly of Pakistan, therefore, by no stretch of reasoning and imagination, it can be claimed that the Civil Service of Pakistan (Composition and Cadre) Rules, 1954 created not a Service of the Federation but an All Pakistan Service. The Civil Service of Pakistan (Composition and Cadre) Rules, 1954 are, therefore, without lawful authority to the extent of their coverage of the posts in connection with affairs of the Provinces.

V. Article 183 (1) of the Constitution of 1956 does not validate the Civil Service of Pakistan (Composition and Cadre) Rules, 1954. Article 183 (2), however, empowers the Parliament to have exclusive power to make laws with respect to All-Pakistan Services. This is an enabling provision for creation of All Pakistan Services through Act of Parliament. It cannot be said that Article 183 assumes existence of All Pakistan Services on the Constitution Day. If that be the case, it has been held in Earl of Shrewsbury Vs. Scott (1859) LJCP 34, p 53, per Cockburn that:

> "If it appears from the wording of an enactment that the legislature was under some misapprehension as to the law on a particular subject, such a misapprehension would not have the effect of making the law which the legislature had erroneously assumed it to be."

It has been observed in Wilberforce, Statute Law, p 13, that:

> "One of the most important consequences of the presumption, that the legislature is presumed to know the

law, is that an erroneous declaration of existing law is wholly inoperative."

It is, therefore, in the fitness of things to conclude that the Constituent Assembly did not assume the existence of the Civil Service of Pakistan as an All Pakistan Service immediately before the Constitution Day. Even if a misapprehension with regard to existence of an All Pakistan Service immediately before the Constitution Day was there, the same was incapable of validating the said misapprehension. The Civil Service of Pakistan (Composition and Cadre) Rules, 1954 can, therefore, neither be assumed to be validated, expressly or impliedly, to the extent these rules are interpreted to be the lawful source of creation of the Civil Service of Pakistan as an All Pakistan Service or reservation of posts in connection with affairs of the Provinces for the Civil Service of Pakistan.

VI.   The express mention of one thing implies the exclusion of another. Article 182 of the Constitution of 1956 grants exclusive power of rule-making in respect of services of the Province and posts in connection with affairs of the Province to the concerned Governor or a person authorized by him. The Civil Service of Pakistan (Composition and Cadre) Rules, 1954 make the said Article 182 inoperative to the extent of posts in connection with affairs of the Province which were purportedly reserved for members of the Civil Service of Pakistan. To this extent, the said rules are void ab initio and, therefore, cannot be assumed to be saved and protected by Article 224 of the Constitution of Islamic Republic of Pakistan, 1956.

VII.   Section 263 of the Government of India Act, 1935 did not make Section 241 of the said Act inoperative by reason of an agreement under that Section. Consent of parties to an agreement cannot confer jurisdiction which has not been vested in the parties by or under a valid provision of the Constitution or a law.

VIII. Subordinate legislation must, in order to be law, and in order to be valid, depend on an Act. In the poetical words of Cecil Carr, delegated legislation "is directly related to Acts of Parliament, related as child to parent." (C. Carr, Delegated Legislation; Three Lectures (1921) p.2). Since neither Section 241 nor Section 263 authorized reservation of posts in connection with affairs of a Province for a Service of the Federation and no Article of the Constitution of 1956 is available to lend validity to the arrangement made to this effect through the Civil Service of Pakistan (Composition and Cadre) Rules, 1954, therefore, these rules were not saved and protected by the Constitution of Pakistan, 1956 to the extent of posts in connection with affairs of a Province.

94.   Article 4 (1) and (2) of the Laws (Continuance in Force) Order, 1958, reads as under:

(1)   Notwithstanding the abrogation of the late Constitution, and subject to any Order of the President or Regulation made by the Chief Administrator of Martial Law, all laws, other than the late Constitution, and all Ordinances, Orders-in-Council, Orders other than Orders made by the President under the late Constitution, such Orders made by the President under the late Constitution as are set out in the Schedule to this Order, Rules,

bye-laws, Regulations, Notifications, and other legal instruments in force in Pakistan or in any part thereof, or having extra-territorial validity, immediately before the Proclamation, shall, so far as applicable and with such necessary adaptations as the President may see fit to make, continue in force until altered, repealed or amended by competent authority.

(2)   In this Article, a law is said to be in force if it has effect as law whether or not the law has been brought into operation."

95.   Article 225 of the Constitution of the Islamic Republic of Pakistan, 1962, reads thus:

(1)   Except as provided by this Article, all existing laws shall, subject to this Constitution, continue in force, so far as applicable and with the necessary adaptations, until altered, repealed or amended by the appropriate legislature.

(2)   In this Article "existing laws" means all laws (including Ordinances, Orders-in-Council, Orders, rules, bye-laws, regulations and Letters Patent constituting a High Court, and any notifications and other legal instruments having the force of law) in force in Pakistan or any part of Pakistan, or having extra-territorial validity, immediately before the commencing day.

96.   Article 280 of the interim Constitution of 1972 dealt with continuance of existing laws in these words:

(1) Except as provided by this Article, all existing laws shall, subject to this Constitution, continue in force, so far as applicable and with the necessary adaptations, until altered, repealed or amended by the appropriate Legislature.

(2) The Proclamation made on the twenty-fifth day of March, 1969 is revoked as from the commencing day, and the Orders specified in the Sixth Schedule and any Orders amending those Orders are repealed with effect from that day but this clause shall not affect any existing law made under those Orders.

(3) All Martial Law Regulations and Martial Law Orders, except the Martial Law Regulations and Martial Law Orders specified in the Seventh Schedule are repealed with effect as from the commencing day, and on the day such Martial Law Regulations and Martial Law Orders so specified shall be deemed to have become an Act of the appropriate Legislature and shall, with the necessary adaptations, have effect as such;
Provided that no Bill to amend or to repeal any of the Martial Law Regulations or Martial Law Orders specified as aforesaid shall be introduced or moved without the previous sanction of the President.

(4) For the purpose of bringing the provisions of any existing law into accord with the provisions of this Constitution other than Part-II of this Constitution, the President may make, by Order, such adaptations, whether by way of modification, addition or omission as he may deem to be necessary or expedient, and any Order so made shall have effect (or be deemed to have had effect) from such date not being a date earlier than the commencing day as may be specified in the Order.

(5) The President may authorize the Governor of a Province to exercise, in relation to the Province, the powers conferred on the

President by clause (4) in respect of laws relating to matters with respect to which the Provincial Legislature has power to make laws.

(6) The powers exercisable under clauses (4) and (5) shall be subject to the provisions of any Act of the appropriate Legislature.

(7) Any court, tribunal or authority required or empowered to enforce an existing law shall, notwithstanding that no actual adaptations have been made in such law by an Order made under clause (4) or clause (5) construe the law with such adaptations which are necessary to bring it into accord with the provisions of the Constitution.

(8) In this Article, "existing laws" means all laws including Ordinances, Orders-in-Council, Orders, rules, byelaws, regulations and Letters Patent constituting a High Court and any other notifications and other legal instruments having the force of law in force in Pakistan or any part of Pakistan, or having extra-territorial validity immediately before the commencing day."

97.   Article 241 of the Constitution of the Islamic Republic of Pakistan, 1973, reads as follows:

> **241. Existing rules, etc., to continue**. Until the appropriate Legislature makes a law under Article 240, all rules and orders in force immediately before the commencing day shall, so far as consistent with the provisions of the Constitution, continue in force and may be amended from time to time by the Federal Government or, as the case may be, the Provincial Government."

98.   Article 268 of the Constitution of the Islamic Republic of Pakistan, 1973, provides as under:

> "(1)   Except as provided by this Article, all existing laws shall, subject to the Constitution, continue in force, so far as applicable and with the necessary adaptations, until altered, repealed or amended by the appropriate Legislature.
>
> (2)   to (6) -------------------------.
>
> (7)   In this Article, "existing laws" means all laws (including Ordinances, Orders- in- Council, Orders, rules, by-laws, regulations and Letters Patent constituting a High Court, and any notifications and other legal instruments having the force of law) in force in Pakistan or any part thereof, or having extraterritorial validity, immediately before the commencing day.
>
> Explanation: - In this Article, "in force", in relation to any law, means having effect as law whether or not the law has been brought into operation."

99.   Section 25(2) of the Civil Servants Act, 1973 (Act No. LXXI of 1973) provided as follows

> "Any rules, orders or instructions in respect of any terms and conditions of service of civil servants duly made or issued by an authority competent to make them and in force immediately before the commencement of this Act shall, in so far as such rules, orders or instructions are not inconsistent with the provisions of this Act, be deemed to be rules made under this Act."

Exactly similar provision was also present in the Civil Service Ordinance, 1973. We have omitted to notice protection accorded to Martial Laws and the actions taken during those periods. We will, however, examine this issue as and where need be.

100.   The Civil Service of Pakistan (Composition and Cadre) Rules, 1954 have been found to be saved and protected by Article 224 of the Constitution of Islamic Republic of Pakistan, 1956, only to the extent of the creation of the Civil Service of Pakistan as a Service of the Federation, reservation of posts in connection with affairs of the Federation for that Service and other matters pertaining to conditions of recruitment and of service of members of that Service. The said Rules are incapable of attracting Section 10 of the Establishment of the West Pakistan Act, 1955, Article 4 (1) and (2) of the Laws (Continuance in Force) Order, 1956, Article 225 of the Constitution of the Islamic Republic of Pakistan, 1962, Article 280 of the interim Constitution of 1972, Article 241 and 268 of the Constitution of the Islamic Republic of Pakistan, 1973 and Section 25(2) of the Civil Servants Act, 1973 to the extent these rules reserve posts in connection with affairs of the Provinces for a Civil Service of the Federation and other encroachments upon exclusive provincial domain. Besides what has been stated hereinabove to identify repugnancy of these rules with the Constitution of Islamic Republic of Pakistan, 1956, these rules are also in contravention of the Constitutions of Pakistan, 1962, 1972 and 1973 as in all the three Constitutions:

1.   There is no concept of reservation of posts in connection with affairs of a Province for a Service of the Federation;

2.   Powers with regard to posts in connection with affairs of a Province have not been vested in the President of Pakistan;

3.   The Civil Service of Pakistan (Composition and Cadre) Rules, 1954 have not been declared to have been deemed to be valid or protected, either expressly or impliedly;

4.   The Civil Service of Pakistan has not been declared an All Pakistan Service;

5.   No provision similar to Section 246 and 263 of the Government of India Act, 1935, is available;

6.   The rules, to be valid and effective, must not be in contravention of any constitutional or legal provision. The protection intended to be accorded to existing laws under a constitutional provision is only available to the laws and rules made by the competent authority which are not in clash with a constitutional or statutory provision. The Civil Service of Pakistan (Composition and Cadre) Rules, 1954 were made by an incompetent authority to the extent these rules cover the posts in connection with affairs of a Province and are also in contravention of a number of other constitutional provisions; these rules are, therefore, not protected and saved under the aforesaid saving clauses of the Constitutions of 1962, 1972 and 1973 to the extent of their repugnance with these constitutional provisions; and

7.   Existing law has to be examined on the principle of pith and substance. It is saved to the extent it is protected by legislative competence of the concerned legislature. Since concept of reservation of posts in connection with affairs of a province was nor protected, therefore, the Civil Service of Pakistan (Composition and Cadre) Rules, 1954 are not protected in their entirety as existing laws. If, under a new Constitution, a federal subject becomes a provincial subject or vice versa, the relevant statues would fall within the legislative competence as per current constitutional provisions. If the subject partially relates to one legislature, competence of the legislature would be to that extent only. Original jurisdictional want in the enacting legislature or other authority does not stand compensated through purported continuance of an existing law.

101.   Section 24 of the General Clauses Act, 1897 reads as follows:

"**Continuation, of orders, etc., issued under enactments repealed and re-enacted.-** Where any Central Act or Regulation is, after the commencement of this Act, repealed and re-enacted with or without modification, then, unless it is otherwise expressly provided, any appointment, notification, order, scheme, rule, form or bye-law made or issued under the repealed Act or Regulation, shall, so far as it is not inconsistent with the provisions re-enacted, continue in force, and be deemed to have been made or issued under the provisions so reenacted, unless and until it is superseded by any appointment, notification, order, scheme, rule, form or bye-law made or issued under the provisions so re-enacted and when any Central Act or Regulation, which, by a notification under any law, has been extended to any local area, has, by a subsequent notification, been withdrawn from and re-extended to such area or any part thereof, the provisions of such Act or Regulation shall be deemed to have been repealed and re-enacted in such area or part within the meaning of this section."

102.   Section 24 of the General Clauses Act, 1897 is not available to save and protect the Civil Service of Pakistan (Composition and Cadre) Rules, 1954 to the extent of reservation of posts in connection with affairs of the Provinces for members of a Service of the Federation, inter alia, for the reason that the Constitutions of Pakistan, 1956, 1962, 1972 and 1973 do not allow such a dispensation and the said rules are irreconcilably inconsistent with these Constitutions. This inconsistency makes the rules invalid to the extent of the clash.

103.   We are, therefore, persuaded to hold that the aforesaid constitutional and statutory provisions saved and protected the Civil Service of Pakistan (Composition and Cadre) Rules, 1954 to the extent as specified hereinbelow:

(a)   creation of the Civil Service of Pakistan as a Service of the Federation;

(b)   reservation of certain posts in connection with affairs of the Federation, as mentioned in the Schedule to these rules, for the said Service of the Federation; and

(c)   determination of conditions of recruitment and of service of the members of the said Service falling within jurisdiction of the Federation.

104.   It is further held that the Civil Service of Pakistan (Composition and Cadre) Rules, 1954 have not been saved and protected in the following respects:

(a)   reservation of posts in connection with affairs of the Provinces for the Civil Service of Pakistan, by whatever name it is known; and

(b)   any and all things in the said rules pertaining or purporting to pertain to conditions of recruitment and of service of members of the Provincial Services and posts in connection with affairs of the Provinces except appointment by transfer of the provincial civil servants in the Civil Service of Pakistan for posts in connection with affairs of the Federation.

Question # 8

Whether the posts specified in the Schedule to the Civil Service of Pakistan (Composition and Cadre) Rules, 1954 are posts common to the Federation and the Provinces or posts in connection with affairs of the Federation and of the Provinces reserved and encadred for a Service of the Federation?

105.   Under the Government of India Act, 1935, there were three main services, namely (i) All India Services; (ii) Services of the Federation; and (iii) Provincial Services. After

disappearance of the All India Services on the appointed day, only Services of the Federation and Provincial Services remained lawfully in the field.

106.   In a Federation, certain institutions perform functions which can be termed neither purely federal nor entirely provincial. Examples of such institutions, in the context of the Constitution of the Islamic Republic of Pakistan, 1973, may include (i) National Finance Commission (constituted under Article 160 of the Constitution); (ii) National Economic Council (constituted under Article 156 of the Constitution); (iii) Judicial Commission of Pakistan (constituted under Article 175A of the Constitution); (iv) Council of Common Interests (established under Article 153 of the Constitution). Functions of these institutions are functions common to the Federation and the Provinces. Services and posts of these institutions are services and posts common to the Federation and the Provinces. Moreover, two or more Provinces may join hands to constitute joint services and create posts in connection with affairs of more than one provinces. Legislative jurisdiction of a Province does not extend to such services or posts or beyond the territorial limits of the Province. In such an eventuality, the Federal Legislature was allowed to legislate on behalf of the Provincial Legislature which also included extension in jurisdiction of a Public Service Commission to serve the joint services and posts. Section 103 of the Government of India Act, 1935, provided that if it appears to the Legislatures of two or more Provinces to be desirable that any of the matters enumerated in the Provincial Legislative List should be regulated in those Provinces by Act of the Federal Legislature, and if resolutions to that effect are passed by all the Chambers of those Provincial Legislatures, it shall be lawful for the Federal Legislature to pass an Act for regulating that matter accordingly, but any Act so passed may, as respects any Province to which it applies, be amended or repealed by an Act of the Legislature of that Province. Similar provision in the Constitution of the Islamic Republic of Pakistan, 1973 is Article 144.

107.   In the above context, posts common to the Federation and the Provinces are the posts in the Service of Pakistan which are left behind after subtracting therefrom posts in connection with affairs of the Federation and of the Provinces. Posts in connection with affairs of the Federation or of the Provinces cannot be termed posts common to the Federation and the Provinces. The idea of posts common to the Federation and the Provinces cannot be employed to support the concept of reservation of specified posts in connection with affairs of a Province for a Service of the Federation or an All Pakistan Service which never lawfully existed in Pakistan with effect from the appointed day and was not in existence on the Constitution Day. It is not legally possible to hold that the Civil Service of Pakistan (Composition and Cadre) Rules, 1954 do not encroach upon the exclusive provincial domain to the extent these deal with posts in connection with affairs of a Province and the posts mentioned in the Schedule to the aforesaid rules are posts common to the Federation and the Provinces. Moreover, two or more Provinces may agree to establish institutions for transaction of their businesses through these joint institutions. Joint venture or pooling of resources may result into economy in expenditure. Examples may be:

1. Textbook Development Body
2. Agriculture Research Institute
3. Police and Civil Service Training Colleges
4. Joint Public Service Commission

Manpower requirements of the joint ventures of more than one Provinces can be met through constitution of services common to the Provinces. Posts in connection with affairs of these joint institutions will not be posts in connection with affairs of a Province. The Federation may also join such common institutions. Legislative competence of a Province does not extend to such matters. In this case, the Provinces may request the Parliament to legislate for them as allowed under Article 144 of the Constitution. A concrete example of such arrangement may be seen in Article 223 of the interim Constitution of 1972, reproduced below:

"1. There shall be a Federal Public Service Commission for the Federation, and a Provincial Public Service Commission for each Province:

Provided that any two Provinces may agree that there shall be one Public Service Commission (hereinafter referred to as Joint Public Service Commission) to serve the needs of both Provinces.

2.   The agreement referred to in clause (1) shall contain such incidental and consequential provisions, including provisions relating to sharing of expenditure connected with the Joint Public Service Commission, as may appear necessary or desirable for giving effect to the purposes of the agreement and shall specify by which Governor or Chief Justice any function which is to be discharged by a Governor of a Province or a Chief Justice under this Chapter shall be discharged in respect of the Joint Public Service Commission, and the Governor or the Chief Justice so specified shall have the power to discharge those functions."

In no case, posts in connection with affairs of the Federation or of a Province can be termed posts common to the Federation and of the Provinces except the posts in connection with affairs of the common constitutional institutions or common entities created through federal statues in consequence of agreements between and on the request of the Provinces.

108.   Always and everywhere, harmonious construction of the Constitution is preferred. If All Pakistan Services are defined as services other than federal and provincial services to man posts which are neither in connection with affairs of the Federation or of the Provinces, then no word of the Constitution relating to services remains inoperative. It is trite law that if two interpretations of a provision are possible, the one which makes it operative should be preferred over the other which may render it inoperative and dysfunctional.

109.   Posts specified in the Schedule to the Civil Service of Pakistan (Composition and Cadre) Rules, 1954 are posts either in connection with affairs of the Federation or of the Provinces. These are not posts common to the Federation and the Provinces.

110.   We accordingly hold that the posts specified in the Schedule to the Civil Service of Pakistan (Composition and Cadre) Rules, 1954 are not posts common to the Federation and the Provinces and, instead, are posts in connection with affairs of the Federation, or, as the case may be, of the Provinces, which have been reserved and encadred for a Service of the Federation.

Question # 9

Whether an All Pakistan Service was lawfully in existence when the Constitution of the Islamic Republic of Pakistan, 1956 came into operation or whether the Parliament has created an All Pakistan Service through a law or has declared a service to be deemed to be an All Pakistan Service till date?

111.   Article 183 (1) of the Constitution of the Islamic Republic of Pakistan, 1956 defined "All-Pakistan Services" to mean the services common to the Federation and the Provinces which were the All-Pakistan Services immediately before the Constitution Day.

112.   The explanation at the end of Article 240 of the Constitution gives an exhaustive definition of the expression "All-Pakistan Service" by enumerating its two essential characteristics, namely:

1. It is common to the Federation and the Provinces; and
2. It was either in existence immediately before the commencing day or may be created by Act of Parliament.

By saying that an All-Pakistan Service is common to the Federation and the Provinces, it is impliedly stated that the Service is neither a Service of the Federation or of a Province nor it deals with posts in connection with affairs of the Federation or of a Province. Such a Service may deal with matters which are neither federal nor provincial but are common to the

Federation and the Provinces e.g. National Economic Council, National Finance Commission, Council of Common Interests, Judicial Commission, Supreme Judicial Council. The Civil Service of Pakistan, created under the Civil Service of Pakistan (Composition and Cadre) Rules, 1954 was a Service of the Federation as was expressly stated in those rules. No law or rules are on record to indicate that an All Pakistan Service was created in the period falling between commencement of the Civil Service of Pakistan (Composition and Cadre) Rules, 1954 and the commencing day of the Constitution of the Islamic Republic of Pakistan, 1973. It is absolutely reasonable and safe to conclude that no All-Pakistan Service was in existence immediately before the commencing day of the Constitution of 1956, 1962, 1972 and of 1973.

113.   The Parliament has not so far created any All-Pakistan Service through an Act of Parliament. Contrary to the expression "by or under Act of Majlis-e-Shoora (Parliament), used in Article 240 (a) and "by or under Act of the Provincial Assembly" employed in Article 240 (b) of the Constitution, the expression used in the explanation to Article 240 is "by Act of Majlis-e-Shoora (Parliament)." It is well-accepted legal maxim that prescription of one is prohibition of another. By expressly declaring that an All Pakistan Service may be created by an Act of the Parliament, creation of such a Service through rules or executive instructions has been ruled out. It is known fact that the Parliament has not enacted a law for creation of one or more All Pakistan Services as was done by the Parliament of India through enactment of the All-India Services Act, 1951 (LXI of 1951).

114.   Rules of statutory construction are applicable on construction of the Constitution. (Knight v. Seltoon 124 Fed 423). It has been held in a case reported as AIR 1939 Lah 587 that an explanation does not enlarge the scope of the original section that it is supposed to explain. It has been held in a case reported as AIR 1991 Bom 196 that:

> "It is well settled that an explanation added to a statutory provision is not a substantive provision in any sense of the term but as the plain meaning of the word itself shows it is merely meant to explain or clarify certain ambiguities which may have crept in the statutory provision."

Thus, the explanation to Article 240 of the Constitution is neither available to make the then Civil Service of Pakistan an All Pakistan Service nor to validate the Civil Service of Pakistan (Composition and Cadre) Rules, 1954 to the extent these encroach upon exclusive provincial domain through reservation of posts in connection with affairs of a Province for members of the Civil Service of Pakistan.

115.   The preamble of the Civil Servants Act, 1973 (Act No. LXXI of 1973) reads as follows:

> "Whereas it is expedient to regulate by law, the appointment of persons to, and the terms and conditions of service of persons in the service of Pakistan, and to provide for matters, connected therewith or ancillary thereto;"

116.   Section 2(1) (b) of the Civil Servants Act, 1973, defines `civil servant' as under: -
> "Civil servant means a person who is a member of an All Pakistan Service or of a civil service of the Federation, or who holds a civil post in connection with the affairs of the Federation, including any such post connected with defence, but does not include: --
> (i)   a person who is on deputation to the Federation from any province or other authority;
> (ii)   a person who is employed on contract, or on work-charged basis or who is paid from contingencies; or
> (iii)   a person who is a "worker" or "workman" as defined in the Factories Act, 1934 (XXV of 1934), or the Workmen's Compensation Act, 1923 (VII of 1923)."

117.   It has been held by the Hon'ble Supreme Court of Pakistan in the case of Registrar, Supreme Court of Pakistan Vs. Wali Muhammad (1997 SCMR 141), as quoted by a seven-judge bench of the Hon'ble Supreme Court in the case of Muhammad Mubeen-us-Salam and others Vs. Federation of Pakistan (PLD 2006 Supreme Court 602) that:

> "On a careful examination of the definitions of 'Service of Pakistan' as given in Article 260 of the Constitution and the `Civil Servant' as mentioned in Civil Servants Act, 1973, it would appear that the two expressions are not synonymous. The expression `Service of Pakistan' used in Article 260 of the Constitution has a much wider connotation than the term `Civil Servant' employed in the Civil Servants Act. While a `Civil Servant' is included in the expression `Service of Pakistan', the vice versa is not true. `Civil Servant' as defined in the Civil Servants Act, 1973 is just a category of service of Pakistan mentioned in Article 260 of the Constitution. To illustrate the point, we may mention here that members of Armed Forces though fall in the category of `Service of Pakistan' but they are not civil servants within the meaning of Civil Servants Act and the Service Tribunals Act."

118.   The Civil Servants Act, 1973 does not deal with the 'Service of Pakistan' in its entirety; it only deals with the civil servants. There is no express or implied provision in this Act which may authorize the Federation to reserve posts in connection with affairs of a Province for a Service of the Federation. The Act does not and cannot assign meanings to the expression "All Pakistan Service" different from that given to it in explanation to Article 240 of the Constitution of 1973. Since no All Pakistan Service was constitutionally in existence on the commencing day of the Constitution of 1973, therefore, the only way to create an All Pakistan Service was an Act of the Parliament. The Civil Servants Act, 1973 cannot be construed as an Act contemplated in explanation to the said Article 240 because:

I.   It does not expressly create an All-Pakistan Service or declare the Civil Service of Pakistan a service deemed to have been created under this Act;

II.   It does not claim to regulate posts in connection with affairs of a Province and does not disturb the dispensation in respect of Provincial Services and posts in connection with affairs of the Provinces, contained in Article 240(b) of the Constitution, by excluding certain posts in connection with affairs of a Province in order to reserve those posts for a Service of the Federation;

III.   Section 25(2) of the Act ibid saves only those rules which are not inconsistent with provisions of the Act. If there are rules which are partly consistent and partly inconsistent with the Act, the consistent parts shall stand saved and the inconsistent parts shall become invalid and ineffective. To the extent of the Civil Service of Pakistan being a Service of the Federation created with the purpose that its members will hold posts in connection with affairs of the Federation, the Civil Service of Pakistan (Composition and Cadre) Rules, 1954 are consistent with constitutional provisions and the Act ibid but these are inconsistent with the constitutional and statutory provisions when these rules attempt to reserve certain posts or certain percentage of posts in connection with affairs of a Province for a Service of the Federation denying the concerned Provincial Services to hold those posts in accordance with law. To the extent of inconsistency and clash, the Civil Service of Pakistan (Composition and Cadre) Rules, 1954 cannot be said to be saved or protected in terms of Section 25(2) of the Act ibid;

IV.   It only determines conditions of appointment and of services and does not create an All Pakistan Service; and

V.   The preamble of the Act cannot be construed to mean that since services and posts of a Province fall within the definition of the 'Service of Pakistan', therefore, the said Act is also applicable thereto and reservation of posts in connection with affairs of a Province for a Service of the Federation is legally justified on that ground. This argument is not legally tenable because it is well-settled that preamble can neither be read as part of a section nor can it operate to annul a section. It cannot restrict or extend scope of an Act or confer power or override enacting part of an Act. The preamble cannot, in the instant case, be construed to invalidate Article 240(b) of the Constitution and the laws / rules framed thereunder. Mere inclusion of members of an All Pakistan Service in the definition of 'civil servant' given in Section 2(1) (b) of the Act cannot ipso facto constitutionalize or legalize reservation of posts in connection with affairs of a Province for members of a Service of the Federation which has been declared so in the Civil Service of Pakistan (Composition and Cadre) Rules, 1954.

119.   In view of the above, it is evident that the Civil Servants Act, 1973, is not the law contemplated in the explanation to Article 240 of the Constitution. Whereas the Federation is at liberty to create as many Services of the Federation through rules to be framed under the said Act, an All Pakistan Service can only be deemed to have been created or created through an Act of the Parliament.

120.   We accordingly hold that no All Pakistan Service was constitutionally in existence when the Constitution of Islamic Republic of Pakistan, 1973, came into force and no such Service has so far been created through an Act of the Parliament.

Question # 10

Whether the Civil Service of Pakistan (Composition and Cadre) Rule, 1954 are in conflict with federal structure of the Constitution to the extent of reservation of posts in connection with affairs of the Provinces for members of a Service of the Federation?

121.   Democracy, federalism, parliamentary form of government, fundamental rights and independence of judiciary are some of the salient and defining features of the Constitution. It is a normal feature of a federation to make the two levels of government autonomous and independent of each other. Not only are the functions and resources kept clearly demarcated but the machinery of public administration too is kept separate and distinct. It has been observed in a book titled "Problems and issues in Administrative Federalism" by Shraram Maheshwari 1992 (page No. 2) that:

"A federal government, in the classical sense, is premised on the doctrine of administrative dualism, that is, each level of government is to be equipped with its own set of administrative instrumentalities and mechanism, and the two levels of government have thus separate and distinct levels of public administration."

122.   Federalism is reduced to a mere meaningless and ineffective decorative declaration of no practical value if a federating unit is denied powers to manage its provincial services and posts in connection with its affairs.

123.   There was a unitary form of Government in India before enactment of the Government of India Act, 1935. Para 48 of the report of the Joint Committee on Indian Constitutional Reform [Session 1933-34] discusses the matter of provincial autonomy in the following words:

"48. The scheme of Provincial Autonomy, as we understand it, is one whereby each of the Governors' Provinces will possess an Executive and a Legislature having exclusive authority within the Province in a precisely defined sphere, and in that exclusively provincial sphere broadly free from control by the Central Government and Legislature. This we conceive to be the essence of Provincial Autonomy, though, no doubt, there is room for wide differences of opinion with regard to the manner in which that exclusive authority is to be exercised. It represents a fundamental departure from the present system, under which the Provincial Governments exercise a devolved and not an original authority. The Act of 1919 and the Devolution Rules made under it, by earmarking certain subjects as "Provincial subjects" created indeed a sphere within which responsibility for the functions of government rests primarily upon the Provincial authorities; but that responsibility is not an exclusive one, since the Governor-General in Council and the Central Legislature still exercise an extensive authority throughout the whole of the Provinces. Under the proposals in the White Paper, the Central Government and Legislature would, generally speaking, cease to possess in the Governors' Provinces any legal power or authority with respect to any matter falling within the exclusive Provincial sphere, though, as we shall explain later, the Governor-General in virtue of his power of supervising the Governors will have authority to secure compliance in certain respects with directions which he may find it necessary to give."

124.   The Secretary of State for India's services were blamed to be a tool in the hands of imperial rulers to control administration of Federal as well Provincial Governments in India. With imperial rule coming to an end on 15th of August, 1947, these services were abolished with the result of introduction of complete administrative federalism in the two new sovereign states and their provinces. It was for the new Dominions to manage public services through the federal and provincial services. Deviation from the principle of administrative federalism in India was justified on the basis of express provisions of Article 312 of the Constitution of India read with entry appearing at serial number 70 of the Union List and All India Services Act, 1951. In absence of provisions similar to the aforesaid legal instruments of India in any of the Constitutions of Pakistan, the federal structure of the Constitution is not lawfully permissible to be destroyed through reservation of posts in connection with affairs of a Province in terms of the Civil Service of Pakistan (Composition and Cadre) Rules, 1954. The said rules, to the extent of reservation of the posts in connection with affairs of a Province, militate against the federal structure of the Constitution.

125.   It is well-established that what cannot be done directly is also not allowed to be done indirectly. No provision of the Constitution of the Islamic Republic of Pakistan, 1973 allows suspension of operation of Article 240(b) of the said Constitution. By reserving certain posts in connection with affairs of a Province for a Service of the Federation vide the Civil Service of Pakistan (Composition and Cadre) Rules, 1954, the said Article 240(b) has been made ineffective to the extent of those posts. Moreover, the Province has exclusive power to orient its spending priorities and make decisions with respect to appropriation of the proceeds of the Provincial Consolidated Fund. Conditions of service of the civil servants who are members of Services of the Federation are determined by and under the Civil Servants Act, 1973. These conditions include remuneration. It has expressly been laid down in Section 1 (2) of the said Act that the Act shall apply to all civil servants wherever they may be. Implication of this statutory provision is that the Province has to disburse moneys on account of pay, allowances, travelling allowance, daily allowance etc. to members of the Federal Services, while they hold posts in connection with affairs of a Province, in accordance with what has been determined by or under that Act. As a result, the Province is

reduced to a mere rubber stamp in case of service conditions and the consequent appropriations required to implement those conditions of service of members of the Services of the Federation. As determination of remuneration payable from the Provincial Consolidated Fund amounts to creation of charge on the Provincial Consolidated Fund, therefore, this power can only be exercised by the Provincial Assembly through a Money Bill in terms of Article 115 of the Constitution. The Civil Service of Pakistan (Composition and Cadre) Rules, 1954 are invalid on this ground alone to the extent of reservation of posts in connection with affairs of a Province for a Service of the Federation purported to be created under these rules as the constitutional power of the purse of the Provinces is taken away to the extent of financial aspects of conditions of service of the federal employees holding posts in connection with affairs of a Province.

126. Rule 12 of the Civil Service of Pakistan (Composition and Cadre) Rules, 1954 reads as follows:

> "No change shall be made in the duties of the holder of any reserved post if, in the opinion of the President, the character of that post would thereby be altered:
>
> Provided that this shall not apply to a temporary change consequential on leave arrangements or to a change not arising from leave arrangements which will not last more than three months."

127. Article 129 of the Constitution declares that executive authority of the Province shall be exercised in the name of the Governor by the Provincial Government, consisting of the Chief Minister and Provincial Ministers, which shall act through the Chief Minister. Article 137 of the said Constitution provides that the executive authority of the province extends to the matters with respect to which the Provincial Assembly has power to make laws. Article 138 of the Constitution ibid says that on the recommendation of the Provincial Government, the Provincial Assembly may, by law, confer functions upon officers or authorities subordinate to the Provincial Government. To assign powers and functions to persons holding posts in connection with affairs of a Province is an exclusive and indivisible domain of the Province in terms of Article 138 of the Constitution. Rule 12 of the Civil Service of Pakistan (Composition and Cadre) Rules, 1954 is in direct conflict with Article 138 of the Constitution read with other relevant constitutional provisions. The conflict is irreconcilable and in such a case the said Rule 12 has to yield and Article 138 of the Constitution shall have effect irrespective of what has been stated in the said Rule 12. In this view of the matter, the said Rule 12 is ultra vires Article 240 (a) of the Constitution and the Civil Servants Act, 1973, and in conflict with Article 240(b) and the laws and the rules framed thereunder and Article 138 of the Constitution. This rule makes the Civil Service of Pakistan (Composition and Cadre) Rules, 1954 unconstitutional and illegal and, hence, without lawful authority and jurisdiction and of no legal effect to the extent pointed out hereinabove.

128. Rule 13 of the Civil Service of Pakistan (Composition and Cadre) Rules, 1954, provides as under:

1. The President may from time to time, and in the case of posts in connection with the affairs of a Province, after consultation with the Governor of that Province, remove any post from the Schedule or include any post therein.

2. A Governor may, if the exigencies of the public service so require, create a cadre post in connection with the affairs of a Province below the rank of a Commissioner of a Division, for a period not exceeding three months. If subsequently the Governor proposes to retain that cadre post for a further period, he shall forthwith make a report to the President of the reasons for the proposal and the period for which he proposes to retain that post and shall act in accordance with such directions as the President may give.

129.   The method of amendment in or substitution of the Schedule of the Civil Service of Pakistan (Composition and Cadre) Rules, 1954 (to the extent of posts in connection with affairs of the Provinces) and identification of the authority having lawful competence therefor and matters connected therewith or ancillary thereto are relevant only if the constitutionality of the concept of reservation of posts in connection with affairs of the Provinces for members of a Service of the Federation is determined. Once the concept of reservation of posts in connection with affairs of the Provinces for Service of the Federation is adjudged to be unconstitutional, illegal and, hence, without lawful authority and jurisdiction and consequently of no legal effect, the superstructures built upon this concept, as enshrined in of the Civil Service of Pakistan (Composition and Cadre) Rules, 1954 and the SRO No. 1237(1)/73 dated 21.08.1973 and the so-called 1993 formula, will find no legs to stand on.

130.   After commencement of the Constitution of the Islamic Republic of Pakistan, 1973, only an Act of the Parliament could lawfully create an All Pakistan Service. That law could provide for reservation of posts common to the Federation and the Provinces for that Service and the mechanism and the authority to add or delete a post so reserved. Posts in connection with affairs of the Federation and of the Provinces do not fall within the ambit of the posts common to the Federation and the Provinces. The dispensation for addition or deletion of a reserved post common to the Federation and the Provinces could be provided by or under that law. Since the requisite law has not been enacted and the Civil Service of Pakistan (Composition and Cadre) Rules, 1954 are invalid to the extent of reservation of posts in connection with affairs of the Provinces for a Service of the Federation, therefore, the Schedule to the Civil Service of Pakistan (Composition and Cadre) Rules, 1954 and the SRO No. 1237(1)/73 dated 21.08.1973 and the 1993 formula are unconstitutional and illegal and are incapable of being given effect to.

131.   As per Rule 11 of the Punjab Civil Servants (Appointment and Conditions of Service) Rules, 1974, and Schedule-II of the Punjab Provincial Management Service Rules, 2004, the share of posts to be reserved for appointment through transfer may be determined from time to time. Whereas the Punjab Civil Servants (Appointment and Conditions of Service) Rules, 1974 are silent on the issue that who will determine this share, the Punjab Provincial Management Service Rules, 2004 assign this role to the competent authority. No functionary of the Federation has any authority for determination of posts in connection with affairs of a Province to be filled in through appointment by transfer. Any dispensation or a formula devised by the Federation, with or without consent of the Provincial Governments, for reservation of posts in connection with affairs of the Provinces to be filled through appointment by transfer or simple posting / transfer of members of a Service of the Federation is without lawful authority and jurisdiction and, hence, of no legal effect.

132.   Rules and executive instructions are distinguishable. Black's Law Dictionary has defined 'Rule' as "Generally, an established and authoritative standard or principle; a general norm mandating or guiding conduct or action in a given type of situation." It has been held in a case reported as Mir Muhd Sharif Vs. AJ&K Govt., (PLD 1986 SC (AJ&K) 87) that "The dictionary meanings of the word 'rule' are: Principles to which action or procedure is intended to conform." The authority delegated vide Section 23 (1) of the Punjab Civil Servants Act, 1974 is restricted to rules only. Determination of posts reserved to be filled through appointment by transfer is permissible only through the rules to be made by the competent authority. The Federation or the President lacks jurisdiction to reserve posts encadred for the Punjab Provincial Management Service for filling through appointment by transfer or to introduce the mode of allowing members of a Service of the Federation to hold those posts on the basis of simple orders of posting / transfer.

133.   What we have observed hereinabove are, prima fascia, distortions in the federal structure of our Constitution. Whenever an exclusive power of the Provinces is exercised or retained by the Federation without constitutional sanction, the federal system suffers injury.

134.   Learned counsel for the petitioners drew our attention towards the observations of Mr. Shraram Maheshwari at page 19, 20 and 21 of his book "Problems and Issues in Administrative Federalism", published in 1992, which read as follows:

"But one must not forget that 'All Pakistan' elements in the unified civil service have won neither universal acceptance nor applause in the country. Indeed, the Report of the Civil Service Commission (1978-79) contained a strong note of dissent by some of its members who questioned the rationale of such groups in a federal polity. The note observed:

"India and Pakistan are the only two federal systems in the world that have country-wide services in addition to central and provincial services. Pakistani country-wide services are even more centralized than the corresponding services in India. Their claim to all the key positions in the provinces as well as in the central government, not on the basis of performance but on the basis of a country-wide service, has given birth to resentment among other services. An additional puzzling aspect is the reason or reasons for which a country-wide service is organized for one kind of government activity but not for others. In order to clarify these issues one may briefly look into history.

Country-wide services were first organized by the British in India at a time when India was practically a unitary state. Originally, they included many services other than the ICS and the Indian Police. There were All India Services for forestry, education, engineering, health etc. Most of them were provincialized with the advance of provincial autonomy. Two of them, the so-called security services, namely ICS and Police, were allowed to retain their All India character. On independence, the Government of Pakistan retained the country-wide character of Police and the Civil Service of Pakistan (successor service of the ICS).

The British rulers had decided to give All India character to the ICS and Police largely for security considerations. The successive Pakistani governments retained the All Pakistan character of the Civil Service of Pakistan and Police presumably in the hope that it will engender national integration. However, a growing body of public opinion favours the provincialization of the All Pakistan Services. Some of the reasons for this opinion are as follows:

a) All Pakistan Services are not in keeping with the federal character of the state. Other federations do not have country-wide services. They have only central and provincial services.

b) Maintenance of law and order and collection of land revenue are, by tradition and by law, provincial subjects. These subjects should, therefore, be managed by provincial services and not by country-wide services.

c) Reservation of key posts in the provincial as well as the Federal Government for the All Pakistan Services is resented by other occupation groups. It is most acutely resented by the officers of the executive branch of the Provincial Civil Service (PCS). The PCS and the DMG / TAG perform substantially the same functions, yet their conditions of service, especially promotion prospects, vary widely. This variation is all the more galling as it is always traced back to the difference in the mode of recruitment than to difference in the level of responsibility and quality of performance. Originally, the difference in the service conditions of the PCS and the ICS was justified on the ground that the style of life and level of comfort of the native was lower than that of the European (Aitchison Commission, 1886). Now that both the PCS and the DMG / TAG are already de facto provincial services, their formal provincialization would only legalize the factual situation. Provincialization of other services (agriculture, engineering, health, education), in deference to provincial autonomy, has posed no threat to national unity. Provincialization of the Police and DMG should, therefore, create no such danger either.

d) The All Pakistan character of DMG / TAG is not an asset for the performance of policy-making function. The practice of not allocating of a DMG officer to one provincial cadre but rotating him between the various provinces and the federal government deprives him of the required depth of experience even though it might add some superficial breadth. Realizing this, even the British rulers posted the All India officers to provincial cadres for a lifelong career. The government of free India has also stuck to this practice. A country-wide service does facilitate communication and coordination through esprit de corps. However, it operates with equally devastating effect in promoting shared attitudes of authoritarianism and paternalistic ideas of "well-being" of the people in a country characterized by a continuous political vacuum; a cohesive, exclusive, closed elite-style country-wide cadre of officers is capable of more harm than good."

(Page 255-257 of the Report as quoted in Problems and Issues in Administrative Federalism by Shraram Maheshwari 1992 (page No. 19, 20 and 21)

135. On the other hand, the respondents claim that the concept of All Pakistan Service is integral to the Federal structure and the same has been recognized and protected under Article 146 and 240 of the Constitution. In fact, this concept, they assert, is indispensable not only to ensure national integration but also to enable the policy makers at the Federal Government level to have sufficient exposure to the problems of the people at grass-root level so that they are not disconnected from the ground realities while making policies at the highest level. It is argued that existence of an All-Pakistan Service, which starts its career at the grass-root level and finally rises at the national level, is not only necessary for national integration but also in the interest of public at large.

136. We do not find it appropriate to comment on the above pieces of opinion as we are not concerned with reasonability or wisdom of a policy option in the given circumstances. We are only interested in the constitutionality or legality of a matter properly brought before us for adjudication.

137. For the reasons, some of which have been noted hereinabove, we find the concept of reservation of posts in connection with affairs of the Provinces for a Service of the Federation incompatible with federal structure of the Constitution. But this conclusion cannot automatically lead to the finding that this dispensation is unconstitutional for being

incompatible with the federal structure of the Constitution. This conclusion may legitimately be drawn for a number of other legal reasons, but an arrangement may be incompatible with federal structure of the Constitution but the same may still be constitutional if the Constitution expressly provides for that. Extent of powers and functions of the Provinces has to be determined by the competent legislature in the prescribed manner and not by the courts. We are not sitting in the courts to substitute decisions and actions lawfully taken by the competent authorities with our own notions of what is the best policy option in a given set of circumstances. We have, however, seen all legal instruments from the Devolution Rules, 1920 to the Constitution as it is today and have found consistency in the entrustment of functions relating to administration of justice, police, land revenue and land records and coordination in district and divisional administration to the respective Provinces in respect of territories of the Provinces and subjects falling within exclusive provincial legislative domain. At provincial level, the Province deals with subjects which fall within its jurisdiction. Officers of the Pakistan Administrative Service while serving in a Province deals with nothing except provincial subjects. The Federation has no constitutional mandate to control provincial, divisional and district administration through officers of a Federal Service or through a said to be an All Pakistan Service. Idea of federal control through running of provincial affairs through officers subordinate to the Federation slaughters the very basis of administrative federalism. We are, therefore, convinced to hold that the Civil Service of Pakistan (Composition and Cadre) Rules, 1954 are void to the extent of control of provincial administration through officers of the Pakistan Administrative Service being in conflict with the federal structure of the Constitution.

Question # 11

Whether appointment by transfer and orders for posting / transfer are synonymous to each other and whether appointment by transfer can be made in absence of recommendation of the selection authority and without observing due competitive selection process?

138.   The Provincial Assembly of the Punjab enacted the Punjab Civil Servants Act, 1974, to regulate by law, the appointment to, and the terms and conditions of the services and posts of the Province of the Punjab. It provides that "All-Pakistan Unified Grades" has the same meaning as in All Pakistan Services (Change in Nomenclature) Rules, 1973. Section 4 of this Act provided that appointments to a civil service of the Province or to a civil post in connection with the affairs of the Province shall be made in the prescribed manner by the Governor or by a person authorized by him in that behalf. As per Section 2 (1) (g) of the Punjab Civil Servants Act, 1974, "prescribed" means prescribed by rules. Rules mean rules framed or deemed to have been framed under Section 23 of the Act ibid. The Punjab Civil Servants (Appointment and Conditions of Service) Rules, 1974 have been framed under Section 23 of the Act ibid. Rule 3 (1) of these rules provides that appointment to posts shall be made by promotion, transfer or initial recruitment, as may be prescribed. Rule 9 ibid provided that appointments by promotions or transfer to posts in various grades shall be made on the recommendations of the appropriate Committee or Board. Rule 10 ibid specifies that only such persons as possess the qualifications and meet the conditions laid down for the purpose of promotion or transfer to a post shall be considered by the Selection Authority. Rule 11 of the Rules ibid reads as follows:

"Appointments by transfer may be made if transfer is prescribed in the relevant service rules as a method of appointment to such post:

1) from one functional unit to another functional unit if the person holds an appointment on regular basis in the same basic scale and rank as that of the post to which appointment by transfer is proposed to be made provided he possesses the qualifications prescribed for initial recruitment to such posts; or

2) from amongst persons holding appointments in Federal Government and other provinces of Pakistan if the person fulfils conditions of appointment to the post to which he is transferred and satisfies such other conditions as may be laid down by the Government in this respect:

Provided that persons holding posts in All Pakistan Unified Grades may be appointed by transfer to a certain number of posts as may be determined from time to time."

139. The Punjab Provincial Management Service Rules, 2004 mainly regulate the Punjab Provincial Management Service. Rule 3 of the Rules ibid declares that the Service shall consist of the posts as specified in Schedule-II of the said Rules. Schedule II, mentioned in Rule 3 supra, is as follows:

"After allocating the share of the All Pakistan Unified Groups (APUG) officers as may be determined from time to time by the Competent Authority and the share of technical services in the Secretariat, the balance of the following posts in different grades shall form cadre strength of PMS in each grade: -

1	PMS: BS- 17	Section Officer / Deputy District Officer & other equivalent posts as per detail at Annex-Part (I).
2	PMS: BS- 18	Deputy Secretary / District Officer & other equivalent posts as per detail at Annex-Part (II).
3	PMS: BS- 19	Additional Secretary / Executive District Officer & other equivalent posts as per detail at Annex-Part (III).
4	PMS: BS- 20	Secretary to Government of the Punjab / District Coordination Officer & other equivalent posts as per detail at Annex-Part (IV).
5	PMS: BS- 21	Secretary to Government of the Punjab / District Coordination Officer & other equivalent posts as per detail at Annex-Part (V).

NOTE:

Share of technical services in the Secretariat posts shall be as under:

i	S.Os in the Secretariat	20%
ii	Deputy Secretaries in the Secretariat	20%
ii	Additional Secretaries in the Secretariat	20%

140. Before proceeding further, it will be advantageous to define necessary terms, e.g. employment, post, officer, appointment, service or services, posting / transfer, selection authority. An attempt to this effect is made hereinbelow:

EMPLOYMENT

"The concept of employment involves three ingredients: (a) employer; (b) employee; and (c) the contract of employment. The employer is one who employs, that is, one who engages the services of other persons. The employee is one who works for another for hire. The employment is the contract of service between the employer and the employee whereunder the employee agrees to serve the employer

subject to his control and supervision. Employment brings in the contract of service between the employer and the employee."
{Chintaman Rao Vs. State of Madhya Pradesh (1958 SCR 1340; Shankar Balajiivaje Vs. State of Maharashtra AIR 1962 SC 517)}

Post

The Supreme Court of Pakistan, in a judgment reported as Muhammad Mubeen-us-Salam and others Vs. Federation of Pakistan (PLD 2006 Supreme Court 602) has cited with approval the following paragraph, which attempts to explain the term "post", from a judgment of the Supreme Court of India reported as State of Assam Vs. Kanak Chandra (AIR 1967 SC 884): -

"16.   In the context of Arts. 309, 310 and 311, a post denotes an office. A person who holds a civil post under a State holds 'office' during the pleasure of the State, except as expressly provided by the Constitution, see Art. 310. A post under the State is an office or a position to which duties in connection with the affairs of the State are attached, an office or a position to which a person is appointed and which may exist apart from and independently of the holder of the post.

Article 310(2) contemplates that a post may be abolished and a person holding a post may be required to vacate the post, and it emphasizes the idea of a post existing apart from the holder of the post. A post may be created before the appointment or simultaneously with it. A post is an employment, but every employment is not a post. A post under the State means a post under the administrative control of the State. The State may create or abolish the post and may regulate the conditions of service of persons appointed to the post."

Officer

"A person who holds an office of trust, authority or command. In public affairs, the term refers esp. to a person holding public office under a national, state, or local government, and authorized by that government to exercise specific function. In corporate law, the term refers esp. to a person elected or appointed by the board of directors to manage the daily operations of a corporation, such as a CEO, president, secretary, or treasurer."

(Black's Law Dictionary, 8th Edition)

Services or service

The Hon'ble Supreme Court of Pakistan, has comprehensively explained the concept of 'service' in a judgment reported as mirza Muhammad Tufail Vs. District Returning Officer (PLD 2007 Supreme Court 16) in the following words:

"11. In this context, i.e., the expression "in the service" to be taken and construed in general sense and not in the restricted sense, it would be advantageous to refer to the meaning given in 79 CJS. P. 1139 which is reproduced hereinbelow: -

"Service or services: - The word 'service' has a multiplicity and a variety of meanings and different significations. It is not a simple word with the simple meaning, leaving no room for construction, but rather it is broad term of description, which varies in meaning according to the sense in which it is used and the context in which it is found, and the sense in which it is used must be determined from the context. Thus, the Courts have found it impracticable to attempt a definition by which to test every case that may arise.

As a noun: - As lexically defined, the word `service' means the act of serving, the act or instance of helping or benefiting; the act of helping another; the deed of one who serves.

The word 'service' is further defined as meaning aid or assistance rendered; a benefit, advantage, or obligations conferred; that which promotes interest or happiness; useful office; avail.

'service' indicates a master-servant relationship, or it implies a submission to the will of another as to direction and control, and when employed to indicate these concepts it is defined as meaning the performance of labour for the benefit of another or at another's command; labour performed in the interest under the direction of others; any work done for the benefit of another; employment in the interest of a person or of a cause.

The word 'service' is also defined as meaning the being employed to serve another; the position of a servant; the state of being a servant; the occupation, condition, or status of a servant; the work of a servant; the work of a slave, hired man, or employee; the attendance of any inferior, hired helper, slave, etc.

Now according to the definition described above, service means being employed to serve another; it implies the submission to the will of another as to direction and control, to do work for another. The determining factor to hold a person to be in the service of a body or authority, implies sub-ordination to that body. There are five tests for such sub-ordination, namely, the power of the authority of the appointment to the office (ii) the power of removal or dismissal of the holder from the office (iii) the payment of remuneration (iv) the nature of functions of the holder of the office, he performs (v) the nature and strength of control and supervision of the authority. The decisive test is that of appointment and removal from service while the remuneration is neutral factor and not decisive. All the aforesaid tests need not be cumulated and not necessarily must co-exist and what has to be considered is the substance of the matter which must be determined by a consideration of all the factors present in a case ad whether stress will be laid on one factor or the other will depend on each particular case."

Appointment:

1. The designation of a person to discharge the duties of an office or trust by the person or persons having authority therefor.

    The action of nominating to or placing in an office; the office itself.

    (KLR Encyclopedia Law Dictionary)

2. The designation of a person, such as a nonelected public official, for a job or duty; esp; the naming of someone to a nonelected public office.

    (Black's Law Dictionary, 8th Edition)

3. "Appointment obviously refers to appointment to an office. The term 'appointment' therefore implies the conception of tenure,

duration, emolument and duties and obligations fixed by law or by some rule having the force of law."
(Sukhandan Thakur v. State of Bihar, AIR 1957 Pat 617)

Transfer / Posting

1. The word 'posting' means assigning someone to a post, that is 'a position' or a 'job', specially one to which a person is appointed.

2. Transfer in relation to service reduced to simple terms means a change of place of employment within an organization, as stated in New Oxford English Dictionary, 1993 Edition, Vol.2, p.3367. It is an incidence of public service and generally does not require the consent of the employee. In most service rules, there are express provisions relating to transfer. (V. Jagannatha Rao and Ors. Vs. State of Andhra Pradesh and Ors. {(2001) 10 SCC 401}).

3. Transfer essentially is a movement to any other place or branch of the organization on a similar post in the same cadre. {B. Varadha Rao Vs. State of Karnataka (AIR 1987 SC 287)}.

Selection Authority

"Selection authority" means the Punjab Public Service Commission, departmental selection board, departmental selection committee or other authority or body on the recommendation of, or in consultation with which any appointment or promotion, as may be prescribed, is made;"
(Section 2 (j) of the Punjab Civil Servants Act, 1974)

Functional Unit

"Functional Unit" means a group of posts or a part of such group sanctioned as a separate unit in or under a Department;"
(Rule 2 (h) of the Punjab Civil Servants (Appointment and Conditions of Service) Rules, 1974)

Cadre

'Cadre' means the strength of a service or part of a service sanctioned as a separate unit.

141. Appointments to posts specified in Schedule-II of the Punjab Provincial Management Service Rules, 2004 are permissible through one of the following methods:

1. Appointment by initial recruitment means appointment of persons, on the recommendation of the Selection Authority, after open advertisement in the press, from amongst the candidates possessing requisite qualifications against posts reserved for initial recruitment in the cadre;

2. Appointment by promotion means appointment of persons from amongst members of the cadre, on the recommendation of the Selection Authority, against posts reserved for promotion in the cadre; and

3. Appointment by transfer means the appointment, on recommendation of the Selection Authority, of persons holding posts under the Federal or Provincial Governments and officers of the All Pakistan Unified Grades, against posts in the Provincial Management Service reserved for filling through appointment by transfer, through the process of inviting applications from all eligible and qualified candidates.

142. Whereas appointment by initial recruitment and promotion is commonly understood correctly, appointment by transfer is often confused with normal posting / transfer.

Appointment by transfer and simple posting / transfer are distinguishable, inter alia, in the following respects:

a. Recommendation of the selection authority is not required for posting / transfer but it is a condition-precedent for appointment by transfer;

b. Transfer / posting is normally from one post encadred for a service / functional unit to another post within the same cadre or from one station of duty to another against the same post. On the other hand, appointment by transfer is always from one service / cadre / functional unit to another;

c. Whereas an officer remains member of his service / cadre / functional unit in case of posting / transfer, he ceases to be a member of his original service / cadre / functional unit upon his appointment by transfer and becomes member of the service / cadre / functional unit to which he is appointed;

d. An officer appointed by transfer has a right to rejoin his previous functional unit if he has lien to this effect. There is no concept of lien in case of posting / transfer;

e. Posting is generally for a period extending upto three years; appointment by transfer is normally till superannuation;

f. Due competitive process amongst eligible and willing officers is necessary for appointment by transfer. There is no such requirement in case of posting / transfer;

g. Upon appointment by transfer, an officer so appointed again becomes a probationer in the new service / functional unit / cadre. This is not the case in the matter of posting / transfer; and

h. Consent of the officer is not required for posting / transfer. On the other hand, appointment by transfer depends upon willingness and merit of the officer.

143.   Whereas members of other functional units of the Province of Punjab and persons holding appointments in the Federal Government and other Provincial Governments who possess the requisite qualifications are eligible to compete for appointment by transfer in the Punjab Provincial Management Service, no specific quota has been fixed for any functional unit; however, there is a reference for allocation of posts for the All Pakistan Unified Grades.

144.   Rule 11 of the Punjab Civil Servants (Appointment and Conditions of Service) Rules, 1974, read with Rule 3 and Schedule-II of the Punjab Provincial Management Service Rules, 2004 has been grossly misconstrued in the sense of simple posting / transfer. Officers of the All Pakistan Unified Grades are posted to hold posts in connection with affairs of the Province without following due competitive procedure of selection by the selection authority. Applications are not invited from all eligible and willing officers of the Federal and other Provincial Governments and of other functional units of the Government of the Punjab to compete for appointment by transfer. Right to trade and profession is a fundamental right under Article 18 of the Constitution. Employment under the Government is a lawful profession. Appointment by transfer without open competition amongst the eligible officers not only amounts to impliedly suspend, take away or abridge fundamental right guaranteed by Article 18 of the Constitution but is also violative of Article 4 (2) (b) of the Constitution which commands that no person shall be prevented from or be hindered in doing that which is not prohibited by law. Making appointments by transfer without open advertisement amounts to preventing eligible and willing officers to enter into a lawful profession on the basis of merit.

145.   The Punjab Civil Servants Act, 1974 has been enacted by the Provincial Legislature in lawful exercise of its power under Article 240 (b) of the Constitution. The Punjab Civil

Servants (Appointment and Conditions of Service) Rules, 1974 and the Punjab Provincial Management Service Rules, 2004 have been framed under Section 23 (1) of the Punjab Civil Servants Act, 1974. It is trite law that express mention of one thing implies the exclusion of another. Except the posts reserved for technical services in the administrative departments, the only method for officers of other functional units to occupy cadre posts of the Punjab Provincial Management Service is to become member of the said Service through appointment by transfer. All other methods including holding such a post on the basis of transfer orders are, therefore, void and of no legal effect. Obviously, a person acts in fraud of law, who, the letter of the law being inviolate, uses the law contrary to its intention.

146. The Civil Service of Pakistan (Composition and Cadre) Rules, 1954 are without lawful authority and jurisdiction to the extent of holding of posts by members of the Pakistan Administrative Service or the Secretariat Group on the basis of transfer orders and not through appointment by transfer as prescribed by or under the Punjab Civil Servants Act, 1974. Non-observance of competitive process for appointment through transfer is void in terms of Article 8 of the Constitution on account of being in contravention of the fundamental right guaranteed by Article 18 of the Constitution.

147. We hold that members of other functional units can become members of the Punjab Provincial Management Service through appointment by transfer to be made by the authorities competent to make appointments in that Service on the recommendation of the selection authority after a transparent and open competition amongst all eligible and willing candidates. We further hold that the fundamental right to trade and profession extends to all willing and eligible members of all federal as well as provincial functional units or functional units of other public entities in the matter of their appointment by transfer to the Punjab Provincial Management Service.

Question # 12

Whether Article 146 of the Constitution allows reservation of posts in connection with affairs of the Provinces for a Service of the Federation?

148. The S.R.O No. 88(I)/2014 dated 10.02.2014 substituted reference to sub-section (1) and (2) of Section 241 of the Government of Indian Act, 1935 in the preamble of the Civil Service of Pakistan (Composition and Cadre) Rules, 1954 with Article 146 of the Constitution. Learned counsel for the petitioners term this action an implied admission by the Federation that sub-section (1) and (2) of Section 241 or Section 263 of the Government of Indian Act, 1935, or any provisions in the subsequent Constitutions of the Islamic Republic of Pakistan similar to the said Sections of the Government of India Act, 1935 cannot lend legality to the aforesaid rules to the extent of reservation of posts in connection with affairs of the Provinces for members of a Service of the Federation. The further averred that it had impliedly been admitted that the only constitutional basis for the aforesaid rules can be Article 146 of the Constitution. The said Article reads as follows:

> **"146. Power of Federation to confer powers, etc., on Provinces, in certain cases. ___**
>
> (1) Notwithstanding anything contained in the Constitution, the Federal Government may, with the consent of the Government of a Province, entrust either conditionally or unconditionally to that Government, or to its officers, functions in relation to any matter to which the executive authority of the Federation extends.
>
> (2) An Act of Majlis-e-Shoora (Parliament) may, notwithstanding that it relates to a matter with respect to which a Provincial Assembly has no power to make laws, confer powers and impose duties upon a Province or officers and authorities thereof.

(3)   Where by virtue of this Article powers and duties have been conferred or imposed upon a Province or officers or authorities thereof, there shall be paid by the Federation to the Province such sum as may be agreed or, in default of agreement, as may be determined by an arbitrator appointed by the Chief Justice of Pakistan, in respect of any extra costs of administration incurred by the Province in connection with the exercise of those powers or the discharge of those duties."

149.   The above Article is a replica of Section 124 of the Government of India Act, 1935, reproduced below:

1.   Notwithstanding anything in this Act, the Governor General may, with the consent of the Government of a Province or the Ruler of a Federated State, entrust either conditionally or unconditionally to that Government or Ruler, or to their respective officers, functions in relation to any matter to which the executive authority of the Federation extends.

2.   An Act of the Federal Legislature may, notwithstanding that it relates to a matter with respect to which a Provincial Legislature has no power to make laws, confer powers and impose duties upon a Province or officers and authorities thereof.

3.   An Act of the Federal Legislature, which extends to a Federated State may confer powers and impose duties upon the State or officers and authorities thereof to be designated for the purpose by the Ruler.

4.   Where by virtue of this section powers and duties have been conferred or imposed upon a Province or Federated State or officers or authorities thereof, there shall be paid by the Federation to the Province or State such sum as may be agreed or, in default of agreement, as may be determined by an arbitrator appointed by the Chief Justice of India, in respect of any extra costs of administration incurred by the Province or State in connection with the exercise of those powers and duties."

150.   Article 146 of the Constitution does not relate to the question of reservation of posts in connection with affairs of the Provinces for members of a Service of the Federation; it does not deal with any matter relating to an All-Pakistan Service; it is also irrelevant to the issue of determination of conditions of recruitment and of service of any federal service or posts in connection with affairs of the Federation and of the Provinces. It simply relates to entrustment of functions of the Federation to the Provinces. To create, regulate and control the Provincial Services and posts in connection with affairs of the Provinces is not a Federal subject, therefore, the said Article 146 is not applicable to the issue of reservation of posts in connection with affairs of the Provinces for members of a Service of the Federation.

151.   It is interesting to note that whenever an arrangement under Article 146 is resorted to, the Federation is under obligation to pay the cost of performance of additional duties assigned to a Province by the Federation. We specifically asked the counsels appearing for the parties in these proceedings to inform us about the estimated cost of the performance of federal functions by the Provinces, any agreement between the Federation and the Provinces over the cost or any award of an arbitrator appointed by the Chief Justice of Pakistan or the cost actually paid by the Federation to the Provinces in respect of the Civil Service of Pakistan (Composition and Cadre) Rules, 1954. We were amused to know that no party is concerned with the cost despite the fact that the Constitution has specifically provided for the same.

152.   In the light of the above discussion, we hold that Article 146 of the Constitution does not authorize the Federation to reserve posts in connection with affairs of the Provinces for the Pakistan Administrative Service or to exercise control over Provincial Services or posts in connection with affairs of the Provinces. As an inescapable consequence of this declaration, the Civil Service of Pakistan (Composition and Cadre) Rules, 1954, to the extent of reservation of posts in connection with affairs of the Provinces and other matters falling within jurisdiction of the Provinces, are declared to be ultra vires Article 146 of the Constitution and are, therefore, held to be without lawful authority and of no legal effect.

Question # 13

Whether the Listed Posts (Substantive Appointments) Act, 1967 (Act XVI of 1967) validated reservation of posts in connection with affairs of the Provinces for a Service of the Federation or not?

153.   The said Act reads as follows:

"LISTED POSTS (SUBSTANTIVE APPOINTMENTS) ACT, 1967
(Act XVI of 1967)

An Act to provide for vesting in the President the power to make substantive apppintment to certain posts in connection with the affairs of a Province

Whereas Article 178 of the Constitution provides that, subject to the Constitution and law, appointments to a civil post in connection with affairs of a Province shall be made, and the terms and conditions of service of a person, not being a member of an All-Pakistan Service, serving in connection with the affairs of a Province shall be prescribed, by the Governor of the Province or a person authorized by the Governor in that behalf:

And whereas it is expedient to provide for vesting in the President the power to make substantive appointment of persons, not being members of the Civil Service of Pakistan, to certain posts in connection with the affairs of a Province which are borne on the cadre of that Service and for matters ancillary thereto;

And whereas the national interest of Pakistabn in relation to the achievement of uniformity within the meaning of clause (2) of Article 131 of the Constitution requires Central legislation in the matter;

It is hereby enacted as follows:-

1.   **Short title and commencement**.- (1) This Act may be called the Listed Posts (Substantive Appointments) Act, 1967.

(2) It shall come into force at once.

2.   **Power to specify a percentage of CSP cadre posts to be filled by others**.- The President may, by rules, prescribe a percentage of the superior posts in connection with the affairs of a Province borne on the cadre of the Civil Service of Pakistan which may be filled by persons who are not members of the Civil Service of Pakistan; and a post which may be filled by such person is hereinafter referred to as the "listed post."

3.   **Power to make substantive appointments to a listed post of certain persons**.- Substantive appointment of a person, not being a member of the Civil Service of Pakistan, to a listed post shall be made by the President after consultation with the Provincial Government concerned and the Central Public Service Commission.

4.   **Validation**.- Any such appointment as is mentioned in section 3 made by the President before the commencement of the Act shall be

deemed to have been made under this Act as if this Act were in force when such appointment was made.

5. **Power to make rules**.- The President may make rules to prescribe-

(a) the percentage of posts referred to in section 2;

(b) the remuneration and other terms and conditions of service of persons appointed under section 3; and

(c) such other matters as may be necessary for carrying out the purposes of this Act."

154. The Province of the Punjab argues that the apportionment of provincial posts amongst members of CSP and PCS was sanctified retrospectively by Act XVI of 1967 which also lends legality to the Civil Service of Pakistan (Composition and Cadre) Rules, 1954. In response to our question regarding the rules envisaged in Section 5 of the Act ibid, it was frankly admitted that no rules were framed by the President under the Act. It was also admitted that no system was devised for implementation of Section 3 of the Act. A list of persons benefiting from the said Section 3 was also not submitted in this Court. Since the powers purported to be vested in the President of Pakistan under Act XVI of 1967 are to be exercised through rules to be framed for carrying out the purposes of the Act, the Act remained inoperative in absence of the rules to be framed under the Act.

155. Preamble of the Civil Service of Pakistan (Composition and Cadre) Rules, 1954, even after amendments introduced in the said rules in 2014, does not refer to the Act XVI of 1967 as an enabling provision for the said rules.

156. No provision similar to Section 246 and 263 of the Government of India Act, 1935 was available in the Constitution of the Islamic Republic of Pakistan, 1962. It was not explained to us that how posts in connection with the affairs of the Provinces could be included in the Listed Posts throgh a Federal Law. No plausible justification was offered to establish that the Act XVI was not irreconciliably inconsistent with Article 178 of the Constitution of the Islamic Republic of Pakistan, 1962, which vested exclusive powers in the Provincial Governors with respect to Provincial Services and posts in connection with affairs of the Provinces. Nothing was placed on record to show existence of valid resolution of the concerned Provincial Assembly authorizing the Central Legislature to legislate on the issue of reservation of posts in connection with affairs of the Province for the Civil Service of Pakistan and vesting in the President of Pakistan powers to make appointments theiragainst. Act XVI of 1967 cannot survive in absence of any of the aforesaid constitutional requirements. It is, therefore, declared to be enacted without lawful authority and is, as a consequence, of no legal effect. Words of Act XVI of 1967 are absolutely incapable of conferring the authority and assigning the duties purported to be conferred and assigned thereby.

Question # 14

Whether prescription of training as a condition-precedent for being eligible to be considered for promotion for officers of the Punjab Provincial Management Service is lawful or not?

157. The petitioners state that promotion of a civil servant in Punjab is governed by Section 8 of the Punjab Civil Servants Act, 1974, and Rule 12 of the Punjab Civil Servants (Appointment and Conditions of Service) Rules, 1974. It has been stated that the expression "qualification" referred to in Section 8 does not include training. Requirement of passing departmental examination could, however, be found in Rule 12 supra, but the requirement of mandatory training as a pre-condition for promotion does not have the backing either of Section 8 or Rule 12 supra, it is argued. It is further submitted that the Notification dated June 4, 2004 has the effect of modifying the substantive provisions of law as well as the Rules, which could not have been done by an executive order. The petitioners have prayed that the Notification dated 04.06.2004, whereby mandatory training for promotion up to grade 21 was prescribed for PCS officers, may be declared without legal

authority and ultra vires the provisions of Section 8 of the Punjab Civil Servants Act, 1974 read with Rule 12 of the Punjab Civil Servants (Appointment and Conditions of Service) Rules, 1974. On the other hand, Province of the Punjab submits that imposition of the condition of training for promotion is neither discriminatory nor does it affect the career prospects of the Provincial Civil Servants.

158.   Section 8(1) of the Punjab Civil Servants Act, 1974 provides that a civil servant shall be eligible to be considered for appointment by promotion to a post reserved for promotion in the service or cadre to which he belongs in a manner as may be prescribed, provided that he possesses the prescribed qualifications. "Prescribed" means prescribed through rules (Section 2(g) of the Act ibid). Rules mean the rules made or deemed to have been made under the Act (Section 2(i) of the Act ibid). The Punjab Civil Servants (Appointment and Conditions of Service) Rules, 1974 are the rules relevant to the subject under consideration Rule 12 whereof reads as follows:

> "Until the rules laying down the qualifications and other conditions for the purposes of promotion are made, no person shall be promoted to a post in higher grade on regular basis unless he has passed such test as may be specified by the appointing authority to be conducted by the selection authority:
>
> Provided that the Government may dispense with the requirement of passing the test in relation to such posts as may be specified."

159.   Section 23 of the Punjab Civil Servants Act, 1974, reproduced below, is also materially relevant to the lis at hand:

> "(1)   The Governor, or any person authorized in this behalf may make such rules as appear to him to be necessary or expedient for carrying out the purposes of this Act.
>
> (2)   Any rules, orders or instructions in respect of any terms and conditions of service of civil servants duly made or issued by an authority competent to make them and in force immediately before the commencement of this Act shall, in so far as such rules, orders or instructions are not inconsistent with the provisions of this Act, be deemed to be rules made under this Act."

160.   Word 'qualification' has not been defined in the Punjab Civil Servants Act, 1974 and the Punjab Civil Servants (Appointment and Conditions of Service) Rules, 1974. Dictionary defines 'qualification' as a condition that must be fulfilled before a right can be acquired. With reference to eligibility of a person for consideration for promotion, what is included in the term 'qualification' and what is not included therein is a question of policy to be determined by the competent authority through law or the rules. What is of interest to us is the question of competence of competent authority to prescribe qualifications for promotion. We intend to address this question in the succeeding paragraphs.

161.   It has been held by the Hon'ble Supreme Court of Pakistan in a case reported as Government of N.W.F.P Vs. Muzzaffar Iqbal (1990 SCMR 1524) that no one can claim a vested right in promotion or in the terms and conditions for promotion to a higher post. It has further been held by the Hon'ble Supreme Court that the Government has the right to enhance the qualifications and standards for recruitment and promotion in order to maintain efficiency in service. The Hon'ble Supreme Court has also held in a case reported as Muhammad Umar Malik Vs. Federal Service Tribunal (PLD 1987 SC 172) that no vested right in promotion or rules determining eligibility for promotion exists. The Hon'ble Supreme Court, in another case, examined the question that whether the right of a civil servant to be considered for promotion is to be ascertained in accordance with the rules prevalent at the time of his appointment and not later rules applicable for promotion on the date of promotion. View of the Service Tribunal holding that rules applicable to a civil servant on date of entry into service with regard to promotion acquired finality qua him was rejected by the Hon'ble Supreme Court for being against law laid down by the

Supreme Court with regard to meaning and scope of terms and conditions of service. It has further been held by the Hon'ble Supreme Court that the rules for promotion do not confer a vested right and these rules can be altered to the disadvantage of a civil servant awaiting promotion. It has been held in a case reported as Muhammad Ashraf Mirza Vs. Government of the Punjab {1988 PLC (C.S.) 400} that promotion is governed by latest law or rules in force at time of actual promotion. Promotion right cannot be claimed on basis of service rules which are found to be repealed by subsequent rules which hold field at time of actual promotion. It was also held in a case reported as Province of Punjab Vs. S. Muhammad Zafar Bukhari (PLD 1997 SC 351) that the rules applicable and conditions required to be satisfied on the date of appointment are to be taken into consideration and not what were on an earlier date. Civil servant can neither have vested right in terms and conditions of a post higher than held by him nor a change in the recruitment rules of higher post can be said to operate against him retrospectively. Persons eligible for promotion cannot claim automatic promotion on the expiry of a certain period after fulfilling eligibility criteria. Promotion is necessarily required to be made on the recommendation of the Selection Authority from amongst eligible persons found fit for promotion. It was held in a case reported as Muhammad Aftab Mahmud Vs. Secretary, Establishment Division {1989 PLC (C.S.) 609} that five years of service in Grade-17 was the minimum requirement for eligibility for promotion to Grade-18 but rendering of five years' service would not ipso facto entitle the incumbent to enter Grade 18 by promotion. Filling of the posts lay within the discretion of concerned authorities. It has also been held by the Hon'ble Supreme Court in a case reported as the Central Board of Revenue Vs. Mr. Asad Ahmad Khan (PLD 1960 SC 81) that the rule of promotion on the basis of seniority-cum-fitness can be changed by the Government to make promotion dependent upon result of departmental examination as the Government is entitled to make rules in interest of efficiency of service.

162.   The conclusion of the above discussion seems to be simple and clear: the competent authority can amend, substitute or novate conditions of appointment in public interest. Conditions of appointment may relate to conditions for initial recruitment, conditions for confirmation, conditions for promotion and conditions for appointment through transfer. Generally, age limits, academic qualifications, experience, trainings, examinations and performance evaluations are some of the key components of the conditions of appointment.

163.   After concluding that training can legitimately be made a condition-precedent for promotion, we now may find an appropriate way for its prescription. In other words, we may endeavour to find an answer to the question that whether, after enactment of the Punjab Civil Servants Act, 1974, conditions of recruitment and of service of the civil servants are permissible to be determined otherwise than through law or rules? Conversely speaking, whether conditions of recruitment and of service of the civil servants can lawfully be determined through executive orders?

164.   Words used in sub-section (1) and (2) of Section 23 of the Punjab Civil Servants Act, 1974 need to be carefully read and understood. Whereas the said sub-section (2) validates, subject to consistency with the Act, all rules, orders or instructions in respect of any terms and conditions of service of civil servants duly made or issued by an authority competent to make them and in force immediately before the commencement of that Act, sub-section (1) thereof envisages only rules to carry out purposes of the Act. Absence of "orders or instructions" in the said sub-section (1) rules out issuance of orders or instructions to carry out purposes of the Act save as may expressly be provided by the Act or the Punjab Civil Servants (Appointment and Conditions of Service) Rules, 1974. It is now universally accepted that prescription of one is prohibition of another. Since Rule 12 of the Punjab Civil Servants (Appointment and Conditions of Service) Rules, 1974 specifically mentions the qualifications and other conditions for the purposes of promotion to be laid down through rules, therefore, the Notification dated 04.06.2004, which admittedly does not fall within the definition of the rules, cannot be given the force of the rules. There is no provision in the Punjab Civil Servants (Appointment and Conditions of Service) Rules, 1974 allowing an executive authority to prescribe the qualifications and other conditions for the purposes of

promotion, therefore, an executive authority cannot exercise that power through an executive order.

165. Right to trade and profession guaranteed by Article 18 of the Constitution is subject to qualifications as may be prescribed by law. Training for appointment through promotion can, therefore, be prescribed through a law. We are convinced to hold that training can be made a condition-precedent for promotion either through law or the rules. Since the Notification of 04.06.2004 is neither a law nor rule or issued under express authority of a law or rules, therefore, the same is declared to have been issued without lawful authority and consequently is of no legal effect.

Question # 15

Whether mere lapse of time has made the Civil Service of Pakistan (Composition and Cadre) Rules, 1954 valid to the extent of reservation of posts in connection with affairs of the Provinces and other matters falling within exclusive provincial domain?

166. Mere lapse of time does not cure illegality of an instrument or action or inaction. Members of the service created under the Civil Service of Pakistan (Composition and Cadre) Rules, 1954 are holding posts in connection with affairs of the Province since 1954. Before these rules, posts in connection with affairs of the Province had been held firstly by members of the Pakistan Administrative Service and thereafter by members of the Civil Service of Pakistan since 15th of August, 1947 in absence of a law or rules. It is, therefore, not impermissible to challenge legality of holding of posts in connection with affairs of the Province by members of a Service of the Federation or to question the validity of the Civil Service of Pakistan (Composition and Cadre) Rules, 1954 merely on ground of lapse of considerable time. It has been held in Fazlul Quader Chaudhary's case (PLD 1963 SC 486) that if a person is holding an office without any lawful authority, his continuance in office is continuing wrong giving rise to a cause of action de die in diem and there can be no question of any laches. Also, there is no estoppel against the Constitution. It was further held in the said case that on questions relating to the constitutionality of actions, the ground of laches cannot prevail, for there can be no estoppel against the Constitution and an act which is unconstitutional cannot become constitutional merely by lapse of time, nor can it vest anyone with any kind of legal right to benefit from such an unconstitutional act. The Civil Service of Pakistan (Composition and Cadre) Rules, 1954, to the extent of reservation of posts in connection with affairs of the Provinces for a Service of the Federation and other matters falling within exclusive provincial jurisdiction are hereby declared to be without lawful authority and of no legal effect.

Question # 16

Whether officers of the Pakistan Administrative Service can be posted on posts other than those specified in the Schedule to the Civil Service of Pakistan (Composition and Cadre) Rules, 1954?

167. The petitioners have submitted that officers belonging to the Pakistan Administrative Service are also posted against posts other than those specified in the Schedule of the Civil Service of Pakistan (Composition and Cadre) Rules, 1954. They contend that this practice is not lawful and has adverse effect on their promotion prospects. The Federation of Pakistan avers that the Federal Government merely places the services of an APS / APUG officer at the disposal of a provincial government as per their request and requirements. Once an APS / APUG officer is placed at the disposal of a provincial government, his further posting against a particular post becomes the sole and exclusive prerogative of that provincial government. Further, the Civil Service of Pakistan (Composition and Cadre) Rules, 1954 do not prohibit posting of the officers of the Pakistan Administrative Service on non-cadre posts. Rule 14 of the Civil Service of Pakistan (Composition and Cadre) Rules, 1954 makes it binding upon an officer of the Pakistan Administrative Service, posted in a Province, to

submit himself to the orders of the Provincial Government under which he is serving and his whole time is at the disposal of the Provincial Government. The Province of the Punjab submits that, every civil servant is liable to serve anywhere, within or outside Pakistan, in any equivalent or higher post, under the Federal Government or any Provincial Government within the contemplation of Section 10 of the Civil Servants Act, 1973. The Pakistan Administrative Service Officers Association is of the view that officers of an All Pakistan Service can be posted against posts other than those mentioned in the Civil Service of Pakistan (Composition and Cadre) Rules, 1954.

168.   The question under consideration pales into insignificance after the declaration made by us on the constitutionality of the Civil Service of Pakistan (Composition and Cadre) Rules, 1954, to the extent of reservation of posts in connection with affairs of the Provinces for the Pakistan Administrative Service. We do not find it necessary to separately deal with this question as our aforesaid declaration comprehensively addresses this issue. We, however, may like to briefly discuss the proposition advanced by the Federation and the Province of the Punjab that absence of prohibition can be a legal ground for an act or omission.

169.   It is settled law that the jurisdiction of the executive must be justified and vindicated by affirmative constitutional or statutory provision or it does not exist. The Hon'ble Supreme Court of Pakistan has held in a case reported as Nawaz Sharif Vs. Federation of Pakistan (PLD 1993 SC 473) that:

> "In view of the express provisions of our written constitution detailing with fullness the powers and duties of the various agencies of the government that it holds in balance there is no room of any residual or enabling powers inhering in any authority established by it besides those conferred upon it by specific words."

170.   It has been held in a case reported as Attorney General for Ceylon Vs. A.D. Silva (PLD 1953 PC 58) that:

> "A public officer had not by reason of the fact that he is in the service of the Crown a right to act for and on behalf of Crown in all matters which concern the Crown and that the right to act for the Crown in any particular matter must be established by reference to statute."

171.   It has been held in cases reported as Federation Vs. Saeed Ahmad (PLD 1974 SC 151) and Sabir Shah Vs. Shad Muhammad (PLD 1995 SC 66), as quoted by Justice (R) Fazal Karim in Chapter 1, para 2 at page number 21 of his book "Judicial Review of Public Actions (Volume-1)" that:

> "The written Constitution is the source from which all governmental power emanates; it defines its scope and ambit so that each functionary should act within his respective sphere. No power can, therefore, be claimed by any functionary which is not to be found within the four corners of the Constitution nor can anyone transgress the limits therein specified. The essential point is that the Constitution is the paramount law and the authority which different organs created by it exercise is derived authority, that is, derived from the Constitution."

172.   There is little doubt, so said Justice Kaikaus in Jamal Shah Vs. Election Commissioner (PLD 1966 SC 1) that "its object was to negative any claim by the Government that it had inherent power to take action which was not subject to law or that it could deal with individuals in any manner which was not positively prohibited by law."

173.   Executive authority is the administration of the government in accordance with law. There is no inherent executive authority and such authority has to be as provided for in the Constitution or the law, as held by the Hon'ble Supreme Court of Pakistan in a case reported as Jamal Shah Vs. Election Commission (PLD 1966 SC 1).

174.   The Government is like a solar system, they say, in which each body revolves on its own axis and travels in its own orbit, while the power which keeps them in due relation to

each other and the central body is that of the Constitution. Whenever an action is taken by an executive functionary, it must be referable to the Constitution or a law made thereunder or rules framed under a law or regulations enforced under the rules or the executive authority expressly derived from any of the above sources. We are, therefore, constrained to hold that absence of prohibition is not a valid source of authority for executive functionaries. This declaration does not require that every move of an executive functionary must have been written in detail in the applicable standing operating procedures; he is at liberty to act reasonably within the four corners of the regulatory framework applicable to him and he must take all necessary and proper measures essential for performance of functions lawfully assigned to him.

175.   The contention that Section 10 of the Civil Servants Act, 1973, legalizes posting of a civil servant against any post needs examination. The said Section 10 reads as follows:

> **"Posting and transfer. -** Every civil servant shall be liable to serve anywhere within or outside Pakistan, in any equivalent or higher post under the Federal Government, or any Provincial Government or local authority, or a corporation or body set up or established by any such Government:
>
> Provided that nothing contained in this section shall apply to a civil servant recruited specifically to serve in a particular area or region:
>
> Provided further that, where a civil servant is required to serve in a post outside his service or cadre, his terms and conditions of service as to his pay shall not be less favourable than those to which he would have been entitled if he had not been so required to serve."

176.   Section 10 of the Civil Servants Act, 1973 relates only to posting / transfer. The Act ibid does not define posting / transfer. The meanings assigned to these expressions by dictionaries and judicial pronouncements are, therefore, required to be kept in view to have a proper and legally tenable understanding of the said Section 10. The Hon'ble Supreme Court of India in B. Varadha Rao Vs. State of Karnataka (AIR 1987 SC 287) has defined transfer as a movement of an employee to any other place or branch of the organization on a similar post in the same cadre. New Oxford English Dictionary, 1993 Edition, Vol.2, p.3367 provides that transfer in relation to service reduced to simple terms means a change of place of employment within an organization. It has been held by the Hon'ble Supreme Court of India in V. Jagannatha Rao and Ors. Vs. State of Andhra Pradesh and Ors. {(2001) 10 SCC 401} that transfer is an incidence of public service and generally does not require the consent of the employee. In most service rules, there are express provisions relating to transfer. The word 'posting' means assigning someone to a post, that is 'a position' or a 'job', specially one to which a person is appointed.

177.   Section 25 of the Civil Servants Act, 1973, reads as follows:

1) The President or any person authorised by the President in this behalf, may make such rules as appear to him to be necessary or expedient for carrying out the purposes of this Act.

2) Any rules, orders or instructions in respect of any terms and conditions of service of civil servants duly made or issued by an authority competent to make them and in force immediately before the commencement of this Act shall, in so far as such rules, orders or instructions are not inconsistent with the provisions of this Act, be deemed to be rules made under this Act.

178.   Recruitment and service rules are framed in respect of each service / functional unit / cadre. Posts reserved to be held by members of the service / functional unit / cadre are specified in those rules. Posting of an employee can be made by a competent authority from one post to another as specified in the applicable rules. The rules are, in fact, practical manifestation of the said Section 10. This section can be operational to the extent specified in the rules and does not operate as a license to militate against or to undo the rules. The

Hon'ble Supreme Court of Pakistan in the case of Masood Ahmed Vs. Taj Muhammad Baloch (1999 SCMR 755) has held that Section 10 does not authorize the competent authority to transfer a civil servant out of cadre.

179.   Legislative competence and power to encadre posts for a particular service / functional unit / cadre are co-extensive. Whereas Federation has full and comprehensive powers to encadre, through rules, posts in connection with affairs of the Federation for any federal service / functional unit / cadre and exercise powers enumerated in the said Section 10 in the prescribed manner, the Federation lacks jurisdiction in respect of posts in connection with affairs of the Provinces for any federal service. When we hold that the Federation does not possess, in our constitutional scheme since 15th of August, 1947 till date, lawful competence to encadre or reserve posts in connection with affairs of the Provinces through the Civil Service of Pakistan (Composition and Cadre) Rules, 1954, it automatically results in the declaration that members of the Pakistan Administrative Service are ineligible to hold posts, through transfer / posting, in connection with affairs of the Provinces as specified in the Schedule to the rules supra or any other posts in connection with affairs of the Provinces except through appointment by transfer in the prescribed manner. When members of a Federal service / functional unit / cadre are appointed by transfer to a Provincial Service, they cease to be members of their parent service / functional unit / cadre and their posting / transfer is regulated by the recruitment and service rules of the relevant Provincial Service.

180.   It is accordingly hereby held that posting of an employee is permissible only against posts reserved for the Service / functional unit / cadre to which he belongs. It is further held that members of the Pakistan Administrative Service have no authority of law to hold posts in connection with affairs of the Provinces irrespective of the fact whether these posts have been reserved for them in the Civil Service of Pakistan (Composition and Cadre) Rules, 1954 or not. This declaration will also be applicable to officers of other services / functional units / cadres of the Federation who hold posts in connection with affairs of the Provinces except through appointment by transfer in the prescribed manner.

181.   During arguments on the aforesaid matters, it was pointed out by the learned counsel for the Pakistan Administrative Service Officers Association that the Federation can post any federal officer against any post, including posts in connection with affairs of the Provinces, on deputation basis. The learned Attorney General for Pakistan was also of the same view. This point, therefore, needs to be examined.

182.   Conditions of recruitment and of service of the federal civil servants are, mainly, determined by or under the Civil Servants Act, 1973. The said Act contains 25 sections which deal with the matters as listed hereinbelow:

Section #	Title / subject-matter
1	Short title, application and commencement
2	Definitions
3	Terms and conditions
4	Tenure of office of civil servants
5	Appointments
6	Probation
7	Confirmation
8	Seniority
9	Promotion
10	Posting and transfer
11	Termination of Service
12	Reversion to a lower post etc.
12A	Certain persons to be liable to removal, etc.
13	Retirement from service
14	Employment after retirement

15	Conduct
16	Efficiency and discipline
17	Pay
18	Leave
19	Pension and Gratuity
20	Provident Fund
21	Benevolent Fund and Group Insurance
22	Right of appeal or representation
23	Saving
24	Removal of difficulties
25	Rules

183. We have not been able to find definition of the term "deputation" or any provision dealing with or allowing deputation of federal civil servants in the Civil Servants Act, 1973 against posts in connection with affairs of the Provinces.

184. The President of Pakistan, in exercise of his powers conferred by section 25 of the Civil Servants Act, 1973, was pleased to make, among others, the Civil Servants (Appointment, Promotion and Transfer) Rules, 1973 Rule 20A whereof reads as follows:

"20A. Appointment on deputation. –

(1) A person in the service of a Provincial Government or an autonomous, semi-autonomous body or corporation or any other organization set-up, established, owned, managed or controlled by the Federal Government who possess the minimum educational qualifications, experience or comparable length of service prescribed for a post shall be eligible for appointment to the said post on deputation for a period of two years on such terms and conditions as may be prescribed by Federal Government in consultation with the lending Organization.

(2) Subject to any rules or orders issued by the Federal Government, a civil servant who fulfils the conditions and is considered suitable may be sent on deputation to an autonomous, semi-autonomous body or corporation established by law or to the Provincial Government on such terms and conditions as may be decided by the lending and borrowing organizations.

(3) In case of appointment under sub-rule (1) or sub-rule (2), pension contribution shall invariably be made by the borrowing organizations."

185. On the other hand, appointment by deputation has been covered under Rule 15 of the Punjab Civil Servants (Appointment and Conditions of Service) Rules, 1974 in these words:

"15. Deputation.- (1) A person in the service of an autonomous or semi-autonomous organization or Federal Government, or other Provinces, or Gilgit-Baltistan, or Azad Jammu & Kashmir, who possesses minimum educational qualification, experience or comparable length of service prescribed for the post, shall be eligible for appointment, on deputation, to the said post for a period not exceeding three years at a time, on such terms and conditions as the Government, in consultation with the lending Government or organization, may determine.

(2) Subject to any other rule or order of the Government, a civil servant, who fulfills the conditions and is considered suitable, may be sent on deputation, for a period not exceeding three years, to an autonomous or semi-autonomous organization or Federal Government, or other Provinces, or Gilgit-Baltistan or Azad Jammu & Kashmir, on such terms and conditions, as the appointing authority, in consultation with the borrowing Government or organization, may determine."

186.   Save some exceptions provided by the Constitution, service matters are dealt with, as required by Article 240(a) of the Constitution, under Act of the Parliament in respect of All Pakistan Services, services of the Federation and posts in connection with affairs of the Federation and under an Act of the Provincial Assembly, in terms of Article 240(b) of the Constitution, in case of services of the Province and posts in connection with affairs of the Province. There is no limit of number of statues the competent legislatures may like to enact to regulate service matters falling within their respective jurisdictions. For the purpose of illustration, we may consider the examples of the Civil Servants Act, 1973 and the Punjab Civil Servants Act, 1974 which are applicable to the civil servants of the Federation and of the Punjab respectively. Sub-section 2 of Section 1 of the Civil Servants Act, 1973 provides that the Act applies to all civil servants wherever they may be. Similar provision is available in the Punjab Civil Servants Act, 1974. A perusal of definition of 'civil servant' given in both the aforesaid statutes indicates that the civil servants of the Federation are not civil servants of the Province when they may be deputed to serve under the Province. Likewise, civil servants of the Province are not civil servants in terms of the Civil Servants Act when they are on deputation to the Federation. In this view of the matter, the principle which emerges is this that the Parliament as well as the Provincial Assembly were well aware of limits of their jurisdictional competence under Article 240 of the Constitution. It appears that it was for this reason that none of the two statues provided for serving of their civil servants under another Government where the applicable Civil Servants Act cannot remain applicable and both the statues clearly stated that they will remain applicable to their respective civil servants wherever they may be. We may see implied prohibition in these provisions that the civil servants cannot be sent on deputation anywhere in case the applicable Civil Servants Act does not remain applicable while they are on such deputation. As employment in the Service of Pakistan is a statutory contract employment and the statue is mainly the Civil Servants Act supplemented by other applicable statues, therefore, civil servants cannot be forced to go on deputation where their statutory contract remains inapplicable. We have seen Government of Pakistan, Establishment Division's O.M.No.1/4/86-R.I. dated 03.04.1986 and O.M.No.F.6(4)-R-2/65 dated 09.02.1966, Establishment Division's U.0.Note No.4/1/74-D.III dated 08.05.1975, Law Division's U.O. Note No. 763/75-Law dated 13.05.1975 and Ministry of Finance's letter No.F.10(23)-E.G. II/48 dated 09.12.1948 and 10.06.1949 and have gathered the impression that a civil servant on deputation to another Government remains under the rule-making control of the lending Government.

187.   Whereas the Civil Servants Acts of 1973 and 1974 expressly provide that the Acts will remain applicable to the civil servants wherever they may be, the rules made thereunder relating to deputation allows determination of terms and conditions of deputation with mutual consent of the lending and borrowing governments. Applicability of the said Acts on their respective civil servants means that terms and conditions with respect to matters covered by or under those statues shall remain intact even if the civil servants are on deputation. If the terms and conditions of service determined by or under the applicable statue are incapable of being operational somewhere, then there is implied prohibition that the civil servants cannot be deputed there. One such eventuality is deputation of civil servants of the Federation to a Province and vice versa. To illustrate the issue, we may find answers to the following questions, the questions may be treated as indicative and not exhaustive:

a) Does a Province is authorized to determine remuneration of federal civil servants while they are on deputation to the Province or does the Federation has jurisdiction to determine remuneration payable from the Provincial Consolidated Fund?

b) Can a federal civil servant become member of the Provident Fund, Benevolent Fund, Group Insurance Scheme, Punjab Government Servants Housing Foundation?

c) Is the Punjab Employees Efficiency, Discipline and Accountability Act, 2006 applicable to the federal civil servants during their deputation to the Province?

d) Does the Accommodation Allocation Rules, 2002, framed under Section 25 of the Civil Servants Act, 1973, become inapplicable to federal civil servants while they are on deputation to the Province?

e) Does the policy of "Compulsory Monetization of Transport Facility for Civil Servants in BS-20 to BS-22" issued by the Cabinet Division of the Federal Government vide communication bearing No. 6/7/2011-CPC dated 12.12.2011 remain applicable to federal civil servants during the period of their deputation under a Province?

f) Whether other laws / rules e.g. the Initial Appointment to Civil Posts (Relaxation of Upper Age Limit) Rules, 1993, the Civil Servants (Appointment, Promotion and Transfer) Rules, 1973, the Civil Servants (Confirmation) Rules, 1993, the Civil Servants (Seniority) Rules, 1993, the Government Servants (Applications for Services and Posts) Rules, 1966, the Service Tribunals Act, 1973, the Revised Leave Rules, 1980, the Federal Services Medical Attendance Rules, 1990 remain applicable to the federal civil servants during their posting / deputation to a Province?

g) Can a provincial civil servant claim to be given accommodation under the Accommodation Allocation Rules, 2002 while on deputation to the Federation?

188. We may answer the above questions hereinbelow, seriatim:

a) It is elementary principle of construction that what cannot be done directly is also not allowed to be done indirectly. Subject to the Constitution, jurisdictional limits of the Federation and of the Provinces in matters pertaining to the Service of Pakistan have precisely and expressly been determined in Article 240 of the Constitution. These limits are not allowed to be ignored under any pretext. Neither a Province is competent to determine conditions of recruitment and of service of the All Pakistan Services, services of the Federation and posts in connection with affairs of the Federation nor the Federation is authorized to undertake such an exercise in respect of the provincial services and posts in connection with affairs of a Province. Determination of remuneration payable from the Federal Consolidated Fund is a creation of a liability or charge in terms of Article 73(2)(d) of the Constitution. Similar is the position with respect to the Provincial Consolidated Fund under Article 115(2)(d) of the Constitution. Remuneration is determined with reference to services or, where certain posts are not encadred for a service, then with reference to holders of a post. In both cases, legislative competence has to be exercised only by the concerned legislature. While exercising legislative jurisdiction, the Parliament as well as the Provincial Assembly of the Punjab have expressly laid down that the respective Civil Servants Acts shall remain applicable to their respective civil servants wherever they may be. In this view of the matter, the question is answered in the negative.

b) The Punjab Province has its own laws / rules with respect to the Provident Fund, Benevolent Fund, Group Insurance Scheme, Punjab Government Servants Housing Foundation Scheme etc. These laws / rules are applicable to provincial services and posts in connection with affairs of the Province and not to federal services and federal civil servants as the legislative competence of the Province does not extend to the federal services or federal civil servants. As a consequence, federal services and federal civil servants cannot escape the federal laws and rules made thereunder on the plea that they are under deputation to a Province. The federal civil servants are, therefore, not lawfully entitled to become members of the Provident Fund, Benevolent Fund, Group Insurance Scheme and the Punjab Government Servants Housing Foundation Scheme and any other similar fund or scheme. Section 2(f)(iii) of the Punjab Government Servants Housing Foundation Act, 2004 (Act X of 2004) which purports to extend the Act to the federal civil servants is in excess of the jurisdiction conferred by Article 240(b) of the Constitution, and, hence, is hereby declared to be without lawful authority and jurisdiction and resultantly of no legal effect ab initio. No procedural mechanism exists to show that how federal civil servants can continue to be members of respective federal funds and schemes applicable to them under federal laws / rules while drawing remuneration from the Provincial Consolidated Fund during the period of their deputation or posting to a Province. We have been informed that the Province of Punjab has made federal civil servants members of the funds and schemes initiated and governed by provincial laws and rules. The learned Advocate General, Punjab has also confirmed that the Province is paying interest on the General Provident Fund accumulations of the federal civil servants from the Provincial Consolidated Fund. We are sad to know the pervasive laxity with which public money is being spent without authority of law.

c) Executive authority of the Province is exercisable through officers subordinate to the Provincial Government. It is not the case of any of the parties before us that the deputation of federal officers to a Province or vice versa is sanctioned and protected under Article 146 or 147 of the Constitution. In absence of such an argument, we do not deem it essential to further discuss or construe the said two Articles. Without discussing in detail, we deem an officer subordinate to the Province who is either in statutory employment contract with the Province or holds an elected office e.g. a Cabinet Minister. Exercise of powers of hiring, firing and disciplinary control are inseparable ingredients of the relationship of subordination. The federal civil servants are neither holders of elected offices of the Province nor are in statutory employment contract with the Province. It has not been disputed by any of the parties in these proceedings that the Province, as a matter of established practice and well-entrenched interpretation of applicable law, does not exercise powers of hiring, firing and disciplinary control of the federal civil servants on posting or deputation to the Province. All the parties are unanimous that the Punjab Employees Efficiency,

Discipline and Accountability Act, 2006 is not applicable to the federal civil servants during their posting or deputation to the Province and the federal civil servants continue to be governed by the Removal from Service (Special Powers) Ordinance, 2000 or the Government Servants (Efficiency and Discipline) Rules, 1973 or any other applicable federal law / rules. We are in agreement with submissions of the parties on the subject but are constrained to hold that executive authority of the Province is not allowed to be exercised by any person (legal as well as natural) who is not under subordination to the Province.

d) The Accommodation Allocation Rules, 2002 have been framed under Section 25 of the Civil Servants Act, 1973 and are applicable, inter alia, to the federal civil servants wherever they may be. It is well-established that prescription of one is prohibition of another. Thus, the Allotment Policy of the S&GAD, 1997 updated version of which was circulated vide Government of the Punjab, Services & General Administration Department's letter No. EO(S&GAD) Policy/2009/688 dated 07.05.2018 is not applicable to the federal civil servants. We do not find it essential to examine legality of this policy in these proceedings but we entertain no doubt in our mind that the said policy is not applicable to any federal civil servant and residential accommodations of the Government of the Punjab or of its autonomous or local bodies are not allowed to be allotted to federal civil servants during their posting or deputation in the Province. In the same manner, provincial civil servants are not allowed to be dealt with under the Accommodation Allocation Rules, 2002 during their deputation to the Federation. We have been informed that residential accommodations of the Province are not only allotted to the federal civil servants but they get the best available accommodations and retain them for years even after ceasing to serve the Province. We may request the legislature to look into the matter for appropriate corrective action.

e) The policy of "Compulsory Monetization of Transport Facility for Civil Servants in BS-20 to BS-22" issued by the Cabinet Division of the Federal Government vide communication bearing No. 6/7/2011-CPC dated 12.12.2011 is purportedly applicable to federal civil servants wherever they may be. We have already held in this judgment that where a stature requires something to be regulated through rules, executive instructions cannot be elevated to the level of rules and, therefore, there remain serious questions on legality of such a policy. This observation, however, does not adversely affect entitlement of the federal civil servants to enjoy benefits of the said policy wherever they may be till such time a final judicial decision is taken declaring the policy of no legal effect. As payments from the Provincial Consolidated Fund are not allowed to be controlled through federal laws / rules / regulations and executive orders / policies, therefore, the said monetization policy is inapplicable to the federal civil servants when they serve under the Province of the Punjab as the Province does not have such a policy. An anomaly so created can only be resolved if we accept that the federal civil servants can be deputed only where the Civil Servants Act and other allied laws, rules, regulations and policies remain applicable to them.

f) All federal laws / rules / regulations / policies e.g. the Initial Appointment to Civil Posts (Relaxation of Upper Age Limit) Rules, 1993, the Civil Servants (Appointment, Promotion and Transfer) Rules, 1973, the Civil Servants (Confirmation) Rules, 1993, the Civil Servants (Seniority) Rules, 1993, the Government Servants (Applications for Services and Posts) Rules, 1966, the Service Tribunals Act, 1973, the Revised Leave Rules, 1980, the Federal Services Medical Attendance Rules, 1990 remain applicable to the federal civil servants during their posting / deputation in a Province. On the same analogy, all provincial laws, rules, regulations, policies etc. continue to apply to the provincial civil servants wherever they may be including during the period they serve the Federation. It is not possible or permissible for the Federation or a Province to abdicate its legislative power and executive authority in respect of employees of other Governments serving under it. It is also not lawfully allowed that the legal dispensation constitutionally conceived under Article 240(a) of the Constitution for the Service of Pakistan be temporarily substituted or novated with the arrangement under Article 240(b) of the Constitution or vice versa. The Constitution has not conceived any eventuality when exclusive jurisdictions under Article 240(a) and (b) of the Constitution are allowed to be disturbed, either temporarily or permanently, for any reason. Inter-governmental deputation is, thus, does not fit in our constitutional scheme.

g) The Federation and the Province have their own remuneration policies. A government is under no legal compulsion to follow the remuneration policy of another. A provincial civil servant in the Punjab may be entitled to an allowance which may not be admissible under the Federation and vice versa. A provincial civil servant may be entitled to receive Executive Allowance but no such allowance is admissible under the Federal Government. If allowed, remuneration of a civil servant can be reduced or enhanced through posting or deputation from one government to another. Such arbitrary reward or punishment is not conceivable under the law. From this angle alone, the concept of inter-governmental deputation creates a legally unsustainable position. For further illustration, we may examine the case of sanction of executive allowance to holders of certain posts in the Province of the Punjab. These posts are held by federal as well as provincial civil servants. The Province lacks authority to determine remuneration of federal civil servants; hence, federal civil servants are not entitled to draw this allowance. There is no constitutional possibility in the dispensation in force right now which may remove this anomaly. Another example of an absurdity caused by holding of the post of the Chief Secretary, Punjab by federal civil servants is grant of one driver and orderly for life, 800 free local calls per month, 800 units of electricity per month, 25 HM of gas per month and 200 liters petrol per month by the Services & General Administration Department of the Government of the Punjab. There will be a big question mark on our understanding of law if we fail to declare it out rightly that the Provinces has no authority of law to determine remuneration and other benefits of federal civil servants and the

Province is not liable to pay anything to or for the benefit of former Chief Secretaries of the Government of the Punjab. We hold and direct that the money spent from the public purse on this account is recoverable from the beneficiary former Chief Secretaries of the Government of the Punjab for credit to the Provincial Consolidated Fund.

189.   For the aforesaid reasons, besides others, we conclude and hold that Rule 20A of the Civil Servants (Appointment, Promotion and Transfer) Rules, 1973 and Rule 15 of the Punjab Civil Servants (Appointment and Conditions of Service) Rules, 1974 are without lawful authority and jurisdiction and, hence, of no legal effect to the extent these rules permit inter-governmental deputations and allow determination of terms and conditions of deputation by the lending and borrowing organizations for being in violation of Article 73,115 and 240 of the Constitution and Section 1(2) of the Civil Servants Act, 1973 and Section 1(2) of the Punjab Civil Servants Act, 1974.

190.   After our finding and declaration as recorded in the preceding paragraph, we deem it essential to find out and lay down the parameters under which deputation is lawfully allowed.

191.   Posts requiring similar skill sets, remuneration and other allied matters are generally grouped together and are collectively labelled as a cadre or service or functional unit. Members of the service are under legal obligation to serve on any post so encadred irrespective of the fact where such post exists. It is not necessary to encadre all posts for one or the other service. In such case, the posts are left open to be filled through deputation or temporary posting of members of a service who possess the requisite qualifications. In this scenario, the rules applicable to the post provide for its filling up through deputation. In other words, deputation is not permissible on a post duly encadred for a service / cadre / functional unit. The rules applicable to the service officers of which may be deputed must also provide for a certain percentage or number of its strength to be deputed on deputation. Whereas posting and transfer does not require consent of the employee, it has consistently been held in Indian jurisdiction that deputation cannot be ordered without consent of the employee. Bhagawati Prasad G. Bhatt Vs. State of Gujarat and Ors {(1977) 1 GLR 562, (1978) ILLJ 215 Guj} provides reasoning leading to this conclusion. In view of statutory employment contract in the Service of Pakistan, deputation may be to an entity of the same government where the employment contract of the employee remains intact. If an entity of the same government has been created through a law and that law also governs conditions of recruitment and of service of employees of that entity and the applicable law does not allow conditions of statutory employment contract of the deputationist to be protected during his deputation to that entity, then even the intra-government deputation will not be allowed.

192.   We now examine whether the purported legal dispensations applicable to some well-known services of the Federation allow for deputation or not. The position which emerges is as follows:

Sr.#	Service / Group	Reference	Position on deputation
1	Pakistan Administrative Service	The Civil Service of Pakistan (Composition and Cadre) Rules, 1954 read with Establishment Division's O.M. No. 2/2/74 ARC dated 23.02.1974	No provision for deputation or reservation of posts for deputation exists in the updated rules. However, original rules of 1954 reserved 15% of the cadre strength as deputation reserve.
2	Pakistan Audit & Accounts Service	Establishment Division's O.M.No.1/2/74-ARC, dated 23-1-1974	No provision for deputation or reservation of posts for deputation

3	Commerce and Trade Group	Establishment Division's O.M. No. 6/2/75-ARC, dated 8-5-1975	No provision for deputation or reservation of posts for deputation
4	Customs and Excise Group	Establishment Division's O.M. No. 5/2/75-ARC, dated 9-5-1975	No provision for deputation or reservation of posts for deputation
5	Foreign Service of Pakistan	Establishment Division's O.M. No. 3/2/74-ARC, dated 8-4-1974	No provision for deputation or reservation of posts for deputation
6	Income Tax Group	Establishment Division's O.M.No.4/2/75-ARC, dated 09-5-1975	No provision for deputation or reservation of posts for deputation
7	Information Group	Establishment Division's O.M. No. 2/8/75-ARC, dated 17-6-1977	10% of the duty posts reserved for training and deputation
8	Military Lands and Cantonment Group	Establishment Division's O.M. No.9/2/75-ARC, dated 11-5-1975	No provision for deputation or reservation of posts for deputation
9	Office Management Group	Establishment Division's O.M. No. 1/2/75-ARC, dated 27-1-1975	Training and deputation reserve @15%.
10	Police Service of Pakistan	The Police Service of Pakistan (Composition, Cadre and Seniority) Rules, 1985	Leave, deputation and training reserve at 40% of the number of senior posts
11	Secretariat Group	Establishment Division's O.M.No. 2/2/75-ARC dated 12-4-1976	No provision for deputation or reservation of posts for deputation

193. Intra-government deputation is permissible only in cases and to the extent as specified in the governing legal dispensation applicable to the civil servants. If deputation has been provided in one set of rules and not in others, we may construe it as a conscious decision of the competent authority to allow or not to allow deputation in a particular case. As the rules or executive instructions applicable to a certain group or service are special rules or executive instructions, therefore, these shall prevail notwithstanding anything to the contrary contained in general rules or instructions. We are, therefore, constrained to hold that intra-government deputation is permissible only if the officer consents to be deputed and the rules governing the officer and the post to be filled through deputation provide for the same and the statutory employment contract remains intact. In all other case, deputation is prohibited. In any case, inter-governmental deputation is simply not conceivable. Our declaration to this effect does not supplant but supplements the dictum of law laid down by the Hon'ble Supreme Court of Pakistan in the case reported as Contempt proceedings against the Chief Secretary, Government of Sindh & others (2013 SCMR 1752).

Question # 17

Whether amendments made from time to time in the Civil Service of Pakistan (Composition and Cadre) Rules, 1954 were lawful?

194. After our declarations regarding constitutionality of the Civil Service of Pakistan (Composition and Cadre) Rules, 1954, made hereinabove, a detailed analysis of the amendments from time to time introduced in the rules supra does not seem to be necessary. Suffice is to make the following declarations in this respect:

a)   Amendments made through executive orders in the Civil Service of Pakistan (Composition and Cadre) Rules, 1954 are void and of no legal effect; and

b)   Jurisdictions to frame rules and make amendments therein are concurrent and co-extensive. As a consequence, amendments not involving reservation of posts in connection with affairs of the Provinces for a Service of the Federation and matters in exclusive jurisdiction of the Provinces are valid if made by the President through rules and not through executive orders and those which relate to these matters are invalid to the same extent as the original rules are.

Question # 18

Whether the creation of the District Management Group through an executive order or office memorandum was lawful?

195.   The Federation of Pakistan submits that creation of the District Management Group through an office memorandum is not violative of Article 240 of the Constitution as the same was lawfully issued by the Federal Government and published in the Estacode; hence, it, being not in conflict with any provision of Civil Servants Act, 1973, has acquired the force of law on the strength of the language of sub-section (2) of Section 25 of the Act. The Province of the Punjab has submitted that creation of the District Management Group (through office memorandum No. 2/2/74 ARC dated 23.02.1974) does not tantamount to creation of an All Pakistan Service, rather it is one of the Groups created within the All Pakistan Service which was already in existence. The Pakistan Administrative Service Officers Association has defended the Establishment Division's said Office Memorandum by saying that it did not create an All Pakistan Service. It only created the District Management Group as an occupational group within an already existing All Pakistan Service. Other occupational groups within the APUG were also created through office memoranda. It has further been stated that Article 240(a) of the Constitution provides that appointments to and the conditions of service of persons in the service of the Federation and All Pakistan Services shall be determined by or under Act of Parliament. The Civil Servants Act, 1973 was enacted by the Parliament pursuant to the aforesaid Article of the Constitution. The said Office Memorandum has statutory force and is covered under the Civil Servants Act, 1973.

196.   Whereas sub-section (1) of Section 25 of the Civil Servants Act, 1973 provides for framing of rules to carry out purposes of the Act, sub-section (2) thereof protects rules, orders and instructions in respect of any terms and conditions of service of civil servants duly made or issued by an authority competent to make them and in force immediately before the commencement of the Act, subject obviously to consistency with the Act. The Office Memorandum No. 2/2/74 ARC dated 23.02.1974 is an executive instrument and was issued after enactment of the Civil Servants Act, 1973. The protection envisaged by sub-section (2) of Section 25 of the Civil Servants Act, 1973 is not available to the said Office Memorandum. Article 240 of the Constitution envisions creation of an All-Pakistan Service as a Service common to the Federation and the Provinces through an Act of the Parliament. No Act has so far been enacted by the Parliament for creation of the said Service. The Civil Servants Act, 1973 cannot, for reasons noted elsewhere in this judgment, be deemed to be an Act required for creation of an All Pakistan Service.

197.   The District Management Group, for all intents and purposes, substituted the Civil Service of Pakistan created under the Civil Service of Pakistan (Composition and Cadre) Rules, 1954. The District Management Group was renamed as the Pakistan Administrative Service in 2012. If contention of the respondents to the effect that the District Management Group was not a Service within the meaning of the Civil Service of Pakistan (Composition and Cadre) Rules, 1954 is accepted, then holding of posts even in connection with affairs of the Federation, as mentioned in the Schedule to the rules supra, becomes without lawful

authority and jurisdiction. The arguments of the respondents, to this extent, have no legal force.

198.   In this view of the matter, it is held that creation of the District Management Group through an Office Memorandum was without lawful authority and, hence, of no legal effect.

Question # 19

Whether non-extension of benefit of the Notification No.1/1/73-RA dated 14.09.1973 to the PCS officers was lawful?

199.   The petitioners submit that Notification No.1/1/73-RA dated 14.09.1973 provided that the government servants who were holding cadre posts on 21.08.1973 stood appointed to the All Pakistan Unified Grades (APUG) but the benefit of this notification was not extended to the PCS officers. The Province of the Punjab argues in this respect that non-appointment of holders (belonging to the Provincial Civil Services) of the cadre posts on 21.08.1973 to the All Pakistan Unified Grades (APUG) was not a violation of the said Notification because it was nomenclature of the Civil Service of Pakistan and the Police Service of Pakistan that was changed to the All Pakistan Unified Grades (APUG) through the said Notification and it was applicable only to members of the All Pakistan Services.

200.   This court has examined the matter. The Establishment Division's Notification No. S.R.O. 1307(1)/73 dated 14.09.1973 notified the Civil Servants (Change in Nomenclature) Rules, 1973 made by the President of Pakistan exercising his powers under section 25 of the Civil Servants Ordinance, 1973 (XIV of 1973), rule 3 thereof reads as follows:

> "Notwithstanding anything contained in any rule, order, resolution or instruction, the names of the Civil Service of Pakistan and the Police Service of Pakistan are, with immediate effect, changed to All-Pakistan Unified Grades and all references to Civil Service of Pakistan and Police Service of Pakistan in any rule, order, resolution or instruction shall be construed as references to All-Pakistan Unified Grades."

201.   The All Pakistan Services (Change in Nomenclature) Rules, 1973 were later repealed through S.R.O. 89(1)/2014 dated 10.02.2014. In view of this repeal, we do not find a live issue to be adjudicated upon and do not deem it necessary to further discuss the matter or make any declaration in respect thereof. For the purpose of academic clarity on the issue raised, we may refer to the dictum of law laid down in Fateh Khan Vs. Ministry of Defence {1984 PLC (C.S.) 1399}.

Question # 20

Whether officers of a federal service can be promoted against posts in connection with affairs of a Province and these officers can be assigned charge of posts higher than their pay scales?

202.   Section 9 of the Civil Servants Act, 1973 reads as follows:

> "**Promotion.** – (1) A civil servant possessing such minimum qualifications as may be prescribed shall be eligible for promotion to a higher post for the time being reserved under the rules for departmental promotion in the service or cadre to which he belongs:".

203.   In absence of constitutional sanction for reservation of posts in connection with affairs of a Province for a federal service, it is not lawful to encadre posts in connection with affairs of a Province for that federal service. It is but logical and inevitable to hold that officers of any federal service including officers of the Pakistan Administrative Service cannot be promoted against posts in connection with affairs of a Province. The purported reservation of posts in connection with affairs of the Provinces for the Pakistan Administrative Service under the Civil Service of Pakistan (Composition and Cadre) Rules, 1954 has already been declared to be without lawful authority and of no legal effect. It is further held that Section 9 of the Civil Servants Act, 1973 allows promotion against posts reserved in the cadre for promotion, impliedly excluding posts reserved for training, leave and deputation from the posts reserved in a cadre for promotion.

204.   The question of appointment / posting of officers in grades higher than those substantively held by them has been settled by the Hon'ble Supreme Court of Pakistan in Province of Sindh and others v. Ghulam Fareed and others (2015 PLC (CS) 151) in which it was held as follows:

> "11. We have inquired from the learned Additional Advocate-General to show us any provision of law and or rule under which a Civil Servant can be appointed on higher grade/post on OPS basis. He concedes that there is no specific provision in the law or rule which permits appointment on OPS basis. He, however, submitted that in exigencies the Government makes such appointments as a stop gap arrangement. We have examined the provisions of Sindh Civil Servants Act and the Rules framed thereunder. We do not find any provision which could authorize the Government or Competent Authority to appointment any officer on higher grade on "Own Pay and Scale Basis". Appointment of the nature, that too of a junior officer causes heart burning of the senior officers within the cadre and or department. This practice of appointment on OPS basis to a higher grade has always been discouraged by this Court, as it does not have any sanction of law, besides it impinges the self-respect and dignity of the Civil Servants who are forced to work under their rapidly and unduly appointed fellow officers junior to them. Discretion of the nature if allowed to be vested in the Competent Authority will offend valuable rights of the meritorious Civil Servants besides block promotions of the deserving officers.
>
> 12. At times officers possessing requisite experience to qualify for regular appointment may not be available in a department. However, all such exigencies are taken care of and regulated by statutory rules. In this respect, Rule 8-A of the Sindh Civil Servants (Appointment, Promotion and Transfer) Rules, 1974, empowers the Competent Authority to appoint a Civil Servant on acting charge and current charge basis... Sub-Rule (4) of the afore-referred Rule 8 further provides that appointment on acting charge basis shall be made for vacancies lasting for more than 6 months and for vacancies likely to last for less than six months. Appointment of an officer of a lower scale on higher post on current charge basis is made as a stop-gap arrangement and should not under any circumstances, last for more than 6 months. This acting charge appointment can neither be construed to be an appointment by promotion on regular basis for any purposes including seniority, nor it confers any vested right for regular appointment. In other words, appointment on current charge basis is purely temporary in nature or stop-gap arrangement, which remains operative for short duration until regular appointment is made against the post. Looking at the scheme of the Sindh Civil Servants Act and Rules framed thereunder, it is crystal clear that there is no scope of appointment of a Civil Servant to a higher grade on OPS basis except resorting to the provisions of Rule 8-A, which provides that in exigencies appointment on acting charge basis can be made, subject to conditions contained in the Rules."

205.   We have perused Rule 11 and 15(iii) of the Civil Service of Pakistan (Composition and Cadre) Rules, 1954, reproduced below:

> "11. The Governor of a Province may direct that two Cadre posts in connection with the affairs of a Province shall be held jointly if he considers this necessary for the purpose of facilitating any leave

arrangement or for a period not exceeding 3 months if he considers this necessary for any other purpose.

15. (iii) An officer so deputed to a Provincial Government shall not be posted in a higher post except with the approval of the Provincial Government and in accordance with the prescribed procedure."

206. We have also found the following letters issued by the Establishment Division of the Federal Government relevant to the question under consideration:

"In the Establishment Division O.M.No.2/25/69-C.I. dated July 31, 1979, instructions were issued that appointments of officers of lower grades to posts in higher grades without observing the prescribed process must cease. It was also laid down that if it was necessary to do so due to exigencies of services the post should be down-graded with the approval of the Establishment Division.

2. In January, 1981, Rule 8-A and 8-B were inserted in the Civil Servants (Appointment, Promotion and Transfer) Rules, *vide* Establishment Division Notification No.S.R.O.41(I)/81 dated 12th January, 1981. Rule 8-A lays down that no promotion on regular basis shall be made in grades 19 to 21 unless the officer has completed the prescribed length of service. Rule 8-B provides for acting charge appointment in case the most senior civil servant otherwise eligible for promotion does not possess the specified length of service, or in the case of a grade 17 post and above, reserved under the rules for initial appointment, no suitable officer of the grade in which the post exists is available. For vacancies of less than 6 months, or in other cases not covered by Rule 8-B, current charge arrangement can be made in accordance with the Establishment Division O.M.No.1/21/76-AR. I/R.II. dated 18th June, 1980, as amended from time to time. With the issue of the instructions relating to acting charge appointments and current charge arrangements, there should be no difficulty in filling vacancies.

3. The Ministries/Divisions and Departments are once again requested to ensure that all appointments to higher posts, whether on regular basis or on acting charge / current charge basis, should, henceforth, be made strictly in accordance with the rules, and after observing the prescribed procedure and that on no account should a person be appointed to a higher post otherwise than in accordance with the rules, or without observing the prescribed procedure.

[Authority. – Establishment Division's O.M. No. 5(1)/81-D. II-R/4 dated 12.12.1981].

Sl. No. 20

"It has been observed with regret that despite repeated instructions issued by the Establishment Division regarding appointment of Government servants against higher posts other than in accordance with rules and prescribed procedure, Ministries/Divisions and Departments of the Federal Government and the Provincial Governments (in the case of officers belonging to Occupational Groups controlled by the Establishment Division) continue to make appointments to higher posts occasionally in disregard of the above instructions. Officers appointed to higher posts without going through the prescribed selection process and approval of the competent authority claim pay and allowances of the higher posts on the basis of judgements of the Federal Service Tribunal and the Supreme Court of Pakistan in a number of such cases. This places the Government in an awkward position as pay and allowances of the higher posts have to be allowed to individuals who have not been regularly promoted and who are sometimes not even qualified or eligible for promotion. It also causes heart-burning and resentment among their seniors who were serving elsewhere or were bypassed at the time of making such irregular appointments.

2. While such irregular appointments are claimed to be made in public interest and under unavoidable circumstances it has once again to be emphasized that appointments to higher posts in disregard of the prescribed rules and procedure should be avoided under all circumstances. Various provisions already exist in the rules for making appointments on acting charge, current charge and additional charge basis, to tide over temporary difficulties. It is, therefore, again reiterated that in future appointments against higher posts should only be made either on a regular basis in the prescribed manner, or on acting charge or current charge basis in accordance with the provisions of Civil Servants (Appointment, Promotion and Transfer) Rules, 1973 and relevant instructions issued by the Government from time to time.

3. Disregard of the above instructions would be viewed seriously and may result in bringing the matter to the notice of the Prime Minister."

[Authority. - Establishment Division's O.M.No.14/4/86-R. I dated 02.05-1988].

207.   Our attention was also drawn towards Section 10 of the Civil Servants Act, 1973 and Section 9 of the Punjab Civil Servants Act, 1974, reproduced below:

Civil Servants Act, 1973

"10.   **Posting and transfer**. –Every civil servant shall be liable to serve anywhere within or outside Pakistan, in any equivalent or higher post under the Federal Government, or any Provincial Government or local authority, or a corporation or body set up or established by any such Government:"

Punjab Civil Servants Act, 1974

"9. **Posting and transfers**

Every civil servant shall be liable to serve anywhere within or outside the province in any post under the Government of the Punjab or the Federal Government or any provincial Government or a local authority or a corporation or a body set up or established by any such Government:

Provided that, where a civil servant is required to serve in a post outside his service or cadre, his terms and conditions of service as to his pay shall not be less favourable than those to which he would have been entitled if he had not been so required to serve."

208.   Learned counsel for the petitioners also informed us that it is a practice in the Government of the Punjab to assign posts of higher grades to the officers of the Pakistan Administrative Service and also to assign them additional charge of posts for indefinite period. He stated that officers of the Pakistan Administrative Service in BS. 17 are posted in the Punjab Civil Secretariat as Deputy Secretary in BS. 18. It is also common to extend this favour to officers of the that Service in all grades. He was of the view that broiler growth of the officers of the Pakistan Administrative Service made possible in this way results into entrustment of posts to those who lack requisite experience to properly discharge duties of the posts assigned to them. Thus, the public stands deprived of its right to be served by the best.

209.   After our declaration that the Civil Service of Pakistan (Composition and Cadre) Rules, 1954 are void to the extent of encadrement of posts in connection with affairs of the

Provinces for the Pakistan Administrative Service, the question of posting of these officers on higher posts or entrustment of charge of more than one posts to them for an indefinite period deserves to be peacefully laid to rest. However, for the purpose of clarity only, we may very briefly attend to this question.

210. Basic pay scales for determination of remuneration of the civil servants and ascertainment of equivalence of posts serve the purpose of indicating both the capability of the civil servant and the level of responsibility attached to a post. Posting of officers of lower grades on posts carrying higher grades theoretically results into incompatibility between skills and abilities of the civil servant and the level of skills and abilities required to efficiently perform functions of a post. A higher post is not the same post with an additional higher Basic Pay Scale. A higher post is a post with higher responsibilities including those of supervision and control over the lower posts. Equal and similar posts are always placed at the same level of responsibility.

211. In view of the dictum of law laid down by the Hon'ble Supreme Court of Pakistan, relevant provisions of the applicable law and rules and executive instructions of the Establishment Division of the Federal Government on the subject and without prejudice to our declarations regarding constitutionality of the Civil Service of Pakistan (Composition and Cadre) Rules, 1954 with respect to posts in connection with affairs of the Province, we do hereby declare and hold as follows:

(a) Posting of civil servants on higher posts in their own pay and scale is not provided in any law / rules;

(b) Provincial Government is not authorized to post federal officers on posts in basic pay scales higher than those of the officers. In pith and substance, such postings amount to promotion and the Province does not have power to promote federal officers against posts in connection with affairs of the Province;

(c) Simple posting to a post in a higher basic pay scale does not entitle a civil servant to claim pay of post. Such entitlement arises only on appointment to a basic pay scale or post through initial recruitment, promotion or by transfer. In no case, a federal civil servant be granted pay of the post higher than his basic pay scale;

(d) Section 10 of the Civil Servants Act, 1973 is not applicable in respect of posts in connection with affairs of the Province. This Section is not attracted in case of posting of federal civil servants on posts in connection with affairs of the Province;

(e) Additional charge of a post in connection with affairs of the Province cannot be assigned to an officer of the Pakistan Administrative Service in excess of a period of three months; and

(f) Federal officers are not allowed to be promoted against posts in connection with affairs of the Provinces. All serving officers promoted against posts in connection with affairs of the Provinces are hereby ordered to be demoted forthwith from the date of promotion.

Question # 21

Whether reservation of posts in connection with affairs of the Provinces for the officers of the Police Service of Pakistan under the Police Service of Pakistan (Composition, Cadre and Seniority) Rules, 1985 is lawful or not?

212. The learned counsel for the petitioners informed us that the Police Service of Pakistan is claimed to be one of the All-Pakistan Services for which all posts in police establishments of all the Provinces in BS. 18 and above and some posts in BS. 17 also have been reserved under the Police Service of Pakistan (Composition, Cadre and Seniority) Rules, 1985. Learned counsel prayed that the constitutionality of the Police Service of

Pakistan (Composition, Cadre and Seniority) Rules, 1985 need to be determined to save Article 240 of the Constitution from misconstructions and to protect public interest likely to be seriously hurt by flawed perception of the constitutional scheme in respect of the Service of Pakistan. Finding prayer of the learned counsel reasonable, we directed him to file a concise statement containing facts and law on the subject after examination of which further step in this regard was to be taken, if need be.

213.   The learned counsel for the petitioners, in compliance of our aforesaid direction, filed the following statement:

(a)   All India Services including Indian Police disappeared on 15th of August, 1947 as a Service because of deletion of constitutional provisions providing for reservation of posts in connection with affairs of a Province. However, members of Indian Police were allowed, subject to acceptance of the concerned Dominion or its respective Provinces, to continue to hold the posts held by them on the appointed day with protection of some conditions of service;

(b)   The concept of reservation of posts in connection with affairs of a Province for a federal service is not available in the Constitutions of Pakistan, 1956, 1962, 1972 and 1973; hence, the Police Service of Pakistan (Probationary services) Rules 1950, the Police Service of Pakistan (Composition and Cadre) Rules, 1969, Establishment Division's O.M. No. 3/2/75-ARC dated 31.05.1975 and the Police Service of Pakistan (Composition, Cadre & Seniority) Rules, 1985 are without lawful authority and, hence, void and of no legal effect to this extent;

(c)   Ever since the making of the Devolution Rules, 1990 Police has been and still is a subject falling within exclusive jurisdiction of Provinces. There is consistent legislative, judicial and executive consensus that policing is a provincial subject. Establishment of the police, its organization, working and monitoring in Provinces has never been a federal concern. Applying the doctrine of pith and substance, the organizational laws of police (the Police Act or the Police Order) are provincial laws even if they incidentally encroach upon the field of criminal procedure, criminal law and the law of evidence;

(d)   The concept of uninterrupted continuation in force of existing laws on change of the Constitution implies simply that the laws shall remain in force subject to conformity to the new Constitution and shall not be held invalid only on the ground that the laws were enacted by a legislature which is not competent to do so under the new Constitution. If the law was enacted under the previous dispensation by a competent legislature to which that competence has been denied under the new Constitution and has been vested in some other legislature, the law shall remain effective with the stipulation that the law in question shall not be amended or repealed by the previous legislature but shall be amended or repealed by the legislature in whose jurisdiction the subject falls under the new Constitution. The protection accorded to the existing laws does not save provisions of the existing laws which are repugnant to, in violation of and in irreconcilable clash with the new Constitution. The Police Service of Pakistan (Probationary

Services) Rules 1950, the Police Service of Pakistan (Composition and Cadre) Rules, 1969, Establishment Division's O.M. No. 3/2/75-ARC dated 31.05.1975 and the Police Service of Pakistan (Composition, Cadre & Seniority) Rules, 1985 to the extent of reservation of posts in connection with affairs of a Province are not protected and saved as existing laws and, therefore, posts in connection with affairs of a Province cannot be encadred or reserved for the Police Service of Pakistan under these rules;

(e)   Determination of conditions of recruitment and conditions of service in respect of posts in connection with affairs of a Province exclusively and indivisibly falls within provincial domain under Article 240 of the Constitution read with Article 115, 138 and the rules framed under Article 119 and 139 (3) of the Constitution;

(f)   Posts created by the Province for performance of policing functions in the Province are posts in connection with affairs of the Province and are not posts common to the Federation and the Provinces;

(g)   All expenditure on police establishment is met from the Provincial Consolidated Fund as authorized through the Authenticated Schedule of Authorized Expenditure; hence, the Federation is not relevant to the question of policing in the Province except in cases where armed or paramilitary forces of the Federation are called in aid of the civil administration. In this case also, normally it is the Province which bears the expenditure through reimbursement of the expenses made by the federal forces;

(h)   The Hon'ble superior courts in Pakistan have held that the fundamental right to life and liberty guaranteed under Article 9 of the Constitution includes right of the public employees to have legitimate expectancy to be promoted in accordance with law. Posts in connection with affairs of a Province in its police establishment are required to be filled in through initial recruitment, promotion or appointment by transfer in accordance with provincial laws and are not lawfully available for promotion of the federal police officers. The Federation violates fundamental right of life of provincial police employees by using posts in connection with affairs of the Province for promotion of federal police officers. Thus, promotions of federal police officers against posts in connection with affairs of a Province attract Article 8 of the Constitution and are utterly void and of no legal sanctity in eyes of law; and

(i)   Members of the Police Service of Pakistan are under subordination of the Federation and the Province does not have powers to hire, fire or take any disciplinary action against these officers. Thus, the constitutional requirement of being subordinate to the Province for conferment of functions and exercise of powers is altogether missing in the case of the officers of the Police Service of Pakistan.

214.   The precise prayer of the learned counsel for the petitioners was that the Police Service of Pakistan (Composition, Cadre & Seniority) Rules, 1985 may be declared to be intra vires to the extent of reservation of posts in connection with affairs of the Federation

and ultra vires so far as encadrement of posts in connection with affairs of the Provinces is concerned. He further prayed that to protect fundamental right to life of the provincial police employees as interpreted by the Hon'ble Supreme Court of Pakistan in a series of reported cases, promotions granted to members of the Police Service of Pakistan against posts in connection with affairs of the Provinces may be declared without lawful authority and, hence, void ab initio.

215.   We found the concise statement filed by the learned counsel for the petitioners relevant to the proceedings in this case. The statement made out a prima fascia case for proceeding further in the matter. We, therefore, directed the learned Attorney General for Pakistan to go through the said concise statement and present case of the Federation on the issues raised therein after affording an opportunity of being heard to the Establishment Division, Interior Division, Law Division and members of the Police Service of Pakistan who want to express themselves on the subject. The learned Attorney General for Pakistan, after doing the needful as directed, submitted a written statement which reads as follows:

> "I have sought instructions from the concerned administrative authorities of the Federation and have heard members of the Police Service of Pakistan who wanted to address me. I have also carefully examined written submissions of the said officers and the administrative authorities. After careful analysis of all legal provisions relevant to the subject, I do hereby humbly respond to the issues raised, seriatim:
>
> (a) Dismemberment of the Indian Police as an All India Service to be administered by the Secretary of State for India on 15.08.1947 is a completed and closed transaction and is irrelevant to the facts and law of today. It is, therefore, not necessary to respond to this observation of the petitioners;
>
> (b) Admitted that there is no enabling provision allowing reservation of posts in connection with affairs of a Province for members of a federal service in the Constitutions of Pakistan, 1956, 1962, 1972 and 1973, yet all these constitutions have provided for All Pakistan Services to man posts common to the Federal and the Provinces. The Police Service of Pakistan is an All Pakistan Service in this constitutional sense;
>
> (c) Though there may be reasons to believe that policing is a provincial subject but All Pakistan Services including the Police Service of Pakistan are within exclusive federal jurisdiction; hence, the Police Service of Pakistan (Composition, Cadre & Seniority) Rules, 1985 suffer from no legal infirmity. Moreover, the Federal Government, vide the Federal Laws (Revision and Declaration) Ordinance 1981, declared the Police Act, 1861 as a valid Federal law. The Federal Government, vide Ordinance 11 of 1985, again amended the Police Act, 1861, adding sub-section (6) to its Section 15-A. In 2001, vide C.E. Order No. 7, the Federal Government yet again introduced several significant amendments in the Police Act, 1861. The Federal Government promulgated the Police Order, 2002 (Chief Executive's Order No. 22 of 2002) on 14th August, 2002 through which the Police Act, 1861 was repealed. The Parliament, vide the Constitution (Seventeenth Amendment) Act, 2003, dated 31st December, 2003, amended Article 270AA(I) of the Constitution, validating the Police Order, 2002, and also placing it, for a period of six years, in Sixth Schedule of the Constitution. The Sixth Schedule contained over thirty laws that could not be amended by the Parliament, without prior sanction of the President. The

Eighteenth Amendment Bill dated 20th April, 2010 deleted the Sixth Schedule of the Constitution. Entry 35 relating to the Police Order, 2002 stood already deleted from the Sixth Schedule on 31st December, 2009, due to the sunset clause of the Seventeenth Amendment. Further, the Eighteenth Amendment inserted a new entry at serial number 32 of the Federal Legislative List (International treaties, conventions and agreements and international arbitration). Moreover, entry 10 in the Federal Legislative List (Part-II) provides legislative competence to the Parliament to legislate on the following:

> "Extension of the powers and jurisdiction of members of a police force belonging to any Province to any area in another Province, but not so as to enable the police of one Province to exercise powers and jurisdiction in another province without the consent of the Government of that Province; extension of the powers and jurisdiction of members of a police force belonging to any Province to railway areas outside that Province."

A combined and harmonious reading of all relevant constitutional provisions lead one to conclude that police is a subject on which the Federation has jurisdiction as it is also relatable to criminal procedure;

(d) As all the constitutions of Pakistan provided for protection of the existing laws and to the All Pakistan Services, therefore, the Police Service of Pakistan (Probationary Services) Rules, 1950, the Police Service of Pakistan (Composition and Cadre) Rules, 1969, Establishment Division's O.M. No. 3/2/75-ARC dated 31.05.1975 and the Police Service of Pakistan (Composition, Cadre & Seniority) Rules, 1985 were validly protected and saved;

(e) Article 240 of the Constitution empowers the Parliament to determine conditions of recruitment and of service of members of the All Pakistan Services. As the Police Service of Pakistan is an All Pakistan Service, therefore, the Federation has competence to determine conditions of recruitment and of service of this Service;

(f) The posts in connection with affairs of a Province encadred for the Police Service of Pakistan are posts common to the Federation and the Province;

(g) Incurrence of expenditure by the Province on policing in the Province does not, in and of itself, invalidate encadrement of posts in connection with affairs of the Province for the Police Service of Pakistan;

(h) Except the posts encadred for the Police Service of Pakistan, provincial employees are promoted to the posts reserved for their promotion in their own cadre. Officers of the Police Service of Pakistan have never been promoted against posts reserved for promotion of provincial police employees in their cadre which does not include superior posts; and

(i) Short of powers to hire, fire and disciplinary control, officers of the Police Service of Pakistan are under full control and subordination of the Province in which they perform their duties. It is misconception that officers of the Police Service of Pakistan are not under superintendence and control of the Province of their duty."

216.   The learned Attorney General for Pakistan has prayed that the prayer made by the petitioners for issuance of declarations and directions be turned down. The learned Advocate General, Punjab has endorsed prayer of the learned Attorney General for Pakistan. On the other hand, some provincial police officers of the Province of Punjab have joined these proceedings and have supported the arguments advanced and the prayer made by the learned counsel of the petitioners.

217.   Before attending to the other specific issues raised in these proceedings, we deem it beneficial to first ascertain what police is and whether this subject falls in jurisdiction of the Parliament or the respective Provincial Assemblies.

218.   The term 'police' has not been defined in the Constituting, Police Act, 1861, Pakistan Penal Code, the Criminal Procedure Code and the Police Order, 2002. Some of the definitions of police given in online dictionaries and encyclopedias are reproduced hereinbelow in order to have a fair idea of what police is.

(i)   Police

A body sanctioned by local, state, or national government to enforce laws and apprehend those who break them.

(https://legal-dictionary.thefreedictionary.com/police)

(ii)   Police

Police is the function of that branch of the administrative machinery of government which is charged with the preservation of public order and tranquility, the promotion of the public health, safety, and morals, and the prevention, detection, and punishment of crimes. See State v. Hine, 59 Conn. 50, 21 Atl. 1024. 10 L. It. A. S3; Monet v. Jones. 10 Smedes & M. (Miss.) 247: People v. Squire, 107 N. Y. 593, 14 N. E. S20, 1 Am. St. Rep. 893; Logan v. State, 5 Tex. App. 314. The police of a state, in a comprehensive sense, embraces its whole system of internal regulation, by which the state seeks not only to preserve the public order and to prevent offenses against the state, but also to establish for the intercourse of citizen with citizen those rules of good manners and good neighborhood which are calculated to prevent a conflict of rights, and to insure to each the uninterrupted enjoyment of his own, so far as is reasonably consistent with a like enjoyment of rights by others. Cooley. Const. Lim. *572. It is defined by Jeremy Bentham in his works; "Police is in general a system of precaution, either for the prevention of crime or of calamities. Its business may be distributed into eight distinct branches: (1) Police for the prevention of offenses; (2) Police for the prevention of calamities; (3) Police for the prevention of epidemic diseases; (4) Police of charity; (5) Police of interior communications; (6) Police of public amusements; (7) Police for recent intelligence; (8) Police for registration." Canal Com'rs v. Willamette Transp. Co., G Or. 222.

TLD Example: Police and other law enforcement agencies are a function of the executive branch of government.

(https://thelawdictionary.org/police/)

(iii)   Police

Police, body of officers representing the civil authority of government. Police typically are responsible for maintaining public order and safety, enforcing the law, and preventing, detecting, and investigating criminal activities. These functions are known as policing. Police are often also entrusted with various licensing and regulatory activities.

However, police scholars have criticized this popular understanding of the word **police**—that it refers to members of a public organization having the legal competence to maintain order and enforce the law—

for two reasons. First, it defines police by their ends rather than by the specific means that they use to achieve their goals. Second, the variety of situations in which police are asked to intervene is much greater than law enforcement and order maintenance. There is now a consensus among researchers, based on a definition first proposed by American sociologist Egon Bittner, that the common feature among all the different agencies engaged in policing is the legal competence to enforce coercive, nonnegotiable measures to resolve problematic situations. Such situations are characterized by two features: their potential for harm and the need to solve them urgently before they develop that potential. Hence, the actual use of coercion or the threat of using it allows police to put a quick, non-negotiated, and conclusive end to problematic situations (e.g., keeping people away from the scene of a fire for their own protection and to allow firemen to do their job).

Following that definition, policing, thus, may be performed by several different professional organizations: public police forces, private security agencies, the military, and government agencies with various surveillance and investigative powers. The best known of these bodies are the public constabulary forces that patrol public spaces, often in marked cars, and whose members wear a uniform. They are the most visible representatives of the civil authority of government, and they provide the model typically associated with police organizations. However, in many Anglo-Saxon countries—such as Australia, Canada, the United Kingdom, and the United States—there are at least twice as many private security agents as public police officers. Furthermore, security and intelligence agencies that generally operate undercover have played an increasingly important role in combating terrorism, especially since the September 11 attacks in the United States in 2001. Policing has, therefore, become a complex undertaking that straddles the traditional institutional and jurisdictional distinctions between public and private, criminal and political.

(https://www.britannica.com/topic/police)

(iv)   Police officers

Police officers enforce the law, investigate crimes, preserve evidence, write reports for government prosecutors, apprehend fugitives, and testify in court.

(https://definitions.uslegal.com/p/police-officer/)

(v)   Police

The police are a constituted body of persons empowered by a state to enforce the law, to protect the lives, liberty and possessions of citizens, and to prevent crime and civil disorder.[1] Their lawful powers include arrest and the legitimized use of force. The term is most commonly associated with the police forces of a sovereign state that are authorized to exercise the police power of that state within a defined legal or territorial area of responsibility. Police forces are often defined as being separate from the military and other organizations involved in the defense of the state against foreign aggressors; however, gendarmerie are military units charged with civil policing.[2] Police forces are usually public sector services, funded through taxes.

(https://en.wikipedia.org/wiki/Police)

(vi)   Definition of **police**

(Entry 1 of 2)

*1*a: the department of government concerned primarily with maintenance of public order, safety, and health and enforcement of laws and possessing executive, judicial, and legislative powers

b: the department of government charged with prevention, detection, and prosecution of public nuisances and crimes

(https://www.merriam-webster.com/dictionary/police)

219.   To our mind, police is an executive entity of the Government which is created through law and is tasked mainly with the duties to maintain public order, enforce the law, investigate crimes, preserve evidence, write reports for government prosecutors, apprehend fugitives, testify in courts and perform relief and regulatory functions to the extent and in the manner prescribed by or under a law. The law under which this executive entity is created, generally, comprehensively covers all aspects of that organization—hierarchical structure, recruitment, training, service matters, physical infrastructure, monitoring and accountability etc. Preambles of the Police Act, 1861 and the Khyber Pakhtunkhwa Police Act, 2017, reproduced below, give a clear idea for what purpose a police organization is created:

Preamble of the Police Act, 1861

"WHEREAS it is expedient to re-organize the police and to make it a more efficient instrument for the prevention and detection of crime;"

Preamble of the Khyber Pakhtunkhwa Police Act, 2017

WHEREAS in pursuance of the Constitution of the Islamic Republic of Pakistan and the laws in force in the Province of the Khyber Pakhtunkhwa, the Police has an obligation to perform its duties and functions in an efficient manner for prevention and detection of crime and maintenance of public order;

AND WHEREAS it is expedient to make the police apolitical and accountable to the people through democratic institutions and civilian oversight bodies;

AND WHEREAS in order to maintain effective internal discipline, achieve high performance standards and ensure across the board service delivery, it is expedient to give operational, administrative and financial autonomy to Police;

AND WHEREAS it is expedient to reconstruct and regulate the Police in order to be responsible, service oriented and responsive to effectively uphold and enforce laws, maintain public order, protect the lives, properties and honour of the people, without any discrimination through modern proactive policing and community participation;"

220.   We have perused the Police Rules, 1934 to have an idea of the fields covered by these rules. To be brief, we only refer to titles of chapters and parts of the chapters in the following table:

Chapter	Title of the Chapter	Parts of the Chapter
1	Organization	Part-I Departmental Organization Part-II Relations between Police and Magistrates
2	Establishment	Part-I Permanent Establishment Part-II Additional Police
3	Buildings	
4	Clothing	
5	Equipment	
6	Arms and ammunition	
7	Mounted Police	

Chapter	Title of the Chapter	Parts of the Chapter
8	Leave	
9	Pensions	
10	Accounts	Part-I General scope Part-II Income Part-III Payment from Treasuries Part-IV Cash Book Part-V Pay and allowances Part-VI Contingent charges Part-VII Travelling allowance Part-VIII Miscellaneous
11	Police officers	Part-I Office routine Part-II Stationery and forms Part-III Gazettes, publications and contracts Part-IV Vernacular office
12	Appointments and enrolments	
13	Promotions	
14	Discipline and conduct	
15	Rewards	
16	Punishments	
17	Headquarters establishments and reserves	
18	Guards and escorts	
19	Training and examination	
20	Inspection and supervision	
21	Preventive and detective organization	
22	The Police Station	
23	Prevention of offences	
24	Information to the Police	
25	Investigation	
26	Arrest, Escape and Custody	
27	Prosecution and court duties	
28	Railway police and other special rules	

221.   Our analysis of the contents of the Police Act, 1861 and the Police Rules, 1934 indicates that, in pith and substance, these legal instruments deal with the subject of police. Viewed in the context of doctrines of pith and substance, colourable legislation and incidental and ancillary powers, if a statute is found in substance to relate to a topic within the competence of the legislature, it should be held to be *intra vires* even though it might incidentally trench on topics not within its legislative competence. The extent of the encroachment on matters beyond its competence may be an element in determining whether the legislation is colourable: whether in the guise of making a law on a matter within its competence, the legislature is, in truth, making a law on a subject beyond its competence. However, where that is not the position, the fact of encroachment does not affect the vires of the law even as regards the area of encroachment. Some cases on the doctrine of pith and substance from Pakistani jurisdiction are Sapphire Textile Mills ltd Vs. Collector of Central Excise and Land Customs Hyderabad (1990 CLC 456 Karachi), Mian Ejaz Shafi and others Vs. Federation of Pakistan (PLD 1997 Karachi 604) and Progress of Pakistan Co. Ltd Vs. Registrar Joint Stock Companies Karachi and Islamic Republic of Pakistan (1958 PLD 887 SC). From Indian jurisdiction reliance can safely be placed on the

124

dictum of law laid down in the case reported as A.S. Krishna Vs. State of Madras (1957 SCR 399), Kartar Singh Vs. State of Punjab {(1994) 3 SCC 569}, Bharat Hydro Power Corpn. Ltd. Vs. State of Assam {(2004) 2 SCC 553}, Southern Pharmaceuticals & Chemicals Vs. State of Kerala {(1981) 4 SCC 391}, State of Rajasthan Vs. G. Chawla {AIR 1959 SC 544}, Thakur Amar Singhji Vs. State of Rajasthan {AIR 1955 SC 504}, Delhi Cloth and General Mills Co. Ltd. Vs. Union of India {(1983) 4 SCC 166} and Vijay Kumar Sharma Vs. State of Karnataka {(1990) 2 SCC 562}. We are inclined to hold that the Police Act, 1861 and its successor laws in various parts of Pakistan and the rules framed or deemed to have been framed thereunder are, in pith and substance, on the subject of police.

222.   After declaring that the Police Act, 1861 and its successor laws in Pakistan are on the subject of police and any incidental encroachment on any other subject through these laws is valid mainly on the basis of doctrine of pith and substance, we may now proceed to find that under whose legislative competence the subject of police falls. This may require us to go back in history to have an insight into the legal evolution on the subject.

223.   Prior to enactment of the Government of India Act, 1919, the British rule in the sub-continent was based upon the principle that the impulse which moved it was to be applied from outside India. The Government of India was to obey the Secretary of State for India; the Provincial Governments were to obey the Government of India. There was unitary form of Government and the Provinces were not constitutional entities but were only administrative sub-divisions of the Government of India. The Provinces (also called local governments) had no powers of their own but were meant to exercise powers devolved upon them. Some municipal bodies with executives of their own were the only faint beginnings of a system designed to be driven by internal combustion. The whole position was succinctly set forth in the following extract from the Report of the Decentralization Commission (Report of the Royal Commission upon Decentralization in India, Vol. 1, pp. 20 and 21)

"The present distribution of functions between the Government of India, also styled the Central or Supreme Government, and the Provincial or Local Governments and Administrations is, stated generally, as follows: -

Amongst the important matters which the former retain in their own hands are those relating to foreign affairs, the defences of the country, general taxation, currency, debt, tariffs, posts and telegraphs, railways, and accounts and auditing. Ordinary internal administration, police, civil and criminal justice, prisons, the assessment and collection of the revenues, education, medical and sanitary arrangements, irrigation, buildings and roads, forests, and the control over municipal and rural boards fall to the share of the Provincial Governments. But even in these matters the Government of India exercise a general and constant control. They lay down lines of general policy, and test their application from the administration reports and returns relating to the main departments under the Local Governments. They also employ expert officers to inspect and advise upon a number of departments which are primarily administered by the Local Governments, including Agriculture, Irrigation, Forests, Medical, Sanitation, Education, Excise and Salt, Printing and Stationery, and Archaeology. These officers are commonly known as Imperial Inspectors-General. The essential point to be borne in mind is thus that at present, even in matters primarily assigned to the Provincial Governments, these act as the agents of the Government of India, who exercise a very full and constant check over their proceedings."

224.   The Police Act, 1861 (Act No. 5 of 1861) of 22nd March, 1861 was a Central Government Act which was applicable in the Provinces. At the time of its enactment, there

was no distribution of legislative powers between the Central and Provincial Legislatures; hence, there was no concept of legislative lists.

225. The Government of India Act, 1919 (9 & 10 Geo. 5, eh. 101) inserted Section 45A and 129A, reproduced below, in the Government of India Act:

"Classification of central and provincial subjects

45A.-(1) Provision may be made by rules under this Act-

(a) for the classification of subjects, in relation to the functions of government, as central and provincial subjects, for the purpose of distinguishing the functions of local governments and local legislatures from the functions of the Governor-General in Council and the Indian legislature;

(b) for the devolution of authority in respect of provincial subjects to local governments, and for the allocation of revenues or other moneys to those governments;

(c) for the use under the authority of the Governor-General in Council of the agency of local governments in relation to central subjects, in so far as such agency may be found convenient, and for determining the financial conditions of such agency; and

(d) for the transfer from among the provincial subjects of subjects (in this Act referred to as "transferred subjects") to the administration of the Governor acting with ministers appointed under this Act, and for the allocation of revenues or moneys for the purpose of such administration.

(2) Without prejudice to the generality of the foregoing powers, rules made for the above-mentioned purposes may-

(i) regulate the extent and conditions of such devolution, allocation, and transfer;

(ii) provide for fixing the contributions payable by local governments to the Governor-General in Council, and making such contributions a first charge on allocated revenues, or moneys;

(iii) provide for constituting a finance department in any province, and regulating the functions of that department;

(iv) provide for regulating the exercise of the authority vested in the local government of a province over members of the public services therein;

(v) provide for the settlement of doubts arising as to whether any matter does or does not relate to a provincial subject or a transferred subject, and for the treatment of matters which affect both a transferred subject and a subject which is not transferred; and

(vi) make such consequential and supplemental provisions as appear necessary or expedient:

Provided that, without prejudice to any general power of revoking or altering rules under this Act, the rules shall not authorise the revocation or suspension of the transfer of any subject except with the sanction of the Secretary of State in Council.

(3)   The powers of superintendence, direction, and control over local governments vested in the Governor-General in Council under this Act shall, in relation to transferred-subjects, be exercised only for such purposes as may be specified in rules made under this Act, but the Governor-General in Council shall be the sole judge as to whether the purpose of the exercise of such powers in any particular case comes within the purposes so specified.

(4)   The expressions "central subjects" and "provincial subjects" as used in this Act mean subjects so classified under the rules. Provincial subjects, other than transferred subjects, are in this Act referred to as "reserved subjects."

Provisions as to rules.

129A.-

(1)   Where any matter is required to be prescribed or regulated by rules under this Act, and no special provision is made as to the authority by whom the rules are to be made, the rules shall be made by the Governor-General in Council, with the sanction of the Secretary of State in Council, and shall not be subject to repeal or alteration by the Indian legislature or by any local legislature.

(2)   Any rules made under this Act may be so framed as to make different provision for different provinces.

(3)   Any rules to which sub-section (1) of this section applies shall be laid before both Houses of Parliament as soon as may be after they are made, and, if an address is presented to His Majesty by either House of Parliament within the next thirty days on which that House has sat after the rules are laid before it praying that the rules or any of them may be annulled, His Majesty in Council may annul the rules or any of them, and those rules shall thenceforth be void; but without prejudice to the validity of anything previously done thereunder:

Provided that the Secretary of State may direct that any rules to which this section applies shall be laid in draft before both Houses of Parliament, and in such case the rules shall not be made unless both Houses by resolution approve the draft either without modification or addition, or with modifications and additions to which both Houses agree, but, upon such approval being given, the rules may be made in the form in which they have been approved, and such rules on being so made shall be of full force and effect, and shall not require to be further laid before Parliament."

226.   In exercise of the powers conferred by Section 45A and 149A of the Government of India Act, the Governor General in Council, with the previous sanction of the Secretary of State for India in Council, made the Devolution Rules, 1920, Rule 3, 6 and 47 whereof read as follows:

Part I. Classification of Subjects.

3

(1).   For the purpose of distinguishing the functions of local governments and local legislatures from the functions of the Governor-General in Council and Indian legislature, subjects shall be classified in relation to functions of Government as central and provincial subjects in accordance with the lists set out in Schedule 1.

(2)   Any matter which is included in the list of provincial subjects set out in Part-II of Schedule 1 shall, to the extent of such inclusion, be excluded from any central subject of which, but for such inclusion, it would form such part.

Transfer of subjects and revocation or suspension of transfer.

6.   The Provincial subjects specified in the first column of Schedule II shall, in the provinces shown against each subject in the second column of the said Schedule, shall be transferred subjects provided that the Governor-General in Council may, by notification in the Gazette of India, with the previous sanction of the Secretary of State in Council, revoke or suspend for such period as he may consider necessary the transfer of any provincial subject in any province, and upon such revocation or during such suspension the subject shall not be a transferred subject.

Part-IV Limitation of control by Governor General in Council over transferred subjects

47.   The powers of superintendence, direction and control over the local Government vested in the Governor General in Council under the Act shall, in relation to the transferred subjects, be exercised only for the following purposes, namely: -
(1)   to safeguard the administration of central subjects; and
(2)   to decide questions arising between two provinces in cases where the provinces concerned fail to arrive at an agreement.

227.   Relevant entries in Part-I and II of the Schedule 1 of the aforesaid Devolution Rules are as follows:

"Schedule 1
Part 1
Central Subjects
1.
(a)   Defence of India and all matters connected with His Majesty's Naval, Military and Air Forces in India, or with His Majesty's Marine Service or with any other Force raised in India other than military and armed police wholly maintained by local governments
(b)   Naval and military works and cantonments
16.   Civil law including laws regarding status, property, civil rights and liabilities and civil procedure.
30.   Criminal law including criminal procedure.
40.   All India Services
41.   Legislation in regard to any provincial subject in so far as such subject is in Part II of this Schedule stated to be subject to legislation by the Indian legislature and any powers relating to such subject reserved by legislation to the Governor General in Council

Part II
Provincial Subjects
8.   Land Revenue administration, as distributed under the following heads, namely: -
a)   assessment and collection of land revenue;
b)   maintenance of land records, survey for revenue purposes, records of rights;

c) laws regarding land tenures, relations of landlords and tenants, collection of rents;

d) Courts of Wards, encumbered and attached estates;

e) Land improvement and agricultural loans;

f) Colonization and disposal of Crown land and alienation of land revenue; and

g) Management of Government estates.

17. Administration of justice, including constitution, powers, maintenance and organization of courts of civil and criminal jurisdiction within the province; subject to legislation by Indian Legislature as regards High Courts, Chief Courts and Courts of Judicial Commissioners and any courts of criminal jurisdiction.

31. Police including railway police; subject in the case of railway police to such conditions as regards limits of jurisdiction and railway contributions to cost of maintenance as the Governor General in Council may determine.

38. Prisons, prisoners (except state prisoners) and reformatories; subject to legislation by the Indian legislature.

46. Control, as defined by Rule 10, of members of All India and provincial services serving within the province and control, subject to legislation by the Indian legislature, of other public services within the province.

49. Imposition by legislation of punishments by fine, penalty and imprisonment for enforcing any law of the province; subject to legislation by the Indian legislature in the case of any subject in respect of which such a limitation is imposed under these rules.

228. Some of the above entries do not relate to police, yet, we have reproduced them hereinabove in order to understand the subject of division of legislative powers. It merits to be noted that the legislative and executive powers devolved through the above rules are not co-extensive; it was possible, as was done in some cases, that certain subjects were declared provincial subjects but legislative competence of the Indian legislature was kept intact and was not devolved. Moreover, as the devolution of powers was through the rules, therefore, this devolution was subject to revocation and revision through amendments in the aforesaid rules. None of the provincial subjects at serial number 8, 17, 31, 38, 46 and 49 of Part-II of the Schedule 1 were noted in the Schedule-II of the Devolution Rules which contained transferred subjects. The arrangement of devolution to the provinces through the Government of India Act, 1919 and division of provincial subjects into transferred and reserved subjects is popularly known as dyarchy. Limited control of All India Services in transferred departments was assigned to the Provincial Governments under the All-India Services (Transferred Department) Replacement Rules in respect of the following services:

(i) the Indian Agricultural Service;

(ii) the Indian Educational Service;

(iii) the Indian Forest Service, in those provinces in which Forests is for the time being a transferred subject;

(iv) the Indian Forest Engineering Service, in those provinces in which Forests is for the time being a transferred subject;

(v) the Indian Service of Engineers (Buildings and Road Branch), in those provinces in which Public Works is for the time being a transferred subject; and

(vi) the Indian Veterinary Service.

229. The Police Act, 1861 was a Central Act but the Devolution Rules, 1920 made the subject of police a provincial subject. This change did not affect validity of the Act but only empowered the provincial legislatures to exercise powers in respect of its repeal or

amendments in it. Whereas entry appearing at serial number 31 of the Part-II of the aforesaid Schedule 1 declares the police a provincial subject, entry at serial number 1 of Part-I of the said Schedule affirmatively excludes military and armed police wholly maintained by local governments from the executive competence of the Governor-General in Council and legislative jurisdiction of the Indian legislature. However, legislative competence of the provincial legislatures on the Police Act, 1861 was not absolute but was subject to the Local Legislatures (Previous Sanction) Rules, Rule 2 whereof reads as follows:

> "A local legislature may not repeal or alter without the previous sanction of the Governor General-
>
> 1. any law made by any authority in British India before the commencement of the Indian Councils Act, 1861; provided that the Governor General in Council may, by notification in the Gazette of India, declare that this provision shall not apply to any such law which he may specify and, if he does so, previous sanction shall not thereafter be necessary to the alteration or repeal of that law; or
>
> 2. any law specified in the Schedule to these rules or any law made by the Governor General in Council amending a law so specified."

230. The laws listed in the Schedule referred to in Rule 2(2) of the Rules supra were 68 in total starting from the Indian Penal Code of 1860 to the Charitable and Religious Trusts Act, 1920 and including the Indian Evidence Act, 1872, the Code of Civil Procedure, 1908 but excluding the Police Act,1861. As the Police Act, 1861 was enacted in March 1861 and the Indian Councils Act, 1861 was passed on 1st August, 1861, therefore, it came under Rule 2(1) because it was enacted prior to enactment of the Indian Councils Act, 1861. The Police Act, 1861 could, therefore, be repealed or amended by a provincial legislature with prior sanction of the Governor General.

231. When a legislature is given powers to enact laws on a subject, it has powers to enact measures to enforce the law and punish the violators. Punishment by way of fine, penalty and imprisonment is meant to ensure enforcement and deter violations. Declaration of acts and omissions as crimes precedes imposition of punishment for offenders. In absence of powers to declare acts and omissions as crimes and to prescribe penal actions therefor, a legislature is reduced to the status of a toothless preacher. Penal law, therefore, falls into jurisdiction of a legislature to the extent it has powers to statutorily attend to a subject. Entry at serial number 49 of Part-II of the Schedule 1 of the Devolution Rules is, therefore, not in conflict with entry at serial number 30 of Part-I of the Schedule which relates to criminal law including criminal procedure. Both entries can co-exist and both the legislatures can legitimately deal with the criminal law and criminal procedure within their allotted spheres. Following the same logic, we cannot say that entry at serial number 17 of the Part-II of the Schedule 1 supra relating to administration of justice prohibits the Central legislature to constitute courts to try offences in respect of its laws. We postpone conclusion of this debate but we must record our observation that only a subject can fall in concurrent jurisdiction and not a law. Each legislature has to exercise its jurisdiction within its own area of competence through its own laws and not by amending or repealing a law made by another legislature. Now we proceed to the see introduction of federal system in India through the Government of India Act, 1935. It goes without saying that the Devolution Rules, 1920 clearly and indisputably made the police a provincial subject.

232. Paragraph 153 of the report of the Joint Committee on Indian Constitutional Reform [Session 1933-34] explains the legal basis of the new federal constitution in these words (we admit that this passage has already been reproduced in this judgment, but its relevance to the question under adjudication convinces us to reproduce the same once again):

> "It is clear that, in any new constitution in which autonomous provinces are to be united under the Crown, not only can the provinces no longer derive their powers and authority by devolution by the

Central Government, but the Central Government cannot continue to be an agent of the Secretary of State. Both must derive their powers and authority from a direct grant by the Crown. The legal basis of a reconstituted Government of India must be, first, the resumption into the hands of the Crown of all rights, authority and jurisdiction in and over the territories of British India, whether they are at present vested in the Secretary of State, the Governor-General in Council or the Provincial Governments and Administrations; and second, their redistribution in such manner as the Act may prescribe between the Central Government on the one hand and the Provinces on the other. A Federation of which the British Indian Provinces are the constituent units will thereby be brought into existence."

233. Section 100 of the Government of India Act, 1935, reproduced below, codified the above logic in these words:

"Subject matter of Federal and Provincial laws

100.-

(1) Notwithstanding anything in the two next succeeding subsections, the Federal Legislature has, and a Provincial Legislature has not, power to make laws with respect to any of the matters enumerated in List I in the Seventh Schedule to this Act (hereinafter called the "Federal Legislative List").

(2) Notwithstanding anything in the next succeeding subsection, the Federal Legislature, and, subject to the preceding subsection, a Provincial Legislature also, have power to make laws with respect to any of the matters enumerated in List III in the said Schedule (hereinafter called the "Concurrent Legislative List").

(3) Subject to the two preceding subsections, the Provincial Legislature has, and the Federal Legislature has not, power to make laws for a Province or any part thereof with respect to any of the matters enumerated in List II in the said Schedule (hereinafter called the "Provincial Legislative List").

(4) The Federal Legislature has power to make laws with respect to matters enumerated in the Provincial Legislative List except for a Province or any part thereof."

234. Section 107 of the Government of India Act, 1935 dealt with the possibility of inconsistency between federal and provincial laws in these words:

"Inconsistency between Federal laws and Provincial or State laws

107.-

(1) If any provision of a Provincial law is repugnant to any provision of a Federal law which the Federal Legislature is competent to enact or to any provision of an existing Indian law with respect to one of the matters enumerated in the Concurrent Legislative List, then, subject to the provisions of this section, the Federal law, whether passed before or after the Provincial law, or, as the case may be, the existing Indian law, shall prevail and the Provincial law shall, to the extent of the repugnancy, be void.

(2) Where a Provincial law with respect to one of the matters enumerated in the Concurrent Legislative List contains any provision repugnant to the provisions of an earlier Federal law or an existing Indian law with respect to that matter, then, if

the Provincial law, having been reserved for the consideration of the Governor-General or for the signification of His Majesty's pleasure, has received the assent of the Governor-General or of His Majesty, the Provincial law shall in that Province prevail, but nevertheless the Federal Legislature may at any time enact further legislation with respect to the same matter:

Provided that no Bill or amendment for making any provision repugnant to any Provincial law, which, having been so reserved, has received the assent of the Governor-General or of His Majesty, shall be introduced or moved in either Chamber of the Federal Legislature without the previous sanction of the Governor-General in his discretion.

(3)   If any provision of a law of a Federated State is repugnant to a Federal law which extends to that State, the Federal law, whether passed before or after the law of the State, shall prevail and the law of the State shall, to the extent of the repugnancy, be void."

235.   Relevant entries of the Seventh Schedule referred to in Section 100 of the Government of India Act, 1935 are as follows:

"SEVENTH SCHEDULE.

LEGISLATIVE LISTS.

LIST I.

FEDERAL LEGISLATIVE LIST

39.   Extension of the powers and jurisdiction of members of a police force belonging to any part of British India to any area in another Governor's Province or Chief Commissioner's Province, but not so as to enable the police of one part to exercise powers and jurisdiction elsewhere without the consent of the Government of the Province or the Chief Commissioner, as the case may be; extension of the powers and jurisdiction of members of a police force belonging to any unit to railway areas outside that unit.

42.   Offences against laws with respect to any of the matters in this list.

53.   Jurisdiction and powers of all courts, except the Federal Court, with respect to any of the matters in this list and, to such extent as is expressly authorised by Part IX of this Act, the enlargement of the appellate jurisdiction of the Federal Court, and the conferring thereon of supplemental powers.

LIST II.

PROVINCIAL LEGISLATIVE LIST

1.   Public order (but not including the use of His Majesty's naval, military or air forces in aid of the civil power); the administration of justice; constitution and organisation of all courts, except the Federal Court, and fees taken therein; preventive detention for reasons connected with the maintenance of public order; persons subjected to such detention.

2.   Jurisdiction and powers of all courts except the Federal Court, with respect to any of the matters in this list; procedure in Rent and Revenue Courts.

3.   Police, including railway and village police.

39.   Land revenue, including the assessment and collection of revenue, the maintenance of land records, survey for revenue purposes and records of rights, and alienation of revenue.

III.
CONCURRENT LEGISLATIVE LIST.
PART I.
1.   Criminal law, including all matters included in the Indian Penal Code at the date of the passing of this Act, but excluding offences against laws with respect to any of the matters specified in List I or List II and excluding the use of His Majesty's naval, military and air forces in aid of the civil power.
2.   Criminal Procedure, including all matters included in the Code of Criminal Procedure at the date of the passing of this Act."

236.   Sub-section (1) of Section 100 of the Government of India Act, 1935 is not subordinate to sub-sections (2) and (3) thereof; it will have effect notwithstanding anything contained in the said sub-sections (2) and (3). In plain words, it means that the Federal legislature would be competent to legislate in respect of offences against laws with respect to any of the entries in the Federal Legislative List and notwithstanding exclusive entrustment of policing functions to the Provinces under entry 1 and 3 of the Provincial Legislative List, it may create offences through federal laws in respect of federal subjects and may create its own police to enforce federal laws. The Federation, thus, has jurisdiction to enact penal laws, establish its own police for enforcement and can also create judiciary for adjudication of cases pertaining to federal laws. As public order in the Provinces is not a federal subject but does fall in Provincial Legislative List vide entry 1 of that List, therefore, whereas the Federation may legislate to provide for public order for areas not falling within territorial jurisdiction of a Province, it lacks jurisdiction to enact penal laws designed to maintain public order and protect person and property of citizens and all others for the time being within territories of a Province. The Pakistan Penal Code is a penal law for ensuring public order in the Provinces. The Federation could use this statute as an existing law in terms of Section 292 of the Government of India Act, 1935 for areas outside territorial limits of the Provinces or could have enacted its own law for those areas. Similar option was also available to the Provinces. The concept of prevailing of federal laws in case of inconsistency with a provincial law contained in Section 107 of the Government of India Act, 1935 becomes operational only if the federal law is on a subject exclusively reserved for the federal legislature and not in any other case. The concurrent jurisdiction extends to subjects only and not to the laws. Laws are to be made by the concerned legislature and law made by one legislature is not subject to repeal or amendment by the other legislature. It is only inconsistency between a law the federal legislature is competent to make with a provincial law which the provincial legislature is not competent to make which gives ascendency to the federal law to the extent of the inconsistency. This harmonious construction enables all provisions of the Government of India Act, 1935 on the subjects of police, criminal law and criminal procedure fully effective and functional within the legislative fields allotted to the Federation and the Provinces. What is relevant for us in this discussion is that the subjects of criminal procedure and criminal law are not available to deny the Provinces their absolute, exclusive and indivisible jurisdiction on the subjects of public order and police within their territorial limits. As the continuation in force of the existing laws was subject to conformity of those laws with the provisions of the Government of India Act, 1935 and there was no requirement of pervious sanction of the Governor General for enactments on the provincial subjects by the concerned legislatures, therefore, the Local Legislatures (Previous Sanction) Rules stood laid to rest being not in conformity with the Government of India Act, 1935.

237.   Relevant provisions of the Constitution of Islamic Republic of Pakistan, 1956 are as follows:

133

"Article 105

Subject to the provisions of the Constitution, Parliament may make laws, including laws having extra-territorial operation, for the whole or any part of Pakistan, and a Provincial Legislature may make laws for the Province or any part thereof.

Article 106

(1)   Notwithstanding anything in the two next succeeding clauses, Parliament shall have exclusive power to make laws with respect to any of the matters enumerated in the Federal List.

(2)   Notwithstanding anything in clause (3), Parliament, and subject to clause (1) a Provincial Legislature also, shall have power to make laws with respect to any of the matters enumerated in the Concurrent List.

(3)   Subject to clauses (1) and (2), a Provincial Legislature shall have exclusive power to make laws for a Province or any part thereof with respect to any of the matters enumerated in the Provincial List.

(4)   Parliament shall have power to make laws with respect to matters enumerated in the Provincial List, except for a Province or any part thereof.

Article 107

If it appears to the Provincial Assemblies to be desirable that any of the matters enumerated in the Provincial List, or any matter not enumerated in any list in the Fifth Schedule should be regulated in the Provinces by Act of Parliament and if resolutions to that effect are passed by the Provincial Assemblies, it shall be lawful for Parliament to pass an Act regulating that matter accordingly, but any Act so passed may, as respects any Province, be amended or repealed by an Act of the Legislature of that Province.

Article 108

Parliament shall have power to make laws for the whole or any part of Pakistan for implementing any treaty agreement or convention between Pakistan and any other country, or any decision taken at any international body, notwithstanding that it deals with a matter enumerated in the Provincial List or a matter not enumerated in any list in the Fifth Schedule:

Provided that no law under this Article shall be enacted except after consultation with the Governor of the Province to which the law is to be applied.

Article 109

Subject to the provisions of Articles 107 and 108, the Provincial Legislature shall have exclusive power to make the laws with respect to any matter not enumerated in any list in the Fifth Schedule, including any law imposing tax not mentioned in any such list; and the executive authority of the Province shall extend to the administration of any law so made.

Article 110

(1)   If any provision of an Act of a Provincial legislature is repugnant to any provision of an Act of Parliament, which Parliament is competent to enact, or to any provision of any existing law with respect to any of the matters enumerated in the Concurrent List, then, subject to the provisions of clause (2), the Act of Parliament, whether passed before or after the Act of the

Provincial Legislature, or, as the case may be, the existing law, shall prevail and the Act of the Provincial Legislature shall, to the extent of the repugnancy, be void.

(2)   Where an Act of a Provincial Legislature with respect to any of the matters in the Concurrent List contains any provision repugnant to the provisions of an earlier Act of Parliament or an existing law with respect to that matter, then, if the Act of the Provincial Legislature, having been reserved for the consideration of the President, has received his assent, the Act of the Provincial Legislature shall prevail in the Province concerned, but nevertheless Parliament may at any time enact any law with respect to the same matter, amending or repealing the law so made by the Provincial Legislature.

Fifth Schedule

Article 106

Federal List

1. Defence of Pakistan and of every part thereof, and all acts and measures connected therewith.
The Naval, Military and Air Forces of the Federation and any other armed forces raised or maintained by the Government of the Federation; armed forces which are not forces of the Federation but are attached to or operating with any of the armed forces of the Federation;
any other armed forces of the Federation, including civil armed forces.

22. Federal Services, and the Federal Public Service Commission; Federal Pensions.

29. Jurisdiction and powers of all courts, except the Supreme Court, with respect to any of the matters in this List; offences against laws with respect to any of the matters in this List.

30. All matters which under the Constitution are within the legislative competence of Parliament, and matters incidental thereto.

Concurrent List

PART I

1.   Civil and Criminal law, including the law of evidence and procedure, limitation, marriage and divorce, minors and infants; adoption, joint family and partition; all matters in respect of which parties in judicial proceedings were immediately before the Constitution Day subject to their personal law; wills, intestacy, succession, and transfer of property (excluding succession to and transfer of agricultural land); registration of deeds and documents; arbitration; contract; partnership; agency; bankruptcy and insolvency; actionable wrongs; legal and medical professions contempt of court; trusts and official trustees.

PART II

19.   Jurisdiction and powers of all courts, except the Supreme Court, with respect to any of the matters in this List; offences against laws with respect to any of the matters in this List.

Provincial List

1.   Public order (but not including the use of naval, military or air forces, or any other armed forces of the Federation in aid of the civil power).

2. Administration of justice; constitution and organization of all except the Supreme Court; procedure in Rent and Revenue courts; fees taken in all courts, except the Supreme Court.
3. Police, including Armed Police, Railway and Village Police.
4. Extension of the powers and jurisdiction of members of a Police force belonging to any province to any area outside that province.
5. Preventive detention for reasons connected with the maintenance of public order; persons subjected to such detention.
8. Land, that is to say, rights in or over land; land tenures, including the relation of landlord and tenant, and the collection of rents; transfer, alienation and devolution of agricultural land; land improvement and agricultural loans; colonization.
10. Land revenue, including the assessment and collection of revenue, the maintenance of land records, survey for revenue purposes and records of rights and alienation or revenues.

238. Legislative jurisdictions were distributed amongst the Central and Provincial Legislatures by the Constitution of the Islamic Republic of Pakistan, 1962 in the following words:

"Article 131

(1) The Central Legislature shall have exclusive power to make laws (including laws having extra-territorial operation) for the whole or any part of Pakistan with respect to any matter enumerated in the Third Schedule.

(2) Where the national interest of Pakistan in relation to
(a) the security of Pakistan, including the economic and financial stability of Pakistan;
(b) planning or co-ordination; or
(c) the achievement of uniformity in respect of any matter in different parts of Pakistan,

so requires, the Central Legislature shall have power to make laws (including laws having extra-territorial operation) for the whole or any part of Pakistan with respect to any matter not enumerated in the Third Schedule.

(3) If-
(a) it appears to the Assembly of a Province to be desirable that a matter not enumerated in the Third Schedule should be regulated in the Province by an Act of the Central Legislature; and
(b) a resolution to that effect is passed by the Provincial Assembly,

the Central Legislature shall have power to make laws having effect in the Province with respect to that matter, but any law made in pursuance of this power may be amended or repealed by an Act of the Provincial Legislature.

(4) The Central Legislature shall have power (but not exclusive power) to make laws for the Islamabad Capital Territory and the Dacca Capital Territory with respect to any matter not enumerated in the Third Schedule.

(5) The Central Legislature shall have power to make laws for any part of Pakistan not forming part of a Province with respect to any matter.

Article 132

A Provincial Legislature shall have power to make laws for the Province, or any part of the Province, with respect to any matter other than a matter enumerated in the Third Schedule.

Article 134

When a Provincial Law is inconsistent with a Central Law, the latter shall prevail, and the former shall to the extent of the inconsistency, be invalid.

THIRD SCHEDULE.

MATTERS WITH RESPECT TO WHICH THE CENTRAL LEGISLATUUE HAS EXCLUSIVE POWER TO MAKE LAWS.

1. Defence of Pakistan and of each part of Pakistan, including

   (a)   the Defence Services of Pakistan, any other armed forces (including civilian armed forces) raised or maintained by the Central Government of Pakistan and any other armed forces attached to or operating with any of the armed forces of Pakistan;

   (b)   military, naval and air force works;

   (c)   industries connected with defence;

   (d)   the manufacture of arms, firearms, ammunition and explosives; and

   (e)   cantonment areas, including-

      (i)   the delimitation of such areas;

      (ii)   local self-government in such areas, the constitution of local authorities for such areas and the functions and powers of such authorities; and

      (iii) the control of housing accommodation (including control of rents) in such areas.

2. External Affairs, including

   (a)   relations and dealings or all kinds with other countries;

   (b)   international organisations and bodies, and the implementation of their decisions;

   (c)   the making and implementation of treaties, conventions and agreements with other countries;

   (d)   diplomatic, consular, trade and other representation in other countries;

   (e)   the declaration of war upon, and the making of peace with, any foreign country;

   (f)   offences against the laws of nations; and

   (g)   foreign and extra-territorial jurisdiction, Admiralty jurisdiction and piracy and offences committed on the high seas and in the air.

33. Central intelligence and investigating organisations.

34. Preventive detention for reasons connected with defence, external affairs or the security of Pakistan, and persons subjected to such detention.

39. The service and execution outside a Province of the processes and the judgments, decrees, orders and sentences of courts, and of other authorities and tribunals, of the Province, and the recognition outside a Province of the laws, records and judicial proceedings of 1he Province.

46. Jurisdiction and powers of courts with respect of any of the matters enumerated in this Schedule.

47.   Offences against laws with respect to any of the matters enumerated in this Schedule.

48.   Matters which under this Constitution are within the legislative competence of the Central Legislature or relate to the Centre.

19.   Mutters incidental or ancillary to any matter enumerated in this Schedule.

239.   Interim Constitution of the Islamic Republic of Pakistan, 1972 covered the subject of distribution of legislative powers in the following words:

"Article 137

Subject to the provisions of this Constitution, the Federal Legislature may make laws (including laws having extra-territorial operation) for the whole or any part of Pakistan, and a Provincial Legislature may make laws for the Province or any part thereof.

Article 138

(1)   Notwithstanding anything in the two next succeeding clauses, the Federal Legislature has, and a Provincial Legislature has not, power to make laws with respect to any of the matters enumerated in List 1 in the Fourth Schedule (hereinafter called the "Federal Legislative List").

(2)   Notwithstanding anything in the next succeeding clause, the Federal Legislature, and subject to the preceding clause, a Provincial Assembly also, have power to make laws with respect to any of the matters enumerated in List III in the said Schedule (hereinafter called the "Concurrent Legislative List").

(3)   Subject to the two preceding clauses, the Provincial Legislature has, and the Federal Legislature has not, power to make laws for a Province or any part thereof with respect to any of the matters enumerated in List II in the said Schedule (hereinafter called the "Provincial Legislative List").

(4)   The Federal Legislature has power to make laws with respect to matters enumerated in the Provincial Legislative List except for a Province or any part thereof.

Vide entry appearing at serial number 3 of the Provincial Legislative List, Police including railway and village police was a provincial subject. On the other hand, criminal law, criminal procedure, civil procedure and evidence were enumerated in the Concurrent Legislative List.

Entry at serial number 40 of the Federal Legislative List was as follows:

"Extension of the powers and jurisdiction of members of a police force belonging to any Province to any area in another Province, but not so as to enable the police of one Province to exercise powers and jurisdiction in another Province without the consent of the Government of that Province; extension of the powers and jurisdiction of members of a police force belonging to any unit to railway areas outside that unit."

240.   Position of the Constitution of the Islamic Republic of Pakistan, 1973 before and after the Constitution (Eighteenth Amendment) Act, 2010 in the Constitution is as follows:

Constitution before the Constitution (Eighteenth Amendment) Act, 2010

Article 142

Subject to the Constitution-

(a) Majlis-e-Shoora (Parliament) shall have exclusive power to make laws with respect to any matter in the Federal Legislative List;

(b) Majlis-e-Shoora (Parliament), and a Provincial Assembly also, shall have power to make laws with respect to any matter in the Concurrent Legislative List;

(c) A Provincial Assembly shall, and Majlis-e-Shoora (Parliament) shall not, have power to make laws with respect to any matter not enumerated in either the Federal Legislative List or the Concurrent Legislative List; and

(d) Majlis-e-Shoora (Parliament) shall have exclusive power to make laws with respect to matters not enumerated in either of the Lists for such areas in the Federation as are not included in any Province.

FOURTH SCHEDULE

[Article 70(4)]

Legislative Lists

1. The defence of the Federation or any part thereof in peace or war; the military, naval and air forces of the Federation and any other armed forces raised or maintained by the Federation; any armed forces which are not forces of the Federation but are attached to or operating with any of the Armed Forces of the Federation including civil armed forces; Federal Intelligence Bureau; preventive detention for reasons of State connected with defence, external affairs, or the security of Pakistan or any part thereof; person subjected to such detention; industries declared by Federal law to be necessary for the purpose of defence or for the prosecution of war.

2. Military, naval and air force works; local self- government in cantonment areas, the constitution and powers within such areas of cantonment authorities, the regulation of house accommodation in such areas, and the delimitation of such areas.

3. External affairs; the implementing of treaties and agreements, including educational and cultural pacts and agreements, with other countries; extradition, including the surrender of criminals and accused persons to Governments outside Pakistan.

40. Extension of the powers and jurisdiction of members of a police force belonging to any Province to any area in another Province, but not so as to enable the police of one Province to exercise powers and jurisdiction in another Province without the consent of the Government of that Province; extension of the powers and jurisdiction of members of a police force belonging to any Province to railway areas outside that Province.

55. Jurisdiction and powers of all courts, except the Supreme Court, with respect to any of the matters in this list and, to such extent as is expressly authorized by or under the Constitution, the enlargement of the jurisdiction of the

Supreme Court, and the conferring thereon of supplemental powers.

56. Offences against laws with respect to any of the matters in this Part.

58. Matters which under the Constitution are within the legislative competence of Majlis- e-Shoora (Parliament) or relate to the Federation.

59. Matters incidental or ancillary to any matter enumerated in this Part.

Concurrent Legislative List

1. Criminal law, including all matters included in the Pakistan Penal Code on the commencing day, but excluding offences against laws with respect to any of the matters specified in the Federal Legislative List and excluding the use of naval, military and air forces in aid of civil power.

2. Criminal procedure, including all matters included in the Code of Criminal Procedure, on the commencing day.

3. Civil procedure, including the law of limitation and all matters included in the Code of Civil Procedure on the commencing day, the recovery in a Province or the Federal Capital of claims in respect of taxes and other public demands, including arrears of land revenue and sums recoverable as such, arising outside that Province.

4. Evidence and oath; recognition of laws, public acts and records of judicial proceedings.

13. Removal of prisoners and accused persons from one Province to another Province.

14. Preventive detention for reasons connected with the maintenance of public order, or the maintenance of supplies and services essential to the community; persons subjected to such detention.

15. Persons subjected to preventive detention under Federal authority.

Constitution after the Constitution (Eighteenth Amendment) Act, 2010

Article 142

Subject-matter of Federal and Provincial laws. Subject to the Constitution—

(a) Majlis-e-Shoora (Parliament) shall have exclusive power to make laws with respect to any matter in the Federal Legislative List;

(b) Majlis-e-Shoora (Parliament) and a Provincial Assembly shall have power to make laws with respect to criminal law, criminal procedure and evidence;

(c) Subject to paragraph (b), a Provincial Assembly shall, and Majlis-e-Shoora (Parliament) shall not, have power to make laws with respect to any matter not enumerated in the Federal Legislative List;

(d) Majlis-e-Shoora (Parliament) shall have exclusive power to make laws with respect to all matters pertaining to such areas in the Federation as are not included in any Province.

Article 143

If any provision of an Act of a Provincial Assembly is repugnant to any provision of an Act of Majlis-e-Shoora (Parliament) which Majlis-e-Shoora (Parliament) is competent to enact, then the Act of Majlis-e-Shoora (Parliament), whether passed before or after the Act of the Provincial Assembly, shall prevail and the Act of the Provincial Assembly shall, to the extent of the repugnancy, be void.

FOURTH SCHEDULE

[Article 70 (6)]

LEGISLATIVE LISTS

Federal Legislative List

PART I

1. The defence of the Federation or any part thereof in peace or war; the military, naval and air forces of the Federation and any other armed forces raised or maintained by the Federation ; any armed forces which are not forces of the Federation but are attached to or operating with any of the Armed Forces of the Federation including civil Armed Forces; Federal Intelligence Bureau; preventive detention for reasons of State connected with defence, external affairs, or the security of Pakistan or any part thereof ; persons subjected to such detention; industries declared by Federal law to be necessary for the purpose of defence or for the prosecution of war.

2. Military, naval and air force works; local self-government in cantonment areas, the constitution and powers within such areas of cantonment authorities, the regulation of house accommodation in such areas, and the delimitation of such areas.

3. External affairs; the implementing of treaties and agreements, including educational and cultural pacts and agreements, with other countries; extradition, including the surrender of criminals and accused persons to Governments outside Pakistan.

32. International treaties, conventions and agreements and International arbitration.

56. Offences against laws with respect to any of the matters in this Part.

58. Matters which under the Constitution are within the legislative competence of Majlis-e-Shoora (Parliament) or relate to the Federation.

59. Matters incidental or ancillary to any matter enumerated in this Part.

PART II

10. Extension of the powers and jurisdiction of members of a police force belonging to any Province to any area in another Province, but not so as to enable the police of one Province to exercise powers and jurisdiction in another province without the consent of the Government of that Province; extension of the powers and jurisdiction of members of a police force belonging to any Province to railway areas outside that Province.

241. A perusal of the constitutional provisions reproduced hereinabove guides us to arrive at, inter alia, the following conclusions:

141

a) Police and public order in areas falling within territorial jurisdiction of the Provinces have never been federal subjects; these subjects either fell in the Provincial Legislative Lists or were not assigned to the Federation through their non-inclusion in the Federal Legislative Lists. The Federation had and continues to have full jurisdiction to legislate on public order and police for areas not forming part of a Province and on subjects within its exclusive legislative jurisdiction;

b) Legislation on public order and police necessarily includes penal law and criminal procedure. Legislation on other subjects by the Federation and the Provinces may also require incrimination of certain undesired acts or omissions and prosecution of the offenders. The Federation as well as the Provinces have jurisdiction to legislate for their respective subject-matters and territories;

c) The concept of concurrent jurisdiction relates to legislative subjects and not laws. Each legislature is competent to enact its own laws within its legislative jurisdiction and a law competently made by a legislature is not subject to repeal or amendment through enactment of any other legislature on the ground of the subject being the same as applicability of statues of a legislature is exclusive and not concurrent. Federal laws on police, public order, criminal law, evidence and criminal procedure shall be applicable in federal territories and in respect of exclusive federal subjects. On the other hand, provincial laws on public order, police, criminal law, evidence and criminal procedure shall be enforceable in the territorial jurisdiction of the Provinces and on subjects not falling within the Federal Legislative List. The constitutional provision regarding prevailing of federal law in case of its inconsistency with a provincial law can be invoked only if it is proved that the Province travelled beyond its jurisdiction and legislated on a subject falling within exclusive federal jurisdiction. Thus, if the provincial legislature legislates on defence, currency, nuclear energy, aircraft and air navigation, copy rights, State Bank of Pakistan or on any other subject enumerated in the Federal Legislative List, the same will be void and of no legal effect whether it is consistent or inconsistent with federal legislation on that subject. With abolition of the concept of Concurrent Legislative List through the Constitution (Eighteenth Amendment) Act, 2010, Article 142 (b) of the Constitution can be made really functional only if it is construed to empower the respective legislatures to enact laws on the subjects listed in that Article in their respective jurisdictions and subjects only. As regards criminal laws, laws on criminal procedure and evidence existing on coming into effect of the Constitution (Eighteenth Amendment) Act, 2010, these were required to be treated as valid laws in their capacity of existing laws which thereafter fell into exclusive jurisdictions of the respective legislatures to the extent of their territorial and subject-matter jurisdictions. This point is relevant to the matter under adjudication as clarity on this issue inevitably leads to the conclusion that exclusive provincial jurisdiction on public order, police and administration of justice within territorial and subject-matter jurisdiction of the Province cannot be encroached upon or objected to on the basis of Article 142(b) of the Constitution. Even otherwise, the doctrine of pith and substance is there to save and protect provincial legislation on police for provincial territories and subjects; and

d) Federation can have resort to entrustment of policing functions in respect of federal laws to the provincial police within territorial jurisdiction of that Province through an arrangement under Article 146 of the Constitution, obviously on payment of expenditure required for policing of federal laws. It is trite law that what is not allowed to be done directly can also not be done indirectly. Offences in respect of federal laws is an exclusive federal subject. The Province cannot assume jurisdiction on this exclusive federal subject under the pretext of legislation on public order or police. If the Federation is competent to create offences on subjects of its legislative competence, then it also has the power to statutorily create executive machinery for enforcement of federal laws. In this view of the matter, the Pakistan Railways Police Act, 1977 (Act No.7 of 1977), the Federal Investigation Agency Act, 1974 (Act No. VII of 1975) and the National Accountability Ordinance, 1999 (XVIII of 1999) are valid pieces of legislation to the extent of offences on subjects falling within exclusive federal legislative jurisdiction and not in case of offences under exclusive provincial domain.

242. After examining constitutional provisions on the subject of police from the Government of India Act to the Constitution (Eighteenth Amendment) Act, 2010, we may now lend our ears to listen to what the superior judiciary has said on the subject of police. The Hon'ble Supreme Court of Pakistan has held in Inspector General of Police vs Mushtaq Warraich and others (1985 PLD 159) that:

> "----the Police Act is now a Provincial Act by reason of the subject— Police, being within the legislative competence of the Provincial Legislature."

A Division Bench of the Hon'ble High Court of Sindh, in its judgment in CP D-7097 of 2016 & CP D-131 of 2017 has held that the legislative competence of "Police" is in the exclusive Provincial domain. The Hon'ble Court quoted with approval the following excerpt from Mr. Peter Hogg's *Constitutional Law of Canada* (5th ed. (loose leaf), 2014):

> "Provincial power over the administration of justice in the province (s.92(14)) is not confined to civil justice. It includes criminal justice as well, despite the allocation to the federal Parliament of power over criminal law and procedure (s.91(27)). In *Di Iorio v.Warden of Montreal Jail* (1976) [[1978] 1 SCR 152] ... [seven of the nine judges explicitly made the point that the administration of justice in the province included criminal justice. Laskin C.J. (with de Grandpre J.) dissented...."

In India, Police has been enumerated in the State List (Provincial List). Thus, in Prakash Singh and Ors Vs. Union of India {(2006) 8 SCC 1}, the Hon'ble Supreme Court of India issued certain directions to the State Governments in respect of the Police Act. In compliance of directions so issued, a number of State legislatures enacted new Police Acts, repealing the Police Act, 1861.

243. On legislative front, we may examine measures of all the four Provinces in respect of the Police Act, 1861, starting from the Province of Khyber Pakhtunkhwa. The Province promulgated the Khyber Pakhtunkhwa Police Ordinance, 2011 (Khyber Pakhtunkhwa Ordinance No. XI of 2011) through which the Police Order, 2002 was repealed. Subsequently, the Khyber Pakhtunkhwa Police Act, 2017 (Khyber Pakhtunkhwa Act No. II of 2017) was enacted in January 2017 through which Khyber

Pakhtunkhwa Ord. No. XI of 2016 was repealed. In Khyber Pakhtunkhwa, the law applicable to the police is the Khyber Pakhtunkhwa Police Act, 2017. However, the rules made under the Police Act, 1861 (V of 1861) have been kept in force until altered, repealed or amended by the appropriate authority. The said Police Act of 2017 deals with establishment of police in the Province and matters connected therewith or ancillary thereto. The Act defines the 'Government' as the Government of Khyber Pakhtunkhwa. It does not assign any role to the Federal Government in police matters of the Province except under Section 15 and 16 of the Act in respect of posting of the Provincial Police Officer from amongst list of police officers provided by the Federal Government and Section 28 regarding recruitment of the Assistant Superintendents of Police through the Federal Public Service Commission. The Police Service of Pakistan has not been mentioned in this Act. Whereas Sections 15, 16 and 28 of the said Act are open to serious constitutional exceptions, what is relevant for us is the conclusion that the said Act has neither been challenged nor held ultra vires the legislative competence of the Province on the ground that police is a federal subject and the Province lacks jurisdiction to enact such a law.

244.   Balochistan is divided into 'A' and 'B' areas. A-Area is policed by regular Police force whereas B-Area is policed by levies. A-Area constitutes five per cent of Balochistan. In A-Area, now the applicable law is the Balochistan Police Act, 2011 (Act No. X of 2011) which was passed by the Provincial Assembly of Balochistan on 19th of August, 2011 and was assented into law by the Governor of Balochistan on 24th of August, 2011. The said Act is, with some modifications, a replica of the Police Act, 1861. The said Act of 2011 repealed the Police Order, 2002 to the extent of Balochistan. The Act does not assign any role to the Federal Government or the Police Service of Pakistan in matters relating to police in the Province. The Act is still in the field and its legality has not been judicially questioned.

245.   In Sindh, the Sindh (Repeal of the Police Order, 2002 and Revival of the Police Act, 1861) Bill, 2011 (Sindh Act No. XXII of 2011) was passed by the Provincial Assembly of Sindh on 13th July, 2011 and assented to by the Governor of Sindh on 14th July, 2011. This Act repealed the Police Order, 2002 to the extent of Sindh Province and revived the Police Act, 1861 with immediate effect as it stood on 13th of August, 2002. The Police (Amendment) Order, 2001 had made substantial changes in the Police Act, 1861 with effect from 14th August, 2001 implying that the Police Act, 1861 was revived inclusive of changes introduced in it through the Police (Amendment) Order, 2001. Vires of the Sindh (Repeal of the Police Order, 2002 and Revival of the Police Act, 1861) Bill, 2011 were challenged in in CP D-7097 of 2016 & CP D-131 of 2017 in the Hon'ble Sindh High Court which was pleased, inter alia, to hold that:

> "It is declared that the Sindh (Repeal of the Police Order, 2002 and Revival of the Police Act, 1861) Act, 2011 is *intra vires* the Constitution, and that, therefore, the Police Act, 1861, as revived and restored by the said Act is the law in force in this Province and not the Police Order, 2002."

The Provincial Assembly of Sindh on 18th of May, 2019 passed the Sindh (Repeal of the Police Act, 1861 and Revival of Police Order, 2002) (Amendment) Bill, 2019 (Sindh Act No. XI of 2019) which was returned by the Governor for reconsideration by the Provincial Assembly in terms of Article 116(2)(a) of the Constitution. The Provincial Assembly of Sindh reconsidered the Bill and passed it again with amendments on 13th of June, 2019 which was sent to the Governor for assent. The said Bill was deemed to have been assented to by the Governor after elapse of ten days as provided in clause (3) of Article 116 of the Constitution. The said Act of 2019 has repealed the Police Act, 1861 and has revived the Police Order, 2002 as it stood on 13th of July, 2011 with amendments. Section 11(1), 12(2) and 116(2) of the said Act of 2019 read as follows:

Section 11(1)

> "The Government shall post the Inspector General of Police out of a panel of three police officers recommended by the Federal Government.
>
> Provided that before a police officer is posted as Inspector General of Police under clause (1) the Federal Government shall place his services at the disposal of the Provincial Government."
>
> **Section 12(2)**
>
> "The Provincial Government or the Federal Government may, for compelling reasons, in consultation with each other, repatriate, or recall the Inspector General of Police, as the case may be."
>
> **Section 116(2)**
>
> "The Federal Government may require the Government to submit reports on such matters as may be specified in the requirements on matters connected with performance of the police officers of the Police Service of Pakistan."

Except the above three provisions, no substantial role of the Federation or of the Police Service of Pakistan has been specified in the Sindh (Repeal of the Police Act, 1861 and Revival of Police Order, 2002) (Amendment) Act, 2019 in matters relating to police in the Sindh. We intend to examine constitutionality of the above three provisions later in this judgment. The Police Act, 1861 was earlier amended by the Province through Sindh Ordinance No. XLII of 1984.

246.   The Punjab Government, vide Act VII of 1975, introduced a Punjab-specific amendment in Section 7 of the Police Act 1861. The said Act of 1861 was again amended through the Police (Punjab Amendment) Ordinance VI11 of 1984. The Punjab has retained the Police Order, 2002 with amendments made through the Punjab Police Order (Amendment) Act, 2013. The Police Order amended by the Punjab does not mention the Police Service of Pakistan but has provisions with regard to posting of the Provincial Police Officer from amongst a panel of officers to be proposed by the Federal Government and recruitment of Assistant Superintendent of police through the Federal Public Service Commission. The amended Police Order, 2002 is in force in the Punjab.

247.   The Police Order, 2002 was issued under the Proclamation of Emergency of 14.10.1999 and the Provisional Constitution Order No. 1 of 1999. The aforesaid Proclamation provided that the Constitution shall remain in abeyance and the whole of Pakistan will come under the control of the Armed Forces of Pakistan. The Provisional Constitution Order No. 1 of 1999 specified that notwithstanding the abeyance of the provisions of the Constitution, Pakistan shall, subject to this Order and any other Orders made by the Chief Executive, be governed, as nearly as may be, in accordance with the Constitution. The Constitution is, therefore, not a valid touchstone to determine legality of the Police Order, 2002 which had lawful effect notwithstanding its repugnancy with the Constitution. Article 2(1) of the Provisional Constitution Order No. 1 of 1999 reads as follows:

> "Notwithstanding the abeyance of the provisions of the Constitution of the Islamic Republic of Pakistan, hereinafter referred to as the Constitution, Pakistan shall, subject to this Order and any other Orders made by the Chief Executive, be governed, as nearly as may be, in accordance with the Constitution."

Article 5(1) of the said Provisional Constitution Order provides as under:

> "Notwithstanding the abeyance of the provisions of the Constitution, but subject to the Orders of the Chief Executive all laws other than the Constitution all Ordinances, Orders, Rules, Bye Laws, Regulations, Notifications, and other instruments in force in any part of Pakistan whether made by the President or the Governor of a Province shall

continue in force until altered, amended or repealed by the Chief Executive or any authority designated by him."

The effect of the holding in abeyance of the Constitution of 1973 through the Provisional Constitution Order was that the Orders of the Chief Executive could lawfully make deviations from the Constitution of 1973. The Police Order, 2002 is one example of exercise of powers in respect of police matters of the Provinces by the Chief Executive which were not available to the Federation under the Constitution of 1973. As the Hon'ble superior judiciary accepted validity of the Proclamation of Emergency of 14.10.1999 and the Provisional Constitution Orders issued thereunder, therefore, the Police Order, 2002 was a valid peace of law till revival of the Constitution of 1973.

However, the Constitution (Seventeenth Amendment) Act, 2003, vide its Section 10, substituted Article 270-AA clause (1) to (3) whereof reads as follows:

(1) The Proclamation of Emergency of the fourteenth day of October, 1999, all President's Orders, Ordinances, Chief Executive's Orders, including the Provisional Constitution Order No. 1 of 1999, the Oath of Office (Judges) Order, 2000 (No. 1 of 2000), Chief Executive's Order No. 12 of 2002, the amendments made in the Constitution through the Legal Framework Order, 2002 (Chief Executive's Order No. 24 of 2002), the Legal Framework (Amendment) Order , 2002 (Chief Executive's Order No. 29 of 2002), the Legal Framework (Second Amendment) Order, 2002 (Chief Executive's Order No. 32 of 2002) and all other laws made between the twelfth day of October, one thousand nine hundred and ninety-nine and the date on which this Article comes into force (both days inclusive), having been duly made or accordingly affirmed, adopted and declared to have been validly made by the competent authority and notwithstanding anything contained in the Constitution shall not be called in question in any court or forum on any ground whatsoever.

(2) All orders made, proceedings taken, appointments made, including secondments and deputations, and acts done by any authority, or by any person, which were made, taken or done, or purported to have been made, taken or done, between the twelfth day of October, one thousand nine hundred and ninety-nine, and the date on which this Article comes into force (both days inclusive), in exercise of the powers derived from any Proclamation, President's Orders, Ordinances, Chief Executive's Orders, enactments, including amendments in the Constitution, notifications, rules, orders, bye-laws or in execution of or in compliance with any orders made or sentences passed by any authority in the exercise or purported exercise of powers as aforesaid, shall, notwithstanding any judgment of any court, be deemed to be and always to have been validly made, taken or done and shall not be called in question in any court or forum on any ground whatsoever.

(3) All Proclamations, President's Orders, Ordinances, Chief Executive's Orders, laws, regulations, enactments, including amendments in the Constitution, notification, rules, orders or bye-laws in force immediately before the date on which this Article comes into force shall continue in force, until altered, repealed or amended by the competent authority.

Explanation: In this clause," competent authority" means, -

(a)   in respect of President's Orders, Ordinances, Chief Executive's Orders and enactments, including amendments in the Constitution, the appropriate Legislature; and

(b)   in respect of notifications, rules, orders and bye-laws, the authority in which the power to make, alter, repeal or amend the same vests under the law."

248.   Section 9 of the Constitution (Seventeenth Amendment) Act, 2003 amended Article 268 of the Constitution resulting into prohibition of repeal of or amendment in certain laws including the Police Order, 2002 (entry at serial number 35 of the Sixth Schedule) without previous sanction of the President before expiry of a period of six years. It was specified that entries 27 to 30 and entry 35 (Police Order, 2002) in the Sixth Schedule shall stand omitted after six years. These 'six years' period came to an end on 31st December, 2009 bringing the Police Order, 2002 within competence of the appropriate legislature for the purpose of its repeal or amendments in it without previous sanction of the President.

249.   Section 96 of the Constitution (Eighteenth Amendment) Act, 2010 substituted Article 270 AA of the Constitution with the following:

(1)   The Proclamation of Emergency of the fourteenth day of October, 1999, the Provisional Constitution Order No. 1 of 1999, the Oath of Office (Judges) Order, 2000 (No. 1 of 2000), Chief Executive's Order No. 12 of 2002, Chief Executive's Order No. 19 of 2002, the amendments made in the Constitution through the Legal Framework Order, 2002 (Chief Executive's Order No. 24 of 2002), the Legal Framework (Amendment) Order, 2002 (Chief Executive's Order No. 29 of 2002) and Legal Framework (Second Amendment) Order, 2002 (Chief Executive's Order No. 32 of 2002), notwithstanding any judgment of any court including the Supreme Court or a High Court, are hereby declared as having been made without lawful authority and of no legal effect.

(2)   Except as provided in clause (1) and subject to the provisions of the Constitution (Eighteenth Amendment) Act, 2010, all laws including President's Orders, Acts, Ordinances, Chief Executive Orders, regulations, enactments, notifications, rules, orders or bye-laws made between the twelfth day of October, one thousand nine hundred and ninety-nine and the thirty-first day of October, two thousand and three (both days inclusive) and still in force shall, continue to be in force until altered, repealed or amended by the competent authority.
Explanation: - For the purposes of clause (2) and clause (6), "competent authority" means, -
(a) in respect of Presidents' Orders, Ordinances, Chief Executive's Orders and all other laws, the appropriate Legislature; and
(b) in respect of notifications, rules, orders and bye-laws, the authority in which the power to make, alter or amend the same vests under the law.

(3)   to (9) -----."

250.   The question whether the validating provisions also have the effect of validating acts done coram non judice or without jurisdiction or mala fide has been addressed in a series of cases by the superior judiciary in Pakistan. In Federation of Pakistan Vs. Saeed Ahmad Khan (PLD 1974 SC 151), State Vs. Zia ur Rahman (PLD 1973 SC 49), Federation of Pakistan Vs. Ghulam Mustafa Khar (PLD 1989 SC 26), Muhammad Bachal Menton Vs. Government of Sind (PLD 1987 Kar 296), Rawalpindi Bar Association Vs. Federation (PLD 2015 SC 401), it has been held that purported validity granted and the ouster of jurisdiction of courts is not

applicable to acts and orders without jurisdiction, coram non judice and mala fide. As the Police Order,2002 was an Order of the Chief Executive issued in exercise of powers assumed under the Proclamation of the 14th day of October, 1999, therefore, we are not in a position to term it without jurisdiction as the constitutional limits on jurisdiction were not attracted to an Order of the Chief Executive. We are not in agreement with the ratio of the cases reported as Sheo Shankar Vs. State of M. P. {AIR 1951 Nag 58 (80) (FB)}, Sagar Mal Vs. The State, AIR 1951 {All 816 (817)}, Binoy Bhusan Vs. State of Bihar {AIR 1954 Pat 346}, Kanpur Oil Mills Harriesganj Vs. Judge, Sales Tax, {(S) AIR 1955 All 99 (104)}, State Vs. Yash Pal {(S) AIR 1957 Punj 91 (92)} and R. L. Aurora Ram Ditta Mal Vs. State of Uttar Pradesh {AIR 1958 All 126 (131 and 132)} which holds that when an enactment is granted continuity as existing law, its constitutionality on the ground of want of power in the legislature which enacted it does not remain open to challenge. This may be so if the competent legislature, directly or indirectly, adopts the existing law. An amendment in the existing law amounts to adoption of law by the legislature in whose jurisdiction the law now falls. A Full Bench of the Hon'ble Sindh High Court in Dr. Nadeem Rizvi and others Vs. Federation of Pakistan and others (PLD 2017 Sindh 347) held as follows:

> "32. Every Constitution establishes its own constitutional dispensation, creating its own legislative and executive bodies, imbuing them with requisite powers and competencies and, if the
> nature of the polity is federal, sharing the same between the two tiers of the State. One question that needs to be addressed is the fate of laws existing on the commencing day of the new Constitution. In terms of the Constitution itself, such laws would of course not be laws at all, since they were made under a different constitutional dispensation. Yet, to discard the existing laws (a possibility that does exist in theory) would be to invite chaos. So, each Constitution provides for continuity and gives due recognition and force to existing laws. This was done in the present Constitution by means of Article 268, but this provision is by no means unique. It had its equivalents in the 1962 Constitution (Article 225), the 1956 Constitution (Article 224), the Indian Constitution (Article 372) and even the Government of India Act, 1935 (s. 292) ...."

251.   The Hon'ble High Court of Sindh in Pakistan International Freight Forwarders Vs. Province of Sindh and another (2017 PTD 1) was pleased to observe as under:

> "49. ... Article 268(1) provided that all laws existing on that date were to continue in force "until altered, repealed or amended by the appropriate Legislature" .... For present purposes, it suffices to note that what it meant was that each "existing law" stood allocated to one or the other of the legislatures created by the Constitution (i.e., Majlis-e-Shoora (Parliament) on the one hand and the Provincial Assemblies on the other) and till such time as the relevant legislature chose to alter, repeal or amend it, the law continued in force in the form it had on the commencing day. But how was this allocation to be made? How was it to be decided that a particular "existing law" fell to the lot of the Federation or the Provinces? In our view, given the federal structure and scheme of the Constitution, the allocation could be only on the basis of the well-known test of "pith and substance". The pith and substance of each "existing law" had to be determined, and here it is important to remember that the legislative source or origin of the statute in any previous constitutional dispensation was irrelevant. In other words, it was irrelevant whether the "existing law" in question would have been regarded as a federal or provincial statute when enacted in terms of whichever constitution was then prevailing. The

"existing law" had to be considered simply as a law in its own right, and its pith and substance determined. If the pith and substance was relatable to any entry on the Federal Legislative List or the Concurrent Legislative List (both Lists of course existed on the commencing day) then the "existing law" stood allocated to the Federation. If the pith and substance was not relatable to any enumerated power, then it stood allocated to the Provinces."

252.   Applying the relevant constitutional provisions, case law and the doctrine of pith and substance to the Police Order, 2002, the situation which emerges after restoration of the Constitution of 1973 is as follows:

(a)   The Order fell into jurisdiction of the Parliament in respect of territories not included in a Province and offences relating to federal subjects created through federal laws with its provisions relating to the Provinces in eclipse till such time these provisions are deleted from the Order through an Act of the Parliament; and

(b)   The Order fell into exclusive jurisdiction of the Provincial Assembly to the extent of policing in territorial limits of the Province and with respect to subjects falling within exclusive provincial jurisdiction with provisions relating to the federal areas and federal subjects in eclipse till such time these provisions are deleted from the Order through an amending Act of the concerned Provincial Assembly. However, provisions relating to role of the Federal Government in the matter of postings and appointments in the Provincial Police is rendered a nullity in eyes of law being an impermissible encroachment on exclusive provincial domain. Powers to repeal or amend the Chief Executive's Orders were vested in the appropriate Legislature and not in the Parliament alone. Appropriate legislature in respect of the police matters of a Province is the concerned Provincial Assembly.

253.   Amendments made in the Police Act, 1861 by the Federation including the one made through the Federal Laws (Revision and Declaration) Ordinance, 1981 may be seen in the above context and may be taken as valid to the extent of the federal subjects and federal territories only. Likewise, amendments made by the provincial legislatures cannot be denied effect to the extent of provincial areas and provincial subjects.

254.   We have examined the argument that there are dozens of international treaties and agreements on policing to which Pakistan is a member and since international treaties and agreements and inter-provincial coordination are federal subjects, therefore, police is a federal subject. Section 106 of the Government of India Act, 1935 negates this argument in the following words:

"Provisions as to legislation for giving effect to international agreements.

106.-

(1)   The Federal Legislature shall not by reason only of the entry in the Federal Legislative List relating to the implementing of treaties and agreements with other countries have power to make any law for any Province except with the previous

consent of the Governor, or for a Federated State except with the previous consent of the Ruler thereof.

(2)   So much of any law as is valid only by virtue of any such entry as aforesaid may be repealed by the Federal Legislature and may, on the treaty or agreement in question ceasing to have effect, be repealed as respects any Province or State by a law of that Province or State.

(3)   Nothing in this section applies in relation to any law which the Federal Legislature has power to make for a Province or, as the case may be, a Federated State, by virtue of any other entry in the Federal or the Concurrent Legislative List as well as by virtue of the said entry."

255.   Article 142 of the interim Constitution of Pakistan, 1972 also deals with the matter in these words:

"(1)   The Federal Legislature shall not by reason only of the entry in the Federal Legislative List relating to implementing of treaties and agreements with other countries, have power to make any law for any Province except with the previous consent of the Governor.

(2)   So much of any law as is valid only by virtue of such entry as aforesaid may be repealed by the Federal Legislature and may on the treaty or agreement in question ceasing to have effect, be repealed as respects any Province by a law of that Province.

(3)   Nothing in this Article applies in relation to any law which the Federal Legislature has power to make for a Province by virtue of any other entry in the Federal or Concurrent Legislative List as well as by virtue of the said entry."

256.   In view of the above, we hold that legislative entries on treaties with other countries, inter-provincial coordination and extension of jurisdiction of provincial police beyond territorial limits of the concerned Province do not make policing in provincial areas and on provincial subjects a federal subject.

257.   After arriving at conclusive finding that police in federal areas and on federal subjects is a federal subject and in provincial areas and on provincial subjects is a provincial subject since coming into force of the Devolution Rules, 1920 till date, we may now endeavour to discover role of the Federal and Provincial authorities and authorities above them in the matter of human resource management of police.

258.   Before introduction of federal system in India through the Government of India Act, 1935, powers with respect to administration in India were distributed among the Secretary of State for India, Central Government and the provincial or local governments. All India Services were neither in the control of Central Government nor in the domain of local or provincial governments. These services were directly under the control of the Secretary of State for India. Indian Police was one of the All India Services. Certain posts under the Central Government and the Provincial Governments were encadred for the Indian Police which were required to be held exclusively by officers of this service.

259.   Though the Government of India Act, 1935 introduced federal system in India and provided for distribution of legislative powers between the Federation and the Provinces yet it retained the concept of Secretary of States for India's All India Services vide its Section 244, reproduced below:

"Services recruited by Secretary of State.

244.-

(1)   As from the commencement of Part III of this Act appointments to the civil services known as the Indian Civil Service, the Indian Medical Service (Civil), and the Indian Police Service

(which last-mentioned service shall thereafter be known as " the Indian Police") shall, until Parliament otherwise determines, be made by the Secretary of State.

(2)   Until Parliament otherwise determines, the Secretary of State may also make appointments to any service or services which at any time after the said date he may deem it necessary to establish for the purpose of securing the recruitment of suitable persons to fill civil posts in connection with the discharge of any functions of the Governor-General which the Governor-General is by or under this Act required to exercise in his discretion.

(3)   The respective strengths of the said services shall be such as the Secretary of State may from time to time prescribe, and the Secretary of State shall in each year cause to be laid before each House of Parliament a statement of the appointments made thereto and the vacancies therein.

(4)   It shall be the duty of the Governor-General to keep the Secretary of State informed as to the operation of this section, and he may after the expiration of such period as he thinks fit make recommendations for the modification thereof. In discharging his functions under this subsection, the Governor-General shall act in his discretion.

260.   Section 246 of the Government of India Act, 1935 provided the concept of reservation of posts for All India Services. The Secretary of State for India was given powers with respect to determination of conditions of appointment and of service of members of the All India Services.

261.   The legal effect of reservation of certain posts in connection with affairs of the Federation and of the Provinces for members of a Secretary of State for India's Service was that notwithstanding distribution of legislation powers between the Federal and the Provincial legislatures, powers with respect to the reserved posts and the Secretary of State for India's Services were neither vested in the Federation nor in the Provinces but were constitutionally reserved for the Secretary of State for India. Such entrustment of powers to the Secretary of State for India ousted jurisdiction of all the Governments in India to the extent of the reserved posts and officers of the Secretary of State for India's Services meant to hold these posts even in respect of subjects falling within legislative competence of the Federal and Provincial legislatures. In this background, the Police Act, 1861 read with the Police Rules, 1934 which spoke of junior and senior ranks excluding jurisdiction of the respective legislatures on senior ranks and reservation of senior ranks for Indian Police was constitutionally valid arrangement.

262.   The Hon'ble Supreme Court of India in Tarak Nath Ghosh Vs. State of Bihar & Ors (1968 AIR 1372) held that:

"When independence was achieved by India, the Secretary of State and the Crown ceased to have any authority in India, so that no Service of the Secretary of State or the Crown could continue thereafter. Under the agreement that was entered into by the new Indian Government with the British Government, provision was made that members of the previous Secretary of State's Service could continue to serve the Government of India or a Provincial Government and certain rights were preserved to them if they continued to do so. There was, however, no provision that the old Secretary of State's Service would continue, so that with the passing of the Indian Independence Act, Secretary of State's Services like the Indian Civil Service and the Indian Police ceased to exist."

263.   The Hon'ble Supreme Court of India further observed in the aforesaid case that:

> "In the latter case of R.P. Kapur (1964 SCR (5) 431), the Court proceeded further to take notice of s. 10 of the Indian Independence Act under which every person appointed by the Secretary of State to a civil service of the Crown in India, who continued on and after the appointed day to serve under the Government of either of the new Dominions or of any Province or part thereof, was entitled to receive the same conditions of service as respects remuneration, leave and pension and the same rights as respects disciplinary matters or, as, the case may be, as respects the tenure of his office, or rights as similar thereto as changed circumstances may permit as that person was entitled to immediately before the appointed day, i.e., August 15, 1947. This, it was clearly recognised by this Court that the Services constituted by the Secretary of State earlier disappeared with the passing of the Indian Independence Act, though persons, who continued to serve thereafter under the Indian Dominion or any Province, were entitled to certain rights in regard to remuneration, leave, pension and disciplinary matters. In view of this decision, it has to be held that, on the passing of the Indian Independence Act, the appellant ceased to
>
> be a member of the Service constituted by the Secretary of State but he continued to serve the Government of India and the Province of Bihar, as a result of which certain rights relating to conditions of service and disciplinary matters, which were earlier applicable to him, were preserved."

264.   We have discussed earlier in this judgment that Schedule to the Pakistan (Provisional Constitution) Order, 1947, omitted Sections 248, 249, 250, 251 and 252 of the Government of India Act, 1935 and Section 10 of the Indian Independence Act, 1947 made inoperative and impliedly omitted Sections 244, 246, 248, 249 and 278 to 284-A from that Act. If we construe Section 263 of the Government of India Act, 1935 as constitutional sanction for reservation of posts and creation of All India Services, then Section 10 of the Indian Independence Act, 1947 comes forward to erase it from the statute book being relatable to Secretary of State for India's Services. The Secretary of State for India became irrelevant to the governance in India with coming into force of the Indian Independence Act, 1947 and lost all his powers in respect of Federal and Provincial Governments in India including his powers with respect to reservation of posts for All India Services. With denial of powers to an entity higher than the Governments and legislatures in India in respect of posts in connection with affairs of the Federation and of the Provinces and Federal and Provincial Services, these powers fell within jurisdictions of the respective Governments in their respective territories and subjects. With demolition of the pillar (Secretary of State for India) on which the edifice of All India Services including the Indian Police was constructed, the federal principle came into operation to allow the Federation and the Provinces to exercise their respective jurisdictions in respect of their Services and posts in connection with their affairs.

265.   We have carefully gone through all constitutional documents starting from the Indian Independence Act, 1947 to the Constitution of the Islamic Republic of Pakistan, 1973 alongwith all amendments in it. We have not found any constitutional sanction for reservation of posts in connection with affairs of the Provinces for a Service of the Federation. We have also examined Section 263 of the Government of India Act, 1935 and have concluded that this Section does not substitute the Sections deleted from the Government of India Act, 1935 vide the Pakistan (Provisional Constitution) Order, 1947 or

impliedly repealed by Section 10 of the Indian Independence Act, 1947. In absence of any positive and affirmative constitutional sanction for reservation of posts in connection with affairs of the Federation and of the Provinces for a Service of the Federation, continuance of the Police Service after 15th of August, 1947 was without lawful authority and was of no legal effect. This constitutional position still holds good.

266. The change brought about by disappearance of the Secretary of State and his All India Services also affected the post-independence concept of All Pakistan Services. Such services were conceived as services manning posts common to the Federation and of the Provinces. These are the posts which are neither purely federal nor provincial but deal with subjects which are common to the Federation and the Provinces e.g. National Finance Commission, National Economic Council, Judicial Commission of Pakistan, Council of Common Interests. So far as policing is concerned, it is exclusive to the Federation in respect of federal areas and federal subjects and to the Provinces in case of provincial areas and provincial subjects.

267. Continuation of the Police Act, 1861 and the Police Rules, 1934 as existing laws in terms of relevant provisions of all the Constitutions of Pakistan does not amount to enhance jurisdictions of the respective legislatures to areas and subjects outside the limits set by the relevant Constitutions. The Federation is not at liberty to claim that a power or jurisdiction entrusted to it in an existing law shall continue to remain vested in it even if the new constitutional scheme has denied it that power and jurisdiction. A Province is also debarred to continue to exercise powers and jurisdictions vested in it under existing laws if those powers and jurisdictions have been taken away through new constitutional dispensation. Protection of an existing law is effective only to cure the lack of jurisdiction of the enacting legislature under the new Constitution, if any, and the said protection cannot be taken as an independent and additional source of jurisdiction. Protection accorded to existing laws is also subject to lawful jurisdiction of the enacting legislature at the time of enactment. It cannot be overemphasized that continuance in force of existing laws is to the extent of their consistency and conformity with the applicable constitutional provisions. In case of clash and inconsistency, the Constitution is destined to prevail.

268. Keeping in view the above discussion, we may now proceed to analyze constitutionality of the Police Service of Pakistan from 15.08.1947 till enforcement of the Police Service of Pakistan (Probationary Service) Rules, 1950. Thereafter, we will examine the Police Service of Pakistan (Probationary Service) Rules, 1950, the Police Service of Pakistan (Composition and Cadre) Rules, 1969, Establishment Division's O.M. No. 3/2/75-ARC dated 31.05.1975 and the Police Service of Pakistan (Composition and Cadre) Rules, 1985.

269. The Indian Independence Act, 1947 abolished the Secretary of State for India's Services. The members of these Services were, however, allowed, under certain conditions, to continue to hold the posts held by them on the appointed day i.e. 15.08.1947. Thus, though officers of the Indian Police who opted to serve Pakistan continued to hold their posts either under the Federal or the Provincial Governments but their status as members of a district Service came to an end. The legal position was this that they fell under Federal jurisdiction if they were holding posts in connection with affairs of the Federation on the appointed day and in provincial domain if they were holding posts in connection with affairs of a Province. No authority higher than the Federation and the Provinces remained in existence on coming into force of the Indian Intendance Act, 1947 and the officers of the Indian Police had to serve under the concerned Government. Continued existence, if any, of members of the Indian Police after the appointed day in Pakistan as members of a distinct Service was, therefore, not backed by the Constitution.

270. The Police Service of Pakistan (Probationary Service) Rules, 1950 were framed by the Governor General under Section 241 of the Government of India Act, 1935 as adapted by the Pakistan (Provisional Constitution) Order, 1947. Salient features of the Service were as follows:

153

a) The Service was to be named the Police Service of Pakistan (PSP);

b) Certain posts in connection with affairs of the Federation and of the Provinces were reserved and encadred for the said Service;

c) Direct recruitment in the Service was to be made on the recommendations of the Central Public Service Commission;

d) Like Indian Police, the Service was to be a provincial cadre whose members were to serve in the Province to which these were allocated at the time of induction into service; and

e) Police officers of the Provincial Governments were made eligible to be inducted into the Service, through appointment by transfer, to the extent specified in the Rules.

271. It was claimed that an understanding between the Federal and Provincial Governments preceded the aforesaid Rules. When we required filing of written understanding or agreement between the Federation and the Provinces in this court, it transpired that the said agreement does not exist in the form of a formal written or signed document.

272. After examining the Police Service of Pakistan (Probationary Service) Rules, 1950, we declare as follows:

a) The said Rules are intra vires Article 241 of the Constitution to the extent of creation of a Federal Service for performance of policing functions in federal territories and in respect of federal functions as Section 141 (1) (a) and (2)(a) empowered the Governor General to make appointments in Services of the Federation and posts in connection with affairs of the Federation and determine conditions of service of persons so appointed;

b) As provisions allowing reservation of posts in connection with affairs of the Federation and of the Provinces for All India Services (after the appointed day to be better labelled as the All Pakistan Services) stood deleted from the Government of India Act, 1935, therefore, there was no constitutional backing for creation of the Police Service of Pakistan as an All Pakistan Service. Without positive constitutional sanction similar to the deleted sections of the Government of India Act, 1935, it was not intra vires Section 241 (1) (a) and (2)(a) of the Government of India Act, 1935 to create the Police Service of Pakistan for holding posts in connection with affairs of a Province as posts reserved for the Service;

c) The said Rules encroached upon the provincial domain exclusively vested in the Provincial Governors under Section 241 (1) (b) and (2)(b) of the Government of India Act, 1935 as posts in connection with affairs of the Provinces were reserved under these rules for the Police Service of Pakistan. To this extent, the rules were ultra vires Section 241 (1) (a) and (2)(a) of the Government of India Act, 1935 and were without lawful authority and consequently were of no legal effect; and

d) Mutual consent of the Federation and of the Provinces cannot fill a constitutional vacuum and cannot compensate absence of lawful competence to deal with a matter. In the instant, even the claimed agreement between the Federation and of the Provinces does not exist because we are forced to assume its non-existence as the same was neither produced before this Court nor any reasonable justification for inability to produce it was submitted to our satisfaction.

273.   In view of the above, the protection given to the existing laws vide Article 224 of the Constitution of Islamic Republic of Pakistan, 1956 was available to the aforesaid Rules to the extent of their consistency with the new Constitution and competence of the Governor General under Section 241 (1) (a) and (2)(a) of the Government of India Act, 1935. As there was no enabling clause in the Constitution of 1956 under which posts in connection with affairs of a Province could be reserved for the Police Service of Pakistan, therefore, these Rules remained without lawful jurisdiction so far as the question of reservation of posts in connection with affairs of the Provinces for the Police Service of Pakistan was concerned. Further, explanation 2 to the Article 224 of the Constitution of 1956 clarifies that "in force" means having effect as law. To have effect as law necessarily requires that the law must have been made by the competent authority within jurisdiction lawfully vested in it. Subject to the extent permissible under the doctrine of pith and substance, a law which is without jurisdiction or which travels beyond the lawful jurisdiction is a law incapable of having effect as a law. To have effect as a law means that the law must be capable of enforcement through court of law in case of dispute. A law made without jurisdiction or in excess of jurisdiction or inconsistent with the applicable constitutional provisions is not enforceable through courts of law to the extent of want of jurisdiction and non-conformity with the Constitution which gives protection to existing laws. Since the Police Service of Pakistan (Probationary Service) Rules, 1950 were without jurisdiction in the matter of reservation of posts in connection with affairs of the Provinces for the Police Service of Pakistan, therefore, to this extent, these Rules lacked the force of law and were of no legal effect.

274.   The fact that the Provinces did not materially objected to the legality of reservation of posts in connection with their affairs for the Police Service of Pakistan does not confer legality to the act which was unlawful and without jurisdiction ab initio.

275.   The Police Service of Pakistan (Composition and Cadre) Rules, 1969 were made by the President of Pakistan under powers conferred upon him vide the Proclamation of 25th of March, 1969, read with the Provisional Constitutional Order issued thereunder. Rule 2(d) of the Rules ibid defined "Service" in these words

>   "Service" means the Police Service of Pakistan constituted by the Ministry of the Interior (Home Division) letter No.10/1/50-Police dated the 11th March, 1950, as a Service common to the Federation and the Provinces in pursuance of an agreement made under section 263 of the Government of India Act, 1935 (26 Gec. 5 c. 2), at the Prime Ministers' Conference held on the 27th December, 1949."

276.   Rule 4 of the Rules supra reads as follows:
>   "(1)   All appointments to the Service shall be made by the President;
>   (a) on the basis of the results of the competitive examinations held for the purpose by the Commission; and
>   (b) on the basis of selection made on the recommendation of the Governor and in consultation with the Commission from amongst the members of the Police Service of Pakistan;
>   Provided that the number of appointment under clause (b) of the members of the Police Service of a Province shall not exceed one-third of the number of Senior Cadre posts in that Province.
>   Explanation. In this sub-rule, "senior cadre posts" means a cadre post shown as a senior post in the Schedule."

277.   The Police Service of Pakistan (Composition and Cadre) Rules, 1969 were based upon the idea of reservation of posts in connection with affairs of the Federation as well as of the Provinces for the Police Service of Pakistan. As the said Rules were framed by the President of Pakistan under powers conferred upon him vide the Proclamation of 25th of March, 1969, read with the Provisional Constitutional Order issued thereunder, therefore,

constitutionality of these Rules is dependent upon the legal validity of said Proclamation and the Order. The Provisional Constitution Order of 4ᵗʰ April, 1969 specified that notwithstanding the abrogation of the 1962 Constitution by the Proclamation of March 25, 1969, and subject to any Regulation or Order made, from time to time, by the Chief Martial Law Administrator, the State of Pakistan shall, except as otherwise provided in the Order, be governed as nearly as may be in accordance with the said Constitution.

278.   The Hon'ble Supreme Court of Pakistan held in Miss Asma Jilani Vs. the Government of the Punjab and another (PLD 1972 Supreme Court 139) that:

> "We may now turn to the methodology of law-making during the Martial Law which was imposed by Yahya Khan on the 26ᵗʰ March 1969. Pakistan came into being with a written Constitution-Government of India Act, 1935 (26 Geo. 5, Ch. 2) and the Indian Independence Act, 1947 (10 & 11 Geo. 6, Ch. 30). These constitutional instruments were, in time, replaced by the Constitution of 1956 which in turn was substituted by the Constitution of 1962. It is still in force either by its own vitality or under the Provisional Constitution Order, 1969. The written Constitution of a State is, according to Kelsen, its basic norm. It regulates all other legal norms. Pakistan has unfortunately suffered long spells of Martial Law, but its basic structure was democratic from its inception. There was distribution of powers between the executive, legislature and judiciary. During Martial Law the legislative powers of the State were usurped by the Executive and attempt made to deny to Courts the exercise of judicial functions. The usurpation of legislative powers of the state by the Chief Martial Law Administrator was, therefore, against the basic norm. The new Legal Order consisting of Martial Law Orders, Martial Law Regulations, Presidential Orders and Presidential Ordinances was, therefore, unconstitutional and *void ab initio*. This Order would have become legal only if the Government of Yahya Khan was recognized by Courts as de jure and the Order he gave to the country was held valid. This question has already been answered in the negative."

279.   The Hon'ble Supreme Court of Pakistan was further pleased to hold in the aforesaid case that:

> "Let us next examine the validity of the Presidential Orders and Ordinances issued by Yahya Khan between 26ᵗʰ March 1969, and 20ᵗʰ December 1971. He assumed the office of President on 31-3-1969 with effect from the 25ᵗʰ March 1969. Under Article 16 of the 1962 Constitution if at any time the President was unable to perform the functions of his office, the Speaker of the National Assembly was to act as President. Muhammad Ayub Khan could not, therefore, transfer the office of the President to Yahya Khan. Indeed, he did not even purport to do so. He simply asked him to perform his constitutional and legal responsibilities. Yahya Khan, therefore, assumed the office in violation of Article 16 of the Constitution to which he had taken oath of allegiance as Commander-in-Chief. It could not, therefore, be postulated that Yahya Khan had become the lawful President of Pakistan and was competent to promulgate Orders and Ordinances in exercise of the legislative functions conferred by the Constitution on the President. All Presidential Orders and Ordinances which were issued by him were, therefore, equally void and of no legal effect."

280.   The Hon'ble Supreme Court in its above cited judgment also observed that:

> "The next question which arises for determination is whether these illegal legislative acts are protected by the doctrine of State necessity.

156

The Laws saved by this rule do not achieve validity. They remain illegal, but acts done and proceedings undertaken under invalid laws may be condoned on the conditions that the recognition given by the Court is proportionate to the evil to be averted, it is transitory and temporary in character does not imply abdication of judicial review."

281.   The Hon'ble Supreme Court also held in the said judgment that:

"It has been the Constitutional practice in the Indo-Pakistan sub-continent that whenever an existing Order ceased to be operative, either legally or illegally, the existing laws have been continued to remain valid by the new dispensation. Beginning from the Government of India Act (Consolidated in 1924) down to the Laws (Continuance in Force) Order, 1958, and the Proclamation of Martial Law by General Agha Muhammad Yahya Khan, the validity of existing laws was continued by this process. The details are as follows: ----

Section 30 of the Government of India Act, 1919 (Consolidated in 1924); section 292 of the Government of India Act, 1935; section 18 of the Indian Independence Act, 1947; Articles 221 and 224 of the Constitution of Islamic Republic of Pakistan, 1956; Paragraph 4 of the Laws (Continuance in Force) Order, 1958; Article 225 of the Constitution of Pakistan, 1962; and paragraph 5 of the Proclamation of Martial Law dated the 25th March 1969. Similar is the provision in Article 372 of the Indian Constitution.

On the 20th of December 1971, Chief Martial Law Administrator and ex-President of Pakistan General Agha Muhammad Yahya Khan stepped down from his offices, and consequently all the existing laws lapsed, and unless they were saved by a competent authority under the subsequent dispensation, they ceased to have any sanction behind them. The 1962-Constitution having already been abrogated by him, the only sanction behind the various Laws that he purported to make was his individual will and with his disappearance from the scene. all the existing Laws including President's Order No. 3 of 1969 and Martial Law Regulation No. 78 lapsed. There is nothing to show, and the learned Attorney-General has been unable to place before us anything from the new dispensation to show, that the existing laws were saved. He has, however, relied upon the proclamation of General Agha Muhammad Yahya Khan dated the 20th December 1971, whereby he transferred power to President Zulfikar Ali Bhutto for the purpose of showing that the existing laws were continued in force. In this Proclamation it has been stated that the Proclamation of the 25th March, 1969 shall have effect subject to the Proclamation of the 20th December, 1971, and inasmuch as the Proclamation of the 25th March, 1969 had saved the existing laws, the Proclamation of the 20th December, 1971, it has been contended, also operated to save the existing laws. It is to be noticed that the Proclamation of the 20th December 1971, itself was by General Agha Muhammad Yahya Khan and it derived its force and validity from his individual will. As soon as, however, this will ceased to exist on account of his exit, the very life line of the Proclamation of 20th December 1971 was cut off. I have, therefore, no hesitation in saying that neither President's Order No. 3 of 1969 nor Martial Law Regulation No. 78 is a valid existing law."

282.   The interim Constitution of 1972 came into force on 21.04.1972. Article 281 of that Constitution, reproduced below, inter alia, accorded validity to the Proclamation of 25th March, 1969 and the legal instruments flowing therefrom:

157

"Validation of laws and acts etc.-

Article 281

"(1)   All Proclamations, President's Orders, Martial Law Regulations, Martial Law Orders, and all other laws made as from the twenty-fifth day of March, 1969 are hereby declared, notwithstanding any judgment of any court, to have been validly made by the competent authority, and shall not be called in question in any court.

(2)   All orders made, proceedings taken and acts done by any authority, or by any person, which were made or purported to have been made, taken or done, on or after the twenty-fifth day of March, 1969 in exercise of the powers derived from any President's Orders, Martial Law Regulations, Martial Law Orders, enactments, notifications, rules, orders or byelaws or in execution of any orders made or sentences passed by any authority in the exercise or purported exercise of powers as aforesaid shall be deemed to be and always to have been validly made, taken or done.

(3)   No suit or other legal proceedings shall lie in any court against any authority or any person for or on account of or in respect of any order made, proceedings taken or act done whether in the exercise or purported exercise of or in compliance with orders made or sentences passed in exercise or purported exercise of such powers."

283.   The validity accorded through Article 281 of the interim Constitution of 1972 to the Proclamation of 25th March, 1969 and the legal instruments flowing therefrom was confined to the acts done. So far as the question of continuance in force of the then existing laws was concerned, it was settled through Article 280 of the interim Constitution of 1972.

284.   Article 290 of the interim Constitution of 1972 defines existing law in these words:
        "existing law" means any such law as is referred to in clause (4) of Article 280".
In view of the above, existing laws included the rules.

285.   We have not found any difference in status of the Police Service of Pakistan (Composition and Cadre) Rules, 1969 as existing law in terms of the interim Constitution of 1972 on the grounds noted in respect of the Police Service of Pakistan (Probationary Service) Rules, 1950 in the context of the Government of India Act, 1935 as adopted through the Pakistan (Provisional Constitution) Order, 1947. The interim Constitution of 1972 did not revive the concept of reservation of posts in connection with affairs of the Provinces for a Federal or an All Pakistan Service. Constitutional sanction for reservation of posts in connection with affairs of the Federation and of the Provinces for an All India or All Pakistan Service is oxygen in absence of which such a Service cannot survive. Notwithstanding absence of concept of reservation of posts in connection with affairs of a Province for a federal service under the Constitution of 1962, the Police Service of Pakistan (Composition and Cadre) Rules, 1969 cannot be held to have been made incompetently as the same were not made under the Constitution of 1962 but were made under the Proclamation of 25th March, 1969 and the Provisional Constitution Orders issued thereunder. Validity of these rules was bound to come under attack upon coming into force of the interim Constitution of 1972. The rules were not consistent with the interim Constitution to the extent of reservation of posts in connection with affairs of the Provinces for the Police Service of Pakistan. Whereas, under the interim Constitution, competence of the Federation to reserve posts in connection with its affairs for the Police Service of Pakistan is unquestioned, it lacks such authority in respect of posts in connection with affairs of a

Province. We, therefore, declare that the Police Service of Pakistan (Composition and Cadre) Rules, 1969 were, after coming into force of the interim Constitution of 1972, intra vires to the extent of constitution of the said Service for federal areas and subjects and reservation of posts in connection with affairs of the Federation therefor and ultra vires so far as these rules encadred posts in connection with affairs of the Provinces for the Police Service of Pakistan. References to Section 263 of the Government of India Act, 1935 and to the Prime Ministers' Conference held on 27th of December, 1949 in Rule 2(d) of the Police Service of Pakistan (Composition and Cadre) Rules, 1969 are also of no legal significance because of absence of provision similar to Section 263 of the Government of India Act, 1935 in the interim Constitution of 1972.

286. In 1975, an occupational group with the nomenclature of Police Group was constituted vide Establishment Division's O.M. No. 3/2/75-ARC dated 31.05.1975, reproduced below:

"In continuation of the Establishment Division O.M. No. 2/2/75/ARC dated 21.02.1975, it has been decided to constitute another occupational group called the Police Group which will comprise all Police posts in Grade-17 and above viz. ASP, SP, DIG, Addl. I. G, I.G, etc. specified in the schedule (Annexure) of the cadre strength of the former PSP (now called All-Pakistan Unified Grades) as may be revised from time to time.

2. The Police Group will be under the administrative control of the Establishment Division and will function within the following framework of rules and procedure.

3. Grade 17.- Recruitment to the posts in Grade 17 (Assistant Superintendents of Police) will continue to be made through the FPSC as hitherto. On selection by the FPSC the probationers will be given integrated training at the Academy for Administrative Training, Lahore. Those allocated to the Police Group will be posted to the Provinces and given further specialized training at the Police Training College, Sihala.

4. Grade 18 and above. - Officiating appointments to Grade 18 were hitherto made by the Provincial Governments. As already decided in the case of the District Management Group, all appointments to Grade 18 will henceforth be made by the Federal Government.

5. Appointments to posts in Grade 18 will be made by promotion of officers of Grade 17 of the Police Group and also of Grade 17 officers of the Provincial Police of the rank of DSP of requisite service and experience who are recommended by the Provincial Governments. Selection for appointment to posts in Grade 18 and above will be made on the recommendations of the Central Selection Board.

6. Secretariat Posts. - The officers of the Police Group will be eligible for appointment to the Secretariat Posts (Deputy Secretary and above) selection for which is made by examination or by horizontal movement of officers of the prescribed length of service in other Groups. Appointment by horizontal movement will be made after assessment of suitability and fitness by the Central Selection Board.

7. Lateral entry. - To bring in fresh blood and to relieve shortages, if any, at various levels, induction in the group may be made by selection from amongst officers of the Armed Forces or by

lateral entry from other sources subject to suitability and fitness being determined by the Selection Board.

8. Seniority. - The inter se seniority of direct recruits to Grade 17 will be determined on the basis of the order of merit assigned to the probationer officers allocated to the Police Group on completion of the training at the Academy for Administrative Training. Seniority in Grade 18 and above would be determined from the date of regular continuous officiation in a Grade. Gradation Lists of Officers in All-Pakistan Unified Grade would be issued by the Establishment Division periodically."

287. Constitution of the Police Group through an executive order reproduced hereinabove is open to serious legal exceptions some of which are as follows:

a) Learned Attorney General for Pakistan was required by us to explain that how the office memorandum of 1975 could be issued, to the extent of federal posts, without repealing the Police Service of Pakistan (Composition and Cadre) Rules, 1969 which were claimed to be in lawful existence as existing law at the time of issuance of the office memorandum of 1975 as both these instruments, in pith and substance, were on the same subject-matter? We must admit that we were unable to understand that why the maxim "prescription of one is prohibition of another" was not applicable on the issue under consideration. Without prejudice to our declaration on legality of the Police Service of Pakistan (Composition and Cadre) Rules, 1969, it is held that issuance of the office memorandum of 1975 attempted to impliedly repeal or at least materially amend the Police Service of Pakistan (Composition and Cadre) Rules, 1969. It is trite law that rules cannot, expressly or impliedly, be repealed or amended through executive orders. The Police Service of Pakistan (Composition and Cadre) Rules, 1969 have been held by us to be ultra vires to the extent of reservation of posts in connection with affairs of the Provinces for the Police Service of Pakistan. What was not legally possible through rules could not be lawfully done through an office memorandum. In this view of the matter, both the instruments were without lawful authority and jurisdiction to the extent of reservation of posts in connection with affairs of the Provinces for the Police Group or the Police Service of Pakistan. The memorandum of 1975 is also legally invalid for the purpose of creation of a Service of the Federation and for reservation of posts in connection with affairs of the Federation for that Service as this was doable through appropriate legal instrument and not through executive orders.

b) Section 25(1) of the Civil Servants Act, 1973 empowered the President or any person authorized by him to make rules for carrying out purposes of the said Civil Servants Act. Whereas Section 25(2) gave the status of rules to lawful orders, rules and instructions made prior to enactment of the said Act, Section 25(1) envisaged only the rules to carry out purposes of the Act. As the office memorandum of 1975 was issued after enactment of the Civil Servants Act, 1973 and it was nothing more than mere executive instructions not relatable to any provision of the Act or the rules framed thereunder, therefore, it could not be treated as rules. This office memorandum was sans any lawful authority and was, therefore, of no legal effect.

    c) Our declaration earlier in this judgment regarding non-existence of the Civil Service of Pakistan as an All Pakistan Service on the day of commencement of the Constitution of 1973 is also applicable to the Police Service of Pakistan. The aforesaid office memorandum attempted to create an All Pakistan Service. In view of express provisions of Article 240 of the Constitution, an All Pakistan Service could only be created through an Act of the Parliament and that too only for posts common to the Federation and the Provinces. Posts in connection with affairs of the Federation and of the Provinces are not, in absence of positive constitutional sanction expressly providing therefor, allowed to be reserved for officers of such a Service or to be treated as posts common to the Federation and of the Provinces.

288. In view of, inter alia, the above reasons, we declare the Establishment Division's O.M. No. 3/2/75-ARC dated 31.05.1975 without lawful authority and jurisdiction and, hence, of no legal effect in its entirety.

289. In 1985, the Police Service of Pakistan (Composition, Cadre and Seniority) Rules, 1985 were made by the President of Pakistan which are reproduced hereinbelow to serve as ready reference:

    "S.R.O. 1033(I)/85.- In exercise of the powers conferred by section 25 of the Civil Servants Act, 1973 (LXXI of 1973), the President is pleased to make the following rules, namely: -

1. **Short title and commencement.** - (1) These rules may be called the Police Service of Pakistan (Composition, Cadre and Seniority) Rules, 1985.

    (2) They shall come into force at once.

2. **Definitions.** - In these rules, unless there is anything repugnant in the subject or context, -

    (a)   "Cadre post" means a post specified in the Schedule;

    (b)   "Commission" means the Federal Public Service Commission;

    (c)   "Schedule" means the schedule to these rules;

    (d)   "Service" means the Police Service of Pakistan referred to in rule 3.

3. **Change in nomenclature and composition.** - (1) Notwithstanding anything contained in the All-Pakistan Services (Change in Nomenclature) Rules, 1973, the Police Group in the All-Pakistan Unified Grades is renamed as the Police Service of Pakistan.

    (2) The Police Service of Pakistan shall consist of:

    (a)   persons appointed or deemed to have been appointed to the Police Service of Pakistan in accordance with the Police Service of Pakistan (Composition and Cadre) Rules, 1969;

    (b)   persons, other than those mentioned in clause (a), appointed to the Police Group whose names appeared in the gradation list issued on the 28th August, 1980 and persons appointed in the Police Group after that date but before the commencement of these rules; and

    (c)   persons appointed to the Service in accordance with these rules.

4. **Cadre Strength.** - (1) The cadre strength of the service shall be as specified in the Schedule.

(2) The President, or a person authorized by him in this behalf, may, from time to time, and in the case of posts in connection with the affairs of a Province after consultation with the Governor of the Province, remove from or include any post in the Schedule.

5. **Initial appointment.** - (1) Initial appointment to the service against cadre posts in basic Grade 17 shall be made on the basis of the results of the competitive examinations held for the purpose by the Commission.

(2) Unless the appointing authority in any case otherwise directs, a person appointed to the Service under sub-rule (1) shall be appointed to the Service as a probationer in accordance with the rules which the Federal Government may make from time to time, including rules and orders relating to training during probation, and shall be required to undergo such departmental training and pass such departmental examinations as may be specified by the Federal Government or the Government of the Province to which he is allocated.

6. **Appointment of officers of Armed Forces.** - Officers of the Armed Forces of the rank of Captain and Major or equivalent shall be eligible for appointment to the Service in accordance with the procedure laid down by Government and against the cadre posts reserved for them from time to time.

7. **Appointment of members of Police cadre of a Province.** - Members of the Police cadre of a Province shall be appointed to the Service on the basis of selection made on the recommendation of the Governor:

Provided that appointment of members of the police cadre of a Province under this rule shall not exceed 40% of the senior cadre posts in that Province as specified in the Schedule.

7-A. **Appointment of members of Pakistan Railway Police.** - Member of the Pakistan Railway Police shall be appointed to the service on the basis of selection made on the recommendation of the Ministry of Railways:

Provided that the appointment of members of the Police cadre of Railways under this rule shall not exceed 40% of the senior cadre posts of Pakistan Railway Police as specified in the Schedule.

8. **Appointment by promotion.** - Members of the Service shall be eligible for promotion to higher posts in accordance with the Civil Servants (Appointment, Promotion and Transfer) Rules, 1973, and the administrative instructions issued from time to time.

9. **General.** - (1) A cadre post shall ordinarily be filled by a member of the Service.

(2) Nothing in sub-rule (1) shall be construed as preventing the posting to a cadre post of a person who is not a member of the Service:

Provided that no such person shall be so posted for a period exceeding twelve months except with the previous sanction of the authority competent to make appointment to the post.

10. **Liability to serve.** - A member of the Service shall be liable to serve anywhere in Pakistan in any post and to hold, if he is so directed, more than one post at the same time.

11. **Seniority. -** (1) The members of the Service referred to in clauses (a) and (b) of sub-rule (2) of rule 3 shall retain the same seniority as is shown in the gradation list as it stood immediately before the commencement of these rules.

(2) Persons appointed to the Service in accordance with these rules shall count seniority from the date of regular appointment against a post in the Service subject to the following conditions, namely: -

(a) persons selected for initial appointment on the basis of the same competitive examination shall on appointment reckon seniority *inter se* in accordance with the merit position obtained in that examination;

(b) officers of the Armed Forces selected for appointment to a cadre post on regular basis in a batch shall on appointment retain their seniority *inter se:*

Provided that officers of the Armed Forces appointed in basic Grade 17 in a year shall be treated as senior to probationers appointed in the same year on the basis of the competitive examination held by Commission;

(c) members of the police cadre of a particular Province selected in a year shall on appointment to the Service take seniority *inter se* as in the Provincial cadre and in keeping with that sequence, each such member shall reckon his date of regular appointment to the Service from the day the respective vacancy arose in the senior cadre posts reserved in that Province for such officers as specified in the schedule:

Provided that, if the date of regular appointment of officers of two or more Provinces be the same, their seniority *inter se* shall be determined on the basis of their date of regular appointment to the post of Superintendent of Police;

(d) officers selected for promotion in the same batch shall on promotion retain their seniority as in the lower post; and

(e) the general principles of seniority set out in the Establishment Division O.M. No. 1/16/69-D. II dated the 31st December, 1970, shall apply in matters not covered by these rules.

12. The Police Service of Pakistan (Composition and Cadre) Rules, 1969, are hereby repealed."

290. The Schedule to the aforesaid Rules encadred a total of 182 posts in BS. 17 and above in connection with affairs of the Punjab Province for the Police Service of Pakistan.

291. In Begum Nusrat Bhutto Vs. Chief of Army Staff and Federation of Pakistan (PLD 1977 SC 657), challenge to the Proclamation of 5th July, 1977 and the Laws (Continuance in Force) Order, 1977 and detentions made thereunder failed. The Proclamation of 5th July, 1977 was revoked with effect from 30th of December, 1985 through the Proclamation of Withdrawal of Martial Law. Clause A of the Proclamation of 05.07.1975 provided that the Constitution of the Islamic Republic of Pakistan shall remain in abeyance. Article 2(1) of the Laws (Continuance in Force) Order, 1977 stipulated that notwithstanding the abeyance of the provisions of the Constitution, Pakistan shall, subject to this Order and any Order made by the President and any Martial Law Regulation or Martial Law Order made by the Chief Martial Law Administrator be governed as nearly as may be, in accordance with the Constitution. Practical effect of Article 2(1) of the Laws (Continuance in Force) Order, 1977 is this that the country was normally to be governed in accordance with the Constitution;

however, deviation from the Constitution was permissible through Martial Law Regulation or Martial Law Order made by the Chief Martial Law Administrator. In other words, in absence of Martial Law Regulation or Martial Law Order to the contrary made by the Chief Martial Law Administrator, the Constitution had to be followed. The Police Service of Pakistan (Composition, Cadre and Seniority) Rules, 1985 were framed by the President of Pakistan under Section 25 of the Civil Servants Act, 1973 (LXXI of 1973). These Rules are not Martial Law Regulation or Martial Law Order made by the Chief Martial Law Administrator. Mere fact that the offices of the President of Pakistan and the Chief Martial Law Administrator were held by one person does not, in and of itself, convert the rules made by the President under a statute into the orders of the Chief Martial Law Administrator. The rules framed by the President of Pakistan in exercise of powers under Section 25 of the Civil Servants Act, 1973 were compulsorily required to remain within four corners of the governing statute which in turn was also had to be in conformity with the Constitution. Where a deviation from the constitutional scheme was intended it could be done through Orders of the Chief Martial Law Administrator. Such Orders could amend the Constitution and sub-constitutional measures could be taken accordingly. There is no dispute that Constitution was amended a number of times through Orders of the Chief Martial Law Administrator. It was possible for the Chief Martial Law Administrator to reintroduce the concept of reservation of posts in connection with affairs of the Federation and of the Provinces as was available in the Government of India Act, 1935 and earlier Government of India Acts. But this was not done. Rule-making power of the President was available for subordinate legislation—only to give effect to the will of the legislature as expressed in the governing statute and not for any other purpose. This rule-making power was not available to fill constitutional gaps and to provide what was not provided by the Constitution.

292.　At present, the Police Service of Pakistan (Composition, Cadre and Seniority) Rules, 1985 are said to be legally validated in terms of Section 19 of the Constitution (Eighth Amendment) Act, 1985 which substituted Article 270-A of the Constitution with the following:

> "270-A Affirmation of President's Orders, etc.
>
> (1)　The Proclamation of the fifth day of July, 1977, all President's Orders, Ordinances, Martial Law Regulation, Martial Law Orders, including the Referendum Order, 1984 (P.O. No 11 of 1984), under which in consequence of the result of the referendum held on the nineteenth day December, 1984, General Muhammad Zia-ul-Haq became the President the day of the first meeting of the Majlis-e-Shoora (Parliament) in joint sitting for the term specified in clause (7) of Article 41, the Revival of the Constitution of 1973 Order, 1985 (P.O. No. 14 of 1985), the Constitution (Second Amendment) Order, 1985(P.O.20 of 1985) the Constitution (Third Amendment) Order, 1985 (P O.No.24 of 1985) and all other laws made between the fifth day of July, 1977 and the date on which Article comes into force are hereby affirmed, adopted and declared notwithstanding a judgment of any court, to have been validly made by competent authority and notwithstanding anything contained in the Constitution shall not be called in question in any Court on any ground whatsoever;
>
> Provided that a President's Order', Martial Law Regulation or Martial Law Order made after the thirtieth day of September, 1985, shall be confined only to making such provisions as facilitate, or are incidental to, the revocation of the Proclamation of the fifth day of July, 1977.

(2)   All order's made, proceedings taken and acts done by any authority or by any person, which were made, taken or done, or purported to have been made, taken or done between the fifth day of July, 1977, and the date on which this Article comes into force in exercise of the powers derived from any Proclamation, President's Orders, Ordinances, Martial Law Regulations, Martial Law Orders, enactments, notifications, rules, orders or bye-laws, or in execution of or in compliance with any order made or sentence passed by any authority in the exercise or purported exercise of powers as aforesaid, shall, notwithstanding any judgment of any Court, be deemed to be and always to have been validly made, taken or done and shall not be called in question in any Court on any ground whatsoever.

(3)   All President's Orders, Ordinances, Martial Law Regulations, Martial Law Orders, enactment, notifications, rules, orders or bye-laws in force immediately before the date on which this Article comes into force shall continue in force until altered, repealed or amended by competent authority.

Explanation. In this clause, "competent authority" means, -

(a)   in respect of President's Orders, Ordinances, Martial Law Regulation Martial Law Orders and enactments, the appropriate Legislature; and

(b)   in respect of notifications, rules, orders and bye-laws, the authority in which the power to make, alter, repeal or amend the same vests under the law.

(4)   ----.

(5)   ----.

(6)   ----."

293.   Relying upon a series of judgments of the superior courts in Pakistan, we have earlier concluded in this judgment that purported validity granted and the ouster of jurisdiction of courts is not applicable to acts and orders without jurisdiction, coram non judice and mala fide. Validity conferred is to acts done or purported to be done in the exercise of or in the purported exercise of powers derived from such legal instruments and to nothing else. Executive actions and legislative instruments are also adjudged on the basis of lawful competence of the persons acting and the legislatures legislating. The principle in this regard is so simple: if an act is within the powers granted, it is valid; if it travels beyond given powers, it is without lawful authority and of no legal effect. Moreover, continuance in force of the existing laws protects laws for which the enacting legislature or authority had powers but in the new constitutional dispensation those powers have been relocated and vested in some other entity. If the enacting legislature or authority lacked powers, in part or full, the existing law remain unprotected to the extent of lack of powers. An existing law is a law in force at the time of coming into force of the new constitutional dispensation. To be in force does not necessarily mean to be in operation; it simply means that the law has effect as law and is judicially enforceable. A law without jurisdiction or in excess of jurisdiction is not judicially enforceable to the extent of lack or excess of jurisdiction. Thus, a law is deemed to be in force only to the extent it is made by the competent legislature on subjects within its jurisdiction and is otherwise valid for being in conformity with the Constitution. When we examine the Police Service of Pakistan (Composition, Cadre and Seniority) Rules, 1985 on the touchstone of jurisdictional competence and conformity with the Constitution, we are certain to, inter alia, observe the following:

(a)   The Federation has lawful competence to create federal services to deal with federal subjects including policing in federal areas and with respect to offences created through federal laws and reserve posts in connection with affairs of the Federation for the Police Service of Pakistan;

(b)   The Federation is authorized to prescribe posting by transfer as one of the methods of recruitment in the Police Service of Pakistan for provincial police officers to the extent and in the manner as it may determine;

(c)   Posts in connection with affairs of the Provinces are not allowed to be reserved for the Police Service of Pakistan as provisions providing such reservation were deleted from the Government of India Act, 1935 when it was adopted as provisional constitution under the Pakistan (Provisional Constitution) Order, 1947. No subsequent constitution revived the concept of reservation of posts. The Police Service of Pakistan (Composition, Cadre and Seniority) Rules, 1985 are, therefore, without lawful authority and of no legal effect to the extent of reservation of posts in connection with affairs of the Provinces for the Police Service of Pakistan. The validity and protection intended to be given to the Police Service of Pakistan (Composition, Cadre and Seniority) Rules, 1985 under Section 19 of the Constitution (Eighth Amendment) Act, 1985 is not legally valid to the extent of reservation of posts in connection with affairs of the Provinces for the Police Service of Pakistan. We declare and hold that the Schedule of the Police Service of Pakistan (Composition, Cadre and Seniority) Rules, 1985 is void and of no legal effect to the extent it contains posts in connection with affairs of the Provinces;

(d)   Police Service of Pakistan is not a service common to the Federation and the Provinces as the Police Service of Pakistan (Composition, Cadre and Seniority) Rules, 1985 do not encadre any posts common to both but only reserves posts either in connection with affairs of the Federation or of the Provinces for the Police Service of Pakistan;

(e)   Officers of the Police Service of Pakistan are not legally allowed to be promoted against posts in connection with affairs of the Provinces. All serving officers of the Police Service of Pakistan who were promoted by calculating posts reserved for promotion in the cadre by including posts in connection with affairs of the Provinces are held to be promoted without lawful authority and are hereby ordered to the demoted forthwith with effect from the date of promotion. Future promotions in the Police Service of Pakistan shall only be made against posts in connection with affairs of the Federation; and

(f)   Determination of remuneration payable from the Provincial Consolidated Fund is creation of a charge on the Provincial Consolidated Fund in terms of Article 115 of the Constitution. The Province lacks jurisdiction to determine remuneration of federal employees. We hold that payment of remuneration to officers of the Police Service of Pakistan during their service in the Province in accordance with the Basic Pay Scales and Fringe Benefits Scheme is quantum meruit and any amount drawn in excess thereof e.g. superior executive allowance and any special allowances not admissible in the Federal Government is without lawful authority and legal effect and, hence, recoverable. We direct the Accountant General Pakistan Revenues and the Accountant Generals of all the Provinces to calculate and effect recovery accordingly with a further direction to submit progress report, through Registrar of this court, each month for our information and, if need be, appropriate orders.

Question # 22

Whether this court can restrain an executive entity to perform functions assigned to it on mere apprehension of some illegality or should the court direct it to do or not to do something on the basis of fears of the petitioners?

294.   Learned counsel for the petitioners informed us that the Prime Minister of Pakistan, in pursuance of decision of the Federal Cabinet dated 28th of August, 2018, had constituted a Task Force on the Civil Service Reforms, comprising 19 members with the following terms of reference:

a) To review the existing reports and material on civil service reforms policies and the federal government restructuring and update the recommendations in light of the new developments and the commitments made in the Election Manifesto.

b) To prepare recommendations and Action Plan for the approval of the Cabinet in respect of: -

i) The design of public service structure for the federal, provincial and local governments including human resource policies and management – recruitment, training, placement, promotion, career planning, performance measurement, compensation and post-retirement benefits.

ii) The adequacy of the current Basic Pay Scale to attract the talent and skills for employment in the public sector.

iii) Legislative requirements to implement the plan

c) To prepare a monitoring mechanism to review the implementation of the approved Action Plan.

d) To comment upon and consider other ancillary matters referred to the Task Force from time to time by the Prime Minister or the Cabinet.

295.   Learned counsel for the petitioners expressed his apprehension that the aforesaid Task Force may deal with matters falling within exclusive jurisdiction of the Provinces and prayed that a direction may be issued to the Task Force to confine its deliberations to the matters within legislative competence of the Federation only. The prayer is turned down as every public entity in the country, including the said Task Force, is bound to follow the Constitution and to function within four corners of the Constitution. A direction of this court is not necessary to follow the Constitution and a mere apprehension of likely violation of the Constitution does not justify issuance of a direction by this court. The said Task Force is a mere recommendatory body whose recommendation will not be binding. The Federal Cabinet may take action on recommendations of the Task Force in accordance with law and submit proposals of the Task Force on any matter falling within exclusive provincial legislative jurisdiction to the respective provincial authorities for consideration and decision as per policy options of the Provinces.

Question # 23

What should be the appropriate order in the facts and circumstances of this case?

296.   We have been cautioned that if the Civil Service of Pakistan (Composition and Cadre) Rules, 1954 and the Police Service of Pakistan (Composition, Cadre and Seniority) Rules, 1985 to the extent these relate to reservation of posts in connection with affairs of the Provinces and inter-governmental deputations are held to be of no legal effect in their entirety, the resultant vacuum will cause chaos and the administrative machinery, especially in the Provinces, will come to a standstill. When asked whether educational institutions, hospitals, law enforcement institutions, entities for conflict resolution, power-generation, irrigation, agriculture and other essential institutions would cease to be functional in absence of specialized knowledge and skills of the PAS or PSP or other federal officers in the Provinces, the answer was in the negative. However, this is not a question of law and, therefore, we need not to dilate upon this question. We are also not inclined to direct or suggest the legislature or the executive to notice the matter for action. We have full faith and confidence that the legislature and the executive are aware of their due role and will certainly do what they deem appropriate keeping in view facts and circumstances of any case requiring their attention. For us, suffice is to say that once unconstitutionality of a legal instrument is established, fear of disruption of the status quo and likely problems associated therewith or reaction of the affected parties cannot deter us to refuse to issue a declaration which preserves, protects and defends the Constitution. It is not within our discretion to accept any justifications which result into disobedience of the Constitution. We endorse and are inclined to follow what was stated by Chief Justice John Marshall in Cohen v. Virginia (1821) 19 US (16 Wheat) 264) that:

> "We have no more right to decline the exercise of jurisdiction which is given, than to usurp that which is not given. The one or the other would be treason to the Constitution"

297.   We do hereby consolidate the declarations already made in this judgment or we intend further to make for ease and convenience of all concerned:

1.   The instant petition is maintainable under Article 184(3) of the Constitution as it raises questions of public importance with reference to enforcement of fundamental rights.

2.   The Indian Civil Service disappeared as such Service on 15th of August, 1947 (the appointed day) and its members (whose option to join the new dominion of Pakistan was accepted) could continue to hold posts held by them immediately before the appointed day but could not, in absence of express constitutional provisions providing for reservation of posts in connection with affairs of the Provinces for a Federal or an All Pakistan Service, function in the Provinces as members of the Pakistan Administrative Service.

3.   The Pakistan Administrative Service or the Civil Service of Pakistan existed and functioned, from the appointed day till coming into force of the Civil Service of Pakistan (Composition and Cadre) Rules, 1954 in complete absence of any constitutional or statutory authority. These rules neither attempt nor are claimed to have filled the constitutional and statutory vacuum under which the Pakistan Administrative Service and the Civil Service of Pakistan worked during the aforesaid period.

4.   The Civil Service of Pakistan (Composition and Cadre) Rules, 1954, suffer from no constitutional or statutory infirmity in respect of the following matters:

    i.   Creation of the Civil Service of Pakistan as a Service of the Federation;

    ii.   Reservation of certain posts in connection with affairs of the Federation for the Civil Service of Pakistan;

iii. Provisions regarding appointments of persons belonging to the Provincial Services in the Civil Service of Pakistan as a Service of the Federation through appointment by transfer; and

iv. Subject to the Constitution, determination of conditions of recruitment and of service of members of the Civil Service of Pakistan as a Service of the Federation to the extent as specified in the said Rules.

5. Reservation of posts in connection with affairs of the Provinces for the Civil Service of Pakistan under the Civil Service of Pakistan (Composition and Cadre) Rules, 1954 is, ab initio, without lawful authority and jurisdiction and, therefore, is of no legal effect.

6. An agreement between the Federation and the Federating Units under Section 263 of the Government of India Act, 1935, could not lawfully make the Governor-General a valid delegate of the Provincial Governors for the purpose of exercise of their rule-making powers with respect to Provincial Services or posts in connection with affairs of the Provinces and powers of reservation of posts in connection with affairs of the Provinces for a Service of the Federation or an All Pakistan Service were not available after deletion of Section 246 of the Government of India Act, 1935.

7. The Civil Service of Pakistan (Composition and Cadre) Rules, 1954 were saved and protected as existing law to the extent as specified hereinbelow:

   (a) creation of the Civil Service of Pakistan as a Service of the Federation;

   (b) reservation of certain posts in connection with affairs of the Federation, as mentioned in the Schedule to these rules, for the said Service of the Federation; and

   (c) determination of conditions of recruitment and of service of the members of the said Service falling within jurisdiction of the Federation.

8. The Civil Service of Pakistan (Composition and Cadre) Rules, 1954 had not been saved and protected as existing law in the following respects:

   (a) reservation of posts in connection with affairs of the Provinces for the Civil Service of Pakistan, by whatever name it is known; and

   (b) any and all things in the said rules pertaining or purporting to pertain to conditions of recruitment and of service of members of the Provincial Services and posts in connection with affairs of the Provinces except appointment by transfer of the provincial civil servants in the Civil Service of Pakistan for posts in connection with affairs of the Federation.

9. The posts specified in the Schedule to the Civil Service of Pakistan (Composition and Cadre) Rules, 1954 are not posts common to the Federation and the Provinces and, instead, are posts in connection with affairs of the Federation, or, as the case may be, of the Provinces, which have been reserved and encadred for a Service of the Federation.

10. No All Pakistan Service was constitutionally in existence when the Constitution came into force and no such Service has so far been created through an Act of the Parliament.

11. The Civil Service of Pakistan (Composition and Cadre) Rules, 1954 are void to the extent of control of provincial administration through officers of the Pakistan Administrative Service being in conflict with the federal structure of the Constitution.

12. Members of other functional units can become members of the Punjab Provincial Management Service through appointment by transfer to be made by the authorities competent to make appointments in that Service on the recommendation of the selection authority after a transparent and open competition amongst all eligible and willing candidates. The fundamental right to trade and profession extends to all willing and eligible members of all federal as well as provincial functional units or functional units of other public entities in the matter of their appointment by transfer to the Punjab Provincial Management Service.

13. Article 146 of the Constitution does not authorize the Federation to reserve posts in connection with affairs of the Provinces for the Pakistan Administrative Service or to exercise control over Provincial Services or posts in connection with affairs of the Provinces. As an inescapable consequence of this declaration, the Civil Service of Pakistan (Composition and Cadre) Rules, 1954, to the extent of reservation of posts in connection with affairs of the Provinces and other matters falling within jurisdiction of the Provinces, are declared to be ultra vires Article 146 of the Constitution and, therefore, are held to be without lawful authority and of no legal effect.

14. Article 146 of the Constitution does not authorize the Federation to reserve posts in connection with affairs of the Provinces for the Pakistan Administrative Service or to exercise control over Provincial Services or posts in connection with affairs of the Provinces.

15. Act XVI of 1967 was enacted without lawful authority and is, therefore, of no legal effect. Words of Act XVI of 1967 are absolutely incapable of conferring the authority and assigning the duties purported to be conferred and assigned thereby.

16. Act XVI of 1967 cannot survive for not being in conformity with the constitutional provisions; it was enacted without lawful authority and is of no legal effect.

17. Training can be made a condition-precedent for promotion either through law or the rules. Since the Notification of 04.06.2004 is neither a law nor rule or issued under express authority of a law or rules, therefore, the same was issued without lawful authority and is of no legal effect.

18. An act which is unconstitutional cannot become constitutional merely by lapse of time.

19. Posting of an employee is permissible only against posts reserved for the Service / functional unit / cadre to which he belongs. Members of the Pakistan Administrative Service have no authority of law to hold posts in connection with affairs of the Provinces irrespective of the fact whether these posts have been reserved for them in the Civil Service of Pakistan (Composition and Cadre)

Rules, 1954 or not. This declaration will also be applicable to officers of other services / functional units / cadres of the Federation who hold posts in connection with affairs of the Provinces except through appointment by transfer in the prescribed manner.

20.   Section 10 of the Civil Servants Act, 1973 does not authorize the competent authority to transfer a civil servant out of cadre.

21.   Rule 20A of the Civil Servants (Appointment, Promotion and Transfer) Rules, 1973 and Rule 15 of the Punjab Civil Servants (Appointment and Conditions of Service) Rules, 1974 are without lawful authority and jurisdiction and, hence, of no legal effect to the extent these rules permit inter-governmental deputations and allow determination of terms and conditions of deputation by the lending and borrowing organizations for being in violation of Article 73,115 and 240 of the Constitution and Section 1(2) of the Civil Servants Act, 1973 and Section 1(2) of the Punjab Civil Servants Act, 1974.

22.   Intra-government deputation is permissible only if the officer consents to be deputed and the rules governing the officer and the post to be filled through deputation provide for the same and the statutory employment contract remains intact. In all other case, deputation is prohibited. In any case, inter-governmental deputation is simply not conceivable.

23.   Amendments made through executive orders in the Civil Service of Pakistan (Composition and Cadre) Rules, 1954 are void and of no legal effect.

24.   Jurisdictions to frame rules and make amendments therein are concurrent and co-extensive. As a consequence, amendments made by the President through rules not involving reservation of posts in connection with affairs of the Provinces for a Service of the Federation and matters in exclusive jurisdiction of the Provinces are valid and those which relate to these matters are invalid to the same extent as the original rules are.

25.   Creation of the District Management Group through an Office Memorandum was without lawful authority and, hence, of no legal effect.

26.   Non-implementation of the Notification No. S.R.O. 1307(1)/73 dated 14.09.1973 is not a live issue and, therefore, does not require adjudication.

27.   Posting of civil servants on higher posts in their own pay and scale is not provided in any law / rules.

28.   Without prejudice to our declarations regarding unconstitutionality of the Civil Service of Pakistan (Composition and Cadre) Rules, 1954 to the extent of reservation of posts in connection with affairs of the Provinces for the Pakistan Administrative Service, Provincial Government is not authorized to post federal officers on posts in basic pay scales higher than those of the officers. In pith and substance, such postings amount to promotion and the Province does not have power to promote federal officers against posts in connection with affairs of the Province.

29.   Simple posting to a post in a higher basic pay scale does not entitle a civil servant to claim pay of post. Such entitlement arises only on appointment to a basic pay scale or post through initial

recruitment, promotion or by transfer. In no case, a federal civil servant be granted pay of the post higher than his basic pay scale.

30. Section 10 of the Civil Servants Act, 1973 is not applicable in respect of posts in connection with affairs of the Province. This Section is not attracted in case of posting of federal civil servants on posts in connection with affairs of the Province.

31. Without prejudice to our declarations regarding unconstitutionality of the Civil Service of Pakistan (Composition and Cadre) Rules, 1954 to the extent of reservation of posts in connection with affairs of the Provinces for the Pakistan Administrative Service, additional charge of a post in connection with affairs of the Province cannot be assigned to an officer of the Pakistan Administrative Service in excess of a period of three months.

32. Federal officers are not allowed to be promoted against posts in connection with affairs of the Provinces. All serving officers promoted against posts in connection with affairs of the Provinces are hereby ordered to be demoted forthwith from the date of promotion.

33. The following provisions of the Civil Service of Pakistan (Composition and Cadre) Rules, 1954 are struck down for being in violation of the Constitution of the Islamic Republic of Pakistan, 1973:

   (a) Sub-rule (2) of Rule 5;
   (b) Sub-rule (1) of Rule 7;
   (c) Sub-rule (2) of Rule 8;
   (d) Rule 9, 10,11, 14 and 15;
   (e) Sub-rule (2) of Rule 16;
   (f) All posts in connection with affairs of the Provinces mentioned in the Schedule to the Rules;
   (g) The phrases "Provincial or" occurring before "Federal sub-Cadre" and "or the Provincial Government as the case may be" occurring after "the Federal Government" in sub-rule (4) of Rule 5;
   (h) The phrase "and the Governor in the case of posts in connection with the affairs of a Province" occurring in sub-rule (1) of rule 8;
   (i) The phrase "and in the case of posts in connection with the affairs of a Province, after consultation with the Governor of that Province" occurring in sub-rule (1) of Rule 13; and
   (j) The phrase "in consultation with Provinces" occurring in rule 17.

34. Police and public order in areas falling within territorial jurisdiction of the Provinces have never been federal subjects; these subjects either fell in the Provincial Legislative Lists or were not assigned to the Federation through their non-inclusion in the Federal Legislative Lists. The Federation had and continues to have full jurisdiction to legislate on public order and police for areas not forming part of a Province and on subjects within its exclusive legislative jurisdiction.

35. Legislation on public order and police necessarily includes penal law and criminal procedure. Legislation on other subjects by the Federation and the Provinces may also require incrimination of certain undesired acts or omissions and prosecution of the offenders. The Federation as well as the Provinces have jurisdiction to legislate for their respective subject-matters and territories.

36. The concept of concurrent jurisdiction relates to legislative subjects and not laws. The doctrine of pith and substance saves and protects provincial legislation on police for provincial territories and subjects.

37. Federation can have resort to entrustment of policing functions in respect of federal laws to the provincial police within territorial jurisdiction of the concerned Province through an arrangement under Article 146 of the Constitution.

38. Applying the relevant constitutional provisions, case law and the doctrine of pith and substance to the Police Order, 2002, the situation which emerges after restoration of the Constitution of 1973 is as follows:

    (a) The Order fell into jurisdiction of the Parliament in respect of territories not included in a Province and offences relating to federal subjects created through federal laws with its provisions relating to the Provinces in eclipse till such time these provisions are deleted from the Order through an Act of the Parliament; and

    (b) The Order fell into exclusive jurisdiction of the Provincial Assembly to the extent of policing in territorial limits of the Province and with respect to subjects falling within exclusive provincial jurisdiction with provisions relating to the federal areas and federal subjects in eclipse till such time these provisions are deleted from the Order through an amending Act of the concerned Provincial Assembly. However, provisions relating to role of the Federal Government in the matter of postings and appointments in the Provincial Police is rendered a nullity in eyes of law being an impermissible encroachment on exclusive provincial domain. Powers to repeal or amend the Chief Executive's Orders were vested in the appropriate Legislature and not in the Parliament alone. Appropriate legislature in respect of the police matters of a Province is the concerned Provincial Assembly.

39. Legislative entries on treaties with other countries, inter-provincial coordination and extension of jurisdiction of provincial police beyond territorial limits of the concerned Province do not make policing in provincial areas and on provincial subjects a federal subject.

40. In absence of any positive and affirmative constitutional sanction for reservation of posts in connection with affairs of the Federation and of the Provinces for a Service of the Federation, continuance of the Police Service after 15th of August, 1947 was without lawful authority and was of no legal effect.

41. After examining the Police Service of Pakistan (Probationary Service) Rules, 1950, we declare as follows:

(a) The said Rules are intra vires Article 241 of the Constitution to the extent of creation of a Federal Service for performance of policing functions in federal territories and in respect of federal functions as Section 141 (1) (a) and (2)(a) empowered the Governor General to make appointments in Services of the Federation and posts in connection with affairs of the Federation and determine conditions of service of persons so appointed;

(b) As provisions allowing reservation of posts in connection with affairs of the Federation and of the Provinces for All India Services (after the appointed day to be better labelled as the All Pakistan Services) stood deleted from the Government of India Act, 1935, therefore, there was no constitutional backing for creation of the Police Service of Pakistan as an All Pakistan Service. Without positive constitutional sanction similar to the deleted sections of the Government of India Act, 1935, it was not intra vires Section 241 (1) (a) and (2)(a) of the Government of India Act, 1935 to create the Police Service of Pakistan for holding posts in connection with affairs of a Province as posts reserved for the Service;

(c) The said Rules encroached upon the provincial domain exclusively vested in the Provincial Governors under Section 241 (1) (b) and (2)(b) of the Government of India Act, 1935 as posts in connection with affairs of the Provinces were reserved under these rules for the Police Service of Pakistan. To this extent, the rules were ultra vires Section 241 (1) (a) and (2)(a) of the Government of India Act, 1935 and were without lawful authority and consequently were of no legal effect; and

(d) Mutual consent of the Federation and of the Provinces cannot fill a constitutional vacuum and cannot compensate absence of lawful competence to deal with a matter. In the instant, even the claimed agreement between the Federation and of the Provinces does not exist because we are forced to assume its non-existence as the same was neither produced before this Court nor any reasonable justification for inability to produce it was submitted to our satisfaction.

42. The Establishment Division's O.M. No. 3/2/75-ARC dated 31.05.1975 is without lawful authority and jurisdiction and, hence, of no legal effect in its entirety.

43. With regard to the Police Service of Pakistan (Composition, Cadre and Seniority) Rules, 1985, we hold as follows:

(a) The Federation has lawful competence to create federal services to deal with federal subjects including policing in federal areas and with respect to offences created through federal laws and reserve posts in connection with affairs of the Federation for the Police Service of Pakistan;

(b) The Federation is authorized to prescribe posting by transfer as one of the methods of recruitment in the Police Service of Pakistan for provincial police officers to the extent and in the manner as it may determine;

(c) Posts in connection with affairs of the Provinces are not allowed to be reserved for the Police Service of Pakistan as provisions providing such reservation were deleted from the Government of India Act, 1935 when it was adopted as provisional constitution under the Pakistan (Provisional Constitution) Order, 1947. No subsequent constitution revived the concept of reservation of posts. The Police Service of Pakistan (Composition, Cadre and Seniority) Rules, 1985 are, therefore, without lawful authority and of no legal effect to the extent of reservation of posts in connection with affairs of the Provinces for the Police Service of Pakistan. The validity and protection intended to be given to the Police Service of Pakistan (Composition, Cadre and Seniority) Rules, 1985 under Section 19 of the Constitution (Eighth Amendment) Act, 1985 is not legally valid to the extent of reservation of posts in connection with affairs of the Provinces for the Police Service of Pakistan. We declare and hold that the Schedule of the Police Service of Pakistan (Composition, Cadre and Seniority) Rules, 1985 is void and of no legal effect to the extent it contains posts in connection with affairs of the Provinces;

(d) Police Service of Pakistan is not a service common to the Federation and the Provinces as the Police Service of Pakistan (Composition, Cadre and Seniority) Rules, 1985 do not encadre any posts common to both but only reserve posts either in connection with affairs of the Federation or of the Provinces for the Police Service of Pakistan;

(e) Officers of the Police Service of Pakistan are not legally allowed to be promoted against posts in connection with affairs of the Provinces. All serving officers of the Police Service of Pakistan who were promoted by calculating posts reserved for promotion in the cadre by including posts in connection with affairs of the Provinces are held to be promoted without lawful authority and are hereby ordered to the demoted forthwith with effect from the date of promotion. Future promotions in the Police Service of Pakistan shall only be made against posts in connection with affairs of the Federation; and

(f) Determination of remuneration payable from the Provincial Consolidated Fund is creation of a charge on the Provincial Consolidated Fund in terms of Article 115 of the Constitution. The Province lacks jurisdiction to determine remuneration of federal civil servants. We hold that payment of remuneration to officers of the Police Service of Pakistan during their service in the Provinces in accordance with the Basic Pay Scales and Fringe Benefits Scheme is quantum meruit and any amount drawn in excess thereof e.g. superior executive allowance and any special allowances not admissible in the Federal Government is without lawful authority and legal effect and, hence, recoverable. We direct the Accountant General Pakistan Revenues and the Accountant Generals of all the Provinces to calculate and effect recovery accordingly with a further direction to submit progress report, through Registrar of this court, each month for our information and, if need be, appropriate orders.

44. A direction of this court is not necessary to follow the Constitution and a mere apprehension of likely violation of the Constitution does not justify issuance of a direction by this court.

298.   In order to effectively resolve the controversy between the parties in the instant proceedings, we deem it necessary to direct that the Federation and the Province of Punjab shall, forthwith, relieve all officers of the Pakistan Administrative Service, Police Service of Pakistan and of other Federal Services holding civil posts in connection with affairs of the Province of the Punjab. The Federation shall also relieve forthwith all provincial employees on deputation to the Federation. A compliance report to this effect shall be submitted to this court, by the Attorney General for Pakistan and the Advocate General, Punjab, within thirty days reckonable from the date of announcement of this judgment. The dictum of law laid down by us in this judgment shall also be applicable to and shall be followed by all other Provinces and authorities in Pakistan. We need not to say that all authorities in the country are under constitutional obligation to act in aid of this court by faithfully implementing its judgments in letter and spirit. It is also obvious that non-compliance of orders of this court has consequences.

299.   We offer apology to persons who retired from service or died during pendency of these proceedings. We are regretful that delay in adjudication of the lis at hand wrongfully prevented them to enjoy what was lawfully due to them. We also find no satisfactory reason which can justify such delay in determination of some questions of law by this court. It goes without saying that justice delayed is justice denied.

300.   The Federation and the Province of Punjab shall pay, in equal proportions, ten million rupees as cost of this petition to the petitioners within fifty working days of announcement of this judgment.

301.   Learned counsels of the parties rendered valuable assistance to this court in the instant proceedings which is gratefully acknowledged.

Sd/

Mr. Jamal Mustafa Kundan

Sd/

Mr. Saleem Anwar Taya

Sd/

Mr. Rasheed Ahmad

Announced in Open Court on 2nd of October, 2019.

Sd/

Mr. Jamal Mustafa Kundan

APPROVED FOR REPORTING

Chapter 2

Meritorious illusions

This Chapter undertakes an in-depth legal study of discrimination against citizens on the ground only of religion, sex, residence, place of birth or disability in the matter of appointments in the service of Pakistan.

IAH 2018 MOOT COURT JUDGMENTS 3

Present: Mr. Jamal Mustafa Kundan
                Mr. Saleem Anwar Taya
                Mr. Rasheed Ahmad

Yasir Qayum Khan and others

------Petitioners

Versus

The Federation of Pakistan and others

-----Respondents

Petitioners	Mr. Faisal Saleem Mufti, Senior Advocate, Supreme Court of Pakistan
	Mr. Ghulam Ali, Senior Advocate, Supreme Court of Pakistan
	Mr. Gul Shahzad Sarwar, Advocate, Supreme Court of Pakistan
	Mr. Nazir Ahmad Bhatti, Advocate, Supreme Court of Pakistan
	Mr. Zahoor Ahmad, Advocate, Supreme Court of Pakistan
Respondents	Mr. Kamran Ali Afzal, Attorney General for Pakistan for the Federation of Pakistan
	Mr. Saleem Anwar Taya, Advocate General, Khyber Pakhtunkhwa for the Province of Khyber Pakhtunkhwa
Dates of hearing	01.08.2019, 16.08.2019, 19.08.2019 to 23.08.2019, 23.09.2019 and 25.11.2019

JUDGMENT

MR. JAMAL MUSTAFA KUNDAN. – This judgment decides a number of petitions each of which has its own set of facts and circumstances. What is common in all of these petitions is the question of constitutionality of discrimination against citizens on the ground only of religion, sex, residence, place of birth or disability in the matter of appointments in the service of Pakistan. As all petitions are mainly relatable to Article 27 of the Constitution of the Islamic Republic of Pakistan, 1973 (hereinafter referred to as the Constitution), therefore, we intend to dispose of all these petitions through this single judgment.

Facts of the case and arguments and prayers of the parties

2.   In response to an advertisement issued by the District Education Officer, Karak in the Khyber Pakhtunkhwa inviting applications for initial recruitment against the post of Primary School Teacher, Mr. Noor Alam Khan Wazir submitted an application. According to him, he possessed all the qualifications with respect to education, training, age and valid domicile of district Karak. Though he had two years of experience of teaching but the teaching experience was not a condition-precedent to compete for the job. His candidature was accepted and he was directed to appear in a screening test to the conducted by the National Testing Service. He appeared in the test and was declared eligible to be called for interview but instead of calling him for the interview, he was informed that since he did not have the computerized national identity card and domicile of the Union Council in which the primary schools having vacant posts were situated and since sufficient number of duly qualified candidates belonging to that Union Council had passed the screening test, therefore, he was not eligible to be called for interview. He submitted a written request for informing him of the legal grounds leading to rejection of his candidature on the basis of not being resident of the concerned Union Council. The District Education Officer, Karak informed him that his candidature was rejected on the basis of Section 3 of the Khyber Pakhtunkhwa (Appointment, Deputation, Posting and Transfer of Teachers, Lecturers,

178

Instructors and Doctors) Regulatory Act, 2011 (Khyber Pakhtunkhwa Act No. XII of 2011) which reads as follows:

"**3.   Appointment, posting and transfer of primary school teachers.** -(1) The vacancy of primary school teacher shall be filled in from the candidates belonging to the Union Council of their permanent residence mentioned in their Computerized National Identity Card and domicile, on merit and if no eligible candidate in that Union Council is available where the school is situate, such appointment shall be made on merit from amongst eligible candidates belonging to the adjacent Union Councils:

Provided that on availability of a vacancy, a primary school teacher, appointed from adjacent Union Council, as referred to in this sub-section, shall be transferred against a vacant post in a school of the Union Council of his residence within a period of fifteen days.

(2)   Upon marriage, the primary school teacher on request may be transferred to the school in the Union Council, where his spouse ordinarily resides, subject to the availability of vacancy.

(3)   The primary school teacher shall be transferred to other school within the Union Council on completion of tenure as may be prescribed or before completion of tenure, subject to the policy of rationalization for maintaining certain student teachers ratio, if any.

(4)   Government shall, within a period not exceeding one year of the commencement of this Act, make arrangement for posting of all the primary school teachers appointed prior to coming into force of this Act, to the schools of their respective Union Councils or adjacent Union Councils, as the case may be."

3.   The following provision of the Recruitment Policy of the Government of Khyber Pakhtunkhwa (issued vide letter No. SOR.I (S&GAD)1-117/91(C), dated 12.10.1993 at page 33 of the Estacode (Revised edition of 2011) of the Government of Khyber Pakhtunkhwa) was also cited to justify recruitment of primary school teachers on the basis of place of residence:

"The Provincial Government have already agreed that recruitment to the post of PTC in Education Department in various districts shall be made on constituency-wise basis. For this purpose, the existing districts have been divided into various zones. Each zone shall correspond to the area of constituency of the Provincial Assembly. However, recruitment to the posts shall, in each case, be 50% on merit in open competition on district basis and 50% on constituency basis."

4.   Mr. Noor Alam Khan Wazir claims that he has fundamental right to compete for jobs under the Government and his place of residence cannot be made a ground to deny him this fundamental right. He avers that the matter is of public importance as all eligible candidates for similar jobs in the Province are being subjected to constitutionally prohibited adverse discrimination on the basis of place of residence. He prays that the said Section 3 be declared void ab initio and be erased from the statute book on the ground of being inconsistence with the fundamental right guaranteed under Article 27 of the Constitution. He submits that rejection of his candidature be declared without lawful authority and of no legal effect and may be set aside and the directions may be issued for fresh interviews of all the eligible candidates irrespective of their place of residence.

5.   Dr. Waleed Ahmad has domicile of Chitral district in the Khyber Pakhtunkhwa. He applied for initial recruitment against the post of a medical officer in a healthcare facility in Peshawar district. He fulfilled the requisite eligibility criteria. The appointment was to be made on ad hoc basis for a period not exceeding one year or the arrival of a candidate

recommended by the Khyber Pakhtunkhwa Public Service Commission, whichever was earlier. His application was rejected summarily on the ground that he did not possess the domicile of Peshawar district and the prohibition contained in Section 4 of the Khyber Pakhtunkhwa (Appointment, Deputation, Posting and Transfer of Teachers, Lecturers, Instructors and Doctors) Regulatory Act, 2011, reproduced below, was attracted in his case:

"**4.   Appointment of doctors, lecturers, instructors, subject specialists and teachers on adhoc basis.-** (1) Government may, through the competent authorities, make adhoc appointment on merit against the vacant posts of doctors, lecturers, instructors, subject specialists and teachers, falling within the purview of Commission, in a district concerned from the domicile holders of that district for a period of one year or till the arrival of recommendees of Commission, whichever is earlier after fulfilling the pre-requisites of giving wide publicity in the press. On assumption of charge of post by recommendee of the Commission, the services of such ad hoc appointee shall stand automatically terminated:

Provided that if no suitable and eligible candidate is available in the district concerned for appointment, then the candidates belonging to the neighbouring districts shall be considered for appointment in the order of their merit.

(2)   Save as the appointment made under proviso of this section, "ad hoc appointee" shall serve in the district of his domicile.

(3)   The post of a doctor, lecturer, instructor, subject specialist or teacher who proceeds on training or long leave may be treated as vacant post for the purpose of contract or contingent appointment till the return of such employee from training or long leave and assumption of charge of the post:

Provided that the period of such training or long leave shall not be less than one year and no appointment on contract or contingent shall be made on the post which may fall vacant for a period less than one year."

6.   Dr. Waleed Ahmad is aggrieved of violation of his fundamental right guaranteed by Article 27 of the Constitution and terming it a matter of public importance prays for just and equitable reliefs keeping in view facts and circumstances of this case besides a declaration on the unconstitutionality of Section 4 of the Khyber Pakhtunkhwa (Appointment, Deputation, Posting and Transfer of Teachers, Lecturers, Instructors and Doctors) Regulatory Act, 2011.

7.   Mr. Allah Ditta applied for initial recruitment against the post of police constable in Mardan district. There was no dispute regarding his eligibility for the post applied for. He has a domicile of Sawabi district. The District Police Officer, Mardan informed him that his application was rejected because of his domicile district in terms of Section 34 of the Khyber Pakhtunkhwa Police Act, 2017 (Khyber Pakhtunkhwa Act No. II of 2017) which reads as under:

"34. Initial recruitment of Constables. - (1) The post of Constable shall be filled in by initial recruitment at the District level by the head of district police through a selection process conducted by an accredited testing agency approved by the Provincial Police Officer.

(2)   The recruitment in the rank of Constable shall be on the basis of district of domicile."

8.   Mr. Allah Ditta attacks the constitutionality of Section 34 of the Khyber Pakhtunkhwa Police Act, 2017 on the ground of its inconsistency with Article 27 of the Constitution and prays for the consequential relief and declarations under Article 184(3) of the Constitution.

9.   Mr. Shahzad Ahmad Khan Bangash appeared in the combined competitive examination conducted by the Khyber Pakhtunkhwa Public Service Commission in 2018 for initial recruitment in the Provincial Management Service. He successfully qualified written portion of the examination and was also declared successful in the interview but was not recommendee for appointment on the ground that the quota reserved for the zone to which he belongs stood occupied by the candidates who had secured more marks in the examination. Upon his inquiry, he came to know that the candidates belonging to other zones who had secured less marks than him were recommended for appointment. He is aggrieved of the fact that despite his comparatively better performance in the examination, he was ignored for appointment and candidates inferior to him in merit were given jobs. He claims that adverse discrimination against him on the ground of his place of residence is nothing except denial of his fundamental right to join service of Pakistan on the basis of his merit. He submits that a series of executive instructions and Rule 12 of the Khyber Pakhtunkhwa Civil Servants (Appointment, Promotion and Transfer) Rules, 1989, reproduced below, are stated to be legal basis of denial of the fundamental right guaranteed by Article 27 of the Constitution:

> "12. **Zonal and Divisional representation: -** (1) Except as otherwise specifically provided in any rule for the time being in force, initial recruitment to posts in Basic Pay Scales 16 and 17 and other posts in Basic Pay Scales 3 to 15 borne on Provincial cadre shall be made in accordance with the Zonal quota specified by Government from time to time:
>
> Provided that initial recruitment to the post of Civil Judge/Judicial Magistrate/Allaqa Qazi (BPS-18) shall also be made in accordance with the zonal quota specified by the Government from time to time.
>
> (2)   Initial recruitment to posts in Basic Pay Scales 3 to 15 borne on divisional or district cadre shall be made from amongst bona fide residents of the division or district concerned, as the case may be.
>
> (3)   Initial recruitment to posts in Basic Pay Scales 1 and 2 or equivalent shall ordinarily be made on local basis."

10.   Our attention was drawn towards zonal allocation formula contained in S&GAD's Notification NO.SOS.III(S&GAD)3-39/70, dated 2.10.1973, as amended from time to time, reproduced below:

> "In exercise of the powers conferred by Article 241 of the Constitution of the Islamic Republic of Pakistan and in supersession of this Department's Notification No. SOS.III (S&GAD)339/70 dated 25th March,1971 the Governor of the North-West Frontier Province is pleased to direct that notwithstanding anything to the contrary contained in any service/ Recruitment Rules under the rule making authority of the Governor of the North-West Frontier Province, vacancies to be filled by initial recruitment and by promotion shall be filled in the following manner: -
>
> 1. In the case of initial recruitment: -
>
> > (a)   there shall be block of 24 vacancies in the former Gazetted Service or post (including un-classified services or Posts) or equivalent status, which shall be filled in the following manner: -
> >
> > (i)   Six such vacancies shall form merit quota and shall be filled on merit from among the candidates domiciled in any part of the North-West Frontier Province including the Federally Administered Tribal Areas attached thereto; and

(ii) the remaining 18 vacancies shall be reserved for bona fide residents of the zones specified in column 2 of the Appendix to this Notification in accordance with the number of posts shown against each zone in column 4 thereof;"

(b) there shall be block of 18 vacancies in non-Gazetted Services or posts in the Secretariat Department and the Headquarters Offices of the Attached Departments which shall be reserved for bona fide residents of the zones specified in column 2 of the Appendix to this Notification in accordance with the number of posts shown against each zone in column 4 thereof;

Provided that where a zone has been further sub-divided into parts specified in column 3 of the said Appendix, the vacancies allocated to that zone shall be made available to each part of the zone in equal shares or by rotation, as the case may be;

Provided further that in the case of vacancy allocated to a zone or, as the case may be, a part of that zone if no suitable candidate from that zone or part is available, the vacancy shall be filled from any other zone or part of that zone, as the case may be, and the vacancy of the latter zone or part of that zone, as the case may be, when available shall be filled from former zone, or as the case may be a part of that zone, where no suitable candidate was available.

2. In the case of vacancies to be filled by promotion in the manner specified in the Service/Recruitment Rules of the Service concerned;

Provided that if in the opinion of the appointing authority no suitable officer/official is available for promotion to any post in the Provincial Secretariat from among the officers/officials constituting the Secretariat Services the vacancies, not exceeding ten per cent of the total cadre strength of the Service concerned, may be filled by transfer or promotion of suitable officers/officials serving in any Department of the Government of the North-West Frontier Province."

11. Various executive orders issued by the Government of the Khyber Pakhtunkhwa on the issue of zanal allocation of posts for the purpose of initial recruitment were also appended with the petition of Mr. Shahzad Ahmad Khan Bangash. It was pointed out that the Khyber Pakhtunkhwa Civil Servants Act, 1973 does not contain any provisions relating to citizenship of civil servants of the Government of the Khyber Pakhtunkhwa. The following Rule 11(1) of the Khyber Pakhtunkhwa Civil Servants (Appointment, Promotion and Transfer) Rules, 1989 was also referred to by the learned counsel for Mr. Shahzad Ahmad Khan Bangash:

"11. **Eligibility.** (1) A candidate for appointment shall be a citizen of Pakistan and bona fide resident of the North-West Frontier Province.
Provided that for reasons to be recorded in writing, Government may, in a particular case, relax this restriction."

12. It has been claimed that the provisions of the rules and the executive instructions regarding residence-based quota are in violation of the Constitution and, hence, void and of no legal effect. Learned counsel for Mr. Shahzad Ahmad Khan Bangash has prayed that this court may declare recruitment on zonal quota basis void and may direct recruitment of the petitioner purely on the basis of merit as determined by the Khyber Pakhtunkhwa Public Service Commission through the competitive examination.

13.   Mr. Jamal Akhtar applied for the post of watchman for night duty in the office of Assistant Commissioner, Takht-e-Nasrati (a tehsil or sub-division of district Karak). His application was rejected on the ground that he belonged to Tehsil Banda Daud Shah of district Karak whereas Rule 12 (3) of the Khyber Pakhtunkhwa Civil Servants (Appointment, Promotion and Transfer) Rules, 1989 prescribes filling of posts in basic pay scales number 1 and 2 or equivalent on local basis. A tehsil was taken as basis to determine whether an applicant was local or not. Since he did not belong to the sub-division Takht-e-Nasrati and since candidates having requisite qualifications were available from the concerned sub-division, therefore, his application was rejected. Mr. Jamal Akhtar is aggrieved of rejection of his application on unconstitutional ground and seeks suitable relief not only for himself but for all other similarly placed citizens.

14.   Mr. Ghulam Safdar Shah applied for initial recruitment against the post of junior clerk in the Law and Parliamentary Affairs Department of the Government of Khyber Pakhtunkhwa. After written test and interview, he was not selected for the post. When he checked the marks obtained by the selected candidates, it transpired that female candidates securing marks less than what he secured were selected. Upon inquiring about the reason of selection of less meritorious female candidates, he was informed that the Government of Khyber Pakhtunkhwa had allocated 10% quota in all jobs for female candidates. The female candidates were also eligible to compete with male candidates on merit quota. Quota for females in initial recruitments was justified on the basis of the following provision of the recruitment policy of the Government of the Khyber Pakhtunkhwa:

> "10% quota has also been fixed for female candidates in all the Provincial services which are filled up through initial recruitment in addition to their participation in the open merit. However, it shall not be applicable to cadres exclusively reserved for females. The vacancies reserved for women for which qualified women candidates are not available shall be carried forward and filled by women."

15.   Learned counsel for Mr. Ghulam Safdar Shah claims that reservation of quota for females in initial recruitment against posts in connection with affairs of the Province is a discrimination on the basis of sex alone which is prohibited under the Constitution. He prays that reservation of quota for female candidates in services be declared void ab initio and directions be issued for recruitment on the sole basis of merit determined through objective criteria.

16.   Mr. Raheel Ahmad Siddiqui applied for the post of Naib Qasid in the office of the Superintendent, District Jail, Peshawar. Though there were 20 posts of Naib Qasid in the District Jail, but the only vacant post at that time was not meant for filling up through open competition on merit. His application was rejected on the ground that he was a Muslim whereas the post was reserved for religious minorities in the district. In this regard, he was informed of the following provision of the recruitment policy of the Government of Khyber Pakhtunkhwa:

> "0.5 per cent quota has been fixed for candidates belonging to minorities in all the Provincial services which are filled in through initial recruitment in addition to their participation in the open merit. However, this reservation shall not apply to: -
> * the percentage of vacancies reserved for recruitment on the basis of merit;
> * Short term vacancies likely to last for less than six months; and
> * Isolated posts in which vacancies occur only occasionally."

17.   Learned counsel for Mr. Raheel Ahmad Siddiqui asserts that reservation of 0.5 per cent quota in government jobs for the non-Muslims, which stands at 0.29 per cent of the total population of the Province, is not only unjustified on other grounds but is also an example of discrimination in services on the sole ground of religion. It is claimed that the said quota was subsequently increased to 5% in August, 2015. He advocates that no

discrimination is permissible on the basis of religion in the matter of jobs under the provincial government. He seeks annulment of quota for religious minorities and provision of an opportunity to prove his merit irrespective of his religion and the religion of those competing him for this job.

18.   The Establishment and Administration Department of the Government of Khyber Pakhtunkhwa advertised a number of posts in B.S. 1 to B.S. 4 in the Secretariat of the Government indicating in the advertisement that 25% of the posts shall be filled in from amongst the candidates who were children of retiring civil servants on superannuation / invalidation. Mr. Ali Raza applied for the post of Naib Qasid. He was not selected but candidates securing marks less than those secured by him were selected because they were children of retired civil servants for which specific quota was fixed in terms of the following executive instructions:

> **"First letter**
> I am directed to refer to the subject cited above and to state that in supersession of all instructions issued in this behalf, the competent authority has been pleased to direct that a quota of 25% falling to the share of initial recruitment in BPS-1 to BPS-4 shall be reserved for appointment of one of the children of a retiring civil servant on superannuation / invalidation; provided that: -
>
> 1)   the appointment shall be made subject to the availability of vacancy.
> 2)   A waiting list showing the name, designation and date of retirement / invalidation of retiring civil servant shall be maintained in the department / office. The merit shall be determined from the date of retirement / invalidation of the civil servant.
> 3)   The child possesses qualification prescribed for the post.
> 4)   In case, the date of retirement / invalidation of two civil servants is the same, the child of the civil servant older in age shall be considered first for appointment.
> 5)   Under-age child of the said civil servant shall be included in the waiting list from the date of retirement / invalidation. However, he shall be considered for appointment after he attains the age prescribed for the posts.
>
> 2.   The competent authority has further been pleased to authorize the Chief Secretary, NWFP to exercise the power of grant of relaxation of ban for initial appointment in cases of appointment of one of the children of retired / invalid civil servant and deceased civil servant died during the service as required in rule 10 (4) of the NWFP Civil Servant (Appointment, Promotion and Transfer) Rules, 1989.
> 3.   I am, therefore, directed to request that the above policy instructions should be followed strictly in letter and spirit.
> (Authority: S&GAD's letter No. SOR-I (S&GAD)4-1/80(Vol-III) dated 23.05.2000)
>
> **Second letter**
> In continuation of this department's circular letter of even number dated 23.5.2000, I am directed to refer to the subject cited above and to say that while submitting summary to the Competent Authority for the recruitment of a child of retiring civil servant in BPS-1 to BPS-4 on superannuation / invalidation, the Administrative Department shall certify that vacancy against which the child of the said civil servant was being recruited is within the prescribed quota.

19.   Learned counsel for Mr. Ali Raza submits that no law / rules / regulations authorize executive authorities to allocate quotas for children of retired or incapacitated civil servants. Such reservation of quotas offends the concept of equality of opportunity and is not consistent with the constitutional provisions. He prays that these quotas be set aside and the authorities be directed to select him for appointment on the basis of marks secured by him in the selection process.

20.   Mr. Qaiser Shah applied for the post of Naib Qasid in an office where there were 102 such posts. His application was rejected on the ground that the posts advertised were reserved for disable persons and since he was a physically and mentally healthy person suffering from no disability, therefore, he was ineligible to compete for posts reserved for disable persons. He was informed that Section 10 of the Disabled Persons (Employment and Rehabilitation) Ordinance, 1981 (Ordinance No. XL of 1981) as amended by the Khyber Pakhtunkhwa Disabled Persons (Employment and Rehabilitation) (Amendment) Act, 2012 makes it compulsory for an establishment to employ disable persons in the proportion of not less than 2% of the total number of its employees. Disable person and establishment were defined in the Disabled Persons (Employment and Rehabilitation) Ordinance, 1981 in these words:

> "disabled person" means a person who, on account of injury, disease or congenital deformity, is handicapped for undertaking any gainful profession or employment in order to earn his livelihood, and includes a person who is blind, deaf, physically handicapped or mentally retarded;
>
> "establishment" means a Government establishment, a commercial establishment or an industrial establishment, in which the number of workers employed at any time during a year is not less than one hundred;"

21.   Learned counsel for Mr. Qaiser Shah admits that his client does not fall within the definition of disable person but he questions the reservation of quota for disabled person on the strength of the argument that such an arrangement is against the concept of equality of opportunity in the matter of appointments in the service of Pakistan. He also avers that being able bodied his client is in better position to perform duties of his post than the persons with disabilities. He prays for setting aside reservation of quota for disable persons fixed under the Khyber Pakhtunkhwa Disabled Persons (Employment and Rehabilitation) (Amendment) Act, 2012 and declaring the said law void ab initio to this extent.

22.   Mr. Johnson Bernard, after passing FSc. in good marks, applied for a job in the University of Engineering and Technology, Peshawar. He appeared in written test and interview and remained successful in both but was not given job. A Muslim candidate succeeded in getting the job despite the fact that he was awarded less marks in the written test, interview and on the basis of academic record. It was stated that since the Muslim candidate was given twenty marks on the basis of being memorizer of the Holy Quran, therefore, he got more marks than those earned by Mr. Johnson Bernard who claims to have good knowledge of Bible but that knowledge is awarded no additional marks. He terms his rejection for the job applied for a discrimination on religious grounds and prays for a declaration regarding the practice of awarding twenty marks on account of learning the Holy Quran by heart void and of no legal effect and a direction to the University for his appointment by withdrawing twenty marks given to the selected candidate. He further says that the practice of award of twenty additional marks to a memorizer of the Holy Quran is not backed by any law and is based solely on executive instructions.

23.   Mr. Yasir Qayum Khan belongs to Abbottabad district in Khyber Pakhtunkhwa. He appeared in the competitive examination conducted by the Federal Public Service Commission for recruitment to various posts in B.S. 17 under the Federal Government. 24.

The said examination is popularly known as CSS (Central Superior Services) Examination. It has been claimed that in the advertisement inviting applications for the CSS examination, 2018, there was no mention of reservation of any regional quota. Only quota reserved for women and minorities was mentioned in the advertisement. General instructions of the Federal Public Service Commission to the candidates contains the following on the subject of citizenship, domicile and regional reserved quotas:

"I.)   The candidate must be a citizen of Pakistan or a person deriving his / her nationality from the State of Jammu and Kashmir.

II.)   A candidate who has acquired the citizenship of Pakistan by registration under the Pakistan Citizenship Act and the rules made thereunder should produce a certificate (attested copy thereof) of citizenship alongwith the requisite documents.

III.)   Seats earmarked for prescribed provincial / regional quotas should be allocated to candidates on the basis of the domicile certificate issued by the competent authority in accordance with the law and the rules.

IV.)   Only those candidates shall be considered for vacancies reserved for Azad Jammu and Kashmir who hold the domicile certificate of this region issued by the competent authority in accordance with the Law & Rules.

V.)   The domicile claimed by a candidate and accepted by the Government at the time of first entry into Government service shall be treated as final throughout his / her service career and no subsequent change in his / her domicile will be recognized for the purpose of terms & conditions of his / her service including his / her allocation and liability to transfer.

VI.)   The domicile once claimed and accepted by the Commission for the purpose of admission to an examination / selection shall be treated final and, no change will be allowed at a subsequent examination / selection.

VII.)   Candidate will submit an undertaking / declaration that he / she is not in possession of any other domicile certificate other than the one claimed in his Online Application for the aforesaid case / post.

VIII.)   The provincial / regional quota as advertised will be observed strictly. Therefore, candidates possessing the required domicile will only be considered for appointment. All candidates must attach with requisite documents, attested copies of self-domicile certificates. Applications of candidates who do not possess prescribed domicile for a post shall be rejected.

IX.)   Posts reserved to be filled on merit shall be opened to all applicants irrespective of their domicile.

X.)   A Sindh (Urban) domicile refers only to the city areas of Karachi, Hyderabad and Sukkur. Cantonment areas are considered as being a part of the city. The areas under the jurisdiction of the District Councils of these districts and the rest of Sindh are Sindh Rural Areas.

XI.)   Federally Administered Tribal Areas include: -

    i.)   Tribal Areas adjoining Peshawar, Bannu, D.I. Khan and Kohat Districts; and

    ii.)   Bajor, Mohmand, Orakzai, Khyber, Kurram, North Waziristan and South Waziristan Agencies.

XII.) A candidate belonging to the Federal or Provincial Tribal Areas should produce alongwith requisite documents a certificate issued and signed by the Political Agent of the area in the prescribed form available on FPSC website.

XIII.) A candidate who has married a person who is not a citizen of Pakistan shall not be eligible for appointment provided that a person who marries an Indian national with the prior permission of the Government may be regarded as being eligible for appointment."

25. Learned counsel for Mr. Yasir Qayum Khan placed on record a letter of the Establishment Division of the Federal Government which reads as follows:

"Merit / Provincial / Regional quotas for recruitment to civil posts

The question of revision of the Provincial / regional quotas for recruitment to the civil posts under the Federal Government has been under consideration of Government for some time. It has been decided that with immediate effect the following merit and provincial / regional quotas shall be observed in filling vacancies reserved for direct recruitment to posts under the Federal Government which are filled on all-Pakistan basis: -

Merit quota 10%

Punjab (including federal area of Islamabad) 50%

Sindh (including Karachi) 19%

The share of Sindh will be further sub-allocated in the following ratio:

Urban areas namely Karachi, Hyderabad and Sukkur 40% of 19% or 7.6%

Rural areas i.e. rest of Sindh excluding Karachi, Hyderabad and Sukkur 60% of 19% or 11.4%

N.W.F.P. 11.5%

Balochistan 3.5%

Northern Areas and Federally Administered Tribal Areas 4%

Azad Kashmir 2%

[Authority. - Estt. Division O.M. No.8/9/72-TRV, dated 31.08.1973]."

26. Learned counsel for Mr. Yasir Qayum Khan further informed us that the following clarifications were issued vide O.M. No.8/15/73-TRV, dated 28.11.1973 of the Establishment Division of the Federal Government:

"(1) Posts in each grade should be considered separately for purposes of allocation of the prescribed merit and Provincial / Regional quotas.

(2) The Provincial / Regional quotas do not apply to posts filled by promotion. These are applicable to direct, including lateral entry, appointments.

(3) Vacancies which cannot be filled by candidates belonging to the Province or region to which the vacancy is allocated should be carried over and re-advertised at a later date.

(4) Posts in the Ministry / Division should be allocated separately from posts in Attached Departments and Subordinate Offices. In other words, the allocation should be made separately for each Department, Office or Institution.

(5) Provincial / Regional quotas do not apply to posts filled by transfer of Government servants to posts in equivalent grades whether on deputation or on secondment as in the case of military officers."

27.   The learned counsel informs us that, as per recruitment policy of the Federal Public Service Commission, the current status of quota applied to recruitments made through the CSS examination is as follows:

- Merit 7.5%
- Punjab (including federal area of Islamabad) 50%
- Sindh (including Karachi) 19%
- The share of Sindh will be further sub-allocated in the following ratio:
    - Urban areas, namely Karachi, Hyderabad and Sukkur 40% of 19% or 7.6%.
    - Rural areas i.e. rest of Sindh excluding Karachi, Hyderabad & Sukkur 60% of 19% or 11.4%)
- Khyber Pakhtunkhwa 11.5
- Balochistan 6%
- Gilgit–Baltistan and Federally Administered Tribal Areas 4%
- Azad Kashmir 2%
- Women Reserved Quota: 10%. Women quota will be calculated from the share of each province / region

28.   The learned counsel for the petitioner claims that the Civil Servants Act, 1973 neither requires nationality of Pakistan for becoming a civil servant of the Federation nor sanctions quota system for posts in connection with affairs of the Federation or posts common to the Federation and of the Provinces. He, however, admits that nationality requirement and quota system have been provided in Rule 13, 14, 15 and 16 of the Civil Servants (Appointment, Promotion and Transfer) Rules, 1973, reproduced below:

"13.   A candidate for appointment shall be a citizen of Pakistan;

Provided that this requirement may be relaxed with the approval of the Establishment Division:

Provided further that, in the case of candidates to be appointed on temporary basis to posts in the Pakistan Missions abroad, such relaxation shall not be accorded for a period exceeding one year at a time.

14.   Vacancies in the undermentioned posts shall be filled on All Pakistan basis in accordance with the merit and provincial or regional quotas prescribed by Government from time to time:

(i)   All posts in basic pay scales 16 and above and equivalent.

(ii)   Posts in basic pay scales 3 to 15 and equivalent in offices, which serve the whole of Pakistan:

Provided that if no suitable person holding the domicile of the Province or Region to which a vacancy has been earmarked and fulfilling the prescribed qualifications is found even after the vacancy has been advertised twice, the appointing authority may fill up the vacancy on open merit on contract in the following manner, namely: -

(i)   contract appointment shall be made initially for a period of one year, and if the post falls under the purview of the Federal Public Service Commission, the Commission shall be informed about contract appointment;

(ii)   if nomination is not received from the Federal Public Service Commission within one year, contract appointment may in the public interest be extended for another year; and

(iii)   the Federal Public Service Commission shall ensure that the nominations of the qualified candidates are made within a period of two years. If Federal Public Service Commission does not find a suitable candidate, it shall advise the appointing authority, for the extension in the contract.

15. Vacancies in posts in basic pay scales 3 to 15 and equivalent in offices which serve only a particular province or region shall be filled by appointment of persons domiciled in the province or region concerned.

16. Vacancies in posts in basic pay scales 1 and 2 and equivalent shall ordinarily be filled on local basis."

29. Our attention was also drawn towards the Establishment Division of the Government of Pakistan's O.M. No. 8/9/72-TRV/R.2 dated 29.09.1973 (Sl. No.49) under which the provincial / regional quotas were made applicable to appointments in or equivalent to BPS-17 and above posts in all autonomous / semi-autonomous bodies under the administrative control of the Federal Government. As such, recruitment to posts upto BPS-16 in autonomous / semi-autonomous bodies located in Islamabad was said to be outside the provincial / regional quotas.

30. Learned counsel for Mr. Yasir Qayum Khan claims that Mr. Yasir Qayum Khan passed the written examination and was also declared successful in the interview but he was not recommended for appointment by the Federal Public Service Commission. The learned counsel states that his client got marks more than those obtained by the candidates from Rural Sindh and Balochistan who were recommended for appointment. He argues that adverse discrimination through reservation of quota on the basis of place of residence, sex and religion has prevented his client to join the profession of his choice on the strength of his meritorious performance in the examination. He claims that such discrimination on the basis of place of residence, sex and religion is patently against the guarantee provided by Article 27 of the Constitution. He prays that quotas in the federal services be declared an abridgment of the fundamental rights and may be held void and of no legal effect. He further prays that direction may be given to the Federal Public Service Commission and the Federation of Pakistan through the Establishment Division that his client be appointed against a post in BS. 17 as per his merit determined on the basis of results of the CSS Examination, ignoring quotas fixed on account of place of birth, place of residence, sex and religion.

31. Before admitting the aforesaid petitions for regular hearing, we thought it proper and expedient to listen to the learned Attorney General for Pakistan and the learned Advocate General, Khyber Pakhtunkhwa and the learned counsels for the petitioners on the maintainability of the petitions under Article 184(3) of the Constitution. Notices were accordingly issued to all concerned for the purpose.

32. Learned Attorney General for Pakistan and the learned Advocate General, Khyber Pakhtunkhwa have frankly admitted that the questions raised in these petitions relate to enforcement of the fundamental right of the petitioners to trade and profession and to get appointments in the Service of Pakistan without discrimination. They, however, vehemently oppose the assertion that the petitions involve any issue of public importance as the grievances agitated are personal to the petitioners. It is asserted that personal grievances cannot be agitated under Article 184(3) of the Constitution even if they relate to enforcement of any one or more of the fundamental rights. It is pointed out by the learned law officers that a question of public importance can be one which has impact on the public at large and not on some individuals or on a small group of citizens. It is stated that in the petitions under adjudication the grievances raised are personal to the petitioners who are individuals and do not form public at large or a large representative group of the public at large. It is averred that Article 184(3) of the Constitution can only be invoked if both the conditions specified therein are satisfied. The jurisdiction under that Article is not exercisable in absence of any one of the specified conditions, it is submitted. They have

prayed that the petitions be dismissed for want of jurisdiction as no question of public importance is involved in these petitions.

33.   On the other hand, leaned counsels for the petitioners argue that a matter does not require thousands or millions of petitioners to qualify to be a matter of public importance. It is not the number of persons or parties directly involved in the litigation which determines public importance of the matter under litigation, the learned counsels contend. They assert that public importance of a matter lies in its potential effect on rights and obligations of public at large. It is argued by them that any question **of law or fact would be a question of public importance in terms of Article 184(3) of the Constitution if its impacts and consequences are substantial, broad-based, transcending the litigation-interests of the parties and bearing upon the public interest. They argue that the questions raised in these constitutional petitions are questions of public importance as these questions transcend the circumstances of the particular cases, and have a significant bearing on the public interest. They further plead the idea that discrimination on the basis of place of residence, sex or religion impacts the whole society and generations to come. Denial of the fundamental right to join public services on grounds expressly prohibited by the Constitution is a question of public importance of this significance that it makes the right to trade and profession and the right guaranteed by Article 27 of the Constitution and even the right to life meaningless, they submit.**

34.   **We have given patient hearing to the rival contentions on the subject. The question that what constitutes a question of public importance in the context of Article 184(3) of the Constitution has very ably been discussed in paragraph 9 of the judgment of the Hon'ble Supreme Court of Pakistan in** Suo Moto Action regarding Islamabad–Rawalpindi Sit-in / Dharna case (PLJ 2019 SC Criminal Cases 190), reproduced hereinbelow:

> "9. In the case of Benazir Bhutto v Federation of Pakistan (PLD 1988 SC 416) this Court held that, "It is only when the element of "public importance" is involved that the Supreme Court can exercise its power to issue the writ". {See also Asad Ali v Federation of Pakistan (PLD 1988 SC 161, 2092)}. In the case of Manzoor Elahi v Federation of Pakistan (PLD 1975 SC 66, 144-145), this Court had deliberated on what is meant by public importance:
>
> > "Now, what is meant by a question of public importance. The term "public" is invariably employed in contradistinction to the terms private or individual, and connotes, as an adjective, something pertaining to, or belonging to, the people; relating to a nation, state, or community. In other words, it refers to something which is to be shared or participated in or enjoyed by the public at large, and is not limited or restricted to any particular class of the community. As observed by the Judicial Committee of the Privy Council in Hamabai Franjee Petit v. Secretary of State for India-in-Council (ILR 39 Bomb. 279), while construing the words public purpose such a phrase this, "whatever else it may mean must include a purpose, that is an object or aim, in which the general interest of the community, as opposed to the particular interest of individuals, is directly and vitally concerned". This definition appears to me to be equally applicable to the phrase "public importance".
>
> The aforesaid definition of public importance, has been consistently followed by this Court. In Suo Moto Case No. 13 (PLD 2009 SC 217 229) the definition as had been enunciated in the cases Manzoor Elahi and Benazir Bhutto (above) was reiterated:

"The public importance of case is determined as observed by this Court in Manzoor Elahi's case (supra) on question affecting the legal rights and liberties of the people at large, even though the individual who may have brought the matter before the Court is of no significance. Similarly, it was observed in Benazir Bhutto's case (supra), that public importance should be viewed with reference to freedom and liberties guaranteed under the Constitution, their protection and invasion of these rights in a manner, which raises a serious question regarding their enforcement, irrespective of the fact whether such infraction of right, freedom or liberty is alleged by an individual or a group of individuals."

In Sohail Butt v Deputy Inspector General of Police (2011 SCMR 698, 704), this Court observed:

"Public importance must include a purpose or aim in which general interest of the community as opposed to the particular interest of the individuals is directly and vitally concerned."

In Watan Party v Federation of Pakistan (PLD 2012 SC 292, 324) this Court said that the scope of public importance had been settled, and it related to the general interest of the community:

"It is settled that public importance must include a purpose or aim in which the general interest of the community as opposed to the particular interest of the individuals is directly and vitally concerned."

Thus, a fortiori, this Court may invoke its power under Article 184 (3) of the Constitution provided the matter is one of public importance and pertains to the enforcement of any of the Fundamental Rights."

35.   Article 184(3) of the Constitution provides as follows:

"Without prejudice to the provisions of Article 199, the Supreme Court shall, if it considers that a question of public importance with reference to the enforcement of any of the Fundamental Rights conferred by Chapter 1 of Part II is involved, have the power to make an order of the nature mentioned in the said Article."

36.   Two threshold questions for invoking original jurisdiction under Article 184(3) are as follows:

(1)   Whether the matter brought before the court is for enforcement of fundamental rights?

(2)   Whether judicial resolution of the matter brought before the court will have impact on the litigating parties only or the public at large will be affected by the determination of the questions raised?

37.   If answer to both of the above questions is in affirmative, then the court is bound to invoke its constitutional jurisdiction. If any of the two elements is missing, then the court has no option except to dismiss the petitions. Hon'ble Justice(retired) Fazal Karim, in Volume-III of his book "Judicial Review of Public Actions" has observed at page 1713 that:

"The words "if it considers that a question of public importance is involved" clearly express the intention that the Supreme Court has jurisdiction under Article 184(3) if, and only if, the case involves a question of public importance. The existence of a question of pubic importance is, therefore, sine qua non (an indispensable requisite or condition) or a condition precedent to the jurisdiction of the Supreme Court. The words "if it considers"
also manifest the intention that the Court has to decide the question of public importance in each case before it enters upon the merits."

38.   No party before us in these proceedings has claimed that right to trade and profession granted by Article 18 of the Constitution does not include the right to compete for jobs in the Service of Pakistan. It has not been controverted that every citizen has a fundamental right not to be discriminated against in respect of any appointment in the service of Pakistan on the ground only of race, religion, caste, sex, residence or place of birth. Article 27 of the Constitution provides this fundamental right in these words:

> **"27. Safeguard against discrimination in services.** - (1) No citizen otherwise qualified for appointment in the service of Pakistan shall be discriminated against in respect of any such appointment on the ground only of race, religion, caste, sex, residence or place of birth:
>
> Provided that, for a period not exceeding forty years from the commencing day, posts may be reserved for persons belonging to any class or area to secure their adequate representation in the service of Pakistan:
>
> Provided further that, in the interest of the said service, specified posts or services may be reserved for members of either sex if such posts or services entail the performance of duties and functions which cannot be adequately performed by members of the other sex:
>
> Provided also that under-representation of any class or area in the service of Pakistan may be redressed in such manner as may be determined by an Act of Majlis-e-Shoora (Parliament).
>
> (2)   Nothing in clause (1) shall prevent any Provincial Government, or any local or other authority in a Province, from prescribing, in relation to any post or class of service under that Government or authority, conditions as to residence in the Province, for a period not exceeding three years, prior to appointment under that Government or authority."

39.   Almost similar provisions in the earlier constitutions of Pakistan and Article 16 of the Constitution of India, 1950 are as follows:

Constitution of Pakistan, 1956

Article 17

(1) No citizen otherwise qualified for appointment in the service of Pakistan shall be discriminated against in respect of any such appointment on the ground only of race, religion, caste, sex, residence or place of birth:

> Provided that for a period of fifteen years from the Constitution Day, posts may be reserved for persons belonging to any class or area to secure their adequate representation in the service of Pakistan.
>
> Provided further that in the interest of the said service, specified posts or services may be reserved for members of either sex.

(2) Nothing in clause (1) shall prevent any Provincial Government or any local or other authority from prescribing, in relation to any class of service under that Government or authority, conditions as to residence in the Province prior to appointment under that Government or authority.

Constitution of Pakistan, 1962

Article 6

2. Equality of Citizens.

All citizens should be equal before the law, be entitled to equal protection of the law and be treated alike in all respects.

This Principle may be departed from where -

In the interest of equality itself, it is necessary to compensate for existing inequalities, whether natural, social, economic or of any other kind;

In the interest of the proper discharge of public functions, it is necessary -

To give to persons performing public functions powers, protections or facilities that are not given to other persons; or

To impose on persons performing public functions obligations or disciplinary controls that are not imposed on other persons; or

It is necessary in the interest of the security of Pakistan or otherwise in the interest of the State to depart from this Principle,

But, where this Principle is departed from, it should be ensured that no citizen gets an undue preference over another citizen and no citizen is placed under a disability, liability or obligation that does not apply to other citizens of the same category.

This Principle shall not be construed as preventing a legislature from making laws different from laws made by any other legislature.

6. Freedom to Follow Vocation.

No law should impose any restriction on the freedom of a citizen to engage in any profession, trade, business, occupation or employment, or otherwise to follow the vocation of his choice.

This Principle may be departed from where it is necessary so to do-

In the interest of the security of Pakistan;

In the interest of decency or morality;

For the purpose of regulating, in the public interest, any profession or trade by a licensing system;

For the purpose of ensuring, in the public interest, that, where a profession or trade requires special qualifications or skill, only persons possessing those qualifications or that skill engage in the profession or trade;

For the purpose of ensuring, in the public interest, that a trade, business, industry or service may be carried on by or on behalf of the State or an organ of the State to the exclusion, in whole or in part, of other persons; or

For the purpose of ensuring, in the public interest, the development of Pakistan and of its resources and industries.

Interim Constitution of Pakistan, 1972

24. Safeguard against discrimination in services and elective offices. - (1) No citizen otherwise qualified for appointment in the service of Pakistan shall be discriminated against in respect of any such appointment on the ground only of race, religion, caste, sex, residence or place of birth:

Provided that, for a period not exceeding ten years from the commencing day, posts may be reserved for persons belonging to any class or area to secure their adequate representation in the service of Pakistan:

Provided further that, in the interest of the said service, specified posts or services may be reserved for members of either sex if such posts or services entail the performance of duties and functions which cannot be adequately performed by members of the other sex:

(2) Nothing in this Article shall prevent any Provincial Government, or any local or other authority in a Province, from prescribing, in relation to any class of service under that Government

or authority, conditions as to residence in the Province, for a period not exceeding three years, prior to appointment under that Government or authority."

Constitution of India, 1950

16.   Equality of opportunity in matters of public employment. -

(1)   There shall be equality of opportunity for all citizens in matters relating to employment or appointment to any office under the State.

(2)   No citizen shall, on grounds only of religion, race, caste, sex, descent, place of birth, residence or any of them, be ineligible for, or discriminated against in respect of, any employment or office under the State.

(3)   Nothing in this article shall prevent Parliament from making any law prescribing, in regard to a class or classes of employment or appointment to an office under the Government of, or any local or other authority within, a State or Union territory, any requirement as to residence within that State or Union territory prior to such employment or appointment.

(4)   Nothing in this article shall prevent the State from making any provision for the reservation of appointments or posts in favour of any backward class of citizens which, in the opinion of the State, is not adequately represented in the services under the State.

(4A)   Nothing in this article shall prevent the State from making any provision for reservation in matters of promotion, with consequential seniority, to any class or classes of posts in the services under the State in favour of the Scheduled Castes and the Scheduled Tribes which, in the opinion of the State, are not adequately represented in the services under the State.

(4B)   Nothing in this article shall prevent the State from considering any unfilled vacancies of a year which are reserved for being filled up in that year in accordance with any provision for reservation made under clause (4) or clause (4A) as a separate class of vacancies to be filled up in any succeeding year or years and such class of vacancies shall not be considered together with the vacancies of the year in which they are being filled up for determining the ceiling of fifty per cent reservation on total number of vacancies of that year.

(5)   Nothing in this article shall affect the operation of any law which provides that the incumbent of an office in connection with the affairs of any religious or denominational institution or any member of the governing body thereof shall be a person professing a particular religion or belonging to a particular denomination."

40.   We entertain no doubt that the questions raised in the constitutional petitions under adjudication in these proceedings relate to enforcement of fundamental rights of the citizens. We are also convinced that the questions raised are of public importance as their impact is sure to be *substantial, broad-based, transcending the litigation-interests of the parties and bearing upon the public interest. The fact that petitioners are few in number is certain to be neutralized by the potential consequences of decision in these cases. These likely consequences have persuaded us to hold that*

the questions raised are of public importance. We, therefore, hold that these
petitions are maintainable under Article 184(3) of the Constitution.

41.   After admitting the petitions for regular hearing, we directed the respondents to file concise statements. For the purpose of brevity, we summarize hereinbelow main points raised by the petitioners against reservation of quota on the basis of place of residence, religion, sex and disability. We first note one thing which is common in all these statements. That common thing is the expiry of the period for which posts could be reserved for a class or area to ensure its adequate representation in the service of Pakistan. It has been argued that the prohibition against adverse discrimination in the matter of otherwise qualified citizens for appointment in the service of Pakistan on the ground only of race, religion, caste, sex, residence or place of birth under Article 27 (1) of the Constitution is absolute and non-violable. The first proviso to that Article originally allows only reservation of posts in the service of Pakistan for a period not exceeding ten years from the commencing day for persons belonging to any class or area to secure its adequate representation. Article 265(2) of the Constitution has declared 14th of August, 1973 as the 'commencing day'. Thus, the period of 10 years specified in the first proviso to Article 27 (1) came to an end on 13th of August, 1983 but on that date the Constitution was in abeyance because of the Proclamation of the fifth day of July, 1977. The Constitution of 1973 was revived in 1985 through the Revival of the Constitution of 1973 Order, 1985 (President's Order No. 14 of 1985). Entry appearing at serial number 4 of the Schedule to the said Order substituted the word "ten" in the first proviso to Article 27 (1) with the word "twenty". The period of twenty years elapsed on 13.08.1993. This period of twenty years was later substituted with a period of forty years vide Section 2 of the Constitution (Sixteenth Amendment) Act, 1999, reproduced below:

> **"2.   Amendment   of   Article   27   of   the   Constitution.**
> In the Constitution of the Islamic Republic of Pakistan, in Article 27, in clause (1), in the first proviso for the word "twenty" the word "forty" shall be substituted and shall be deemed always to have been so substituted."

42.   Statement of objects and reasons of the Constitution (Sixteenth Amendment) Act, 1999 reads as under:

> "Article   27   of   the   constitution   provides   safeguards   against discrimination   in   services.   In   order   to   provide   opportunity   and representation to all classes of persons and areas in services, clause (1) of the said Article provides that for a period not exceeding twenty years from the commencing day of the Constitution, certain posts may be reserved for persons belonging to any class or areas. It has been felt that since equal opportunity of education and other facilities are not yet available to all citizens of Pakistan, the period of twenty years specified in clause (1) of Article 27 ibid be extended to forty years.
> The Bill seeks to achieve the aforesaid object."

43.   It has been pointed out that the said period of forty years expired on 13th of August, 2013 whereafter there is no constitutional sanction for reservation of posts for persons belonging to any class or area in the service of Pakistan even if that class or area has inadequate representation in the service of Pakistan. Even during currency of the said period of forty years, adverse discrimination on the basis of race, religion, caste, sex, or place of residence or place of birth was not permissible. Posts could legitimately be reserved for a class but a class could not be defined on the criteria of race, religion, caste, sex, place of residence or place of birth, it has been asserted. It has further been averred that adequate representation of persons belonging to an area in the service of Pakistan may allow prescription of residence for a reasonable period in that area a necessary qualification for availing the benefits of reservation of posts but place of birth cannot be allowed to be taken as material and determinant factor in the matter of determination of residence. It is

195

claimed that reservation of quotas for persons belonging to various areas in the service of Pakistan after 13th of August, 2013 is void and of no legal effect being in violation of the fundamental right guaranteed by Article 27 of the Constitution. As the argument of expiry of the constitutionally sanctioned period for reservation of posts for persons belonging to classes and areas is common, therefore, we will read this argument in respect of all petitions under adjudication in these proceedings.

44.   The second common argument of the petitioners relates to the definition of class. It has been submitted that the Black's Law Dictionary, 8th Edition defines class in these words:

> "class, n.1. A group of people, things, qualities, or activities that have common characteristics or attributes <a class of common-stock shares> <the upper-middle class>.
>
> protected class. A class of people who benefit from protection by statute, such as Title VII of the Civil Rights Act of 1964, which prohibits discrimination based on race, sex, national origin, or religion. [Cases: Civil Rights 1007, 1107, 1152, 1165. C.J.S. Civil Rights §§ 2–5, 7–9, 11–13, 18, 22, 26–27, 30–31, 33–37, 41–42, 44, 67, 88.]".

https://www.yourdictionary.com/class has given the following definition of class:

> 1. "a number of people or things grouped together because of certain likenesses or common traits; kind; sort; category
> 2. *a group of people considered as a unit according to economic, occupational, or social status; esp., a social rank or caste:* the working **class**, the middle **class**
> 3. high social rank or caste
> 4. the division of society into ranks or castes."

45.   It has been argued that race, religion, caste, sex, residence or place of birth are such attributes which can be used to create classes but classification on these common attributes is not permissible to be made a ground for discrimination in the matter of appointments in the service of Pakistan. It is vehemently stressed that if immutable characteristics (characteristics impossible or difficult to change, such as race, gender, caste, religion, place of birth) are taken as grounds of classification, such classification in not a valid basis of denial of fundamental right of equality of opportunity and to have equal protection of law. Learned counsel for the petitioners do not object to classification on the basis of educational, social and economic factors but are of the view that Article 27 (1) of the Constitution categorically rules out classification on any of the grounds enumerated in that Article. It has been submitted that holding otherwise would permanently deny citizens opportunity to realize their full potential and enjoy status, power, economic gains and opportunity of public service which flow from employment in the service of Pakistan as they will be discriminated against on the basis of immutable characteristics. The learned counsels say that the use of the expression "on the ground only of" in Article 27 (1) of the Constitution needs to be given full effect. In this regard, they have referred to paragraph 655 of the judgment of the Hon'ble Supreme Court of India in Indra Sawhney etc. Vs Union of India and others etc. (AIR 1993 SC 477, 1992 Supp 2 SCR 454), reproduced below:

> "655. Would the consequences be different if race, religion or caste etc. are coupled with some other factors? In other words, what is the effect of the word, 'only' in Article 16(2). In the context it has been used it operates, both, as permissive and prohibitive. It is permissive when State action, legislative or executive, is founded on any ground other than race, religion or caste. Whereas it is prohibitive if it is based exclusively on any of the grounds mentioned in Article 16(2). Javed Niaz Beg and Anr. v. Union of India and Anr., furnishes best illustration of the former. A notification discriminating between candidates of North Eastern States, Tripura, Manipur etc. on the one hand and others for IAS examination and exempting them from offering

language paper compulsory for everyone was upheld on linguistic concession. When it comes to any State action on race, religion or caste etc. the word, 'only' mitigates the constitutional prohibition. **That is if the action is not founded, exclusively, or merely, on that which is prohibited then it may not be susceptible to challenge.** What does it mean? Can a State action founded on race, religion, caste etc. be saved under Article 16(2) if it is coupled with any factor relevant or irrelevant? What is to be remembered is that the basic concept pervading the Constitution cannot be permitted to be diluted by taking cover under it. Use of word, 'only' was to avoid any attack on legitimate legislative action by giving it colour of race, religion or caste. At the same time, it cannot be utilised by the State to escape from the prohibition by taking recourse to such measures which are race, religion or caste-based by sprinkling it with something other as well. For instance, in State of Rajasthan v. Pradip Singh, , where exemption granted to Muslims and Harijans from levy of cost for stationing additional police force was attempted to be defended because the notification was not based 'only' on caste or religion but because persons belonging to these communities were found by the State not to have been guilty of the conduct which necessitated stationing of the police force it was struck down as discriminatory since it could not be shown by the State that there were no law abiding persons in other communities. Similarly, identification of backward class by such factors as dependence of group or collectivity on manual labour, lower age of marriage, poor schooling, living in kuccha house etc. and applying it to caste would be violative of Article 16(2) not only for being caste-based but also for violation of Article 14 because it excludes other communities in which same factors exist only because they are not Hindus. Further the group or collectivity, thus, determined would not be caste coupled with other but on caste and caste alone."

46.   The learned counsels for the petitioners contend that direct or indirect use of race, religion, caste, sex, residence or place of birth as a basis of classification for the purpose of appointment in the service of Pakistan has been prohibited by Article 27 (1) of the Constitution. They say that what is not allowed to be done directly is also not allowed to be done indirectly. The prohibition contained in Article 27 (1) of the Constitution cannot be bypassed under any pretext or on reasons in combination with race, religion, caste, sex, residence or place of birth.

47.   Learned counsels for the petitioners state that Article 27 (1) of the Constitution guarantees prohibition of adverse discrimination in the matter of appointments in the service of Pakistan to those citizens who are otherwise qualified for appointment. According to them, West's Encyclopedia of American Law, 2nd edition defines qualification in these words:

> "A particular attribute, quality, property, or possession that an individual must have in order to be eligible to fill an office or perform a public duty or function.
> For example, attaining the age of majority is a qualification that must be met before an individual has the capacity to enter into a contract.
> The term qualification also refers to a limitation or restriction that narrows the scope of language (such as that contained in a statute) that would otherwise carry a broader meaning."

48.   They also refer to the definition of 'qualification and 'qualified' given in the Black's Law Dictionary (8th ed. 2004), reproduced below:

> "QUALIFICATION

qualification. 1. The possession of qualities or properties (such as fitness or capacity) inherently or legally necessary to make one eligible for a position or office, or to perform a public duty or function <voter qualification requires one to meet residency, age, and registration requirements>. [Cases: Officers and Public Employees 35. C.J.S. Officers and Public Employees § 58.] 2. A modification or limitation of terms or language; esp., a restriction of terms that would otherwise be interpreted broadly <the contract contained a qualification requiring the lessor's permission before exercising the right to sublet>.3. CHARACTERIZATION (1). — qualify, vb.
QUALIFIED

qualified, adj.1. Possessing the necessary qualifications; capable or competent <a qualified medical examiner>.2. Limited; restricted <qualified immunity>. — qualify, vb."

49.   Relying upon https://thelawdictionary.org/qualifications/, the learned counsels say that 'qualifications' is the term that describes a person's attributes that are needed for a certain job or position. They argue that Article 18 of the Constitution guarantees that subject to such qualifications, if any, as may be prescribed by law, every citizen shall have the right to enter upon any lawful profession or occupation, and to conduct any lawful trade or business. They contend that service of Pakistan is a lawful profession. They say that education, experience, age, training, license of or registration with professional or regulatory bodies and recommendation of selection authority after due open competition may be termed as reasonable qualifications for the purpose of appointment in the service of Pakistan. The only other permissible qualification can be requirement of residence in a Province for a period not exceeding three years in respect of the provincial services and posts in connection with affairs of the Province or a bona fide occupational qualification, defined in the Black's Law Dictionary (8th ed. 2004) in the following words:
"BONA FIDE OCCUPATIONAL QUALIFICATION

bona fide occupational qualification. An employment qualification that, although it may discriminate against a protected class (such as sex, religion, or national origin), relates to an essential job duty and is considered reasonably necessary to the operation of the particular business. Such a qualification is not illegal under federal employment-discrimination laws. —

Abbr. BFOQ. [Cases: Civil Rights 1118, 1529. C.J.S. Civil Rights §§ 25, 161–162.]

"The bona fide occupational qualification is a complete defense. It is invoked when the defendant makes a distinction expressly forbidden by Title VII, such as the refusal to hire women or women with preschool-age children, the reassignment of pregnant employees, or the exclusion of particular ethnic groups from particular jobs.... The employer's motivation for excluding the protected class is not significant in evaluating the BFOQ defense. The inquiry focuses on the necessity of using an expressly forbidden classification. The fact that the employer adopted the exclusion for invidious reasons, rather than for the business consideration on which the defense is based, is not material. Thus, if the exclusion, in fact, is proved to be necessary it may be used, even if invidiously motivated." Mack A. Player, Employment Discrimination Law § 5.29, at 282–83 (1988)."

50.   It is argued that the phrase "otherwise qualified for appointment in the service of Pakistan" used in Article 27 (1) of the Constitution refers to qualifications, if any, prescribed by law, and prohibition of discrimination on the basis of race, religion, caste, sex, residence or place of birth necessarily implies that none of these attributes can be made a qualification

for appointment in the service of Pakistan. It is submitted that if a class is made on the basis of common attributes as enumerated in Article 27 (1) of the Constitution, it would amount to make the attribute used for classification a necessary qualification for appointment in the service of Pakistan. What is prohibited by Article 27 (1) of the Constitution is not the classification based upon race, religion, caste, sex, residence or place of birth but use of that classification in the matter of appointments in the service of Pakistan, it is pointed out. When a classification is made on the basis of prohibited grounds and that classification is used in the matter of appointments in the service of Pakistan it simply converts the common attribute used for classification into a necessary qualification for appointment. As the immutable characteristics such as race, caste, religion, place of birth and gender are impossible or extremely difficult to change, therefore, making them qualifications for appointment would amount to require the candidates to acquire a qualification which they are not able to acquire through use of labour, intelligence or with the help of anyone else. Such an arrangement is definite to frustrate efforts of individuals or communities to better their lots through obtaining their share from the national wealth as per their merit. Learned counsels for the petitioners term service of Pakistan national wealth to which every citizen has a fundamental right proportionate to his proven comparative merit.

51.	Learned counsels for the petitioners further contend that citizens deserve to be served by the best. They argue that efficiency and productivity of state machinery is adversely affected if less meritorious persons are preferred our those who are more meritorious. They assert that some posts require highest level of intelligence and skill and discrimination in favour of candidates inferior in talent and skill in the matter of appointments to these posts results into collective punishment to the whole society as the society stands deprived of the benefits it can have from the intelligence, labour and skills of best of the best. They contend that state is not debarred to invest for betterment of backward classes and to provide social security to the deserving but appointments in the service of Pakistan are not to be treated as social security or measures for protection of backward classes. An appointment in the service of Pakistan is a selection of a person to perform duties assigned to a post. Every appointment is directed for achievement of this goal. Economic gain, social status, power and opportunity to serve the nation are inevitably attached to appointments in the service of Pakistan but these are not the direct objective of selection of persons for appointment in the service of Pakistan. It is, therefore, in the fitness of things that the selection must be based only on the ability to perform as ascertained through open competitive process, free from reservations, the learned counsels plead.

52.	Learned counsels for the petitioners contend that no law can be made against provisions of the Constitution. They say that neither the Constitution nor the Civil Servants Act, 1973 and the Khyber Pakhtunkhwa Civil Servants Act, 1973 make possession of domicile of a particular area a condition-precedent for appointment in the service of Pakistan. What Article 27(2) of the Constitution allows is permission to a Provincial Government or any local or other authority in a Province to prescribe conditions as to residence in the Province, for a period not exceeding three years, prior to appointment under that Government or authority. They argue that domicile and residence are two different concepts. It is stated that by specifically mentioning conditions as to residence, any possibility for prescription of domicile as a qualification for appointment in the service of Pakistan has been ruled out as prescription of one is prohibition of another. It is claimed that the prescription of condition of possession of a valid domicile of a particular area for appointment in the service of Pakistan is a travel beyond the mandate given by Article 27 (2) of the Constitution and the Civil Servants Act, 1973 and the Khyber Pakhtunkhwa Civil Servants Act, 1973. It is claimed that the condition of domicile is, therefore, without backing of lawful authority and is of no legal effect in the matter of appointments for All Pakistan Services, services of the Federation and posts in connection with affairs of the Federation.

53.   The learned counsels contend that the Constitution allows reservation of posts for persons belonging to any class or area to secure their adequate representation in the service of Pakistan. Before reservation of posts for persons belonging to any class or area, the fact of inadequate representation of persons belonging to that class or area has to be established to the satisfaction of the concerned legislature. The permission of reservation of posts is only to ensure adequate representation and will cease to be available soon after achievement of the goal of that adequate representation. Reservation cannot be in excess of what is required to make representation of a class or an area adequate. Reservation of posts, therefore, can be transient and self-liquidating measure which has been allowed to compensate for lingering effects of past injustices to persons belonging to a class or area. The learned counsels argue that quota system was introduced in Pakistan by the first Prime Minister of Pakistan, Mr. Liaquat Ali Khan in civil service through an executive order dated 1st of September, 1948 with the reservation of posts in the civil service for various areas in the following ratio:

Areas	Percentage of population	Share in Quota (Percent)
East Bengal	56.75	42
West Punjab	28	24
Sindh, Balochistan, NWFP, Khairpur	14.05	17
Potential Migrants	Unknown	15
Karachi	1.2	2
Total	100	100

The above formula was substituted with the following quota system for the Central Superior Services in the year 1949:

East Bengal (40%)
Punjab and Bahawalpur (23%)
Merit (20%)
Sindh, Balochistan, NWFP and tribal agencies (15%)
Karachi (2%)

54.   Learned counsels for the petitioners assert that there was no enabling provision in the Government of India Act, 1935 as adopted through the Pakistan (Provisional Constitution) Order, 1947 which could allow reservation of posts for any class or area in the service of Pakistan. Later, Article 17 of the Constitution of Pakistan, 1956 allowed reservation of posts in the service of Pakistan for a class or area for a period of fifteen years only. In 1970, quota of Sindh was bifurcated into quota for urban and rural Sindh. The learned counsels argue that quota system is in operation since 1948 till date. They are of the view that existence of quota system for a period in excess of seventy years is more than enough to ensure adequate representation of persons belonging to any under-represented class or area. A temporary measure allowed to correct historical imbalances in representation of some classes or areas in the service of Pakistan must not be perpetuated so as to nullify the object of elimination of discrimination in the matter of appointments in the service of Pakistan. They say that meaningful efforts to ensure level playing field for all for seventy years must have made the quota system an ugly feature of our past. They advance the legal theory that extension in period of quota for any further period is likely to convert a transient self-liquidating measure into a permanent feature of the Constitution which runs counter to the constitutional spirit of equality of opportunity for all citizens in the matter of appointments in the service of Pakistan. They say that culture of spoon-feeding kills the spirit of competition which is the engine for growth, poverty-alleviation, institution-building and evolution of human society. The learned counsels prayer that quota system may be declared to be offensive to the fundamental principles on which our Constitution is based.

55. Learned counsels for the petitioners contend that each race, area, religion, caste and sex has persons and families who have sufficient resources at their disposal, enjoy best possible facilities and cannot be labelled backward socially, educationally, economically or on any other criteria. If posts are reserved for persons belonging to a class based on race, area, religion, caste and sex, the creamy layer of that class would reap the benefits of reservation and overwhelming majority of that class will continue to be deprived. If a class is defined on the basis of social, economic and educational status of citizens with adequate safeguards to exclude creamy layer therefrom, then reservation of posts for a bare minimum period may be beneficial for the backward. To illustrate, they refer to example of a resident of Balochistan who is appointed in the Pakistan Administrative Service or the Police Service of Pakistan against the quota reserved for Balochistan. He was affluent even before joining the service. Thereafter, his children are provided best education and other facilities to realize their full potential. The learned counsels question the wisdom of provision of spoon-feeding of quota to these children. They assert that such quota in fact perpetuates inequalities and breeds injustices without any material benefit to the majority or the country as a whole. The quota system, besides being without legally valid justification, is also offensive to reason and national policy objectives, the learned counsels argue. The learned counsels for the petitioners further contend that reservation of posts for backward classes is a known policy of the Indian Constitution but, save a few exceptions, requirement of residence has been dispensed with under the Public Employment (Requirement as to Residence) Act, 1957 and this was done to save the reservation policy from degenerating into a tool in the hands of the creamy layers to further consolidate and expand their gains.

56. Learned counsels for the petitioners contend that quota system, if based on the ground only of race, religion, caste, sex, residence or place of birth, is a collective punishment for competent persons belonging to a class which may be minority in numbers but may outperform other classes in knowledge and skills. The quota system limits prospects of growth and upward mobility of such minority despite its educational superiority over others, it is asserted. As quota reserved for merit is very limited, therefore, excellence of minority would be unable to guarantee its share in the service of Pakistan what is proportionate to its excellence, the learned counsels argue. In this way, the learned counsels allege, quota system perpetuates handicaps to excellence and merit in the matter of appointments in the service of Pakistan. Adequate representation in the service of Pakistan, the learned counsels assert, means representation directly proportionate to merit of a class and not number of members of a class. In this view of the matter, the learned counsels stress, quota system is not in interest of justice and national prosperity as it compromises ability of the nation to compete with other countries because of comparatively inferior manpower quality of those who transact the governmental business.

57. The learned counsels for the petitioners further argue that first proviso to Article 27 (1) of the Constitution speaks of inadequate representation with reference to appointments in the service of Pakistan. They say that appointments are made through initial recruitment, by promotion or transfer. They contend that where promotion is made on the basis of seniority, the quota for initial recruitment automatically gets reflected in posts reserved for promotion in a cadre. But in cases of promotion on the basis of selection on merit, representation at the stage of initial recruitment is likely to be disturbed as selection on merit would result into promotion of more meritorious persons in the service of Pakistan, it is stated. The learned counsels claim that promotions by the Government of Khyber Pakhtunkhwa and the Government of Pakistan in basic pay scale 19 and above are exclusively based on the principle of selection on merit and quota system is not applicable on promotions. It is claimed that non-application of quota system on promotion is attributed to the requirement of administrative efficiency as only more meritorious officers are expected to perform better and better performance is deemed to be in public interest. The learned counsels contend that quota system is also not applied to appointment by transfer on the ground of administrative efficiency. The counsels contend that the argument of

201

administrative efficiency is applicable to initial recruitments also and the same argument must be used to substitute quota-based system with a merit-driven system for initial recruitments in the service of Pakistan. They pray that quota system be declared incompatible with fundamental constitutional values which put premium on equality, merit, performance and excellence.

58.   After the above summary of common points raised in the written statements of the petitioners and oral submissions of their counsels, we may now give a curious look to specific points raised by each petitioner and his counsel.

59.   The following arguments specific to various petitions have been submitted:

Case of Mr. Noor Alam Khan Wazir

a) The case falls within the category of discrimination in the matter of appointments in the service of Pakistan on the basis of residence as ascertained through the domicile of the candidate. Such discrimination is constitutionally invalid;

b) The requirement of domicile of the concerned Union Council or, in case of non-availability of a suitable candidate from the concerned Union Council, of the adjacent Union Council has no nexus or rational relationship with the requirement to ensure adequate representation of a class or area in the service of Pakistan;

c) The policy of appointment of primary school teachers on the basis of residence has statutorily been adopted for the stated purpose of ensuring availability of teachers in the schools. The purpose behind the policy is to neutralize administrative and political pressures which the teachers exert to get them transferred to schools nearest to their residences to get rid of fatigue caused by and the expenditure to be incurred on travelling. Posting / transfer is not a right of an employee. The administration has to achieve administrative discipline and efficiency keeping in view the constitutional requirements. No fundamental right of citizens, including right not to be discriminated against on impermissible grounds in the matter of appointments in the service of Pakistan, can be taken away on the pretext of ensuring presence of teachers in schools;

d) Whereas discrimination on the basis of domicile of a candidate is prohibited, there is no legal infirmity in school-specific appointments. In case of school-specific appointments, all eligible and willing residents of the Province can compete for appointment against any post in a school but once appointed transfer would not be permissible, save on just exceptions to be statutorily determined. Thus, the policy objective of ensuring presence of teachers in schools is achievable without abridgment of fundamental right of the citizens not to be discriminated against in the matter of appointments in the service of Pakistan on the basis of place of birth or residence; and

e) Section 3 of the Khyber Pakhtunkhwa (Appointment, Deputation, Posting and Transfer of Teachers, Lecturers, Instructors and Doctors) Regulatory Act, 2011 and provisions of the recruitment policy of the Government of Khyber Pakhtunkhwa relating to recruitment of teachers on the basis of domicile of a particular district, Union Council or constituency of the Provincial Assembly are void and of no legal effect being in violation of Article 27 of the Constitution.

Case of Dr. Waleed Ahmad

a) Peshawar is capital of Khyber Pakhtunkhwa. It has more healthcare facilities in the public sector than any other district in the Province. Number of posts in these healthcare facilities is higher than posts in any other district. Number of posts in healthcare facilities in Peshawar is higher than what should be its share on the basis of size of its population. As a result, condition of domicile of Peshawar district for being eligible to compete for appointment as doctor on ad hoc basis causes adverse discrimination against willing and qualified doctors of all other districts in the Province;

b) The object of recruitment of doctors on ad hoc basis is to select best doctors for provision of professional medical services. A classification based upon domicile of a district has no nexus with the object intended to be achieved. The Hon'ble Supreme Court of India has held in Minor P. Rajendran Vs. State of Madras & Ors (1968 AIR 1012) that:

> "We may add that we do not mean to say that territorial classification is always bad under all circumstances. But there is no doubt that district-wise classification which is being justified on territorial basis in these cases is violative of Art. 14, for no justification worth the name in support of the classification has been made out."

Case of Mr. Allah Ditta

Besides being ultra vires Article 27(2) of the Constitution, restriction of recruitment of constables to holders of domicile of the concerned district does not ensure representation of all districts in the police force proportionate to their populations as number of vacancies of police constables in a district is not based upon population of the district; hence, a constitutionally prohibited adverse discrimination ensues which cannot be allowed to persist.

Case of Mr. Shahzad Ahmad Khan Bangash

a) The Khyber Pakhtunkhwa Civil Servants Act, 1973 does not provide for zonal or divisional representation in the matter of appointments in the services of the Province and posts in connection with affairs of the Province. In absence of such a provision in the parent statute, the rules framed under the said Act are not allowed to provide which has not been provided in the Act. Rules provide procedure and are incapable of creation of substantive rights or disabilities;

b) Zonal quota has not been fixed statutorily. The object of determination of zonal quota cannot lawfully be achieved through executive instructions; and

c) In view of definition of bona fide residence given in Corpus Juris Secundum, Volume 28, page 5, the condition of bona fide residence in the Province imposed on candidates for appointment vide Rule 11(1) of the Khyber Pakhtunkhwa Civil Servants (Appointment, Promotion and Transfer) Rules, 1989 means the residence with domiciliary intent. It has been held in Viggiano v. Civ. Serv. Com., City of Phila, 74 Pa. Commw. 191, (Pa. Cmmw. Ct. 1983) and McCarthy v. Philadelphia Civil Service Commission, 19 Pa. Commw. 383, 339 A.2d 634 (1975), aff'd, 424 U.S. 645 (1976) that bona fide residence is synonymous with domicile or sole legal residence. Article 27(2) of the Constitution does not allow imposition of the condition of domicile in the matter of appointments in the services of a Province or posts in connection with affairs of a Province. The said Article only allows condition of residence in the Province for a prescribed minimum duration prior to appointment and limits the maximum duration to be prescribed not to exceed three years. Thus, the Article 27(2) of the Constitution speaks of durational residence and not of domiciliary residence.

Case of Mr. Jamal Akhtar

Rejection of application of Mr. Jamal Akhtar on the ground that he is not a resident of the area in which the concerned office exists is discrimination on the basis of residence. As he is resident of the Province, therefore, his candidature cannot be rejected on the basis of his residence in another local area. Moreover, there is no definition of a local area in the Khyber Pakhtunkhwa Civil Servants Act, 1973 and the rules framed thereunder. The Khyber Pakhtunkhwa Local Government Act, 2013 defines local area in these words:

"For the purpose of this Act Village, Neighbourhood, Tehsil, Town, District and City District shall be local areas for local governments."

In absence of a legal definition of local area under the Khyber Pakhtunkhwa Civil Servants Act and the rules framed thereunder, the condition of residence in a local area is unenforceable being vague and imprecise. State employees cannot be given unfettered discretion in the matter of fundamental rights of citizens through resorting to definitions to suit their personal liking and disliking as has been done in the instant case.

Case of Mr. Ghulam Safdar Shah

Second proviso to Article 27 (1) of the Constitution allows reservation of posts for a particular sex in cases of posts or services which entail the performance of duties and functions which cannot be adequately performed by members of the other sex. A determination and declaration must precede reservation of quota for women that the duties assigned to the posts cannot adequately be performed by males. In absence of such a declaration, posts cannot be reserved for females. In the instant case, quota for women has been fixed without any declaration that the duties of the posts can only be satisfactorily performed by women. Moreover, Article 25(2) of the Constitution command that there shall be no discrimination on the basis of sex. Reservation of quota for women in the service of Pakistan is a discrimination on the basis of sex. What needs to be understood is the reality that the Article 25(2) of the Constitution has prohibited discrimination on the basis of sex and any discrimination shall be in favour of one sex at the cost of the other sex. Thus, the question of adverse or protective and benevolent discrimination is of no practical implication so far as prohibition of discrimination on the basis of sex in the matter of appointments in the service of Pakistan is concerned.

Case of Mr. Raheel Ahmad Siddiqui

a) To treat religious minorities a separate class for the purpose of reservation of quota for them for appointments in the service of

Pakistan is discrimination on the basis of religion which has been prohibited by Article 27 (1) of the Constitution;

b) The quota reserved for minorities far exceeds the share proportionate to their population. Whereas minorities are 0.29 per cent of the total population of the province, the quota reserved for them is 5%. Thus, the quota cannot be taken as a measure to compensate for their under representation in the service of Pakistan but is a tool to ensure their over representation in the service of Pakistan. Thus, the quota is against the intents and purposes of first proviso to Article 27 (1) of the Constitution which allows the concept of reservation of posts for persons belonging to a class or area to ensure their adequate representation in the service of Pakistan; and

c) Preamble to our Constitution declares that provision shall be made to safeguard the legitimate interests of minorities and backward and depressed classes. Article 36 of the constitution commands that the State shall safeguard the legitimate rights and interests of minorities, including their due representation in the Federal and Provincial services. These noble goals are allowed to be achieved without adverse or protective discrimination on the basis of religion. Discrimination on the basis of religion is not necessary to safeguard legitimate interests of the minorities. Short of resorting to discrimination on the ground of religion, state is free to take all measures deemed necessary and expedient for welfare of the minorities and protection of their legitimate interests.

Case of Mr. Ali Raza

a) Reservation of 25% posts in B.S. 1 to B.S. 4 for children of civil servants retired on superannuation or invalidation is a discrimination not on the basis of race, religion, caste, sex, residence or place of birth but the classification is irrelevant to the purpose of recruitment in the service of Pakistan. A classification cannot be termed lawful unless there is a nexus between the classification and object to be achieved. Appointments are made to select best candidates for performance of duties assigned to a post. Reservation of posts for retired civil servants has no nexus with the objective to be achieved through appointments in the service of Pakistan. The reservation is legally invalid as it is based on irrelevant grounds; and

b) The Khyber Pakhtunkhwa Civil Servants Act, 1973 and the rules framed thereunder do not provide for reservation of quotas on the basis of profession or employment of parents of the candidates aspiring to join service in BS. 12 to BS.4. Mere executive instructions are not a lawful instrument to introduce the concept of reservation of certain posts for children of retired civil servants.

Case of Mr. Qaiser Shah

Reservation of posts for disable persons results into denial of opportunity to healthy and fit persons to serve the society. The state is at liberty to take whatever measures it wants to facilitate or subsidize dignified living of those suffering from bodily infirmities or mental illnesses but it has no right to through away public jobs on account of its misplaced sympathy for persons with disabilities who lack capacity to efficiently perform duties attached with posts in connection with affairs of the Province.

Case of Mr. Johnson Bernard

Grant of additional marks on account of memorization of the Holy Quran while ascertaining relative merit of a candidate in the matter of his appointment in the services of the Province or posts in connection with affairs of the Province is an example of discrimination on the basis of religion. Non-Muslim candidates are thrown out of competition when a memorizer of the Holy Quran competes with them. No comparative advantage on account of proficiency in religious knowledge is extended to non-Muslim candidates. This discrimination is void being in violation of Article 27 (1) of the Constitution.

Case of Mr. Yasir Qayum Khan

a) Article 18 of the Constitution requires prescription of qualifications for a profession through law. Service of Pakistan is a lawful profession. Law means enactment of the Parliament in respect of All Pakistan Services, services of the Federation and posts in connection with affairs of the Federation. The law applicable to the case of Mr. Yasir Qayum Khan is the Civil Servants Act, 1973. This law does not prescribe the condition of nationality of Pakistan or domicile of Pakistan for joining an All Pakistan Service or a Service of the Federation or for holding a post in connection with affairs of the Federation. Such conditions cannot be prescribed through rules which are meant to be procedural in nature;

b) Whereas Rule 14 of the Civil Servants (Appointment, Promotion and Transfer) Rules, 1973 provides for filling of all posts in basic pay scales 16 and above and equivalent in accordance with the merit and provincial or regional quotas prescribed by Government from time to time, no provision in these rules provide for quota on gender basis. Thus, 10% quota reserved for women is without backing of the rules;

c) Quota for various regions has not been statutorily fixed. It has not been fixed even through rules. Delegation of power to the Government to do so without spelling out legislative policy amounts to abdication of legislative power which is prohibited;

d) Practical abandonment of the principle of merit in the matter of appointments in the service of Pakistan has cost the nation very dearly, administrative efficiency being the first casualty. Absence of administrative efficiency limits citizens' right to live and enjoy a dignified life and does not ensure proper return on tax payers' money; and

e) The quota system has become a permanent feature of our national life and is just like opium influence of which has disabled the desire to summon the best in the nation to provide all areas similar infrastructure and facilities for full realization of potential of all the citizens. The sooner we get rid of quota, the better.

60.   The leaned Advocate General, Khyber Pakhtunkhwa and the learned Attorney General for Pakistan explained concise statements of the Province of Khyber Pakhtunkhwa and the Federation of Pakistan respectively. Main points of these statements are as follows:

a) It is utterly misconceived that reservation of posts for persons belonging to a class or area automatically results into slaughter of merit and absence of competence. Quota system limits competition within persons belonging to the specified class or area but the persons aspiring to compete must compulsorily possess basic eligibility in terms of education, training, experience, age, professional certification etc. Thus, only those who meet the eligibility criteria are allowed to apply for quota reserved for any class or area. Then follows a fair competition among the candidates belonging to the specified class or area. Only those are selected for appointment who cross the threshold requirements and the candidates who fail to qualify this test of minimum competence are rejected. Ability to successfully meet the minimum standards of selection process is a reliable assurance that the selected candidates have the requisite competence to efficiently perform duties assigned to posts. Brilliance required to conceive theory of relativity or excellence needed for discovery and invention is obviously not expected from a state employee whose role is of executive nature and this role can satisfactorily be performed if the selected candidate possess prudence of an ordinary man.

b) Equal opportunity or equality of opportunity in the matter of appointments in the service of Pakistan means that citizens must be able to compete on equal terms or on a level playing field and careers be open to talent alone. To achieve this objective, the Constitution has neutralized factors of race, religion, caste, sex, residence or place of birth by prohibiting discrimination on the basis of these factors. On the other hand, our Constitution has based its theory of equality of opportunity on a justified presumption that equality between unequals or one law for the lion and the ox is oppression. Social and economic background of a citizen decisively affects his prospects to acquire qualifications and competencies to get success in competition for appointment in the service of Pakistan. Past or present differences in social and economic status of citizens are of such material importance that an open competition is sure to result into inhuman perpetuation of dominance of those who have over those who do not. Employment in the service of Pakistan offers social and economic benefits. Classes of citizens that have adequate representation in the service of Pakistan have a definitive competitive edge over those classes that are under-represented in the service of Pakistan. It is necessary to give fair access to opportunities to qualifications to underrepresented classes to make the equality of opportunity substantive and just. The process to ensure provision of equal facilities to the classes underrepresented in the service of Pakistan takes considerable time. Till the nation achieves its goal to provide equal educational and other facilities to all the citizens, those who are socially, economically and educationally inferior to others be protected through quota system. This protective discrimination is not against the idea of equality of opportunity but is a necessary transient measure to make the equality of opportunity fair and real for all. This is a tool to help those who legitimately need help to have real chance of getting their share in the national wealth coming from their adequate representation in the service of Pakistan. Equal opportunity in its literal form, un-mitigated by temporary protective shield of reservation of quota for those who have been rendered uncompetitive by centuries of discrimination, deprivation and degradation, would be a guaranteed way to legitimize inequalities on permanent basis. Emphasis on equality of opportunity does not require mere verbal gymnastics or empty slogans or an orator's rhetoric; it needs concrete measures of which quota system is a perfect transient option. Intent and purpose of Article 27(1) of the Constitution and its first proviso is the same; both are for ensuring fair equality of opportunity to all citizens in the matter of appointments in the service of Pakistan. Quota for the backward classes is the necessary and unavoidable cost the nation has to pay for some time in order to put in place a real and fair system to ensure equality of opportunity. In the words of Judge Tanaka of the International Court of Justice:

> ".... The principle is that what is equal is to be treated equally and what is different is to be treated differently, namely proportionately to the factual difference. This is what was indicated by Aristotle as justitia commutative and justitia distributiva.
>
> ...the principle of equality before the law does not mean the absolute equality, namely equal treatment of men without regard to individual concrete circumstances, but it means the relative equality, namely the principle to treat equally what are equal and unequally what are unequal.
>
> .... To treat unequal matters differently according to their inequality is not only permitted but required...."
> (South West Africa Cases (Second Phase), ICJ Rep. p. 6, 305-6.)

It has been held by the Hon'ble Supreme Court of India in Ahmedabad St. Xavier's College Society and Anr. Vs. State of Gujarat ([1975] 1 SCR 173) that:

> "It is obvious that "equality in law precludes discrimination of any kind; whereas equality, in fact, may involve the necessity of differential treatment in order to attain a result which establishes an equilibrium between different situations."

Article 27(1) of the Constitution and its first proviso have to be read together to make up the ideal of equality effective and real. Article 27(1) of the Constitution does not prohibit discrimination in the matter of appointments in the service of Pakistan in its entirety; it only prohibits discrimination on the ground only of race, religion, caste, sex, residence or place of birth. Discrimination on other grounds is not prohibited. What first proviso to Article 27 (1) allows is essentially discrimination on grounds other than those listed in the said Article 27(1). In this view of the matter, reservation of posts in the service of Pakistan for backward classes and areas for a defined period fits well in the constitutional scheme of fair equality of opportunity for all citizens.

c) As regards expiry of the period of 40 years specified in first proviso to Article 27 (1) of the Constitution, the Court is expected to exercise judicial restraint and may not strike down quota system as it will result into catastrophic consequences and may cause anarchy and widespread unrest which has the potential to escalate to violent protests by the classes likely to be adversely affected by discontinuation of the quota system. The court has exercised judicial restraint in countless cases of national importance.

d) The Constitution envisages rules of business for the federal and provincial governments. Subjects within jurisdictions of the respective governments are assigned to various entities of those governments.

Business relating to those subjects is transacted by the concerned entities. Whereas some may see legislation a preferred way of conferring executive powers and regulating their exercise, it is not unconstitutional to take actions in absence of a law on the subject. Legislative and executive powers are co-extensive. The executive can exercise executive powers on any subject which falls within legislative competence of the concerned legislature even in absence of enabling legislation. Fixation of quota through executive orders is, therefore, not unconstitutional or illegal or irregular merely on the ground that it has not been provided for or fixed by the concerned legislature through a proper enactment.

e) Rules framed under a law are not required to be explanatory or procedural in nature. The rules can create substantive rights or impose duties on the citizens if the rules are in furtherance of the objects and purposes of the main statute and are supplementary in nature and are not intended to supplant the main statute. Moreover, executive orders cannot be issued in contravention of the statutory rules but these could be issued to supplement the statutory rules. Thus, fixation of quota through executive orders is lawful.

f) Article 34 of the Constitution commands that steps shall be taken to ensure full participation of women in all spheres of national life. Women form a class as distinguished from men who form another class. Though like men, women are a multiclass sex, yet they are not adequately represented in the service of Pakistan when compared with representation of men. In this sense, women form a distinct class which needs to be favoured through appropriate protective discrimination in order to ensure its adequate representation in the service of Pakistan. Women are treated as a class not because of gender but because of educational, social and economic backwardness of women and, hence, prohibition of discrimination is not attracted in case of reservation of posts in the service of Pakistan for women. The same argument is applicable to classification on grounds of religion and disability.

g) Pakistan is a federal republic. Article 37(f) of the Constitution directs the state to enable the people of different areas, through education, training, agricultural and industrial development and other methods, to participate fully in all forms of national activities, including employment in the service of Pakistan. Article 38(g) orders to ensure that the shares of the Provinces in all Federal services, including autonomous bodies and corporations established by, or under the control of, the Federal Government, shall be secured and any omission in the allocation of the shares of the Provinces in the past shall be rectified. Reservation of quota for different areas in the service of Pakistan is essential for national integrity and balanced development of all areas of the country.

h) Residence and domicile are identical concepts. Article 27(2) of the Constitution expressly authorizes the Provinces and their authorities to prescribe the condition of residence in the concerned Province as a condition-precedent for being eligible to apply to compete to join provincial services or hold posts in connection with affairs of the Provinces. Similar power is inherently available to the Federation which is fully competent to prescribe the condition of domicile of a particular area as a necessary qualification for appointment in the service of Pakistan.

i) The argument that a creamy layer of classes for which posts are reserved in the service of Pakistan snatches away the benefits of reservation applies with equal force to the selection based upon open competition. In open competition, it is usually the creamy layer of society which succeeds in reaping the fruits of merit-based appointments in the service of Pakistan. Unless man develops a system which neutralizes all factors except ability and effort of a citizen, we have to accept and live with the reality that those who are better positioned to acquire requisite qualifications will continue to outperform others.

j) As initial recruitment against reserved posts enables promotion on seniority-cum-fitness basis, therefore, similar ratio is automatically maintained in appointments made through promotion. Such ratio may disturb in case of posts to be filled in through promotion by selection on merit. As reservation of quota in promotion has not been deemed appropriate, therefore, the same has expressly been rejected in the applicable policies. The question, being a question of policy, does not fall within jurisdiction of the court which does not need to be answered by the court being a moot question.

61. Specific arguments given by the respondents in respect of individual cases are as follows:

Case of Mr. Noor Alam Khan Wazir

a) All eligible residents of a Union Council are entitled to compete for appointment as primary school teacher; hence, there is no discrimination between similarly placed candidates belonging to the concerned Union Council. Candidates belonging to other Union Councils have similar rights in the matter of appointment as primary school teachers in their respective Union Councils;

b) The object of recruitment of primary school teachers having domicile of the concerned Union Council is to ensure availability of teachers in the schools. Thus, the condition of domicile of the respective Union Council has direct and rational nexus to the objective intended to be achieved;

c) Exigencies of service and public interest make imperfect pragmatism preferable over legal or intellectual perfection. Though posting / transfer is a matter of administrative discretion and not a right of an employee, yet the administration is unable to resist political and other pressures. Experience has taught that a statutory provision for recruitment of local residents as primary school teachers is of great help in ensuring availability of teachers in the schools. Seeing positive effect of the policy, it has been further fine-tuned and now recruitments are being made which are school-specific and non-transferable;

d) Allowing all eligible persons domiciled in the Province to compete for all jobs wherever they may be in the Province would cause problems which are feared to adversely affect fundamental right of the citizens guaranteed by Article 25A of the Constitution; and

e) Section 3 of the Khyber Pakhtunkhwa (Appointment, Deputation, Posting and Transfer of Teachers, Lecturers, Instructors and Doctors) Regulatory Act, 2011 and provisions of the recruitment policy of the Government of Khyber Pakhtunkhwa relating to recruitment of teachers on the basis of domicile of a particular district, Union Council or constituency of the Provincial Assembly are not in violation of Article 27 of the Constitution and are, therefore, valid.

Case of Dr. Waleed Ahmad

a) Purpose of the Khyber Pakhtunkhwa (Appointment, Deputation, Posting and Transfer of Teachers, Lecturers, Instructors and Doctors) Regulatory Act, 2011, inter alia, is to ensure presence of doctors in the hospitals. Recruitments from amongst the eligible candidates belonging to the district in which hospitals situate ensures that the doctors recruited devote themselves to duty instead of going from pillar to post to get themselves transferred to district of their origin or of choice. Slight disproportionality of posts available in a district with the population of that district is necessary collateral abnormality which merits to be tolerated as the benefits of this dispensation outweigh the ill effects of the disproportionality.

b) Judgements of the Hon'ble Supreme Court of India and of any other foreign court are not legally binding on courts in Pakistan. Our courts have made no declaration against recruitments on the basis of domicile of the district in which a hospital exists. We have to make our own decisions keeping in view our peculiar facts and circumstances and the legal regime applicable thereto.

Case of Mr. Allah Ditta

As specified in Article 8(3) of the Constitution, the prohibitions contained in Article 8(1) & (2) are not applicable to members of the Armed Forces, or of the police or of such other forces as are charged with the maintenance of public order, for the purpose of ensuring the proper discharge of their duties or the maintenance of discipline among them. The Province is not debarred to make a law which may contain inconsistencies with any of the fundamental rights to the extent specified in Article 8(3) of the Constitution. Section 34 of the Khyber Pakhtunkhwa Police Act, 2017, therefore, can lawfully abridge fundamental right guaranteed by Article 27 of the Constitution in respect of police employees.

Case of Mr. Shahzad Ahmad Khan Bangash

Article 27(2) of the Constitution allows the Provincial Government, or any local or other authority in a Province, from prescribing, in relation to any post or class of service under that Government or authority, conditions as to residence in the Province, for a period not exceeding three years, prior to appointment under that Government or authority. The condition of domicile for appointment to provincial services or posts in connection with affairs of the Province has constitutional sanction and, therefore, cannot be attacked on any legal ground.

Case of Mr. Jamal Akhtar

Local area is so obvious expression that everyone has fair idea what it means in facts and circumstances of a case. If low-paid jobs in a locality are offered to those not belonging to that area, travel expenses will consume a lion's share of selected person's remuneration. This will not be in public interest for more reasons than one. Reservation of low-paid jobs for eligible local candidates is, therefore, justified as it is not only in public interest but has the cover of rule 12(3) of the Khyber Pakhtunkhwa Civil Servants (Appointment, Promotion and Transfer) Rules, 1989.

Case of Mr. Ghulam Safdar Shah

Equality clause enshrined in Article 25 of the Constitution does not preclude special measures to be taken for protection of women and children. Further, Article 34 of the Constitution commands that steps shall be taken to ensure full participation of women in all spheres of national life. Reservation of quota for women in the service of Pakistan is a special measure for protection of women which also ensures the purpose of their full participation in national life. This quota is, therefore, not exceptionable on any legal ground.

Case of Mr. Raheel Ahmad Siddiqui

Besides making special efforts for protecting and promoting legitimate interests of the religious minorities through education, training and socio-economic development, it is also deemed necessary for national integration that religious minorities be given adequate representation in the service of Pakistan. Reservation of quota for religious minorities is a protective discrimination to ensure adequate representation of the minorities. This noble cause must not be allowed to be defeated on grounds of mere technicalities and unnecessary hair-splitting.

Case of Mr. Ali Raza

Reservation of 25% posts in B.S. 1 to B.S. 4 for children of civil servants retired on superannuation or invalidation is a welfare measure for low-paid employees. This measure is essential to boost morale of the employees and keep them motivated. There is no discrimination within the similarly placed retired civil servants. This benign discrimination is in public interest and must be allowed to be continued.

Case of Mr. Qaiser Shah

a) Disability is a reasonable basis to form a separate class. What is prohibited by Article 27 (1) of the Constitution is discrimination on the ground only of race, religion, caste, sex, residence or place of birth in the matter of appointments in the service of Pakistan. Other reasonable classifications are allowed and are part of constitutional scheme to ensure real and fair equality of opportunity. Moreover, Pakistan ratified the UN Convention on the Rights of Persons with Disabilities, 2006 (CRPD) in 2011 which promotes, protects and ensures full enjoyment of all human rights by all persons with disabilities, and promotes respect to their inherent human dignity. The CRPD provides that persons with disabilities include those who have long-term physical, mental, intellectual or sensory impairments which in interaction with various barriers may hinder their full and effective participation in society on an equal basis with others. Keeping in view disadvantages associated with disability in the matter of competing for appointments in the service of Pakistan, special quota for disable persons has statutorily been fixed under the Disabled Persons (Employment and Rehabilitation) Ordinance, 1981 and other special arrangements have been provided through the Special Citizens Act, 2008 (Act No. 24 of 2008). These measures are in line with international commitments of Pakistan and the objectives of our constitutional scheme; and

b) As per 1998 national census data, persons with disabilities constitute 2.49% of the population of Pakistan. The quota reserved for disables in the service of Pakistan is proportionate to their population.

Case of Mr. Johnson Bernard

Objectives Resolution envisions Pakistan as a country wherein the Muslims shall be enabled to order their lives in the individual and collective spheres in accordance with the teachings and requirements of Islam as set out in the Holy Quran and Sunnah. Article 31 of the Constitution gives the following principle of policy:

> (1) Steps shall be taken to enable the Muslims of Pakistan, individually and collectively, to order their lives in accordance with the fundamental principles and basic concepts of Islam and to provide facilities whereby they may be enabled to understand the meaning of life according to the Holy Quran and Sunnah.
>
> (2) The State shall endeavour, as respects the Muslims of Pakistan, —
>
>> (a) to make the teaching of the Holy Quran and Islamiat compulsory, to encourage and facilitate the learning of Arabic language and to secure correct and exact printing and publishing of the Holy Quran;
>>
>> (b) to promote unity and the observance of the Islamic moral standards; and
>>
>> (c) to secure the proper organisation of zakat, ushr, auqaf and mosques."

Allocation of additional marks to Muslim candidates on the basis of their learning by heart the whole of Quran is for promotion of Islamic way of life and teachings of the Holy Quran. It is not an instance of any adverse discrimination against any religious minority but is a simple measure to encourage memorization of the Holy Quran.

Case of Mr. Yasir Qayum Khan

a) Quota system is being followed in the matter of appointments in the service of Pakistan since 1948. There is national consensus on desirability of continuation of the quota system. This consensus has not so far been reflected in the Constitution after 2013 due to political reasons but needful is sure to be done in near future. The court may exercise judicial restraint in the larger interest of national integrity; and

b) Reservation of quota for different classes and regions is based upon valid classification which has direct and rational nexus to the results intended to be achieved thereby. The classification attempts to ensure adequate representation of backward classes and regions in the service of Pakistan.

62. Heard. Record perused.

63. The question regarding maintainability of these petitions has already been attended to with the conclusion that these petitions are maintainable. Other questions which arise in these proceedings and require conclusive judicial determination, in our view, are as follows:

1. Whether discrimination in respect of any appointment in the service of Pakistan is permissible on the ground only of race, religion, caste, sex, residence or place of birth or a combination of more than one of these grounds?

2. Whether the Federation can impose the condition of domicile of Pakistan for appointments of citizens in the service of Pakistan and whether the condition of residence in a Province for a period not exceeding three years prior to appointment to a provincial service and posts in connection with affairs of a Province means domicile of that Province or mere residence? Are residence and domicile synonymous?

3. Whether posts in the service of Pakistan can be reserved for persons with disabilities after the expiry of the period of forty years specified in the first proviso to Article 27(1) of the Constitution?

4. Whether reservation of posts in the service of Pakistan for women is a discrimination on the basis of gender or a special measure for protection of women?

5. Whether reservation of posts in the service of Pakistan for religious minorities and allocation of additional marks for memorizers of the Holy Quran is discrimination on the basis of religion?

6. Whether a citizen has fundamental right guaranteed by Article 27 of the Constitution in the matter of initial recruitment in police force of the Federation or of a Province?

7. Whether allocation of special quota for children of retired civil servants is based upon intelligible differentia having rational nexus to the purpose intended to be achieved?

8. Whether reservation of posts for a class which otherwise may be in accordance with the Constitution be made through executive orders?

9. What should be the order of the court in the facts and circumstances of these cases and whether the principle of judicial restraint is different from the doctrine of necessity?

64.   Now we attempt to find answers to the questions raised, seriatim hereinbelow.

Question # 1

Whether discrimination in respect of any appointment in the service of Pakistan is permissible on the ground only of race, religion, caste, sex, residence or place of birth or a combination of more than one of these grounds?

65.   Man is a social animal. He lives and loves to live in the society of humans. Crossing different stages of evolution, man has developed the concept of a modern state. This state guarantees certain rights which are inviolable and every citizen is entitled to enjoy these rights, known as basic human rights or the fundamental human rights. One of the fundamental rights is right to life. Life is not understood to mean an animal existence or mere physical survival but a dignified life with opportunities to pursue happiness and realize full potential of a citizen, to the extent possible within available resources of the state. The right to life is made meaningful with the aid of right to trade and profession. The right to trade and profession is fortified, inter alia, through elimination of discrimination in the matter of employments under the state. A man may realize his potential and may derive pleasure from exercise of skill if he is allowed to adopt profession of his choice. Subject to reasonable qualifications and conformity to permissible regulatory framework, he may opt for any profession he likes. Factors which are not in his control or which are extremely difficult to change are usually excluded from the qualifications prescribed as conditions-precedent to adopt a profession. Usually these factors are race, religion, caste, sex, residence or place of birth. No disqualification is allowed to be caused on the basis of one or a combination of these factors. A man can enjoy no real or substantive equality of opportunity if he is discriminated against on the basis of factors which are not within his control. As a common practice, such discrimination is prohibited in the Constitution of a state.

66.   Structure of a state, composition and character of its main organs and powers and responsibilities of citizens and entities of a state are usually determined in the Constitution. State entities are organizations which are created for achievement of public purposes and are generally financed from taxes collected from the citizens. These state entities are composed of humans who exercise powers of the state and get remuneration and enjoy

social and economic benefits associated with state employment in return. Recruitments of citizens as state employees are guided mainly by the following considerations:

a) Recruitment is not an end in itself; it is a means to hire services of persons for performance of certain functions and exercise of certain powers;

b) Selection of best candidates for employment is possible through affording fairly equal opportunity to all eligible and willing candidates;

c) Selection of the best candidates is necessary for organizational efficiency which is deemed beneficial for the whole society;

d) For making selection of the best candidates possible and to make the talent a determinant criterion, factors such as race, caste, religion, place of birth, gender etc. are neutralized and are made irrelevant for the purpose of selection for appointment; and

e) Where factors such as race, caste, religion, place of birth, gender etc. adversely impact ability of citizens to have substantively and fairly equal opportunity to compete with persons having better environment because of socio-economic status of their families, classes of citizens disadvantageously placed are given protective treatment to make the competition really fair. For this purpose, classification is made on the basis of factors other than race, caste, religion, place of birth, gender etc. and such classification aims at neutralization, to the extent possible, of these factors and other past or present disabilities.

67. In the context of appointments in the service of Pakistan, Article 27(1) read with Article 25(2) of the Constitution prohibit discrimination on the ground only of race, religion, caste, sex, residence or place of birth. There are three provisos to the said Article 27(1) which are as follows:

1. Provided that, for a period not exceeding forty years from the commencing day, posts may be reserved for persons belonging to any class or area to secure their adequate representation in the service of Pakistan:

2. Provided further that, in the interest of the said service, specified posts or services may be reserved for members of either sex if such posts or services entail the performance of duties and functions which cannot be adequately performed by members of the other sex:

3. Provided also that under-representation of any class or area in the service of Pakistan may be redressed in such manner as may be determined by an Act of Majlis-e-Shoora (Parliament)."

68. Before proceeding further, it would be advisable to understand the purpose and scope of a proviso to an Article of the Constitution or to a section of an Act. For this purpose, the following academic works and judicial pronouncements are thought to be helpful:

(i) Craies said in his book 'Statute Law' (7th Edition) that:

"The effect of an excepting or qualifying proviso, according to the ordinary rules of construction, is to except out of the preceding portion of the enactment, or to qualify something enacted therein, which but for the proviso would be within it...The natural presumption is that, but for the proviso, the enacting part of the section would have included the subject-matter of the proviso."

(ii)   Odgers observed in 'Construction of Deeds and Statutes' (5th Edition) that:

> "Provisos-These are clauses of exception or qualification in an Act, excepting something out of, or qualifying something in, the enactment which, but for the proviso, would be within it."

(iii)   Vepa P. Sarathi has collected the following principles in regard to a proviso at pages 294-295 of his book 'Interpretation of Statutes': -

> "(a)   When one finds a proviso to a section the natural presumption is that, but for the proviso, the enacting part of the section would have included the subject-matter of the proviso.
>
> (b)   A proviso must be construed with reference to the preceding parts of the clause to which it is appended.
>
> (c)   Where the proviso is directly repugnant to a section, the proviso shall stand and be held a repeal of the section as the proviso speaks the later intention of the makers.
>
> (d)   Where the section is doubtful, a proviso may be used as a guide to its interpretation; but when it is clear, a proviso cannot imply the existence of words of which there is no trace in the section.
>
> (e)   The proviso is subordinate to the main section.
>
> (f)   A proviso does not enlarge an enactment except for compelling reasons.
>
> (g)   Sometimes an unnecessary proviso is inserted by way of abundant caution.
>
> (h)   A construction placed upon a proviso which brings it into general harmony with the terms of section should prevail.
>
> (i)   When a proviso is repugnant to the enacting part, the proviso will not prevail over the absolute terms of a later Act directed to be read as supplemental to the earlier one.
>
> (j)   A proviso may sometimes contain a substantive provision."

(iv)   Lord Wright held in (1939) 4 All.ER 471 that:

> "It is said that, where there is a proviso, the former part, which is described as the enacting part, must be construed without reference to the proviso. No doubt there may be cases in which the first part is so clear and unambiguous as not to admit in regard to the matters which are there clear any reference to any other part of the section. The proviso may simply be an exception out of what is clearly defined in the first part, or it may be some qualification not inconsistent with what is expressed in the first part."

(v)   The Hon'ble Supreme Court of Pakistan has held in Baksh Elahi Vs. Qazi Wasif Ali (1985 SCMR 291) that:

> "It has been held in some cases, as pointed out by Crawford in his book "Statutory Construction" that three functions are to be ascribed to the proviso, namely (1) to exempt something from the enacting clause (2) to qualify or restrain its generality and (iii) to exclude some possible misinterpretation of it as extending to cases not intended by the legislature."

(vi)   The Hon'ble Supreme Court of India held in A.N. Sehgal Vs. Raje Ram Sheoran (1992 Supp (1) SCC 304) that:

> "14. It is a cardinal rule of interpretation that a proviso to a particular provision of a statute only embraces the field which is covered by the main provision. It carves out an exception to

the main provision to which it has been enacted by the proviso and to no other. The proper function of a proviso is to except and deal with a cause which would otherwise fall within the general language of the main enactment, and its effect is to confine to that case. Where the language of the main enactment is explicit and unambiguous, the proviso can have no repercussion on the interpretation of the main enactment, so as to exclude from it, by implication, what clearly falls within its express terms."

(vii)   It was held by the Hon'ble Supreme Court of India in Abdul Jabar Butt Vs. State of Jammu & Kashmir {[1957] SCR 51} that:

> "It is a fundamental rule of construction that a proviso must be considered with relation to the principal matter to which it stands as proviso." Therefore, it is to be construed harmoniously with the main enactment."

(viii)   The Hon'ble Supreme Court of India held in Jabalpur Vs. Hanuman Prasad ([1967] I S.C.R. 831) that:

> "It is well-recognised that a proviso is added to a principal clause primarily with the object of taking out of the scope of that principal clause what is included in it and what the legislature desires should be excluded."

(ix)   The Hon'ble Supreme Court of India held in Hindustan Ideal Insurance Co. Ltd. Vs. Life Insurance Corporation of India (AIR 1963 SC 1083) that:

> "28. There is no doubt that where the main provision is clear its effect cannot be cut down by the proviso. But where it is not clear the proviso, which cannot be presumed to be a surplusage, can properly be looked into to ascertain the meaning and scope of the main provision."

(x)   It was held in Province of Bombay Vs. Hormusji Manekji (AIR 1947 PC 200) that:

> "It is a familiar principle of statutory construction that where you find in the same section express exceptions from the operative part of the section, it may be assumed, unless it otherwise appears from the language employed, that these exceptions were necessary, as otherwise the subject-matter of the exceptions would have come within the operative provisions of the section."

(xi)   https://legal-dictionary.thefreedictionary.com/Proviso says this on the subject of 'proviso':

> "3. A proviso differs from an exception. 1 Barn. k Ald. 99. An exception exempts, absolutely, from the operation of an engagement or an enactment; a proviso defeats their operation, conditionally. An exception takes out of an engagement or enactment, something which would otherwise be part of the subject-matter of it; a proviso avoids them by way of defeasance or excuse. 8 Amer. Jurist, 242; Plowd. 361; Carter 99; 1 Saund. 234 a, note; Lilly's Reg. h.t.; and the cases there cited. Vide, generally Amer. Jurist, No. 16, art. 1; Bac. Ab. Conditions, A; Com. Dig. Condition, A 1, A 2; Darw. on Stat. 660"

69.   It was held by the Hon'ble Supreme Court of India in Indra Sawhney etc. Vs Union of India and others, etc. (AIR 1993 SC 477, 1992 Supp 2 SCR 454) at paragraph 56 of the judgment that:

> "Question 2(a). Whether Clause (4) of Article 16 is an exception to Clause (1)?
>
> 56. In Balaji it was held - "there is no doubt that Article 15(4) has to be read as a proviso or an exception to Articles 15(1) and 29(2)". It was observed that Article 15(4) was inserted by the First Amendment in the light of the decision in Champakam, with a view to remove the defect pointed out by this Court namely, the absence of a provision in Article 15 corresponding to Clause (4) of Article 16. Following Balaji it was held by another Constitution Bench (by majority) in Devadasan - "further this Court has already held that Clause (4) of Article 16 is by way of a proviso or an exception to Clause (1)". Subbarao, J., however, opined in his dissenting opinion that **Article 16(4) is not an exception to Article 16(1) but that it is only an emphatic way of stating the principle inherent in the main provision itself.** Be that as it may, since the decision in Devadasan, it was assumed by this Court that Article 16(4) is an exception to Article 16(1). This view, however, received a severe set-back from the majority decision in State of Kerala and Ors. v. N.M. Thomas. Though the minority (H.R. Khanna and A.C. Gupta, JJ.) stuck to the view that Article 16(4) is an exception, the majority (Ray, C.J., Mathew, Krishna Iyer and Fazal Ali, JJ.) held that **Article 16(4) is not an exception to Article 16(1) but that it was merely an emphatic way of stating a principle implicit in Article 16(1).** (Beg. J. took a slightly different view which it is not necessary to mention here). The said four learned Judges - whose views have been referred to in para 41 - held that **Article 16(1) being a facet of the doctrine of equality enshrined in Article 14 permits reasonable classification just as Article 14 does.** In our respectful opinion, the view taken by the majority in Thomas is the correct one. **We too believe that Article 16(1) does permit reasonable classification for ensuring attainment of the equality of opportunity assured by it. For assuring equality of opportunity, it may well be necessary in certain situations to treat unequally situated persons unequally. Not doing so, would perpetuate and accentuate inequality.** Article 16(4) is an instance of such classification, put in to place the matter beyond controversy. The "backward class of citizens" are classified as a separate category deserving a special treatment in the nature of reservation of appointments / posts in the services of the State. Accordingly, we hold that **Clause (4) of Article 16 is not exception to Clause (1) of Article 16. It is an instance of classification implicit in and permitted by Clause (1).** The speech of Dr. Ambedkar during the debate on draft Article 10(3) [corresponding to Article 16(4)] in the Constituent Assembly - referred to in para 28- shows that a substantial number of members of the Constituent Assembly insisted upon a "provision (being) made for the entry of certain communities which have so far been outside the

administration", and that draft Clause (3) was put in recognition and acceptance of the said demand. It is a provision which must be read along with and in harmony with Clause (1). **Indeed, even without Clause (4), it would have been permissible for the State to have evolved such a classification and made a provision for reservation of appointments/posts in their favour. Clause (4) merely puts the matter beyond any doubt in specific terms.** Regarding the view expressed in Balaji and Devadasan, it must be remembered that at that time it was not yet recognised by this Court that Article 16(1) being a facet of Article 14 does implicitly permit classification. Once this feature was recognised, the theory of Clause (4) being an exception to Clause (1) became untenable. **It had to be accepted that Clause (4) is an instance of classification inherent in Clause (1).** Now, just as Article 16(1) is a facet or an elaboration of the principle underlying Article 14, Clause (2) of Article 16 is also an elaboration of a facet of Clause (1). If Clause (4) is an exception to Clause (1) then it is equally an exception to Clause (2). Question then arises, in what respect is Clause (4) an exception to Clause (2), if 'class' does not means 'caste'. Neither Clause (1) nor Clause (2) speak of class. Does the contention mean that Clause (1) does not permit classification and, therefore, Clause (4) is an exception to it? Thus, from any point of view, the contention of the petitioners has no merit." (Emphasis supplied).

70. Seeking guidance from the above, we may learn that a proviso:
  (i)   is restricted to the subject matter of the enacting clause;
  (ii)   does not destroy or nullify the enacting clause;
  (iii) needs to be construed in harmony with the enacting clause so as both are given effect to and nothing is rendered a mere surplusage; and
  (iv)   may qualify application of the enacting clause in certain conditions with a view to rule out chances of misinterpretation of the clause by emphatically stating what may, though implied or present, not be so obvious.

71. When we apply the above lessons to Article 27 of the Constitution, we find that:
  a) The subject-matter of Article 27(1) is prohibition of discrimination in the matter of appointments in the service of Pakistan;
  b) The discrimination prohibited by Article 27(1) of the Constitution is the discrimination on the ground only of race, religion, caste, sex, residence or place of birth;
  c) The said Article 27(1) does prohibit discrimination on the grounds enumerated in the Article for appointments in the service of Pakistan but does not prohibit classification on those grounds. A classification on the grounds listed in the Article may be valid for any other purpose but same would be void so far as it is intended to be used as a criterion for discrimination in the matter of appointments in the service of Pakistan;
  d) A classification made on grounds other than those enumerated in Article 27(1) of the Constitution for provision of real, substantive and fair equal opportunity in the matter of appointments in the service of Pakistan shall be construed to be in furtherance of objects and purposes of that Article and not as an exception to the principle stated therein;
  e) A classification made on grounds other than those enumerated in Article 27(1) of the Constitution can only be resorted to for the purpose of

ensuring adequate representation of a class or area in the service of Pakistan;

f) The classification resorted to for ensuring adequate representation must be based upon intelligible differentia and must have rational nexus to the purpose being intended to be achieved and may exclude creamy layer of the class or area which more often than not snatches away the benefits of reservation of posts;

g) Any reservation of posts in the service of Pakistan for a class or area is not allowed to exceed what is adequate representation. However, it is for the legislature to determine what is adequate representation for a class or area in the service of Pakistan; and

h) Whether reservation of posts in the service of Pakistan for a class or area to ensure adequate representation is restricted to undo lingering effects of historical underrepresentation of that class or area or to ensure, on permanent basis, their continued adequate representation in the service of Pakistan? Prima facie, the provision seems to be temporary for the purpose of provision of equally good education and other enabling facilities to the disadvantaged class so that it may not suffer from any handicaps and all enjoy equal opportunities for realization of their potentials. How long the reservation of posts for a particular class or area is sufficient to achieve the goal of adequate representation is a question which is not justiciable being a question of policy. The legislature may take a decision which suits to its wisdom and policy objectives.

72. What has been prohibited by Article 27(1) of the Constitution cannot be deemed to be allowed through its first proviso. The prohibition contained in the Article 27(1) is absolute and inviolable. The first proviso attempts to achieve equality of opportunity in the matter of appointments in the service of Pakistan by mitigating adverse effects of factors other than those enumerated in the enacting clause. These factors may be backwardness in terms of education, social status, economic worth or any other intelligible differentia. Whatever the intelligible differentia be, it will separate those intended to be adequately represented in the service of Pakistan from others. Article 27(1) does not disallow such a reasonable classification in the matter of appointments in the service of Pakistan if the same does not destroy or nullify the intent of the Article. The first proviso to Article 27(1) is, therefore, an emphatic way of stating what is already inbuilt in the Article. Since classification based upon the ground only of race, religion, caste, sex, residence or place of birth for the purpose of discrimination in the matter of appointments in the service of Pakistan has expressly been prohibited under the Article, therefore, the first proviso cannot be interpreted to allow classification or discrimination on the basis of religion, gender, caste, place of birth or residence.

73. What is clarified by the first proviso is that reservation of posts in the service of Pakistan for a class is permissible only to ensure its adequate representation in the service of Pakistan. If a classification is made on the basis of educational, social or economic backwardness, persons constituting a class may be residing in different geographic or administrative areas. Though on the touchstone of the intelligible differentia used for defining a class for the purpose of ensuring its adequate representation in the service of Pakistan, persons belonging to different areas will fall within the same class, yet this class can be used to ensure adequate representation of members of the class residing in different areas of the country. Sub-division of a class on the basis of area in which its members reside is not a sub-division on the ground of place of residence, but is just a further fine-tuning of the classification based on an intelligible differentia simply to ensure fair competition within the sub-division. Such a measure ensures proportionate distribution of fruits of reservation of posts intended to be achieved through adequate representation of a class in the service of Pakistan. The purpose underlying sub-division of a class on the basis

of area is not to use place of residence as a ground of discrimination in the matter of appointments in the service of Pakistan but to make the equal opportunity more precisely fair. If we literally interpret the word 'area' in the first proviso, it will nullify the prohibition against discrimination on the basis of place of residence in the enacting clause. It would be absurd to assume that the legislature partially nullifies the enacting clause through adding a proviso thereto. Under the golden rule for statutory interpretation, where the literal rule gives an absurd result, which Parliament could not have intended, the judge can substitute a reasonable meaning in the light of the statute as a whole. We may focus on giving effect to the purpose of the legislation. We, therefore, hold that the first proviso to Article 27(1) does not introduce discrimination in the matter of appointments in the service of Pakistan on the basis of place of residence and it does only permit classification on grounds other than those mentioned in the Article 27(1) and reservation of posts for persons belonging to a class on the basis of residence in a particular area is meant to ensure proportionate representation and more fair and really equal opportunity within the class.

74.   The second proviso to Article 27(1) of the Constitution is explanatory and exhibits abundance of caution on the part of the framers of the Constitution to avoid any misconception of Article 27(1). Use of gender or sex for discrimination in the matter of appointments in the service of Pakistan has been prohibited by Article 27(1). If in case it is found that a particular job can adequately be performed by persons belonging to a particular sex, persons belonging to the other sex may be disqualified to compete for the job. This disqualification is caused not by a desire to discriminate against a sex but to ensure that duties attached to a post are discharged adequately and efficiently. The second proviso, therefore, does not militate against the Article 27(1) and is in harmony with the said Article. What it contains is the express sanction for use of gender as a bona fide occupational qualification in order to ensure adequate and efficient performance of duties by persons in the service of Pakistan.

75.   The third proviso to Article 27(1) of the Constitution reinforces the first proviso. It was not specified in the first proviso that which authority would provide for ensuring adequate representation of a class or area in the service of Pakistan. The third proviso has assigned this duty to the Parliament which is tasked with the function to redress the issue of under-representation of any class or area in the service of Pakistan through an Act of the Parliament. This Act would remain within the parameters specified in Article 27 (1) read with provisos thereto. In other words, the enactment envisaged in the third proviso shall be for furtherance of objects and purposes of the Article and shall be subject to the limitations spelled out therein.

76.   The Hon'ble Supreme Court of Pakistan has very scholarly shed light on Article 27 of the Constitution in Mushtaq Ahmad Mohal and Others Vs. the Honourable Lahore High Court, Lahore and Others (1997 SCMR 1043). Some relevant excerpts from the headnotes of the aforesaid judgment, reproduced below, are of valuable help in our effort to understand the said Article for the purpose of judicial determination of the questions under consideration:

> "Clause (1) of Article 27 of the Constitution (which relates to one of the Fundamental Rights guaranteed by the Constitution), enjoins that no citizens otherwise qualified for appointment in the service of Pakistan shall be discriminated against in respect of any such appointment on the ground only of race, religion, caste, sex, residence or place of birth. The original first proviso to the above clause provided that for a period not exceeding ten years from the commencing day, posts may be reserved for persons belonging to any class or area to secure their adequate representation in the service of Pakistan. The above period of ten years was substituted by twenty years through President's Order No. 14 of 1985. The said period of twenty years had

expired on 13.08.1993 as the Constitution was enforced on 14.08.1973. Proviso 2 to above clause lays down that in the interest of the service of Pakistan, specified posts or services may be reserved for members of either sex if such posts or services entail the performance of duties and functions which cannot be adequately performed by members of the other sex. By virtue of clause (2) of the Article any Provincial Government, or any local authority in a Province has been empowered to prescribe the requirement of residence in the Province for a period not exceeding three years in relation to any post or class of service."

"Clause (1) of Article 27 of the Constitution guarantees that every citizen will have equal opportunity for appointment in the service of Pakistan if otherwise qualified. Whereas clause (2) thereof also guarantees equal opportunity to all the citizens with the condition that any Province or local authority may prescribe the requirement of three years' residence in the Province concerned in order to ensure that the locals of that Province should have preferential right to have a job as compared to an outsider, who has no domicile and has not been residing for a period of three years in that Province. This condition has been provided apparently in order to ensure the Provincial autonomy which the Constitution guarantees to the Federating Units."

"Article 27 of the Constitution is to be read in conjunction with, inter alia, Articles 2A, 18 and 25 of the Constitution. Article 25 of the Constitution guarantees that all citizens are equal before law and are entitled to equal protection and that they shall not be discriminated on the basis of sex alone. Inter alia the above Articles of the Constitution are designed, intended and directed to bring about an egalitarian society based on Islamic concept of social justice."

"The period of 20 years contained in first proviso to clause (1) of Article 27 of the Constitution has already expired and, therefore, there cannot be any justification to violate the express mandate of clause (1) of Article 27 of the Constitution that no citizen otherwise qualified for appointment in the service of Pakistan shall be discriminated against in respect of any such appointment on the ground only of race, religion, caste, sex, residence or place of birth."

"It is manifest that the Holy Quran, inter alia, enjoins that there is no difference between the individuals of mankind on the basis of race, colour and territory and that all human beings are equal in the eyes of Allah. The fittest person who is strong and trustworthy is to be employed. It is evident that the concept of zone or quota system runs counter not only to the above clause (1) of Article 27 read with Article 2A and Article 25 of the Constitution, but also to the Commandment of Allah as ordained in the Holy Quran. The quota system has not served Pakistan interest but on the contrary, it has generated parochial and class feelings resulting into disunity."

"The well-established rule of interpretation is that whereas a provision relating to a fundamental right will be construed liberally so that its benefit and protective umbrella are extended rather than restricted, any exception to a fundamental right will be construed strictly, so that the exception will apply to cases clearly falling within its language and the effect of the exception will not be extended by implication or analogy."

77. Concise statements filed by the petitioners have specifically mentioned that after expiry of the period of forty years as noted in the first proviso to Article 27(1) of the Constitution, reservation of posts in the service of Pakistan for a class or area with the purpose to ensure its adequate representation is void and of no legal effect. Learned counsels of the petitioners have vehemently emphasized on this point. The learned Attorney General for Pakistan and the learned Advocate General, Khyber Pakhtunkhwa have not been able to offer any acceptable legal justification for continued implementation of the quota system or reservation of posts for persons belonging to a class or area in the service of Pakistan after 13.8.2019. Being a court of law, we are concerned with legality of a matter. Reasonability or wisdom or preference of one policy option over others in a given case are issues beyond our jurisdiction and capacity. We do not deem it appropriate even to discuss policy options and give our views thereon. Whatever be the wisdom of a given policy option, we are bound to give it effect if it is properly enacted by the competent legislature and conforms to the Constitution and does not suffer from any fatal legal infirmity. The arguments other than those directed to address the issue of legality of the quota system may be of value and relevance for the executive and the legislature but are irrelevant for us because we are here to decide cases in accordance with existing laws and not on the basis of our policy preferences. We are, therefore, constrained to hold that:

a) No discrimination has ever been permitted by the Constitution in the matter of appointments in the service of Pakistan on the ground only of race, religion, caste, sex, residence or place of birth; and

b) Reservation of posts for persons belonging to a class or area to ensure their adequate representation in the service of Pakistan is void and of no legal effect after the expiry of the period of forty years on 13.08.2013 even if the classification is made on grounds other than those enumerated in Article 27(1) of the Constitution and the classification is based upon intelligible differentia which has rational nexus to the object of ensuring adequate representation and is implemented through an Act of Parliament in respect of All Pakistan Services, services of the Federation and posts in connection with affairs of the Federation and through a provincial law in case of provincial services and posts in connection with affairs of a Province.

Question #2

Whether the Federation can impose the condition of domicile of Pakistan for appointments of citizens in the service of Pakistan and whether the condition of residence in a Province for a period not exceeding three years prior to appointment to a provincial service and posts in connection with affairs of a Province means domicile of that Province or mere residence? Are residence and domicile synonymous?

78. The Civil Servants Act, 1973 and the Khyber Pakhtunkhwa Civil Servants Act, 1973 do not prescribe citizenship or domicile as a necessary qualification for being eligible to compete for appointment in the service of Pakistan. An attempt was made through the Civil Servants (Amendment) Bill, 2013 to add the following proviso to Section 9(1) of the Civil Servants Act but the Bill was not passed by the Parliament:

223

"Provided further that a civil servant holding dual nationality or citizenship of any foreign country shall not be entitled for promotion to posts in Basic Pay Scale 20 or equivalent and above."

79.   On the other hand, Sections 10, 12 and 10 of the Pakistan Army Act, 1952, the Pakistan Air Force Act, 1953 and the Pakistan Navy Ordinance, 1961 respectively provide that no person who is not a citizen of Pakistan shall, except with the consent of the Federal Government signified in writing, be eligible for appointment in the armed forces. As per Article 62 read with Article 63 and 113 of the Constitution, citizenship of Pakistan is a condition-precedent for eligibility to run for elections to membership of the Parliament or of a Provincial Assembly. A person who is not a citizen of Pakistan is ineligible for appointment as judge of the Supreme Court or of a High Court (Article 177 and 193 of the Constitution). Citizenship of Pakistan is also a necessary qualification for election to the office of the President of Pakistan (Article 41(2) of the Constitution). As per Article 260 of the Constitution, "citizen" means a citizen of Pakistan as defined by law. Citizenship falls within exclusive legislative jurisdiction of the Parliament. Pakistan enforced its citizenship law (the Pakistan Citizenship Act, 1951) on 13th of April, 1951. There was no law on citizenship before independence of Pakistan. Section 17 of the Pakistan Citizenship Act, 1951 provided for domicile in these words:

> "**17.   Certificate of domicile. -** The Federal Government may, upon an application being made to it in the prescribed manner containing the prescribed particulars grant a certificate of domicile to any person in respect of whom it is satisfied that he has ordinarily resided in Pakistan for a period of not less than one year immediately before the making of the application, and has acquired a domicile therein."

80.   Domicile has not been defined in the Pakistan Citizenship Act, 1951; however, its Section 3(c) states that the term 'domicile' has been used within the meaning of Part II of the Succession Act, 1925 (XXXIX of 1925). Rule 23 of the Pakistan Citizenship Rules, 1952 provides as follows in respect of domicile:

> "**23. Certificate of domicile.**
>
> The Federal Government, the Provincial Government or any District Magistrate authorized by the Provincial Government in this behalf may on application made to it in this behalf issue a certificate of domicile in Form P-I in the manner following: -
>
> (a)   An application for a certificate of domicile shall be made in Form P in duplicate, shall be accompanied by an affidavit affirming the truth of the statement made in it and affirming further that the applicant had not migrated to India after the first day of March 1947 or that, having so migrated, and returned to Pakistan under a permit for resettlement or permanent return issued by an officer authorized by the Government of Pakistan.
>
> (b)   Any authority to whom an application is presented may demand such evidence as it may consider necessary for satisfying itself that the facts stated in the application are correct and that the applicant has been continually resident in Pakistan for a period not less than one year and intends to live permanently in Pakistan.
>
> (c)   The authority shall pass such order son the application as it deems fit."

81.   Section 10 of the National Database and Registration Authority Ordinance, 2000 (VIII of 2000) speaks of issuance of national identity cards to the citizens in these words:

> "**10.   National Identity Cards**. — (1) The Authority shall issue or renew, or cause to be issued or renewed, in such manner and on

224

terms and conditions, subject to every citizen who has attained the age of eighteen years and got himself registered under section 9, a card to be called National Identity Card in such form, with such period of validity upon payment of such fee in such form and manner as may be prescribed:"

82.   Rule 5 of the National Database and Registration Authority (National Identity Card) Rules, 2002 requires that all citizens shall get themselves registered with the Authority. A citizen has been defined in these words in Rule 2(1)(d) to mean a citizen of Pakistan who has attained the age of eighteen years and includes both a resident and a non-resident citizen. Rule 4 of the Rules ibid provides that a citizen shall be a non-resident citizen if he, –

    (a)   is an emigrant or intending emigrant;
    (b)   is, or is intending to be, resident abroad;
    (c)   holds nationality or citizenship of any other country or state pursuant to sub-section (3) of section 14 of the Pakistan Citizenship Act, 1951 (II of 1951); or
    (d)   holds an emigrant or resident visa, permanent or otherwise, or equivalent authorization, permit or status, as the case may be, of a foreign state or country.

83.   The Hon'ble Supreme Court of Pakistan held in Syed Mehmood Akhtar Naqvi Vs. Federation of Pakistan (PLD 2012 SC 1089) that:

    "We may clarify that section 14(1) of the Citizenship Act, 1951, confers upon Pakistani citizens the right to hold the citizenship of certain other countries without having to forego their Pakistani citizenship. The right, therefore, of Pakistani citizens to hold dual citizenship, as per law, remains very much a statutory right vested in them."

84.   A person who is not a citizen of Pakistan has been defined as a foreigner in Section 2(a) of the Foreigners Act, 1946 (XXXI of 1946). Paragraph 10 of the Foreigners Order, 1951, issued under Section 3 of the Foreigners Act, 1946, imposed restrictions on foreigners in respect of their employment in Pakistan in these words:

    "**10. Restrictions on employment. -** No foreigner shall, without the general or special permission in writing of the civil authority, enter any premises relating to, or be employed in, or in connection with-
    (1)   Any undertaking for the supply to Government or to the public of light, petroleum, powers or water, or-
    (2)   Any other undertaking which may be specified by the Central Government in this behalf."

85. Article 27(1) of the Constitution, inter alia, rules out use of residence or place of birth for discrimination in the matter of appointments in the service of Pakistan. When the Civil Servants Act, 1973 is seen in this background and is read with the Foreigners Act, 1946 and paragraph 10 of the Foreigners Order, 1951, absence of requirement of citizenship and domicile for appointment in the service of Pakistan to the extent of the Federation becomes understandable. This absence may be attributed to the legislative policy of not ruling out employment of foreigners except to the extent specified in paragraph 10 of the Foreigners Order, 1951. The legislature might have conceived situations in which employment of foreign talent may be necessary and an absolute prohibition on employment of foreigners in the service of Pakistan may not be in national interest.

86.   What is relevant for our discussion in the light of the legal provisions supra may be summarized as follows:

    a)   There is no constitutional or statutory prohibition of employment of foreigners in the service of Pakistan except against posts in the armed forces or in an undertaking for the supply to Government or to the public of light, petroleum, powers or water, or any other undertaking to be specified by the Federal Government;

b) Citizenship of a Pakistani remains intact even if a citizen obtains dual nationality of other specified countries or resides outside Pakistan in any country with domiciliary intent;

c) Making domicile of Pakistan a necessary qualification for being eligible to compete for appointment in the service of Pakistan implies ineligibility of citizens of Pakistan and citizens with dual nationality not domiciled in Pakistan; and

d) It needs to be ascertained that whether what has not been prohibited by the Constitution and the applicable statutes can legitimately be prohibited through the rules framed under purported authority of the statues?

87.   The conditions of citizenship and domicile of Pakistan have been imposed in respect of the civil servants of the Federation through the Civil Servants (Appointment, Promotion and Transfer) Rules, 1973. Conditions of citizenship of Pakistan and bona fide residence of the Province have been introduced through Rule 11(1) of the Khyber Pakhtunkhwa Civil Servants (Appointment, Promotion and Transfer) Rules, 1989 for persons aspiring to become civil servants of the Province. We need to examine legality of both of the above provisions in the light of the following principle of interpretation which is so well-settled that there seems to be no need to fortify it with quotations from cases decided on the basis of this principle:

> "Statutory rule cannot enlarge the scope of the section under which it is framed and if a rule goes beyond what the section contemplates, the rule must yield to the statute. The authority of executive to make rules and regulations, in order to effectuate the intention and policy of the Legislature, must be exercised within the limits of mandate given to the rule making authority and the rules framed under an enactment must be consistent with the provisions of said enactment. The rules framed under a statue, if are inconsistent with the provisions of the statute and defeat the intention of Legislature expressed in the main statue, same shall be invalid. The rule-making authority cannot clothe itself with power which is not given to it under the statute and thus the rules made under a statute, neither enlarge the scope of the Act nor can go beyond the Act and must not be in conflict with the provisions of statute or repugnant to any other law in force."

88.   It goes without saying that written constitution is the fundamental and paramount law of the land and all other laws, be they the result of primary or subordinate legislation, must conform to it. "Craies on Statute Law" (7th Edition page 320) states that the settled law is that the subordinate legislation, if it has a meaning or effect inconsistent with the Act authorizing it, it is pro tanto ultra vires. Further, the Hon'ble Supreme Court of Pakistan held in Mehmood Tahsin Vs. Ejaz Hussain (PLD 1965 SC 618) that where an expression has been used but not defined in the enabling Act, that expression is presumed to have been used in its ordinary sense and the rules cannot give it an artificial meaning. The Hon'ble Supreme Court of Pakistan has also held in Pakistan Vs. Aaran Petro Chemical Industry (2003 SCMR 370) that subordinate legislation must be consistent not only with the enabling enactment, but also must not contravene any other enactment.

89.   When viewed in the context of the aforesaid principles of interpretation, the Civil Servants (Appointment, Promotion and Transfer) Rules, 1973 seem to be travelling beyond what is contemplated in the parent statue to the extent of prescription of conditions of citizenship and domicile for being eligible to join All Pakistan Services, civil services of the

Federation or to hold civil posts in connection with affairs of the Federation. Some of the reasons leading to this conclusion are as follows:

a) The Civil Servants Act, 1973 does not require the qualifications of citizenship and domicile for being eligible to join the All Pakistan Services, civil services of the Federation or to hold civil posts in connection with affairs of the Federation The rules framed under a law cannot require that what has not been specified in the law;

b) The rules are inconsistent with the Foreigners Act, 1946 and paragraph 10 of the Foreigners Order, 1951, so far as appointments in the service of Pakistan are concerned. The Foreigners Order, 1951 prohibit employment of foreigners in certain undertakings already specified or to be specified in future but the aforesaid rules impose a blanket prohibition;

c) Rules are meant to elaborate the law and provide procedural details but are not conceived as sources of creation of substantive rights or imposition of duties. The rules under consideration have done which cannot fairly be termed a legitimate attempt to further the intents and purposes of the governing statue;

d) Clause (1) of Article 4 of the Constitution commands that to enjoy the protection of law and to be treated in accordance with law is the inalienable right of every citizen, wherever he may be, and of every other person for the time being within Pakistan. Clause (2) of the said Article 4 is significant as it does not use the term 'citizen' but uses the term 'person' when it commands that

    a) no action detrimental to the life, liberty, body, reputation or property of any person shall be taken except in accordance with law;

    b) no person shall be prevented from or be hindered in doing that which is not prohibited by law; and

    c) no person shall be compelled to do that which the law does not required him to do.

The term law used in the aforesaid Article 4 means the law enacted by the competent legislature. In Federation Vs. United Sugar Mills (PLD 1977 SC 397), the Hon'ble Supreme Court of Pakistan held that both in Article 4 and Article 8 of the Constitution, "law" means positive law, that is to say, a formal pronouncement of the will of a competent law-giver. In other words, "law" there means law made by legislation only. If prescription of citizenship and domicile are qualifications possession of which is a condition-precedent to be eligible to join the service of Pakistan, then, these qualifications can only be prescribed through an enactment. Article 18 of the Constitution also prescribes determination of qualifications for a trade or profession, if any, through law. It is well-established that prescription of one is prohibition of another. As the Constitution requires prescription of qualifications through law, therefore, these cannot be prescribed through subordinate legislation or the rules as the rules are meant only to give effect to the applicable law and not to offer what has been denied or prohibited by the law; and

e) The fundamental right guaranteed by Article 27 of the Constitution is for citizens and not for citizens domiciled in Pakistan only. A citizen of Pakistan can retain his citizenship even if he obtains nationality of certain other countries and if he resides in any country with domiciliary intent. So long citizenship of a person is intact, he cannot be discriminated against in the matter of appointments in the service of Pakistan to the extent of All Pakistan Services, services of the Federation and posts in connection with affairs of the Federation on the ground that he is not domiciled in Pakistan or does not possess a certificate of domicile. Doing so would be denial of a valuable fundamental right of a citizen. No executive or legislative instrument can allow such denial and discrimination. The fundamental rights as enshrined in a written constitution are "limitations upon all the powers of government, legislative as well as executive and judicial.' (Hurtado v. California (1884) 110 US 516, 531-2, 28 L Ed 232, 237). They "impose a fetter on the exercise by the legislature, the executive and the judiciary of the plentitude of their respective powers." (Hinds v. The Queen (1976) 1 All ER 353, 369). It was held in Muhammad Nawaz Sharif Vs. Federation of Pakistan (PLD 1993 SC 473, 557) that:

> "Fundamental rights in essence are restraints on the arbitrary exercise of power by the State in relation to any activity that an individual can engage (in)."

Hon'ble Justice(Retired) Fazal Karim has observed in his book "Judicial Review of Public Actions", Volume-III at page 743 that:

> "This is, as we shall see, what the words "Subject to the Constitution", with which Articles 141 and 142 of the Constitution begin, means. They mean that the power to legislate generally on the matters enumerated in the legislative lists is subject to the Constitution, that is, subject to the limitations imposed by the Constitution, e.g. the limitations in the form of fundamental rights.
>
> Thus, the object of guaranteeing the fundamental rights by entrenching them in the Constitution, with an express prohibition against legislative interference with these rights read with the provisions in Article 199, clause (2) and Article 184, clause (3), of the Constitution for the enforcement of these rights by means of judicial review, clearly is that these rights are to be paramount to ordinary law. Lest there be any doubt about it, it has been thought necessary to provide expressly in Part II, Chapter 1, Article 8, that laws inconsistent with or in contravention of the fundamental rights shall to the extent of inconsistency and contravention be void and that "the rights conferred by this chapter shall not be suspended except as expressly provided by the Constitution", for example, by Article 233."

Rules which are inconsistent with any of the fundamental rights are, therefore, void.

90. Whereas Parliament is competent to prescribe, through law, citizenship of Pakistan as a necessary qualification for appointment in the service of Pakistan to the extent of All Pakistan Services, services of the Federation and posts in connection with affairs of the Federation as has been done in the case of appointments in the armed forces, it has no power to prescribe the condition of domicile of Pakistan for the purpose as it would amount to taking away the fundamental right guaranteed by Article 27 of the Constitution in respect of the citizens of Pakistan domiciled out of Pakistan. This might had been possible had permanent residence abroad had any effect on citizen's fundamental rights in Pakistan. In view of the legal position explained in the preceding

paragraphs, we have no option except to hold that prescription of the condition of domicile through Rule 14, 15 and 16 of the Civil Servants (Appointment, Promotion and Transfer) Rules, 1973 as one of constituents of eligibility for appointment to All Pakistan Services, services of the Federation or for holding civil posts in connection with affairs of the Federation is void and of no legal effect.

91. Article 27(2) of the Constitution states that nothing in Article 27(1) shall prevent any Provincial Government, or any local or other authority in a Province, from prescribing, in relation to any post or class of service under that Government or authority, conditions as to residence in the Province, for a period not exceeding three years, prior to appointment under that Government or authority. What needs to be noted is that the requirement is of residence and not of domicile and residence is required to be in the Province and not in a particular district, division or region of the Province and that the maximum duration of the residence to be prescribed in not allowed to exceed three years prior to appointment.

92. Article 15 of the Constitution guarantees to every citizen a fundamental right to remain in, and, subject to any reasonable restriction imposed by law in the public interest, enter and move freely throughout Pakistan and to reside and settle in any part thereof. We may attempt to learn what does the term 'residence' convey.

93.   The Hon'ble Supreme Court of India held in Union of India and others Vs. Doodh Nath Prasad (AIR 2000 SC 525) that:

> "13. The word "reside" has been defined in the Oxford Dictionary as "dwell permanently or for a considerable time to have once settled or usual abode; to live in or at a particular place." The meaning, therefore, covers not only the place where the person has a permanent residence but also the place where the person has resided for a "considerable time."
>
> 14. In Black's Law Dictionary, 5th Edition, the word "reside" has been given the following meaning:
>
> "Live, dwell, abide, sojourn, stay, remain, lodge; to settle oneself or a thing in a place, to be stationed, to remain or stay, to dwell permanently or continuously, to have a settled abode for a time, to have one's residence or domicile; specifically, to be in residence, to have an abiding place, to be present as an element, to inhere as a quality, to be vested as a right."
>
> In the same dictionary the word 'residence' has been defined as under:
> "Personal presence at some place of abode with no present intention of definite and early removal and with purpose to remain for undetermined period, not infrequently, but not necessarily combined with design to stay permanently. Bodily presence and the intention of remaining in a place, to sit down, to settle in a place, to settle, to remain, and is made up of fact and intention, the fact of abode and the intention of remaining, and is a combination of acts and intention. Residence implied something more than mere physical presence and something (sic) than domicile."
>
> 15. If the two meanings referred to above are to be read along with the word "ordinarily", it becomes clear that a person, before he can be said to be "ordinarily residing" at a particular place, has to have an intention to stay at that place for a considerably long time. It would not include a flying visit of a short or casual presence at that place."

94.   It was held by the Hon'ble Supreme Court of India in Dr. Yogendra Bharadwaj Vs. State of U.P. And others (AIR 1991 SC 356) that:

"17. Residence is a physical fact. No volition is needed to establish it. Unlike in the case of a domicile of choice, animus manendi is not an essential requirement of residence. Any period of physical presence, however short, may constitute residence provided it is not transitory, fleeting or casual. Intention is not relevant to prove the physical fact of residence except to the extent of showing that it is not a mere fleeting or transitory existence. To insist on an element of volition is to confuse the features of 'residence' with those of 'domicile'."

95.   It was also declared by the Hon'ble Supreme Court of India in Bhagwan Dass and another Vs. Kamal Abrol and others (AIR 2005 SC 2583) that:

"12. From the aforesaid analysis it is apparent that the word 'residence' is generally understood as referring to a person in connection with the place where he lives, and may be defined as one who resides in a place or one who dwells in a place for a considerable period of time as distinguished from one who merely works in a certain locality or comes casually for a visit and the place of work or the place of casual visit are different from the place of 'residence'. There are two classifications of the meaning of the word 'residence'. First is in the form of permanent and temporary residence and the second classification is based on de facto and de jure residence. The de facto concept of residence can also be understood clearly by the meaning of the word 'residence' as given in the Black's Law Dictionary, 8th Edition. It is given that the word 'residence' means bodily presence as an inhabitant in a given place. Thus, de facto residence is also to be understood as the place where one regularly resides as different to the places where he is connected to by mere ancestral connections or political connections or connection by marriage."

96.   In Reg v. Barnet L.B.C., Ex p. Shah, [1983] 2 A.C. 309, the House of Lords held that a person was ordinarily resident in the United Kingdom, if he normally resided lawfully in that country from choice and for a settled purpose. If a person resided there for the specific and limited purpose of education, he was ordinarily resident in that country, even if his permanent residence or real home was outside that country or his future intention or expectation was to live outside that country.

97.   Residence must be voluntary. "Enforced presence by reason of kidnaping or imprisonment, or a Robinson Crusoe existence on a desert island with no opportunity of escape, may be so overwhelming a factor as to negative the will to be where one is". Per Lord Scarman, Reg v. Barnet L.B.C., Ex. p. Shah, [1983] 2 A.C. 309 at 344.

98.   As regards domicile, the Wikipedia states as follows:

"In law, domicile is the status or attribution of being a lawful permanent resident in a particular jurisdiction. A person can remain domiciled in a jurisdiction even after he has left it, if he has maintained sufficient links with that jurisdiction or has not displayed an intention to leave permanently (i.e. if that person has moved to a different state but has not yet formed an intention to remain there indefinitely).

Traditionally many common law jurisdictions considered a person's domicile to be a determinative factor in the conflict of laws and would, for example, only recognize a divorce conducted in another jurisdiction if at least one of the parties were domiciled there at the time it was conducted.

Where the country is federated into separate legal systems, citizenship and domicile will be different. For example, one might have United States citizenship and a domicile in Kentucky, Canadian citizenship and

230

a domicile in Quebec, or Australian citizenship and a domicile in Tasmania.

One can have dual nationality but not more than one domicile at a time. A person may have a domicile in one state while maintaining nationality in another country.

Unlike nationality, no person can be without a domicile even if stateless.

A person can have only one domicile at any given time.

Each state of the United States is considered a separate sovereign within the U.S. federal system, and each, therefore, has its own laws on questions of marriage, inheritance, and liability for tort and contract actions."

(https://en.wikipedia.org/wiki/Domicile_(law)

99.   Some definitions of domicile, relevant judicial pronouncements and other opinions, reproduced hereinbelow, may help us in properly understanding the issues under adjudication in these proceedings:

(i)   **"Domicile is the place where a person has fixed his ordinary dwelling, without a present intention of removal."**

(https://www.upcounsel.com/legal-def-domicile)

(ii)   "The permanent residence of a person; a place to which, even if he or she were temporary absent, they intend to return."

(http://www.duhaime.org/LegalDictionary/D/Domicile.aspx)

(iii)   "Domicile is the place where a person has his / her permanent principal home to which, whenever he / she is absent, he / she returns or intends to return. Domicile is important because it is used in determining in what state a probate of a dead person's estate is filed, what state can assess income or inheritance taxes, where a party can begin divorce proceedings, or whether there is "diversity of citizenship" between two parties which may give federal courts jurisdiction over a lawsuit. Where a person has several "residences" evidence may need to be examined to determine which is the state of domicile. A person may have only one domicile at a single point in time. A business has its domicile in the state where its headquarters is located. For tax purposes, a business' domicile is often a principal place of business."

(https://definitions.uslegal.com/d/domicile/)

(iv)   "Domicile means the place or country which is considered by law to be a person's permanent home."

(A.V. Dicey, in 'The Law of Domicile as a Branch of the Law of England).

(v)   "The word 'Domicile' has not been defined under the Citizenship Act, 1951. The Black's Law Dictionary (Seventh Edition), defines the word 'Domicile' as a person's true, fixed, principal, and permanent home, to which that person intends to return and remain even though currently residing elsewhere. --also termed permanent abode.

The above discussion leads us to the conclusion that the domicile certificate is a, prima facie, proof of the place of permanent residence of a person, who intends to permanently reside at a particular place."

{Muhammad Khalil & another Vs. Executive District Officer, Revenue, Pishin & another (PLD 2011 Quetta 21)}

(vi)   "For the acquisition of a domicile of choice, there must be a combination of residence and intention of permanent or indefinite residence before that change can become effective."

{Dicey's Conflict of Laws, 6th Edition, page 89. Joan Mary Carter v. Albert William Carter (PLD 1961 SC 616). Miss Amtul Naseer Sami v. Secretary Health, Government of Balochistan (1975 SCMR 265)}

(vii)   "The law attributes to every person at birth a domicile which is called a domicile of origin. This domicile, may be changed and a new domicile, which is called a domicile of choice, acquired but the two kinds of domicile differ in the following respects:

(1)   The domicile of origin is received by operation of law at birth, the domicile of choice is acquired later by the actual removal of an individual to another country accompanied by his animus manendi.

(2)   The domicile of origin is retained until the acquisition of a domicile of choice; it cannot be divested by mere abandonment and is never destroyed though it remains in abeyance during the continuance of domicile of choice, the domicile of choice is lost by abandonment whereupon the domicile of origin is acquired; the domicile of choice; when is once lost, is destroyed but may be acquired anew by fulfilling the same conditions as are required in the first instance."

(Halsbury's Laws of England 3rd Edition Vol.7, page 14)

(viii)   "The word `domicile' is to identify the personal law by which an individual is governed in respect of various matters such as the essential validity of a marriage, the effect of marriage on the proprietary rights of husband and wife, jurisdiction in divorce and nullity of marriage, illegitimacy, legitimation and adoption and testamentary and intestate succession to moveables. "

{Dr. Pradeep Jain Etc. Vs. Union of India and Ors. Etc (1984 AIR 1420, 1984 SCR (3) 942)}

(ix)   "Each person who has, or whom the law deems to have, his permanent home within the territorial limits of a single system of law is domiciled in the country over which the system extends; and he is domiciled in the whole of that country even though his home may be fixed at a particular spot within it."

"In federal states some branches of law are within the competence of the federal authorities and for these purposes the whole federation will be subject to a single system of law and an individual may be spoken of as domiciled in the federation as a whole; other branches of law are within the competence of the states or provinces of the federation and the individual will be domiciled in one state or province only."

(Paragraph 422 of Halsbury's Laws of England (4th Edition) Volume 8)

(x)   "English law determines all questions in which it admits the operation of a personal law by the test of domicile. For this purpose, it regards the organisation of the civilised world in civil societies, each of which consists of all those persons who live in

any territorial area which is subject to one system of law, and not its organization in political societies or states, each of which may either be co-extensive with a single legal system or may unite several systems under its own sovereignty".
(Paragraph 242 of Halsbury's Laws of England (4th Edition) Volume 8)

(xi)   "The area contemplated throughout the Rules relating to domicile is a country or territory subject to one system of law. The reason for this is that the object of this treatise, in so far as it is concerned with domicile, is to show how far a person's rights are affected by his having his legal home or domicile within a territory governed by one system of law, i.e. within a given country, rather than within another. If, indeed, it happened that one part of a country, governed generally by one system of law, was in many respects subject to special rules of law, then it would be essential to determine whether D was domiciled within such particular part, e.g. California in the United States; but in this case, such part would be pro tanto a separate country, in the sense in which that term is employed in these Rules".
(Dicey's Conflict of Laws, 6th Edition, page 83)

(xii)   "Thus, domicile is that attribute of a person's status which according to International Law determines the personal laws by which he is governed and on which his personal laws depend."
(George Udny v John Henry Udny of Udny [1869] UKHL 2 Paterson 1677, (1869) LR 1 HL 441 (3 June 1869), pp. 1686–1687)

(xiii)   "It is no doubt true that there are countries which though politically one unit have different personal laws, in different areas thereof. In such a case the sub-unit which is governed by one system of law is the area of domicile. Thus, for instance, as has been pointed out, though Great Britain is one single political unit, the personal laws in Scotland are different and, therefore, Scotch domicile is recognised."
{Dr. Pradeep Jain Etc. Vs. Union of India and Ors. Etc (1984 AIR 1420, 1984 SCR (3) 942)}

(xiv)   "That the domicile and permanent residence Certificate are two entire distinct concepts."
{Mehmood Ul Hassan Khan Vs. Dow University of Health Sciences through Vice-Chancellor {PLJ 2008 Karachi 10 (DB)}

(xv)   "7. At the very outset, it may be noted that the Province of Balochistan has multiethnic / linguistic population i.e. Baloch, Pashtun, Hazara and Settlers. The Local certificates are issued to the persons, who belong to one of the indigenous tribes of Balochistan and such tribes have been duly notified by the Home and Tribal Affairs Department, Government of Balochistan, permanently residing in a particular area of the Province and their reference could also be found in the Gazetteer of Balochistan, whereas, domicile certificates are issued to those who do not belong to indigenous tribes of Balochistan, but, otherwise, are permanently residing in Balochistan (commonly known as `settlers'). There is no difference or discrimination between a local and settler for the purpose of applying against any reserved seat or post and the only requirement is to produce a local / domicile certificate issued by the respective Deputy Commissioner of the concerned districts."

{Mubashar Mehmood and another Vs. Home and Tribal Affairs through Secretary Civil Secretariat and others (PLD 2018 Balochistan 49)}

100.   A perusal of the above may lead us to note that domicile denotes a person's true, fixed, principal, and permanent home, to which that person intends to return and remain even though currently residing elsewhere. Intention to reside at a place permanently or without present intention of change of place of residence is the essential requirement of domicile. Domicile of origin can be changed with domicile of choice. The domicile is a concept of private international law which is used mainly to determine that what laws shall apply to marriage, divorce and succession of a person and where legal proceedings in relation thereto shall be entertained.

101.   Pakistan is a federal republic with distribution of legislative powers between the Federation and the Provinces. The Federation also has powers of a Province in the Federal capital or other areas not forming part of a Province. Marriage, divorce and succession are provincial subjects. Duties in respect of succession to property was a federal subject vide entry appearing at serial number 45 of Part-1 of the Federal Legislative List in the Fourth Schedule to the Constitution but this entry was omitted by the Constitution (Eighteenth Amendment) Act, 2010 (10 of 2010), s. 101. With this omission, there is no doubt that the subject of succession fell within exclusive provincial domain. Now the Provinces are competent to repeal or amend the Succession Act, 1925 (Act No. XXXIX of 1925). Similarly, the Muslim Family Laws Ordinance, 1961 (VIII of 1961), the West Pakistan Muslim Personal Law (Shariat) Application Act, 1962 (V of 1962), the Hindu Marriage Act, 2017 (Act No. VII of 2017), enacted by the Parliament under authority derived from resolutions of the Provincial Assemblies of the Punjab, Balochistan and Khyber Pakhtunkhwa under Article 144 of the Constitution and the Sindh Hindus Marriage Act, 2016 (Sindh Act No. IX of 2016) are laws within provincial legislative domain. There is no constitutional requirement that all the Provinces and the Federation may enact exactly similar laws. Each jurisdiction can enact what seems to be the best in its wisdom. Here domicile will determine which legal dispensation is applicable and where legal proceedings are to be initiated in matters relating to marriage, divorce and succession. In this view of the matter, each jurisdiction has to be treated as a separate legal system. A domicile certificate contains permanent address of the applicant. This address will indicate which jurisdiction will be attracted in the case of matters relating to marriage, divorce and succession of the person holding the domicile. As nationality, citizenship and naturalization are federal subjects and domicile certificates are issued under Section 17 of the Pakistan Citizenship Act, 1951 read with Rule 23 of the Pakistan Citizenship Rules, 1952, therefore, these certificates can only be issued by the Federation and not by the Provinces.

102.   The question of domicile was considered in John Oswald Horatio Neale Vs. Mrs. Margrate Eilen Neale (PLD 1957 Dacca 363) in which a couple domiciled in British India, applied to the courts in Pakistan for dissolution of marriage. The court refused to exercise its jurisdiction as the couple was simply residing in the Pakistani territories and there was no intent to abandon the domicile of origin, or adopt the domicile of Pakistan. The court held that mere residence in a country does not prove a domicile of choice and the following two essential conditions must co-exist to establish this factum:

    i.   that a person has abandoned his domicile of origin or that his domicile of origin is in abeyance; and

    ii.   that he has adopted the country in which he resides as his home, that is to say, he intends living in the country in which he resides as his home, and does not intend going back to his country of origin. The residence, animus manendi (intent of remaining) and lack of animus revertendi (intent of returning) to the former domicile are necessary ingredients for establishing sui juris. The residence without the animus manendi and, animus manendi without the proof of residence are insufficient to claim citizenship and this principle is unequivocally encapsulated in the Act (Section 3).

103.   Whereas Article 27(2) of the Constitution allows imposition of the condition of residence in the Province prior to appointment, the Khyber Pakhtunkhwa Civil Servants (Appointment, Promotion and Transfer) Rules, 1989 impose the condition of bona fide residence which is synonymous to domicile. Section 3 and 4 of the Khyber Pakhtunkhwa (Appointment, Deputation, Posting and Transfer of Teachers, Lecturers, Instructors and Doctors) Regulatory Act, 2011 and Section 34 of the Khyber Pakhtunkhwa Police Act, 2017 also prescribe the condition of domicile for being eligible for appointments specified therein.

104.   Residence and domicile are not identical. Article 27(2) of the Constitution allows prescription of residence not exceeding three years prior to appointment and not of domicile. The requirement of domicile may make the fundamental right guaranteed under Article 15 ineffective. If a citizen is allowed to reside in any part of the country but is made ineligible to compete for jobs under a provincial entity for want of domicile of that Province, the fundamental rights granted by Article 15 and Article 18 get materially squeezed to an extent not permitted by the Constitution. To guard against misconceptions, the Constitution uses the word 'residence' and not 'domicile' in clause 1 as well as 2 of Article 27. The requirement under clause 2 of Article 27 is a requirement of durational residence not exceeding three years. For issuance of domicile of choice, the requirement is of durational residence of one year with intent to reside indefinitely. A citizen can reside in a Province for an indefinite period without being in any legal compulsion to acquire domicile from that Province. If a Province has statutorily prescribed a minimum duration of residence (not exceeding three years in any case) in that Province as one of the conditions of eligibility to compete for appointments in services of that Province or posts in connection with affairs of that Province, and a citizen proves his residence in that Province for the minimum period prescribed, he shall not be denied eligibility on the ground that he has domicile of another jurisdiction in the country as domicile and residence are not synonymous. Every word used in the Constitution needs to be given full effect. Use of word 'residence' in Article 27 of the Constitution rules out the possibility of its substitution with the word 'domicile' through any sub-constitutional or executive instrument.

105.   After concluding that the condition of domicile is not allowed to be made a requirement for eligibility for appointment in provincial services or posts in connection with affairs of the Province but a condition of durational residence is permissible, we may examine whether the Constitution allows to make residence in a particular area or administrative sub-division of a Province necessary for becoming eligible for appointment to posts on provincial level or in cadres maintained at district, divisional or zonal level. To be more specific, we may find the answer to the question whether a resident of a Province for the prescribed minimum period can be discriminated against in the matter of appointments in any of the entities of that Province on the basis of his residence at a particular place? We have not been able to find anything in the Constitution which may authorize the provincial legislature or the executive to require a person to reside in any particular district or area of the Province as a condition-precedent to be eligible to compete for appointment in provincial services or posts in connection with affairs of the Province. The requirement of minimum durational residence in the Province and necessity of residing in a particular district or area are not identical requirements. What Article 27(2) of the Constitution authorizes is the requirement to be resident in that Province for a minimum prescribed period prior to appointment. A Province has its known territorial boundaries. A person who resides in these territories resides in the Province. If his residence is for the prescribed minimum period,

then he is eligible to get appointment if otherwise qualified and on merit. His candidature cannot be rejected on the basis alone of his being or not being resident of a particular district or area of the Province if the fact of his durational residence is proved.

106.   We have seen the judgment reported as Mubashar Mehmood and another Vs. Home and Tribal Affairs through Secretary Civil Secretariat and others (PLD 2018 Balochistan 49)} and a number of judgments of the Hon'ble Sindh High Court regarding the Sindh Permanent Residence Certificate Rules, 1971. With respect, we observe that the respective provincial legislatures are competent to enact laws to prescribe the condition of durational residence in the Province and to provide for matters connected therewith or ancillary thereto. The executive has no power to prescribe the condition of residence through executive orders even if issued under the name of rules. We have also observed that Section 17 of the Pakistan Citizenship Act, 1951 authorizes the Federal Government to issue domiciles. Rule 23 of the Pakistan Citizenship Rules, 1952 authorizes the Provincial Government or any District Magistrate authorized by the Provincial Government in this behalf, in addition to the Federal Government, to issue certificates of domicile. This rule enlarges the scope of the Act by including in the rules which is not expressly or impliedly included in the Act. Thus, the rules are void and of no legal effect to the extent of their travel beyond the territory envisaged by the Act. If the Federation intends the Provincial Governments or the District Magistrates to issue domiciles on its behalf, it may resort to an arrangement under Article 146 of the Constitution on payment of expenditure to be incurred by the Province for the purpose. We have also seen Rule 23 of the Pakistan Citizenship Rules, 1952 in the light of the dictum of law laid down by the Hon'ble Supreme Court of Pakistan in the Mustafa Impex case (PLD 2016 SC 808) wherein the expression 'federal government' has been defined. We asked the learned Attorney General for Pakistan to produce a single domicile certificate issued by the Federal Government or the Government of Khyber Pakhtunkhwa or a District Magistrate in the Khyber Pakhtunkhwa during the year 2019 or to advise the Government to remove redundancies from the relevant laws / rules.

107.   In the light of the above discussion, we hold that:

    a) The condition as to residence in the Province, for a period not exceeding three years, prior to appointment in a provincial service or posts in connection with affairs of the Province means the requirement of minimum durational residence in the Province statutorily prescribed:

    b) A bona fide residence or domicile or residence in a particular district or area of the Province are not permitted as conditions as to residence allowed to be prescribed under Article 27(2) of the Constitution. Prescribed minimum period of physical presence will constitute residence provided it is not transitory, fleeting or casual;

    c) Rule 11 and 12 of the Khyber Pakhtunkhwa Civil Servants (Appointment, Promotion and Transfer) Rules, 1989, Section 3 and 4 of the Khyber Pakhtunkhwa (Appointment, Deputation, Posting and Transfer of Teachers, Lecturers, Instructors and Doctors) Regulatory Act, 2011 and Section 34 of the Khyber Pakhtunkhwa Police Act, 2017 are void to the extent of prescription of the condition of domicile; and

    d) Domicile certificates issued by the Provincial Government or the District Magistrates or other provincial employees in the Provinces are invalid being ultra vires Section 17 of the Pakistan Citizenship Act, 1951. The Federal Government may, however, resort to arrangements under Article 146 of the Constitution for issuance of domiciles in the Provinces.

Question # 3

Whether posts in the service of Pakistan can be reserved for persons with disabilities after the expiry of the period of forty years specified in the first proviso to Article 27(1) of the Constitution?

108.   We are in agreement with the argument that disability is an attribute on the basis of which a class can be formed for the purpose of ensuring adequate representation of persons with disabilities in the service of Pakistan. By specifically prohibiting discrimination against citizens in the matter of appointments in the service of Pakistan on the ground only of race, religion, caste, sex, residence or place of birth, other reasonable grounds for protective discrimination have not been ruled out. Disability is one of those reasonable grounds. Reservation of posts in the service of Pakistan for persons with disabilities under the Disabled Persons (Employment and Rehabilitation) Ordinance, 1981 and the Khyber Pakhtunkhwa Disabled Persons (Employment and Rehabilitation) (Amendment) Act, 2012, was, therefore, constitutionally valid till 13.08.2013 i.e. before expiry of the constitutionally fixed period of forty years. After expiry of that period, reservation of posts for persons with disabilities is without constitutional mandate. We are aware of responsibilities of Pakistan under the UN Convention on the Rights of Persons with Disabilities, 2006 (CRPD) which was ratified by Pakistan in 2011. But we are not convinced that ratification of a UN Convention authorizes the Federation to abridge fundamental rights of the citizens under the pretext of a UN Convention. We hold that in case of an irreconcilable clash between provisions of the Constitution and obligations of the state under a convention of the United Nations or treaties with any other multilateral or foreign entity, the provisions of the Constitution shall prevail. The state is debarred to enact any law in contravention of the fundamental rights. It is also prohibited to do so in the name of its international obligations. Article 8 of the Constitution provides the basic test that any law or custom or usage having the force of law is void to the extent of its inconsistency with the fundamental rights. We are unable to subscribe to the theory that what the state is expressly prohibited to do is allowed to be done if it is a requirement of a UN Convention. In fact, the state is not authorized to enter into any international or bilateral arrangement which contravenes any of the fundamental rights or otherwise is against any express or implied provision of the Constitution. If it is absolutely necessary to enter into an international or bilateral arrangement which may not be in accordance with the Constitution, a constitutional amendment enabling that arrangement must precede acceptance of that arrangement by the Federation.

109.   On 14.08.2013, the provisions of the Disabled Persons (Employment and Rehabilitation) Ordinance, 1981 and the Khyber Pakhtunkhwa Disabled Persons (Employment and Rehabilitation) (Amendment) Act, 2012 became void to the extent of reservation of posts in the service of Pakistan for persons with disabilities. We, however, reject prayer of the learned counsel for Mr. Qaiser Shah to declare the above laws void ab initio. The Hon'ble Supreme Court of Pakistan has elaborated the term 'void' in its judgment reported as Dr. Mobashir Hassan Vs. Federation (PLD 2010 SC 265) in these words:

> "55.   As far as the term 'void' is concerned, it has been defined in Black's Law Dictionary, 7th Edo. (1999), as "of no legal effect; null". Corpus Juris Secundum, Vol.92 at pp 1021 to 1022 defines 'void" as follows: -
>
>> "The word 'void' may be used in what is variously referred to as its literal, absolute, primary, precise, strict, and strictly accurate sense, and in this sense it means absolutely null; null and incapable of confirmation or ratification; of no effect and incapable of confirmation; of no force and effect; <u>having no legal forte</u> or binding effect, having no legal or binding force; incapable of being enforced by law; of no legal force or effect whatever; that which has no force and effect; without legal efficacy, without vitality or legal effect; ineffectual; nugatory;

unable in law to support the purpose for which it was intended".
(emphasis added).

56. The expression 'void' has also been commented upon in Province of East Pakistan v. Md. Mehdi Ali Khan, PLD 1959 SC 387, Syed Abul A 'la Maudoodi v. Government of West Pakistan, PLD 1964 SC 673, Bhikaji Narain v. State of MP., AIR 1955 SC 781. This Court in Haji Rehmdil v. Province of Balochistan, 1999 SCMR 1060 defines that "term `void' signifies something absolutely null, incapable of ratification or confirmation and, thus, having no legal effect whatsoever". Similarly, the word `void ab initio' has been defined in Black's Law Dictionary, 7th Edn. (1999), as "null from the beginning".

110. It was held by the Hon'ble Supreme Court of Pakistan in Province of East Pakistan Vs. Md. Mehdi Ali Khan (PLD 1959 SC 387) that the law in violation of a fundamental right "is void only to the extent of such contravention, and not void ab initio like legislation which suffers from the incident of an inherent lack of power".

111. It was further held by the Hon'ble Supreme Court of Pakistan in Syed Abul Ala Maudoodi Vs. Govt. of West Pakistan (PLD 1964 SC 673) with reference to a law in conflict with a fundamental right that:

"It only means that such a law becomes unenforceable so long as a conflict with a fundamental right exists and if the fundamental right for some reason or other disappears, the law becomes operative again. It is really a state of hibernation rather than one of death."

112. As the Disabled Persons (Employment and Rehabilitation) Ordinance, 1981 and the Khyber Pakhtunkhwa Disabled Persons (Employment and Rehabilitation) (Amendment) Act, 2012 were enacted before expiry of the prescribed period of forty years, therefore, these went into state of hibernation on 14.08.2013 and became void due to inconsistency with Article 27 of the Constitution to the extent of reservation of posts in the service of Pakistan for persons with disabilities. These laws are not void ab initio to the extent of reservation of posts in the service of Pakistan and shall stand revived when fundamental rights are suspended in accordance with the Constitution or the period of forty years specified in Article 27 is extended. Moreover, the Disabled Persons (Employment and Rehabilitation) Ordinance, 1981 is applicable to an establishment as defined in Section 2 (f) of the Ordinance ibid, reproduced below:

"establishment" means a Government establishment, a commercial establishment or an industrial establishment, in which the number of workers employed at any time during a year is not less than one hundred;".

113. As is evident from the above definition, reservation of posts for persons with disabilities is not restricted to posts in the service of Pakistan only; this reservation is also applicable on establishments in the private sector. The fundamental right enshrined in Article 27 of the Constitution relates only to the reservation of posts in the service of Pakistan and no other posts. The Parliament or a Provincial Assembly are, therefore, well within their lawful jurisdiction if they reserve quota for persons with disabilities in private sector. It needs to be clarified that if a law is made in contravention of a fundamental right after the commencing day of the Constitution, the same shall be void ab initio being in violation of prohibition on legislation which takes away or abridges any of the fundamental rights.

114. We are convinced of the desirability of measures for welfare of the persons with disabilities. All measures required for dignified living of persons with disabilities must be taken by the state. But our sympathy for persons with disabilities does not allow us to legitimize violations of the Constitution. Welfare measures for persons with disabilities must remain within the constitutional limits. It pains us to declare that reservation of posts in the service of Pakistan under the Disabled Persons (Employment and Rehabilitation) Ordinance,

1981 and the Khyber Pakhtunkhwa Disabled Persons (Employment and Rehabilitation) (Amendment) Act, 2012 is void with effect from 14.08.2013.

Question # 4

Whether reservation of posts in the service of Pakistan for women is a discrimination on the basis of gender or a special measure for protection of women?

115. Use of gender as a common attribute to constitute a class within the contemplation of first proviso to Article 27(1) of the Constitution so as to ensure its adequate representation in the service of Pakistan not only violates the prohibition contained in Article 27(1) but is also not consistent with the intents and purposes of second proviso to the said Article. It may legitimately be argued that women lag behind men in terms of education and socio-economic status and this comparative backwardness entitles them to be treated as a class but in view of prohibition embodied in Article 27(1) sex is not allowed to be taken as determinant factor in classification and the consequent discrimination against other classes in the matter of appointments in the service of Pakistan. Like men, women are also a multiclass sex. Women of every level of achievement are available in every society. If backwardness is the criteria for formation of a class, then citizens falling within that criteria shall be construed as a class irrespective of gender, race, caste, place of residence or place of birth. It would be the backwardness which shall be taken as the determinant factor and not gender or sex.

116. Article 25(2) of the Constitution imposes a comprehensive and absolute prohibition on discrimination on the basis of sex. First proviso to Article 27(1) cannot be construed so as to nullify Article 25(2) and Article 27(1) of the Constitution. The question of intelligible differentia and its nexus to the objectives sought to be achieved arises when classification is made on the basis of common attributes other than those enumerated in Article 27(1) of the Constitution.

117. The second proviso to Article 27(1) of the Constitution makes the matter crystal clear by clarifying that specified posts or services may be reserved for members of either sex if such posts or services entail the performance of duties and functions which cannot be adequately performed by members of the other sex. This is the only scenario in which gender is allowed to be used as a criterion for definition of a class. In this case, a declaration to the effect that functions assigned to the specified posts or specified classes of posts in a particular service can adequately be performed only by a particular sex must precede reservation of those posts for that sex. In absence of such a declaration, reservation of posts for a sex is not permissible under the Constitution.

118. In order to properly understand true import of Article 27 of the Constitution in the context of second proviso thereto, we may peruse the following provision of the Civil Rights Act of 1964 of the United States of America:

> "DISCRIMINATION BECAUSE OF RACE, COLOR, RELIGION, SEX, OR NATIONAL ORIGIN
>
> SEC. 703.
>
> (a) It shall be an unlawful employment practice for an employer--
>
> > (1) to fail or refuse to hire or to discharge any individual, or otherwise to discriminate against any individual with respect to his compensation, terms, conditions, or privileges of employment, because of such individual's race, color, religion, sex, or national origin; or
> >
> > (2) to limit, segregate, or classify his employees in any way which would deprive or tend to deprive any individual of employment opportunities or otherwise adversely affect his status as an employee, because of such individual's race, color, religion, sex, or national origin.

(b)   It shall be an unlawful employment practice for an employment agency to fail or refuse to refer for employment, or otherwise to discriminate against, any individual because of his race, color, religion, sex, or national origin, or to classify or refer for employment any individual on the basis of his race, color, religion, sex, or national origin.

(c)   It shall be an unlawful employment practice for a labor organization--

(1)   to exclude or to expel from its membership, or otherwise to discriminate against, any individual because of his race, color, religion, sex, or national origin;

(2)   to limit, segregate, or classify its membership, or to classify or fail or refuse to refer for employment any individual, in any way which would deprive or tend to deprive any individual of employment opportunities, or would limit such employment opportunities or otherwise adversely affect his status as an employee or as an applicant for employment, because of such individual's race, color, religion, sex, or national origin; or

(3)   to cause or attempt to cause an employer to discriminate against an individual in violation of this section.

(d)   It shall be an unlawful employment practice for any employer, labor organization, or joint labor-management committee controlling apprenticeship or other training or retraining, including on-the-job training programs to discriminate against any individual because of his race, color, religion, sex, or national origin in admission to, or employment in, any program established to provide apprenticeship or other training.

(e)   Notwithstanding any other provision of this title, (1) it shall not be an unlawful employment practice for an employer to hire and employ employees, for an employment agency to classify, or refer for employment any individual, for a labor organization to classify its membership or to classify or refer for employment any individual, or for an employer, labor organization, or joint labor-management committee controlling apprenticeship or other training or retraining programs to admit or employ any individual in any such program, on the basis of his religion, sex, or national origin in those certain instances where religion, sex, or national origin is a bona fide occupational qualification reasonably necessary to the normal operation of that particular business or enterprise, and (2) it shall not be an unlawful employment practice for a school, college, university, or other educational institution or institution of learning to hire and employ employees of a particular religion if such school, college, university, or other educational institution or institution of learning is, in whole or in substantial part, owned, supported, controlled, or managed by a particular religion or by a particular religious corporation, association, or society, or if the curriculum of such school, college, university, or other educational institution or institution of learning is directed toward the propagation of a particular religion."

119. In the case under adjudication in these proceedings, the posts are those duties of which can adequately be performed by either sex or even by trans genders. Nothing is on record to show that sex is a bona fide occupational qualification reasonably necessary for adequate performance of duties assigned to the posts against which recruitment was made. Reservation of a percentage of these posts for a particular gender is, thus, not supported under the second proviso to Article 27(1) and the same attracts bar under Article 25(2) and Article 27(1) and is not protected under the first and second provisos to Article 27(1) of the Constitution.

120. Since the practice of reservation of posts for women fails to qualify the constitutional requirement of a fair classification not based upon sex or the requirement of adequate performance of duties of a post in the interest of a service, therefore, the question of determination of adequacy of representation of women in the service of Pakistan pales into insignificance and we are not inclined to attend to this aspect of the matter in these proceedings.

121. We have examined the arguments that the equality clause enshrined in Article 25 of the Constitution does not preclude special measures to be taken for protection of women and children and that it is a principle of policy (Article 34 of the Constitution) to take steps to ensure full participation of women in all spheres of national life. Article 25(3) and Article 34 allow special measures to facilitate women to realize their potential to the extent possible. When we seek guidance from Article 37(f) of the Constitution, we may find that such special measures may include capacity building through education, training, agricultural and industrial development and other methods to enable the women to participate fully in all forms of national activities, including employment in the service of Pakistan. These facilitative and protective measures cannot be conceived to include permission to make discrimination in the matter of appointments in the service of Pakistan on the basis of sex. Moreover, a principle of policy cannot be used as a pretext to usurp fundamental rights of the citizens. The Constitution has to be read as a whole and be construed harmoniously so as to give effect to each and every word of the Constitution. Article 25(3) of the Constitution is not available to nullify Article 27 of the Constitution. There is no clash between these two Articles and both can co-exist without a need to do violence against each another. Special measures can be taken for protection of women without violating the bar imposed by Article 27(1) of the Constitution. We are, therefore, convinced to hold that reservation of posts in the service of Pakistan for women on the sole ground of sex is not a special measure for the protection of women and children as contemplated by Article 25(3) of the Constitution.

122. The above discussion leads us to hold that reservation of posts for women in the service of Pakistan, other than the posts duties of which cannot adequately be performed by the other sex, is void ab initio being a discrimination on the basis of sex prohibited by Article 25(2) and Article 27(1) of the Constitution and not covered under the first and second provisos to Article 27(1) of the Constitution.

Question # 5

Whether reservation of posts in the service of Pakistan for religious minorities and allocation of additional marks for memorizers of the Holy Quran is discrimination on the basis of religion?

123. We have earlier held in this judgment that citizens are not allowed to be discriminated against in the matter of appointment in the service of Pakistan on the grounds enumerated in Article 27(1) of the Constitution. Religion is one of those grounds. Prohibition of discrimination on those grounds automatically precludes classification of citizens on those grounds for the purpose of appointments in the service of Pakistan. Religion is, therefore, not a valid attribute for reservation of posts in the service of Pakistan for citizens belonging to a particular religion. State has to be religion-neutral so far as appointments in the service of Pakistan are concerned. A person otherwise qualified is not allowed to be discriminated

against on the basis of his religion. Where a post requires religious knowledge and belief of a particular religion as a necessary qualification for adequate performance of duties of that post e.g. memorization of the Holy Quran for teachers employed for enabling Muslim students to learn Quran by heart, the condition of religion may not go against intents and purposes of Article 27(1) of the Constitution and may be declared consistent with the spirit of Article 22 of the Constitution as holding otherwise would cause absurdities. In all other cases, religion is an irrelevant factor in the matter of appointments in the service of Pakistan.

124.   Promotion of teachings of Islam and efforts to enable Muslims to order their lives in accordance with the fundamental principles and basic concepts of Islam and to provide facilities whereby they may be enabled to understand the meaning of life according to the Holy Quran and Sunnah do not justify discrimination on religious grounds in the matter of appointments in the service of Pakistan. Award of additional marks to Muslim candidates on account of memorization of the Holy Quran is an instance of adverse discrimination on the basis of religion as no corresponding credit is given to non-Muslims for their proficiency in their religious teachings.

125.   Article 260(3) of the Constitution, reproduced below, provides the following definitions of a Muslim and non-Muslim:

> "(3)   In the Constitution and all enactments and other legal instruments, unless there is anything repugnant in the subject or context, —
>
> (a)   "Muslim" means a person who believes in the unity and oneness of Almighty Allah, in the absolute and unqualified finality of the Prophethood of Muhammad (peace be upon him), the last of the prophets, and does not believe in, or recognize as a prophet or religious reformer, any person who claimed or claims to be a prophet, in any sense of the word or of any description whatsoever, after Muhammad (peace be upon him); and
>
> (b)   "non-Muslim" means a person who is not a Muslim and includes a person belonging to the Christian, Hindu, Sikh,   Budhist or Parsi community, a person of the Quadiani group or the Lahori group (who call themselves 'Ahmadis' or by any other name), or a Bahai, and a person belonging to any of the scheduled castes."

126.   Our attention has been drawn towards a judgment reported as 2005 MLD 1053. In that case, the petitioner who was an Ahmadi was promoted as Superintendent (BS-16) in the Auqaf Organization. The said order of promotion was re-called on 06.08.1996 on the ground that proviso to section 5(1) of the Punjab Waqf Properties Ordinance, 1979 (IV of 1979) as inserted therein by Punjab Ordinance No. XIII of 1984, did not permit promotion of a non-Muslim as an officer. The petitioner approached the High Court in Writ Petition No. 13894 of 1996 which was allowed vide order dated 18.09.2000 after finding that the petition was condemned unheard. It was held by the Hon'ble Court that:

> "The guarantee against discrimination on the ground of religion is absolute and not subject to reasonable qualification or restriction. The exceptions to that said guarantee have been provided by the Article itself. Therefore, the proviso to section 5(1) added to the Punjab Waqf Properties Ordinance, 1979 (IV of 1979) by the Punjab Ordinance NO. XIII of 1984 is repugnant to the Article 27 and is, thus, void by virtue of operation of Article 8 of the Constitution."

127.   Leaned counsel for Mr. Raheel Ahmad Siddiqui argued that the quota reserved for non-Muslims in the Khyber Pakhtunkhwa far exceeds the share proportionate to their

population. He submitted that whereas non-Muslims are 0.29 per cent of the total population of the Province, the quota reserved for them is 5%. Thus, the quota cannot be taken as a measure to compensate for their under representation in the service of Pakistan but is a tool to ensure their over representation in the service of Pakistan. We asked the learned Advocate General, Khyber Pakhtunkhwa to offer views of the Provincial Government on the authenticity of the figures quoted by the learned counsel for Mr. Raheel Ahmad Siddiqui. The learned Advocate General confirmed these figures. The disproportionality of the quota reserved for non-Muslims can be a good ground to attack the quota if it is otherwise found valid. The quota for non-Muslims in the service of Pakistan is a discrimination on the basis of religion. Same is the case with award of additional marks to memorizers of the Holy Quran. We are, therefore, constrained to hold that reservation of quota for the non-Muslims in the appointments in the service of Pakistan and the award of additional marks on account of memorization of the Holy Quran are void ab initio.

Question # 6

Whether a citizen has fundamental right guaranteed by Article 27 of the Constitution in the matter of initial recruitment in police force of the Federation or of a Province?

128. We have already held in this judgment that discrimination against citizens on the basis of domicile of a particular district in the matter of appointments in the provincial services and posts in connection with affairs of a Province is void being in violation of Article 27(1) of the Constitution and in excess of the authority conferred by Article 27(2) of the Constitution. The learned Advocate General, Khyber Pakhtunkhwa has defended discrimination in the matter of recruitments in the police in the Province on the basis of district of domicile pleading that the prohibitions contained in Article 8(1) & (2) of the Constitution are not applicable to members of the Armed Forces, or of the police or of such other forces as are charged with the maintenance of public order, for the purpose of ensuring the proper discharge of their duties or the maintenance of discipline among them. What he wants to say is that the fundamental right guaranteed by Article 27 of the Constitution is not enforceable to the extent of members of the Armed Forces, or of the police or of such other forces as are charged with the maintenance of public order. We may peruse Article 8 of the Constitution, reproduced below, to see the strength in the argument of the learned Advocate General, Khyber Pakhtunkhwa:

"**8. Laws inconsistent with or in derogation of Fundamental Rights to be void. -**

(1)   Any law, or any custom or usage having the force of law, in so far as it is inconsistent with the rights conferred by this Chapter, shall, to the extent of such inconsistency, be void.

(2)   The State shall not make any law which takes away or abridges the rights so conferred and any law made in contravention of this clause shall, to the extent of such contravention, be void.

(3)   The Provisions of this Article shall not apply to—

(a)   *any law relating to members of the Armed Forces, or of the police or of such other forces as are charged with the maintenance of public order, for the purpose of ensuring the proper discharge of their duties or the maintenance of discipline among them*; or

(b)   any of the —

(i)   laws specified in the First Schedule as in force immediately before the commencing day or as amended by any of the laws specified in that Schedule;

(ii) other laws specified in Part I of the First Schedule;

and no such law nor any provision thereof shall be void on the ground that such law or provision is inconsistent with, or repugnant to, any provision of this Chapter.

(4) Notwithstanding anything contained in paragraph (b) of clause (3), within a period of two years from the commencing day, the appropriate Legislature shall bring the laws specified in Part II of the First Schedule into conformity with the rights conferred by this Chapter:

Provided that the appropriate Legislature may by resolution extend the said period of two years by a period not exceeding six months.

Explanation. – If in respect of any law Majlis-e-Shoora (Parliament) is the appropriate Legislature, such resolution shall be a resolution of the National Assembly.

(5) The rights conferred by this Chapter shall not be suspended except as expressly provided by the Constitution."

(emphasis supplied)

129. A plain reading of the above Article makes it clear that Article 8(1) and (2) are inapplicable, inter alia, to **any law relating to members of the Armed Forces, or of the police or of such other forces as are charged with the maintenance of public order, for the purpose of ensuring the proper discharge of their duties or the maintenance of discipline among them.** Thus, the extent of non-applicability of the Article 8(1) and (2) is restricted to the limited purpose of ensuring the proper discharge of their duties or the maintenance of discipline among members of the Armed Forces, or of the police or of such other forces as are charged with the maintenance of public order. There is no question of abridgment of fundamental rights guaranteed by Article 18 and 27 of the Constitution in the matter of appointments through initial recruitments in the Armed Forces, or the police or such other forces as are charged with the maintenance of public order. All citizens, otherwise qualified, have a fundamental right not to be discriminated against in the matter of appointment in the armed forces or law enforcing agencies on the ground only of race, religion, caste, sex, residence or place of birth. It is only when an appointment is made of duly qualified citizens through a non-discriminative and transparent open competitive process, then the fundamental rights become inapplicable to the extent of maintenance of discipline and for ensuring proper discharge of duties. Since the matter under adjudication in these proceedings pertains to initial recruitment in the police force of the Khyber Pakhtunkhwa on the basis of domicile of the district in which vacancy occurs and has nothing to do with maintenance of discipline in the police or proper discharging of duties, therefore, fundamental rights of the citizens are firmly intact. As an inescapable consequence of this finding, we do hereby declare that citizens have a fundamental right to compete for recruitment in the police force of the Federation or of a Province without being subjected to discrimination on the basis of domicile of a particular district. A Province may, however, prescribe condition of residence in the Province for a period not exceeding three years prior to such appointment.

Question # 7

Whether allocation of special quota for children of retired civil servants is based upon intelligible differentia having rational nexus to the purpose intended to be achieved?

130. Welfare of employees to maintain their morale and to reap the benefits of resultant better efficiency and productivity may be a legitimate interest of the Province. Suitable measures found necessary to achieve the purpose can be taken by the Province. We are

244

vitally concerned with legality of the measures and their nexus to the objectives intended to be achieved.

131. Appointments to the provincial services and posts in connection with affairs of the Province are made to ensure efficient performance of functions attached with the posts. Efficient performance of these functions requires selection of the best available candidates to be chosen on the basis of open competitive procedure. Appointments in absence of due open competitive process results into appointment of less meritorious candidates and abridges the fundamental right to trade and profession guaranteed by Article 18 of the Constitution to the extent of citizens excluded from the competition.

We have noted that reservation of posts for children of civil servants retiring on superannuation or due to invalidation is not a classification prohibited by Article 27(1) of the Constitution but the same is not covered by the first proviso to Article 27(1) as the object stated to be achieved is not to ensure adequate representation of a class in the service of Pakistan. The civil servants do not form a separate class for the purpose of ensuring its adequate representation in the service of Pakistan as all civil servants are already represented in the service of Pakistan. Civil servants are a microscopic minority when viewed in comparison with those who don't have any representation in the service of Pakistan. If civil servants and non-civil servants are deemed to be two separate classes within the contemplation of first proviso to Article 27(1) of the Constitution, then it is non-civil servants who need to be favoured with protective discrimination in order to ensure their adequate representation in the service of Pakistan. During hearing of the rival contentions, we required the parties to support their submission with empirical data. It transpired that both parties were basing their arguments on assumptions and empirical data on the subject was not available with them in compiled and presentable form.

132. We are skeptical about the necessity of the reservation of posts for the children of the retired civil servants. A measure may be deemed necessary only if intended result cannot be achieved without it. Mere desirability or assumed importance of a measure are not enough to make a measure necessary. In our view, it is not necessary for welfare or morale boosting of the retired civil servants that posts in the service of Pakistan be reserved in BS. 1 to BS. 4 for their children. What a civil servant can expect from his employment as a civil servant is the remuneration-pay during service and pension after retirement. The Government may enhance this remuneration for welfare of the civil servants. Other benefits may also be extended to the civil servants through law. It is not understandable that how a low-paid job of one child of a retired civil servant is necessary for welfare of the concerned retired civil servant. In presence of other suitable options, we don't agree with the argument of desirability or necessity of reservation of posts for children of the retired civil servants. Even if its necessity or desirability is accepted, its legality is the material thing on the basis of which we are under oath to decide cases brought before us. Welfare measures for the civil servants can be taken without doing violence against any of the fundamental rights of the citizens. In the instant case, the reservation of posts has been found in violation of Article 18 and 27 of the Constitution.

133. The Khyber Pakhtunkhwa Civil Servants Act, 1973 and the rules framed thereunder do not provide for reservation of quotas on the basis of profession or employment of parents of the candidates aspiring to join a provincial service or hold a post in connection with affairs of the Province. We agree with the argument that mere executive instructions, in absence of a law and the rules sanctioning such a dispensation, are not a lawful instrument to introduce the concept of reservation of certain posts for children of retired civil servants, even if the concept clears the constitutional barriers.

134. The Hon'ble Supreme Court of India, in D. N. Chanchala Vs. State of Mysore and Ors. Etc. (971 AIR 1762, 1971 SCR 608) has held as follows:

> "In two other decisions, Umesh Chandra v. V. N. Singh ([1967] 1 L.
> R. 46 Put. 616) and Kerala v. Jacob, (AIR 1964 Ker. 316) a provision
> authorising special preference to the children of the employees of the

University who had rendered meritorious service to the University, and a provision for reservation for children of registered medical practitioners in medicine were struck down, the first on the ground that it would lead to favouritism and patronage, and the second on the ground that the classification was not a rational one. Ram Chandra v. State (AIR 1961 M.P. 247) is yet another case where the High Court, dealing with rules providing for 3% of the seats for children of bona fide political sufferers as defined in M. P. Freedom Fighters Pension Rules, 1959, observed, though it declined to set them aside on other grounds, that "the preferential treatment accorded to them (the children of political sufferers) is based upon irrelevant and wholly extraneous considerations because there is no rational relation between the political suffering of a person and the education imparted to his descendants in a medical college with the object of promoting efficiency in the medical profession".

135.   We are, accordingly, convinced to hold that allocation of special quota for children of retired civil servants is not based upon intelligible differentia, has no rational nexus to the purpose intended to be achieved and can reasonably be termed unlawful favouritism and patronage. The same is held to be void and of no legal effect.

Question # 8

Whether reservation of posts for a class which otherwise may be in accordance with the Constitution be made through executive orders?

136.   This court has held in its judgment reported as Ali Waqar and others versus Province of the Punjab and others (IAH 2019 MOOT COURT JUDGMENTS 2) that:

> "37.   This court, in its judgment reported as Azhar Hussain and others vs. Federation of Pakistan and others (IAH 2019 MOOT COURT JUDGMENTS 1) has observed as under:
>
>> "169. It is settled law that the jurisdiction of the executive must be justified and vindicated by affirmative constitutional or statutory provision or it does not exist. The Hon'ble Supreme Court of Pakistan has held in a case reported as PLD 1993 SC 473 that:
>>
>>> "In view of the express provisions of our written constitution detailing with fullness the powers and duties of the various agencies of the government that it holds in balance there is no room of any residual or enabling powers inhering in any authority established by it besides those conferred upon it by specific words."
>>
>> 170. It has been held in PLD 1953 PC 58 that:
>>
>>> "A public officer had not, by reason of the fact that he is in the service of the Crown, a right to act for and on behalf of Crown in all matters which concern the Crown and that the right to act for the Crown in any particular matter must be established by reference to statute."
>>
>> 171. It has been held in cases reported as Federation v. Saeed Ahmad-PLD 1974 SC 151, 165 and Sabir Shah v. Shad Muhammad--- PLD 1995 SC 66, 256, as quoted by Justice (R) Fazal Karim in Chapter 1, para 2 at page number 21 of his book "Judicial Review of Public Actions (Volume-1-First Edition)" that:
>>
>>> "The written Constitution is the source from which all governmental power emanates; it defines its scope and

ambit so that each functionary should act within his respective sphere. No power can, therefore, be claimed by any functionary which is not to be found within the four corners of the Constitution nor can anyone transgress the limits therein specified. The essential point is that the Constitution is the paramount law and the authority which different organs created by it exercise is derived authority, that is, derived from the Constitution."

172. There is little doubt, so said Justice Kaikaus in Jamal Shah v. Election Commissioner, PLD 1966 SC 1, 52, that "its object was to negative any claim by the Government that it had inherent power to take action which was not subject to law or that it could deal with individuals in any manner which was not positively prohibited by law."

173. Executive authority is the administration of the government in accordance with law. There is no inherent executive authority and such authority has to be as provided for in the Constitution or the law, as held by the Hon'ble Supreme Court of Pakistan in a case reported as PLD 1966 SC 1."

38. It has been held in PLD 1973 Karachi 132, 147 that:

"Now it is elementary in our system of law that the executive has no power except such as has been given to it, and that anything done, which in any manner adversely affects a citizen or any other person for the time being in the country, must have the warrant of power duly conferred by law and would otherwise be illegal."

39. In above view of the matter, if a department entrusted with certain business of the Provincial Government intends to create an executive entity in furtherance of objects and purposes of the Provincial Government or to operationalize an institution envisaged in the Constitution through provision of machinery, conferment of functions, powers and detailing other matters connected therewith or ancillary thereto, it will initiate process for legislation. If a certain matter pertains to more than one departments, an elaborate procedure for inter-departmental consultation has been provided in the Punjab Government Rules of Business, 2011. Rendering assistance in policy formulation and legislation and undertaking subordinate legislation are essentially executive functions. Once a decision in respect of creation of an executive entity is taken, the requisite draft law shall be introduced in the Provincial Assembly by the Government in terms of Article 138 of the Constitution with the clear stipulation that the said entity will be subordinate to the Provincial Government. The mandatory condition of subordination of all provincial executive entities to the Provincial Government is at the heart of doctrine of joint responsibility of the Cabinet to the Provincial Assembly. This objective is obtained through placing an entity under an administrative department and making a minister in-charge of that department who is answerable to the Provincial Cabinet. The Provincial Cabinet is collectively answerable to the Provincial Assembly whose members are accountable to the electorate----to the men in the street. As an

inescapable consequence of this arrangement, the law must provide a meaningful role to the minister concerned in respect of major policy decisions and executive actions so that he may be held responsible for acts and omissions of the departments and entities under his control. The Hon'ble Supreme Court of India, in A. Sanjeev Naidu v. State of Madras (AIR 1970 SC 1102, 1106) has held that:

> "The cabinet is responsible to the legislature for every action taken in any of the ministries. That is the essence of joint responsibility."

Clause (4) of Article 91 of the Constitution of Pakistan enacts this doctrine. "The cabinet, together with the Ministers of State, shall be collectively responsible to the National Assembly." In the Provinces, the same cabinet system obtains. This is reflected in Articles 105 and 130(4) of the Constitution.

137.   We have a written constitution which vests legislative powers in the legislature, judicial powers in the judiciary and executive powers in the executive. The legislature derives its powers from substantive provisions and Article 142 of the Constitution, reproduced below:

> "142.   Subject-matter of Federal and Provincial laws. Subject to the Constitution. —
>
> (a)   Majlis-e-Shoora (Parliament) shall have exclusive power to make laws with respect to any matter in the Federal Legislative List;
>
> (b)   Majlis-e-Shoora (Parliament) and a Provincial Assembly shall have power to make laws with respect to criminal law, criminal procedure and evidence;
>
> (c)   Subject to paragraph (b), a Provincial Assembly shall, and Majlis-e-Shoora (Parliament) shall not, have power to make laws with respect to any matter not enumerated in the Federal Legislative List;
>
> (d)   Majlis-e-Shoora (Parliament) shall have exclusive power to make laws with respect to all matters pertaining to such areas in the Federation as are not included in any Province."

138.   Source of power of the judiciary has been specified in Article 175 (2) of the Constitution in these words:

> "No court shall have any jurisdiction save as is or may be conferred on it by the Constitution or by or under any law.

139.   The executive derives its powers from the Constitution and the laws made thereunder. The Hon'ble Supreme Court of Pakistan has authoritatively and unambiguously laid down the following dictum of law in its judgment reported as Pakistan Muslim League Vs. Federation of Pakistan (PLD 2007 SC 642):

> "There is no inherent power in the Executive, except what has been vested in it by law, and that law is the source of power and duty, therefore, executive action would necessarily have to be such that it could not possibly violate a Fundamental Right. The only power of the executive to take action would have to be derived from law."

140.   The following argument of the learned Attorney General for Pakistan does not appeal to our judicial mind:

> "The Constitution envisages rules of business for the federal and provincial governments. Subjects within jurisdictions of the respective governments are assigned to various entities of those governments. Business relating to those subjects is transacted by the concerned entities. Whereas some may see legislation a preferred way of

conferring executive powers and regulating their exercise, it is not unconstitutional to take actions in absence of a law on the subject. Legislative and executive powers are co-extensive. The executive can exercise executive powers on any subject which falls within legislative competence of the concerned legislature even in absence of enabling legislation. Fixation of quota through executive orders is, therefore, not unconstitutional or illegal or irregular merely on the ground that it has not been provided for or fixed by the concerned legislature through a proper enactment."

141. The Rules of Business of the Federal and Provincial Governments in Pakistan are made under the Constitution for allocation and transaction of their businesses through assigning subjects falling with legislative competence to different executive entities (Divisions in the Federations and Departments in the Provinces). These entities initiate needed executive measures for legislation on the subjects assigned to them. Powers and functions are derived from the legislative instruments and not from the Rules of Business. The argument that since legislative and executive powers are co-extensive and, therefore, what can be done through legislation can also be done through executive instructions even in absence of an enabling law is without merit. We reject this argument. Whenever the executive acts in matters other than external affairs, it must have a valid law or command of the Constitution as a lawful justification for its action.

142. When we say that there is a trichotomy of powers in Pakistan, we impliedly rule out the possibility of exercise of the legislative powers by the executive except to the extent of temporary law-making through ordinances expressly authorized by the Constitution. Subordinate legislation or rule-making is not exercise of legislative power. It is rendering executive assistance to the legislature for giving effect to the legislative intent as enacted in the law. Authorization by the legislature to the executive to render assistance through rule-making is valid only if it is for implementation of the enacted legislative policy. If there is no enacted legislative policy, rule-making power would become impermissible abdication of legislative power.

143. We have seen the applicable federal and provincial laws and have neither found any legislative policy nor any authorization to the executive to introduce concept of reservation of posts in the service of Pakistan for any class on any ground. In absence of statutory authorization, rules are simply incompetent to do what essentially can only be done through statues, subject, obviously, to constitutional validity of the statutes.

144. The principle of responsible government is based upon the theory that what the executive does is the execution of laws made by the legislature and the cabinet is answerable to the legislature not only in the matter of rendering needed assistance in legislation but also its performance in execution. The principle on which a responsible government is based was noted a century ago in the book titled "DYARCHY" published by the OXFORD UNIVERSITY PRESS in 1920 in these words:

> "§ I. In order to sketch the constitution of the executive, it is necessary first of all to consider the functions which the new governments would have to discharge.
> These may be divided into two classes.
> I. In the first place there are the administrative functions which may involve legislation from time to time. Education is an instance. In this connection it is important to note that, under the existing system, educational policy is embodied in executive resolutions and regulations. Under a system of responsible government, it will have to be embodied in education Acts passed by the Assembly. A change of policy will involve a legislative amendment of the education Act."

145. Third proviso to Article 27(1) of the Constitution assigns the Parliament to redress the issue of under-representation of any class or area in the service of Pakistan through its

enactment. Such an enactment may cover the question of adequate representation of a class or area in the service of Pakistan to the extent of All Pakistan Services, services of the Federation and posts in connection with affairs of the Federation. Following this analogy, a Provincial Assembly may address the same question in respect of provincial services and posts in connection with affairs of the Province through a provincial law. Such laws will be a proper legal dispensation if otherwise in accordance with the Constitution. What needs to be noted in this discussion is that the executive does not possess any power to do so on its own.

146. Quotas in the service of Pakistan have been fixed by the Federal Government and the Government of Khyber Pakhtunkhwa through executive instructions. We hold that such a fixation of quotas through executive orders is invalid on this ground alone. If we conceive, for the purpose of arguments only, a situation in which Constitution clearly allows reservation of posts in the service of Pakistan for a class of citizens for a defined period, then the posts shall either be reserved statutorily or through the rules strictly in accordance with the enacted legislative policy. Reservation of posts through executive orders is simply inconceivable in our present constitutional scheme. All executive instructions issued by various authorities of the Federation and of the Province of Khyber Pakhtunkhwa in respect of quota system are, therefore, hereby held to be void and of no legal effect.

Question # 9

What should the order of the court in the facts and circumstances of these cases and whether the principle of judicial restraint is different from the doctrine of necessity?

147. We have given due consideration to the submissions of the learned Attorney General for Pakistan and the learned Advocate General, Khyber Pakhtunkhwa requesting this court to exercise judicial restraint in the matter of constitutional validity of the quota system in the matter of appointments in the service of Pakistan after 13.08.2013 i.e. after expiry of the period of forty years. Before attending to these submissions, we may see some of the definitions of the expressions "judicial restraint" and "judicial activism" downloaded from the online resources:

1. judicial restraint. 1. A restraint imposed by a court, as by a restraining order, injunction, or judgment. 2. The principle that, when a court can resolve a case based on a particular issue, it should do so, without reaching unnecessary issues. [Cases: Appeal and Error 843; Federal Courts 756. C.J.S. Appeal and Error §§ 705–706.] 3. A philosophy of judicial decision-making whereby judges avoid indulging their personal beliefs about the public good and instead try merely to interpret the law as legislated and according to precedent. — Also termed (in senses 2 & 3) judicial self-restraint. Cf. JUDICIAL ACTIVISM.
   (Black's Law Dictionary, 8th Edition).

2. Judicial restraint refers to the doctrine that judges' own philosophies or policy preferences should not be injected into the law and should whenever reasonably possible construe the law so as to avoid second guessing the policy decisions made by other governmental institutions such as Congress, the President and state legislatures. This view is based on the concept that judges have no popular mandate to act as policy makers and should defer to the decisions of the elected "political" branches of the Federal government and of the states in matters of policy making so long as these policymakers stay within the limits of their powers as defined by the US Constitution and the constitutions of the several states.
   The deference to lawmakers exhibited by exercising judicial restraint is opposed to the concept of judicial activism. The activist seeks to determine what is "just," not necessarily what is intended by law. In the

250

area of constitutional law, the judicial activist views the U.S. Constitution as a living, dynamic document which must necessarily be interpreted to meet the needs of modern times.

(https://definitions.uslegal.com/j/judicial-restraint/)

3. Judicial restraint, a procedural or substantive approach to the exercise of judicial review. As a procedural doctrine, the principle of restraint urges judges to refrain from deciding legal issues, and especially constitutional ones, unless the decision is necessary to the resolution of a concrete dispute between adverse parties. As a substantive one, it urges judges considering constitutional questions to grant substantial deference to the views of the elected branches and invalidate their actions only when constitutional limits have clearly been violated.

(https://www.britannica.com/topic/judicial-restraint)

4. The term judicial restraint refers to a belief that judges should limit the use of their power to strike down laws, or to declare them unfair or unconstitutional, unless there is a clear conflict with the Constitution. This concept relies heavily on the uniform adherence to case law, which encompasses decisions rendered by other judges on prior, similar cases. To explore this concept, consider the following judicial restraint definition.

(https://legaldictionary.net/judicial-restraint/)

On the other hand, judicial activism is defined thus:

5. "judicial activism, n. A philosophy of judicial decision-making whereby judges allow their personal views about public policy, among other factors, to guide their decisions, usu. with the suggestion that adherents of this philosophy tend to find constitutional violations and are willing to ignore precedent."

(Black's Law Dictionary, 8th Edition).

6. Judicial activism is the view that the Supreme Court and other judges can and should creatively (re)interpret the texts of the Constitution and the laws in order to serve the judges' own visions regarding the needs of contemporary society. Judicial activism believes that judges assume a role as independent policy makers or independent "trustees" on behalf of society that goes beyond their traditional role as interpreters of the Constitution and laws. The concept of judicial activism is the polar opposite of judicial restraint."

(https://definitions.uslegal.com/j/judicial-activism/)

148. From the definitions reproduced hereinabove, we may learn that judicial restraint does not mean a licence to allow disobedience of the Constitution. When, after due diligence, it becomes clear that a certain law or practice is in violation of the Constitution, this court has no discretion to refuse to make necessary declarations and issue consequent directions for the reasons, inter alia, that the Constitution is being misconstrued for a reasonable period of time and such misinterpretation suits interests of some segments of the society or the legislature is not in a position to evolve consensus required for amendments in the Constitution or there is danger of adverse outbursts against correct enunciation of law by this court. We are under oath to preserve, protect and defend the Constitution. We lack power to delay or deny correct interpretation of the Constitution in cases involving questions of public importance having substantial impact on the society as a whole. Accepting requests of the learned law officers for exercise of judicial restraint when there remains no doubt about the true intents and purposes of the Constitution in a matter under adjudication amounts to reviving the condemnable doctrine of necessity which we have buried deep in the graveyard of history. We have, therefore, no option except to reject prayers of the learned law officers which are not for exercise of judicial restraint in the sense this expression is used and understood by legal fraternity all over the world. These

prayers are in fact for revival of the doctrine of necessity with an expectation from us to do for what we have no jurisdiction or mandate. The solution to the problems and answers to difficult questions may lie in other organs of the state. We are here to implement the Constitution and, subject to the Constitution, laws as they are today and not as they are expected to be in future or in accordance with our notions of what they should be. It is held in categorical terms that the doctrine of judicial restraint does not furnish any legal justification for disobedience of the Constitution for any reason and for any period of time. We are bound to reject the argument of exercise of judicial restraint as it is being used as euphemism for the doctrine of necessity.

149. Before attending to individual cases in these proceedings, we deem it appropriate to consolidate declarations made by us earlier in this judgment so that these declarations may guide us in disposal of the individual cases. These declarations shall have effect as envisaged in Article 189 of the Constitution and are repeated hereinbelow for the purpose of clarity:

1. A petition under Article 184(3) of the Constitution is maintainable if it relates to enforcement of any of the fundamental rights of a citizen and contains questions adjudication of which may have ***substantial and broad-based impact transcending the litigation-interests of the parties and the likely results of the petition may be of importance for the public at large even if the petition is submitted by a single citizen in respect of his personal grievance.***

2. No discrimination has ever been permitted by the Constitution of the Islamic Republic of Pakistan, 1973 in the matter of appointments in the service of Pakistan on the ground only of race, religion, caste, sex, residence or place of birth.

3. Reservation of posts for persons belonging to a class or area to ensure their adequate representation in the service of Pakistan is void and of no legal effect after the expiry of the period of forty years on 13.08.2013 even if the classification is made on grounds other than those enumerated in Article 27(1) of the Constitution and the classification is based upon intelligible differentia which has rational nexus to the object of ensuring adequate representation and is implemented through an Act of Parliament in respect of All Pakistan Services, services of the Federation and posts in connection with affairs of the Federation and through a provincial law in case of provincial services and posts in connection with affairs of a Province.

4. Prescription of the condition of domicile through Rule 14, 15 and 16 of the Civil Servants (Appointment, Promotion and Transfer) Rules, 1973 as one of constituents of eligibility for appointment to All Pakistan Services, services of the Federation or for holding civil posts in connection with affairs of the Federation is void and of no legal effect.

5. The condition as to residence in the Province, for a period not exceeding three years, prior to appointment in a provincial service or posts in connection with affairs of the Province means the requirement of minimum durational residence in the Province statutorily prescribed.

6. A bona fide residence or domicile or residence in a particular district or area of the Province are not permitted as conditions as to residence allowed to be prescribed under Article 27(2) of the

Constitution. Prescribed minimum period of physical presence will constitute residence provided it is not transitory, fleeting or casual.

7. Rule 11 and 12 of the Khyber Pakhtunkhwa Civil Servants (Appointment, Promotion and Transfer) Rules, 1989, Section 3 and 4 of the Khyber Pakhtunkhwa (Appointment, Deputation, Posting and Transfer of Teachers, Lecturers, Instructors and Doctors) Regulatory Act, 2011 and Section 34 of the Khyber Pakhtunkhwa Police Act, 2017 are void to the extent of prescription of the condition of domicile.

8. Domicile certificates issued by the Provincial Government or the District Magistrates or other provincial employees in the Provinces are invalid being ultra vires Section 17 of the Pakistan Citizenship Act, 1951. The Federal Government may, however, resort to arrangements under Article 146 of the Constitution for issuance of domiciles in the Provinces.

9. Reservation of posts in the service of Pakistan under the Disabled Persons (Employment and Rehabilitation) Ordinance, 1981 and the Khyber Pakhtunkhwa Disabled Persons (Employment and Rehabilitation) (Amendment) Act, 2012 is void with effect from 14.08.2013.

10. Reservation of posts in the service of Pakistan for women on the sole ground of sex is not a special measure for the protection of women and children as contemplated by Article 25(3) of the Constitution.

11. Reservation of posts for women in the service of Pakistan, other than the posts duties of which cannot adequately be performed by the other sex, is void ab initio being a discrimination on the basis of sex prohibited by Article 25(2) and Article 27(1) of the Constitution and not covered under the first and second provisos to Article 27(1) of the Constitution.

12. Reservation of quota for non-Muslims in the appointments in the service of Pakistan and the award of additional marks on account of memorization of the Holy Quran are void ab initio.

13. Citizens have a fundamental right to compete for recruitment in the police force of the Federation or of a Province without being subjected to discrimination on the basis of domicile of a particular district.

14. Allocation of special quota for children of retired civil servants is not based upon intelligible differentia, has no rational nexus to the purpose intended to be achieved and can reasonably be termed unlawful favouritism and patronage. The same is void and of no legal effect.

15. Fixation of quotas through executive orders is invalid. If we conceive, for the purpose of arguments only, a situation in which Constitution clearly allows reservation of posts in the service of Pakistan for a class of citizens for a defined period, then the posts shall either be reserved statutorily or through the rules strictly in accordance with the enacted legislative policy. All executive instructions issued by various authorities of the Federation and of the Province of Khyber Pakhtunkhwa in respect of quota system are void and of no legal effect.

150. In addition to the above declarations, we declare and order the following in respect of individual cases of the petitioners:

1. The recruitment process undertaken by rejection of candidature of Mr. Noor Alam Khan Wazir is void and is hereby set aside. Recruitment process be initiated afresh. Punitive costs of Rs. 5,00,000/ (Five hundred thousand rupees only) are imposed upon the Province of Khyber Pakhtunkhwa to be paid to the petitioner by the Chief Secretary, Government of Khyber Pakhtunkhwa not later than sixty days of announcement of this judgment. The petition is allowed in these terms.

2. The recruitment process undertaken by rejection of candidature of Dr. Waleed Ahmad is void and is hereby set aside. Recruitment process be initiated afresh. Punitive costs of Rs. 10,00,000/ (One million rupees only) are imposed upon the Province of Khyber Pakhtunkhwa to be paid to the petitioner by the Chief Secretary, Government of Khyber Pakhtunkhwa not later than sixty days of announcement of this judgment. The petition is allowed in these terms.

3. Rejection of candidature of Mr. Allah Ditta is held to be void and the recruitment process is set aside and is ordered to be initiated afresh in accordance with our declarations in this judgment. The Province of Khyber Pakhtunkhwa is burdened with punitive costs of Rs. 5,00,000/ (Five hundred thousand rupees only) to be ensured to be paid by the Provincial Police Officer, Khyber Pakhtunkhwa to the petitioner not later than sixty days of announcement of this judgment. The petition is allowed in these terms.

4. Recommendations of the Khyber Pakhtunkhwa Public Service Commission on the basis of results of the combined competitive examination, 2018 made in accordance with zonal quota and quota for women are held to be void and are set aside. The Khyber Pakhtunkhwa Public Service Commission is directed to make recommendations on the basis of results purely on merit disregarding any quotas and the Government of Khyber Pakhtunkhwa is directed to make appointments accordingly. The Government of Khyber Pakhtunkhwa shall pay punitive costs of Rs. 10,00,000/ (One million rupees only), through the Chairman, Khyber Pakhtunkhwa Public Service Commission not later than sixty days of announcement of this judgment to Mr. Shahzad Ahmad Khan Bangash. The petition is allowed in these terms.

5. Rejection of candidature of Mr. Jamal Akhtar on the basis of his residence is held to be void and the recruitment process is set aside with direction to initiate the process afresh. The Government of Khyber Pakhtunkhwa is burdened with a punitive cost of Rs. 5,00,000/ (Five hundred thousand rupees only) to be paid by the Chief Secretary, Government of Khyber Pakhtunkhwa to the petitioner not later than sixty days of announcement of this judgment. The petition is allowed in these terms.

6. The recruitments made by preferring women over Mr. Ghulam Safdar Shah are held to be void. The respondents are directed to make recruitments on the basis of results of the selection process already undertaken exclusively on merit. The Secretary to the Law and Parliamentary Affairs Department of the Government of Khyber Pakhtunkhwa is hereby burdened with a punitive cost of Rs. 5,00,000/ (Five hundred thousand rupees only) to be paid by him personally to the petitioner not later than sixty days of

announcement of this judgment. The petition is allowed in these terms.

7. Rejection of candidature of Mr. Raheel Ahmad Siddiqui is held to be void and the recruitment process is set aside, to be initiated afresh with punitive costs of Rs. 5,00,000/ (Five hundred thousand rupees only) to be ensured to be paid by the Chief Secretary, Government of Khyber Pakhtunkhwa to the petitioner not later than sixty days of announcement of this judgment. The petition is allowed in these terms.

8. Recruitments made on the basis of results of the competitive selection process by allocating quota to children of the retired civil servants are held to be void and the departmental authorities are directed to prepare fresh merit lists ignoring quotas of any kind on the basis of marks obtained by the candidates and make recruitments accordingly solely on the basis of merit. Punitive costs of Rs. 5,00,000/ (Five hundred thousand rupees only) are hereby imposed upon the Government of Khyber Pakhtunkhwa to be ensured to be paid by the Chief Secretary, Government of Khyber Pakhtunkhwa to the petitioner not later than sixty days of announcement of this judgment. The petition is allowed in these terms.

9. Rejection of candidature of Mr. Qaiser Shah is held to be void with direction to the respondents to initiate the recruitment process afresh and make recruitments purely on merit by not allocating quota to any class including women, minorities and persons with disabilities. The Government of Khyber Pakhtunkhwa is hereby burdened with a punitive cost of Rs. 5,00,000/ (Five hundred thousand rupees only) to be ensured to be paid by the Chief Secretary, Khyber Pakhtunkhwa to the petitioner not later than sixty days of announcement of this judgment. The petition is allowed in these terms.

10. Allocation of additional marks to memorizers of the Holy Quran is held to be void and the Vice Chancellor of the University of Engineering and Technology, Peshawar is directed to prepare fresh merit list by not adding any additional marks to the memorizers of the Holy Quran. Punitive costs of Rs. 5,00,000/ (Five hundred thousand rupees only) are hereby imposed upon the Vice Chancellor of the University of Engineering and Technology, Peshawar to be paid, out of funds of the University, to Mr. Johnson Bernard not later than sixty days of announcement of this judgment. The petition is allowed in these terms.

11. The recommendations of the Federal Public Service Commissions on the basis of results of the CSS Examination, 2018 prepared keeping in view quota for various regions and classes and the consequent appointments made by the Federation are held to be void. The Federal Public Service Commission is directed to prepare fresh recommendations based upon results of the examination already conducted purely on merit with no quota for any region or class and the Federation is directed to make appointments accordingly within thirty days of announcement of this judgment. The Federation is burdened with a punitive cost of Rs. 20,00,000/ (Two million rupees only) to be paid to Mr. Yasir Qayum Khan through the Chairman, Federal Public Service Commission not later

than sixty days of announcement of this judgment. The petition is allowed in these terms.

151.   Persons appointed in consequence of the recruitments held to be void hereinabove shall not be required to refund amounts drawn as remuneration as a consideration of services rendered. The amounts drawn as remuneration are held to be the quantum meruit. Holding otherwise would make their employments forced labour which is prohibited by the Constitution. Moreover, the persons recruited on the basis of void rules or executive instructions cannot be held responsible for conceiving or implementing policies in violation of the fundamental rights.

152.   Learned counsels for the petitioners and the learned law officers rendered valuable assistance to this court in the instant proceedings which is hereby gratefully acknowledged.

Sd/
Mr. Jamal Mustafa Kundan
Sd/
Mr. Saleem Anwar Taya
Sd/
Mr. Rasheed Ahmad

Announced in Open Court on 10th of December, 2019.

Sd/
Mr. Jamal Mustafa Kundan

APPROVED FOR REPORTING

Chapter 3

Rules relax

This Chapter, inter alia, answers the following questions:

1. Whether a petitioner is entitled to withdraw a petition under Article 199 (1) (b) (ii) of the Constitution and whether a person can be termed stranger to proceedings under that Article for the purpose of appeal against an order passed on the request of the petitioner?

2. Whether a civil servant is a holder of a public office?

3. On what grounds a civil servant can be declared to be holding a public office without lawful authority?

4. Whether conditions of recruitment can lawfully be relaxed in favour of an individual or a group of individuals?

5. Whether services of persons recruited on ad hoc basis in the prescribed manner can be regularized through relaxation of rules?

6. Whether persons can be appointed in the service of Pakistan on political grounds?

Present: Mr. Jamal Mustafa Kundan
               Mr. Saleem Anwar Taya
               Mr. Rasheed Ahmad

Dr. Ahsan Saleem

------Petitioner

Versus

The Province of Punjab and others

-----Respondents

Petitioner	Mr. Faisal Saleem Mufti, Senior Advocate, Supreme Court of Pakistan
Respondents	Mr. Kamran Ali Afzal, Attorney General for Pakistan for the Federation of Pakistan
	Mr. Saleem Anwar Taya, Advocate General, Punjab for the Province of the Punjab
	Mr. Aleem Akhtar Kiani for the private respondent
Dates of hearing	04.12.2019, 05.12.2019, 06.12.2019

JUDGMENT

MR. JAMAL MUSTAFA KUNDAN. –This is an appeal under Article 185(3) of the Constitution against an order of a Division Bench of the Hon'ble Lahore High Court through which an order of the learned Single Bench of the Lahore High Court disposing of a writ petition filed under Article 199 (1) (b) (ii) of the Constitution to challenge legality of appointment of a civil servant was upheld as the petitioner had withdrawn his petition and the learned Single Bench had no option except to dispose of the petition on the basis of its withdrawal. The learned Division Bench dismissed the intra court appeal on the ground that it was filed by a stranger to the proceedings before the Single Bench and that the withdrawal of the writ petition by the petitioner did not left any live issue to be decided by the court. The learned Division Bench advised the appellant before it to consider the possibility of filing a new writ petition against the respondents instead of becoming an appellant in a case to which he was stranger in the proceedings before the Single Bench. Aggrieved of order of the leaned Division Bench, the appellant is before us with a prayer for grant of leave to appeal.

Facts of the case

2.   Facts necessary for adjudication of this appeal may be summarized in the following words:

    a)   Mr. Shakeel Ahmad (the respondent) worked as Senior Accountant in Water and Sanitation Agency, Faisalabad for about one year. Thereafter, he was appointed as Assistant Director in the Faisalabad Development Authority where he worked for eleven months. Then he was appointed as Public Relations Officer in the Punjab Sports Board for about two years from where he was declared surplus and was placed in the Surplus Pool of the Services & General Administration Department. He was absorbed as District Food Controller but his services were terminated, during probation period, on allegation of misconduct. He filed an appeal against termination of his services in the Punjab Service Tribunal which was dismissed.

    b)   The respondent submitted an application, recommended by a member of the Provincial Assembly of the Punjab, to the Chief Minster, stating therein:

            "This is a request for your kind consideration of my qualification for the post of Treasury Officer lying vacant in the Finance Department.

Briefly, I am MBA (Finance) degree holder and have about seven years' experience to my credit in different capacities; testimonials are attached for your kind perusal, please."

c) On receipt of the aforesaid application, the Secretary to the Chief Minister issued the following directive to the Secretary to Government of the Punjab, Finance Department (the appointing authority):

"On presentation of the enclosed application, Chief Minister has been pleased to approve appointment on ad hoc basis of Mr. Shakeel Ahmad as Treasury Officer in Finance Department against initial recruitment quota."

d) The appointing authority issued offer of appointment to the respondent stating therein:

"In compliance of the Chief Minister's orders, you are hereby offered the post of Treasury Officer / District Accounts Officer (BS-17) on ad hoc basis in accordance with Rule 22 of the Punjab Civil Servants (Appointment & Conditions of Service) Rules, 1974 on the following terms and conditions: ----."

e) One of the conditions of ad hoc appointment in respect of the respondent as communicated to him in the offer of appointment was as follows:

"For regular appointment to the post, requisition has been placed with the Punjab Public Service Commission and the Commission will advertise the posts in due course. You will have to compete before the Commission with other candidates in accordance with the rules. If you do not compete before the Commission or are not selected by the PPSC, your services will stand terminated forthwith."

f) The respondent again submitted an undated application, recommended by a Member of the Provincial Assembly (MPA), to the Chief Minister for regularization of his ad hoc appointment. The Additional Secretary, Chief Minister's Secretariat issued two directives on this application:

First Directive

"On presentation of the enclosed application, Chief Minister has been pleased to observe that services of Mr. Shakeel Ahmad, Treasury Officer (Ad hoc), Finance Department may be regularized as per precedent enclosed."

Second Directive

"Chief Minister has been pleased to approve the regularization of ad hoc appointment of Mr. Shakeel Ahmad, Treasury Officer, Finance Department in relaxation of all rules and procedures."

g) The respondent was informed by the appointing authority about the action taken on his application submitted to the Chief Minister and the directives issued thereon, in the following words:

"Subject: Request for regularization of services as Treasury Officer in relaxation of policy / rules

Please refer to your application dated Nil addressed to the Chief Minister on the above noted subject.

2.   Summary was submitted to the Chief Minister who has been pleased to desire that you may be advised to appear before the Punjab Public Service Commission for regular appointment to the post of Treasury Officer."

h)   The respondent failed to appear before the Public Service Commission. Despite his failure and in violation of the last and final orders of the Chief Minister communicated to the respondent, the appointing authority regularized ad hoc appointment of the respondent.

i)   Some years later, on the direction of the Provincial Cabinet, the appointing authority issued a show-cause notice to the respondent proposing penalty of compulsory retirement / removal from service on the charges of recruitment on ad hoc basis followed by regularization without open advertisement and relaxation in upper age limit.

j)   The respondent submitted a written reply to the appointing authority contending therein that he was appointed in relaxation of all rules and procedures by the Chief Minister who had statutory power to do so in terms of Section 22 of the Punjab Civil Servants Act, 1974 and Rule 23 of the Punjab Civil Servants (Appointment & Conditions of Service) Rules, 1974. He further submitted that he possessed requisite qualifications for the post, had passed the departmental examination and his performance was good and the matter of his appointment had become a past and closed transaction. He requested that proposed action may not be taken against him.

k)   After considering written defence of the respondent, the appointing authority, through a written order, declared that appointment of the respondent was not processed in the prescribed manner. Without exonerating him from the charges leveled against him, his appointment was declared administratively, technically and legally valid. The respondent, thereafter, continued to hold the public office and is still working as such.

l)   Dr. Ahsan Saleem filed a writ petition under Article 199 (1) (b) (ii) of the Constitution in the Lahore High Court, Lahore. The appointing authority and the said Mr. Shakeel Ahmad were arrayed as respondents. The respondents filed reports and para-wise comments. The petitioner filed rejoinder. The respondent filed written reply to the rejoinder which was followed by submission of written arguments by the rival parties in the case. The case lingered on for two years during which both sides presented their oral arguments. On direction of the High Court, the petitioner also appeared in person to verify that he had filed the writ petition. Then the petitioner's counsel sought permission of the court to withdraw the petition which was granted and the petition was disposed of on the basis of withdrawal by the petitioner.

m)   The appellant herein filed an intra court appeal in terms of Section 3 of the Law Reforms Ordinance, 1972 which was dismissed in limine on the ground that the appellant was a stranger to the proceedings and, therefore, was not competent to file an intra court appeal.

Arguments of the petitioner

3.   The arguments advanced in favour of the writ petition of Dr. Ahsan Saleem can be summarized thus:

i.   Appointment of the respondent on political grounds without open advertisement, and not on merit determined through objective criteria, is void ab initio in terms of Article 8 (1) and (2) of the Constitution being in contravention of Article 18 read with Article 2A, Article 4 (2) (b), Article 25, Article 27 and in excess of executive authority conferred by Article 137 of the Constitution. Since legislative measures in contravention of fundamental rights are void, therefore, executive actions in contravention of fundamental rights are also void and the Chief Minister cannot suspend, take away or abridge fundamental rights through relaxation of all rules / procedures.

ii. The respondent lacks the requisite qualifications: -
   a. to compete for the post of Treasury Officer; and
   b. for appointment as Treasury Officer.

The qualifications required to compete for this post are: -
   a. Degree of graduation from a recognized university; and
   b. Age not below 21 years and not above 25 years.

The qualifications required for appointment to this post are: -
   a. Qualifications required to compete for appointment to the post;
   b. Recommendation of the Selection Authority on the basis of merit determined through objective criteria after written test and interview; and
   c. Medical fitness certificate from the competent authority.

The respondent lacks qualification of proper age to compete for the post and the qualification of recommendation of the Selection Authority for appointment to the post. These qualifications cannot lawfully be dispensed with by the Chief Minister through relaxation of all rules / procedures because: -

   a) Powers under Section 22 of the Punjab Civil Servants Act, 1974 and Rule 23 of the Punjab Civil Servants (Appointment and Conditions of Service) Rules, 1974 can be exercised in respect of a civil servant and not in favour of one aspiring for entry into civil service.

   b) Rule 5 (1) (i) of the West Pakistan Provincial Treasury and Accounts Service Rules, 1962 prescribes that initial recruitment shall be made on the recommendation of the Public Service Commission. Rule 12 ibid provides that any of these rules may, for reasons to be recorded in writing, be relaxed in individual cases if Government is satisfied, in consultation with the Public Service Commission, that a strict application of the rule would cause undue hardship to the individual concerned. The case of the respondent is not a case of hardship. No consultation was made with the Commission.

   c) The Punjab Delegation of Powers (Relaxation of Conditions of Service) Rules, 1989 restricted the power of the Chief Minister to relax rules for recruitment to posts in BS-1 to BS-5 only. These were the applicable rules at the time of ad hoc and regular appointment of the respondent. The Chief Minister could not exercise his executive powers in violation of these rules.

iii. When the case for regularization of services of the respondent was submitted to the Chief Minister, the Chief Minister was pleased to advise the respondent to appear before the Punjab Public Service Commission for regular appointment to the post of Treasury Officer. Instead of implementing final and lawful orders of the Chief Minister, the appointing authority appointed the respondent on regular basis. This was in flagrant violation of Rule 5 (2) read with Part-A of Schedule VII of the Punjab Government Rules of Business, 1974, which requires that all cases of relaxation of service rules shall be submitted to the Chief Minister before issuance of orders. Since the elements of justice and equity are altogether missing in the case of the respondent, therefore, orders of the Chief Minister regarding relaxation of all rules / procedures are without lawful authority and are of no legal effect and notwithstanding these orders being in the field, the respondent is neither qualified to compete for nor qualified for appointment to the post of Treasury Officer.

iv. The appointing authority was not competent in law to make appointment of the respondent on ad hoc basis without fulfilling the conditions precedent specified in Rule 22 of the Punjab Civil Servants (Appointment and Conditions of Service) Rules, 1974. Even if he is accepted, for the sake of argument, competent in law to make recruitment on ad hoc basis without fulfilling the said conditions precedent, the ad hoc appointment of the respondent was for a maximum period of one year. The appointing authority was also not competent in law to appoint the respondent on regular basis except in the prescribed manner and on the recommendation of the Punjab Public Service Commission in view of Section 2 (j) read with Section 2 (2) and Section 4 of the Punjab Civil Servants Act, 1974 and Rule 16 of the Punjab Civil Servants (Appointment and Conditions of Service) Rules, 1974. Regularization made in contravention of the prescribed procedure could not be equated with that of legal regularization and in absence whereof the status of the ad hoc appointee could not be changed unless regularized legally by adopting the prescribed procedure. The condition of recommendation of the Selection Authority for regular appointment can be waived off neither under Section 22 of the Punjab Civil Servants Act, 1974 nor under Rule 23 of the Punjab Civil Servants (Appointment and Conditions of Service) Rules, 1974. The regular appointment of the respondent, in absence of recommendation of the Selection Authority, is invalid and incurably bad and a petition for a writ of quo warranto is maintainable because the appointment was made by a person not competent in law to appoint the respondent on regular basis.

Defence offered by the respondent and the appointing authority

4. In defence, the appointing authority and the respondent presented the following arguments:

i. The Hon'ble High Court lacks jurisdiction due to bar contained in Article 212 of the Constitution as the matter pertains to terms and conditions of service of a civil servant.

ii. The petitioner is not an aggrieved person; hence, the writ petition is liable to be dismissed on this ground alone.

iii. The petitioner is a tool in the hands of departmental colleagues of the respondent and the petition merits to be dismissed as it has been filed with mala fides and is aimed at blackmailing the respondent.

iv. The petitioner has other adequate remedy of approaching the appointing authority of the respondent for redressal of his grievances in respect of appointment of the respondent.

v. The respondent does not hold a constitutional or statutory post; hence, he cannot be termed holder of a public office and therefore, 199 (1) (b) (ii) of the Constitution is not attracted in his case.

vi. Work and conduct of the respondent is extremely satisfactory and there is no complaint against him. On the other hand, his performance has been acknowledged through grant of honouraria and merit certificates.

vii.	The appointing authority has reviewed appointment of the respondent and declared it legally valid; hence, the same is a past and closed transaction and is not open to challenge because of laches.
viii.	No fundamental right has been violated in the matter of appointment of the respondent on ad hoc basis and subsequent regularization. Assumptions regarding violation of Article 2A, 18, 25 and 27 are far-fetched and incorrect.
ix.	The Chief Minister is competent to relax rules and he exercised his lawful power keeping in view hardship of the respondent.
x.	There have been thousands of cases of regularization of ad hoc appointments by the Government of the Punjab. Case of the respondent is not the first or only case of regularization of ad hoc appointment.
xi.	The respondent had qualifications required for the post and the appointing authority was fully competent to appoint the respondent.
xii.	As the orders regarding appointment of the respondent on ad hoc basis and the regularization of ad hoc appointment have been acted upon and are in operation since two decades, therefore, the respondent has acquired a vested right and no authority is competent to rescind these orders.
xiii.	Termination of services of the respondent at this belated stage will cause extreme hardship as the respondent has become over-age and cannot join any other service and has no other source of income to feed and finance his family. Termination of services of the respondent is sure to cause economic ruination of his family.

Legal analysis of the preliminary objections

5. In reply to the preliminary objections raised by the respondent, the petitioner submitted that Article 212 of the Constitution, the doctrine of laches, the doctrine of the past and closed transaction and the principle of locus standi are not applicable to proceedings under Article 199 (1) (b) (ii) of the Constitution as holding a public office without lawful authority is a continuing wrong giving rise to a cause of action de die in diem and quo warranto proceedings are addressed to preventing a continued exercise of authority unlawfully asserted, rather than to correct what has already been done. Moreover, the principle of locus poenitentiae is not available to perpetuate an illegality. Further, jurisdiction of this Hon'ble Court under Article 199 (1) (b) (ii) of the Constitution remains intact even if a departmental authority issues an order in favour of a person who has no authority of law to hold a public office.

6. As the learned Single and Division Benches of the Hon'ble High Court had not attended to the preliminary objections, therefore, we find it appropriate to adjudicate upon these objections before proceeding further in the matter.

7. Relevant portion of Article 199 (1) of the Constitution will guide our discussion in this case which is reproduced hereinbelow to serve as ready reference:

> "Subject to the Constitution, a High Court may, if it is satisfied that no other adequate remedy is provided by law, -
> (a)   on the application of any aggrieved party, make an order-
> (i)   directing a person performing, within the territorial jurisdiction of the Court, functions in connection with the affairs of the Federation, a Province or a local authority, to refrain from doing anything he is not permitted by law to do, or to do anything he is required by law to do; or
> (ii)   declaring that any act done or proceeding taken within the territorial jurisdiction of the Court by a person performing functions in connection with the affairs of the

Federation, a Province or a local authority has been done or taken without lawful authority and is of no legal effect; or

(b)   on the application of any person, make an order-

    (i)   directing that a person in custody within the territorial jurisdiction of the Court be brought before it so that the Court may satisfy itself that he is not being held in custody without lawful authority or in an unlawful manner; or

    (ii)   requiring a person within the territorial jurisdiction of the Court holding or purporting to hold a public office to show under what authority of law he claims to hold that office; or

(c)   on the application of any aggrieved person, make an order giving such directions to any person or authority, including any Government exercising any power or performing any function in, or in relation to, any territory within the jurisdiction of that Court as may be appropriate for the enforcement of any of the Fundamental Rights conferred by Chapter 1 of Part 11."

8.   The preliminary objections relate to locus standi of the petitioner, inordinate delay in filing of the petition and jurisdictional bar under Article 212 of the Constitution. As regards locus standi of the petitioner, Article 199 (1) (b) (ii) of the Constitution empowers the High Court to issue an order, on the application of any person, requiring a person within the territorial jurisdiction of the Court holding or purporting to hold a public office to show under what authority of law he claims to hold that office. The petitioner does not need to be an aggrieved person to file a writ petition under Article 199(1)(b)(ii) of the Constitution. The Hon'ble Supreme Court of Pakistan has held in Malik Asad Ali and others Vs. Federation of Pakistan through Secretary, Law, Justice and Parliament Affairs, Islamabad and others (PLD 1998 Supreme Court 161) that:

"The language of Article 199(1)(b)(ii) is plain and unambiguous, and it entitles any person to seek information in the nature of quo warranto against a person holding or purporting to hold a public office."

"As to the locus standi of the appellant the Constitution itself is quite clear and entitled 'any person' to make the application under Article 199(1) (b) (ii). Even in the case of an unwritten Constitution it has been held that a stranger and a member of the public acting in good faith can apply for a writ of quo warranto. Vide R. v. Speyer (1916) 1 KB 595, wherein at page 609 it has been observed that such remedy is available to private persons."

9.   It has been held by the Hon'ble Supreme Court of Pakistan in a case reported as Capt. (Retd.) Muhammad Naseem Hijazi Vs. Province of Punjab through Secretary, Housing and Physical Planning and 2 others (2000 SCMR 1720) that:

"Under Article 199(1) (b) (ii) of the Constitution of the Islamic Republic of Pakistan, the High Court in exercise of its Constitutional jurisdiction is competent to enquire from any person, holder of a public office to show that under what authority he is holding the said office. In such-like cases where a Writ in the nature of quo warranto is instituted the duty of the petitioner is to lay an information before the Court that such and such officer has no legal authority to retain such office. For a petitioner who acts, in fact, as an informer is not required to establish his locus standi to invoke the jurisdiction of the Court. Writ of quo warranto in its nature is an information laying against persons who claimed or usurped an office, franchise or liberty and was intended to inquire by what authority he supported his claim in order that right to office may be determined. It is necessary for the issuance of writ that the office should be one created by the State of character or by statute and that the duty should be of a public nature. Writ of quo warranto could be moved by "any person who even may not be an aggrieved party but is holding a public office created by character or statute by the State". Any person can move the High Court to challenge the unauthorized occupation of a public office. On any such application Court is not only to see that the incumbent is holding the office under the order of a Competent Authority but it is to go beyond that and see as to whether he is legally qualified to hold the office or to remain in the office. The Court has also to see if statutory provisions have been violated in making the appointment. The invalidity of appointment may arise not only from want of qualifications but also from violation of legal provision for appointment.

It may also be observed that on question of locus standi of the respondent to challenge the appointment of petitioner reliance can also be placed on Al-Jehad Trust through Raeesul Mujahideen Habib-ul-Wahabb-ulKhairi and others v, Federation of Pakistan and others (PLD 1996 SC 324) and Malik Asad Ali and others v. Federation of Pakistan through Secretary Law, Justice and Parliament Affairs, Islamabad and others (PLD 1998 SC 161)."

10. It was held by the Hon'ble Supreme Court of India in the University of Mysore and another Vs. C. D. Govinda Rao and another {[1964] 4 SCR 575} that:

"As Halsbury has observed:

"An information in the nature of a quo warranto took the place of the obsolete writ of quo warranto which lay against a person who claimed or usurped an office, franchise, or liberty, to inquire by what authority he supported his claim, in order that the right to the office or franchise might be determined."

Broadly stated, the quo warranto proceeding affords a judicial remedy by which any person, who holds an independent substantive public office or franchise or liberty, is called upon to show by what right he holds the said office, franchise or liberty, so that his title to it may be duly determined, and in case the finding is that the holder of the office has not title, he would be ousted from that office by judicial order. In other words, the procedure of quo warranto gives the Judiciary a weapon to control the Executive from making appointment to public office against law and to protect a citizen from being deprived of public office to which he has a right. These proceedings also tend to protect the public from usurpers of public office, who might be allowed to continue either with the connivance of the Executive or by reason of its apathy. It will, thus, be seen that before a person can effectively claim a writ of quo warranto, he has to satisfy the Court that the office in question is a public office and is held by a usurper without legal authority, and that inevitably would lead to the enquiry as to whether the appointment of the alleged usurper has been made in accordance with law or not."

11. It appears that Article 199(1) (b) (ii) of the Constitution intends to authorize every person, whether he is a citizen or not, to challenge legality of title of a holder of public office to hold that office. A person does not need to be an aggrieved person for invoking jurisdiction of a High Court under Article 199(1) (b) (ii) of the Constitution. The preliminary

objection of the respondent on the locus standi of the petitioner is, therefore, not legally tenable and is hereby held to be invalid.

12.   As regards the preliminary objections based upon the doctrine of laches, theory of the past and closed transaction and the principle of locus poenitentiae, we may observe that holding a public office without lawful authority is a continuing wrong, hence, the doctrine of laches and the doctrine of the past and closed transaction are not applicable to proceedings under Article 199(1) (b) (ii) of the Constitution. Quo warranto proceedings are addressed to preventing a continued exercise of authority unlawfully asserted, rather than to correct what has already been done. Where the alleged usurpation has terminated, quo warranto will be denied. (People v. City of Whittier (1933) 133 Cal. App. 316, 324; 25 Ops. Cal. Atty. Gen. 223 (1955).)   By the same token, because quo warranto serves to end a continuous usurpation, no statute of limitations applies to the action. (People v. Bailey (1916) 30 Cal. App. 581, 584, 585.)

13.   The jurisdiction of the Hon'ble High Court cannot be considered to be ousted just because a certain act has been performed and it has become a past and closed transaction. Holding a public office cannot be claimed to have become a past and closed transaction till such time the office is held by a person having no lawful authority therefor. Holding otherwise would, in fact, defeat the very purpose for which Article 199(1) (b) (ii) has been written in the Constitution. As regards the principle of locus poenitentiae, it is not available to perpetuate an illegality and is irrelevant in quo warranto proceedings. It is also incorrect to assert that since the appointing authority has reviewed appointment of the respondent and has not taken any adverse action against the respondent, therefore, jurisdiction of the High Court under Article 199(1) (b) (ii) of the Constitution stands ousted. No departmental action can take away jurisdiction of the High Court under the said under Article 199(1) (b) (ii).

14.   Justice (R) Fazal Karim, in his book "Judicial Review of Public Actions" (First Edition), at page 1140, has stated that: -

> "Malik Asad Ali case (PLD 1998 SC 161) decides also that in considering the question whether the court should, in its discretion, grant the relief, the doctrine of past and closed transaction, the doctrine of laches, the fact that the persons directly affected had not challenged the appointment and their conduct amounted to acquiescence, and the length of time for which the respondent had held the office or the time that remained to him, are not relevant."

15.   The Hon'ble Supreme Court of Pakistan has held in Fazlul Quader Chaudhary and others Vs. Mr. Muhammad Abdul Haque (PLD 1963 SC 486) that:

> "If the Ministers were holding office without any lawful authority, their continuance in office was in the nature of a continuing wrong giving rise to a cause of action de die in diem, and, therefore, there could be no question of any laches. In any event, on questions relating to the constitutionality of actions, the ground of laches cannot prevail, for there can be no estoppel against the Constitution and an act which is unconstitutional cannot become constitutional by lapse of time, nor can it vest anyone with any kind of legal right to benefit from such an unconstitutional act."

16.   It was held by the Hon'ble Supreme Court of India in Central Electricity Supply Utility of Orissa Vs. Dhobei Sahoo and Others (A.I.R. 2014 S.C. 246) that:

> "Sometimes a contention is raised pertaining to doctrine of delay and laches in filing a writ of quo warranto. There is a difference pertaining to personal interest or individual interest on one hand and an interest by a citizen as a relator to the court on the other. The principle of doctrine of delay and laches should not be allowed any play because the person holds the public office as a usurper and such continuance is

to be prevented by the court. The Court is required to see that the larger public interest and the basic concept pertaining to good governance are not thrown to the winds."

17.   It   was   held   in Pradeep P. Prajapati Vs. Principal Secretary and others [2012 (2) GLH 781] that:

"If a genuine petition for a writ of quo warranto is rejected solely on the ground of delay, then it necessarily means that such a person would continue to hold such a public office regardless of the right of such a person to hold such an office."

"We may furthermore notice that while examining if a person holds a public office under valid authority or not, the court is not concerned with technical grounds of delay or motive behind the challenge, since it is necessary to prevent continuance of usurpation of office or perpetuation of an illegality. [See Dr. Kashinath G. Jalmi and Another v. The Speaker and Others (1993) 2 SCC 703]."

"Thus, the cause of action for a writ of quo warranto is "de dei in dium". In other words, the usurper's continuance in office affords a fresh cause of action every day and each hour till he is ousted. There is, therefore, no question of delay so far as this writ is concerned. The petition for issuance of writ of quo warranto cannot be dismissed only on the ground of delay."

18.   In view of the above, the preliminary objections regarding laches, past and closed transaction and the principle of locus poenitentiae are held to be irrelevant to proceedings under Article 199(1) (b) (ii) of the Constitution.

19.   It was argued on behalf of the respondent, that the jurisdictional bar under Article 212 of the Constitution is attracted as the matter pertains to conditions of service of the respondent and a remedy in respect thereof lies exclusively in the Punjab Service Tribunal. Article 212 of the Constitution does not bar the High Court to entertain a petition filed under Article 199 (1) (b) (ii) of the Constitution. Jurisdiction of Service Tribunal can be invoked by a civil servant aggrieved by final order of a departmental authority in respect of terms and conditions of his service. The Punjab Service Tribunals Act, 1974 does not provide a remedy identical to that provided by Article 199 (1) (b) (ii) of the Constitution. It has been held in I.A. Sharwani and others Vs. Government of Pakistan (1991 SCMR 1041) that:

"9. From the above-quoted Article 212 of the Constitution and section 4 of the Act, it is evident that the jurisdiction of the Courts is excluded only in respect of the cases in which the Service Tribunal under subsection (1) of section 4 has the jurisdiction. It must, therefore, follow that if the Service Tribunal does not have jurisdiction to adjudicate upon a particular type of grievance, the jurisdiction of the Court remains intact."

20.   It has been held by the Hon'ble Lahore High Court in Dr. Muhammad Azhar Vs. Dr. Tariq Mahmood Malik and 2 others (2002 PLC (C.S.) 57) that:

"The question is whether the very induction into the service of the private respondent is valid or not. Such a question does not fall within the purview of Article 212(2) of the Constitution. Needless to explain that once a person has been validly inducted into service and has become member of the same, the question thereafter arising in concerning the terms and conditions will be examined by the Service Tribunal and not by the High Court."

21.   Article 199 (1) (b) (ii) of the Constitution provides a window for public interest litigation in the matter of holding public offices. If a civil servant is aggrieved of holding a public office by someone without valid authority of law and seeks relief in the form of ousting him from office so that he may be able either to occupy that office or to get any

other relief, the proper forum for him would be the Service Tribunal. In such a case, the order under which the alleged usurper holds a public office would serve as final order for the purpose of preferring an appeal. All other persons have the only remedy provided by Article 199 (1) (b) (ii) of the Constitution; they are not allowed to approach the Service Tribunal as no question of their service is there and no final order is in field to challenge. A person can question title of a holder of a public office to hold the office through instituting proceedings under Article 199 (1) (b) (ii) of the Constitution. Thus, it has been held in Girjesh Shrivastava Vs. State of Madhya Pradesh {(2010) 10 SCC 707)}, Duryodhan Sahu (Dr.) Vs. Jitendra Kumar Mishra {(1998) 7 SCC 273}, B. Srinivasa Reddy, Dattaraj Nathuji Thaware Vs. State of Maharashtra, {(2005) 1 SCC 590) and Ashok Kumar Pandey Vs. State of W.B ((2004) 3 SCC 349) that except for a writ of quo warranto, public interest litigation is not maintainable in service matters. We are constrained to hold that no other adequate remedy is provided by law to challenge legality of appointment of the respondent except proceedings under Article 199 (1) (b) (ii) of the Constitution and Article 212 of the Constitution does not bar the Hon'ble High Court to exercise its constitutional jurisdiction under Article 199 (1) (b) (ii).

22.   We allowed leave to appeal to consider the following questions of law:

1.   Whether a petitioner is entitled to withdraw a petition under Article 199 (1) (b) (ii) of the Constitution and whether a person can be termed stranger to proceedings under that Article for the purpose of appeal against an order passed on the request of the petitioner?

2.   Whether a civil servant is a holder of a public office?

3.   On what grounds a civil servant can be declared to be holding a public office without lawful authority?

4.   Whether conditions of recruitment can lawfully be relaxed in favour of an individual or a group of individuals?

5.   Whether services of persons recruited on ad hoc basis in the prescribed manner can be regularized through relaxation of rules?

6.   Whether persons can be appointed in the service of Pakistan on political grounds?

7.   What would be the appropriate order in the facts and circumstances of this case?

Question # 1

Whether a petitioner is entitled to withdraw a petition under Article 199 (1) (b) (ii) of the Constitution and whether a person can be termed stranger to proceedings under that Article for the purpose of appeal against an order passed on the request of the petitioner?

23.   In a petition under Article 199 (1) (b) (ii) of the Constitution, the petitioner informs the High Court that a person is holding a public office without lawful authority. If, on the basis of information provided, the High Court finds that a prima facie case is made out against the respondent, the Court directs the respondent to prove his lawful entitlement to the public office. If the respondent fails to prove his lawful entitlement to the public office, the Court declares the office vacant and directs that it be filled in accordance with law. Thus, the proceedings under Article 199 (1) (b) (ii) of the Constitution are not for a direct relief to the petitioner or for enforcement of any of his legal or fundamental rights. Interest of the petitioner is to ensure that public offices are held by legally qualified persons selected through due process. These proceedings are in the nature of public interest litigation as these are aimed at the good cause of ensuring rule of law in the matter of holding public offices.

24.   A petitioner in proceedings under Article 199 (1) (b) (ii) of the Constitution cannot be termed 'dominus litis' as his role is that of a mere informer; he is not master of the petition. Once he informs the High Court about illegalities in the matter of holding a public office by the respondent, he does an irreversible act. This action is what is a lighted match to a train of gunpowder. He cannot make the High Court to unlearn what it has learnt through the writ petition. Once the Court has learnt that sufficient cause exists to require a holder of a public office to establish his legal title to the public office being held by him, it is under oath to preserve, protect and defend the Constitution through appropriate action in accordance with law. It becomes immaterial thereafter whether the petitioner wants to continue to pursue his petition or not. Application for withdrawal of a quo warranto petition is inconsequential as role of the petitioner ends after he brings into the notice of the court that holder of a post lacks qualifications to hold that post or his appointment suffers from some other fatal illegality. Rest is for the court to do. His request for withdrawal indicates only that the court will have to adjudicate the matter in absence of assistance and support of the petitioner except that already rendered. Withdrawal of the petition neither makes an illegality legal nor takes away jurisdiction of the court in the matter or relieves the court of its responsibility to exercise its powers under Article 199 (1) (b) (ii) of the Constitution. On the other hand, the court has no authority to direct an unwilling petitioner to continue to assist the court. If a petitioner is unwilling to pursue his petition, for any reason, it is of no material consequence if the court rejects his application to withdraw the petition and continue to proceed in the case in his absence. Legality of holding a public office does not, obviously, depend on assertions to be made by a petitioner; it rests on the fact whether the appointment conforms to the applicable legal dispensation or not.

25.   The question of withdrawal of the petitioner from a public interest litigation was considered by the Hon'ble Supreme Court of India in Sheela Barse Vs. Union of India and Ors. (AIR 1988 SC 2211) wherein, while rejecting application for withdrawal of the petition, it was held:

> "The question agitated relates, on the contrary, to the aspect whether a public-minded person who brings such an action is entitled, as of right, to withdraw the proceedings from the court. Applicant asserts that this Court cannot refuse leave for withdrawal. The proceedings, it is contended, are the result of a "voluntary action of a citizen" and that, as a corollary, the proceedings cannot be continued except with applicant's participation. The applicant relies on what she calls "a citizen's right to be a petitioner-in-person in a public interest litigation". As stemming from this premise, applicant contends that not only that leave for withdrawal cannot be refused but also that the main petition cannot be continued by any other citizen or organisation."
>
> "The third-this pertains to the claim that nobody else can go on with this litigation-is that the proceedings were initiated as a result of the voluntary action on the part of a citizen and that that citizen is entitled to withdraw them. The applicant claims that she as representing "other conscientious citizens, social workers and activists is duty bound to sustain the citizens' right to be petitioners-in-person" and that, therefore, the petition cannot be continued against the wishes and without the participation of the applicant."
>
> "12. The first ground, therefore, does not justify the withdrawal of this public interest litigation. If we acknowledge any such status of a Dominus Litis to a person who brings a public interest litigation, we will render the proceedings in public interest litigations vulnerable to and susceptible of a new dimension which might, in conceivable cases, be used by person for personal ends resulting in prejudice to the public weal."

26.   It was held in S.P. Anand Vs. H.D. Deve Gowda (AIR 1997 SUPREME COURT 272) that:

> "Here we must mention that in PIL cases, the petitioner is not entitled to withdraw his petition at his sweet-will unless the court sees reason to permit withdrawal. In granting the permission the Court would be guided by considerations of public interest and would also ensure that it does not result in abuse of the process of law. Courts must guard against possibilities of such litigants settling the matters out of the court to their advantage and then seeking withdrawal of the case. There are umpteen ways in which the process can be abused and the courts must be aware of the same before permitting withdrawal of the petition."
>
> (Explanation: PIL means public interest litigation. Explanation supplied).

27.   The Hon'ble Supreme Court of India held in Dr. B. Singh Vs. Union of India and Others, {(2004) 3 SCC 363} that:

> "The court has to act ruthlessly while dealing with imposters and busybodies or meddlesome interlopers impersonating as public spirited holy men. They masquerade as crusaders of justice. They pretend to act in the name of pro bono publico, though they have no interest to the public or even of their own to protect."

28.   The most effective way to discourage busybodies who intend to use proceedings under Article 199 (1) (b) (ii) of the Constitution for their personal gains and private benefits is to hold that despite their application to withdraw the writ petition, the court will proceed in the matter till its logical conclusion in accordance with law. If courts are swayed by their misplaced sympathy, the blackmailers will continue to pursue their petitions till the stage the respondent comes to deal with them on their terms and then apply to the court to allow withdrawal of the petition "in interest of justice."

29.   If there is a prima facie good case to invoke powers of the High Court under Article 199(1)(b)(ii) of the Constitution and the case nears conclusion in the form of judgment by the court and the case is allowed to be withdrawn by the petitioner, it will facilitate blackmailers to institute new petitions in the name of other petitioners on the same facts and law points. There is no legal prohibition if a fresh writ petition is filed against a person holding a public office without lawful authority. Permission to withdraw a petition under Article 199 (1)(b)(ii) of the Constitution may, in this way, result into misuse of process of the court for unlawful personal gains.

30.   The High Court is not at liberty to terminate proceedings under Article 199 (1)(b)(ii) of the Constitution even on application of the petitioner in cases in which legality of holding a public office is in doubt. Once facts on file present a prima facie good case, permission by the court to withdraw the petition would amount to allow continued illegal usurpation of the public office. If the information given is not credible or does not offer sufficient grounds to proceed further, the court may dismiss the petition and impose costs on the petitioner for wasting public-paid time of the court. Frivolous or ill-motivated litigation deserves no sympathy. It does not, however, imply that the High Court can refuse to exercise its powers under Article 199 (1)(b)(ii) of the Constitution in cases in which it is proved that the holder of a public office lacks lawful authority to hold that office on the ground of alleged mala fides of the petitioner. Good or bad intentions of a petitioner does not affect lawful entitlement of a person to hold a public office. If a public office is held without lawful entitlement, alleged mala fides of the petitioner cannot convert it into lawful and authorize the High Court to perpetuate a patent illegality on the pretext of the alleged mala fides. The Hon'ble Supreme Court of India has held in Dr. Kashinath G. Jalmi Vs. The Speaker and others {(1993) 2 SCC 703} that:

"35. We may also advert to a related aspect. Learned counsel for the respondents were unable to dispute, that any other member of the public, to whom the oblique motives and conduct alleged against the appellants in the present case could not be attributed, could file such a writ petition even now for the same relief, since the alleged usurpation of the office is continuing, and this disability on the ground of oblique motives and conduct would not attach to him. This being so, the relief claimed by the appellants in their writ petitions filed in the High Court being in the nature of a class action, without seeking any relief personal to them, should not have been dismissed merely on the ground of laches. The motive or conduct of the appellants, as alleged by the respondents, in such a situation can be relevant only for denying them the costs even if their claim succeeds, but it cannot be a justification to refuse to examine the merits of the question raised therein, since that is a matter of public concern and relates to the good governance of the State itself."

31.   In cases involving rights of petitioners, the petitioner is 'dominus litis' and his voluntary decision to withdraw his petition may ordinarily end the proceedings as others are not likely to be affected by dismissal of the petition on the ground of its withdrawal by the petitioner. But in public interest ligation such as proceedings under Article 199 (1)(b)(ii) of the Constitution the petitioner is not 'dominus litis'. His decision to withdraw the petition has no effect on legality of title of a person to hold a public office. The jurisdiction vested in the High Court under Article 199 (1)(b)(ii) of the Constitution is to ensure that public offices are not held without lawful authority. It is not a personal grievance of the petitioner the redressal of which is attempted to by the High Court in quo warranto proceedings but is the alleged illegal usurpation of a public office which is intended to be terminated by the High Court under Article 199 (1)(b)(ii) of the Constitution. So long the cause of action exists, the need and duty to act to bring to an end illegal usurpation of a public office and to get it filled in in accordance with law will continue to call the High Court to perform its constitutional duty through action under Article 199 (1)(b)(ii) of the Constitution. A High Curt shall not be relieved of its constitutional duty if a petitioner prays for withdrawal of his petition. In quo warranto proceedings, the petitioner is just an informer and the public at large is the 'dominus litis'. If the petitioner applies for withdrawal of his petition, the real 'dominus litis' cannot be denied the right to intervene in the proceedings to safeguard the public interest of ensuring that public offices are held lawfully and not otherwise. In this view of the matter, every person is 'dominus litis' in quo warranto proceedings and no one is stranger to these proceedings at any stage of the case. If a person has right to join proceedings under Article 199 (1)(b)(ii) of the Constitution before the High Court at initial stage, he can also join or initiate intra court appeal against judgment of a single bench of the High Court. Taking the argument to its logical end, it is reasonable to say that any person is legally competent to file a civil petition for leave to appeal to the Hon'ble Supreme Court even if he was not a party to the proceedings before the Single and Division Benches of the High Court.

32. We find it lawful to hold that proceedings under Article 199 (1)(b)(ii) of the Constitution shall not be abated on application of the petitioner for withdrawal of the petition. The proceedings shall continue in absence of the petitioner. In cases where the petitions under Article 199 (1)(b)(ii) of the Constitution are disposed of on the sole ground of withdrawal of the petition by the petitioner, any person can file an intra court appeal or a civil petition for leave to appeal even if he was not a party to the proceedings in earlier stages of the case.

33.   Our declaration hereinabove does not mean that the High Court is not competent to exercise due diligence to check and discourage frivolous litigation. If a petition under Article 199 (1)(b)(ii) of the Constitution is found to be frivolous and without merits by the High Court, it is necessary to dismiss it in limine with deterrent punitive costs on the petitioner.

The respondent may be ordered to prove his lawful entitlement to hold a public office only when a prima facie case is made out necessitating such an order. After requiring the respondent to prove his lawful entitlement to hold a public office, it is necessary for the High Court to authoritatively adjudicate upon lawfulness of holding of the public office by the respondent. Not doing what is necessary is, obviously, unnecessary and, therefore, prohibited. Courts must not be allowed to be used as tools in the hands of blackmailers. On the other hand, if holding of a public office is proved to be without lawful authority, it must come to an end forthwith and the court is not permitted to refuse to exercise its jurisdiction under Article 199 (1)(b)(ii) of the Constitution under the pretext of alleged mala fides of the petitioner or under an erroneous assumption that it has discretion to exercise or refuse to exercise its powers under Article 199 (1)(b)(ii) of the Constitution. As a High Court is a court of law, it has to act when legal grounds to act exist and has no power to act in absence of legal grounds to act. Once it is proved that legal grounds to act exist, the High Court has no discretion to refuse to act as doing so would go against its oath to preserve, protect and defend the Constitution. And it would surely be misuse of authority to act when legal grounds to act are missing. Let us put six feet under the erroneous theory of discretion of the High Court in proceedings under Article 199 (1)(b)(ii) of the Constitution as spirit of this Article commands that the High Court shall act when found that a public office is held without lawful authority and it shall certify lawfulness of holding a public office where no fatal illegality in the title of a person to hold a public office is found. Discretion is nothing but selection of one of the lawful options in a given case. Where there is no option except to hold whether a public office is held with or without lawful authority, there is no option to refuse to make an express judicial declaration in the matter. Exercise of judicial power of the state is a duty to be performed by the courts without fail. When we say that the High Court has no discretion to refuse to give judicial verdict on lawfulness of holding a public office by a person, we mean to rule out the possibility of both express or implied refusal. Express refusals may be very rare. Often, the refusal is implied and is embodied in unjustified delay in adjudication. Examples are not very rare when proceedings under Article 199 (1)(b)(ii) of the Constitution against a parliamentarian are prolonged till completion of the tenure of the respondent and then are terminated on the ground that after new elections the petition has become infructuous. Instances have also been brought into our notice in which persons holding tenure posts were allowed to complete their tenures and the proceedings were kept pending in absence of any just and equitable cause. Similarly, proceedings are lingered on till doomsday i.e. till the holder of public office retires from service on attaining the age of superannuation. If a time limit has not been fixed for disposal of a petition under Article 199 (1)(b)(ii) of the Constitution, then the case has to be decided within reasonable time and absence of time limit cannot be construed as a license to unreasonably delay the case so as no live matter remains for adjudication. Whereas each case may require time for disposal depending upon peculiar facts and legal issues involved, we may reasonably hope that quo warranto proceedings under Article 199 (1)(b)(ii) as well as Article 184(3) of the Constitution shall be concluded not later than 100 working days from the date of institution of these proceedings.

Question # 2

Whether a civil servant is a holder of a public office?

34.   Article 199 (1)(b)(ii) of the Constitution empowers a High Court to order a person holding or purporting to hold a public office to show under what authority of law he claims to hold that office. Thus, this power is exercisable only if a person holds or purports to hold a public office. Constitution of Pakistan, 1973 does not define 'public office'. It is, therefore, necessary to consult definitions of 'office', 'public', 'public office', 'holder of public office' and 'service of Pakistan', reproduced hereinbelow, for accurately and precisely understanding what is meant by 'public office':

Office

(a) "An office is a right to exercise a public function or employment and to take the fees and emoluments belonging to it."
(https://legal-dictionary.thefreedictionary.com/Office)

(b) office. 1. A position of duty, trust, or authority, esp. one conferred by a governmental authority for a public purpose <the office of attorney general>. [Cases: Officers and Public Employees 1. C.J.S. Officers and Public Employees §§ 1–9, 12–17, 21.] 2. (often cap.) A division of the U.S. government ranking immediately below a department <the Patent and Trademark Office>. [Cases: United States 29. C.J.S. United States §§ 52, 57.] 3. A place where business is conducted or services are performed <a law office>.

alienation office. English law. An office for the recovery of fines levied upon writs of covenant and entries.

lucrative office. 1. A position that produces fee revenue or a salary to the officeholder. 2. A position that yields a salary adequate to the services rendered and exceeding incidental expenses; a position whose pay is tied to the performance of the office's duties. [Cases: Officers and Public Employees 30.1. C.J.S. Officers and Public Employees §§ 37–39, 44.]

ministerial office. An office that does not include authority to exercise judgment, only to carry out orders given by a superior office, or to perform duties or acts required by rules, statutes, or regulations.

office of honor. An uncompensated public position of considerable dignity and importance to which public trusts or interests are confided. [Cases: Officers and Public Employees 1. C.J.S. Officers and Public Employees §§ 1–9, 12–17, 21.]
(Black's Law Dictionary, 8th Edition)

(c) "an office or an employment of profit was an office or employment which was a subsisting, permanent, substantive position, which had an existence independent of the person who filled it and which went on and was filled in succession by successive holders".

"A position or place to which certain duties are attached, especially one of a more or less public character."

(Great Western Railway Co. v. Bater [1920] 3 KB 266)

Public

public, adj.1. Relating or belonging to an entire community, state, or nation. [Cases: Municipal Corporations 721. C.J.S. Municipal Corporations §§ 1557–1559.] 2. Open or available for all to use, share, or enjoy. 3. (Of a company) having shares that are available on an open market. [Cases: Corporations 3. C.J.S. Corporations §§ 5–7, 62.]

public, n.1. The people of a nation or community as a whole <a crime against the public>. 2. A place open or visible to the public <in public>.
(Black's Law Dictionary, 8th Edition)

Public Office

(a) "public office" includes any office in the service of Pakistan and membership of an Assembly."
(Article 242 of the Constitution of Pakistan, 1962)

(b) "public office" includes any office in service of Pakistan and membership of an Assembly."

(Article 290 of the Interim Constitution of Pakistan, 1972)

(c) public office. A position whose occupant has legal authority to exercise a government's sovereign powers for a fixed period. [Cases: Officers and Public Employees 1. C.J.S. Officers and Public Employees §§ 1–9, 12–17, 21.]

(Black's Law Dictionary, 8th Edition)

(d) "Public Office" defined. 55-6 V. c.40 S.4 A position whose occupant has legal authority to exercise a government's sovereign powers for a fixed period. Position involving exercise of governmental functions [S.6(f), T.P. Act (4 of 1882)]; an office where public business is transacted. [O.XIII, R.5(2), CPC (5 of 1908)].

(Major Law Lexicon, 4th Edition, 2010)

(e) "A Public office is the right, authority and duty created and conferred by law, by which an individual is vested with some portion of the sovereign functions of the government to be exercised by him for the benefit of the public, for the terms and by the tenure prescribed by law. It implies a delegation of a portion of the sovereign power. It is a trust conferred by public authority for a public purpose, embracing the ideas of tenure, duration, emolument and duties. A public officer is thus to be distinguished from a mere employment or agency resting on contract, to which such powers and functions are not attached. The common law rule is that in order for the writ to lie, the office must be one of a public nature. The determining factor, the test, is whether the office involves a delegation of some of the solemn functions of government, either executive, legislative or judicial, to be exercised by the holder for the public benefit."

(The Law of Extraordinary Legal Remedies by Forrest G. Ferris and Forrest G. Perris. JR. of the St. Louis Bar)

(f) "The meanings of 'public office' and 'public officer' vary according to the context in which the terms are used. In general, a public officer may be said to be one who discharges a duty in the performance of which the public is interested; a person is more likely to be such an officer if he is paid out of a fund provided by the public, but it does not necessarily follow that the fund must belong to the central government. Tenure of a public office is not inconsistent with having the status of employee under a contract of employment; but the occupants of certain public offices, such as that of a police officer, are not regarded as having the status of servants.

(Halsbury's Laws of England, Fourth Edition, 2001, Reissue, Volume 1(1). Page 14).

(g) "Winfield in Law Quarterly Review, Volume 61 at page 464 has in an interesting article discussed what a public office is. He mentions two judicial definitions: In 1914, Lawrence, J. said that a public officer is an officer who discharges any duties, in the discharge of which the public are interested, more clearly so, if he is paid out of a fund provided by the public. Best, C. J. in 1828 described a public officer as everyone who is appointed to discharge a public duty and receives a compensation in whatever shape, whether from the Crown or otherwise. The C. J. lays too much emphasis on remuneration of some sort, for some public officers discharge their duties gratuitously for example, the Lord Lieutenant of a country or

Justice of the Peace, and both definitions use the very word which they purport to explain. He concludes that the chief characteristics of a public officer seem to be that is a post, the occupation of which involves the discharge of duties towards the community, or some section of it, and that usually those duties are connected with Government, whether central or local."

{As quoted in Allah Ditta v. Muhammad Munir & others (PLD 1966 (W.P.) Lahore 770)}

(h) "The term 'public office' is defined in Article 290 of the Interim Constitution as including any office in the Service of Pakistan and membership of an Assembly. The phrase 'Service of Pakistan' is defined, in the same Article, as meaning any service, post or office in connection with the affair of the Federation or of a Province and includes an All-Pakistan Service, any defence service and any other service declared to be a Service of Pakistan by or under Act of the Federal Legislature or of a Provincial Legislature but does not include service as a Speaker, Deputy Speaker or other member of an Assembly. Reading the two definitions together, it becomes clear that the term 'public office', as used in the Interim Constitution, is much wider than the phrase 'Service of Pakistan', and although it includes any office in the Service of Pakistan, it could not really refer to the large number of posts or appointments held by state functionaries at various levels in the hierarchy of Government. As early as 1846, the House of Lords in Henry Farran Darley v. Reg. (6), expressed the view that "a proceeding by information in the nature of quo warranto will lie for usurping any office, whether created by Charter of the Crown alone, or by the Crown with the consent of Parliament, provided the office be of a public nature and a substantive office, and not merely the function or employment of a deputy or servant held at the will and pleasure of others". Their Lordships held the office of Treasurer of the public money of the county of the city of Dublin to be an office for which an information in the nature of a quo warranto would lie. In other words, their Lordships excluded, from the purview of the term 'public office', the large number of servant of the Crown who were not holding any statutory, representative or elective office.

In the light of the foregoing discussion, the position of a public limited company, in relation to the applicability of the various clauses of Article 201 of the Interim Constitution, or Article l99 of the permanent Constitution of 1973, may be summed up by saying that while it cannot ordinarily be regarded as a person performing functions in connection with the affairs of the Federation, a Province or a local authority simply for the reason that its functioning is regulated by a statute; yet nevertheless the offices held by its Directors and its Chief Executive, which term would include a Managing Director, must be regarded as public offices inasmuch as they involve the performance of public duties which are of the greatest importance to the public interest in the field of the operation of public joint stock companies under the Company Law. As a consequence, although a joint-stock company may not be amenable to the issuance of a writ under clauses (2)(a)(i) and (2)(a)(ii) of Article 201 of the Interim Constitution, but its Directors and the Chief Executive are within the purview of clause (2)(b)(ii) of the said Article which permits the High Court to issue a writ in the nature of quo warranto, requiring a person within its territorial jurisdiction holding or purporting to hold a public office to show under what authority of law he claims to hold that office".

{Salahuddin & others Vs. Frontier Sugar Mills & Distillery Ltd (PLD 1975 Supreme Court 244)}

(i) The term "officer' is one inseparably connected with an office, and so it may be said that one who holds a public office, as that term is hereinafter defined, is a public officer, and that where there is no office, there can be no public officer. A public officer is such an officer as is required by law to be elected or appointed, who has a designation or title given him by law, and who exercises functions concerning the public, assigned to him by law. The duties of such officer do not arise out of contract or depend for their duration or extent upon the terms of a contract."

(American Jurisprudence, Volume 42, Page.879)

(j) "PUBLIC OFFICE.

(1) An employ in an incorporated company, such as the Bank of Scotland, was a "public office, or employment of profit," within Sched. E to the Income Tax Acts 1842 (c. 35) and 1853 (c. 91) (Tennant v. Smith [1892] A.C. 150); so, of a national schoolmaster, "because the salary is paid by persons whose position as managers of the school is recognized by Act of Parliament, and is paid out of sums of money principally contributed from the taxes of the country in order that the persons to whom it is paid may discharge a duty which is recognized as part of the PUBLIC SERVICE" (PER Pollock B., Bowers v. Harding [1891] 1 Q.B. 560.)

(2) A bursar of an Oxford college, who was not on the foundation and received a salary, held such a "public office" (Langston v. Glasson [1891] 1 Q.B. 567). A person assessable on a "public office, or employment," had to be assessed under Sched. E, and could not be assessed under Case 2, Sched. D. as on an "employment or VOCATION" (per Lord Watson, Tennant v. Smith, supra).

(3) In Pickles v. Foster [1913] 1 K.B. 174, it was held that under r. 3, s. 146 of the Income Tax Act 1842 (c. 35), the office or employment of the profit had to be exercised within the United Kingdom, and did not include the case of a person employed by an English company who exercised his functions entirely abroad.

(4)

(a) As regards the Income Tax Act 1918 (c. 40), Sched. E, see Ricketts v. Colquhoun, 95 L.J.K.B. 82. See also Great Western Railway v. Bater [1992] 2 A.C. 1, cited OFFICE, in which case the question was fully discussed, and it was held that a clerk employed by a railway company did not hold a "public office."

(b) The office of director of an English private company was a "public office in the United Kingdom" within the meaning of Sched. E., r. 6, whether the director resided in England or not. The office of director was situate where the company was, and in the above-mentioned rule the expression "public office" included the office of a director of any company incorporated under the Companies Act 1929 (c.23) (MacMillan v. Guest [1942] A.C. 561).

(c) A foreign journalist in England whose salary was payable abroad was not within the rule (Bray v. Colenbrander [1952] 2T.L.R. 499).

(d) "Payable . . . by any public office "(Income Tax Act 1918 (c. 40), Sched. 3, r. 4(1)): on the true construction of the War Damage Act 1943 (c.21) the War Damage Commission is a "public office" within the meaning of the rule (I.R.C. v. Bew Estates; I.R.C v. Westbury [1956] Ch. 407).

(5) A commission in the Territorial Forces was held to be a "public office" for the purposes of a condition in a will providing for forfeiture on under taking any "public office." The condition was held to be contrary to public policy (Re Edgar, 83 S.J. 154).

(6) "Public annual office" (Public Accounts Act 1692 (c. 11), s.6), included the office of assessor and collector of land or assessed taxes, or of a churchwarden (R. v. Anderson, 9 Q.B. 663, cited SERVED); so, semble, of a clerk to Land Tax Commissioners (R. v. St. Martin-inthe-Fields Commissioners, 1 T.R.146).

(7) Semble the mastership of a city company is a public office of trust (R. v. Neal, Cunn. 267).

(Stroud's Judicial Dictionary of Words and Phrases, Fifth Edition)

(k) "In general, the term "public office" embraces the ideas of tenure, duration, emolument, powers, and duties; and it has been defined as a public station or employment conferred by the appointment of government, or the right, authority, and duty created and conferred by law, by which for a given period an individual is invested with part of the sovereign functions of the government."

(Corpus Juris Secundum, Volume LXVII)

Holder of public office

(a) "Public office holder" refers to any person working in the public sector, whether in parliamentary, government or municipal institutions. An elected official or person appointed to work in the public administration can be a public office holder."

(https://www.commissairelobby.qc.ca/en/public-office-holder/types-of-public-office-holders/)

(b) "Holder of public office" means a person who—

(i) has been the President of Pakistan or the Governor of a Province;

(ii) is, or has been the Prime Minister, Chairman Senate, Speaker of the National Assembly, Deputy Speaker National Assembly, Federal Minister, Minister of State, Attorney General and other Law Officer appointed under the Central Law Officers Ordinance, 1970 (VII of 1970), Advisor to the Prime Minister, Special Assistant to the Prime Minister, Federal Parliamentary Secretary, Member of Parliament, Auditor General, Political Secretary, Consultant to the Prime Minister and holds or has held a post or office with the rank or status of a Federal Minister or Minister of State;

(iii)	is, or has been, the Chief Minister, Speaker Provincial Assembly, Deputy Speaker Provincial Assembly, Provincial Minister, Advisor to the Chief Minister, Special Assistant to the Chief Minister, Provincial Parliamentary Secretary, Member of the Provincial Assembly, Advocate General including Additional Advocate General and Assistant Advocate General, Political Secretary, Consultant to the Chief Minister and who holds or has held a post or office with the rank and status of a Provincial Minister;
(iv)	is holding, or has held, an office or post in the service of Pakistan, or any service in connection with the affairs of the Federation, or of a Province, or of a local council constituted under any Federal or Provincial law relating to the constitution of local councils, cooperative societies or in the management of corporations, banks, financial institutions, firms, concerns, undertakings or any other institution or organization established, controlled or administered by or under the Federal Government or a Provincial Government, other than a member of any of the armed forces of Pakistan except a person who is, or has been a member of the said forces and is holding, or has held, a post or office in any public corporation, bank, financial institution, undertaking or other organization established, controlled or administered by or under the Federal Government or a Provincial Government or, notwithstanding anything contained in the Pakistan Army Act, 1952 (XXXIX of 1952) or any other law for the time being in force, a person who is a civilian employee of the Armed Forces of Pakistan;
(v)	has been the Chairman or Vice-Chairman of a Zila council, a municipal committee, a municipal corporation or a metropolitan corporation constituted under any Federal or Provincial law relating to local councils; and
(va)	is or has been a District Nazim or Naib Nazim, Tehsil Nazim or Naib Nazim or Union Nazim or Naib Nazim. "Explanation" For the purpose of this sub-clause, the expressions "Chairman" and "Vice-Chairman" shall include "Mayor" and "Deputy Mayor" as the case may be, and respective councilors therein.
(vi)	has served in and retired or resigned from or has been discharged or dismissed from the Armed Forces of Pakistan. {Section 5(m) of the National Accountability Ordinance, 1999 (XVIII of 1999)}.

Service of Pakistan

"Service of Pakistan" means any service, post or office in connection with the affairs of the Federation or of a Province, and includes an All-Pakistan Service, service in the Armed Forces and any other service declared to be a service of Pakistan by or under Act of Majlis-e-Shoora (Parliament) or of a Provincial Assembly, but does not include service as Speaker, Deputy Speaker, Chairman, Deputy Chairman, Prime Minister, Federal Minister, Minister of State, Chief Minister, Provincial Minister, Attorney-General, Advocate-General, Parliament Secretary or Chairman or member of a Law Commission, Chairman or member of the Council of Islamic Ideology, Special Assistant to the prime Minister,

Adviser to the Prime Minister, Special Assistant to a Chief Minister, Adviser to a Chief Minister or member of a House or a Provincial Assembly."

(Article 260 of the Constitution of Pakistan)

35. A careful analysis of the aforesaid definitions may lead us to conclude that a public office for the purpose of Article 199 (1)(b)(ii) of the Constitution means an office under the Federal, a Provincial or a local government or in or under any executive, legislative or judicial entity of the state and includes all posts in the service of Pakistan and other posts or offices in the public sector specifically excluded from the definition of 'service of Pakistan' in Article 260 of the Constitution. Though payment of remuneration to holder of a public office is a routine, yet remuneration is not the determinant factor and a person shall remain holder of a public office even if he is not in receipt of remuneration. A public office exists independent of its holder. It may be created by or under the Constitution. When an office is created under a statute, it may either be created directly in the statute or through rules in accordance with the legislative policy contained in the statute. Qualifications possession of which is essential to hold a public office are determined through law (Article 18 of the Constitution). Powers and functions attached to an office in connection with affairs of a Province are also determined statutorily. (Article 138 of the Constitution). To qualify to be a public office, it is not necessary that that office must be of permanent nature and it may not be for a certain period of time. Succession in office is also not a necessary attribute of a public office; an office may be created for a specific person which may abolish when that person ceases to exist or quits the office. There may arise situations requiring creation of a ceremonial office to which no substantial duties are attached but holder of the office is held entitled to certain benefits.

36. A civil servant does fall within the definition of persons in the service of Pakistan. He holds an office for performance of duties attached thereto by or under a law and receives remuneration fixed for holder of that office. These duties are of public nature and are not personal or private to anyone. Performance of these duties is for the purpose of achieving intended public purposes. His appointment is for a substantial period of time i.e. till he attains the age of superannuation or otherwise is prematurely removed from service. He gets remuneration from the public purse. A civil servant is, therefore, hereby held to be a public servant for the purpose of Article 199 (1)(b)(ii) of the Constitution. The respondent in the instant case is a civil servant who holds an office in connection with affairs of the Province. It is held that the respondent is a holder of a public office and proceedings under Article 199 (1)(b)(ii) of the Constitution can be initiated against him.

Question # 3

On what grounds a person in the service of Pakistan can be declared to be holding a public office without lawful authority?

37. Public offices are created for achieving defined public purposes. It is in public interest to ensure that holders of public offices are able to perform functions attached with the public offices and must not suffer from a disability which render them unfit to perform those functions. For this purpose, qualifications are prescribed for persons aspiring to hold a public office. Black's Law Dictionary, 8th Edition, defines 'qualification' and 'qualified' in these words:

> "qualification. 1. The possession of qualities or properties (such as fitness or capacity) inherently or legally necessary to make one eligible for a position or office, or to perform a public duty or function <voter qualification requires one to meet residency, age, and registration requirements>. [Cases: Officers and Public Employees 35. C.J.S. Officers and Public Employees § 58.] 2. A modification or limitation of terms or language; esp., a restriction of terms that would otherwise be interpreted broadly <the contract contained a qualification requiring

the lessor's permission before exercising the right to sublet>.3. CHARACTERIZATION (1). — qualify, vb."

qualified, adj.1. Possessing the necessary qualifications; capable or competent <a qualified medical examiner>.2. Limited; restricted <qualified immunity>. — qualify, vb."

38.   Justice (Retired) Fazal Karim has observed at page 1165 of his book "Judicial Review of Public Actions", 2nd Edition, that:

> "'Qualification' means that which makes a person fit to do an act; it relates to the fitness or capacity of a person for a particular pursuit or profession. It should, therefore, be quite appropriate to refer by qualifications to the competence or the positive qualities needed for carrying on a profession and to regard the obstacles in the carrying on a profession as disqualifications. Every profession requires for the efficient performance of the duties involved in it (i) knowledge, (ii) skill and (iii) a moral standard. In short, whatever goes to his competence or makes a person fit to discharge the duties involved in his profession is a qualification. On the other hand, if a person is debarred from entering a profession though he is admittedly quite competent to discharge his duties for some reason not connected with his competence that is a disqualification. For example, a person may be disqualified because he has served under a foreign government or because he belongs to a particular tribe or his father was a rebel or because he has already sufficient income from lands or he is a shareholder of a company and so on. He may be the most competent person for carrying on a profession yet he may be debarred because of some other attributes which he possesses that will be a disqualification. The case of Government of Pakistan v. Akhlaque Hussain (PLD 1965 SC 527) affords a striking example. It was a case in which the respondent was a person in all respects qualified to practise law but was disqualified to do so because he had been a Judge of the High Court."

39.   A full bench of the Hon'ble Supreme Court of Pakistan has held in Mushtaq Ahmad Mohal and others Vs. The Honourable Lahore High Court, Lahore and others (1997 SCMR 1043) that:

> "If may be observed that even otherwise, the Constitutional requirement, inter alia, enshrined in Article 18 of the Constitution which enjoins that 'Subject to such qualifications, if any, as may be prescribed by law, every citizen shall have the right to enter upon any lawful profession or occupation, and to conduct any lawful trade or business' includes the right of a citizen to compete and participate for appointment to a post in any Federal or a Provincial Government Department or an attached department or autonomous bodies / corporations etc. on the basis of open competition, which right he cannot exercise unless the process of appointment is transparent, fair, just and free from any complaint as to its transparency and fairness."

40.   Restricting our discussion to the offices or posts held by persons in the service of Pakistan, we may see that these offices are created, in some cases, by the Constitution itself e.g. offices of judges in the superior judiciary specifying qualifications, selection authority and appointing authority. Statues also create offices and specify necessary details with respect to qualifications, selection authorities and appointing authorities. Where it is deemed appropriate to prescribe qualifications, selection authorities and appointing authorities through rules, legislative policy is spelt out in the statute and the executive is tasked with the duty to execute it through subordinate legislation.

41. As per Section 2(j) of the Punjab Civil Servants Act, 1974 (Punjab Act No. VIII of 1974), "selection authority" means the Punjab Public Service Commission, departmental selection board, departmental selection committee or other authority or body on the recommendation of, or in consultation with which any appointment or promotion, as may be prescribed, is made. Appointing authority is a person holding an office in which legal power to appoint a person is vested. These definitions of selection authority and appointing authority are relevant for the civil servants as contemplated in the Punjab Civil Servants Act, 1974.

42. In cases in which the appointing authority is not deemed to have sufficient time or organizational capability to carry out selection process and select the best available candidates for public offices, it is assisted through advice of a selection authority. The appointing authority requests the selection authority to recommend candidates for appointment. Our Constitution has provided the institution of Public Service Commission to act as selection authority for certain posts in the service of Pakistan. Where a selection authority is designated for certain post in the service of Pakistan, the appointing authority is legally competent to appoint a person through initial recruitment on the advice of the selection authority. Advice of the selection authority precedes exercise of power to appoint; it is a condition-precedent for appointment through initial recruitment. Posts excluded from the purview of the Public Service Commission are filled in on the recommendation of departmental selection committees or boards. There may be cases in which recommendation of the selection authority is not deemed necessary and, therefore, the appointing authority is given the task of observing due process in selection of candidates for appointment and then appointing them in the prescribed manner.

43. Whether selection process is carried out by the selection authority or the appointing authority, two things have to be ensured, namely:

(a) Save exceptions provided by the Constitution, no citizen otherwise qualified for appointment in the service of Pakistan shall be discriminated against in respect of any such appointment on the ground only of race, religion, caste, sex, residence or place of birth; and

(b) All willing and eligible persons shall be given an opportunity to compete for appointment and only the best performing candidates shall be selected for appointment.

44. Qualifications for eligibility and appointment are not identical. Black's Law Dictionary, 8th Edition has defined eligible and ineligible in these words:

> "ELIGIBLE
> eligible, adj. Fit and proper to be selected or to receive a benefit; legally qualified for an office, privilege, or status. — eligibility, n.
> INELIGIBLE
> ineligible, adj. (Of a person) legally disqualified to serve in office. [Cases: Officers and Public Employees 18. C.J.S. Officers and Public Employees §§ 21–22.] — ineligibility, n."

45. An eligible person is allowed to prove his merit in the selection process. If there is one post, the person found to be the best in the selection process shall be recommended for appointment. Mere being eligible is not enough for appointment; eligibility is only for the purpose of participation in the selection process. Normally, eligibility qualifications, in the context of the civil servants of the Province of Punjab, are as follows:

(a) prescribed education;

(b) age not less than minimum or more than maximum prescribed age;

(c) work experience, if required, including but not limited to research publications;

(d) citizenship of Pakistan, if prescribed;

(e) residence in the Province, if prescribed;

(f) registration with or license of the regulatory body e.g. Pakistan Medical and Dental Council, Bar Council; and

(g) any other requirement applicable to all persons aspiring to compete for appointment.

46.   Qualifications for appointment to join services of the Province as civil servants or posts in connection with affairs of the Province may be as follows:

(a) eligibility qualifications;

(b) recommendation of the selection authority, if prescribed or determination of merit of the persons by the appointing authority after observing due process;

(c) medical fitness certificate required vide rule 3.2 of the Civil Service Rules (CSR);

(d) undertaking regarding no marriage with a foreign national required by Rule 19(2) of the Punjab Civil Servants (Appointment and Conditions of Service) Rules, 1974; and

(e) any other condition-precedent prescribed. (We may like to clarify here that registration of a criminal case or conviction of a citizen is not a lawful ground to deny him the fundamental right guaranteed by Article 18 of the Constitution. It is, therefore, unnecessary to call for Police report before appointing a person in the service of Pakistan.)

47.   The selection process has to be fair, just and open to all willing and eligible persons. There must be no restriction on any willing and eligible person to compete for appointment. If a person is not informed of existence of a post or office, eligibility criteria, qualifications for appointment, procedure of selection and intention of the selection authority to select or of the appointing authority to appoint, it would amount to prohibiting a person from doing that which is not prohibited by law. Article 4(2)(b) of the Constitution leaves no measure of ambiguity in this regard.

48.   Conditions of appointment and of service of persons in the service of Pakistan pertaining to provincial services and posts in connection with affairs of the Province are required to be determined by or under an Act of the Provincial Assembly. For the civil servants in the Punjab, the requisite enactment is the Punjab Civil Servants Act, 1974. It spells out legislative policy on the subject and allows framing of rules to carry out the purposes of the Act. All laws and rules are notified in the official Gazette. With publication of something in the official Gazette, it is assumed that the public at large has duly been informed of that thing. Official Gazette is a public document and any person can have its copy. Thus, all necessary details regarding public offices viz. designation of the post, qualifications, selection authority, appointing authority, prospects of promotion are publically accessible to all. What is not knowable through the publically-accessible documents is the existence of vacancy and intention of the appointing authority to fill the vacancy either on its own or on the recommendation of the appointing authority. If the appointing authority has to carry out selection process on its own, it invites applications from the eligible persons through advertisement in the press and selects persons on the basis of merit determined through known criteria. If the recruitment is to be made on the recommendation of the selection authority, the appointing authority sends requisition to the selection authority for initiating due process. In this case, selection authority invites applications from the eligible and willing persons through open advertisement in the press. Merit of the candidates is determined in accordance with known and non-discriminate criteria and those found meritorious are recommended for promotion.

49.   Whether it is the selection authority or the appointing authority, all willing and eligible persons have a fundamental right to compete for appointment and to be appointed if found superior to others on merit. The method so far found suitable for inviting persons to compete for appointments is the advertisement in the press. If this method is not adopted, it would not only amount to violation of Article 4(2)(b) of the Constitution but would be

denial of the fundamental right to trade and profession guaranteed by Article 18 of the Constitution besides being a material effort to abridge fundamental right to life. As the Constitution has to be read harmoniously, therefore, discrimination in the matter of appointments in the service of Pakistan is prohibited not merely on the grounds listed in Article 27(1) of the Constitution but also in case the eligible and willing persons are kept ignorant of availability of a public office or post which they can hold if they prove their merit.

50.   The Hon'ble Supreme Court of Pakistan has held in Abdul Jabbar Memon and others (1996 SCMR 1349), reiterated in Obaidullah Vs. Habibullah (PLD 1997 SC 835) that:

> "While inquiring into various complaints of violation of Fundamental / Human Rights, it has been found that the Federal Government, Provincial Governments, Statutory Bodies and the Public Authorities have been making initial recruitments, both ad hoc and regular, to posts and offices without publicly and properly advertising the vacancies and at times by converting ad hoc appointments into regular appointments. This practice is prima facie violative of Fundamental Right (Article 18 of the Constitution) guaranteeing to every citizen freedom of profession. Subject to notice to all concerned and subject to final orders after full hearing in the matter, it is ordered as an interim measure that the violation of this Fundamental / Human Right shall be discontinued forthwith."

51.   It was held by the Hon'ble Supreme Court of Pakistan in Mushtaq Ahmad Mohal Vs. Honourable Lahore High Court, Lahore (1997 SCMR 1043) that:

> "It may be observed that even otherwise, the Constitutional requirement, inter alia, enshrined in Article 18 of the Constitution which enjoins that "Subject to such qualifications, if any, as may be prescribed by law, every citizen shall have the right to enter upon any lawful profession or occupation, and to conduct any lawful trade or business" includes the right of a citizen to compete and participate for appointment to a post in any Federal or a Provincial Government department or an attached department or autonomous bodies/corporations etc. on the basis of open competition, which right he cannot exercise unless the process of appointment is transparent, fair, just and free from any complaint as to its transparency and fairness. The above objective enshrined in our Constitution cannot be achieved unless due publicity is made through public notice for inviting applications with the aid of the leading newspapers having wide circulation."

52.   It was held by the Hon'ble Supreme Court of India in Union Public Service Commission Vs. Girish Jayanti Lal Vaghela & Others [2006 (2) SCALE 115] that:

> "Article 16 which finds place in Part III of the Constitution relating to fundamental rights provides that there shall be equality of opportunity for all citizens in matters relating to employment or appointment to any office under the State. The main object of Article 16 is to create a constitutional right to equality of opportunity and employment in public offices. The words "employment" or "appointment" cover not merely the initial appointment but also other attributes of service like promotion and age of superannuation etc. The appointment to any post under the State can only be made after a proper advertisement has been made inviting applications from eligible candidates and holding of selection by a body of experts or a specially constituted

committee whose members are fair and impartial through a written examination or interview or some other rational criteria for judging the inter se merit of candidates who have applied in response to the advertisement made. A regular appointment to a post under the State or Union cannot be made without issuing advertisement in the prescribed manner which may in some cases include inviting applications from the employment exchange where eligible candidates get their names registered. Any regular appointment made on a post under the State or Union without issuing advertisement inviting applications from eligible candidates and without holding a proper selection where all eligible candidates get a fair chance to compete would violate the guarantee enshrined under Article 16 of the Constitution (See B.S. Minhas Vs. Indian Statistical Institute and others AIR 1984 SC 363)."

53. The Hon'ble Lahore High Court, Lahore in its judgment in W. P. No. 29005-2012 titled Barrister Sardar Mohammed Ali Vs. the Federation of Pakistan, etc. has held at paragraphs 29 and 35 that:

"29. It is well settled that the entire process of recruitment leading to appointment to a "public office" can be judicially reviewed under article 199(1)(b)(ii) of the Constitution. The process has to pass the test of law, which includes the settled principles of due process, openness, fairness, participation and transparency. Appointment to a "public office" is a public trust reposed by the people of Pakistan in the Competent Authority. It is a key institutional decision and marks the future progress, growth and development of the public institution, which is to be manned by the prospective incumbent to the said public office. This trusteeship in the hands of the Competent Authority (the Executive) cannot be discharged in whimsical, temperamental, partial and preferential manner. The recruitment process must be above board, devoid of even the slightest taint of favourtisim. The Court is under an obligation to judicially review the integrity of the selection process to a public office. -----."

35. The participatory recruitment process, through open public advertisement, to fill public sector posts has been time and again mandated by the Supreme Court of Pakistan. Reliance is also placed with advantage on Munawar Khan v. Niaz Muhammad and 7 others, (1993 SCMR 1287), Abdul Jabbar Memon and others, (Human Rights Case) (1996 SCMR 1349), Government of N.W.F.P. through Secretary, Forest Department, Peshawar and others, v. Muhammad Tufail Khan, (PLD 2004 S.C. 313), Mushtaq Ahmad Mohal and others v. The Honourable Lahore High Court, Lahore and others, (1997 SCMR 1043), Obaid Ullah and another v. Habib Ullah and others, (PLD 1997 S.C. 835) and Abdur Rashid v. Riaz ud Din and others, (1995 SCMR 999)."

54. The purpose of initial recruitments to public offices through open advertisement in the press is twofold:

a) ensuring equality of opportunity to all citizens; and
b) selection of the best available candidates for holding public offices so that their performance may further public interest and promote organizational efficiency.

55. The requirement of giving all otherwise qualified persons an opportunity to compete for public employments is a basic ingredient of our constitutional scheme regarding initial recruitments in the service of Pakistan. This requirement is fulfilled through inviting

applications for initial recruitments by means of advertisements in the press. In this way, right to trade and profession is protected and avenues of favourtisim, nepotism and backdoor recruitments are plugged so that the state is served by the best and merit alone becomes determinant factor in giving jobs in the public sector. The constitutional requirement of public advertisements for initial recruitments in the public sector must be read as a necessary requirement or inviolable condition of due selection process. Any initial recruitment against a public office made without inviting applications from eligible and willing citizens through public advertisements is void in terms of Article 8 of the Constitution. Executive is to execute laws. Legislature is prohibited to legislate in contravention of any of the fundamental rights. Thus, any executive or legislative measure which, directly or indirectly, amounts to taking away, abridging or denying fundamental rights to citizens are void and of no legal effect. The requirement of open advertisement and competitive selection process for appointments in the service of Pakistan through initial recruitment must be read as integral part of the Constitution, laws, rules and executive instructions relating to such appointments.

56.   In view of the above discussion, a person shall be held to be holding a public office with lawful authority if he:

    (a)   possess qualifications to compete for recruitment to the public office and to hold a public office;

    (b)   has been recommended by the selection authority for appointment after open competitive process or has been selected by the appointing authority after due process;

    (c)   has been appointed by the competent appointing authority; and

    (d)   applicable laws / rules which create and regulate the public office do not suffer from any fatal legal infirmity.

57.   Performance or conduct of a holder of a public office are irrelevant factors in proceedings under 199(1)(b)(ii) of the Constitution. Motives of the appointing authority are also irrelevant in quo warranto proceedings. It was also held in P.L. Lakhanpal Vs A.N. Ray and Ors. (ILR 1974 Delhi 725) that:

> "It is indisputable that mala fide action is no action in the eye of law. But to my mind, the mala fide of the appointing authority or, in other words, the motives of the appointing authority in making the appointment of a particular person are irrelevant in considering the question of issuing a writ of quo warranto.

> What works in the mind of the appointing authority in appointing a particular person is irrelevant and does not fall to be considered in a proceeding of quo warranto and in determining the title of the person who has been appointed.

> To the same effect is the statement in Volume 74, Corpus Jurisdiction Secundum at page 265 that, -   "So, also, where respondent's title rests on an appointment, the court will not go back of the power of appointment to inquire into.................... his reasons and motives for making the appointment..."

58.   We will examine lawfulness of holding a public office by the respondent in the light of the criteria noted hereinabove when we will adjudicate upon this appeal.

Question # 4

Whether conditions of recruitment can lawfully be relaxed in favour of an individual or a group of individuals?

59.   Article 240 of the Constitution, reproduced below, deals with appointments to and conditions of service of persons in the service of Pakistan:

> "**240. Appointments to service of Pakistan and conditions of service. -** Subject to the Constitution, the appointments to and the

conditions of service of persons in the service of Pakistan shall be determined-

    (a)   in the case of the services of the Federation, posts in connection with the affairs of the Federation and All-Pakistan Services, by or under Act of Majlis-e-Shoora (Parliament); and

    (b)   in the case of the services of a Province and posts in connection with the affairs of a Province, by or under Act of the Provincial Assembly.

Explanation. - In this Article, "All-Pakistan Service" means a service common to the Federation and the Provinces, which was in existence immediately before the commencing day or which may be created by Act of Majlis-e-Shoora (Parliament)."

60.   The Provincial Assembly has enacted the Punjab Civil Servants Act, 1974 (Punjab Act No. VIII of 1974) Section 22 whereof reads as follows:

"Nothing in this Act or in any rule shall be construed to limit or abridge the power of the Governor to deal with the case of any civil servant in such manner as may appear to him to be just and equitable:

Provided that, where this Act or any rule is applicable to the case of a civil servant, the case shall not be dealt with in any manner less favourable to him than that provided by this Act or such rule."

61.   Rule 22 of the Punjab Civil Servants (Appointment and Conditions of Service) Rules, 1974, reproduced below, allows the Chief Minister to relax rules in any individual case of hardship:

"The Chief Minister may, for special reasons to be recorded in writing, relax any of the rules in any individual case of hardship, to the extent prescribed by him."

62.   Before proceeding further, we may clearly understand that conditions of recruitment and conditions of service are distinct. The Hon'ble Supreme Court of India in a case reported as Suraj Parkash Gupta & Others Vs State of J & K & Others (AIR 2000 SC 2386) has held that:

"30. The decisions of this Court have recently been requiring strict conformity with the recruitment rules for both direct recruits and promotees. The view is that there can be no relaxation of the basic or fundamental rules of recruitment. In Keshav Chandra Joshi v. Union of India (1992 Supp (1) SCC 272) the Rule permitted relaxation of conditions of service and it was held by the three Judge Bench that the rule did not permit relaxation of recruitment rules. The words 'may consult the PSC' were, it was observed, to be read as 'shall consult PSC' and the rule was treated mandatory. In Syed Khalid Rizvi v. Union of India ([1993] Suppl. 3 SCC 575 at 603), decided by a three Judge Bench, a similar strict principle was laid down. The relevant Rule - Rule 3 of the Residuary Rules (see p. 603) (para 33) in that case did permit relaxation of "rules". Even so, this Court refused to imply relaxation of recruitment rule and observed:

"The condition precedent, therefore, is that there should be appointment to the service in accordance with rules and by operation of the rule, undue hardship has been caused, ---. It is already held that conditions of recruitment and conditions of service are distinct and the latter is preceded by an appointment according to Rules. The former cannot be relaxed."

31. Similarly, in State of Orissa v. Sukanti Mohapatra {[1993] 2 SCC 486}, it was held that though the power of relaxation stated in the rule was in regard to 'any of the provisions of the rules', this did not permit relaxation of the rule of direct recruitment without consulting the Commission and the entire ad hoc service of direct recruit could not be treated as regular service. Similarly, in Dr. M.A.Haque v. Union of India {[1993] 2 SCC 213} it was held that for direct recruitment, the rules relating to recruitment through the Public Service Commission could not be relaxed. In Jammu and Kashmir Public Service Commission v. Dr. Narinder Mohan {[1994] 2 SCC 630}, it was held that the provisions of the J & K Medical Recruitment Rules could not be relaxed for direct recruitment. Backdoor direct recruitments could not be permitted. See also Dr. Arundhati Ajit Pargaonkar v. State of Maharashtra {1994 Suppl. (3) SCC 380}. In Dr. Surinder Singh Jamwal and Anr. v. State of J &K {[1996] 9 SCC 619}, this Court directed the direct recruits to go before the Public Service Commission."

63.   It has also been held by the Hon'ble Gauhati High Court in a case reported as Dr. M. Laitphlang and Ors. Vs State of Meghalaya and Ors. {(2004) 2 GLR 546} that:

"25. While considering the above aspects of the matter, it needs to be pointed out, at the very outset, that the concept of appointment, absorption and / or promotion in service in relaxation of relevant recruitment rules has undergone a prominent development. The present view is that there can be no relaxation of the basic and fundamental rules of recruitment. Moreover, strict conformity with the recruitment rules is insisted both for direct recruits as well as promotees. (Ref: Suraj Prakash Gupta v. State of J&K, reported in (2000) 7 SCC 561. Thus, the service jurisprudence, now, clearly draws a distinction between the conditions of recruitment and conditions of service. In other words, in the realm of service jurisprudence, a distinction is, now, drawn between the conditions of recruitment and the conditions of service. While the conditions of service may be relaxed, conditions of recruitment cannot be so relaxed. In other words, the provisions for relaxation, in general, contained in recruitment rules cannot be resorted to for relaxing the conditions of recruitment, the only exception being, when the recruitment rules, in question, contain provisions for relaxation of the conditions of recruitments. The minimum period of qualifying service for promotion, which recruitment rules impose, is really a condition of recruitment and such a condition, not being a condition of service, cannot, generally, be relaxed unless the Rules in themselves provide for otherwise (J. C. Yadav v. State of Haryana, reported in (1990) 2 SCC 189). A Division Bench of this Court have set the matter at rest in the case of Ananda Ram Borah v. State of Assam, reported in 2003 (2) GLT 78, by observing and laying down as follows :

".... The question, which call for determination by this Court is, whether the power to relax the Rule would go to the extent of relaxing conditions of recruitment also or it can be only to the extent of relaxing the conditions of service? Can a direct recruit for recruitment to the post of LDA avoid competitive examination? Can the Government exercise power of relaxation of Rule of recruitment requiring a direct recruit to appear in the competitive examination and such relaxation of the recruitment Rules is permissible? In Keshab Chandra Joshi v. Union of

India, reported in 1992 Suppl. SCC 272, the Apex Court has emphasized the need of strict compliance of the recruitment Rules for both direct recruits and promotees. It is held that there cannot be any relaxation of the basic or fundamental Rules of recruitment. That was a case where the Rule permitting relaxation of conditions of service came for consideration and it was held by a three Judges Bench that the Rule did not permit relaxation of the recruitment Rules. In Syed Khalid Rizvi v. Union of India, 1993 Supp (3) SCC 575, the Apex Court observed:

> "The condition precedent, therefore, is that there should be an appointment to the service in accordance with Rules and by operation of the Rules, undue hardship has been caused...it is already held that the condition of recruitment and conditions of service are distinct and the latter is preceded by an appointment according to Rules. The former cannot be relaxed."

Thus, according to the Apex Court there is distinction between the conditions of recruitment and conditions of service. Appointment has to be made in accordance with the recruitment Rules and, thereafter, there may be a relaxation in the service condition. Similarly, in State of Orissa v. Sukanti Mohapatra (1993) 2 SCC 486, it was held that though the power of relaxation stated in the Rule was in regard to "any of the provisions of the Rules," this did not permit relaxation of the Rule of direct recruitment without consulting the Commission and the entire ad-hoc service of a direct recruit could not be treated as regular service. In M.A. Haque (Dr.) v. Union of India (1993) 2 SCC 213 and in Jammu and Kashmir Public Service Commission v. Dr. Narinder Mohan, (1994) 2 SCC 630, it has been emphatically laid down that the Rule relating to recruitment could not be relaxed. The judgment in the matter of Suraj Prakash Gupta (supra) has also reiterated the principle laid down by the Apex Court that there cannot be any relaxation of the conditions of recruitment. The conditions of recruitment and conditions of service are distinct. The Government has the power to relax conditions of service, whereas the conditions of recruitment cannot be relaxed even though the Rule intends to do so." (emphasis is supplied).

26. We express our complete agreement with the position of law laid down in Ananda Ram Borah (supra) subject to only one clarification that if the recruitment rules, in themselves, provide for relaxation of conditions of recruitment, the conditions of recruitment may be relaxed, provided that such relaxation does not make the conditions of recruitment nugatory and that interpretation of such provisions of relaxation contained in the recruitment rules must not be liberal, but very strict."

64.   Section 1 (2) of the Punjab Civil Servants Act, 1974 says that this Act applies to all civil servants wherever they may be. Rule 1 (3) of the Punjab Civil Servants (Appointment & Conditions of Service) Rules, 1974 provides that these rules shall apply to all civil servants. Powers under Section 22 of the Punjab Civil Servants Act, 1974 and Rule 23 of the Punjab Civil Servants (Appointment & Conditions of Service) Rules, 1974 can be exercised in respect of a civil servant and not in favour of other persons. Recruitment rules are for the purpose of selection of willing and eligible persons for appointment in the service of Pakistan as civil servants of the Province. Candidates aspiring to become civil servants cannot be

given any favour through relaxation of rules under Section 22 of the Punjab Civil Servants Act, 1974 or Rule 23 of the Punjab Civil Servants (Appointment & Conditions of Service) Rules, 1974. It was held in a case reported as Ghulam Muhammad Vs. Azad Govt. and two others (1995 SCR 162) that:

> "The reasoning of Service Tribunal is not sustainable because relaxation under section 22 of the Civil Servants Act, which has been relied upon by Sardar Rafique Mehmood, is exercisable only in respect of a civil servant but not a person who has ceased to be a civil servant or aspires to be one."

65.   It was held in a case reported as Abdul Shakoor Vs. Mrs. Shamim Khalil and 5 others (2004 P L C (C.S.) 7) that:

> "Mr. M. Tabassum Aftab Alvi, the learned counsel representing the petitioner, while pleading the case, banked upon rule 24 of the Rules which, according to him, does not provide relation of rules for 'civil servant' alone. It is correct that aforesaid words do not appear in the rule, but it would be sufficient to mention that the aforesaid Rules are framed under the Act where this power is exercisable by the Government in respect of a civil servant, therefore, no rule can be framed or read against the spirit of parent statute. It follows that the petitioner for the purposes of this matter was not a civil servant and the Government could not make any relaxation in this regard. It is also important to mention that keeping in view the provisions of the Act and the Rules, the notification must show to have recorded reasons for exercising the aforesaid power in any individual case which is just and equitable. The proposition finds support from case-law reported as Miss Azra Hafiz and 10 others v. Israr Hussain Mughal (1997 PLC (C S.) 297)."

66.   It was held in a case reported as Miss Shamaila Mahmood Vs. Mukhtar Ahmed and others (1998 PLC (C.S) 51) that:

> "Contents of the passages reproduced above may be summarized thus: when a set of rules is framed under Section 23 of the Civil Servants Act, it has to be construed that it has been framed to carry out the purposes of the said Act. If in any rule, a special power is granted to override or relax the rules, this power will be deemed to be for carrying out the purposes of Section 22 of Civil Servants Act, namely to advance the ends of justice and equity. This purpose shall be deemed to be incorporated in every rule under the Civil Servants Act which gives the power of relaxation of rules or overriding them. The question as to what is just and equitable depends on facts of each case and if exercise of this power is challenged in a case, the reason on which the order is passed will be judicially scrutinized by courts of law."

67.   It was held in Javed Iqbal Khawaja and others Vs. Azad Government of the State of Jammu and Kashmir through its Chief Secretary, Muzaffarabad and others (PLD 1994 Azad J&K 26) that:

> "It is evident that the provisions of section 22 are enforceable by the Government in exercise of its authority (i) to the case of civil servants; and (ii) this power is to be exercised in just and equitable manner. A person becomes a civil servant when he is appointed to any service of the State in due course of law.   Thus, the discretion of the Government postulated under section 22 of the Act, shall be available post facto to the induction of person in civil service. The discretion of the Government does not come in play at the stage of an initial recruitment.   Since the authority of the Government operates post

facto to the appointment of a person to civil service, it cannot be construed that the Government is empowered to appoint a, person to civil post, in derogation to the scheme of law enunciated in the Act."

68.   It was held in Abdul Shakoor and others Vs. Azad Government of the State of Jammu and Kashmir through Chief Secretary and others (2004 P L C (C.S.) 208) that:

"Mr. M. Tabassum Aftab Alvi, attempted to create an exception that though section 22 of the Civil Servants Act, 1976, refers to the word `civil servant' but in rule 24 of the AJ&K Civil Servants (Appointments and Conditions of Service) Rules, 1977, no such word has been used. According to the learned Advocate this is a willful omission on the part of the rule making authority to cover the situation like present one. Mr. Abdul Rashid Abbasi, controverting the arguments, contended that the rule cannot be read in isolation or in derogation of the phraseology used in the parent Act. I am of the opinion that this, submission of Mr. Abdul Rashid Abbasi, is again in line with the pronouncements of the superior Courts. It is settled position that where the rules are framed under an enactment then the provision of the Act shall be given effect to and rules cannot defeat the intentions of the legislature expressed in the parent statute nor rule making authority can clothe itself with the power which is not given to it under the parent Act. Assuming, for the sake of arguments, that the Government has the power to relax the rules, even in those cases relaxation could only be ordered for carrying out the purpose of the Act and in just and equitable manner. The proposition came under consideration in "Azad Govt. and others v. Muhammad Younas Tahir and others" (1994 CLC 2339). At page 397 of the report, the scope of power of the Government with reference to section 22 of the Civil Servants Act, 1976, has thoroughly been examined. The relevant portion of the judgments is as under: --

"It is evident from the provisions reproduced above that the powers under section 22 of the Civil Servants Act are to be exercised irrespective of the provisions contained in the Act or Rules, provided the same are `just and equitable'. What would be 'just and equitable' in a particular case depends upon the circumstances of each case and no hard and fast rule can be laid down in that regard. It may be stated that in the instant case I fully agree with the view taken by my brother Mr. Justice Basharat Ahmad Shaikh that the order made by the Government in favour of Miss Shamaila, respondent, under section 22 of the Civil Servants Act is not in consonance with spirit of law, although on somewhat different grounds. Consequently, the order passed by the Government is not sustainable because nothing has been brought on the record that when writ petition entitled ' Muhammad Yunus Tahir v. Azad Govt. of the State of Jammu and Kashmir and others' was already pending what prompted the Government to exercise powers under section 22 of the Civil Servants Act to the detriment of Muhammad Yunus Tahir, petitioner, who was also an ad hoc appointee as Sub Judge. No material has been brought on the record that said order was 'just and equitable' as envisaged under section 22 of the Civil Servants Act." (underlining is mine)

Be that at it may, it has finally been concluded by the apex Court in Kh. Ghulam Muhammad's case (1995 SCR 162) that power under section 22 of the Civil Servants Act, 1976, could be exercised in respect of civil servant and not in favour of one who is aspiring for entry into civil service. It is useful to reproduce the relevant observation of the apex Court which is to the following effect: --

"the reasoning of Service Tribunal is not sustainable because relaxation under section 22 of the Civil Servant Act, which has been relied upon by Sardar Rafique Mehmood, is exercisable only in respect of a civil servant but not a person who has ceased to be a civil servant aspires to be one. Section 22 reads as follows:

"22. Saving: -Nothing in this Act or in any rules shall be construed to limit or abridge the power of the Government to deal with the case of any civil servant in such manner as may appear to it to be just and equitable; "

Under section 22 an order which is just and equitable can be passed. The Service Tribunal observed that the Government considered the difficulties of respondent No.3 and relaxed the service rules. We have seen that no such difficulties are referred to in it, although it is claimed that the Government can pass any order to meet any injustice. No situation or justification is on the record to justify the impugned order as just or equitable. It is now well-settled that the power under section 22 cannot be exercised in such a way that it may adversely affect the seniority of any other civil servant, for instance the appellant, because such an order would not be just or equitable."

The same view was followed in Sheikh Manzoor's case 1995 PLC (C.S.) 59 and thereafter in Mir Abdul Hamid's case 1997 PLC (C.S.) 805. In the latter authority it was opined that residuary power available to the Government under section 22 could only be exercised for the advancement and for the ends of justice and equity and not otherwise. This proposition was also considered in Miss Shamaila Mehmood's case (1998 PLC (CS) 51). This is a direct authority on the point. Facts of the case were that Shamalia Mehmood was appointed as Sub-Judge by relaxing legal experience and qualification under a Government order issued under section 22 of the AJ&K Civil Servants Act, 1976 and rules made thereunder. This appointment was challenged by Mukhtar Ahmed and others, through a writ petition and the writ was accepted in view of the result of the judgment in Muhammad Younus Tahir's case, referred hereinabove. On appeal the apex Court again examined the scope of section 22 of the Civil Servants Act, 1976 and opined as under: --

"14. Contents of the passages reproduced above may be summarized thus. When a set of rules is framed under section 23 of the Civil Servants Act it has to be construed that it has been framed to carry out the purposes of the Civil Servants Act. If in any rule a special power is granted to override or relax the rules this power will be deemed to be for carrying out the purposes of section 22 of the Civil Servants Act, namely, to advance the ends of justice and equity. This purpose shall be deemed to be incorporated in every rule under the Civil Servants Act which gives the power of relaxation of rules or overriding them. The question as to what is just and equitable depends on facts of each case and if exercise of this power is challenged in a case the reason on which the order is passed will be judicially scrutinized by Courts of law.

As is evident from the above referred case-law, the relaxation cannot be ordered for the benefit of one individual and to deprive the other. Especially so when the fundamental rights of the citizen are involved. This view lends support from a judgment of this Court in Arshad Hussain Chaudhry's case (1998 PLC (C.S.) 1229)."

69.   It was held in Miss Shamaila Mahmood Vs. Mukhtar Ahmad and 6 others (1998 PLC (C.S.) 51) that:

> "I took the view that section 22 of the Civil Servants Act is not available for exempting any person from the requirement of selection through the Public Service Commission. Consequently, it was held that.
>
> > "13. The overriding powers given in different service rules have been examined by this Court in a recent judgment pronounced in Civil Appeal No.16 of 1997 titled Mir Abdul Hamid v. Azad Government of the state of Jammu and Kashmir and 2 others (1997 PLC (C. S.) 805). The case arose out of a dispute relating to the allotment of a Government residence. One of the points which fell for determination in that case was the scope of power given to the Prime Minister of Azad Jammu and Kashmir in sub-rule (3) of Rule 6-A of the Azad Jammu and Kashmir Allocation (Accommodation) Rules 1981. The sub-rule runs as follows: --
> >
> > "3. Notwithstanding anything contained in these rules or any other rules for the time being in force, the Chief Executive shall have the powers to allot a house to a Government servant at his discretion at any time."
>
> The ratio laid down in Mir Abdul Hamid's case in respect of such powers is directly applicable to the present case. I may, therefore, quote the relevant portion of that judgment:
>
> > "17. While interpreting the power granted in the above extracted sub-rule, we may observe that laws are made and rules are framed for being implemented and not for being violated. This is the concept of law in every State which is governed by a written constitution. The framing of Accommodation Rules is referable to the Azad Jammu and Kashmir Civil Servants Act. Power to make rules is provided in subsection (1) of section 23, which lays down that
> >
> > "(1) The Government or any other person authorised in this behalf, may make such rules as appear to him to be necessary or expedient for carrying out the purposes of this Act."
>
> On a plain reading, rules can only be framed for carrying out the purposes of the parent Act.
>
> 18. Sub-rule (3) of rule 6-A, already reproduced, gives powers to the Chief Executive to override all rules. Such powers, wherever given in any service rules, are only referable to section 22 of the Azad Jammu and Kashmir Civil Servants Act which is as follows: -
>
> > "22. Saving. -Notwithstanding in this Act or in any rules shall be construed to limit or abridge the power of the Government to deal with the case of any civil servant in such manner as may appear to it to be just and equitable:

Provided that, where this Act or any rule is applicable to the case of a civil servant, the case shall not be dealt with in any manner less favourable to him than that provided by this Act or such rule."

19.   It has been held by this Court in Sh. Manzoor Ahmed v. Azad Government and another 1995 PLC (C.S.) 59 that power under section 22 of the Azad Jammu and Kashmir Civil Servants Act has to be exercised to advance the ends of justice and equity and not to give an undue advantage to a civil servant in contravention of the relevant law. Under section 23 the Government is only empowered to make rules for carrying out the purpose of the Azad Jammu and Kashmir Civil Servants Act. Therefore, if a rule confers discretionary power which is exercisable to override the rules, it has to be construed that such powers have been conferred for carrying out the purposes of section 22 of the Civil Servants Act, namely, to advance ends of justice and equity. In our view, this purpose must be deemed to be incorporated in sub-rule (3) under discussion and all other provisions of this type. Therefore, sub-rule (3) of rule 6-A of the Accommodation Rules must be construed accordingly with the result that the Chief Executive can pass an order only to advance ends of justice and equity. The question as to what is just and equitable cannot be answered by laying down a hard and fast definition. Even otherwise, it is not possible to address to this question in vacuum. This depends on the facts of each case. Even the dictates of justice and equity may be different in different situations and what is just and equitable in one case may not necessarily be just and equitable in another case. Therefore, each case has to be examined by the Chief Executive on its own merits in light of persuading reasons. We may add that since a writ petition lies to challenge such an order, reasons must be such that can stand the scrutiny of judicial review."

70.   Statutes are enacted to further the objects and purposes of the Constitution. Flesh is added to bones of the statutes through rules, regulations and executive instructions having the force of law. All sub-constitutional legislative instruments are meant to ensure that dictates of the Constitution are followed in letter and spirit. The details contained in the legislative instruments are as sacred as the Constitution itself if these are for the sole purpose of implementation of the Constitution including the fundamental rights guaranteed by the Constitution. One of the fundamental rights is the right to trade and profession and assurance regarding non-discrimination in the matter of appointments in the service of Pakistan to eligible and willing citizens. If relaxation of rules for the purpose of recruitments in the service of Pakistan in favour of a certain individual is allowed, it would amount to abridge fundamental rights of all other qualified citizens who intend to compete for employment in the service of Pakistan. What may be claimed to be just and equitable in respect of an individual is unjust and inequitable for all others. In simple words, it would have the effect of suspension of a valuable fundamental right of all other eligible citizens just to extend a special favour to an individual. We need not to give arguments in favour of the proposition that what cannot be done directly is not allowed to be done indirectly. The legislature and the executive are debarred to legislate or to act in contravention of the fundamental rights; these rights are guaranteed by the Constitution and are not allowed to be taken away, abridged or denied, temporarily or permanently, through enactments or executive orders as it would be suspension of the relevant provisions of the Constitution. (Here, we are not speaking of suspension of the fundamental rights during the period of a state of emergency).   To explain, we may refer to the fundamental right to trade and profession which citizens can enjoy in respect of appointments in the service of Pakistan and

which cannot be exercised if recruitment is not made after due advertisement in the press. The requirement to invite applications through advertisement in the press is a requirement expressly written in the rules but this requirement is in effect to implement Article 18 read with Article 25 and 27 of the Constitution. Though the executive instrument regarding relaxation of the rules inviting applications through open advertisement will say only to relax the rules but in reality it would be offending Article 18 read with Article 2A, 4 (2) (b), 25, 27 and 137 of the Constitution. This argument requires a little bit elaboration.

71. Article 2A of the Constitution intends enforcement of Qur'an and Sunnah within the framework of the principles and provisions of the Objectives Resolution through courts of law. (Shaukat Hussain Vs. Rubina (PLD 1989 Kar 513), Qamar Raza Vs. Tahira Begum (PLD 1988 Kar 169), Habib Bank Ltd Vs. Muhammad Hussain (PLD 1987 Kar. 612). The Objectives Resolution guarantees fundamental right of equality of opportunity. If recruitments are made without open competition or through relaxation of conditions of recruitment in favour of a selected few and not for all, those who are kept ignorant of the recruitment process or not given favour of relaxation of recruitment rules are subjected to adverse discrimination which has been prohibited by the Constitution.

72. Article 4 (2) (b) of the Constitution says that no person shall be prevented from or be hindered in doing that which is not prohibited by law. Making appointments without open advertisement amounts to preventing eligible and willing citizens to enter into lawful professions. This constitutional requirement is not allowed to be dispensed with under any circumstances, not even during emergency when fundamental rights stand suspended.

73. Employment in the service of Pakistan is a lawful profession which every citizen otherwise qualified has a right to join and this fundamental right cannot be denied to him if he proves his merit. In order to prove his merit, he has to be given information of the intent of the public authorities to make recruitments and the basis of determination of the relative merit of the candidates. If recruitments are made without open competition, it amounts to annulment of the fundamental right of the willing and eligible citizens to get employment in the service of Pakistan on the basis of merit. When read with Article 4 (2) (b) of the Constitution and the dictum of law laid down by the Hon'ble Supreme Court of Pakistan in Mushtaq Ahmad Mohal Vs. Honourable Lahore High Court, Lahore (1997 SCMR 1043), it becomes crystal clear that it is a constitutional requirement to make recruitments in the service of Pakistan after due open competitive process and without any adverse discrimination.

74. The fundamental right of equality of citizens guaranteed by Article 25 of the Constitution stands violated if some citizens are informed to apply for appointment in the service of Pakistan and all others are denied this opportunity or persons are appointed without submission of applications. Recruitments made without open advertisement amount to adverse discrimination against those kept ignorant of the process of recruitment.

75. Article 27 of the Constitution provides that no citizen otherwise qualified for appointment in the service of Pakistan shall be discriminated against in respect of any such appointment on the ground only of race, religion, caste, sex, residence or place of birth. First proviso to this Article provides that, for a period not exceeding forty years from the commencing day, posts may be reserved for persons belonging to any class or area to secure their adequate representation in the service of Pakistan. If recruitments are made without open advertisement, citizens are divided into two classes; one that has knowledge of the recruitment process and is in a position to apply for appointment if otherwise qualified; and the second that has no information of the recruitment process and thus unable to apply for the appointment even if willing, eligible and meritorious. Multi-layered blindfold is not enough to claim that Article 27 of the Constitution allows such absurd classification; one has to be brainless and constitutionally blind to make such an assertion.

76. Article 137 of the Constitution states that subject to the Constitution, the executive authority of the Province shall extend to the matters with respect to which the Provincial Assembly has power to make laws. The Provincial Assembly has no power to make any law

to suspend, take away or abridge any of the fundamental rights. Legislative and executive powers are co-extensive. Since the Provincial Assembly has no power to legislate against fundamental rights, the provincial executive has no power to take away fundamental right guaranteed by Article 18 of the Constitution under the pretext of relaxation of the recruitment rules.

77.   Public Service Commission is an important institution in our constitutional scheme of public employments. Certain posts are required to be filled in on the recommendation of the Public Service Commission. These requirements are embodied in the relevant rules. Public Service Commission recommends candidates for appointment after observance of the due process. While dealing with the concept of recommendation, a three- Judge Bench of the Supreme Court of India in A. Pandurangam Rao Vs. State of Andhra Pradesh and others[AIR 1975 SC 1922] has stated that the literal meaning of the word "recommend" is quite simple and it means "suggest as fit for employment". As regards recruitment rules relating to appointments on the basis of recommendations of the Public Service Commission, the Jammu & Kashmir High Court observed in Mukhtar-Ul-Aziz Vs State of J and K and Ors. {2005 (2) JKJ 583} that:

> "38. It is true that direct recruitment to gazetted posts bypassing the Public Service Commission has not been approved in cases such as Dr. M.A. Haque v. Union of India, (1993) 2 SCC 213, J&K Public Service Commission v. Dr. Narinder Mohan, (1994) 2 SCC 630, Surinder Singh Jamwal v. State of J&K, (1996) 9 SCC 619 and in Suraj Parkash Gupta v. State of J&K (supra). In the last one it was held that if direct recruitment is permitted without consulting the Public Service Commission there would be total chaos in the recruitment process and it will lead to backdoor appointment at the risk and faces of Government."

78.   It was held in Javed Iqbal Khawaja and others Vs. Azad Government of the State of Jammu and Kashmir through its Chief Secretary, Muzaffarabad and others (PLD 1994 Azad J&K 26) that:

> "The Government was not empowered to refuse to refer to the Commission all posts in Grade-16 and above, in order to fill the same. In that case, the Commission would become perfunctory and redundant. Of course, that cannot be the scheme of the Constitution or law of civil service;"

79.   Public Service Commission has been conceived as an independent institution which acts as a professional recruiting agency. This institution cannot be reduced to a mere nugatory through relaxation of recruitment rules to allow recruitments without consultation with the Public Service Commission in cases in which recommendation of the Commission is required under law / rules. Appointing authority lacks power to appoint in absence of recommendation of the Public Service Commission if it has been prescribed that appointment shall only be made after consultation with the Public Service Commission. In State of Uttar Pradesh Vs. Singhara Singh (AIR 1964 SC 358), the Hon'ble Supreme Court of India relied upon the well-known case of Nazir Ahmed (AIR 1936 PC 253), wherein the principle has been laid down that where a power is given to do a certain thing in a certain way, the thing must be done in that way or not at all and that other methods of performance are necessarily forbidden. We may quote paragraph 8 of the said judgment as under:

> "8. The rule adopted in Taylor v. Taylor (1876) 1 Ch D 426 is well recognised and is founded on sound principle. Its result is that if a statute has conferred a power to do an act and has laid down the method in which that power has to be exercised, it necessarily prohibits the doing of the act in any other manner than that which has

been prescribed. The principle behind the rule is that if this were not so, the statutory provision might as well not have been enacted."

80.   The same principle was followed by the Hon'ble Supreme Court of Pakistan in Atta Muhammad Qureshi Vs. The Settlement Commissioner, Lahore Division, Lahore and 2 others (PLD 1971 SC 61). Chief Justice John Marshal has also held in Marbury v. Madison [(1803) 5 US (1 Cranch) 137] that;

> "To what purpose are powers limited and to what purpose is that limitation committed to writing, if these limits may, at any time, be passed by those intended to be restrained? The distinction between a Government with limited and unlimited powers is abolished, if these limits do not confine the persons on whom they are imposed, and if the acts prohibited and acts allowed, are of equal obligation."

81.   Thus, if consultation with the Public Service Commission is a requirement for appointment, the appointing authority shall not appoint a candidate without consulting the Public Service Commission.

82.   There may arise situations when duly qualified candidates are not available and it becomes necessary to relax conditions of recruitment in order to make recruitments. In such a condition, the requirement of inviting applications through open advertisement are not allowed to be relaxed. Other conditions (academic qualifications, experience, age etc.) may be relaxed if express provision for relaxation of the recruitment rules has been made in the rules for all eligible persons and not for a selected few and a decision to this effect must form part of the press advertisement through which applications are invited for recruitment. We reiterate for the purpose of clarity that recruitment rules cannot be relaxed for some; whenever recruitment rules are relaxed, these shall be relaxed for all and public at large shall be informed of the relaxation through open advertisement in the press.

83.   We have concluded from the above discussion that:

    (a) the requirement of inviting applications through open advertisement in the press cannot be dispensed with under any circumstances as it would be in contravention of Article 2A, 4 (2) (b), 18, 25, 27 and 137 of the Constitution and, hence, void in terms of Article 8 of the Constitution;

    (b) where the applicable law or rules requires consultation with the Public Service Commission as a condition-precedent for appointments in the service of Pakistan, appointments are not allowed to be made without consulting the Public Service Commission under the pretext of relaxation of the rules;

    (c) other conditions of recruitment cannot be relaxed in favour of an individual or a group of individuals; and

    (d) whenever it is deemed necessary in public interest to relax conditions of recruitment, these may be relaxed if express provision therefor exists and the benefit of such relaxation shall be given to all and this decision shall form part of open advertisement in the press through which applications are invited for recruitment.

84.   Section 22 of the Punjab Civil Servants Act, 1974 and Rule 23 of the Punjab Civil Servants (Appointment & Conditions of Service) Rules, 1974 can be resorted to to ensure justice and equity to the civil servants in cases in which strict application of the rules may result into undue hardship. The aforesaid provisions are applicable to civil servants only and are related to conditions of service and not conditions of appointment. The powers to relax conditions of service are exercisable only for just and equitable purposes and not as tools to favour a civil servant or for anything which may be adverse discrimination for other civil servants. It has been held in a case reported as Abdul Shakoor Vs. Mrs. Shamim Khalil and 5 others (2004 PLC (C.S.) 7) that:

"Relaxation of Rules by Government---Notification must show reasons for exercising such powers in any individual case which are just and equitable, otherwise same would be ultra vires."

85.   It has been held in a case reported as Dr. Muhammad Azhar Vs. Dr. Tariq Mahmood Malik and 2 others (2002 PLC (C.S.) 57) that:

> "Section 22 of the Punjab Civil Servants Act and Rule 23 of the Punjab Civil Servants Act (Appointments and Conditions of Service) Rules, 1974 were interpreted by the Hon'ble Supreme Court in Muhammad Iqbal Khokhar's case (PLD 1991 SC 35) and laid down the following principle: --
>
>> "The power of relaxation of rules vested in the Governor / Chief Ministers basically intended to correct serious cases to remove injustice. This power is exercised only in genuine cases to remove injustice and inequity which may stand in the way of civil servant or individual."
>
> The aforesaid view was upheld by the Hon'ble Supreme Court in Abdul Qayyum's case (PLD 1992 SC 184). Similar view was taken qua the administrative body in Akram Bus Services' case (PLD 1963 SC 564) and laid down the following view: --
>
>> "The aforesaid section 22 of the Act and Rule 23 do not permit the Chief Minister / Governor to relax the Rules and Regulations through omnibus order. It is a condition precedent for the Governor to pass Order under section 22 to keep in view that it is just and equitable. According to the Black's Law Dictionary the words 'just' and 'equitable' mean as under: --
>> "Just. Conforming to or consonant with what is legal or lawful; legally right; lawful.
>> Equitable. Just; conformable to the principles of justice and right. Existing in equity, available or sustainable by action in equity, or upon the rules and principles of equity."
>
> The word 'just' means according to the law as per principle laid down by the Hon'ble Supreme Court in the following judgments: --
> PLD 1987 SC 447 (Utility Stores Corporation Pakistan Ltd.'s case and (1993 SCMR.1370) Shai Brothers Pvt. Ltd.'s case.
> The word 'equity' has been defined by Snellas as "something equivalent to natural justice or morality". The word 'equity' has been interpreted in Muhammad Hussain's case (PLD 1970 Azad J&K 97) and laid down the following principle:
>
>> "equity in any given situation means what would be fair in that situation."
>
> Rule 23 was considered by the Division Bench of this Court in Writ Petition No.6387 of 1990, decided on 31-5-2001 and laid down the following principle: --
>
>> "It may be added that there is no power of relaxation of the rules 'in their entirety'. We declare that law maker has conferred no such authority on the Government. The absorption of all these respondents vide the impugned notifications is, therefore, declared to have been made without lawful authority and consequently of no legal effect. We are fortified in the above conclusions by a D.B. judgment of Balochistan High Court reported as Muhammad Afzal etc. v. Government of Balochistan etc. (1995 PLC (C.S.) 567) cited by Ch. Khurshid Ahmad, Advocate........."

The Chief Minister or for that matter any other competent authority has to give reasons which could show the application of mind. We would like to add that Pakistan is a democratic society where there is no room for a king. Even the elected Chief Minister has to abide by law and remain subservient to the same. Discretion to bypass the law as a whole may be vesting in the kings but not in democratically elected Chief Minister nor any other authority in a democratic society."

86.   The High Court of Sindh in Constitution Petition No. D-385 of 1991 (Mr. Liaquat Ali Baloch Vs. Government of Sindh and others) has observed that no doubt Section 24 of Sindh Civil Servants Act gives a blank cheque to the Government to deal with a civil servant in such a manner as may appear to it to be just and equitable, there must be some rational for it and discretion so conferred upon the Government may only be used judicially and not arbitrarily. Moreover, the appointments made without observing formalities and proper procedure have been held violative of Fundamental Human Rights by the Supreme Court of Pakistan.

87.   The Hon'ble Supreme Court of Pakistan was pleased to hold in Ch. Muhammad Akram Vs. Registrar, Islamabad High Court and others (PLD 2016 SC 961) that:

"It would be advantageous to interpret the term "just and equitable".

In Corpus Juris Secundum, Volume L, the term "just" has been defined as under: -

"conforming to, or consonant with, what is legal or lawful; conformable to laws; conformable to rectitude and justice; conformed to rules or principles of justice; conforming to the requirements of right or of positive law; correct; right; legally right; rightful; right in law or ethics; due; lawful; legitimate; equitable; fair; honest; true; impartial in accordance with law and justice; not doing wrong to any; not transgressing the requirements of truth and propriety;

48. In Words and Phrases, Permanent Edition, Volume 23A, the term "just" has been defined as under: -

"The term "just" may apply to law as well as ethics. In certain cases, it denotes that which is right and fair according to positive law. The word "just" means a right, and more technically a legal right – a law. This "jus dicere" was to pronounce the judgment; to give the legal decision."

49. The term "equitable" has been interpreted in Words and Phrases, Permanent Edition Volume 15, as under: -

"The term "equitable" is defined as meaning according to natural right or natural justice; marked by the due consideration for what is fair, unbiased, or impartial."

50. The term "undue" used in Section 16 of the Islamabad High Court Rules, has been defined in Words and Phrases, Permanent Edition, Volume 43, as under: -

"Undue" means not appropriate or suitable, improper, unreasonable, unjustifiable, illegal, going beyond what is appropriate, warranted or natural"

51. From the perusal of the above definitions in conjunction with the above-quoted Rules of Lahore High Court and Islamabad High Court, it can safely be held that absolute power to relax a certain service Rule has not been conferred on the Chief Justices of both the High Courts and this power is limited only to be exercised where it does not encroach upon the statutory rights of the other persons or employees. These two Rules cannot be interpreted in such a manner

as to bestow an absolute power upon the Chief Justices to deal with the case of a person / employee in a manner they like. The Chief Justices can exercise powers under these Rules only in a manner that may not cause injustice or prejudice to any individual / employee. In the case in hand, the learned Chief Justice of Islamabad High Court has exercised a power beyond the scope of the Rules and relaxed them under the garb of "relaxation of Rules" which cannot be permitted in any circumstances, especially when it impinges upon the statutory rights of the citizens and other employees of the High Court. Rules can only be relaxed if the rules permit their relaxation, and the conditions stipulated for relaxation are strictly met. Admittedly, the conditions for relaxation of the Rules which are "just and equitable" and "undue hardship" have not been met in relaxing the Rules for making appointments and absorptions in the Islamabad High Court.

53. This Court in the case of Ali Azhar Khan Baloch vs. Province of Sindh (2015 SCMR 456), while interpreting Section 24 of the Sindh Civil Servants Act, has held as under: -

> "137. ....The Competent Authority can exercise powers under section 24 of the Act, by relaxing rules, if there is a vacuum in law, but such powers cannot be exercised under the garb of the term "Relaxation of Rules" with the intent to by-pass the mandate of law for extending favours to a person or an individual, offending and impairing the statutory rights of other Civil Servants. The Competent Authority, by an executive order, cannot frame Rules in exercise of powers under section 24. The authority conferred under section 24 of the Act is confined to hardship cases, without negating the vested rights of the other Civil Servants and / or causing prejudice to their interests."

54. While discussing section 23 of the Civil Servants Act, 1973 in the case of Peer Mukarram-ul-Haq Vs Federation of Pakistan (2014 SCMR 1457) this Court was pleased to observe that:

> "15. We may further observe that scope of section 23 is very limited. This section empowers the Competent Authority (President) to deal with the case of a Civil Servant in such a manner as may appear to him to be 'just' and 'equitable', but such powers are not unbridled."

55. Scope of powers of Governor under section 22 of the Punjab Civil Servants Act, also (pari materia to section 24 of the Sindh Civil Servants Act) were discussed in the case of Muhammad Iqbal Khokhar Vs. Govt of Punjab (PLD 1991 SC 35) and it was observed that:

> "This power permits the Governor, as the Chief Executive of the Province at the apex, to deal with serious cases relating to civil servants in such manner as may appear to him to be just and fair, which otherwise cannot be sorted out by the Chief Minister or the Punjab Government under the various powers vested in them by the different rules existing from time to time relating to relaxation. This section is primarily a saving section, basically intended to correct serious cases, where unusual factors place a civil servant in serious disability, which requires correction on the basis of equity and justice by the Governor himself, sitting at the apex of the executive

hierarchy. Amendments, additions and substitutions effected in the rules from time to time, mergers in and transfers from one service to another, etc., create a host of problems, where civil servants placed under serious disability and hardship call for a fair and equitable resolution of their difficulties. To meet these genuine cases, the Governor has been granted this special savings power to deal with such cases, so as to remove injustice and inequity which may stand in the way of a civil servant in securing his just rights. In short, it is a power rarely used, unless to serve justice or correct grave injustice, and perhaps never used arbitrarily to reward a person or to grant him an undue privilege over the right of another."

88.   The Hon'ble Supreme Court of India was pleased to observe in J.C. Yadav and Ors. Vs. State of Haryana and Ors. {(1990) 2 SCC 189} that:

"...........The relaxation of the rules may be to the extent the State Government may consider necessary for dealing with a particular situation in a just and equitable manner. The scope of rule is wide enough to confer power on the State government to relax the requirement of rules in respect of an individual or class of individuals to the extent it may consider necessary for dealing with the case in a just and equitable manner. The power of relaxation is generally contained in the Rules with a view to mitigate undue hardship or to meet a particular situation. Many a time strict application of service rules create a situation where a particular individual or a set of individuals may suffer undue hardship and further there may be a situation where requisite qualified persons may not be available for appointment to the service. In such a situation the Government has power to relax requirement rules. The State Government may in exercise of its powers issue a general order relaxing any particular rule with a view to avail the services of requisite officers. The relaxation even if granted in a general manner would ensure to the benefit of individual officers."

89.   It was held by the Hon'ble Supreme Court of India in Ashok Kumar Uppal Vs. State of J&K and Ors. {(1998) 4 SCC 179} that:

"Power to relax Recruitment Rules may or any other Rule made by the State Government, under Article 309 of the Constitution of which the corresponding provision is contained in Section 124 of the Constitution of Jammu and Kashmir, is conferred upon the Government to meet any emergent situation where injustice might have been caused or is likely to be caused to any individual employee or class of employees or where the working of the Rule might have become impossible. Under service jurisprudence as also the Administrative Law, such a power has necessarily to be conceded to the employer particularly the State Government or the Central Government who have to deal with hundreds of employees working under them in different departments including the Central or the State Secretariat."

90.   In view of the above discussion, we are constrained to hold that Section 22 of the Punjab Civil Servants Act, 1974 and Rule 23 of the Punjab Civil Servants (Appointment & Conditions of Service) Rules, 1974 allow relaxation of the service rules to save civil servants from undue hardship and to promote justice and equity. These provisions cannot be used to make backdoor appointments or to relax qualifications or to by-pass the due process for selection for appointments in the service of Pakistan.

300

91.   Proceedings under Article 199 (1) (b) (ii) of the Constitution are held to be maintainable on the ground of recruitments without open advertisement in the press inviting applications for recruitment and on the basis of absence of recommendations of the Public Service Commission where consultation with the Public Service Commission is a requirement. The Hon'ble Supreme Court of Pakistan has held in Capt. (Retd.) Muhammad Naseem Hijazi Vs. Province of Punjab through Secretary, Housing and Physical Planning and 2 others (2000 SCMR 1720) that "the invalidity of appointment may arise not only from want of qualifications but also from violation of legal provisions for appointment."

Question # 5

Whether services of persons recruited on ad hoc basis in the prescribed manner can be regularized through relaxation of rules?

92.   Rule 22 of the Punjab Civil Servants (Appointment and Conditions of Service) Rules, 1974, which deals with ad hoc appointments, reads as follows:

> "(1)   When a post is required to be filled, the appointing authority shall forward a requisition to the selection authority immediately after decision is taken to fill the post.
>
> (2)   After forwarding a requisition to the selection authority, the appointing authority may, if it considers necessary in the public interest, fill the post on ad hoc basis for a period not exceeding one year pending nomination of a candidate by the selection authority:
>
> Provided;
>
> 1. the vacancy is advertised properly in the newspapers;
> 2. the appointment is made of a person duly qualified in accordance with the provisions of the rules and orders applicable to the post;
> 3. the selection is made on the basis of merit determined by objective criteria;
> 4. the appointment order certifies that a requisition has been sent to the selection authority; and
> 5. the appointment is made subject to revocation at any time by the competent authority;
>
> Provided further that ad hoc appointment shall not confer any right on the persons so appointed in the matter of regular appointment to the same post nor the service will count towards seniority in the grade."

93.   Services & General Administration Department of the Government of the Punjab has issued the following clarification regarding ad hoc appointments vide its letter bearing No. SOR.I(S&GAD)16-12/85 dated 17th of October, 1986:

> "I am directed to say that according to Rule 22 of the Punjab Civil Servants (Appointment and Conditions of Service) Rules, 1974, it is necessary for an Appointing Authority to forward a requisition to the Selection Authority before making an appointment on ad hoc basis. A question has arisen whether or not in cases where the Appointing Authority is himself the Head of the Departmental Selection Committee, it would be necessary to forward a requisition to the Selection Authority before making any such appointment. It is clarified that in such a situation it is not necessary for the Appointing Authority to forward a requisition to the Selection Authority before making an ad hoc appointment. However, it would be more desirable if instead of making ad hoc appointment, the post is filled in on regular basis

> because the formalities prescribed under the rules for ad hoc / regular appointments are almost similar."

94.   Following the spirit of the aforesaid letter, it can be inferred that appointment on ad hoc basis is permissible in case the selection authority is not headed by the appointing authority as it would be absurd for the appointing authority to send requisition to himself and then make recruitments by following the same procedure which is applicable to regular appointments. Conversely speaking, appointment on ad hoc basis is allowed if the appointing authority is the Public Service Commission or a committee or board not headed by the appointing authority. Normally selection authorities in case of posts not falling within the purview of the Public Service Commission are headed by the appointing authorities. In any case, ad hoc appointments can be made only after advertisement in the press through a competitive process from amongst duly qualified candidates. Ad hoc appointments are transient in nature and are necessarily required to be terminated on expiry of the maximum period prescribed for ad hoc appointment or on availability of candidates recommended by the selection authority for appointment, whichever is earlier. Ad hoc appointments are a stop-gap arrangement which is resorted to in cases in which it is deemed in public interest to immediately fill in a vacant post and it is feared that postponing filling in of the post till receipt of recommendations of the selection authority would adversely affect public business.

95.   The provision relating to ad hoc appointments is relatable to conditions of recruitment; conditions attached to ad hoc appointments viz. open advertisement in press and selection of duly qualified candidates on the basis of merit determined through objective criteria are meant to protect fundamental right to trade and profession of the citizens and to obviate adverse discrimination in the matter of appointments in the service of Pakistan. Section 22 of the Punjab Civil Servants Act, 1974 and Rule 23 of the Punjab Civil Servants (Appointment and Conditions of Service) Rules, 1974 are not available to relax provisions regarding ad hoc appointments after competitive process and determination of relative merit of the duly qualified candidates through objective criteria.

96.   Whether ad hoc appointments can be regularized through executive or legislative instruments? Certain ad hoc appointees were declared as "validly selected" and "regularly appointed" without going through the prescribed selection procedure under existing laws through the Azad Jammu and Kashmir Civil Servants (Regularisation of Ad hoc Appointments) Act, 1992. This law was held to be against the fundamental rights and was declared unconstitutional in a case reported as Azad Government and others Vs. Muhammad Younas Tahir and others (1994 CLC 2339). By the Regularisation Act the persons holding posts on ad hoc basis as well as persons holding discretionary posts were treated to have been regularly appointed. The aforementioned statute was struck down as being inconsistent with fundamental rights Nos. 15 and 17 as well as to the Civil Servants Act, Public Service Commission Act and rules made there under. Right No. 15 in the Interim Constitution Act of the Azad Jammu and Kashmir guarantees that all State subjects are equal before law and are entitled to equal protection of law while right No. 17 provides safeguard against discrimination in services.
97.   It was held in Javed Iqbal Khawaja and others Vs. Azad Government of the State of Jammu and Kashmir through its Chief Secretary, Muzaffarabad and others (PLD 1994 Azad J&K 26) that:

"10. On August 18, 1992, an Act called as Azad Jammu and Kashmir Civil Servants (Regularisation of Ad hoc Appointment) Act, 1992, was enforced with immediate effect. Under section 3 of the Act, it was postulated that notwithstanding anything contained in any law or rule, decree, order or judgment of Court, all civil servants holding ad hoc appointment till the date of commencement of the Act, shall be deemed to have been validly selected and appointed to the post held by them on regular basis, with effect from the date of commencement of the Act. The relevant provisions are reproduced: --

> "3. Regularisation of services of certain civil servants. - Notwithstanding anything contained in any law or rule, or in any decree, order or judgment of a Court, all civil servants holding ad hoc appointment till the date of commencement of this Act, shall be deemed to have been validly selected and appointed to the post held by them on regular basis, with effect from the date of commencement of this Act:
>
> Provided that--
>
> (i)   such civil servants possess the educational qualification and experience prescribed for the posts; and
>
> (ii)   the Commission has in respect of the post held by such civil servant, not recommended any other person on or before the commencement of this Act."

In Sardar Muhammad Abdul Qayum Khan's case (PLD 1983 SC (AJ&K) 95), at page 115, it was observed: -

> "....it becomes all the more necessary for the Courts to be at guard to see that the authority does not transgress its limits and legislation made by such an authority encroaches not upon the rights of the citizens especially fundamental rights which have been enshrined in the Constitution Act, 1974. The opinion of such an authority to prevail against fundamental rights of the citizens over whom the authority is to exercise executive responsibility is not recognised by the Constitution."

51. Section 48 of the Interim Constitution Act conceived the Scheme of Constitution of the Public Service Commission, in order to raise civil service in a prescribed method of law. The Civil Servants Act, Public Service Commission Act and other relevant laws, nowhere suggest that the recommendation of the Public Service Commission, for appointment of civil servants to posts, shall not be obligatory on the Government or the appointing authority. It was wrong to suggest that the recommendation of Public Service Commission was optional. It may be accepted that in special cases, the recommendation of the Commission may not be carried through restrictively, in the larger interest of the State or civil service itself. Such special and exemplary eventualities are always kept in view by the Legislature. To meet such eventualities, saving clause is always added to each statute. Exceptions to ordinary course of law always carry special qualifications, high-merit and appropriate requirements to meet an extraordinary situation. In the present case, it is least suggestible that such an eventuality was there. And in order to meet the necessity, thus, the Government and the Legislature were compelled to introduce the impugned legislation. Neither the impugned legislation nor the explanation furnished by the respondents in their written statements indicates to such exceptional or extraordinary situation.

58. It is noticed elsewhere that an ad hoc appointment is, equally to be made in the prescribed manner. We have, in detail, examined the scheme of ad hoc appointment to a civil post. It also carries certain qualifications, experience and conditions. The system is again prescribed under law. However, the period of ad hoc appointment has been prescribed as 6 months or to be extended by another 6 months. Under law, a regular appointment and an ad hoc appointment are made in different manner except that qualifications, experience and appointing authority in both cases, is common. Rest of the conditions and manner of appointment is altogether different. Therefore, the manner of an ad hoc appointment cannot be construed as in pari materia to regular appointment in civil service. It is, therefore, least permissible under law to acknowledge an ad hoc appointment as regular appointment in the civil service. Any scheme or step in that direction, would amount to an illegality. This position is not denied by the learned counsel for the respondents.

Thus, like an employer, the Government or appointing authority is entitled to pick and choose from amongst large number of candidates offering themselves for employment, but it has to make a choice from such candidates by virtue of equitable and uniform method. Moreover, in order to ensure that all citizens are provided equal chance or opportunity to avail appointment in the civil service, an equal opportunity has to be provided to all qualified and suitable candidates, without discrimination or liking or disliking. So long as an applicant, alongwith others, has been given his chance, it cannot be said that he did not have an equal opportunity alongwith others, who may have been selected in preference to him. Therefore, the test of selection of candidates is to be based upon some reasonable principle which has nexus, with requisite qualifications, experience, efficient performance of duties and obligations of particular office. If the selective test is not based on these principles, the rule of equal opportunity for employment under the State would be violated.

The aforesaid authorities support the proposition that the legislature or executive authority cannot legislate or act in derogation to the prescribed measure. An enactment which contains no norms or guideline, to carry out its objective, is not sustainable. Likewise, the executive authority cannot assume an uncontrolled power in the matter of recruitment of civil servants or exercise discretion in other administrative matters. It has to act in a prescribed manner and such manner has to be universal in its application and effect, particularly, in the case of persons who enjoy alike status or qualifications. Therefore, there can be no argument in support of proposition to give uncontrolled authority to Government or an appointing authority, to make ad hoc appointments and to get the same regularized by enactment of the Assembly.

85. The impugned enactment has been found quite inconsistent and in contravention to the provisions of section 4(15) and (17) of the Interim Constitution Act, in addition to the provisions of Civil Servants Act, Public Service Commission Act and Rules framed thereunder. It is also derogatory to the scheme of civil services provided under sections 48 and 49 of the Interim Constitution Act. It cannot be allowed to perpetuate its effect. It is, therefore, struck down. The ad hoc appointments desired to be regulated by virtue of these provisions

shall remain ad hoc appointment in nature and character. Consequently, all orders and notifications whereby ad hoc appointments of respondent-civil servants have been regulated, are declared null and void and of no legal effect. These appointments are to be regulated in accordance with law. Here, it may be observed that since various persons holding ad hoc appointments may have passed the upper limit of age of initial recruitment, they may not be punished due to enforcement of the impugned enactment and its consequences. Therefore, the Government may, in exercise of its powers, relax the upper limit of age of such persons, to enable them to avail an opportunity of appearance in tests / examinations held by the Commission."

98.   The Hon'ble Supreme Court of Pakistan has held in a case reported as Nazar Hussain and others Vs. Deputy District Education Officer and others (2003 PLC (C.S.) 956) that:

> "Regularization made in contravention of prescribed procedure could not be equated with that of legal regularization and in absence whereof the status of ad hoc or temporary appointees could not be changed unless regularized legally by adopting the prescribed procedure---Where the said procedure had not been followed, no legal right whatsoever had been created in favour of the ad hoc appointees which could refrain the Competent Authority from retracing the steps taken by them and accordingly the Competent Authority could remove the ad hoc appointees from service without assigning any reason and even without a show-cause notice and mere by afflux of time no ad hoc / temporary appointment could be converted to regular appointment till the prescribed procedure was followed. In this regard, we are fortified by the dictum laid down in Pakistan v. Muhammad Himayatullah (PLD 1969 SC 407), Dr. Muhammad Yunis v. Province of Sindh (1989 PLC (C.S.) 8), Fayaz Hussain Shah v. Province of Sindh (1991 PLC (C.S.) 447) Province of Punjab v. Azhar Abbas (2002 SCMR 1)."

99.   It was held by the Hon'ble Supreme Court of India in Surinder Prasad Tiwari Vs. U.P. Rajya Krishi Utpadan Mandi Parishad & others, {2006 (7) SCC 684} that:

> "Equal opportunity is the basic feature of our Constitution. ...Our constitutional scheme clearly envisages equality of opportunity in public employment. .... This part of the constitutional scheme clearly reflects strong desire and constitutional philosophy to implement the principle of equality in the true sense in the matter of public employment.
> In view of the clear and unambiguous constitutional scheme, the courts cannot countenance appointments to public office which have been made against the constitutional scheme. In the backdrop of constitutional philosophy, it would be improper for the courts to give directions for regularization of services of the person who is working either as daily-wager, ad hoc employee, probationer, temporary or contractual employee, not appointed following the procedure laid down under Articles 14, 16 and 309 of the Constitution."

100.   It was observed by the Hon'ble Supreme Court of India in State of Karnataka & others Vs. G.V. Chandrashekhar {JT 2009 (4) SC 367} that:

> "The High Courts acting under Article 226 of the Constitution, should not ordinarily issue directions for absorption, regularisation, or permanent continuance unless the recruitment itself was made regularly and in terms of the constitutional scheme. Merely because an

employee had continued under cover of an order of the court, which we have described as "litigious employment" in the earlier part of the judgment, he would not be entitled to any right to be absorbed or made permanent in the service."

101.   In State of Bihar Vs. Upendra Narayan Singh & others {(2009) 5 SCC 65}, the Hon'ble Supreme Court of India held that any regular appointment made on a post under the State or Union without issuing advertisement, inviting applications from eligible candidates and without holding a proper selection where all eligible persons get a fair chance to compete is in violation of guarantee enshrined under Article 226 of the Constitution. Ad hoc / temporary / daily wage employees are not entitled to claim regularisation in service as a matter of right. If an illegality or irregularity has been committed in favour of any individual or a group of individuals or a wrong order has been passed by a judicial forum, others cannot invoke the jurisdiction of the higher or superior Court for repeating or multiplying the same irregularity or illegality or for passing wrong order.

102.   The Hon'ble Supreme Court of India was pleased to direct in State of Rajasthan and others Vs. Daya Lal & others {2011(2) SCC 429} that:

> "The High Courts, in exercising power under Article 226 of the Constitution will not issue directions for regularization, absorption or permanent continuance, unless the employees claiming regularization had been appointed in pursuance of a regular recruitment in accordance with relevant rules in an open competitive process, against sanctioned vacant posts. The equality clause contained in Articles 14 and 16 should be scrupulously followed and Courts should not issue a direction for regularization of services of an employee which would be violative of constitutional scheme."

103.   It was held in State of U. P. and others Vs. Rekha Rani, {JT 2011 (4) SC 6} that:

> "12. It has been held in a recent decision of this Court in State of Rajasthan vs. Daya Lal, 2011 (2) SCC 429 following the Constitution Bench decision of this Court in State of Karnataka vs. Umadevi (2006) 4 SCC 1 that the High Court in exercise of its power under Article 226 cannot regularize an employee."

104.   The Hon'ble Supreme Court of India held in Brij Mohan Lal Vs. Union of India {(2012) 6 SCC 502} that:

> "A Constitution Bench of this Court has clearly stated the principle that in matters of public employment, absorption, regularization or permanent continuance of temporary, contractual or casual daily wage or ad hoc employees appointed and continued for long in such public employment would be de hors the constitutional scheme of public employment and would be improper. It would also not be proper to stay the regular recruitment process for the concerned posts."

105.   It was held by the Hon'ble Supreme Court of India in University of Rajasthan and others Vs. Prem Lata Agarwal and others {(2013) 3 SCC 705} that:

> ".... the Constitution Bench, after survey of all the decisions in the field relating to recruitment process and the claim for regularization, in paragraph 43, has held that consistent with the scheme for public employment, it is the duty of the court to necessarily hold that unless the appointment is in terms of the relevant rules, the same would not

confer any right on the appointee. The Bench further proceeded to state that merely because a temporary employee or a casual wage worker is continued for a time beyond the term of his appointment, he would not be entitled to be absorbed in regular service or made permanent, merely on the strength of such continuance, if the original appointment was not made by following a due process of selection as envisaged by the relevant rules."

106.   It was held by the Hon'ble Supreme Court of India in Secretary, State of Karnataka and Ors. Vs. Umadevi and Ors. {(2006) 4 SCC 1} that:

"3. But, sometimes this process is not adhered to and the Constitutional scheme of public employment is by-passed. The Union, the States, their departments and instrumentalities have resorted to irregular appointments, especially in the lower rungs of the service, without reference to the duty to ensure a proper appointment procedure through the Public Service Commission or otherwise as per the rules adopted and to permit these irregular appointees or those appointed on contract or on daily wages, to continue year after year, thus, keeping out those who are qualified to apply for the post concerned and depriving them of an opportunity to compete for the post. It has also led to persons who get employed, without the following of a regular procedure or even through the backdoor or on daily wages, approaching Courts, seeking directions to make them permanent in their posts and to prevent regular recruitment to the concerned posts. Courts have not always kept the legal aspects in mind and have occasionally even stayed the regular process of employment being set in motion and in some cases, even directed that these illegal, irregular or improper entrants be absorbed into service. A class of employment which can only be called 'litigious employment', has risen like a phoenix seriously impairing the constitutional scheme. Such orders are passed apparently in exercise of the wide powers under Article 226 of the Constitution of India. Whether the wide powers under Article 226 of the Constitution is intended to be used for a purpose certain to defeat the concept of social justice and equal opportunity for all, subject to affirmative action in the matter of public employment as recognized by our Constitution, has to be seriously pondered over. It is time, that Courts desist from issuing orders preventing regular selection or recruitment at the instance of such persons and from issuing directions for continuance of those who have not secured regular appointments as per procedure established. The passing of orders for continuance tends to defeat the very Constitutional scheme of public employment. It has to be emphasized that this is not the role envisaged for High Courts in the scheme of things and their wide powers under Article 226 of the Constitution of India are not intended to be used for the purpose of perpetuating illegalities, irregularities or improprieties or for scuttling the whole scheme of public employment. Its role as the sentinel and as the guardian of equal rights protection should not be forgotten.

4. This Court has also on occasions issued directions which could not be said to be consistent with the Constitutional scheme of public

employment. Such directions are issued presumably on the basis of equitable considerations or individualization of justice. The question arises, equity to whom? Equity for the handful of people who have approached the Court with a claim, or equity for the teeming millions of this country seeking employment and seeking a fair opportunity for competing for employment? When one side of the coin is considered, the other side of the coin has also to be considered and the way open to any court of law or justice, is to adhere to the law as laid down by the Constitution and not to make directions, which at times, even if do not run counter to the Constitutional scheme, certainly tend to water down the Constitutional requirements. It is this conflict that is reflected in these cases referred to the Constitution Bench.

5. The power of a State as an employer is more limited than that of a private employer inasmuch as it is subjected to constitutional limitations and cannot be exercised arbitrarily (See Basu's Shorter Constitution of India).----- If rules have been made under Article 309 of the Constitution, then the Government can make appointments only in accordance with the rules.----. Therefore, when statutory rules are framed under Article 309 of the Constitution which are exhaustive, the only fair means to adopt is to make appointments based on the rules so framed."

107. A Constitution Bench of the Hon'ble Supreme Court of India held in State of Punjab Vs. Jagdip Singh & Ors. (1964 (4) SCR 964) that:

"In our opinion, where a Government servant has no right to a post or to a particular status, though an authority under the Government acting beyond its competence had purported to give that person a status which it was not entitled to give, he will not in law be deemed to have been validly appointed to the post or given the particular status."

108. It was held in State of Haryana Vs. Piara Singh and Others [1992) 3 SCR 826] that:

"The normal rule, of course, is regular recruitment through the prescribed agency but exigencies of administration may sometimes call for an ad hoc or temporary appointment to be made. In such a situation, effort should always be to replace such an ad hoc / temporary employee by a regularly selected employee as early as possible. Such a temporary employee may also compete along with others for such regular selection / appointment. If he gets selected, well and good, but if he does not, he must give way to the regularly selected candidate. The appointment of the regularly selected candidate cannot be withheld or kept in abeyance for the sake of such an ad hoc / temporary employee."

109. A three Judge Bench of the Hon'ble Supreme Court of India held in State of Himachal Pradesh Vs. Suresh Kumar Verma {(1996 (1) SCR 972} that:

"It is settled law that having made rules of recruitment to various services under the State or to a class of posts under the State, the State is bound to follow the same and to have the selection of the candidates made as per recruitment rules and appointments shall be made accordingly."

110.   It was held by the Hon'ble Supreme Court of India in Ashwani Kumar and others Vs. State of Bihar and others (1996 Supp. (10) SCR 120) that:

> "The so called regularizations and confirmations could not be relied on as shields to cover up initial illegal and void actions or to perpetuate the corrupt methods by which these 6000 initial entrants were drafted in the scheme."

111.   It was further held by the Hon'ble Supreme Court of India in Ashwani Kumar and others Vs. State of Bihar and others (1996 Supp. (10) SCR 120) that:

> "27. In A. Umarani Vs. Registrar, Cooperative Societies and Others (2004 (7) SCC 112), a three judge bench made a survey of the authorities and held that when appointments were made in contravention of mandatory provisions of the Act and statutory rules framed thereunder and by ignoring essential qualifications, the appointments would be illegal and cannot be regularized by the State. The State could not invoke its power under Article 162 of the Constitution to regularize such appointments. This Court also held that regularization is not and cannot be a mode of recruitment by any State within the meaning of Article 12 of the Constitution of India or anybody or authority governed by a statutory Act or the Rules framed thereunder. Regularization furthermore cannot give permanence to an employee whose services are ad hoc in nature. It was also held that the fact that some persons had been working for a long time would not mean that they had acquired a right for regularization.
>
> 28. Incidentally, the Bench also referred to the nature of the orders to be passed in exercise of this Court's jurisdiction under Article 142 of the Constitution. This Court stated that jurisdiction under Article 142 of the Constitution could not be exercised on misplaced sympathy. This Court quoted with approval the observations of Farewell, L.J. in Latham vs. Richard Johnson & Nephew Ltd. (1913 (1) KB 398)"
>
>> "We must be very careful not to allow our sympathy with the infant plaintiff to affect our judgment. Sentiment is a dangerous will o' the wisp to take as a guide in the search for legal principles."

112.   In R.N. Nanjundappa Vs T. Thimmiah & Anr. [(1972) 2 S.C.R. 799], the Hon'ble Supreme Court of India held that:

> "If the appointment itself is in infraction of the rules or if it is in violation of the provisions of the Constitution, illegality cannot be regularized. Ratification or regularization is possible of an act which is within the power and province of the authority, but there has been some non-compliance with procedure or manner which does not go to the root of the appointment. Regularization cannot be said to be a mode of recruitment. To accede to such a proposition would be to introduce a new head of appointment in defiance of rules or it may have the effect of setting at naught the rules."

113.   It has authoritatively been held by the Hon'ble Supreme Court of India in Secretary, State of Karnataka and Ors. Vs. Umadevi and Ors. {(2006) 4 SCC 1} that:

> "In B.N. Nagarajan & Ors. Vs. State of Karnataka & Ors. [(1979) 3 SCR 937], this court clearly held that the words "regular" or "regularization" do not connote permanence and cannot be construed so as to convey an idea of the nature of tenure of appointments. They

are terms calculated to condone any procedural irregularities and are meant to cure only such defects as are attributable to methodology followed in making the appointments. This court emphasized that when rules framed under Article 309 of the Constitution of India are in force, no regularization is permissible in exercise of the executive powers of the Government under Article 162 of the Constitution in contravention of the rules. These decisions and the principles recognized therein have not been dissented to by this Court and on principle, we see no reason not to accept the proposition as enunciated in the above decisions. We have, therefore, to keep this distinction in mind and proceed on the basis that only something that is irregular for want of compliance with one of the elements in the process of selection which does not go to the root of the process, can be regularized and that it alone can be regularized and granting permanence of employment is a totally different concept and cannot be equated with regularization."

114.   We have felt it necessary to quote the aforesaid cases in order to revive the jurisprudence in service matters which has seriously been damaged by litigious employments. Superior courts in Azad Kashmir and India have consistently held that appointments made on ad hoc basis without open advertisement and transparent competitive selection process from amongst eligible candidates cannot be converted into regular appointments through executive order or legislative instrument or by courts in exercise of their writ jurisdiction. If it is held that ad hoc appointments can be converted into regular appointments by executive orders or through enactments or on the basis of court orders even if made by incompetent appointing authority without advertisement and open and fair competitive selection from amongst eligible candidates, then it would impliedly mean that the fundamental rights relating to public appointments can be suspended otherwise than through imposition of state of emergency. Our constitutional scheme has not envisaged any such situation and does not allow abridgment, suspension or denial of fundamental rights of the citizens in any situation in the matter of appointments in the service of Pakistan. Even if fundamental rights are suspended during state of emergency, Article 4 of the Constitution gives a citizen an inalienable right to be treated in accordance with law and a person cannot be prevented to do that which is not prohibited by law or to do that which is not required of him to be done by a law. The superior courts in Azad Kashmir and in India have not tolerated or encouraged litigious employments. We have observed with pain that this is not so frequent in Pakistan where courts are generally swayed by emotions and are generous in granting prayers for regularization of services of contract, ad hoc, work-charged and daily-wage workers. Article 8 of the Constitution commands that the state shall not make any law which abridges or takes away any of the fundamental rights. What is prohibited to be done through legislation is also not allowed to be done through executive orders or use of judicial power of the state. In order to make the matter crystal clear and to obviate chances of misuse of executive, legislative and judicial power of the state in the matter of appointments on regular basis in the service of Pakistan, we declare, hold and direct as follows:

   a) Appointments made in the service of Pakistan without open advertisement and fair competitive selection process are incurably bad and cannot be declared or deemed to be lawful or regular through enactment, executive order or judicial pronouncement;

   b) Appointment of a person in the service of Pakistan who does not fulfil the eligibility criteria by an appointing authority, irrespective of the fact whether that authority is competent or not, is not curable through any post-appointment measure even if made after open advertisement and due competitive selection process;

c) Where the Public Service Commission is the selection authority, the appointing authority cannot appoint a person in the service of Pakistan in absence of recommendation of the Public Service Commission and requirement of recommendation of the Public Service Commission cannot be dispensed with under the pretext of relaxation of the rules; and

d) Ad hoc, contract, work-charged and daily-wage employees cannot be regularized as regularization is not a mode of appointment and regularization of such employees takes away fundamental right to trade and profession and non-discrimination in the matter of appointments in the service of Pakistan of the otherwise qualified citizens. All legislative, executive and judicial measures to regularize such employees would be void within the meaning of Article 8(1) of the Constitution. This declaration may not be interpreted to mean that contract appointments not backed by a law are valid.

115. Learned counsel for the petitioner has pointed out the Hon'ble judges in the Hon'ble superior judiciary are public servants. He submitted that in accordance with Section 6(21) of the Pakistan Penal Code, every judge is a public servant. It has been held in a case reported as 1993 PSC (Crl) 443 that "Every judge" includes Judges of High Court and Supreme Court also. He informed that Article 218 of the Constitution of the Islamic Republic of Pakistan, 1956, reproduced below, excluded judges of the superior courts from the definition of the 'service of Pakistan':

"service of Pakistan" means any service or post in connection with the affairs of the Federation or of a Province, and includes any defence service, and any other service declared as a service of Pakistan by or under an Act of Parliament or of a Provincial Legislature, but does not include service as Governor-General, President, Governor, Speaker or Deputy Speaker, of the National or a Provincial Assembly, Minister of the Federal or a Provincial Government, Minister of State or Deputy Minister of the Federal Government, Deputy Minister or Parliamentary Secretary of a Provincial Government, Judge of the Supreme Court or a High Court, or Comptroller and Auditor-General; and "Servant of Pakistan" shall be construed accordingly;"

116. Learned counsel for the petitioner also invited our attention to Article 241 of the Constitution of the Islamic Republic of Pakistan, 1962 which defined the service of Pakistan in these words:

"service of Pakistan" means any service, post or office in connection with the affairs of the Centre or of a Province, and includes an All-Pakistan Service, any defence service and any other service declared to be a service of Pakistan by or under an Act of the Central Legislature or of a Provincial Legislature, but does not include service as Speaker, Deputy Speaker or other member of an Assembly or as a Parliamentary Secretary;"

117. Learned counsel for the petitioner argued that the Hon'ble judges of the Hon'ble superior courts were outside the definition of the service of Pakistan in the Constitution of 1956. In the Constitution of 1962, a departure was made and the judges of the superior courts were not specifically excluded from the definition of the service of Pakistan. The same is the position in Article 268 of the Constitution of 1973. The counsel prayed that appointment of the Hon'ble judges of the Hon'ble superior courts may be ordered to be made through a process in which every eligible and willing citizen is given an opportunity to

prove his merit. He further averred that remuneration of judges of the superior courts in Pakistan is very attractive and to substantiate his claim he referred to a news story which appeared in the Express Tribune, Pakistan on 14th of September, 2017 (available at https://tribune.com.pk/story/1505831/superior-court-judges-bag-rs159m-salary/) which reads as follows:

"ISLAMABAD: The salaries of 134 Supreme Court and high court judges can reach up to Rs. 159 million a month, besides assigned chauffer driven cars, 500 litres of fuel and Rs. 65,000 or above as house rent, wrote Law and Justice Minister Zahid Hamid to the Senate in reply to a question from Senator Karim Ahmed Khawaja.

Apex court judges

According to details shared with the Senate, the chief justice of Pakistan withdraws about Rs. 846,549 as a month's salary and is also granted Rs. 370,597 as superior judicial allowance. Furthermore, if the chief justice is not provided official residence, he is also entitled to receive Rs. 68,000 as house rent.

Pakistan's top judge makes Rs. 8.9 million annual salary

Similarly, every judge of the Supreme Court receives Rs. 799,699 per month as salary, Rs. 370,597 as superior judicial allowance and house rent compensation in the case official residence is not provided. Each judge hence receives Rs. 1.17 million, without the inclusion of house rent.

As there are 15 judges associated with the apex court, just the total of their salaries and judicial allowance amounts to a staggering Rs. 17.5 million per month, which comes to Rs. 18.71 million if the chief justice's salary is also added to the total.

Other benefits for judges include a medical allowance of 15 per cent, two chauffer driven cars, one present in Islamabad and the other in whatever province that the judge may be in to perform his duty. Judges are only supposed to bear the cost of petrol if it exceeds 600 litres a month.

Judges also receive Rs. 5,000 as daily allowance, while receiving concessions on tickets for official tours. They, however, have to pay for the tickets of their families and receive no exemption from paying taxes.

Punjab's top judge gets Rs. 1.05 m per month

High courts

The document further stated that high court chief justices receive Rs. 784,608 per month as salary and an additional Rs. 296,477 as their superior judicial allowance and Rs. 65,000 as house rent if official residence is not provided.

There are five chief justices, including the one for Gilgit Baltistan and they collectively draw Rs. 6.48 million per month.

Similarly judges in the high court draw up to Rs. 754,432 per month as salary, Rs. 296,477 as superior judicial allowance and are compensated if official residence is not provided.

President orders raises for superior court judges

As per the official website, there are 128 high court judges across Pakistan, including those in the Gilgit Baltistan area, and their collective monthly expenses come to Rs. 134 million a month.

Each high court chief justice and judge is allowed one chauffer driven car, 500 litres of petrol, free medical care and Rs. 4,400 as a daily allowance. If the judges in question are travelling for work, they are allowed to ask for Rs. 12 per km travelled."

118. Besides above, the Hon'ble judges are given pension and other post-retirement privileges which are better than those offered to any civil servant in the service of Pakistan, the learned counsel submitted. He argued that every eligible citizen has a fundamental right to compete for appointment to the lucrative post of such judge and to be appointed as judge once he proves his merit in the due open selection process and enjoy lawful monetary and other benefits flowing from such employment.

119. We have given an opportunity to the learned law officers to assist the court on the contention raised by the learned counsel for the petitioner. The learned Attorney General for Pakistan and the Advocate General, Punjab have admitted that the Hon'ble judges of the Hon'ble superior courts in Pakistan are public servants and do fall within the definition of service of Pakistan. They have, however, contended that the principle of equality of opportunity and the constitutional requirement to make appointments in the service of Pakistan after open advertisement and due competitive selection process are not applicable in the matter of selection and appointment of Hon'ble judges of the Hon'ble superior judiciary. They have also argued that though the Judicial Commission of Pakistan is a selection authority for recommending citizens for appointment as judges in the superior courts, yet the Commission is fully authorized to recommend citizens on the basis of its private and personal knowledge. They are of the view that since the Hon'ble Chief Justice of Pakistan has the exclusive power to nominate a citizen for appointment as a judge in the superior courts, therefore, the nation must have full faith in his wisdom in the matter and may expect him to nominate the best citizens. They have asserted that the Hon'ble Chief Justice does not form his opinion regarding a citizen before nominating him for employment as a judge in the superior judiciary on the basis of hearsay or to favour someone. But the learned law officer failed to explain the institutional arrangements and processes employed for selection and determination of merit of the candidates for judgeship in the superior judiciary.

120. It is trite law that entitlement of a person to hold a public office can be called in question before a High Court or in the Supreme Court through direct quo warranto proceedings and no such challenge is allowed to be entertained collaterally. Moreover, this Court is expected to decide questions of law for the country and not to decide individual cases without reference to such principles of law. We have attempted to enunciate the law in the matter of appointments in the service of Pakistan after due competitive process. As judges of the superior courts do fall within the definition of service of Pakistan, therefore, we are under oath to decide cases in respect of judges of the superior courts in accordance with law enunciated by us. Let everyone be assured that whenever a case is properly and directly brought before us to challenge lawfulness of holding office of a judge in the superior judiciary without open advertisement and observing due competitive process, we will not hesitate, delay or refuse to decide the case in accordance with law. We are not here to decide academic or moot questions. As quo warranto proceedings are not allowed to be initiated by way of collateral challenge, therefore, we regret our inability to adjudicate upon the lis raised by the learned counsel for the petitioner to the extent of judges of the superior judiciary. We acknowledge that what the Hon'ble Supreme Court of Pakistan has held in Chief Secretary Punjab and others Vs. Abdul Raoof Dasti, (2006 P L C (C.S) 1278) is still relevant and applicable:

"It is our misfortune that when we are looking for individuals to serve our own-selves, we search for the best of doctors, the best of architects, the best of lawyers, the best of engineers, the best of cooks, the best of butlers and so on but when it comes to selecting similar individuals to serve the public, we get swayed by nepotism, by petty personal interests and by other similar ulterior and extraneous considerations and settle for the ones not worthy of serving the public in the requisite manner. We need to remind ourselves that choosing persons for public service was not just providing a job and the consequent livelihood to the one in need but was a sacred trust to be discharged by the ones charged with it, honestly, fairly, in a just and transparent manner and in the best interest of the public. The individuals so selected are to be paid not out of the private pockets of the ones appointing them but by the people through the public exchequer. Therefore, we must keep it in mind that not selecting the best as public servants was a gross breach of the public trust and was an offence against the public who had right to be served by the best. It is also blatant violation of the rights of those who may be available and whose rights to the said posts are denied to them by appointing unqualified or even less qualified persons to such posts. Such a practice and conduct is highly unjust and spreads a message from ones in authority that might was right and not vice versa which message gets gradually permeated to the very gross-root level leading ultimately to a society having no respect for law, justice and fair play. And it is the said evil norms which ultimately lead to anarchic and chaotic situations in the society. It is about time we suppressed such-like evil tendencies and eliminate them before the same eliminate us all."

121.   The Indian Supreme Court also considered the issue of appointments in Channabasavih's case (AIR 1965 SC 1293) and relevant observation, quoted with approval in a case reported as Ghulam Murtaza Vs. Headmaster Ch. Inayatullah and others (1998 PLC (C. S.) 274), is as follows: -

> "It is very unfortunate that these persons should be uprooted after they had been appointed but if equality and equal protection before the law have any meaning and if our public institutions are to inspire that confidence which is expected of them we would be failing in our duty if we did not, even at the cost of considerable inconvenience to Government and the selected candidates, do the right thing."

122.   Let someone knock the door of this court in direct quo warranto proceedings and we will decide the case without delay. To no one, we sell, deny or delay justice and we will never hesitate to enunciate law. We will not be found underweight when time comes to weigh us. We will prove that we are loyal to our oath to preserve, protect and defend the Constitution at any cost.

123.   Learned counsel for the petitioner has also contended that thousands of persons were recruited in the Punjab Police and Revenue Department without open competition under the pretext of relaxation of all rules and procedures. He has alleged that recruitment of criminals in the Punjab Police has resulted into institutionalized evasion of the institution of Police in the Province as the officers recruited in relaxation of all rules and procedures are incorrigible and they have effectively and comprehensively destroyed the Police as disciplined law-enforcement agency and this fact is known to all. Same is the position with Revenue Department. He has prayed that the nation will continue to suffer till these officers are terminated from their services and all are assured that the constitutional scheme of public employments has some sanctity. We have considered these submissions. Prima facie, these raise serious questions. We hope that courts shall take judicial notice of these

appointments whenever these are challenged under 199 (1)(b)(ii) or 184(3) of the Constitution. Indirect or collateral challenge to entitlement of a person to hold a public office is not permissible. Law will take its own course when allegedly void appointments are challenged through appropriate judicial proceedings.

Question # 6

Whether persons can be appointed in the service of Pakistan on political grounds?

124.   Powers to make appointments in the service of Pakistan are vested in state functionaries who are required to appoint duly qualified persons after observance of due process. The appointing and the selection authorities apply their mind to the facts and circumstances of each case and make or recommend appointments of persons of proven merit determined through open competitive process. If appointments are made or recommended not on the basis of merit but on the basis of connections of the candidates with politicians, it would mean that the appointing or the selection authority has not properly exercised powers vested in him in public interest. Powers are given to holders of public offices for achievement of public purposes and not for personal or private gains or to promote dynastic rulership of the politicians. It has been stated by the Hon'ble Supreme Court of India in Kumari Shrilekha Vidyarthi Etc. Vs. State of U.P. And Ors (1991 AIR 537) that:

> "In Wade's Administrative Law, 6th Ed., after indicating that `the powers of public authorities are essentially different from those of private persons', it has been succinctly stated at p. 400-401 as under:
>
>> ".... The whole conception of unfettered discretion is inappropriate to a public authority, which possesses powers solely in order that it may use them for the public good. There is nothing paradoxical in the imposition of such legal limits. It would indeed be paradoxical if they were not imposed. Nor is this principle an oddity of British or American law: it is equally prominent in French law. Nor is it a special restriction which fetters only local authorities: it applies no less to ministers of the Crown. Nor is it confined to the sphere of administration: it operates wherever discretion is given for some public purpose, for example where a judge has a discretion to order jury trial. It is only where powers are given for the personal benefit of the person empowered that the discretion is absolute. Plainly this can have no application in public law. For the same reasons, there should in principle be no such thing as unreviewable administrative discretion, which should be just as much a contradiction in terms as unfettered discretion. The question which has to be asked is what is the scope of judicial review, and in a few special cases the scope for the review of discretionary decisions may be minimal. It remains axiomatic that all discretion is capable of abuse, and that legal limits to every power are to be found somewhere."

125.   It was held by the Hon'ble Supreme Court of India in Ramanna Dayaram Shetty Vs. International Airport Authority of India (AIR 1979 SC 1628) that:

> "It must, therefore, be taken to be the law that where the Government is dealing with the public, whether by way of giving jobs or entering into contracts or issuing quotas or licences or granting other forms of largesse, the Government cannot act arbitrarily at its sweet will and, like a private individual, deal with any person it pleases, but its action must be in conformity with standard or norms which is not arbitrary, irrational or irrelevant. The power or discretion of the Government in

the matter of grant of largesse including award of jobs, contracts, quotas, licences, etc. must be confined and structured by rational, relevant and non-discriminatory standard or norm and if the Government departs from such standard or norm in any particular case or cases, the action of the Government would be liable to be struck down".

"There is a basic difference between the acts of the State which must invariably be in public interest and those of a private individual, engaged in similar activities, being primarily for personal gain, which may or may not promote public interest. Viewed in this manner, in which we find no conceptual difficulty or anachronism, we find no reason why the requirement of Article 14 should not extend even in the sphere of contractual matters for regulating the conduct of State activity."

126.   It has been declared by the Hon'ble Supreme Court of India in State of U.P. Vs. U.P. State Law Officers Association {(1994) 2 SCC 204} that:

"17. The Government or the public body represents public interests, and whoever is in charge of running their affairs, is no more than a trustee or a custodian of the public interests. The protection of the public interests to the maximum extent and in the best possible manner is his primary duty. The public bodies are, therefore, under an obligation to the society to take the best possible steps to safeguard its interest. This obligation imposes on them the duty to engage the most competent servants, agents, advisers, spokesmen and representatives for conducting their affairs. Hence, in the selection of their lawyers, they are duty-bound to make earnest efforts to find the best from among those available at the particular time. This is more so because the claims of and against the public bodies are generally monetarily substantial and socially crucial with far-reaching consequences."

127.   It was held by the Hon'ble Supreme Court of Pakistan in Munawar Khan Vs. Niaz Muhammad and 7 others (1993 SCMR 1287) that:

"8. As regards the allocation of quota of posts to the local MPAs or MNAs for recruitment to the posts, we find it offensive to the Constitution and the law on the subject. The Ministers, the Members of National and Provincial Assemblies, all are under an oath to discharge their duties in accordance with the Constitution and the law. The service laws designate, in the case of all appointments, a departmental authority competent to make such appointments. His judgment and discretion is to be exercised honestly and objectively in the public interest and cannot be influenced or subordinated to the judgment of anyone else including his superior. In the circumstances, allocation of such quotas to the Ministers / MNAs / MPAs and appointments made thereunder are all illegal ab initio and have to be held so by all Courts, Tribunals and authorities."

128.   It was held by the Hon'ble Lahore High Court, Lahore in a case reported as Ghulam Murtaza Vs. Headmaster Ch. Inayatullah and others (1998 P L C (C. S.) 274) that:

"9. It is observed with regrets that respondents allowed their authority to be misused by the M.N.A. / M.P.A. who had no such powers. The Punjab Civil Servants Act or the Rules made thereunder did not authorise the M.N.A. / M.P.A. to pass such-like orders for appointment of respondent No.3. Respondents Nos. 1 and 2 while appointing respondents No. 3 in accordance with the wishes of M.N.A. / M.P.A.

acted without lawful authority as it was a case of dictatorial exercise of powers and not independent discharge of function. Such an exercise of powers under the dictate of public representatives has been held to be invalid in a number of judgments decided by the superior Courts of Pakistan and outside. In this regard reliance can be placed on the following judgments: --

Ghulam Mohy-ud-Din's case (PLD 1964 SC 829); Syed Fayyaz Hussain Qadri's case (PLD 1972 Lah. 316); Aman Ullah Khan's case (PLD 1990 SC 1092); Abaidullah's case (1993 SCMR 1195); Gardhandas Bhanji's case (AIR 1952 SC 100): Orion Paper Mill's case (AIR 1970 SC 1498); and Sacm Labour Union's case (1946) 2 All ER 201)."

129.   The Hon'ble Supreme Court of India has defined the spoils system as a system of distribution of offices on political consideration or party lines and has denounced it as unconstitutional in a number of judgments some of which are Mohan Lal Tripathi Vs. District Magistrate, Rae Bareilly (AIR 1993 SC 2042), Hargovind Pant Vs. Raghukul Tilak and Ors. (AIR 1979 SC 1109), Mundrika Prasad Singh Vs. State of Bihar (AIR 1979 SC 1871) and State of Mysore Vs. R.V Bidap, AIR (1973 SC 2355).

130.   So far as employments in the service of Pakistan are concerned, the selection and appointing authorities are not allowed to abdicate their lawful powers and be puppets in the hands of politicians. When the Constitution conceives that a particular matter be determined by the people themselves or their elected representatives, it clearly says so. Members of the Provincial Assemblies and of the National Assembly are directly elected by the citizens. Members of the Senate are elected by elected members of the Assemblies. The Prime Minister and the Chief Ministers are elected by the National Assembly and concerned Provincial Assemblies respectively. It is the Prime Minister and the Chief Ministers who select members of their respective Cabinets. They are also authorized to appoint their Advisors and Special Assistants. Governors are appointed by the President on the advice of the Prime Minister. Recommendations of the Judicial Commission of Pakistan are confirmed or rejected by the Parliamentary Committee. Beyond these offices, there is no role of the politicians except to give legislative policy to regulate all matters with respect to conditions of appointment and of service of the civil servants and others in the service of Pakistan. These are laws and the rules under which powers have been given to the selection and appointing authorities. In other words, it is legislative policy that these authorities must exercise powers given to them justly, fairly and after observing due process. If these powers are exercised by the politicians and the civil servants just put their thumb impressions on everything dictated by the politicians, then the concept of the rule of law is put six feet under. Such a position is inconceivable in any civilized society. There may be no prohibition if, through appropriate constitutional amendments, certain civil posts are placed at the disposal of the political executive as is the case in United States of America. Till then, powers have to be exercised by those to whom these have been given by the Constitution, laws and rules. Exercise of powers of the appointing and selection authorities by the politicians is without lawful authority and of no legal. If selection and appointment is made upon recommendations of politicians, it is nothing except exercise of powers of the selection and appointing authorities by the recommending politicians. We are constrained to hold that exercise of powers of the selection and appointing authorities in the matter of appointments of the civil servants by the politicians through recommending candidates and coercing civil servants to issue orders accordingly is void and of no legal effect.

Question # 7

What would be the appropriate order in the facts and circumstances of this case?

131.   Our determination of questions of law relating to this case hereinabove will make our task easier to make an appropriate order when law is applied to the facts and

circumstances of this case. We recapitulate hereinbelow our declarations of law in this case to proceed further in the matter:

i. Article 199(1) (b) (ii) of the Constitution intends to authorize every person, whether he is a citizen or not, to challenge legality of title of a holder of public office to hold that office. A person does not need to be an aggrieved person for invoking jurisdiction of a High Court under Article 199(1) (b) (ii) of the Constitution.

ii. Holding a public office without lawful authority is a continuing wrong, hence, the doctrine of laches and the argument of the past and closed transaction are not applicable to proceedings under Article 199(1) (b) (ii) of the Constitution.

iii. The principle of locus poenitentiae is not available to perpetuate an illegality and is irrelevant in quo warranto proceedings.

iv. No departmental action can take away jurisdiction of the High Court under Article 199(1) (b) (ii) of the Constitution.

v. Jurisdictional bar contained in Article 212 is not applicable to proceedings under Article 199(1) (b) (ii) of the Constitution.

vi. The High Court is not at liberty to terminate proceedings under Article 199 (1)(b)(ii) of the Constitution even on application of the petitioner in cases in which legality of holding a public office is in doubt.

vii. Good or bad intentions of a petitioner does not affect lawful entitlement of a person to hold a public office. If a public office is held without lawful entitlement, alleged mala fides of the petitioner cannot convert it into lawful and authorize the High Court to perpetuate a patent illegality on the pretext of the alleged mal fides.

viii. Proceedings under Article 199 (1)(b)(ii) of the Constitution shall not be abated on application of the petitioner for withdrawal of the petition. The proceedings shall continue in absence of the petitioner. In cases where the petitions under Article 199 (1)(b)(ii) of the Constitution are disposed of on the sole ground of withdrawal of the petition by the petitioner, any person can file an intra court appeal or a civil petition for leave to appeal even if he was not a party to the proceedings in earlier stages of the case.

ix. If a petition under Article 199 (1)(b)(ii) of the Constitution is found to be frivolous and without merits by the High Court, it is necessary to dismiss it in limine with deterrent punitive costs on the petitioner.

x. Once it is proved that legal grounds to act exist, the High Court has no discretion to refuse to act as doing so would go against its oath to preserve, protect and defend the Constitution. And it would surely be misuse of authority to act when legal grounds to act are missing.

xi. If a time limit has not been fixed for disposal of a petition under Article 199 (1)(b)(ii) of the Constitution, then the case has to be decided within reasonable time and absence of time limit cannot be construed as a license to unreasonably delay the case so as no live matter remains for adjudication. Whereas each case may require time for disposal depending upon peculiar facts and legal issues involved, we may reasonably hope that quo warranto proceedings under Article 199 (1)(b)(ii) as well as under Article 184(3) of the Constitution shall be concluded not later than 100 working days from the date of institution of these proceedings.

xii. A public office for the purpose of Article 199 (1)(b)(ii) of the Constitution means an office under the Federal, a Provincial or a local government or in or under any executive, legislative or judicial entity of the state and includes all posts in the service of Pakistan and other posts or offices in the public sector specifically excluded from the definition of 'service of Pakistan' in Article 260 of the Constitution.

xiii. A person shall be held to be holding a public office with lawful authority if he:

    a) possess qualifications to compete for recruitment to the public office and to hold a public office;

    b) has been recommended by the selection authority for appointment after open competitive process or has been selected by the appointing authority after due process;

    c) has been appointed by the competent appointing authority; and

    d) applicable laws / rules which create and regulate the public office do not suffer from any fatal legal infirmity.

xiv. The requirement of inviting applications through open advertisement in the press cannot be dispensed with under any circumstances as it would be in contravention of Article 2A, 4 (2) (b), 18, 25, 27 and 137 of the Constitution and, hence, void in terms of Article 8 of the Constitution.

xv. Where the applicable law or rules requires consultation with the Public Service Commission as a condition-precedent for appointments in the service of Pakistan, appointments are not allowed to be made without consulting the Public Service Commission under the pretext of relaxation of the rules.

xvi. Other conditions of recruitment cannot be relaxed in favour of an individual or a group of individuals.

xvii. Whenever it is deemed necessary in public interest to relax conditions of recruitment, these may be relaxed if express provision therefor exists and the benefit of such relaxation shall be given to all and this decision shall form part of open advertisement in the press through which applications are invited for recruitment.

xviii. Section 22 of the Punjab Civil Servants Act, 1974 and Rule 23 of the Punjab Civil Servants (Appointment & Conditions of Service) Rules, 1974 allow relaxation of the service rules to save civil servants from undue hardship and to promote justice and equity. These provisions cannot be used to make backdoor appointments or to relax qualifications or to by-pass the due process for selection for appointments in the service of Pakistan.

xix. Appointments made in the service of Pakistan without open advertisement and fair competitive selection process are incurably bad and cannot be declared or deemed to be lawful or regular through enactment, executive order or judicial pronouncement.

xx. Appointment of a person in the service of Pakistan who does not fulfil the eligibility criteria by an appointing authority, irrespective of the fact whether that authority is competent or not, is not curable through any post-appointment measure even if made after open advertisement and due competitive selection process.

xxi. Ad hoc, contract, work-charged and daily-wage employees cannot be regularized as regularization is not a mode of appointment and regularization of such employees takes away fundamental right to trade and profession and non-discrimination in the matter of appointments in the service of Pakistan of the otherwise qualified citizens. All legislative, executive and judicial measures to regularize such employees would be void within the meaning of Article 8(1) of the Constitution.

xxii. Exercise of powers of the selection and appointing authorities in the matter of appointments of the civil servants by the politicians through recommending candidates and coercing civil servants to issue orders accordingly is void and of no legal effect.

132. We have applied the above enunciation of law on the facts and circumstances of this case. Facts on file prove that:

1. Appointment of the respondent was initially made on ad hoc basis without inviting applications through advertisement in the press and observing due competitive process.

2. The West Pakistan Provincial Treasury and Accounts Service Rules, 1962 did not provide for recruitment on ad hoc basis and these rules were not relaxed in consultation with the Public Service Commission.

3. The respondent was appointed on ad hoc basis on the recommendation of an MPA and not on merit determined by objective criteria after written test and interview.

4. The respondent was not a civil servant when he was recruited on ad hoc basis.

5. There was no request for relaxation of rules in the first application of the respondent. The first directive of the Chief Minister was silent about relaxation of rules and the offer of appointment issued to the respondent by the appointing authority was issued under Rule 22 of the Punjab Civil Servants (Appointment & Conditions of Service) Rules, 1974 and not under Rule 23 ibid. Rule 22 ibid deals with recruitment on ad hoc basis whereas Rule 23 ibid deals with relaxation of rules. Rules and procedures have, therefore, not been relaxed for ad hoc appointment of the respondent. The appointing authority has stated, in his para-wise-comments submitted in the High Court, that:

"The orders of the appointments passed by the competent authority i.e. the Chief Minister in relaxation of all rules and procedures were as a result of a conscious decision of the Chief Minister on the basis of hardship in term of Rule 23 ibid. The orders of the Chief Minister manifest independent application of mind given the fact that the Finance Secretary as the Appointing Authority had separately resisted the appointments on ad hoc and regular basis by initiating two separate summaries bringing out the position of Rules with regard to the appointment of the officer. But the Chief Minister over-ruled the said positions and ordered the appointments, notwithstanding, by invoking his powers under Sections 22 and 23 of the Punjab Civil Servants Act, 1974. This implies a well thought out decision and constitute sufficient reasons for the purpose of the said appointment."

Recruitment of the respondent on ad hoc basis implies that the Chief Minister over-ruled the appointing authority on the first summary submitted to him. On second summary, the respondent was advised to appear before the Public Service Commission for regular appointment. This order of the Chief Minister was communicated to the respondent by the appointing authority. The appointing authority has not claimed filing of a third application by the respondent to the Chief Minister or issuance of third directive by the Chief Minister or submission of a third summary to the Chief Minister. It is, therefore, incorrect to assume that the Chief Minister relaxed all rules and procedures for regular appointment of the respondent. Under Rule 5 (2) read with Part-A of Schedule VII of the Punjab Government Rules of Business, 1974, all cases of relaxation of service rules are required to be submitted to the Chief Minister before issuance of orders. Since it has been proved that no third summary was initiated, therefore, the claim of relaxation of all rules and regulations for the purpose of regularization of services of the respondent is incorrect.

6. The qualifications required to compete for selection for this post are: -

    1. Degree of graduation from a recognized university (Rule 7 (1) of the West Pakistan Provincial Treasury and Accounts Service Rules, 1962); and
    2. Age not below 21 years and not above 25 years (Rule 6 (1) of the West Pakistan Provincial Treasury and Accounts Service Rules, 1962).

The qualifications required for regular appointment to this post are: -

    1. Qualifications required to compete for selection to the post;
    2. Recommendation of the Selection Authority on the basis of merit determined through objective criteria after open advertisement, written test and interview (Rule 5 (1) (i) of the West Pakistan Provincial Treasury and Accounts Service Rules, 1962 read with Section 2 (1) (j), Section 2 (2) and Section 4 of the Punjab Civil Servants Act, 1974 and Rule 16 and 17 of the Punjab Civil Servants (Appointment & Conditions of Service) Rules, 1974);
    3. Medical fitness certificate; and
    4. Declaration regarding marriage with foreign nationals.

The respondent lacks qualification of proper age to compete for selection to the post. Rule 12 of the West Pakistan Provincial Treasury and Accounts Service Rules, 1962 provides that any of these rules may, for reasons to be recorded in writing, be relaxed in individual cases if Government is satisfied, in consultation with the Public Service Commission, that a strict application of the rule would cause undue hardship to the individual concerned. There is no provision for ad hoc appointment in these rules. The rules were not relaxed in consultation with the Public Service Commission. The West Pakistan Provincial Treasury and Accounts Service Rules, 1962 are special rules whereas the Punjab Civil Servants (Appointment & Conditions of Service) Rules, 1974 are general rules. It has been held in a case reported as Neimat Ali Goraya and 3 others Vs. Jaffar Abbas and others (1996 PLC (C.S.) 878) that "Where both laws applied to a particular case, then to the extent of application of special law in that case, provisions of general law stand displaced". Moreover, the Punjab Delegation of Powers (Relaxation of Conditions of Service) Rules, 1989 restricted the power of the Chief Minister to relax rules for recruitment to posts in BS-1 to BS-5 only. These were special and applicable rules at the time of ad hoc and regular appointment of the respondent. The Chief Minister could not issue executive orders in violation of these rules. The Punjab Civil Servants (Appointment & Conditions of Service) Rules, 1974 are general rules whereas the Punjab Delegation of Powers (Relaxation of Conditions of Service) Rules, 1989 are special rules exclusively dealing with relaxation of conditions of service. It has been held in a case reported as 1996 PLC (C.S.) 878 that in case of existence of general and special laws on the same subject, the special laws prevail. Further, the relaxation in the upper-age limit for more than ten years sanctioned in favour of the respondent was to enable the respondent to "compete against the post of Treasury Officer in the Finance Department" and was not meant for any other purpose, including the purpose of recruitment without competition. The said relaxation was used for recruitment without competition for which it was not meant.

7. The Order issued by the appointing authority does not exonerate the respondent from the charges levelled against him and expressly admits that his appointment was not processed in the prescribed manner.

8. The appointing authority was competent to appoint the respondent on regular basis only on recommendation of the Selection Authority in the same manner as the President of Pakistan can appoint judges of superior courts only on the recommendation of the Judicial and Parliamentary Commissions and advice of the Prime Minister and not otherwise.

133.   Applying law to the admitted and proved facts in this case, we find that appointment of the respondent is void ab initio in terms of Article 8 of the Constitution being in contravention of fundamental right guaranteed by Article 18 read with Article 2A, 4 (2) (b), 25, 27 and 137 of the Constitution because it has been made without open advertisement and on the recommendation of an MPA and not on merit determined through objective criteria. It has also been proved that the Chief Minister did not relax all rules and regulations for the purpose of ad hoc appointment of the respondent. Even if we accept, for the purpose of argument only, that all rules and regulations were relaxed by the Chief Minister in favour of the respondent for the purpose of his appointment, such order of the Chief Minister is void being in violation of the fundamental rights. Even otherwise, recruitment rules are not allowed to be relaxed to favour an individual and the service rules can only be relaxed in favour of a civil servant for just and equitable causes and only to the extent of protecting a civil servant from hardship caused by strict application of a rule. Moreover, in case an appointing authority is competent to appoint only on the recommendation of the selection authority, rules cannot be relaxed to make that authority competent to appoint someone in absence of recommendation of the selection authority.

134.   For the aforesaid reasons, the appeal is allowed and the petition for quo warranto is hereby granted. The respondent (Mr. Shakeel Ahmad) is found disqualified from and is hereby adjudged guilty of unlawfully holding the office of the District Accounts Officer and is hereby ousted and excluded therefrom with a direction to the appointing authority to make appointment on the post so vacated in accordance with law.

135.   So far as legal validity of actions of the respondent as usurper of a public office are concerned, the de **facto** doctrine comes to rescue us. De facto has been defined in these words:

> "As a matter of fact; something which, while not necessarily lawful, exists in fact."

136.   This doctrine has been dealt with at https://encyclopedia.lexroll.com/encyclopedia/de-facto-doctrine/ in the following words:

> "The **de facto** doctrine (aka, "**de facto** officer doctrine") validates, on grounds of public policy and prevention of a failure of public justice, the acts of an official who functions under color of law even though it is later discovered that the legality of that person's appointment or election to office is deficient. "The **de facto** doctrine springs from the fear of the chaos that would result from multiple and repetitious suits challenging every action taken by every official whose claim to office

could be open to question, and seeks to protect the public by insuring the orderly functioning of the government despite technical defects in title to office." 63A Am. Jur. 2d, **Public Officers and Employees** § 578, pp. 1080-1081 (1984).

"A person will be held to be **de facto** officer when, and only when, he is in possession, and is exercising the duties, of an office; his incumbency is illegal in some respect; he has at least a fair color of right or title to the office, or has acted as an officer for such a length of time, and under such circumstances of reputation or acquiescence by the public and public authorities, as to afford a presumption of appointment or election, and induce people, without inquiry, and relying on the supposition that he is the officer he assumes to be, to submit to or invoke his action; and, in some, although not all, jurisdictions, only when the office has a **de jure** existence." 45 CJ, **Officers** § 366, p. 1053."

137. Albert Constantineau wrote **in A Treatise on the De Facto Doctrine in its Relation to Public Officers and Public Corporations** (Toronto: Canada Law Book, 1910), pages 3-6 that:

"The **de facto** doctrine is a rule or principle of law which, in the first place, justifies the recognition of the authority of governments established and maintained by persons who have usurped the sovereign authority of the State, and assert themselves by force and arms against the lawful government; secondly, which recognizes the existence of, and protects from collateral attack, public or private bodies corporate, which, though irregularly or illegally organized, yet, under colour of law, openly exercises the powers and functions of regularly created bodies; and, thirdly, which imparts validity to the official acts of persons who, under colour of right or authority, hold office under the aforementioned governments or bodies, or exercise lawfully existing offices of whatever nature, in which the public or third persons are interested, where the performance of such official acts is for the benefit of the public or third persons, and not for their own personal advantage....

"Again, the doctrine is necessary to maintain the supremacy of the law and to preserve peace and order in the community at large, since any other rule would lead to such uncertainty and confusion, as to break up the order and quiet of all civil administration. Indeed, if any individual or body of individuals were permitted, at his or their pleasure, to challenge the authority of and refuse obedience to the government of the state and the numerous functionaries through whom it exercises its various powers, or refuse to recognize municipal bodies and their officers, on the ground of irregular existence or defective titles, insubordination and disorder of the worst kind would be encouraged, which might at any time culminate in anarchy."

138. It has been observed at https://definitions.uslegal.com/d/de-facto-officer/ that:

"De Facto Officer refers to an officer holding a colorable right or title to the office accompanied by possession. The lawful acts of an officer de facto, so far as the rights of third persons are concerned, when done within the scope and by the apparent authority of office, are valid and binding.

The de facto officer doctrine confers validity upon acts performed by a person acting under the color of official title even though it is later discovered that the legality of that person's appointment or election to office is deficient.

The following is case law defining the term De Facto Officer.

"An officer de facto is one whose acts, though not those of a lawful officer, the law, upon principles of policy and justice, will hold valid so far as they involve the interests of the public and third persons, where the duties of the office were exercised:

First, without a known appointment or election, but under such circumstances of reputation or acquiescence as were calculated to induce people, without inquiry, to submit to or invoke his action, supposing him to be the officer he assumed to be;

Second, under color of a known and valid appointment or election, but where the officer had failed to conform to some precedent requirement or condition, as to take an oath, give a bond, or the like;

Third, under color of a known election or appointment, void because the officer was not eligible, or because there was a want of power in the electing or appointing body, or by reason of some defect or irregularity in its exercise, such ineligibility, want of power, or defect being unknown to the public;

Fourth, under color of an election or appointment by or pursuant to a public unconstitutional law, before the same is adjudged to be such".
[Jersey City v. Dep't of Civil Serv., 57 N.J. Super. 13, 27 (App. Div. 1959)]"

139. The principle of de facto exercise of power by a holder of judicial office was recognized by the Hon'ble Supreme Court of India in Gokaraju Rangaraju Vs. State of A.P. (AIR 1981 SC 1473) in these words: -

"17. In our view, the de facto doctrine furnishes an answer to the submissions of Shri Phadke based on section 9 of Criminal Procedure Code and Article 21 of the Constitution. The Judges who rejected the appeal in one case and convicted the accused in the other case were not mere usurpers or intruders but were persons who discharged the functions and duties of Judges under colour of lawful authority. We are concerned with the office that the Judges purported to hold. We are not concerned with the particular incumbents of office. So long as the office was validly created, it matters not that the incumbent was not validly appointed. A person appointed as a Sessions Judge, Additional Sessions Judges or Assistant Sessions Judge, would be exercising jurisdiction in the Court of Session and his judgments and orders would be those of the Court of Session. They would continue to be valid as the judgments and orders of the Court of Session, notwithstanding that his appointment to such Court might be declared invalid. On that account alone, it can never be said that the procedure prescribed by law has not been followed. It would be a different matter if the constitution of the Court itself is under challenge. We are not concerned with such a situation in the instant cases. We, therefore, find no force in any of the submissions of the learned counsel. "

140. It has been observed in Cooley's "Constitutional Limitations"' (8ᵗʰ Edition Vol.2 p.1357) that:

"No one is under obligation to recognize or respect the acts of an intruder, and for all legal purposes they are absolutely void. But for the sake of order and regularity, and to prevent confusion in the conduct of public business and in security of private rights, the acts of officers de facto are not suffixed to be questioned because of the want of legal authority except by some direct proceeding instituted for the purpose by the State or by someone claiming the office de jure, or except when the person himself attempts to build up some right, or claim some privilege or emolument, by reason of being the officer which he claims to be. In all other cases the acts of an officer de facto are as valid and effectual, while he is suffered to retain the office, as though he were an officer by right and the same legal consequences will flow from them for the protection of the public and of third parties. This is an important principle, which finds concise expression in the legal maxim that the acts of officers de facto cannot be questioned collaterally".

141.   In view of the above, we are persuaded to hold that if a person is held not lawfully entitled to hold a public office, his acts as such holder of public office would be valid if otherwise lawful and shall not be declared invalid merely on account of defects in his title to the public office.

142.   The appellant in these proceedings shall be paid Rs. 10,000,00/ (One million rupees) as costs by the respondent within fifty days of announcement of this judgment.

143.   The respondent shall not be liable to refund remuneration and other benefits drawn in consideration of his employment as a District Accounts Officer as requiring him to refund the amounts drawn would amount to extracting forced labour from a citizen which is prohibited under the Constitution. The remuneration drawn by the respondent is hereby held to be quantum meruit.

144.   Before parting with the judgment, valuable assistance rendered by the learned counsels of the opposing parties is hereby acknowledged with gratitude.

Sd/
Mr. Jamal Mustafa Kundan
Sd/
Mr. Saleem Anwar Taya
Sd/
Mr. Rasheed Ahmad

Announced in Open Court on 13th of December, 2019.

Sd/
Mr. Jamal Mustafa Kundan

APPROVED FOR REPORTING

Chapter 4

Stolen purse

This Chapter examines the constitutionality of:

a. entrustment of treasury functions of the plaintiff to the CGA through Section 5(b) of the Controller General of Accounts (Appointment, Functions and Powers) Ordinance, 2001 (Ordinance No. XXIV of 2001, hereinafter referred to as the CGA Ordinance);

b. assigning of accounting functions of the Provincial and District Governments to the Controller General of Accounts (CGA) under Section 5 (a) of the CGA Ordinance;

c. non-payment of cost incurred by the plaintiff on performance of treasury functions of the defendant;

d. non-separation of accounting and auditing functions after promulgation of the CGA Ordinance and the Auditor General's (Functions, Powers and Terms and Condition of Service) Ordinance, 2001 (Ordinance No. XXIII of 2001, hereinafter referred to as the AG Ordinance); and

e. holding of posts in connection with affairs of the plaintiff by employees of the defendant through posting / transfer or on deputation.

Present: Mr. Jamal Mustafa Kundan
                 Mr. Saleem Anwar Taya
                 Mr. Rasheed Ahmad

Province of the Punjab

------Plaintiff

Versus

Federation of Pakistan

-----Defendant

Plaintiff	Mr. Zahoor Ahmad, Advocate General, Punjab
Defendant	Mr. Shahanshah Faisal Azeem, Attorney General for Pakistan for the Federation of Pakistan
	Mr. Tariq Mehmood Awan, Senior Advocate, Supreme Court of Pakistan for the private defendant
Dates of hearing	04.12.2019, 16.12.2019, 27.12.2019

JUDGMENT

MR. SALEEM ANWAR TAYA. –This plaint has been filed by the Province of the Punjab against the Federation of Pakistan under Article 184(1) of the Constitution of the Islamic Republic of Pakistan, 1973 (hereinafter referred to as the Constitution) to assail the constitutionality of:

f. entrustment of treasury functions of the plaintiff to the CGA through Section 5(b) of the Controller General of Accounts (Appointment, Functions and Powers) Ordinance, 2001 (Ordinance No. XXIV of 2001, hereinafter referred to as the CGA Ordinance);

g. assigning of accounting functions of the Provincial and District Governments to the Controller General of Accounts (CGA) under Section 5 (a) of the CGA Ordinance;

h. non-payment of cost incurred by the plaintiff on performance of treasury functions of the defendant;

i. non-separation of accounting and auditing functions after promulgation of the CGA Ordinance and the Auditor General's (Functions, Powers and Terms and Condition of Service) Ordinance, 2001 (Ordinance No. XXIII of 2001, hereinafter referred to as the AG Ordinance); and

j. holding of posts in connection with affairs of the plaintiff by employees of the defendant through posting / transfer or on deputation.

Issues raised and arguments given by the plaintiff

2.   The plaintiff furnishes the following grounds in support of his plaint:

As regards treasury functions

k. The authority to operate bank accounts of the federal and provincial governments has been vested in the CGA through Section 5 (b) of the CGA Ordinance. This authority is commonly known as treasury function which includes receiving or disbursing or authorizing the State Bank of Pakistan (SBP) to receive or disburse moneys on behalf of a government. Whereas the Federation has full powers to assign its treasury functions to any of its functionaries or entities, it has no constitutional authority to assume to itself treasury functions of the Provinces through any sub-constitutional measure without getting Article 119 of the Constitution amended. Treasury functions of the Provinces exclusively and indivisibly fall within jurisdiction of the respective Provincial Governments under Section 151 of the Government of India Act, 1935, Article 95 of the Constitution of 1956, Article 87 of the Constitution of 1962, Article 124 of the interim Constitution of 1972 and Article 119 of the Constitution of 1973.

l. No federal functionary can operate bank accounts of the plaintiff for the purpose of withdrawal of moneys therefrom as Federation is not a party to the agreement between the SBP and the plaintiff under which the SBP maintains bank accounts of the plaintiff and provides the banking services.

m. No entry in the Federal Legislative List or any substantive provision of the Constitution authorizes the defendant to assume treasury functions of the plaintiff. The treasury functions of the Provinces had never been assigned to the Auditor General under any legal arrangement.

n. The plaintiff, in exercise of its authority under Article 119 of the Constitution, has established Treasuries / District Accounts Offices (DAOs), Sub-Treasuries and the Inspectorate of Treasuries and Accounts (the Inspectorate) for performance of its treasury functions and executive control of these offices has been assigned to the Finance Department in terms of the Punjab Government Rules of Business, framed under Article 139 of the Constitution. The defendant has no constitutional authority to assume ownership or control of the provincial entities created for performance of treasury functions.

o. Assumption of treasury functions of the plaintiff by the defendant is not only in violation of Article 119 of the Constitution but it also hurts the federal structure of the Constitution. In such an eventuality, authority of the plaintiff to manage its finances decreases to an objectionable extent, as it loses control over the machinery, which is entrusted with the work of authorization of payments from its bank accounts under the Authenticated Schedule of Authorized Expenditure approved in terms of Article 123 of the Constitution. Absence of this control is definite to result into financial and administrative indiscipline.

p. In case of assumption of treasury functions of the plaintiff by the defendant, the Public Accounts Committees of the Provincial Assembly is rendered incompetent to initiate action on account of grave irregularities, misappropriations and frauds or facilitation thereof by the office of the CGA --- a federal entity--- as the Public Accounts Committees can take remedial and corrective measures in respect of provincial employees and entities and not against federal employees or entities. Such incompetency does not fit in the constitutional scheme under which power of the purse has been vested in the Provincial Assembly.

q. Payments into Provincial Consolidated Fund and withdrawal therefrom are regulated in terms of the Rules framed or deemed to have been framed under Article 119 of the Constitution and not under Section 5 (b) of the CGA Ordinance. The Auditor General or the President of Pakistan cannot assume powers vested in the Provincial Assembly or the Governor of the Province under Article 119 of the Constitution in the pretext of prescribing pre-audit checks for payments from the Provincial Consolidated Fund and Public Account of the Province.

Authority of the Province under Article 119 of the Constitution cannot be surrendered to the Auditor General or the CGA or even the President of Pakistan. This idea is offensive to the spirit of federalism and provincial autonomy. The defendant lacks constitutional jurisdiction to prescribe the so-called pre-audit checks for the Provincial Consolidated Fund and Public Account of the Province. Section 5(b) of the CGA Ordinance is void to the extent of treasury functions of the Province and pre-audit checks in respect thereof being an unconstitutional encroachment on exclusive provincial domain.

r. All the four Provinces have established their Treasuries / Sub-Treasuries and organizations for their monitoring and superintendence. Rules of Business of the all the Provinces assign business relating to these offices to the respective Finance Departments of the Provincial Governments. Legality of these arrangements has never been challenged judicially or before any other forum.

s. If the above constitutional position is not accepted, then operation of bank accounts of the plaintiff through its employees becomes illegal. As a logical consequence, control of the plaintiff through its Finance Department over its Treasuries / DAOs and the Inspectorate loses legal legs to stand on. Article 5 of the Constitution commands that loyalty to the State is the basic duty of every citizen and obedience to the Constitution and law is the inviolable obligation of every citizen wherever he may be and of every other person for the time being within Pakistan. If a government functionary has to make a decision on an issue which has specifically been covered both by the Constitution and a law / set of rules and the relevant provisions are in irreconcilable clash and incapable of having simultaneous effect, the government functionary has to decide to make decision which either conforms to the Constitution or to the law / rules. If he implements the law / rules ignoring the Constitution which is the fundamental and supreme law, he will be guilty of violation of Article 5 of the Constitution. If he implements the Constitution and ignores the law / rules, he would be exhibiting his loyalty and obedience to the Constitution. Anyone aggrieved of his decision may approach the judiciary to challenge the interpretation of the Constitution made by the executive. Until an interpretation made by the executive is corrected / nullified by the judiciary, the same will remain in field. To sum up, if there is an irreconcilable clash between provisions of an ordinary law and those of the Constitution, one can either obey the Constitution and disregard the law or obey the law and violate the Constitution. Constitution, being the supreme and fundamental law, must be obeyed and any law in violation of it must always be ignored. In the matter under adjudication, it is not possible to harmonize Section 5 (b) of the CGA Ordinance to the extent it assigns treasury functions of the Provincial Government to the CGA and Article 119 of the Constitution and the rules competently framed thereunder and to remove the inconsistency. The two provisions cannot be given simultaneous effect and cannot co-exist. It is well-settled principle of law that in case of irreconcilable clash between provisions of the Constitution and those of a law, the provisions of the Constitution prevail and those of the law yield to the Constitution to the extent of clash. Therefore, the words 'and Provincial Governments' occurring in Section 5 (b) of the CGA Ordinance are void and of no legal effect being inconsistence to Article 119 of the Constitution. It is trite law that the legislation made by the Parliament or validation of Ordinances issued without jurisdiction or in excess of jurisdiction is void to the extent of incompetence of the Parliament to legislate or validate. Section 5 (b) of the CGA Ordinance to the extent it provides for performance of treasury functions of the Provincial Governments by the CGA may, therefore, be declared void and of no legal effect.

As regards accounting functions

a. Written records of public moneys received or disbursed are maintained by the public sector entities that receive or disburse moneys. This function has never been entrusted to the Auditor General ever since coming into force of the "Rules regarding the Auditor General in India" made by the Secretary of State in Council under Section 96D (1) of the Government of India Act. Individual accounts of public entities which receive or disburse public moneys are compiled by those entities through their internal arrangements. The defendant has nothing to do with these internal accounting arrangements of the plaintiff and its local governments.

b. The Government of India Act, 1935 and Constitutions of Pakistan, 1956, 1962, 1972 and 1973 provided that the Auditor General shall perform such functions in respect of accounts of the Federation and of the Provinces as may be determined through an Order of the Governor General or President of Pakistan or an Act of the Parliament. The function of preparation of government-wide accounting reports remained assigned to the Auditor General till 30th of June, 2001. Article 169 of the Constitution, 1973 confines the power of the Parliament and that of the President to determine the functions and powers of the Auditor General in relation to the accounts of the Federation, Provinces and bodies or authorities established by them. The Parliament or the President, who had the authority to direct the Auditor General to keep the accounts of the Federation and of the Provinces, could also direct him not to keep such accounts. Entrustment of accounting functions of the Federation and of the Provinces to the Auditor General through the Pakistan (Audit and Accounts) Order, 1973 suffered from no constitutional infirmity. It needs, however, to be noted that the said Article 169 confines the power of the Parliament and that of the President to "determine" the functions and powers of the Auditor General in relation to the accounts of the Provinces. Once the power to keep the accounts of a Province is taken away from the Auditor General through a statute, that power cannot be conferred on any other authority or functionary by a federal law. The moment, therefore, these powers and functions are denied him, the authority to keep the provincial accounts vests in the Provinces under Article 142 (c) of the Constitution read with the Fourth Schedule thereto.

c. Local Governments in the Province constitute third tier of public administration; these are created and managed under provincial laws. Section 5(a) of the CGA Ordinance, inter alia, assigns functions of preparation and maintenance of accounts of the District Governments to the CGA. The CGA Ordinance does not define the word 'accounts'; it, however, defines "appropriation accounts" and "finance accounts" in its Section 2 (a) and 2 (d) respectively in the following words:

(a) "appropriation accounts" means accounts relating to expenditure brought in to account during a financial year to several items specified in the schedule of expenditures authenticated under the Budgetary Provisions Order, 2000 (Chief Executive's Order No. 6 of 2000)

(d) "Finance Accounts" means the accounts exhibiting annual receipts and disbursements as well as balances of assets and liabilities of the Federal Government as on the thirtieth June of a financial year."

The Budgetary Provisions Order, 2000 is applicable to the Federal Consolidated Fund, Public Account of the Federation, Provincial Consolidated Fund and Public Account of the Province and is irrelevant to a Local Fund of a District Government or of any other local government. As Section 5(a) of the CGA Ordinance purports to be applicable to accounts of a District Government and the definition of "Appropriation Accounts" does not include Local Fund of a District Government, therefore, Appropriation and Finance Accounts of the District Governments or of any other local government do not fall within purview of the CGA.

d. District Governments in the Provinces are creation of provincial laws; every aspect and function of these governments including treasury and accounting functions, with the sole exception of prescription of principles and methods of maintenance of accounts by the Auditor General with the approval of the President, has to be performed in accordance with the Provincial laws only. Local Government is not a Federal subject and the defendant is not competent to legislate on any issue relating to the District Governments. The Provincial legislature, through Section 114 of the Punjab Local Government Ordinance, 2001 (Ordinance XIII of 2001) assigned accounting and treasury functions of the District Governments to the respective District Accounts Officers (DAOs) / Treasury Officers (TOs) / Accountant General (AG, Punjab). The Punjab Local Government Act, 2013 (XVIII of 2013) entrusted accounting and treasury functions of District Health and Education Authorities to the respective DAOs / AG, Punjab and of other local governments to other provincial employees. The Punjab Local Government Act, 2019 (Act XIII of 2019) does not assign any role to the CGA in the matter of keeping and maintaining accounts of the local governments. The Federal Government has no authority of law to assume to itself accounting functions of the local governments and assign these functions to any federal functionary including the CGA. The CGA Ordinance is void also in respect of keeping and maintaining accounts of the local governments through the CGA because of its clash with the competently enacted provincial legislation and for being in violation of Article 142 of the Constitution read with constitutional provisions governing the local governments.

e. Pakistan is a federal republic. The Constitution distributes legislative and executive powers between the Federation and the federating units. Jurisdiction of the Province in subjects falling within its purview is complete and exclusive. The Federation cannot interfere with or control exercise of exclusive legislative and executive powers of the Province under the guise of keeping and maintaining accounts of the Province and its local governments. The Federation may impose reporting requirements on the Provinces with respect to accounting information relating to the Province and its local governments but no stretch of reasoning or imagination can empower it to assume the function of keeping and maintaining accounts of the Province and its local governments. A federal claim on exclusive jurisdiction to keep and maintain provincial and local accounts makes the federal structure of the Constitution nugatory. In case a federal entity keeps and maintains provincial and local accounts, the Province will be dependent on that entity for their day-to-day accounting information requirements for prudent financial management and will not be in a position to take action if information is not provided or provided with unjustified delay or the information is incorrect or contains material errors. The purported entrustment of accounting functions of the provincial and local governments to the CGA does not fit well in the federal scheme of the Constitution and merits to be declared ultra vires the Constitution on this ground alone.

As regards reimbursement of the cost incurred by the plaintiff on performance of treasury functions of the defendant

a. Prior to enactment of the Government of India Act, 1935, there was a unitary form of Government in which Treasuries and Sub-Treasuries used to perform treasury functions of the Central Government as well as of the local governments (Provinces). Section 151 of the Government of India Act, 1935 assigned treasury functions of the Provinces to the respective Provincial Governments. The Federal Government did not establish its separate infrastructure for performance of its treasury functions and assigned this duty to the Provincial Treasuries under Section 124 of the Government of India Act, 1935. This arrangement continues to exist till date in terms of Article 146 of the Constitution of Pakistan, 1973. All constitutional provisions from 1935 till date require that there shall be paid by the Federation to the Province such sum as may be agreed or, in default of agreement, as may be determined by an arbitrator appointed by the Chief Justice, in respect of any extra costs of administration incurred by the Province in connection with the exercise of the powers or the discharge of the duties by the Province on behalf of the Federation. The plaintiff is performing treasury functions of the defendant within its territorial limits but the defendant has not yet paid even a single penny to the plaintiff on account of extra cost incurred by the plaintiff.

b. Notwithstanding promulgation of the CGA Ordinance and entrustment of treasury functions of the defendant to the CGA, the defendant has failed to establish its organizational capability for performance of its treasury functions in the Province of the Punjab and the plaintiff continues to be burdened with duties of performance of federal treasury functions in the Province. The Hon'ble Supreme Court may like to declare law on the legal validity of the arrangements for performance of federal treasury functions in the Province after promulgation of the CGA Ordinance.

As regards separation of accounting and auditing functions

a. Till such time the Constitution is appropriately amended to empower the Province to audit its accounts through a Provincial Auditor General, auditorial functions of the Province stand exclusively assigned to the Auditor General of Pakistan. The Province is deprived of auditorial services of the requisite quality because of conflict of interest as a single service (Pakistan Audit and Accounts Service, hereinafter referred to as the PA&AS) has been assigned accounting and auditing functions. Officers who are assigned auditorial functions can also be tasked to maintain accounts. Continued existence of the PA&AS as a combined service both for audit and accounts after separation of auditing and accounting functions through the CGA Ordinance deprives the Province of the specialized services of a professional pool of officers exclusively for audit. It is loud and clear that the CGA Ordinance was promulgated to separate accounting and auditing functions. Legislative intent unambiguously expressed in the CGA Ordinance for separation of accounting functions from auditorial functions does not allow conflict of interest through tolerating continued existence of the PA&AS as it used to be before promulgation of the said Ordinance. The Supreme Court may make the declaration that Auditor General can audit accounts of the Province only through officers employed exclusively for audit.

b. Deputation of auditors on accounting and other posts also causes problems which are inescapable consequences of conflict of interest. In such situations, an auditor may happen to audit transactions to which he might had been associated during his deputation or posting. Judges have been prohibited to hold executive posts through deputation or posting / transfer. Similar principle merits to be applied to auditors who must not perform any duty except audit. The Province is adversely affected if auditors are not confined to their auditorial functions. The Supreme Court may make a declaration that deputation / posting / transfer of auditors subordinate to the Auditor General on posts relating to accounts and other executive functions including financial management is against the concept of separation of audit from accounts.

As regards holding of posts in connection with affairs of the Province by federal employees

a. Posting of Divisional Accountant or the Divisional Accounts Officer in works divisions of the Public Works Departments by the Director General Accounts Works, Punjab (DGAW) is without lawful authority and jurisdiction being in violation of Article 119, 129, 137, 139, 147 and 240 of the Constitution and the laws / rules framed thereunder. All matters relating to posts in connection with affairs of the Province fall within exclusive legislative jurisdiction of the Province. Legislative and executive powers are co-extensive. On the other hand, Article 97 of the Constitution commands that the executive authority of the federation shall extend to the matters with respect to which Parliament has power to make laws. Since the Federation lacks power to legislate on posts in connection with affairs of the Province, therefore, it has no executive power of appointments / postings / transfers on posts in connection with affairs of the Province. As the posts of Divisional Accountant or the Divisional Accounts Officer in works divisions of the Public Works Departments of the Province are posts in connection with affaitrs of the Province, therefore, no federal functionary has any power to post federal employees on these posts.

b. Rule 14 (a) of the Punjab Departmental Financial Rules is not saved as existing law because of its inconsistency with the Constitution; hence, this Rule is void and of no legal effect.

c. No posts with the nomenclature of Director, Audit & Accounts (Works) exists in the Punjab; hence, Rule 2.14 (a) of the Punjab Departmental Financial Rules has lost its effectiveness and has become redundant. The DGAW cannot use this rule to post federal employees on posts in connection with affairs of the Province.

d. Section 23 (2) of the Punjab Civil Servants Act, 1974 (Punjab Act No. VIII of 1974) protects only such rules, orders or instructions in respect of any terms and conditions of service of civil servants duly made or issued by an authority competent to make them and in force immediately before the commencement of the Punjab Civil Servants Act to the extent these rules, orders or instructions were not inconsistent with the provisions of the Act ibid. The Act does not assign any role to federal functionaries in respect of posts in connection with affairs of the Province. The post of the Divisional Accountant or the Divisional Accounts Officer is a post in connection with affairs of the Province. Rule 2.14 (a) of the Punjab Departmental Financial Rules assigns role in the matter of posting of the Divisional Accountant to the Director, Audit & Accounts (Works). This Rules does not have the protection of Section 23 (2) of the Punjab Civil Servants Act, 1974 and is, therefore, of no legal effect being inconsistent with the Punjab Civil Servants Act, 1974.

e. Remuneration to incumbents of post of the Divisional Accountant or the Divisional Accounts Officer is paid from the provincial exchequer. The Federation or its employees are not empowered to upgrade this post as up-gradation causes financial burden on the Provincial Consolidated Fund. No federal functionary has any authority of law to directly or indirectly burden the Provincial Consolidated Fund or a local fund of the Province. The Supreme Court may like to declare that no federal employee is empowered to make appointments or postings to posts in connection with affairs of a Province or to re-designate or up-grade or hold such a post.

3. The plaintiff has placed on record photocopies of a number of letters written by the Governor, Chief Minister and the Secretary to the Government of the Punjab, Finance Department which were addressed to the President of Pakistan, Prime Minister of Pakistan, Federal Finance Minister and Federal Finance Secretary demanding exclusive control of the Province over the administrative machinery responsible for performance of accounting and treasury functions of the Province. It was alleged that these letters were rarely responded to by the Federation and a pervasive evasive attitude of the Federation has made the issue a dispute within the meaning of Article 184(1) of the Constitution. It was also averred that non-handing over of the administrative machinery of the Federation for performance of accounting and treasury functions of the Province to the Province is a valid cause of action making the plaint maintainable. It was argued that the cause of action occurred in 1965 when a District Accounts Offices Scheme (DAOs Scheme) was introduced and this cause got reinforced when the CGA Ordinance was promulgated in 2001. The cause of action, it was argued, continues to exist today, giving a cause of action de die in diem. It was vehemently stressed that the principle of laches is not applicable to continuing wrongs and each day a wrong continues furnishes a fresh cause of action. It was further asserted that the principle of laches is not available to perpetuate an unconstitutionality. It was also stated that existence of a live justiciable dispute is not necessary for obtaining declaratory judgments

from the Supreme Court under Article 184(1) of the Constitution. It was argued that rights and obligations of the litigants can be made crystal clear through having resort to judicial declarations even in absence of a cause of action in conventional meaning which is a pre-requisite for normal adversarial judicial proceedings.

4.	The Punjab Civil Accounts Welfare Association submitted an application claiming itself to be a necessary party to these proceedings as outcome of the proceedings was of material interest to it. It prayed for joining these proceedings as respondent.

5.	The defendant has filed a written statement giving grounds to rebut the claims and assertions of the plaintiff. It has been argued that mere difference of opinion on an issue does not elevate that issue to be a dispute within contemplation of Article 184(1) of the Constitution. It is claimed that absence of a live dispute or a justiciable cause of action converts court proceedings into efforts to find answers to moot questions. It is averred that the academic exercise to find answers to moot questions does not constitute exercise of judicial power of the state and the judiciary is not authorized to indulge into such an exercise. It is claimed that other alternate constitutional institutions e.g. Council of Common Interests, National Economic Council, National Finance Commission are available to resolve problems arising out of conflicting views of the Federation and of the Federating Units on any issue. The plaintiff has, it is alleged, not made any concrete effort to get the issues resolved through resort to these constitutional institutions. It is also argued that vires of a federal law can be challenged by any aggrieved person through proceedings under Article 199 of the Constitution before a High Court. It is submitted that a Province is a person for the purpose of invoking constitutional jurisdiction of a High Court under Article 199 of the Constitution. There is no express or implied prohibition in filing a writ petition by a Province to call in question constitutional validity of a federal law, it is argued. Having said all this, it has been submitted that the Federation does not wish to avail itself of any technical defence and is most anxious to know the views of this Court on the various provisions of the CGA Ordinance so that it should not do anything which, in the opinion of this Court, is unconstitutional.

Arguments of the defendant

6.	On merits, the defendant has made written submissions which are summarised hereinbelow.

As regards treasury functions

a.	Section 5(b) of the CGA Ordinance empowers the CGA to authorize payments and withdrawals from the Consolidated Funds and Public Accounts of the Federal and Provincial Governments against approved budgetary provisions, after pre-audited checks as Auditor General may, with the approval of the President, from time to time, prescribe. Operation and effectiveness of a federal law cannot be interfered with by a Province. The arrangements for performance of treasury functions of the Federal and Provincial Governments in Pakistan prior to promulgation of the CGA Ordinance have undergone a sea change and now these functions are necessarily required to be performed exclusively by the CGA as laid down in the CGA Ordinance.

b.	Pre-audit is part of accounting. As accounting of the Provincial and District Governments has been assigned to the CGA, therefore, the CGA has to apply pre-audited checks before authorizing disbursements from the Provincial Consolidated Fund and the District Funds. No other body or person has any authority of law to do so.

c. Pre-audit by the CGA does not offend the provincial autonomy or encroach upon the exclusive provincial jurisdiction under Article 119 of the Constitution; it is assistance provided by the Federation to the Provinces to maintain financial discipline and to ensure that laws / rules / procedures and instructions relating to financial management and treasury operations are implemented in letter and spirit. Bulk of the receipts of the Provincial Consolidated Fund is provided by the Federation from the Federal Consolidated Fund. The Federation is justified in entrusting pre-audit of operations of the Provincial Consolidated Fund to the CGA with a view to ensure that public funds are utilized for public welfare with economy, efficiency and effectiveness.

d. The CGA is not authorized to generate claims for drawl of money from the Provincial Consolidated Fund or Public Account of the Province or to draw cash from the SBP or from any of the agents of the SBP. These are the provincial employees who prepare claims for withdrawal of money from the Provincial Consolidated Fund or Public Account of the Province and draw cash from the Bank in accordance with the authorizations given by the CGA after pre-audit. In this view of the matter, the CGA only assists the plaintiff through applying pre-audit checks and authorizing payments through issuance of pre-audit cheques.

As regards accounting functions

a. In view of Articles 168,169,170 and 171 of the Constitution read with item 58 of Federal Legislative List, the CGA Ordinance and the AG Ordinance, audit and accounts are federal subjects and a Province has no jurisdiction in the matter of its accounts and audit. Accounts means written records of all transactions having financial implication.

b. Local governments, autonomous bodies and all other entities of the Province do fall within the definition of "Province" as used in Article 169 of the Constitution; hence, it is perfectly constitutional to assign the federal function of keeping and maintaining accounts of the District Governments to the CGA through a federal law.

c. Accounts of all entities of the Province are required to be maintained by the CGA. After promulgation of the CGA Ordinance, Province and its entities are not authorized to maintain their accounts through their own administrative machinery. The existing provincial employees working in the DAOs are now under the administrative control of the CGA with protection of their terms and conditions of service under Section 10 of the CGA Ordinance. Same is the case of other provincial employees keeping and maintaining accounts of bodies and authorities of the Province including local governments. All provincial laws making arrangements of keeping and maintaining accounts of the provincial entities by provincial employees are of no legal effect being in contravention of the CGA Ordinance as Article 143 of the Constitution lays down that in case of inconsistency between a Federal and a Provincial law, the Federal law shall prevail to the extent of the inconsistency.

d. Keeping and maintaining accounts of the Federation and of the Federating units by a single federal entity is in national interest and is necessary for national integration and for having a wholesome picture of the national economy and financial performance of all tiers of government in the country.

e. Section 6 (3) of the CGA Ordinance makes the CGA administrative head of all accounting organizations subordinate to him with full authority for transfer and posting within his organization. The CGA will not be in a position to effectually perform duties assigned to him under the CGA Ordinance if administrative control of the provincial accounting organizations is denied to him.

As regards reimbursement of the cost incurred by the plaintiff on performance of treasury functions of the defendant

a. It is not disputed that the defendant is performing a prescribed part of treasury functions of the plaintiff through the AG, Punjab at Lahore since 1935. Coverage of performance of these functions was extended to the whole of the Province through the DAOs Scheme. At present, subordinates of the AG, Punjab are posted in each DAO in the Punjab. Expenditure on remuneration of the federal employees in the office of the AG, Punjab and the DAOs is borne by the defendant. The defendant has, thus, compensated the plaintiff for the extra expenditure incurred by it in performance of federal treasury functions through incurring expenditure on performance of provincial treasury functions by the federal employees.

b. The defendant has incurred an expenditure of Rs. 5,533.5 Million on PIFRA ('Project to Improve Financial Reporting and Auditing') through raising a loan mainly from the World Bank. This Project is for the benefit of the plaintiff also but the loan is repayable by the defendant alone. The infrastructure built under the Project is being used by the plaintiff free of cost. In this way, the defendant has paid to the plaintiff more than what may be payable on account of performance of federal treasury functions by the provincial machinery in the Punjab.

As regards separation of accounting and auditing functions

a. Notwithstanding promulgation of the CGA and the AG Ordinances, the overall superintendence and control of the Auditor General in all matters relating to audit and accounts remains intact. It is the Auditor General who has been conceived as a constitutional office to deal with audit and accounts. No sub-constitutional measure can takeaway jurisdiction of the Auditor General to have control over audit as well as accounts. The separation of audit and accounts is to the extent specified in the CGA Ordinance i.e. the CGA has authority of posting / transfer within organizations subordinate to him and not beyond this. Only an Act of the Parliament can completely effect the separation of audit and accounts. Validation of the CGA and the AG Ordinances by the Parliament through Article 270 AA of the Constitution only cures the defect in the manner in which these pieces of legislation were enacted; these Ordinances cannot be elevated to the status of the Acts of the Parliament. It is, therefore, incorrect to assume that with the promulgation of the two Ordinance an absolute or irreversible separation has been effected between audit and accounts.

b. The Auditor General of Pakistan, through a Notification No. 114/DG (A)/9-2/97 dated 16.07.2001 notified the following in the Gazette of Pakistan:

> "S.R.O, (1)/2001. WHEREAS it is expedient to separate accounting functions for ensuring independence of audit;
> NOW, THEREORE, in pursuance of section 3 of the Controller General of Accounts (Appointment, Functions and Powers) Ordinance, 2001 (XXIV of 2001), the Auditor General of Pakistan is pleased to transfer all accounting functions in respect of accounts of the Federation and the Provinces to the Controller General of Accounts who shall prepare and maintain such accounts and submit the same to the Auditor General for appropriate action in terms of Article 171 of the Constitution of the Islamic Republic of Pakistan and section 7 of the Auditor-General' s (Functions, Powers and Terms and Conditions of Service) Ordinance, 2001 (XXIII of 2001)."

The above Notification transfers only the function of preparation and maintenance of accounts to the CGA; this Notification does not transfer the administration and control of the PA&AS to the CGA. The separation of audit from accounts only means keeping of accounts by the CGA and conduct of audit by the Auditor General; it does not imply air-tight compartmentalization of the PA&AS into audit and accounts. Administration of the PA&AS by the Auditor General is, therefore, not against the spirit of separation of audit and accounts. In line with this reasoning, the Notification of 16.07.2001 transfers the function of maintenance of accounts to the CGA and nothing more.

c. Efforts to provide for coordination between audit and accounts by the Auditor General do not clash with the idea of separation of audit and accounts. The Auditor General constituted a high level Forum for Inter-Functional Audit and Accounts Coordination (FIFAAC) under his patronage through a letter bearing No. 494/49-AR-I/C:/2001 dated 27.12.2001 with the following terms of reference:

   i. To resolve any issue(s) relating to implementation of the Auditor General's and Controller General of Accounts Ordinances, 2001 in terms of identified linkages: resolution of audit observations, setting up and evaluation of internal controls, timings in attestation exercise etc.
   ii. To resolve any issues relating to the audit and accounts linkages in the devolution set-up.
   iii. To attend to any unresolved issues in the audit and accounts components of PIFRA specially in terms of linkages.
   iv. To resolve any HRM issues between the two functions.
   v. To take up any matter requiring high level policy intervention.
   vi. and intervention between the two institutions on matters of mutual interest.

The following officers were made members of the aforesaid Forum:
   1. Deputy Auditor General (Senior)
   2. Controller General of Accounts.
   3. Deputy Auditor General (GA.-I)
   4. Accountant General Punjab
   5. Deputy Auditor General AP&M

6. PD PIFRA

The above and any other bodies to put in place institutional mechanisms to ensure useful coordination between audit and accounts do not clash with the in-principle policy decision of separation of audit and accounts.

d. On 14.03.2013, the Finance Division of the Federal Government issued the following Order:

"F.No.7(2)-Policy-I/2002. WHEREAS the Establishment Division is undertaking a detailed exercise for separating the cadres of Accounts and Audit in accordance with the Auditor-General's (Functions, Terms and Conditions of Service) Ordinance, 2001 (XXIII of 2001) and the Controller-General of Accounts (Appointment, Functions and Powers) Ordinance, 2001 (XXIV of 200l);

AND WHEREAS, Auditor General of Pakistan being the administrative head of the Audit and Accounts Group shall not laterally intervene into transfer and posting in any office under the control of the Controller General of Accounts;

AND WHEREAS it is imperative to enforce functional authority of the Federal Government (Ministry of Finance) in relation to Controller General of Accounts' office and offices working under him and the authority of the Controller General of Accounts as stipulated in sub-section (3) of section 6 of the Controller-General of Accounts (Appointment, Functions and Powers) Ordinance, 2001 (XXIV of 200l);

NOW, THEREFORE, in exercise of the powers conferred by the Controller-General of Accounts (Appointment, Functions and Powers) Ordinance, 2001 (XXIV of 200l) and all other powers enabling the Federal Government in this regard, it is notified that the Controller General of Accounts shall be the administrative head of the offices subordinate to him with full authority for transfer and posting within his organization."

The above order of the Finance Division speaks of non-interference of the Auditor General in postings / transfers within offices subordinate to the Controller General of Accounts. Till such time the PA&AS is separated into audit and accounts, its administrative control vests in the Auditor General. Continued exercise of administrative control over the PA&AS by the Auditor General is legal during the transition leading to complete separation of audit and accounts through an Act of the Parliament.

e. The Hon'ble Lahore High Court, Lahore, in its judgment reported as Rana Fazal-e-Haq Vs. Director General of Accounts (PLD 2003 Lah 726) has only ruled in favour of administrative control of the CGA over the accounting organizations but has not made any declaration against administrative control of the Auditor General over the PA&AS.

As regards holding of posts in connection with affairs of the Province by federal employees

a. Rule 2.14 (a) of the Punjab Departmental Financial Rules empowers the Director, Audit & Accounts (Works) to post a Divisional Accountant in works divisions of the Province. This rule is still in force and until the said Rule is amended or substituted, no objection can be raised over exercise of lawful powers of the Director, Audit & Accounts (Works) regarding postings of the Divisional Accountants.

b. It is correct that the Manual of Standing Orders of the Auditor General of Pakistan published in 2017 does not provide for the Divisional Accountants' Organization but Chapter VII of the previous edition of the Manual of Standing Orders specifically dealt with the Divisional Accountants' Organization on matters including recruitment, confirmation, promotion, selection grade, training, departmental examination, emergency cadre, performance evaluation reports and posting / transfer. Even though the Manual of Standing Orders of 2017 does not contain anything on the subject and there is no other legal instrument providing for the Divisional Accountants' Organization, yet the Organization continues to exist and perform its duties and, therefore, deserves to be retained in public interest.

c. Post of Divisional Accountant or Divisional Accounts Officer is a post in connection with affairs of the Province. Article 147 of the Constitution authorizes the Province to entrust its functions to officers of the Federal Government. The Director General Accounts Works is a federal officer. The function of posting of the Divisional Accountants or Divisional Accounts Officers has been assigned to him by the Province under rules framed in terms of Article 119 of the Constitution. Thus, requirements of Article 147 of the Constitution stand fulfilled.

d. As the Divisional Accountants' Organization is under control and superintendence of the Federation, therefore, the Federation has lawful competence to re-designate or upgrade posts of the Divisional Accountants notwithstanding the fact that the financial effect of this measure has necessarily to be borne by the Province. Orders of the Federal Government regarding up-gradation of the post of the Divisional Accountant from BS. 16 to BS. 17 and its re-designation as the Divisional Accounts Officer have been implemented by the Province which amounts to ratification of the aforesaid re-designation and upgradation. Vested rights created in consequence of the upgradation and its implementation by the Province makes the matter a past and closed transaction leaving no room for its reopening at this belated stage.

e. Rule 2(f) of the Punjab Treasury Rules reads as follows:

> "Accountant-General" / "Director-General, Audit & Accounts (Works)" mean the head of the office of audit and accounts subordinate to the Auditor General of Pakistan, who keeps the accounts of the Province or of Federation and exercises audit functions in relation to those accounts on behalf of the Auditor-General of Pakistan;".

The DGAW within the above definition and, therefore, is entitled to exercise powers vested in him vide Rule 2.14 (a) of the Punjab Departmental Financial Rules. It is unnecessary hair-splitting to object to powers of the DGAW on the ground of change in designation.

f. It is not necessary to regulate the Divisional Accounts Officers through rules to be framed under Section 25 (1) of the Civil Servants Act, 1973 (Act No. LXXI of 1973) as Chapter VII of the Manual of Standing Orders of the Auditor General is saved and protected under Section 25(2) of the Act ibid.

g. Under Section 6 (2) (d) of the CGA Ordinance, departmental accounting organizations are under the control of the CGA. Section 6(3) of the CGA Ordinance makes the CGA administrative head of all the offices subordinate to him with full authority for transfer and posting within his organization. Section 9 of the CGA Ordinance provides as under:

> "9. Delegation of powers. -- The Controller General may, by general or special order, direct that all or any of his powers under this Ordinance shall, under such conditions, if any, as may be specified, be exercisable by any officer or officers of his organization."

The DGAW is subordinate to the CGA and he can exercise powers of the CGA in the matter of postings / transfers of the Divisional Accounts Officers.

7. Heard. Record perused.

Questions requiring adjudication

8. Facts and circumstances of the instant plaint raise the following questions for our adjudication:

1. Whether this plaint is maintainable under Article 184(1) of the Constitution and whether private persons are eligible to become parties to proceedings under Article 184(1) of the Constitution and whether private persons are competent to invoke jurisdiction of a High Court under Article 199 of the Constitution on an issue which is capable of being litigated by a Government as a dispute between the Governments before the Supreme Court under Article 184(1) of the Constitution?

2. Whether Section 5 (b) of the CGA Ordinance, to the extent it assigns treasury functions of the Provinces to the CGA, is in violation of Article 119 of the Constitution or whether the President of Pakistan or the Auditor General are constitutionally empowered to prescribe pre-audit checks in respect of payments from the Provincial Consolidated Fund and Public Account of the Province?

3. Whether accounting functions of the Provinces can be assigned to a federal functionary other than the Auditor General of Pakistan?

4. Whether the Province is entitled to receive amount spent by it on performance of treasury functions of the Federation?

5. Whether administration of the PA&AS as a joint audit and accounts service by the Auditor General is lawful after statutory separation of accounting and auditing functions?

6. Whether the Federation has lawful authority to post or depute federal employees on posts in connection with affairs of the Provinces?

9. The paragraphs that follow contain our answers to the aforesaid questions and the reasons leading to the answers given.

Question # 1

Whether this plaint is maintainable under Article 184(1) of the Constitution and whether private persons are eligible to

become parties to proceedings under Article 184(1) of the Constitution and whether private persons are competent to invoke jurisdiction of a High Court under Article 199 of the Constitution on an issue which is capable of being litigated by a Government as a dispute between the Governments before the Supreme Court under Article 184(1) of the Constitution?

10.   Federalism may be integrative or devolutionary. Integrative federalism is a political order which, over time, aims at stronger unity among previously independent political communities. Devolutionary federalism, on the other hand, attempts at a redistribution of powers of a previously unitary state. A perusal of the report of the Joint Committee on Indian Constitutional Reform (Session 1933-1934), on the basis of which the Government of India Act, 1935 was drafted, indicates that federal system introduced through the said Act was devolutionary; this system substituted the then existing unitary form of government. Paragraph 153 of Volume-I, Part-I of the report of the aforesaid Committee clarifies this point in these words:

> "It is clear that, in any new constitution in which autonomous provinces are to be united under the Crown, not only can the provinces no longer derive their powers and authority by devolution by the Central Government, but the Central Government cannot continue to be an agent of the Secretary of State. Both must derive their powers and authority from a direct grant by the Crown. The legal basis of a reconstituted Government of India must be, first, the resumption into the hands of the Crown of all rights, authority and jurisdiction in and over the territories of British India, whether they are at present vested in the Secretary of State, the Governor-General in Council or the Provincial Governments and Administrations; and second, their redistribution in such manner as the Act may prescribe between the Central Government on the one hand and the Provinces on the other. A Federation of which the British Indian Provinces are the constituent units will thereby be brought into existence."

11.   The foundation of the devolutionary federalism introduced through the Government of India Act, 1935 was distribution of legislative powers between the Federation and the Federating Units. Paragraph 229 of Volume-I, Part-I of the report of the above-referred Committee vividly explains this principle in these words:

> "229. We have already explained that the general plan of the White Paper, which we endorse, is to enumerate in two lists the subjects in relation to which the Federation and the Provinces respectively will have an exclusive legislative jurisdiction and to enumerate in a third list the subjects in relation to which the Federal and each Provincial Legislature will possess concurrent legislative powers the powers of a Provincial Legislature in relation to the subjects in this list extending, of course, only to the territory of the Province. The result of the statutory allocation of exclusive powers will be to change fundamentally the existing legislative relations between the Centre and the Provinces. At present the Central Legislature has the legal power to legislate on any subject, even though it be classified by rules under the Government of India Act as a Provincial subject, and a Provincial Legislature can similarly legislate for its own territory on any subject, even though it be classified as a Central subject for the Act of each Indian Legislature, Central or Provincial, requires the assent of the Governor-General and that assent having been given, "section 84 (3),

of the Government of India Act provides that "the validity of any Act of the Indian Legislature or any local Legislature shall not be open to question in any legal proceedings on the ground that the Act affects a Provincial subject or a Central subject as the case may be." If our recommendations are adopted, an enactment regulating a matter included in the exclusively Provincial List will hereafter be valid only if it is passed by a Provincial Legislature, and an enactment regulating a matter included in the exclusively Federal List will be valid only if it is passed by the Federal Legislature; and to the extent to which either Legislature invades the province of the other, its enactment will be ultra vires and void. It follows that it will be for the Courts to determine whether or not in a given enactment, the Legislature has transgressed the boundaries set for it by the exclusive List, federal or provincial, as the case may be. The questions which may arise as to the validity of legislation in the concurrent field are more complicated and we shall discuss them in later; but here also, disputes as to the validity of legislation will in the last resort rest with the Courts."

12.   A system which distributes legislative powers of the state between the Federation and the Federating Units is bound to cause disputes with regard to legislative competence and other matters. This apprehension was expressed by the Joint Committee on Indian Constitutional Reform (Session 1933-1934) at paragraph 230 of Volume-I, Part-I of its report in the following words:

"230. But we do not disguise the fact that these proposals would open the door of litigation of a kind which has hitherto been almost unknown in India; nor we have forgotten that the Statutory Commission expressed the hope that the provisions of the existing Act which we have mentioned above would be preserved. As we shall explain, our recommendations would have the effect of preserving, in the limited sphere of the concurrent field, the main features of the existing system; but we feel no doubt that the White Paper correctly insists upon a statutory allocation of exclusive jurisdictions to the Centre and the Provinces respectively as the only possible foundation for the Provincial Autonomy which we contemplate. We are fully sensible of the immense practical advantages of the present system and of the uncertainties and litigation which have followed elsewhere from a statutory delimitation of competing jurisdictions; but we are satisfied that a relationship between the Centre and the Provinces, in which each depends in the last resort for the scope of its legislative jurisdiction on the decision of the Central Executive as represented by the Governor General, would form no tolerable basis for an enduring Constitution and would be inconsistent with the whole conception of the autonomous Provinces."

13.   Paragraph 322 of the report of the Joint Committee on Indian Constitutional Reform (Session 1933-34), Vol. 1, Part II reads as follows:

"A Federal Court is an essential element in a Federal Constitution. It is at once the interpreter and guardian of the Constitution and a tribunal for the determination of disputes between the constituent units of the Federation. The establishment of a Federal Court is part of the White Paper scheme, and we approve generally the proposals with regard to it. We have, however, certain comments to make upon them, which we set out below."

14.   The aforesaid Committee proposed the following, at paragraph 324 of its report, to deal with legal resolution of disputes between the Federation and the Federating Units or between the Federating Units:

"324.   It is proposed that the Federal Court shall have an original jurisdiction in

(i)   any matter involving interpretation of the Constitution Act or determination of any rights or obligations arising thereunder, where the parties to the dispute are (a) the Federation and either a Province or a State, or (b) two Provinces or two States or a Province or a State;

(ii)   any matter involving the interpretation of, or arising under, any agreement entered into after the commencement of the Constitution Act between the Federation and a Federal Unit or between Federal Units, unless the agreement otherwise provides.

The jurisdiction is to be an exclusive one, and in our opinion rightly so, since it would be altogether inappropriate if proceedings could be taken by one Unit of the Federation against another in the Courts of either of them. For that reason, we think that, where the parties are Units of the Federation or Federation itself, the jurisdiction ought to include not only the interpretation of the Constitution Act, but also the interpretation of federal laws, by which we mean any laws enacted by the Federal Legislature."

15.   Accepting proposals of the aforesaid Joint Parliamentary Committee, the British Parliament enacted the Government of India Act, 1935 Section 204 whereof provided as follows:

"(1)   Subject to the provisions of this Act, the Federal Court shall, to the exclusion of any other court, have an original jurisdiction in any dispute between any of the following parties, that is to say, the Federation, any of the Provinces if and in so far as the dispute involves any question (whether of law or fact) on which the existence or extent of a legal right depends; provided that the said jurisdiction shall not extend to—

(a)   a dispute to which a State is a party, unless the dispute-

(i)   concerns the interpretation of this Act or of an Order in Council made thereunder, or of the legislative or executive authority vested in the Federation by virtue of the Instrument of Accession of that State; or

(ii)   arises under an agreement made under Part VI of this Act in relation to the administration in that State of a law of the Federal Legislature or otherwise concerns some matter with respect to which the Federal Legislature has power to make laws for that State; or

(iii)   arises under an agreement made after the establishment of the Federation, with the approval of His Majesty's Representative for the exercise of the functions of the Crown in its relations with Indian States, between that State and the Federation or a Province, being an agreement which expressly provides that the said jurisdiction shall extend to such a dispute;

    (b)   A dispute arising under any agreement which expressly provides that the said jurisdiction shall not extend to such a dispute.

(2)   The Federal Court in the exercise of its original jurisdiction shall not pronounce any judgment other than declaratory judgment."

16.   Different Constitutions of Pakistan dealt with the question of adjudication of disputes between the Federation and the Federating Units or between the Federating Units in the following words:

Article 129 of the Constitution of 1956

(1)   Any dispute between the Federal Government and one or both Provincial Governments, or between the two Provincial Governments, which under the law of the Constitution is not within the jurisdiction of the Supreme Court, may be referred by any of the Governments involved in the dispute to the Chief Justice of Pakistan, who shall appoint a tribunal to settle the dispute.

(2)   Subject to the provisions of any Act of Parliament, the practice and procedure of any such tribunal, including the fees to be charged and the award of costs, shall be determined by rules made by the Supreme Court and approved by the President.

(3)   The report of the tribunal shall be forwarded to the Chief Justice, who shall determine whether the purpose for which the tribunal was appointed has been carried out, and shall return the report to the tribunal for re-consideration if he is of opinion that the purpose has not been carried out; and when the report is in order the Chief Justice shall forward the report to the President who shall make such order as may be necessary to give effect to the report.

(4)   Effect shall be given in a Province to any order made under this Article by the President, and any Act of the Provincial Legislature which is repugnant to the order shall, to the extent of the repugnancy, be void.

(5)   An order by the President under this Article may be varied by the President in accordance with an agreement made by the parties concerned."

Article 156 of the Constitution of 1956

(1)   Subject to the provisions of the Constitution, the Supreme Court shall, to the exclusion of any other court, have original jurisdiction in any dispute between--

    (a)   The Federal Government and the Government of one or both Provinces; or

    (b)   The Federal Government and the Government of a Province on the one side, and the Government of the other Province on the other; or

    (c)   The Governments of the Provinces, if and in so far as the dispute involves –

        (i)   any question, whether of law or of fact, on which the existence or extent of a legal right depends; or

        (ii)   any question as to the interpretation of the Constitution.

(2)   The Supreme Court in the exercise of its original jurisdiction shall not pronounce any judgment other than a declaratory judgment.

Article 57 of the Constitution of 1962

(1)   The Supreme Court shall, to the exclusion of every other court, have original jurisdiction in any dispute between one of the Governments and one or both of the other Governments.

(2)   In the exercise of the jurisdiction conferred on it by this article, the Supreme Court shall pronounce declaratory judgments only.

(3)   In this article, "the Governments" means the Central Government and the Provincial Governments."

Article 185 of the interim Constitution of 1972

(1)   The Supreme Court shall, to the exclusion of every other court, have original jurisdiction in any dispute between any two or more Governments.

(2)   In the exercise of the jurisdiction conferred on it by this Article, the Supreme Court shall pronounce declaratory judgments only.

(3)   In this Article, "Governments" means the Federal Government and the Provincial Governments."

Article 184 of the Constriction of 1973

(1)   The Supreme Court shall, to the exclusion of every other court, have original jurisdiction in any dispute between any two or more Governments.
       Explanation:-In this clause, "Governments" means the Federal Government and the Provincial Governments.

(2)   In the exercise of the jurisdiction conferred on it by clause (1), the Supreme Court shall pronounce declaratory judgments only.

(3)   Without prejudice to the provisions of Article 199, the Supreme Court shall, if it considers that a question of public importance with reference to the enforcement of any of the Fundamental Rights conferred by Chapter I of Part II is involved have the power to make an order of the nature mentioned in the said Article.

17.   Article 131 of the Constitution of India (as amended by the Constitution (7th Amendment) Act, 1956), reproduced below to serve as ready reference, deals with adjudication of disputes between the Governments: -

"**131. Original jurisdiction of the Supreme Court.** – Subject to the provisions of this Constitution, the Supreme Court shall, to the exclusion of any other court, have original jurisdiction in any dispute –

(a) between the Government of India and one or more States; or

(b) between the Government of India and any State or States on one side and one or more other States on the other; or

(c) between two or more States

if and in so far as the dispute involves any question (whether of law or fact) on which the existence or extent of a legal right depends:

Provided that the said jurisdiction shall not extend to a dispute arising out of any treaty, agreement, covenant, engagement, sanad or other similar instrument which, having been entered into or executed before the commencement of this Constitution, continues in operation after such commencement, or which provides, that the said jurisdiction shall not extend to such a dispute.".

18.   Before proceeding further, we may understand what a dispute is and how its existence is proved.

19.   West's Encyclopedia of American Law, edition 2 (https://legal-dictionary.thefreedictionary.com/Dispute) defines 'dispute' in these words:

> "A conflict or controversy; a conflict of claims or rights; an assertion of a right, claim, or demand on one side, met by contrary claims or allegations on the other. The subject of litigation; the matter for which a suit is brought and upon which issue is joined, and in relation to which jurors are called and witnesses examined. A labor dispute is any disagreement between an employer and his or her employees concerning anything job-related, such as tenure, hours, wages, fringe benefits, and employment conditions."

20.   Black's Law Dictionary, 8th Edition, defines dispute as a controversy, especially one that has given rise to a particular lawsuit. Hon'ble Lahore High Court, Lahore, in a case reported as Kh. Muhammad Sharif Vs. Federation of Pakistan (1989 CLC 1387) has declared that:

> "Word 'dispute' in Article 184 is wide enough to include all the disputes, jurisdictional, administrative and fiscal".

21.   The Permanent Court of International Justice (PCIJ) gave the following broad definition of dispute in Mavrommatis Palestine Concessions, Judgment No. 2, 1924, P.C.I.J., Series A, No. 2, p. 11:

> "A dispute is a disagreement on a point of law or fact, a conflict of legal views or of interests between two persons."

22.   A dispute is also referred to as present divergence of interests and opposition of legal views. The question of existence or non-existence of a dispute has to be resolved as a preliminary jurisdictional question as jurisdiction of the Supreme Court under Article 184(1) of the Constitution depends upon a positive finding with regard to existence of a dispute between the parties specified in the Article 184(1). Existence of a dispute is a condition-precedent for invoking original jurisdiction under Article 184(1).

23.   The International Court of Justice held in South West Africa, Preliminary Objections, Judgment, I.C.J. Reports 1962, p. 328 that:

> "In other words, it is not sufficient for one party to a contentious case to assert that a dispute exists with the other party. A mere assertion is not sufficient to prove the existence of a dispute any more than a mere denial of the existence of the dispute proves its nonexistence. Nor is it adequate to show that the interests of the two parties to such a case are in conflict. It must be shown that the claim of one party is positively opposed by the other."

24.   Existence of a dispute cannot be denied on the ground that a party has failed to respond to assertions of the other party or has accepted its arguments and has only failed to provide the remedy or relief demanded by the other party. Christoph Schreuer has observed in his treatise on "What is a Legal Dispute?" (www.univie.ac.at › intlaw) that:

> "But an acknowledgement of the other side's position unaccompanied by a remedy or even a simple failure to respond will not exclude the existence of a dispute. The decisive criterion for the existence of a dispute is not an explicit denial of the other party's position but a failure to accede to its demands."

25.   A dispute can be adjudicated by a court of law only if it is a legal dispute. Even where the existence of a dispute is admitted, its legal nature may be contested as courts are not authorized to deal with political disputes or questions of policy. Courts can

adjudicate upon only the legal disputes. http://www.businessdictionary.com/definition/legal-dispute.html defines legal dispute in the following words:

> "Disagreement over the existence of a legal duty or right, or over the extent and kind of compensation that may be claimed by the injured party for a breach of such duty or right."

26.   As to the meaning of the expression "legal right", we may gainfully consult Salmond, Jurisprudence, 10th Ed, page 230 which defines legal right as an interest recognised and protected by a rule of legal justice – an interest, the violation of which would be a legal wrong done to him whose interest it is, and respect for which is a legal duty. The Federal Court of India defined this expression in a case reported as U.P. Vs. G. G. in Council (AIR 1939 FC 58) in these words:

> "The term "legal right", used in section 204, obviously means a right recognised by law and capable of being enforced by the power of a State, but not necessarily in a court of law. It is a right of an authority recognised and protected by a rule of law, a violation of which would be a legal wrong to his interest and respect for which is a legal duty, even though no action may actually lie. The only ingredients seem to be a legal recognition and a legal protection."

27.   It is not necessary that the Government coming to the court must have a legal right vested in itself. It is sufficient if it denies the legal right asserted by the opposite party – which also must be a Government. [State of Rajasthan Vs. Union of India, (1977) 3 SCC 592, 634, 635 (Beg CJ), 637-642, (Chandrachud, J) 647 – 649, (Bhagwati & Gupta JJ); AIR 1977 SC 361].

28.   The fact that a legal question also has political aspects is not sufficient to deprive it of its character as a legal question. Political nature of the motives which may be said to have inspired a party to institute a plaint or the potential political implications of the judgment are of no relevance if the dispute sought to be adjudicated upon is a legal one. The Hon'ble Supreme Court of India held in State of Rajasthan Vs. Union of India (AIR 1977 SC 1361) and State of Karnataka Vs. Union of India (AIR 1978 SC 68) that if a right arising under the Constitution is at issue, then article 131 can be invoked, even if the subject matter might have provoked political controversy. On the other hand, it was held by the Hon'ble Supreme Court of India in State of Bihar Vs. Union of India (AIR 1970 SC 1446) that disputes which do not involve any questions of legal right, e.g. where the disputes have an exclusively political dimension, are not covered by article 131. It is also well-established in international law that whatever its political aspects, the Court cannot refuse to admit the legal character of a question which invites it to discharge an essentially judicial task, namely, an assessment of the legality of the possible conduct of States with regard to the obligations imposed upon them by international law. Reliance in this regard is placed on the dictum of law laid down by the International Court of Justice in cases reported as Advisory Opinion, 1948, I.C.J. Reports 1947 1948, pp. 61 62; Advisory Opinion, I.C.J. Reports 1950, pp. 6 7; Advisory Opinion, I.C.J. Reports 1962, p. 155 and I.C.J. Reports 1996 (I), p. 234, para. 13.

29.   Article 184(1) of the Constitution does not require that exchange of opposing legal opinions between the parties specified in that Article or observance of a particular procedure of exchange of these opinions must precede invoking of the jurisdiction of the Supreme Court. What is of essence in proving existence of a dispute is the existence of conflicting views on questions of law or fact or conduct of the parties. Mere conduct of a party is also sufficient to prove existence of a dispute. When we say that conduct of a party can constitute a dispute, we mean to say that prior communication of opposing views on a legal dispute or even awareness of one party of the opposite views of the other party is not a condition-precedent to institute a plaint under Article 184(1) of the Constitution. It was, perhaps, for this reason that it was held by the Hon'ble Supreme Court of India in State of

Seraikella Vs. Union of India and another (1951 AIR 253) that requirement of service of a notice under Section 80 of the Code of Civil Procedure would not be attracted in case of invoking original jurisdiction of the Supreme Court for adjudication of disputes between the Governments. If communication(s) on questions of law or fact is on record prior to institution of proceedings under Article 184(1) of the Constitution and relief demanded by one party is denied or withheld by the other party, there will absolutely be no dispute regarding existence of a dispute within the meaning of Article 184(1) of the Constitution.

30.   The Hon'ble Supreme Court of India has held in State of Bihar Vs. Union of India (AIR 1970 SC 1446) that legal right which is the subject of dispute must arise in the context of the Constitution and the Federalism it sets up. It was held by the Hon'ble Supreme Court of India in State of Karnataka Vs. Union of India (AIR 1978 SC 68) that:

> "It has to be remembered that Article 131 is traceable to Section 204 of the Government of India Act. The jurisdiction conferred by it, thus, originated in what was part of the federal structure set up by the Government of India Act, 1935. It is a remnant of the federalism found in that Act. It should, therefore, be widely and generously interpreted for that reason too so as to advance the intended remedy. It can be invoked, in my opinion, whenever a State and other States or the Union differ on a question of interpretation of the Constitution so that a decision of it will affect the scope or exercise of governmental powers which are attributes of a State. It makes no difference to the maintainability of the action if the powers of the State, which are Executive, Legislative, and Judicial, are exercised through particular individuals as they necessarily must be. It is true that a criminal act committed by a Minister is no part of his official duties. But, if any of the organs of the State claim exclusive power to take cognizance of it, the State, as such, becomes interested in the dispute about the legal competence or extent of powers of one of its organs which may emerge."

31.   It was further observed by the Hon'ble Supreme Court of India in Union of India Vs. State of Rajasthan (AIR 1984 SC 1675) that:

> "On a careful consideration of the whole matter in the light of the decisions of this Court referred to above, we feel that Article 131 of the Constitution is attracted only when a dispute arises between or amongst the States and the Union in the context of the constitutional relationship that exists between them and the powers, rights, duties, immunities, liabilities, disabilities etc. flowing therefrom. Any dispute which may arise between a State in the capacity of an employer in a factory, a manufacturer of goods subject to excise duty, a holder of a permit to run a stage carriage, a trader or businessman carrying on business not incidental to the ordinary functions of Government, a consumer of railway services etc. like any other private party on the one hand and the Union of India on the other cannot be construed as a dispute arising between the State and the Union in discharge of their respective executive powers attracting Article 131 of the Constitution. It could never have been the intention of the framers of the Constitution that any ordinary dispute of this nature would have to be decided exclusively by the Supreme Court."

32.   Article 184(1) of the Constitution specifies the subject-matter and parties to proceedings falling within its exclusive original jurisdiction. The parties competent to invoke original jurisdiction of the Hon'ble Supreme Court are the Federal Government and the Provincial Governments. In view of definition of the Federal Government given by the Hon'ble Supreme Court of Pakistan in the Mustafa Impex case (PLD 2016 SC 808), any

349

matter which affects or is likely to affect working of a Government in accordance with the Constitution may legitimately be a subject-matter of proceedings under Article 184(1) of the Constitution. Federation is represented by the Federal Government and a Province is represented by the Provincial Government. In accordance with Article 174 of the Constitution, the Federation and the Provinces are competent to sue and be sued. These are the only competent parties under Article 184(1) of the Constitution. In Indian jurisdiction, it has been held in State of Bihar Vs. Union of India (AIR 1970 SC 1446), State of Rajasthan & Ors. etc. Vs. Union of India & Ors. [(1977) 3 SCC 592], State of Karnataka Vs. Union of India & Anr. [(1977) 4 SCC 608] and Union of India v. State of Rajasthan (AIR 1984 SC 1675) that Article 131 of the Constitution of India is inapplicable if any of the parties is other than the Government of India or of a State. The declaration of the Hon'ble Supreme Court of India in State of Bihar Vs. Union of India (AIR 1970 SC 1446) to the effect that Article 131 of the Constitution does not apply, if the other party is a public sector corporation, is per incuriam as a corporation is nothing more than an executive arm of the Government and cannot be viewed as an entity not forming part of the Government.

33.   As regards the subject-matter of disputes between the Governments falling within exclusive jurisdiction of the Hon'ble Supreme Court of Pakistan under Article 184(1) of the Constitution, it may relate mainly to constitutional relationship that exists between the Governments and the powers, rights, duties, immunities, liabilities, disabilities etc. flowing therefrom. It was held by the Hon'ble Supreme Court of India in Union of India Vs. State of Rajasthan (AIR 1984 SC 1675) that disputes exclusively pertaining to ordinary business or commercial transactions are outside article 131. Pakistan is governed by a written Constitution which provides for trichotomy of powers with distribution of legislative powers between the Federation and the Provinces. Legislative and executive powers are co-extensive. If the Federation or a Province has no legislative power on a subject, it lacks executive power to the extent of lack of legislative power. Exercise of legislative power is constitutional only if the enactment:

> (a) is within the legislative competence of the legislature making it;
> (b) does not contravene any of the fundamental rights guaranteed by the Constitution; and
> (c) is not against any provision of the Constitution.

34.   Viewed in the above context, an indicative list of subject-matter of the disputes to be adjudicated by the Hon'ble Supreme Court of Pakistan under Article 184(1) may be as follows:

> (a) Whether a particular enactment or any part thereof falls within the legislative competence of the enacting legislature or not? (Article 141, 142 and 144 of the Constitution).

> (b) Whether a particular enactment or any part thereof hurts the Federation or a Province and is void for being inconsistent with the fundamental rights or any provision of the Constitution or not?

> (c) Whether restrictions imposed on inter-provincial trade or discrimination in the matter of imposition of taxes is sustainable under Article 151 of the Constitution or not?

> (d) Whether federal enactments in respect of services of a Province or posts in connection with affairs of a Province are valid in presence of Article 240 of the Constitution or not?

> (e) Whether a Federal or Provincial law can discriminate in the matter of having residence in or acquisition of property situated in or carrying on of business in territorial jurisdiction of the Federation or of a Province on the basis of domicile of a particular area or not?

(f) Whether, in presence of Article 27 of the Constitution, residence or place of birth can be used to discriminate in the matter of appointments in the Service of Pakistan or not?

(g) Matters relating to taxation of income or property of a Government by another Government under Article 163, 165 or 165-A of the Constitution.

(h) Matters relating to grants by one Government to another under Article 164 of the Constitution including matching grants.

(i) Matters relating to the National Finance Commission, National Economic Council, Council of Common Interests etc. except complaints to the Council of Common Interests relating to water supplies.

(j) Matters relating to net proceeds of the Federal duty of excise on natural gas and oil levied and collected by the Federal Government and other related matters under Article 161 (1) of the Constitution.

(k) Matters relating to net hydel profits under Article 161(2) of the Constitution.

(l) Disputes arising out of arrangements made under Article 146 and 147 of the Constitution except determination of amount payable by the Federation to a Province in terms of Article 146 of the Constitution.

(m) Matters relating to contracts between the Governments.

(n) Matters relating to acquisition of land for federal purposes under Article 152 of the Constitution.

(o) Matters relating to precedence of a Province in which a well-head of natural gas is situated over other consumers of that gas in terms of Article 158 of the Constitution.

(p) Matters concerning programmes, institutions, posts, laws etc. common to the Federation and the Provinces or to two or more Provinces.

(q) Matters relating to debt and guarantees as enumerated in Article 167 of the Constitution.

(r) Matters relating to taxes forming divisible pool of taxes in which Provinces are interested as specified in Article 162 of the Constitution.

(s) International commitments of the Federation on subjects falling within legislative and executive competence of the Provinces.

(t) Matters relating to electricity as specified in Article 157 of the Constitution except those matters required to be determined by an arbitrator to be appointed by the Chief Justice of Pakistan.

(u) Matters pertaining to broadcasting and telecasting as enumerated in Article 159 of the Constitution.

(v) Matters relating to directions of the Federation to the Provinces under Article 149 of the Constitution and matters pertaining to Article 148 of the Constitution.

(w) Matters relating to ownerless property and other matters (Article 172), emergency and allied issues (Article 232, 234 and 235), working of armed forces in aid of civil administration (Article 245), principles and methods of maintenance of accounts (Article 170), reports of the Auditor General (Article 171), assistance to the Election Commission of Pakistan (Article 220) and monopoly of the Federation or of a Province on a trade, business, industry or service {Article 253(b)}.

(x) Matters concerning harmonious exercise of executive authority of the Federation and of the Provinces.

35.   The above is an indicative and not an exhaustive list. Any and all matters having relationship with constitutional status, powers and duties of the Federation and of the Provinces may be brought before the Hon'ble Supreme Court of Pakistan under Article 184(1) of the Constitution for adjudication by the parties specified in the said Article. No one except a Government can be arrayed as a disputant under Article 184(1) of the Constitution.

36.   There may be occasions when a person (legal or natural) is aggrieved of an enactment or a matter which may reasonably be a subject-matter of litigation under Article 184(1) of the Constitution but the parties specified in that Article do not get the dispute adjudicated upon by the Hon'ble Supreme Court. A private person is debarred to invoke the constitutional jurisdiction of the Hon'ble Supreme Court under Article 184(1) of the Constitution. Does Article 199 of the Constitution provide an alternative dispute-resolution window to such private person if he is aggrieved of a matter which is capable of being litigated by a Government in the Supreme Court of Pakistan under Article 184(1) of the Constitution?

37.   Article 199 of the Constitution, inter alia, empowers an aggrieved person / party to make an application to a High Court for issuance of a direction to a person performing functions in connection with affairs of the Federation, a Province or a local authority to refrain from doing anything he is not permitted by law to do, or to do anything he is required by law to do or for a declaration that any act done or proceeding taken was done or taken without lawful authority or for issuance of appropriate orders for enforcement of any of the fundamental rights. To be an aggrieved person / party is a condition-precedent to invoke constitutional jurisdiction of a High Court for the aforesaid purposes. Aggrieved person would be the one who had been denied legal right by someone who had legal duty to perform relating to that right (PLD 1998 Lah. 376). Person invoking constitutional jurisdiction of High Court has to show that he has suffered some personal injury to his property, body, mind or reputation; person suffering such injury would be "aggrieved person / party" in terms of Article 199 of the Constitution. (PLD 1991 SC ref. 1996 MLD 1238 (a).). James L.J. in ex-parte Sidebotham ((1880) 14 Ch. D. 458) attempted a definition of the term "person aggrieved" in the following words:

> "A 'person aggrieved' must be a man who has suffered a legal grievance, a man against whom a decision has been pronounced which has wrongfully deprived him of something or wrongfully refused him something, or wrongfully affected his title to something."

38.   Article 4 of the Constitution provides that to enjoy the protection of law and to be treated in accordance with law is the inalienable right of every citizen wherever he may be, and of every other person for the time being within Pakistan. The said Article further provides that

(a)   no action detrimental to the life, liberty, body, reputation or property of any person shall be taken except in accordance with law;

(b)   no person shall be prevented from or be hindered in doing that which is not prohibited by law; and

(c)   no person shall be compelled to do that which the law does not required him to do.

39.   Article 5 of the Constitution commands that obedience to the Constitution and law is the inviolable obligation of every citizen wherever he may be and of every other person for the time being within Pakistan. The executive, judiciary and legislature are under oath to preserve, protect and defend the Constitution. All laws are required to be in strict conformity with the Constitution. If a person is aggrieved of the provisions of a law which require him to do or not to do something or attempts to take away, abridge or suspend any of his fundamental rights, that citizen cannot be debarred to knock the doors of a High Court under Article 199 of the Constitution and obtain an appropriate direction, declaration or order necessary to protect his legal rights in the facts and circumstances of his case. Vires of any law can also be challenged by an aggrieved person, inter alia, on the ground of the law being enacted without or in excess of legislative jurisdiction. All said and done, a person cannot be forced to suffer injury to any of his rights and liberties on the basis of a law which is shown to be against the Constitution for being without legislative jurisdiction, clash with fundamental rights or inconsistency with any express or implied provision of the Constitution. Order XXVIIA of the Code of Civil Procedure, 1908 requires notice to be given to the Attorney General for Pakistan in a case involving substantial question as to the interpretation of constitutional law (Professors E.C.S. Wade and Godfrey Phillips say in Constitutional Law, 8th Ed. page 4 that: "There is no hard and fast definition of constitutional law. In the generally accepted use of the term it means the rules which regulate the structure of the principal organs of government and their relationship to each other, and determine their principal functions.") if the question concerns the Federal Government and to the Advocate General if the question of law concerns a Provincial Government. Order XXVIIA of the Code of Civil Procedure, 1908 will lose its substance if it is interpreted to be irrelevant in case of jurisdictional challenge to a Federal or a Provincial law under Article 199 of the Constitution. If vires of a law is not allowed to be challenged by a private aggrieved person through proceedings under Article 199 of the Constitution, then, there remains no justification for Order XXVIIA of the Code of Civil Procedure, 1908 as Governments are always represented in the Supreme Court in proceedings under Article 184(1) of the Constitution through the Attorney General or, as the case may be, the Advocate General. The possibility that a Government can initiate proceedings under Article 184(1) of the Constitution on a subject-matter does not deprive an aggrieved person to protect his rights and liberties through proceedings under Article 199 of the Constitution.

40.   The condition of being an aggrieved person / party excludes a majority of the matters falling under Article 184(1) from the purview of Article 199 of the Constitution. An indicative list of cases capable to be entertained under Article 184(1) of the Constitution, which we have attempted hereinabove, is enough to illustrate that, more often than not, only the Governments are concerned with these matters and it would be extremely difficult for a person other than a Government to prove his locus standi in those matters. But in cases in which a person establishes his locus standi to the satisfaction of the High Court, it would not be in interest of justice to shut the doors of judicial resolution of a justiciable issue merely on the ground that the same or similar issue can be agitated by a Government before the Hon'ble Supreme Court of Pakistan under Article 184(1) of the Constitution. An aggrieved person does not merit to be forced to bear injury to his valuable legal rights because of inaction of the Governments to get an issue judicially settled through proceedings under Article 184(1) of the Constitution. It seems to be for this reason that the Hon'ble Supreme Court of India held in State of Bihar Vs. Union of India (AIR 1970 SC

353

1446) that a dispute in which a private party is involved must be brought before a court, other than the Supreme Court of India, having jurisdiction over the matter.

41.   It needs to be noticed that there is a condition-precedent to be an aggrieved person / party, in certain cases, to be able to file an application under Article 199 of the Constitution. There is no such condition in Article 184(1) of the Constitution. A Government can be in dispute with another Government without being aggrieved person / party within the meaning of Article 199 of the Constitution. In other words, being a disputant within the meaning of Article 184(1) of the Constitution and being an aggrieved person / party as contemplated in Article 199 of the Constitution are not synonymous. Every aggrieved person / party may be termed disputant but every disputant is not necessarily required to be an aggrieved person / party. It was held by the Hon'ble Supreme Court of India in State of Karnataka Vs. Union of India (AIR 1978 SC 68) that:

> "While interpreting the Article one is perhaps unconsciously influenced to import the notion of cause of action which is germane in a suit and read this Article as limited only to cases where some legal right of the plaintiff is infringed and consequently it has a cause of action against the defendant. But there is no reference to a suit or cause of action in Art. 131. That Article confers jurisdiction on the Supreme Court with reference to the character of the dispute which may be brought before it for adjudication. The requirement of cause of action, which is so necessary in a suit, cannot be imported while construing the scope and ambit of Art."

42.   The Hon'ble Supreme Court of India also clarified in the aforementioned case that:

> "It may also be noted that, on a proper construction of Article 131, it is not necessary that the plaintiff should have some legal right of its own to enforce, before it can institute a suit under that article. It is not a sine qua non of the applicability of article 131 that there should be infringement of some legal right of the plaintiff."

43.   It was further held in the aforesaid judgment that:

> "The Constitution aims at maintaining a fine balance not only between the three organs of power, the legislature, the executive and the judiciary, but it is designed to secure a similar balance between the powers of the Central Government and those of the State Governments. The legislative lists in the Seventh Schedule contain a demarcation of legislative powers between the Central and State Governments. The executive power of the Central Government extends to matters with respect to which Parliament has the power to make laws while that of the State extends to matters with respect to which the State legislature has the power to make laws. Part XI of the Constitution is devoted specially to the delineation of relations between the Union and the States. That is a delicate relationship, particularly if different political parties are in power at the Centre and in the States. The object of article 131 is to provide a high powered machinery for ensuring that the Central Government and the State Governments act within the respective spheres of their authority and do not trespass upon each other's constitutional functions or powers. Therefore, a challenge to the constitutional capacity of the defendant to act in an intended manner is enough to attract the application of article 131, particularly when the plaintiff claims that right exclusively for itself. If it fails to establish that right, its challenge may fail on merits but the proceeding cannot be thrown out on the ground that the impugned order is not calculated to affect or impair a legal right of the plaintiff. In an ordinary civil suit, the rejection of a right asserted by the defendant

cannot correspondingly and of its own force establish the right claimed by the plaintiff. But proceedings under article 131 are adjudicatory of the limits of constitutional power vested in the Central and State Governments. The claim that the defendant (the Central Government here) does not possess the requisite power involves the assertion that the power to appoint the Commission of Inquiry is vested exclusively in the plaintiff (the State Government here). In a civil suit the plaintiff has to succeed on the strength of his own title, not on the weakness of his adversary's because the defendant may be a rank trespasser and yet he can lawfully hold on to his possession against the whole world except the true owner. If the plaintiff is not the true owner, his suit must fail. A proceeding under article 131 stands in sharp contrast with an ordinary civil suit. The competition in such a proceeding is between two or more governments--either the one or the other possesses the constitutional power to act. There is no third alternative as in a civil suit wherein the right claimed by the plaintiff may reside neither in him nor in the defendant but in a stranger. A demarcation and definition of constitutional power between the rival claimants and restricted to them and them alone is what a proceeding under article 131 necessarily involves. That is how in such a proceeding, a denial of the defendant's right carries with it an assertion of the plaintiff's."

44.   In view of the above, proceedings under Article 184(1) of the Constitution can be initiated by a Government even in absence of a present cause of action. In other words, a Government can have resort to get disputes adjudicated upon by the Hon'ble Supreme Court of Pakistan even if it does not fulfil the criteria of being an aggrieved person or party. This conclusion leads us to explore the idea of declaratory judgments. For the purpose, we may see what a judgment stands for. Quoting Henry Campbell Black from A Treatise on the Law of Judgments§ 1, at 2 (2nd ed. 1902), the Black's Law Dictionary, 8th Edition, explains meaning of a judgment in the following words:

> "An action is instituted for the enforcement of a right or the redress of an injury. Hence a judgment, as the culmination of the action, declares the existence of the right, recognizes the commission of the injury, or negatives the allegation of one or the other. But as no right can exist without a correlative duty, nor any invasion of it without a corresponding obligation to make amends, the judgment necessarily affirms, or else denies, that such a duty or such a liability rests upon the person against whom the aid of the law is invoked."

45.   On the other hand, the same dictionary defines the expression "Declaration of Rights" as an action in which a litigant requests a court's assistance not because any rights have been violated but because those rights are uncertain. It defines declaratory judgment as a binding adjudication that establishes the rights and other legal relations of the parties without providing for or ordering enforcement. We may observe that if a party discloses an immediate and demonstrable concern to its right, even though based mainly upon hypothetical facts, it may get a declaratory judgement if the applicable law empowers the court to make declaratory judgments. Article 184(2) specifies that the Supreme Court can make only declaratory judgments in exercise of its jurisdiction under that Article. In this view of the matter, jurisdiction of the Hon'ble Supreme Court under Article 184(1) of the Constitution extends to disputes having alleged violation of rights as well as disputes relating to uncertain rights or apprehension of injury to legal rights of the Governments. To illustrate, we assume that the Federation has resolved to enact a Federal law under which it intends to assume control of certain provincial property, functions and employees. Once enacted, the Province would be in awkward dilemma to choose between complying with the law at the cost of sacrifice of its constitutional rights and violating it at its own peril as the

law may be declared to be constitutionally valid by the Supreme Court. Another example may be of institutions to be built by a Province at the cost of billions of rupees which may ultimately be declared beyond the legislative and executive domain of the Province. There are numerous case scenarios in which it would be in public interest to ascertain constitutional powers of a Government before spending or allocating public resources for a purpose or an entity. It was observed by Chief Justice John Marshall in McCulloch v. Maryland, 17 U.S. (Wheaton) 316 1819), p. 40 that "...the question respecting the extent of the powers actually granted, is perpetually arising, and will probably continue to arise, so long as our system shall exist". Declaratory judgment may be an effective tool to guard against or minimize ill effects of jurisdictional clashes or uncertainties in respect of jurisdictions.

46.   Our Constitution has not given a definition of declaratory judgment. https://en.wikipedia.org/wiki/Declaratory_judgment defines the expression in these words:

> "A declaratory judgment, also called a declaration, is the legal determination of a court that resolves legal uncertainty for the litigants. It is a form of legally binding preventive adjudication by which a party involved in an actual or possible legal matter can ask a court to conclusively rule on and affirm the rights, duties, or obligations of one or more parties in a civil dispute (subject to any appeal)."

47.   https://www.britannica.com/topic/declaratory-judgment offers the following definition of declaratory judgment:

> "Declaratory judgment, in law, a judicial judgment intended to fix or elucidate litigants' rights that were previously uncertain or doubtful. A declaratory judgment is binding but is distinguished from other judgments or court opinions in that it lacks an executory process. It simply declares or defines rights to be observed or wrongs to be eschewed by a plaintiff, a defendant, or both, or expresses the court's determination of a contested question of law, without ordering that anything be done. Although a declaratory judgment must deal with a real as opposed to a hypothetical dispute, it is not necessary for an actual wrong, giving rise either to criminal liability or to a claim for civil damages, to have been done or even threatened or contemplated. The Declaratory Judgment Act established its use in U.S. law in 1934."

48.   https://definitions.uslegal.com/d/declaratory-judgment/ defines the declaratory judgment in these words:

> "A declaratory judgment is a judgment of a court which determines the rights of parties without ordering anything be done or awarding damages. By seeking a declaratory judgment, the party making the request is seeking for an official declaration of the status of a matter in controversy. A petition for a declaratory judgment asks the court to define the legal relationship between the parties and their rights with respect to the matter before the court. A declaratory judgment is binding but is distinguished from other judgments or court opinions in that it doesn't provide a method of enforcement."

49.   Declaratory judgments do not presuppose a legal wrong, nor are they followed by coercive relief as they simply declare a right, duty, relation, immunity, disability, etc. In the words of Prof. Borchard, distinctive characteristic of declaratory judgments lies in the fact that they constitute merely an authentic confirmation of already existing relations. Concerning the uses of the declaratory judgment, Prof. Borchard observes as follows:

> "As a measure of preventive justice, the declaratory judgment probably has its greatest efficacy. It is designed to enable parties to ascertain

and establish their legal relations so as to conduct themselves accordingly, and thus to avoid the necessity of future litigation."

50.   Whereas Article 184(1) & (2) provides settlement of controversies and relief from uncertainty and insecurity with respect to rights, duties and relations through declamatory judgments, Article 199 of the Constitution can be invoked, save in case of writs of habeas corpus and of quo warranto, only by an aggrieved person / party. Mere apprehension of being aggrieved in future does not grant locus standi to a person to file an application under Article 199 of the Constitution. Moreover, judgments to be delivered by a High Court in exercise of its jurisdiction under Article 199 of the Constitution are not declaratory judgments. It goes without saying that, if authorized by or under the Constitution, making declaratory judgments do fall within the purview of courts as it is exercise of judicial power of the state and cannot be dismissed as mere legal essays or advisory opinions or moot exercises.

51.   Resort to declaratory judgments of the Hon'ble Supreme Court of Pakistan under Article 184(1) of the Constitution needs not be taken as a hostile or unfriendly act on the part of the Government knocking doors of the Apex Court. Apart from other constitutional institutions for consensus-building and dispute-resolution, judicial resolution of disputes is also necessary for harmonious existence and continuity of a federal system. Inevitability of disputes between Governments in a federal set-up demands an institution for judicial settlement of the disputes, if need be. Dicey has observed in his book "Introduction to the Study of the Law of the Constitution" that acceptable distribution of powers between the Centre and units is an essential feature of the federalism, stating further that:

"That a federal system again can flourish only among communities imbued with a legal spirit and trained to reverence the law is as certain as can be any conclusions of political speculation. Federalism substitutes litigation for legislation, and none but a law-fearing people will be inclined to regard the decision of a suit as equivalent to the enactment of a law."

52.   When Supreme Court gives a declaratory judgment under Article 184(2) of the Constitution, it enunciates law in terms of Article 189 of the Constitution. Such enunciation makes the Constitution clear by filling the gaps or by dissipating ambiguities or by simply interpreting and construing it. All courts are bound to follow this law. Thus, declarations under Article 184 (2) of the Constitution are not mere statements of academic interest. Article 190 of the Constitution orders that all executive and judicial authorities throughout Pakistan shall act in aid of the Supreme Court. The Constitution does not conceive an eventuality in which the law laid down by the Supreme Court is to be disregarded by anyone. All in the country are bound to act in aid of the Supreme Court. When the Supreme Court announces that an act is without lawful authority, it loses its legal sanctity forthwith. When an act is declared legal, all objections thereagainst and controversies in relation thereto disappear. A Prime Minister is thrown out of his office when Hon'ble Judges of the Supreme Court utter words requiring him to vacate his office. On the other hand, a Prime Minister thrown out of his office is welcomed back to his office immediately after the Supreme Court issues orders to this effect. When the Hon'ble Supreme Court gives a declaratory judgment under Article 184(2) of the Constitution, the only way to avoid its implementation is to amend the provisions of the Constitution on the basis of which the judgment has been given. The requirement of judgments under Article 184(1) of the Constitution to be of declaratory nature only may be understood with reference to cause of action or locus standi of the Government approaching the Hon'ble Supreme Court and the judgment may not be taken inferior as to its legal validity or effect.

53.   Some Hon'ble Courts in Pakistan consider it, in some cases, essential to link exclusive jurisdiction of the Hon'ble Supreme Court of Pakistan under Article 184(1) of the Constitution with the Council of Common Interests. Article 154 (1) of the Constitution tasks the Council of Common Interests to formulate and regulate policies in relation to matters in

Part-II of the Federal Legislative List and to exercise supervision and control over related institutions. Article 154(7) of the Constitution provides that if the Federal Government or a Provincial Government is dissatisfied with a decision of the Council, it may refer the matter to Parliament in a joint sitting whose decision in this behalf shall be final. Article 155 of the Constitution, reproduced below, also makes the Council of Common Interests competent to entertain complaints as to interference with water supplies:

> "155. Complaints as to interference with water supplies. __
>
> (1)   If the interests of a Province, the Federal Capital or the Federally Administered Tribal Areas, or any of the inhabitants thereof, in water from any natural source of supply or reservoir have been or are likely to be affected prejudicially by —
>
> (a)   any executive act or legislation taken or passed or proposed to be taken or passed, or
>
> (b)   the failure of any authority to exercise any of its powers with respect to the use and distribution or control of water from that source,
>
> the Federal Government or the Provincial Government concerned may make a complaint in writing to the Council.
>
> (2)   Upon receiving such complaint, the Council shall, after having considered the matter, either give its decision or request the President to appoint a commission consisting of such persons having special knowledge and experience in irrigation, engineering, administration, finance or law as he may think fit, hereinafter referred to as the Commission.
>
> (3)   Until Majlis-e-Shoora (Parliament) makes provision by law in this behalf, the provisions of the Pakistan Commissions of Inquiry Act, 1956, as in force immediately before the commencing day shall apply to the Council or the Commission as if the Council or the Commission were a Commission appointed under that Act to which all the provisions of section 5 thereof applied and upon which the power contemplated by section 10A thereof had been conferred.
>
> (4)   After considering the report and supplementary report, if any, of the Commission, the Council shall record its decision on all matters referred to the Commission.
>
> (5)   Notwithstanding any law to the contrary, but subject to the provisions of clause (5) of Article 154, it shall be the duty of the Federal Government and the Provincial Government concerned in the matter in issue to give effect to the decision of the Council faithfully according to its terms and tenor.
>
> (6)   No proceeding shall lie before any court at the instance of any party to a matter which is or has been in issue before the Council, or of any person whatsoever, in respect of a matter which is actually or has been or might or ought to have been a proper subject of complaint to the Council under this Article."

54.   The Hon'ble Supreme Court of Pakistan was pleased to hold in a case reported as Federation of Pakistan Vs. United Sugar Mills Ltd ((PLD 1977 SC 397) that:

> "Again in one significant aspect, the Federal Executive Authority has been abridged under the Constitution and has been entrusted to a newly created institution called the Council of Common Interests. It is a body quite apart from the Federal Executive (See Article 153-156). The administration of matters falling in Part II of the Federal Legislative List (Railways, mineral oil, natural gas etc.) and item 34 of the Concurrent

List (electricity) are entrusted to the Council of Common Interests. This is a body consisting of the representatives of the Federal Government and the four Provinces. Any dispute arising between one or more Provinces inter se or between the Federation or a Province regarding aforesaid subjects is referable to the Parliament in joint session for final decision. This constitutional arrangement also abridges the original jurisdiction of the Supreme Court under Article 184 and correspondingly new power essentially quasi-judicial in character has been conferred on the Parliament in joint sitting."

55.   It was held by the Hon'ble Supreme Court of Pakistan in a case reported as Godoon Textile Mills and others Vs. WAPDA and others (1997 SCMR 641) that:

"In our view Article 153, 154, 155, 160 and 161 of the Constitution provide an inbuilt self-adjudicatory and self-executory mechanism in the constitutional set-up. The object seems to be to generate sense of participation among the Federating Units on sensitive issues of national importance referred to in the above Articles, and to ensure

(i)   resolving of any dispute arising between one or more Federating Units inter se or between the Federation and a Federating Unit;

(ii)   payment of the net proceeds of the Federal duty on natural gas levied at and collected by the Federal Government to the Federating Units to which the well-heads of natural gas are situated;

(iii)   payment of net profits earned by the Federal Government or any undertaking established or administered by the Federal Government from the bulk-generation of power at a hydro-electric station to the Federating Unit in which the hydro-electric station is situated;

(iv)   carrying out direction issued by the Parliament in its joint session to the C.C.I."

56.   Legislative, judicial and executive powers are distinctly different from one another. Powers of formulating and regulating policies in relation to matters in Part-II of the Federal Legislative List and exercising supervision and control over related institutions vested in the Council of Common Interests under Article 154 (1) of the Constitution are not judicial powers. Under the doctrine of separation of powers, judiciary lacks competence to exercise legislative or executive powers. On the other hand, legislature and the executive cannot exercise judicial power of the State. Clause 2 of Article 175 of the Constitution embodies the basic principle that no court shall have any jurisdiction save as is or may be conferred on it by the Constitution or by or under any law. The jurisdiction-ousting Article 155 (6) relates only to complaints relating to interference with water supplies. Adjudication of all other legal disputes between the Governments does fall within the exclusive jurisdiction of the Hon'ble Supreme Court of Pakistan under Article 184(1) of the Constitution.

57.   The question that whether a private person can approach a court on a matter which can legitimately be raised by a Government before the Hon'ble Supreme Court of Pakistan under Article 184(1) of the Constitution has received mixed response from the superior courts in Pakistan. In Lucky Cement Limited through General Manager Vs. Federation through Secretary, Ministry of Petroleum and Natural Resources (2011 PLD 57 Peshawar High Court), the Hon'ble High Court dismissed an objection that the matter being raised was a dispute between the Governments falling within exclusive jurisdiction of the Supreme Court and entertained the writ petition filed by a private party under Article 199 of the Constitution. In the case of Murree Brewery Company Limited and others Vs. Province of Punjab and the Province of Sindh (Constitutional Petition No. 19 of 1995 decided on 28th of

May, 1995 through an agreement between the parties) under Article 184 (1) of the Constitution, no objection about competence of the private parties to invoke original jurisdiction of the Supreme Court under Article 184(1) was raised. It was held by the Hon'ble Balochistan High Court in a case reported as Senator Dr. Abdul Hayee Vs. Government of Pakistan (PLD 1997 Quetta 37) that:

> "I am afraid that the argument raised by learned counsel to say that instant petition be dismissed is not based on any recognized principle of rejecting petition. In this behalf it is to be seen that solely for the reason that Honourable Supreme Court is ceased with the matter, in which neither the petitioner nor respondents 3 and 4 are party, will not divest this Court from exercising jurisdiction, because under Article 184(1) of the Constitution, there is no express provision which excludes this Court from exercising jurisdiction in the matter which is prior in time and was already sub judice before filing of the suit by the Provincial Government of Balochistan. There is no doubt that a private party is debarred to seek remedy before the Honourable Supreme Court under Article 184 of the Constitution and except approaching this Court under Article 199 of the Constitution, no other remedy is available to him, therefore, the relief cannot be denied to him, merely for the reason that another party subsequent to filing of instant constitutional petition has invoked the original jurisdiction of Hon'ble Supreme Court. In this behalf, it is to be mentioned that even under general rule of res sub judice, a suit which is prior in time will not be abated because another Hon'ble Court has concurrent jurisdiction in respect of same remedy, but it can only be availed by the parties specified in the statute which confers jurisdiction on said Court."

58. On the other side of the divide, there is also a number of cases some of which are as follows:

a) It was held by the Hon'ble Federal Court of Pakistan in a case reported as Province of Punjab Vs. Federation of Pakistan (PLD 1956 FC 72) that despite provision of machinery for adjudication of cases relating to Income Tax and the Profits Tax under the Income Tax Act, 1922 and the Excess Profits Tax Act, 1940, a dispute between the Federal Government on one hand and a Provincial Government on the other regarding liability of the later to tax demand raised by the former was within exclusive jurisdiction of the Federal Court under Section 204 of the Government of India Act, 1935.

b) It was held by a three-judge bench of the Hon'ble Lahore High Court, Lahore in a case reported as Haider Mukhtar and others Vs. Government of Punjab and others (PLD 2014 Lahore 214) that a private party cannot invoke the constitutional jurisdiction of High Court for adjudication of a matter that involved a dispute under Article 184(1) of the Constitution. In this case, a plaint of the Government of the Punjab on the same subject-matter was pending in the Supreme Court under Article 184(1) of the Constitution. In this case, reliance was placed on a full bench judgment reported as Khalid Mahmood and others Vs. Federation of Pakistan through Secretary, Ministry of Finance, Islamabad and 74 others (PLD 2003 Lah 629).

c) A single bench of the Hon'ble Lahore High Court, Lahore dismissed a writ petition filed by the Government of the Punjab against the Federal Land Commission in a case reported as Province of Punjab through Secretary, Government of Punjab Vs. Member, Federal Land Commission (2010 YLR 1846 Lahore High Court, Lahore) on the ground that the subject-matter of the petition constituted a dispute within the meaning of Article 184(1) of the Constitution.

d) In Province of Punjab through Secretary Colonies Vs. Waziran Bibi (PLD 1976 Lah. 1135), petition of the Government of the Punjab was dismissed on the ground that the controversy between the parties qualified to be a dispute between the Governments in terms of Article 184(1) of the Constitution.

e) In the Commissioner of Income Tax, Lahore Vs. Messrs. Jallo Rosin & Turpentine Factory, Lahore (PLD 1976 Lah. 1135), it was held that the adjudication of disputes between the Federal Government and a Provincial Government exclusively falls within the jurisdiction of the Hon'ble Supreme Court under Article 184(1) of the Constitution.

f) It was held by the Hon'ble Lahore High Court, Lahore in a case reported as Kh. Muhammad Sharif Vs. Federation of Pakistan (1989 CLC 1387) that:

> "Apart from what has been said above, the grievance agitated by the petitioner essentially raises a dispute of the nature envisaged in Article 184 of the Constitution i.e. a dispute between the Federal Government on the one hand and the Provincial Governments on the other. Such a dispute is determinable by the Supreme Court of Pakistan, which has exclusive jurisdiction under Article 184 of the Constitution, which in its relevant aspect reads as under (citation omitted).
>
> The word 'dispute' in the afore-quoted provision, though not defined, is wide enough to include all the disputes, jurisdictional, administrative and fiscal. The words "to the exclusion of every other court" place it beyond doubt that the Supreme Court has exclusive jurisdiction to determine a dispute between the Federal Government and the Provincial Governments and the jurisdiction of this Court is expressly ousted. Needless to observe that the jurisdiction of this Court under Article 199 is subject to the Constitution and, therefore, the jurisdiction-ousting provision of Article 184 must prevail. It may also pertinently be observed that if the grievance / dispute sought to be agitated by the petitioner had been brought before us by an aggrieved Province, we would certainly have no jurisdiction to entertain it in view of the express provision of Article 184 of the Constitution. That being so, the dispute which necessarily falls within the exclusive jurisdiction of the Supreme Court cannot be allowed to be raised by a private party in proceedings under Article 199 of the Constitution because the principle is well settled that a thing which cannot be done directly can also not be allowed to be done indirectly."

59. Giving another set of cases, it was held in Pakistan Railways Vs. Karachi Development Authority (2003 SCMR 563) and Chief Secretary, Government of Punjab Vs. Commissioner of Income Tax (PLD 1976 Lah. 258) that a dispute between a local authority of the Provincial Government and the Federal Government does not fall within the purview of Article 184(1) of the Constitution. In simple words, a local authority was held to be outside the definition of the concerned Government for the purpose of Article 184(1) of the Constitution.

60.	There is also a set of cases dealing specifically with the issues which are subject-matter of the plaint under adjudication here. Governor of the Punjab issued an Order bearing No. SO (B&E-1) 7-1/2003 dated 12th September, 2005 through which the following posts in the Punjab Treasuries & Accounts Service were re-designated / un-graded:

Sr.No	Existing Designation	New Designation	Existing BS	New BS
1	Chief Inspector of Treasuries	Chief Inspector of Treasuries and Accounts	19	20
2	Inspector of Treasuries	Inspector of Treasuries and Accounts	18	19
3	Treasury Officer/ District Accounts Officer	Treasury Officer/ District Accounts Officer	17	18
4	Assistant Treasury Officer	Assistant Treasury Officer/ Sub-Treasury Officer / Assistant Treasury Officer (Works & Services)	16	17
5	Assistant Accountant	Assistant Accountant	15	16
6	Sub-Accountant	Sub-Accountant	13	14

61.	Legality of the aforesaid Order was assailed through the following writ petitions in the Hon'ble Lahore High Court:

Sr.#	Writ Petition #	Title of the case	Bench
1	17087/2005	Javed Iqbal and others Vs. the Secretary, Finance Department and others	Lahore
2	17503/2005	Muhammad Abdul Latif Shahid khan Joya and others V the Secretary Finance Department and others	Lahore
3	17856/2005	Shamas-ud-Din and others Vs. Government of Pakist and others	Lahore
4	5962/2005	Bashir Ahmad Qamar and another Vs. the Secreta Finance Department and others	Multan
5	12/2006	Mian Abdul Sami and others Vs. the Principal Secreta and others	Rawalpindi
6	465/2006	Ch. Shakeel Ahmad and another Vs. the Princip Secretary and others	Bahawalpu

62.	All the six writ petitions were aimed at getting the aforementioned up-gradations nullified on the ground that performance of accounting and treasury functions of the Provinces and control of district and provincial accounts offices and provincial employees working therein was an exclusive domain of the CGA under the CGA Ordinance. The Federal Government, in its reports and para-wise comments, endorsed the viewpoint of the petitioners. On the other hand, Government of the Punjab got these petitions consolidated at the principal seat of the High Court in Lahore and raised the preliminary objection that the subject-matter of the writ petitions was a dispute between Government of Pakistan and the Government of the Punjab. It was contended by the Government of the Punjab that the Hon'ble Supreme Court had exclusive jurisdiction in the matter and the High Court was not competent to invoke its jurisdiction under Article 199 of the Constitution as the lis before the High Court, in pith and substance, pertained to a dispute between the Government of the Federation and the Government of a Federating Unit. The Hon'ble Single Bench of the Lahore High Court, through a consolidated unreported judgment delivered on 6th of July, 2006, held as follows:

> "15. Article 184(1) in essence confers jurisdiction in the Honourable Supreme Court of Pakistan in the matter enumerated therein. Of course, in terms of Article 184 of the Constitution, such jurisdiction is exclusive, but nevertheless it confers jurisdiction and must be

interpreted in the said context. The obvious interpretation of such provision will be that where jurisdiction vests in the Supreme Court under Article 184(1) of the Constitution, hence, this Court has no jurisdiction in the matter. Thus to accept the contentions of the counsels for the respondents would prima facie imply not only holding that this Court has no jurisdiction to decide the instant Constitutional Petition, but also to hold that said petition lies before the Apex Court. Thus, the petition would be required to be returned in terms of Order 7 Rule 10 C.P.C for filing it before the appropriate forum.

16. Incidentally, in Kh. Sharif's case, supra, it was not held that the Constitutional Petition could or should have been filed before the Apex Court. In fact, the Constitutional Petition was dismissed and not returned for filing it before the Apex Court. It is also noticed with great interest that it is not the case by any of the counsels before this Court that this petition could be filed by the present petitioners before the Apex Court perhaps because of the literal interpretation of Article 184(1) of the Constitution of Islamic Republic of Pakistan would suggest that such proceedings can only be initiated by either the Government of the Federation or the Government of a Federating Unit. Thus, even in the eventuality of a dispute between the Government of Federation and the Government of a Federating Unit which impacts rights of citizens and neither of the two Governments choose to invoke the jurisdiction of the Supreme Court of Pakistan under Article 184(1) of the Constitution of Islamic Republic of Pakistan, the private citizens would be rendered remediless and condemned to a legal no man's land which perhaps could not have been the intention of the framers of the Constitution of Islamic Republic of Pakistan, 1973.

17. In view of the above resume of facts and reasons, I am not persuaded to out rightly dismiss the Constitutional Petition. Article 184(1) of the Constitution of Islamic Republic of Pakistan needs to be revisited and re-interpreted in the context of the jurisdiction of this Court to entertain Constitutional Petition under Article 199 of the Constitution filed by the private individuals. In view of this Court's decision rendered in Kh. Sharif's case ibid, I feel that it would be appropriate that this crucial question be determined by a larger Bench of this Court. Consequently, case is referred to the Honourable Chief Justice of this Court for constitution of a larger Bench to decide the issue, whether this Court under Article 199 of the Constitution has the jurisdiction to entertain a petition filed by private individual involving a dispute between the Government of the Federation or a Federating Unit."

63.   A larger Bench of the Hon'ble Lahore High Court comprising of three judges, constituted in pursuance of the aforementioned reference of a single bench, took almost ten years to deliver the judgment in the aforesaid six writ petitions on 18.06.2015, relevant excerpts thereof are as follows:

"After hearing the learned counsel for the parties at length on this issue, we find that the Petitioners are no longer aggrieved by the Impugned Notification before the Court as their basic grievance regarding the up-gradation of certain posts pursuant to the Impugned Notification has been redressed by the FST. The Petitioners pleaded discrimination before the FST relying specifically on the Impugned Notification. The FST accepted their plea and upgraded their posts. Hence, the posts of the Petitioners were upgraded on the strength of their argument of discrimination. Given that they have taken the benefit of the Impugned Notification for up-gradation of their posts, they cannot now pursue their challenge to the same Notification for being illegal and have the Notification set aside to the detriment of all those who benefited from the Notification. In this regard, their prayer to set aside the Impugned Notification is against the principles of equity and natural justice as all beneficiaries of the Impugned Notification are not before this Court as they have not been impleaded as party. As such now the Petitioners are not aggrieved by the Impugned Notification and **dispute between the Federal Government and the Provincial Government with respect to the promulgation of the Ordinance is a matter to be put before the august Supreme Court of Pakistan under Article 184 (I) of the Constitution by the parties.** (emphasis supplied).

Under the circumstances, these petitions are dismissed."

64.   When the matter reached the Hon'ble Supreme Court of Pakistan, the Hon'ble Apex Court was pleased to dispose it of through the following order on 02.04.2019:

"**GuIzar Ahmed, J**. We have heard the petitioner in Civil Petition No.2568 of 2015, who has appeared in-person as well as the learned counsel for the petitioner in Civil Petition No.2569 of 2015. They state that the anomaly created by the Controller General of Accounts (Appointment, Functions and Powers) Ordinance, 2001 whereby all the powers relating to Finances of the Government of Pakistan so also of the Provinces have been conferred upon the Controller General which is contrary to the scheme of the Constitution of Islamic Republic of Pakistan itself, where under Article 169 thereof Auditor General of Pakistan performs the functions of such office in dealing with the finances of the Government and further the Controller General has also been given powers to deal with the question of finances of the Provinces, which situation has created a bit of anomaly and causing some heartburning into the establishment of Controller General Office and Provincial Offices dealing with finances.

2. Both the learned Additional Attorney General as well as Additional Advocate General Punjab make a categorical statement before the Court that this anomaly / issue shall be considered and dealt with by the respective Governments and a solution to that will be found and addressed and grievances in this respect of the petitioners will also be resolved accordingly. However, both the Governments shall also look at the personal grievances of the petitioner though he has received the benefit of the impugned notification dated 12.09.2005.

3. The petitioner appearing in-person as well as the learned counsel for the petitioner in CP.2569 of 2015 feel satisfied with the above statement made by the learned Additional Attorney General as well as the learned Additional Advocate General Punjab and state that both these petitions in such terms be disposed of.

4. Both these petitions stand disposed of accordingly. It is, however, observed that this exercise will be conducted and concluded by the respective Governments preferably within a period of six months."

65.   Fourteen years of litigation on the CGA Ordinance in the aforesaid cases made one thing certain: it is not judicially certain whether private parties are competent to initiate proceedings under Article 184(1) or 199 of the Constitution in a matter which has potential of being a dispute between the Governments? A number of other cases is still pending adjudication on the issue of constitutionality of the CGA Ordinance. We may hasten to

clarify that non-adjudication of the constitutionality of the CGA Ordinance is not exactly what made the great Chief Justice John Marshal (as cited by Justice Van Devanter in Evans v. Gore — 64 L Ed 887, 891) to observe that:

> "1 have always thought, from my earliest youth till now, that the greatest scourge an angry Heaven ever inflicted upon an ungrateful and a sinning people was an ignorant, a corrupt or a dependent judiciary."

It would also be unfair to refer to Bracton (c. 1235) who said:

> "The seat of judgment is like the throne of God. Let unwise and unlearned not presume to ascend it, lest he should confound darkness with light and light with darkness, lest with a sword in the hand, as it were, of a madman he should slay the innocent and set free the guilty, and lest he should tumble down from on high, as from the throne of God, in attempting to fly before he has acquired wings....".

66. With respect to jurisdictional competence, we have carefully analysed constitutional evolution on the subject of adjudication of disputes between the Governments, entire relevant case law of India and Pakistan, rival submissions of the parties to these proceedings as well as arguments of the private party which prayed to become a party in this case. After a threadbare examination and in-depth study of all legal aspects of the lis at hand, we are persuaded to hold that:

a) Only the Federal Government or a Provincial Government is competent to invoke constitutional jurisdiction of the Hon'ble Supreme Court of Pakistan under Article 184(1) of the Constitution. A Government includes all of its entities including its local governments;

b) Being an aggrieved person is not a condition-precedent to initiate proceedings under Article 184(1) of the Constitution;

c) Except disputes concerning complaints as to interference with water supplies under Article 155 of the Constitution, all legal disputes can be brought by a Government before the Supreme Court under Article 184(1) of the Constitution;

d) No person except a Government can be a plaintiff or a defendant in proceedings under Article 184(1) of the Constitution;

e) A declaratory judgment under Article 184(2) of the Constitution carries the strength of Article 189 of the Constitution to the extent it decides a question of law or is based upon or enunciates a principle of law and all executive and judicial authorities throughout Pakistan are bound to act in aid of the Supreme Court accordingly; and

f) An aggrieved person may invoke constitutional jurisdiction of a High Court under Article 199 of the Constitution even if the subject-matter of the litigation may qualify to be a potential dispute between the Governments provided the same matter is not already under adjudication in terms of Article 184(1) of the Constitution and no other alternate remedy has been provided to the aggrieved person by or under the Constitution.

67. The above declarations of this Court are sufficient to dismiss the application of the private party for implication as a defendant in this case, and the same application is hereby dismissed accordingly.

68. Existence of a justiciable dispute is necessary to invoke constitutional jurisdiction of the Supreme Court under Article 184(1) of the Constitution. Before holding the plaint maintainable under Article 184(1) of the Constitution, we directed the plaintiff to list out the issues which are subject-matter of the dispute and to put on record its past efforts to raise or resolve the dispute. In reply, the learned Advocate General, Punjab stated that the issues raised in the instant plaint are the issues which are subject-matter of the dispute. He submitted that the issues relate to constitutional powers of the Province and are materially important in constitutional relationship of the Province with the Federation. He was of the

view that these issues are of the nature for which Article 184(1) of the Constitution provides an exclusive adjudicatory mechanism. As regards efforts of the plaintiff to raise and resolve the dispute, he referred to letters addressed by the provincial functionaries to the federal functionaries, legal opinions of provincial and federal law officers and of others on the subject, different decisions made at various levels, court cases etc. to prove existence of a dispute between the parties.

69.   Learned Advocate General, Punjab placed certified copies of the following letters in the case file for our perusal:

    a. The Chief Minister, Punjab addressed a demi official letter to the Federal Finance Minister vide No. NO.AS(IMPL.)/CMO/14/0T-4 dated 18.11.2014, wherein it was stated:

> "Finance Act, 2014 has introduced certain amendments in clause 'b' of Section 5 of the CGA Ordinance. These are fine in relation to the Federal Government. So far as Provincial Government is concerned, its power under Article 119 of the Constitution to perform its treasury functions (to operate its bank accounts for the purpose of withdrawal of moneys therefrom) is exclusive, inalienable and indivisible. The Federal Government can neither assume treasury functions of the provinces nor these powers of the provinces can be subjected to any restraints except those specified in the regulatory framework enforced under Article 119 of the Constitution.
>
> I, therefore, request you to kindly review and have Section 5 of the Finance Act, 2014, amended so as to limit its application to the Federal Government. Detailed reasons of this request are contained in the enclosed statement."

    b. In a letter bearing No. SO (TT) 6-4/2012 pt. I dated 10.10.2013 addressed by the Finance Department of the Government of the Punjab to the Accountant General, Punjab, inter alia, it was stated that:

> "It is further stated that the subject matter and the issues dealt with in Articles 118 to 126 and 170(1) of the Constitution are mutually exclusive. Accounting arrangements are necessarily required to be in such a form and manner that these are able to comprehensively capture and truly depict all treasury transactions of monetary nature envisaged in the rules framed under Article 119 ibid and not be in conflict with Articles 118 to 126 and other relevant Articles of the Constitution; thus, accounting arrangements prescribed in the APPM, by the Auditor General of Pakistan under Article 170(1) are beyond the mandate of the said Article if these are inconsistent with financial arrangements made under Article 118 to 126 ibid. In case of clash between provisions of rules framed under Article 119 of the Constitution and those of the manuals issued under Article 170(1) of the Constitution, the provisions of rules shall prevail if the subject matter pertains to treasury functions and those of the manuals if the issues covered relate to accounting functions."

    c. The Chief Minister, Punjab wrote to the Prime Minister of Pakistan vide No. ASG / CMS /04/OT-5/51204 dated 07.10.2004 in which it was stated that:

> "I seek your kind intercession in directing the Ministry of Finance, Government of Pakistan to implement the decisions of the Federal Cabinet dated 6th November, 2002 regarding the provincialization of accounts. These decisions were predicated to suitably amending the Controller General of Accounts Ordinance, 2001, an action which seemingly has not been undertaken, till date.

I am adding that denial of ownership of provincial accounting functions to the respective Provincial Governments has been a subject of controversy for nearly three decades. With the separation of audit and accounts functions, a long standing demand of the Provincial Governments was redeemed. However, the promulgation of the Controller General of Accounts Ordinance, 2001 with its emphasis on centralization of accounts, in essence, forestalled the logical policy initiative relating to provincialization of accounts. While the Provincial Governments have been making periodic references to the Ministry of Finance, an appropriate response is still awaited.

I seek your kind support in the early resolution to this outstanding issue."

d. Governor of the Punjab addressed the following letter to the Federal Finance Minister vide No. PSG-1/2001 dated 25.04.2001:

"I am addressing you on the subject to bring-home a very serious concern of the Punjab Government. This is about the proposed initiative to place the provincial accounts under the Federal Government through the Controller General of Accounts and take-over of the District Accounts Offices (DAOs) by the Ministry of Finance.

While the Punjab Government fully supports the separation of Audit & Accounts, this move taken in the name of separation is actually an aberration with far-reaching constitutional and administrative implications. Not only that the Provincial Government would lose control over the management of its public finances, but this step to centralize the accounting functions of the proposed district governments would be a total negation of the philosophy of the Devolution.

I must add that the decision to separate Audit and Accounts as per constitutional provisions, actually redeemed the long-standing-stance of the Punjab Government. The proposed initiative has, however, added a serious distortion to it in that, instead of placing provincial accounts under the executive authority of the province (a widely accepted accounting principle) the same are being taken away from it. Thus a positive initiative taken over 30 years ago to establish DAOs and to give control to the Provinces on their accounts is now being reversed / centralized. This would indeed be a highly retrogressive step. It is also a paradox that largest stake-holder being the Provincial Government has not even been given the opportunity to react to the recommendations of H.U. Beg's Committee which reportedly form the basis of the said move.

I am adding details of the constitutional, administrative, financial and other repercussions inherent in the matter for your consideration. I would strongly urge that the issue be urgently reviewed and finally decided only after full consultation with the Provincial Governors."

e. The Governor, Punjab sent a letter, bearing No. PSG-1/2001 dated 24.05.2001, to the Chief Executive of Pakistan stating therein that:

"I have learnt through media reports that the Federal Cabinet has recently approved two Ordinances, sponsored by the Ministry of Finance relating to the separation of Audit and Account-keeping functions, and inter-alia placement of provincial accounts under the

Controller General of Accounts, a federal office under the Ministry of Finance. The Ministry did not give the Provinces an opportunity to express their views, which the Federal Cabinet could have considered while taking the decision.

This move, while redeeming a long-standing demand of the provincial governments (separation of audit and accounts) has added a serious aberration to the issue, which negates the well-considered and principled standpoint of the provincial governments, that the account-keeping being an executive function be made over to the provinces, and that the respective Accountants General be placed under the provincial governments. This position is not only constitutionally desirable but is also widely accepted on principle. Besides, it also fits into the scheme of the Devolution Plan.

My communication on the subject bearing No.PSG-1/2001 of April 25, 2001, addressed to the Minister of Finance (copy enclosed) has, perhaps, not been given any consideration. If the new arrangement is put in place, it would severely undermine the implementation of the Devolution Plan, as the provinces, would have no control over their accounts, and instead be looking upon a federal office in the districts about their financial matters. I am afraid this shall erode the scheme of devolution and would actually centralize a key function.

The provincial governments have been contesting this issue for the last 30-odd years. I had written to the Finance Minister in the hope that we would be able to achieve consensus on the issue. However, the provinces despite being the major stakeholders were not consulted. As a matter of fact, one learnt of the latest developments from the media reports.

May I, therefore, request that the promulgation of the Ordinance may kindly be deferred until the Ministry of Finance has consulted the Provinces and their views have been placed before you? You may like to decide at that stage if the Federal Cabinet should give the matter fresh consideration with the participation of representatives from the Provincial Governments."

f. Mr. Salman Siddique, Finance Secretary of Government of the Punjab wrote the following letter bearing No. IT (FD) 3-34/68-Vol-IX dated 21.07.2003, to the Federal Finance Secretary:

"Kindly refer to your letter No. F. No. 1 (PF) 1/2001-669, dated 23rd May, 2003, on the subject noted above.

2. The matter has been examined in the light of the d.o. letter dated 16th April, 2003, addressed by the Auditor General of Pakistan to the Secretary, Government of Pakistan, Finance Division, Islamabad.

3. The Auditor General has expressed his views / concerns mainly on the following issues: -

  i) Ownership of audit and accounting functions with reference to Articles 169 and 170 of the Constitution of the Islamic Republic of Pakistan;

  ii) The purview and competence of the Ministry of Finance in bringing matters relating to audit and accounts before the Federal Cabinet;

iii) The matter relating to CGA Ordinance, and the decisions taken thereon by the NRB on 15th April, 2002, and their approval by the Federal Cabinet on 6th November, 2002.

4. These issues are discussed hereunder in their historical, constitutional / legal and administrative perspectives, seriatim: -

ISSUE NO.1:

5.

(i) This issue has not arisen as a result of any sudden development. The present position is essentially to be seen in the backdrop of years of deliberations. The point of view adduced by the Auditor General leads us once again back to square one.

(ii) The audit of the federal and provincial governments is the function of the Auditor General of Pakistan in terms of the existing constitutional provisions, and the Auditor General's Ordinance, 2001, In a federal set-up, however, audit of provincial governments must be a provincial subject, as is the case in almost all federations.

(iii) So far as accounting is concerned, no clear or precise definition of accounts has been given in the CGA Ordinance, 2001. This has perhaps been done with an intent to perpetually keep the ownership issue nebulous.

(iv) At the heart of the issue is the desire of the Pakistan Audit Department to snatch the power of the provinces to operate their bank accounts through their own officers. However, the function of regulating payments into and withdrawals out of the Provincial Consolidated Fund and Public Account of the province (commonly known as the "treasury function") is the exclusive prerogative of the province. It is the inherent and inalienable function of the Provincial Government. This function is performed in accordance with the Punjab Treasury and Subsidiary Treasury Rules and other rules framed under Article 119 of the Constitution. No entity or authority, except the provincial government, has any right or locus-standi to operate the PCF or the P.A. of the province for the purpose of withdrawal of moneys therefrom. **AN EXPOSE ON THE HISTORICAL PERSPECTIVE OF THE TREASURY AND ACCOUNTING FUNCTIONS IS ADDED AT ANNEX: A.**

6 In view of the above, it can be concluded that the CGA Ordinance, 2001 is a defective piece of law. Section 5(b) of the CGA Ordinance, which authorizes the CGA to authorize withdrawals from the Provincial Consolidated Fund and Public Account of the province, after pre-audit checks, prescribed by the Auditor General of Pakistan, militates against Article 119 of the Constitution. The provincial governments have, therefore, rightfully taken strong exception to this legal infirmity in the CGA Ordinance. This perception has been taken note of by the MOF, and the NRB. Realizing the validity of this perception, the MOF agreed to a status-quo vis-à-vis the CGA Ordinance, while the NRB, after detailed discussions with all the stake-holders, took certain vital decisions on 15th April, 2002, declaring the accounting function to be a provincial subject. However, neither the CGA nor the Auditor

General of Pakistan are seem ready to accept this decision and are trying to drag the issue back to its starting point by re-opening a settled matter. A detailed position paper showing the legal and administrative shortcomings in the CGA Ordinance is added at **Annex: B**.

7. In case of the Provincial Government, it is imperative that its accounts should be maintained by its own Accountant General, and not by a representative of the Federation. The Controller General of Accounts could be responsible for Federal Accounts only, and his authority ought not to be stretched to include the provincial accounts. Therefore, the decisions taken by the NRB on 15th August 2002, which were later ratified by the Federal Cabinet on 6th November 2002, are a step in the right direction. Appropriate amendments in the CGA Ordinance shall resolve this controversy once for all.

8. The Principal Accounting Officer (the Administrative Secretary), the Drawing and Disbursing Officer and the Treasury Officer are equally answerable to the Public Accounts Committee in respect of Audit Paras. But in the context of the CGA Ordinance, the Controller General of Accounts, being a federal functionary, will not be available to the Public Accounts Committee for accountability.

ISSUE NO. 2

9. The argument of the Auditor General that the prescribed procedure was not observed in submitting the issue relating to CGA Ordinance to the Federal Cabinet is not tenable, as the case in question was placed on agenda of the meeting of the Federal Cabinet of 6th November 2002 at the behest of the NRB; after it had earlier discussed the matter with all stake-holders and a consensus was reached regarding the issues viz.;

    (i)   that the provincial accounts were a provincial subject;

    (ii)   that accounts shall be taken over by the provinces as from 1st July, 2006, after necessary capacity building;

    (iii)   that the provinces shall request the Federal Government to perform their accounting functions till June 2006, under Article 147 of the Constitution; and

    (iv)   that the CGA Ordinance, 2001 shall be amended accordingly.

10. These decisions were taken in a meeting held on 15th April, 2002 in the NRB, duly represented by the Federal Secretary General, Finance, the CGA and the representatives of the Auditor General and the provinces. Therefore, the submission of the case to the Federal Cabinet for its approval to the unanimous recommendations of all the stake-holders was a rightful step. Moreover, the validity of the decisions of the Federal Cabinet cannot be challenged on the ground that the Auditor General of Pakistan was not consulted by the Federal Cabinet before making these decisions.

ISSUE NO. 3

11. This issue has the same genesis and rationale as discussed above Issue No. 2. Accordingly, the following steps are now warranted to finalize the matter: -

<blockquote>

<ol type="i">
<li>the accounting function of the provinces should be declared a provincial subject;</li>
<li>the MOF should take concrete steps to get the CGA Ordinance, 2001 appropriately amended to being it in line with the related constitutional provisions in the light of the viewpoint of provincial governments;</li>
<li>the Accountant General, Punjab be placed under the provincial government; and</li>
<li>thereafter, the provinces may ask the Federal Government to take up its accounting functions only (excluding treasury functions) up till 30th June, 2006, whereafter the provinces shall take them over with effect from 1st July, 2006.</li>
</ol>

12. It is considered view of the Government of the Punjab that the solutions offered above are administratively sound and legally viable. Further appropriate action is requested accordingly."

</blockquote>

g. Additional Finance Secretary (Budget) of the Government of the Punjab addressed the following letter bearing No. SO (TT) 3-34/68/PT-VII dated 13.08.2001:

<blockquote>

"Kindly refer to your letter No. 59/104/Policy/CGA/2001, dated 9.7.2001, addressed to the Chief Secretary, Punjab, on the subject cited above.

In this regard, it is to invite your kind attention to the fact that the Governor of the Punjab has separately addressed two demi-official letters dated April 25, 2001 and May 24, 2001 to the Minister for Finance, Government of Pakistan and the Chief Executive/President of Pakistan respectively, raising initial concerns of the Punjab Government in the matter of promulgation of CGAs (Appointment, Function and Powers) Ordinance 2001, vis-à-vis its legal administration and technical ramifications. The response to the said communications is awaited.

Meanwhile, the issue has been further examined in this department in the light of the subsequent developments, whereby, it is considered that the Punjab Government may like to further bring out the legal and administrative infirmities, inherent in the new law, to the notice of the Ministry of Finance.

Till such time that the matter is reviewed, and the issues sorted out mutually, it is proposed that there should be no administrative or structural changes in the present setup and functioning of the District Accounts Offices in the Punjab. This is all the more advisable in view of the parallel implementation of the new setups of the District Governments under the Devolution Plan, and for ensuring that this critical phase is not overtaken by subsidiary issues, thus adversely affecting the maintenance of accounts etc.; in the changed scenario."

</blockquote>

h. Lt. Gen. S. Tanwir H. Naqvi (R), the then Chairman, National Reconstruction Bureau of the Federal Government wrote a letter bearing No. NRB/P/DO-1 dated 09.04.2001 to the Federal Finance Minister, inter alia, stating therein that:

<blockquote>

"The second area is the separation of accounts from audit and the decentralization of accounting as per the constitution to the provinces under provincial accountants' general not subordinated to the Federal Accountant General, who should deal exclusively with Federal

</blockquote>

accounting and be subordinated directly to the Finance Division. I say this because there appears to be a move initiated by the Auditor Generals department to centralize all accounting presently done by District Accounts Officers under the Controller General of Accounts. This would be against 'devolution' and 'decentralization' and manifestly against the constitution in both letter and spirit. I am attaching a comprehensive e-mail 1 got on this subject very recently."

i. Finance Department of the then Government of NWFP, vide letter No. S. O (W&M) 3-5/FD/PIFRA/Vol: VI dated 28.03.2001, intimated to the Federal Finance Secretary that:

"2) It is placed on record that the views of Finance Secretary, Punjab, are fully endorsed. The report of H.U. Beg Committee or the proposal being firmed up at the level of the Ministry of Finance regarding separation of Audit and Accounts have not been shared with the Provincial Government. Unless the Provincial Governments are made privy to above reports/proposal, it would be difficult to offer our considered views even if the Provincial Government are represented in the Cabinet.

3) It is therefore requested that a copy of the report of H.U. Beg Committee and formal proposal of the Ministry of Finance regarding separation of Audit and Accounts may kindly be provided to this department on priority."

j. Finance Secretary of the Government of Balochistan addressed a d.o. letter dated 08.08.2001 to the Federal Secretary General Finance stating that:

"The Provincial Government examined the Ordinance issued by the Federal Government regarding appointment of Controller General of Accounts. The Provincial Government is of the view that such appointment for controlling the Federal Accounts will be all right. However, bringing the Provincial management of Accounts under the ambit of the new Controller General will be a violation of the constitution of Pakistan. The constitution provides that any item not included in the Federal or Concurrent list will be a Provincial subject. Similarly, Articles 119 to 126 of the constitution specifically authorize the Provincial Governments to keep and regulate their accounts at their own.

2. The proposed Ordinance being violative of the constitution of Pakistan is not implementable. Provincial Government requests the Federal Government to amend the Ordinance accordingly and place the local Accountant General at the disposal of the Provincial Government for administrative and operational purposes.

3. The Provincial Government will cooperate with the Controller General of Accounts, Islamabad in coordination of overall accounting patterns in country."

70.   We have gone through the aforesaid letters. We directed the learned Attorney General for Pakistan to submit replies of these letters. After seeking instructions from the defendant, he has informed us that only one letter (letter of the Chief Minister, Punjab bearing No. NO.AS(IMPL.)/CMO/14/0T-4 dated 18.11.2014) was responded to by the Federal Finance Division in which assurance was given that the Federation had no intention to assume treasury functions of the plaintiff but no consequential action was taken to amend the CGA Ordinance accordingly. The learned Attorney General also stated that the

Federation is under no legal obligation to respond to each and every letter of the Provinces and others and no-response or silence is also a reply.

71.   The learned Advocate General, Punjab informed us that the following Committees considered the issue of performance of accounting functions of the Provinces:

a. Provincial Administration Commission constituted in February 1960 recommended as follows:

> "While for obvious reasons, external audit of Government accounts has to be independent of Provincial Government's control, it is not necessary or desirable that the provincial accounts should be maintained by an independent body. In all business and administrative organizations, maintenance of accounts is one of the functions of the organization itself and not of an external independent agency. Moreover, it is manifestly undesirable that the accounting organization should also be responsible for external audit of the accounts maintained by it. We consider that it is absolutely essential that external audit and accounts should be separated. The accounting organization should be squarely under the administrative control of the Provincial Government."

b. The A.G.N. Qazi Committee was constituted in 1984 with the following terms of reference:

a) To examine and recommend what should be the appropriate status for the Auditor-General as well as the Pakistan Audit Department, keeping in view the provisions of the Constitution and other relevant factors.

b) To review the functioning of the Audit Department and recommend whether a team of outside consultants should be commissioned by the AGP to suggest ways and means for effecting improvements in the working and performance of the organization.

The Committee, inter alia, recommended that:

> "The institution of treasuries and sub-treasuries should be abolished and all payment and custodial work should be transferred to National Bank of Pakistan branches and the work of sale of revenue and non-judicial stamps be transferred to post offices."
>
> With the exception of those accounts where responsibility for initial accounting lies with the respective departments, all initial accounting should be carried out by the District Accounts Offices and in those districts which do not have them, such offices should be opened. All the District Accounts Offices should be under the direct control of the Auditor-General and all the employees who are in Provincial service may be taken on the Federal pay-roll."

c. In February, 2000, the Federal Government constituted a committee comprising the following:

Sr. No.	Name	Status
1	Mr. H. U. Beg (Retired civil servant)	Chairman
2	Mr. M.A. Lodhi, Executive Director, Institute of Cost and Management	Member

	Accountants of Pakistan. (Retired civil servant)	
3	Minan Tayyab Hassan, (Retired civil servant)	Member
4	Khawaja Amjad Saeed, Member Council, Institute of Cost and Management Accountants of Pakistan.	Member
5	Mr. Mujahid Eshai, Member Council, Institute of Chartered Accountants of Pakistan.	Member
6	Mr. Najam I. Choudhury, Ferguson & Ferguson	Member
7	Mr. Shahzado Shaikh, Project Director/PIFRA	Member/Secretary

The terms of reference of the committee were as follows:

(A) To review and examine the existing system / functions of the audit and accounts within the purview of the Auditor General of Pakistan in line with constitutional provisions and other laws and rules including issues pertaining to his independence as a Supreme Audit Institution in line with international best practices;

(B) To suggest an action plan and an organizational set up for separation of Audit from Accounts in line with the Project to Improve Financial Reporting and Auditing (PIFRA);

(C) To examine and recommend whether as a result of separation of Audit from Accounts under PIFRA, the accounts of the provinces should be provincialized or not;

(D) To examine and suggest how auditing and accounting functions will be separated at District Accounts Offices level and their administrative control;

(E) To make recommendations regarding proposed organizational set up of accounts and audit offices, its financial implications and the role and administrative control of the officers of the Accounts Group consequent to separation;

(F) To suggest a time frame and phasing of the above reforms and address all Constitutional/Legal/Regulatory/Administrative and procedural issues;

(G) To formulate recommendations for establishing adequate internal controls in the Ministries and subordinate entities including authorities.

Report and recommendations of the H.U. Beg Committee have not been shared with the plaintiff.

d. Higher Government Think Tank of the National Reconstruction Bureau (NRB) was constituted for devolution of federal powers to the Provinces which, inter alia, recommended that:

"One recent development is the establishment of the office of the Controller General of Accounts as an Attached Department of the Finance Division. The Provinces have objected to this arrangement. It seems that constitutionally Provincial Accounts fall under the domain of the Provincial Finance Departments. The proposal of the Provinces may, therefore, be accepted."

e. In June 2006, the Prime Minister of Pakistan approved constitution of a task force headed by Mr. Sharifuddin Pirzada, Senior Advisor to the Prime Minister with Advisor to the Prime Minister on Finance, Auditor General of Pakistan, Secretary Law and Finance Secretary as members to propose suitable amendments in the CGA Ordinance. It has been alleged that the report of this task force has not been shared with the plaintiff.

72.   Learned Advocate General Punjab has also placed on record legal opinions of the Federal Ministry of Law, Attorney General for Pakistan, Law and Parliamentary Affairs Department of the Government of the Punjab and office of the Advocate General, Punjab on the subject of performance of treasury and accounting functions of the plaintiff by the defendant. We will see these valuable pieces of legal opinions as and where required. For the moment, suffice is to say that the lis at hand has been legally analysed by all available executive legal offices of the Federation and of the plaintiff Province.

73.   The learned counsel of the plaintiff also informed us that the following decisions made by various executive authorities have not been able to resolve the lis at hand:

a. The following summary was prepared by the Finance Division of the Federal Government for consideration and orders of the Federal Cabinet:

Subject: -   **Provincialisation of District accounts offices**

The Scheme of District Accounts Offices was introduced in Punjab, NWFP and part of Sindh on experimental basis in 1967. It envisaged simplification of accounting procedure and decentralization of accounts of district level. The Scheme saved considerable time in processing monetary transactions and account keeping. The District Account Offices are managed from Provincial Treasuries and Pakistan Audit Department. The Provincial Governments and Pakistan Audit Department are exercising control on their respective staff.

2.   A Committee headed by AGN Kazi constituted to review working of the Audit Department recommended transfer of control of District Accounts Offices to the Auditor General of Pakistan (Annex I). The recommendations were considered by the Cabinet in its meeting of 8th February, 1987 (Annex II) and decided that the proposal of placing the District Accounts Offices under the direct control of the Auditor General of Pakistan should further be examined in consultation with the Provincial Governments before its implementation (Annex III).

3.   In pursuance of the above decision, Provincial Governments were consulted before implementing the decision. They have not agreed to the transfer of control of District Accounts Offices to the Auditor General of Pakistan but instead have demanded provincialisation of Accounts. The matter was discussed in a meeting of Provincial Finance Secretaries on 15th September, 1993 under the chairmanship of Finance Secretary which was also attended by the acting Auditor General of Pakistan. It was unanimously agreed that District Accounts Offices be placed under the administrative control of Provincial Finance Departments and the new system may come into force with effect from 1st July, 1994. It was also decided to recommend that the institution of District Accounts Offices should also be created in the Province of Sindh and Balochistan.

4.   Pakistan Audit Department arranged a presentation to the Adviser to the Prime Minister for Finance and Economic Affairs wherein it was agreed that the transfer of control of District Accounts Offices be

linked with PAD's modernization project and implemented under a phased manner.

5.   In view of the above, it is, therefore, proposed that in the first phase administrative control of the District Accounts Offices in Punjab may be transferred to Provincial Government with effect from 1st July, 1994, followed by NWFP. It is also recommended that the institution of District Accounts Offices may also be created in Sindh and Balochistan which would subsequently be transferred to respective Provincial Governments.

6.   Approval of the Cabinet is solicited to the recommendations contained in para 5 of the Summary.

7.   Adviser to the Prime Minister for Finance and Economic Affairs has seen and approved the submission of Summary to the Cabinet.

(QAZI M. ALIMULLAH)

Finance Secretary

Islamabad, March 22, 1994."

It has been claimed that the aforesaid summary was on the agenda of the Federal Cabinet but the summary was withdrawn on personal intervention of the then Auditor General for unknown reasons.

b. A meeting held in the NRB on 4th of February 2002 to deliberate upon the CGA Ordinance, 2001 made the following decisions:

    i.   Constitutional amendments may be required to legalize the CGA Ordinance.

    ii.   Provincial A.G.'s may be placed operationally / administratively under the respective Provincial Governments. For technical matters and compilation of the Accounts of the Federation, the A.G.'s shall coordinate with the CGA. This activity can be done immediately.

    iii.   Ultimately through Civil Services Reforms, provincialize the entire Accounting Cadre.

    iv.   Separate service cadres be created for Accounts and for Audit through Civil Services Reforms.

The aforesaid meeting was chaired by Barrister Shahida Jamil, Federal Minister for Law, Justice and Human Rights, and attended by Malik Hakim Khan, Additional Secretary, Law Division, Mr. Moeen Afzal, Secretary General, Finance Division, Mr. Younis Khan, Secretary, Finance Division, Dr. Waqar Masood, Additional Secretary, Finance Division, Lt. Gen (R) S. Tanwir H. Naqvi, Chairman, NRB, Dr. Gulraz Ahmad, Member-1, NRB, Justice (R) Amjad Ali, Member-II, NRB, Mr. Danyal Aziz, Consultant, NRB, Mr. Riaz Khan, Consultant, NRB, Mr. Muhammad Naeemul Haq, Consultant, NRB, Mr. Muhammad Yousuf Memon, Consultant, NRB, Mr. Salman Siddique, Secretary, Finance Department (Punjab), Mr. Nawaz Leghari, Additional Secretary, Finance Department (Sind),Hafiz Matiullah, Additional Secretary, Finance Department (NWFP),Mr. Farooq Akhtar, Deputy Secretary, Finance Department (NWFP),Mr. Jalil Khan Dotani, Provincial Minister for Finance (Baluchistan) and Mr. Saleem Sethi, Secretary, Finance Department (Baluchistan).

c. A meeting held in the NRB on April 15, 2002 attended, among others, by Minister of Finance Punjab and Sindh, Secretary General Finance, besides representatives of Ministry of Finance, Auditor General of Pakistan, Controller General of Accounts and Provincial Secretaries of Finance and Provincial Accountant Generals, inter alia, made the following decisions:

    i.   The accounts will be provincialized by July 1, 21006. This period would be considered as a transition period. The Provinces under Article 147 of the Constitution would assign the accounting function to the Federal

Government. They will send a request to the Federal Government in this regard. NRB will prepare a suitable draft to ensure consistency. The Provincial Ordinances need to be promulgated by October, 2005.

ii. During the transition phase the CGA will be responsible for all accounting functions of the Federal, Provincial and local governments. The staff would continue to serve in their present posts irrespective of the service to which they belong. Staff belonging to Provincial Government services providing accounting and auditing functions should be protected and their role is to be clearly reflected in the amendments. A final solution to the service issues would be arrived at under the Civil Service Reforms.

iii. After the transition period the Provincial Accountant Generals will be placed under the administrative control of the Provincial Government. A right response relationship will need to be developed between the CGA and the Provincial AGs.

iv. The amended CGA Ordinance must address both the transition phase and the post transition phase. It must also include the treatment of the various services.

v. The Tehsil/Town Accounts Officer should be primarily responsible for the TMA accounting under the centralized hierarchy. The amended CGA Ordinance must clearly define the TMA accounting system.

vi. The Local Fund Audit staff will be absorbed in the Internal Control and Audit Offices to be setup in the local governments.

vii. The Auditor General will be responsible for the auditing function for all levels of governments.

d. The Federal Cabinet in its meeting held on November 6, 2002, made the following decisions:

(1) The Provincial and District Government accounts to be maintained exclusively by the Provincial Governments with effect from 1st July, 2006.

(2) The Provincial Governments to request the Federal Government, under Article 147 of the Constitution, to maintain the Provincial and District Government accounts till June, 2006 on behalf of the Provincial Governments.

(3) The Controller General of Accounts Ordinance, 2001 may be amended appropriately to reflect the above position as proposed by NRB.

e. The Prime Minister of Pakistan, vide his orders dated 17.06.2006, approved the proposal at paragraph 6 of the following Summary (bearing No. 4(8)/2003-Policy-2463/FS/06 dated 03.06.2006) for the Prime Minister, submitted by the Federal Finance Division:

"Subject: **PROVINCILIZATION OF ACCOUNTS**

Preparation and maintenance of accounts of the Federation and Provinces was being made by the Office of the Auditor General of Pakistan under Article 169 of the Constitution (Annex-I) read with Presidential Order 21 of 1973. The function was, however, transferred to the Controller General of Accounts (CGA) from 1st July, 2001 by promulgating CGA Ordinance, 2001 (Annex-II). Accordingly, the preparation and maintenance of accounts of the Federation and Provinces is being done by the CGA since then.

2. The National Reconstruction Bureau (NRB), however, considered it appropriate that the accounts of the Provinces should be maintained by

the respective Provincial Governments. NRB also consulted the Attorney General for Pakistan on the subject who expressed the views that if the accounting function is taken away from the Auditor General, the same lapses to the Provinces and cannot be transferred to the Controller General of Accounts. With the consent of the Provincial Governments (views of Provincial Governments of Punjab and NWFP at Annex-III), NRB raised the issue before the Cabinet in a presentation made on 6th November, 2002. The Cabinet decided (Annex-IV) that the Provincial and District Government accounts to be maintained exclusively by the Provincial Governments with effect from 1st July, 2006 and the CGA Ordinance, 2001 may be amended appropriately to reflect the above position.

3. The Auditor General of Pakistan has expressed his views that the Provinces have no locus standi and that the centralization of the accounting function in the CGA are entirely in consonance with the provisions of the Constitution. This position has been upheld by the Ministry of Law, Justice & Human Rights which has opined (Annex-V) that the accounts of the Federation and Provinces is a Federal subject, the Federal Parliament has exclusive powers to make laws on the subject and any law made by the Provincial Legislature regarding the aforesaid subject shall be void.

4. In order to resolve the issue and discuss the legal implications of the Cabinet decision, on the instructions of the Prime Minister, a meeting was held in the Office of Attorney General in which Advisor to Prime Minister on Finance, Auditor General and Secretary Finance participated. The Attorney General, in line with his earlier opinion, stated that the Federal Legislature cannot appoint any functionary for the maintenance of provincial accounts other than Auditor General. The Auditor General may, however, delegate his powers to another functionary of the Federal Government for which the Auditor General Ordinance, 2001 may be amended if so wished by the Government. In his opinion, the CGA Ordinance, 2001 was in conflict to the Constitution with regard to maintenance of provincial accounts and needed to be amended. The Auditor General holds the view that the amendments in the Ordinances have to be carefully thought through.

5. There is also the fact that there is a divergence of views that needs to be resolved before amending the Ordinances. However, there is time constraint imposed by the sunset clause of the Cabinet decision according to which the provincial and district accounts are to be maintained exclusively by the Provincial Governments with effect from the 1st of July, 2006. The Provincial Governments have already initiated steps to take over the function from July, 2006.

6. It is, therefore, proposed that:

a. The Cabinet decision dated 6th November, 2002 is held in abeyance by the Prime Minister under Rule 15(1)(a) of the Rules of Business, 1973 until the controversy is resolved; and

b. A task force headed by Mr. Sharifuddin Pirzada, Senior Advisor to the Prime Minister with Advisor to the Prime Minister on Finance, Auditor General of Pakistan, Secretary Law and Finance Secretary as members may be constituted to propose suitable amendments in the law.

7.The Advisor to the Prime Minister on Finance, Revenue, Economic Affairs and Statistics has seen and authorized submission of this summary."

Constitution of the aforesaid task force was accordingly notified by the Federal Finance Division vide its communication bearing No. 4/8/03-P-I dated 21.06.2006. The plaintiff is not aware of working or report of this task force.

74.   We have seen with interest the executive decisions on the subject and are bewildered to observe the attitude and maturity with which the issue has been tackled. One may gather the impression that the decisions were aimed at avoidance of resolution of the dispute and not for dispute-resolution. A clear lack of sense of responsibility to resolve the dispute is more than visible and pervasive evasive attitude is what is floating on the surface of the record of this case. We refrain to further comment on the attitude of the rival parties in this case as our advice or observations are not likely to have the effect of producing a wholly different attitude overnight. A sense of responsibility, they say, is an attribute of character born of experience, not a garment to be put on or discarded at will, according to the particular function which the wearer may be attending at the moment. Learned Law Officers of the plaintiff as well as of the defendant have frankly admitted before us that the Federation and the Province of Punjab have done nothing to honour their commitment recorded by the Hon'ble Supreme Court of Pakistan in its order announced on 02.04.2019 through which Civil Petitions No.2568 and 2569 of 2015 were disposed of and the Governments were expected to resolve the dispute preferably within six months. The learned Advocate General, Punjab has blamed that non-responsive attitude of the defendant with respect to the dispute regarding the CGA Ordinance has forced the plaintiff to invoke the constitutional jurisdiction of the Hon'ble Supreme Court under Article 184(1) of the Constitution.

75.   The material placed on record and arguments of the learned Advocate General, Punjab and of the learned Attorney General for Pakistan have convinced us that a dispute has been in existence between the plaintiff and the defendant since decades on the issues raised in the instant plaint. The dispute concerns competing claims of the parties with respect to their constitutional jurisdictions on the matters explained in the instant plaint. The dispute is of the nature for which the Constitution has vested exclusive original jurisdiction in the Hon'ble Supreme Court of Pakistan under its Article 184(1). In view of the subject-matter of the dispute and the parties being only the Governments, no other court in Pakistan has jurisdiction to adjudicate upon this dispute. We are, therefore, convinced to hold and do hereby hold that the instant plaint is maintainable under Article 184(1) of the Constitution.

Question # 2

> **Whether Section 5 (b) of the CGA Ordinance, to the extent it assigns treasury functions of the Provinces to the CGA, is in violation of Article 119 of the Constitution or whether the President of Pakistan or the Auditor General are constitutionally empowered to prescribe pre-audit checks in respect of payments from the Provincial Consolidated Fund and Public Account of the Province?**

76.   Functions of the CGA have been specified in Section 5 of the CGA Ordinance (as it was before amendment through the Finance Act, 2014), reproduced below:

 a)   to prepare and maintain the accounts of the Federation, the Provinces and District Governments in such forms and in accordance with such methods and principals as the Auditor General may, with the approval of the President, prescribe from time to time;

 b)   to authorize payments and withdrawals from the Consolidated Fund and Public Accounts of the Federal and Provincial

Governments against approved budgetary provisions, after pre-audited checks as Auditor General may, from time to time, prescribe;

c) to prepare and maintain accounts of such organizations and authorities established, set up or controlled by the Federation or Provinces as may be assigned to him by the President or, as the case may be, the Governor of the Province;

d) to lay down the principals governing the internal financial control for Government Departments in consultation with the Ministry of Finance and the Provincial Finance departments as the case may be;

e) to render advice on accounting procedure for new schemes, programmes or activities undertaken by the Government concerned;

f) to submit accounts compiled by him or any other person responsible in that behalf, after the close of each financial year, to the Auditor General, showing under the respected heads, the annual receipts and disbursements for the purpose of Federation and of each Province within the time frame provided by the Auditor General;

g) to provide, in so far as the accounts compiled by him permit, to the Federal Government or, as the case may be, the Provincial Government or District Government such information as such Governments may from time to time require;

h) develop and maintain an efficient system of pension, provident funds and other retirement benefits in consultation with the concerned Governments;

i) to co-ordinate and ensure resolution of audit observations of the Audit Department with concerned departments; and

j) to prescribe syllabus, standards and provide facilities for the training of officers and staff under his administrative control.

77. Section 6 of the Finance Act, 2014, provided as under:
"In the Controller General of Accounts (Appointment, Functions and Powers) Ordinance, 2001 (XXIV of 2001), in section 5, in clause (b), —

(a) after the word "may" the commas and words ", with the approval of the President," shall be inserted; and

(b) for the semi colon, at the end, a colon shall be substituted and thereafter the following proviso shall be added, namely: -
"Provided that in case of exigency Ministry of Finance or Finance Departments, as the case may be, may authorize payments directly from the State Bank of Pakistan and submit such information to Controller General to enable him to record the transactions;".

78. After enactment of the Finance Act, 2014, Section 5 (b) of the CGA Ordinance reads as under:
"to authorize payments and withdrawals from the Consolidated Fund and Public Accounts of the Federal and Provincial Governments against approved budgetary provisions, after pre-audited checks as Auditor General may, **with the approval of the President**, from time to time, prescribe;
Provided that in case of exigency Ministry of Finance or Finance Departments, as the case may be, may authorize payments directly from the State Bank of Pakistan and submit such

***information to Controller General to enable him to record the
transactions;"***

79.   Starting his arguments, learned Advocate General, Punjab stated that he would not repeat the arguments written in the plaint but would submit additional material to substantiate and fortify those arguments. He invited our attention to paragraph 48 of the report of the Joint Committee on Indian Constitutional Reform (Session 1933-1934), reproduced below:

> "48. The scheme of Provincial Autonomy, as we understand it, is one whereby each of the Governors' Provinces will possess an Executive and a Legislature having exclusive authority within the Province in a precisely defined sphere, and in that exclusively provincial sphere broadly free from control by the Central Government and Legislature. This we conceive to be the essence of Provincial Autonomy, though no doubt there is room for wide differences of opinion with regard to the manner in which that exclusive authority is to be exercised. It represents a fundamental departure from the present system, under which the Provincial Governments exercise a devolved and not an original authority. The Act of 1919 and the Devolution Rules made under it, by earmarking certain subjects as "Provincial subjects," created indeed a sphere within which responsibility for the functions of government rests primarily upon the Provincial authorities; but that responsibility is not an exclusive one, since the Governor General in Council and the Central Legislature still exercise an extensive authority throughout the whole of the Provinces. Under the proposals in the White Paper, the Central Government and Legislature would, generally speaking, cease to possess in the Governors' Provinces any legal power or authority with respect to any matter falling within the exclusive Provincial sphere, though as we shall explain later, the Governor-General in virtue of his power of supervising the Governors will have authority to secure compliance in certain respects with directions which he may find it necessary to give."

80.   Learned Advocate General, Punjab, stated that a brief journey into history is essential for proper understanding of the lis at hand, terming history self-knowledge and claiming this self-knowledge the first step in wisdom. He stated that prior to enactment of Government of India Act, 1935, there was a unitary form of government in India. The distribution of legislative powers between the Provinces and the Centre was necessitated more with a view to administrative convenience than to determine areas of exclusive legislative competence. The Provinces enjoyed almost the same status, as is presently that of the local governments. Elaborating the legal position prevailing before enactment of the Government of India Act, 1935, he stated that:

    i.   There was one public account for both the Central and Provincial Governments. (Section 20(3) of the Government of India Act, 1915 read with Rule 14(1), 16, 21 and 22 of the Devolution Rules, 1920).

    ii. The Provinces were not allowed to incur debt without prior written permission of the Governor General. (Rule 3(1) of the Local Government (Borrowing) Rules, 1920). Even the Provinces were allowed to establish their Finance Departments vide Rule 36(1) of the Devolution Rules, 1920.

    iii. The Governor General in Council, who was the custodian of the Public Account, acting under Rule 16 of the Devolution Rules, 1920 and with the previous sanction of the Secretary of State for India in Council, issued Treasury Orders, 1922 prescribing the procedure to be followed in the payment of moneys into and in the withdrawal, transfer and disbursement of moneys from the Public Account and the custody of moneys standing in that Account. Under these Treasury Orders, the authority to order withdrawals from the public account was vested in the officers of the Indian Audit Department. In cases in which the Auditor General of India was unable to post his own officers to work as Treasury Officers, the officers of district administration were allowed to act as Treasury Officers subject to strict supervision and control by the Indian Audit Department. Every payment made by those Treasury Officers was necessarily required to be scrutinized (post-audited) by the Principal Auditor (the provincial head of the Indian Audit Department, who was entrusted accounting, auditing and treasury functions of Central and Provincial Governments). The authority of the Auditor General of India under the "Rules regarding the Auditor General in India", made by the Secretary of State for India in Council under Section 96D (1) of the Government of India Act, was, however, restricted to conducting audit of Central and Local Governments and compiling the Finance and Revenue Accounts. The Rules regarding the Auditor General in India did not assign treasury functions of the Local Governments (Provincial Governments) to the Auditor General.

iv. There was no effective control of the legislative assemblies of the Provinces over the budget of their respective Provinces. The Governor of a Province had power to incur expenditure notwithstanding refusal of the provincial legislature to authorize that expenditure. (Section 72(d) of the Government of India Act, 1915).

v. The revenues of India were vested in the Secretary of State for India in Council, who was custodian of the revenues of India. The Central and Provincial Governments performed duties with respect to revenues of India on behalf of the Secretary of State for India in Council.

81. The learned Advocate General, Punjab stated that the Government of India Act, 1935 substituted unitary form of government with a federal system. Under the federal system, he explained, the Provinces were given constitutional status and powers and jurisdictions of Federation and of the Federating Units (Provinces) were precisely defined in the Government of India Act, 1935. On adoption of the federal principle, which was a substantive and fundamental policy shift, requisite consequential measures were taken. He listed some of those measures which were as follows:

i. Cash balance of the Provinces was separated from the cash balance of the Federal Government with exclusive and indivisible jurisdiction of the Provinces over operation of their bank accounts through provincial treasuries and sub-treasuries. The Provinces were authorized vide Section 151 of the Government of India Act, 1935 to regulate their public accounts and manage their treasury functions in accordance with the rules to be framed by the Governor of the respective Province. It was specifically laid down in the Treasury Rules framed by the Governor of the Punjab that the Auditor General had no responsibility with regard to functioning of treasuries and sub-treasuries (authorizing withdrawals from the bank account of the Provincial Government).

ii.	The Provincial Governments were given authority to appoint Provincial Auditor General vide Section 167 of the Government of India Act, 1935.

iii.	Section 163 of the Government of India Act, 1935 authorized the Provincial Governments to borrow on the guarantee of their public accounts subject to legislation of the legislative assembly of the Province.

iv.	The revenues of India were no longer vested in the Secretary of State in Council. Under the Government of India Act, 1935, the Federal and Provincial Governments became custodians of their respective revenues.

82.	Learned Advocate General, Punjab read out constitutional provisions relating, inter alia, to treasury functions of the Provinces, starting from the Government of India Act, 1935 to Article 119 of the Constitution of 1973, reproduced below:

Section 151 (1) of the Government of India Act, 1935

Rules may be made by the Governor-General and by the Governor of a Province for the purpose of securing that all moneys received on account of the revenues of the Federation or of the Province, as the case may be, shall, with such exceptions, if any, as may be specified in the rules, be paid into the public account of the Federation or of the Province, and the rules so made may prescribe, or authorize some person to prescribe the procedure to be followed in respect of the payment of moneys into the said account, the withdrawal of moneys therefrom, the custody of moneys therein, and any other matters connected with or ancillary to the matters aforesaid.

Article 95 of the Constitution of Pakistan, 1956

The custody of the Provincial Consolidated Fund, the payment of moneys into such Fund, the withdrawal of moneys therefrom, the custody of public moneys other than those credited to such fund received by or on behalf of the Provincial Government, their payment into the public account of the Province, and the withdrawal of moneys from such Account, and all matters connected with or ancillary to matters aforesaid, shall be regulated by Act of the Provincial Legislature and, until provision in that behalf is so made, by rules made by the Governor.

Article 87 of the Constitution of Pakistan, 1962

The custody of the Provincial Consolidated Fund of a Province, the payment of moneys into, and withdrawal of moneys from that Fund, and all other transactions relating to that Fund, and the custody of other moneys received by or on behalf of the Provincial Government and all transactions relating to those moneys, and all matters ancillary to or connected with any of the aforesaid matters, shall be regulated by or under an Act of the Provincial Legislature or, subject to any such Act, by rules made by the Governor of the Province.

Article 124 of the interim Constitution of Pakistan, 1972

The custody of the Provincial Consolidated Fund, the payment of moneys into that Fund, the withdrawal of moneys from that Fund, and the custody of other moneys received or deposited under clause (2) or clause (3) of the last preceding Article, their payment into the Public Account of the Province, and the withdrawal of such moneys from such Account, and all matters connected with or ancillary to the aforesaid matters, shall be regulated by or under Act of the Provincial Assembly or, until provision in that behalf is so made, by rules made by the Governor.

Article 119 of the Constitution of Pakistan, 1973

The custody of the Provincial Consolidated Fund, the payment of moneys into that Fund, the withdrawal of moneys therefrom, the custody of other moneys received by or on behalf of the Provincial Government, their payment into, and withdrawal from, the Public Account of the Province, and all matters connected with or ancillary to the matters aforesaid, shall be regulated by Act of the Provincial Assembly or, until provision in that behalf is so made, by rules made by the Governor.

83.   It was stated by the learned Advocate General, Punjab that the Governor of the Punjab framed the Punjab Treasury Rules in exercise of his powers under Section 151 of the Government of India Act, 1935 which were originally issued vide Punjab Government's Notification No. 843-F-37/13037 dated 1st April, 1937. These rules primarily provide machinery and procedure to regulate receipts into and withdrawals from the Provincial Consolidated Fund and Public Account of the Province. Banking business of the Government of the Punjab is controlled in accordance with the procedure provided in these rules by the machinery specified therein. Other rules framed under Section 151 of the Government of India Act, 1935, namely, the Punjab Financial Rules, Departmental Financial Rules, Budget Manual and Delegation of Financial Powers Rules deal with financial management and allied issues and provide guidance to the departmental authorities and others. The bank account of the Government of the Punjab is, however, operated mainly under the Punjab Treasury Rules by the Treasury Officers. It was specifically laid down in the Punjab Treasury Rules that the Auditor General had no responsibility with regard to functioning of treasuries and sub-treasuries. Rule 5 of the Punjab Treasury Rules provided as follows:

"No portion of the responsibility for the proper management and working of Treasuries shall devolve upon the officers of the Pakistan Audit Department."

Rule 1.1, reproduced below, of the Punjab Subsidiary Treasury Rules also reinforces the Rule 5 supra:

"The responsibility for the proper management and working of the Treasuries rests entirely with the District Officers acting under the orders of the Government."

84.   The learned Advocate General, Punjab further stated that the Treasuries & Sub-Treasuries used to make payments from the Provincial Consolidated Fund and Public Account of the Province. Net receipts and payments used to be reported to the Accountant General along with vouchers. It was function of the Accountant General to audit the vouchers and consolidate the receipts and expenditure, on gross basis, under the various heads of accounts, to reconcile the compiled accounts with the departmental authorities and to prepare Appropriation Accounts and Finance Accounts in addition to making inter-governmental or inter-departmental transfers and adjustments.

85.   The learned law officer of the plaintiff argued that no legal instrument relating to audit and accounts granted any powers to the Auditor General with respect to treasury functions. He referred to the following to substantiate his assertion:

(a) In exercise of the powers conferred by section 96D (1) of the Government of India Act, the Secretary of State in Council, with the concurrence of the majority of votes at a meeting of the Council held on the 4th day of January 1921, made the Rules regarding the Auditor General in India under which the Auditor General had no power in respect of treasury business of the Provinces.

(b) The Government of India (Audit and Accounts) Order, 1936, the Pakistan (Audit and Accounts) Order, 1952 and the Pakistan (Audit and Accounts) Order, 1973 did not assign treasury functions of the Federation or of the Provinces to the Auditor General. The AG Ordinance also does not assign any treasury functions to the Auditor General. It is the CGA Ordinance which has assigned treasury functions of the Federal and Provincial Governments to the CGA vide its Section 5(b).

86.   The learned Advocate General, Punjab brought into our notice Rule 6 of the Punjab Treasury Rules, reproduced below:

> "The Office of the Accountant General may, with the consent of, and subject to such conditions as may be prescribed by the Auditor General of Pakistan, perform all or any prescribed part of the duties of a Treasury in respect of claims against the Government that may fall due for disbursement and moneys that may be tendered for credit to the Consolidated Fund or the Public Account of the Province, at the headquarters of the Government at Lahore."

87.   It has vehemently been argued by the learned Advocate General, Punjab that the treasury functions assigned to the AG, Punjab vide Rule 6 of the Punjab Treasury Rules were restricted to "any prescribed part of the duties of a Treasury in respect of claims against the Government that may fall due for disbursement and moneys that may be tendered for credit to the Consolidated Fund or the Public Account of the Province, at the headquarters of the Government at Lahore" and there was no express or implied provision of entrustment of these powers in respect of other districts of the Province to the AG, Punjab. He further stated that paragraph 3 of the preface to the first edition of the Punjab Treasury Rules read as follows:

> "Some of these Treasury Rules, (for example rules, 4,5,10,11,16, and 30) require the Finance Minister to issue subsidiary rules, and instructions with regard to certain matters in consultation with the Accountant-General, Punjab, or the Reserve Bank of India. These Subsidiary Rules and instructions issued by the Finance Minister are contained in Part II and have been entitled "Subsidiary Treasury Rules". Logically, these Subsidiary Rules should have been issued alongwith the Treasury Rules and should have come into force from 1st April, 1937----- the date on which the Treasury Rules came into force. As, however, the framing of the detailed rules to fit in with the new statutory position was a very complicated matter and was to take some time, it was declared through the notification of Finance Department bearing No. 843-F-37/13034, dated 1st April, 1937 that the relevant rules previously prescribed by the Punjab Government, Government of India and the Auditor-General (as contained in the Civil Account Code-Volumes I and II, Public Works Account Code, Forest Account Code, Resource Manual, Punjab Treasury Manual, etc.) which were in force prior to 1st April, 1937, would remain in force and would, so far as they were not inconsistent with the provisions of the Treasury Rules (Punjab) be

treated as the instructions issued by the Finance Minister under the various Treasury Rules. With the issue of the Subsidiary Treasury Rules, as contained in this Hand Book, the notification referred to above should be treated as cancelled and so also the relevant portions of the Codes and Manuals mentioned above. Consequently, with the issue of these rules, those rules or portions of the rules in the Codes and Manuals, which have been superseded by these rules, (see the memorandum at the end of the book) will no longer be used, quoted, or referred to."

88.   He stated that the Subsidiary Treasury Rules are valid to the extent of their consistency with the Punjab Treasury Rules. As Rule 6 of the Punjab Treasury Rules restricts entrustment of a prescribed part of treasury functions of the Province to the office of the AG, Punjab to the extent of Lahore district only, therefore, the Subsidiary Treasury Rules cannot go beyond the limit set by the said Rule 6. He further averred that constitutional validity of the said Rule 6 was a question which he would like to address later in his arguments.

89.   The learned Advocate General, Punjab informed us that at paragraph 34 of "Proposals for Departmentalization of Accounts prepared under the directions of the Comptroller and Auditor General of Pakistan", published in 1962 by the Superintendent, Government Printing Press, West Pakistan, Lahore, it was proposed that:

> "To overcome the difficulties discussed above, it is proposed that the treasuries be placed under the Financial Commissioners Accounts (who would be officers of Provincial Government) and converted into Pay and Accounts Offices. The functions of these Pay and Accounts Offices would be: -
>
> (a)   the pre-audit of all claims on account of pay, travelling allowance, contingencies, etc., in respect of the gazetted officers and non-gazetted establishments employed in the district;
>
> (b)   the maintenance of the provident fund accounts of the non-transferable staff of the District;
>
> (c)   the disposal of pension claims, issue of pension payment orders and audit of pension payments;
>
> (d)   the maintenance of deposit registers of the district;
>
> (e)   the compilation of the monthly account of payment and receipts relating to the district classified for each department; and
>
> (f)   the payment of various civil advances and permanent advances."

90.   It was stated by the learned Advocate General, Punjab that the Comptroller and Auditor General of Pakistan, through his letter No. 369–Reorg/8–65 dated 16th August, 1965, informed the Secretary Finance of the Government of West Pakistan that:

> "I have the honour to invite a reference to para 7(iii) of the minutes of the meeting of the Secretaries' Sub-Committee (copy enclosed) held on 6th July, 1965 regarding the organization of Pay and Accounts Offices. It was decided that in each province two treasuries (one large and the other small) should be reorganized on the pattern proposed by the Comptroller & Auditor General. It is accordingly proposed to set up pay and accounts offices as an experimental measure at Hyderabad (which is a large treasury) and at Gujranwala (which is a small treasury) with effect from 01.11.1965.

2.   The functions of the proposed Pay and Accounts Offices to be set up in place of the treasuries will be: –

    (a)   Pre–audit of all personal claims on account of pay, TA. etc. of non–gazetted Estt. employed in the District and contingent staff of the district.

    (b)   Maintenance of provident fund accounts of the C.S.P. Officers, Class-I Officers & other gazetted officers and non–gazetted staff of the district.

    (c)   Disposal of pension claims, issue of pension payment orders and audit of pension payments in respect of non–gazetted staff of the district.

    (d)   Maintenance of deposit registers of the district.

    (e)   Payment of various temporary advances and permanent advances.

    (f)   Payment of claims of gazetted government servants on the authority of the Accountant General/Comptroller.

    (g)   Compilation of the monthly accounts of payments and receipts relating to the district classified by each major head/department.

    (h)   Local audit of the accounts of the disbursing officers in the district.

    (i)   Custody of stamps and other valuables which are now in charge of the Treasury Officer.

3.   The total staff required for each of the above Pay and Accounts Offices is given in Appendices "A", "B", "C" & "D". This staff will be drawn from two sources viz. Pakistan Audit Department and the Treasuries to the extent indicated in Appendix "E" & "F". After adjustment of the staff available in the Try, and that to be transferred from the Accounts Offices, the total requirement of additional staff required for the two Pay & Accounts Offices is also given in the above Appendixes. The additional costs of scheme on the above basis will be Rs.50300 recurring and Rs.28500 non–recurring (Appendix 'C').

4.   Although the experiment is proposed to be conducted from 01.11.1965, the additional staff has been provided with effect from 01.10.1965 to make necessary preparatory arrangements for undertaking the experiment and to allow staff moving from Karachi and Lahore to collect the necessary documents, arrange for the carriage of furniture and records. This period also includes joining time.

5.   A review of the working of the reorganized treasuries will be carried out at the end of six months to determine whether the experiment should be extended, modified or abandoned altogether.

6.   According to the instructions contained in the d.o. letter No. (A&A.I)1/12/63–624–63 dated 16.08.1963 from the Chief Secretary to Government of West Pakistan to the address of Commissioner, Lahore Division, copy inter alia endorsed to this office, the Gujranwala Treasury will continue to remain under the control of the Deputy Comm. Gujranwala legally and technically, actual supervision and control will be exercised by an officer nominated by the Finance Secretary and the Accountant General, West Pakistan will continue to give the Treasury Officer directions connected with audit and accounting matters. Similar position will prevail as regards the Hyderabad Office. Accordingly, the entire staff of Pay & Accounts Office will be borne on the strength of West Pakistan Govt. Formal sanction to

the creation of the entire strength of the Pay and Accounts Offices (less the existing number of posts at the Treasuries) as detailed below, may be accorded by the Provincial Govt."

91.   We directed the learned Attorney General for Pakistan to apprise us of the consequential changes in the accounting policies and procedures prescribed by the Auditor General of Pakistan to reflect the changes introduced through the aforesaid DAOs Scheme which was subsequently implemented in all districts of the Punjab except Lahore. He informed us that the Auditor General had prescribed the Account Code-Volume-I to IV in accordance with which accounts were required to be maintained. He admitted that no changes were made in any volume of the Account Code to provide legal cover to the changed accounting arrangements as a result of implementation of the DAOs Scheme. He also frankly admitted that the accounts were required to be maintained in such form as determined, with approval of the President of Pakistan, by the Comptroller and Auditor General. Referring to Article 197 of the Constitution of Pakistan, 1962 *("The accounts of the Centre and of the Provinces shall be kept in such form as the Comptroller and Auditor-General, with the approval of the President, may determine."),* he informed us that neither approval of the President of Pakistan to the accounting arrangements of the DAOs Scheme nor any consequential amendments in the Account Code were available on record of the Federal Government. Answering a query raised by us, the learned Attorney General for Pakistan stated that Article 197 of the Constitution of Pakistan, 1962 did not assign any role in the matter of determination of accounting policies and procedures to any authority except the Comptroller and Auditor-General and the President of Pakistan. He admitted that the Secretaries' Sub-Committee which approved the DAOs Scheme in its meeting held on 6th of July, 1965 had no authority of law to order any change in the accounting policies and procedures. He further admitted that even the Comptroller and Auditor-General had no constitutional power to effect any change in accounting policies and procedures without approval of the President of Pakistan.

92.   On the other hand, we directed the learned Advocate General, Punjab to submit a written report on the amendments in the Punjab Treasury Rules as the DAOs Scheme assigned role in performance of treasury functions of the Province in all districts of the Punjab to the AG, Punjab whereas Rule 6 of the Punjab Treasury Rules restricted entrustment of treasury functions to the AG, Punjab to Lahore district only. We were of the prima facie view that appropriate amendments in the Punjab Treasury Rules were necessary to give legal cover to the DAOs Scheme for assignment of treasury functions of the Province to the federal employees in the districts other than Lahore. We also directed him to see whether there was a constitutional provision in the Constitution of 1962 comparable to Article 147 of the Constitution of 1973 under which a Province could assign its functions to the Federation.

93.   The written report submitted by the learned Advocate General, Punjab, in compliance of our aforesaid order, was unbelievable for us. The report stated that Section 124 of the Government of India Act, 1935, Article 127 of the Constitution of 1956, Article 143 of the Constitution of 1962, Article 147 of the interim Constitution of 1972 and Article 146 of the Constitution of 1973 provided for entrustment of functions of the Federation to the Provinces but there was no provision comparable to Article 147 of the Constitution of 1973 in any earlier Constitution. Under Article 147 of the Constitution of 1973, the Government of a Province is authorized to entrust, to the Federal Government, or to its officers, functions in relation to any matter to which the executive authority of the Province extends. In absence of any enabling provision similar to Article 147 of the Constitution of 1973 in any earlier constitutional document from the Government of India Act, 1935 to the interim Constitution of 1972, neither the Province was authorized to entrust its functions to the Federation nor the Federation had any authority of law to accept such arrangement. It is not

absence of prohibition which makes an act or omission lawful; it is positive conferment of power which determines legality of an act or omission. In this view of the matter, Rule 6 of the Punjab Treasury Rules was void ab initio. Even if we ignore, for the purpose of arguments only, constitutional invalidity of the said Rule 6, it was restricted to entrustment of prescribed part of treasury functions of the Province to the AG, Punjab in Lahore district only. Partial or complete entrustment of treasury functions in respect of other districts of the Punjab to the AG, Punjab required amendments in the Punjab Treasury Rules and other allied rules. It has been admitted that no such amendments were made in the Punjab Treasury Rules.

94.   Before Eighteenth Amendment in the Constitution, Article 147 of the Constitution of 1973 read as follows:

> "Notwithstanding anything contained in the Constitution, the Government of a Province may, with the consent of the Federal Government, entrust, either conditionally or unconditionally, to the Federal Government, or to its officers, functions in relation to any matter to which the executive authority of the Province extends."

95.   Present version of the said Article 147, as amended by the 18th Amendment in the Constitution, is as under:

> "Notwithstanding anything contained in the Constitution, the Government of a Province may, with the consent of the Federal Government, entrust, either conditionally or unconditionally, to the Federal Government, or to its officers, functions in relation to any matter to which the executive authority of the Province extends:
> Provided that the Provincial Government shall get the functions so entrusted ratified by the Provincial Assembly within sixty days."

96.   We required the learned Attorney General for Pakistan and the learned Advocate General, Punjab to state whether the Provincial Government and the Federal Government entered into any arrangement for entrustment of a role in performance of treasury functions of the Government of the Punjab in districts other than Lahore to the federal employees subordinate to the AG, Punjab after commencement of the Constitution of 1973 in terms of its Article 147. Both of them stated that nothing was on record to show that such arrangement was made.

97.   Before promulgation of the CGA Ordinance, it was the DAOs Scheme which used to be cited as lawful authority for performance of treasury functions of the Province of Punjab in districts other than Lahore by the officers deputed by the office of the AG, Punjab. The DAOs Scheme made changes in accounting procedures and processes without corresponding amendments in the Account Code. Federal employees subordinate to the AG, Punjab were deputed in the districts to perform treasury functions in collaboration with the treasury establishment of the Province. Besides absence of enabling constitutional provision for the purpose, clash of the DAOs Scheme with Account Code and the Punjab Treasury Rules and lack of jurisdiction of the Secretaries' Sub-Committee made this Scheme a nullity in eyes of law. It can also not be given protection as existing law under Article 268 of the Constitution of 1973 because of being without constitutional cover and inconsistent with the Account Code and the Punjab Treasury Rules. It is, therefore, held to be void ab initio in its entirety.

98.   Provincial and federal employees started to perform treasury functions of the Province in the District Treasuries which were renamed as the District Accounts Offices under the DAOs Scheme. The provincial employees were under the administrative control of the Finance Department whereas federal employees were also initially under administrative control of the Province as posting orders of the federal employees in the District Accounts Offices were used to be issued, in consultation with the AG, Punjab by the Finance Department. Later on, the AG, Punjab started to issue posting orders of federal employees on his own creating a situation which is known as duality of control over the DAOs. This duality of control caused problems and each party demanded its exclusive control over the

389

DAOs. The learned Attorney General for Pakistan informed us that the O&M Division of the Federal Government, through u.o. No.25/7/69-Mech-VI dated 22.11.1979, sought advice from the Law Division of the Federal Government on the following questions:

    i.   Whether, in view of the provisions of the Constitution and the Pakistan Audit and Accounts Order cited above, the Provincial Governments are legally in a position to make the demand of handing over of the administrative control of the DAOs to them?

    ii.   Whether in view of the above provisions, and the 'dual responsibility' of the Auditor General and the Provincial Governments, the operational control of the day-to-day functioning and discipline of the District Accounts Offices (including writing of the ACRs of the officers) should be the responsibility of the Auditor General, or whether he should be mainly concerned with overseeing that the accounts are kept in proper from and order, leaving such administrative matters as management of personnel etc. to the Provincial Governments.

99.   We have gone through the opinion tendered by the Law Division through a communication dated 27.02.1980 which is as follows:

    i.   As long the preparation of the accounts continues to be the function of the Accountant General, an officer of Pakistan Audit and Accounts Department under the Auditor General of Pakistan and again that the DAOs have at the same time to deal with transactions of both the Federation and of the provinces at the district level, Provincial Governments are not legally correct to claim the transfer of the administrative control of DAOs from the Pakistan Audit Department to them as a right. Further, demands contained in para 2(ii)(iii) of the Provincial Governments also do not suit in the frame of the constitutional and legal administration of the DAOs.

    ii.   Query on the point is not clear. As long the duality of the preparation of accounts and audit are both to be performed by DAOs at the district level and that officers of the Pakistan Audit and Accounts Department are posted in the DAOs, it appears proper that the office of Auditor General continues to associate itself with the administration and management of the DAOs and that the comments offered by the Auditor General of Pakistan in para 3 reflect a correct legal picture."

100.   We do not deem it necessary to analyse in detail the reasons given for the aforesaid legal advice of the Law Division and to point out their infirmities as it would be a wastage of our precious time to do so in respect of a worthless piece of opinion based upon illogical reasons. We, however, have not been able to refrain ourselves from indicating that the opinion of the Law Division was based upon the following patently erroneous assumptions and one would need a malti-layered blindfold to believe in these assumptions:

    i.   No provision exists in the Constitutions of Pakistan (1956, 1962 and 1973) similar to Section 151 of the Government of India Act, 1935;

    ii.   Payments made by the Treasuries are provisional; and

    iii.   Accounting includes operation of the bank accounts of the Provincial Governments.

101.   We have been informed that the CGA Ordinance was promulgated on 17th of May, 2001 which came into force on 1st of July, 2001. The CGA wrote a letter bearing No: 59 / 104 / Policy / CGA / 2001 dated 09.07.2001 to the Chief Secretary, Punjab, stating therein:

    "Controller General of Accounts Ordinance, 2001 has come into force with effect from 1st July, 2001. In pursuance of Section 6(1) of this Ordinance, the Controller General of Accounts shall have such offices at

Federal, Provincial and District level and such officers working in these offices under him as may be notified for this purpose by the Federal Government and the respective Provincial Governments. At the district level, the payments and accounts are being dealt with by the District Accounts Officers and the Treasury Officers. As the accounting function at District and Provincial level has entirely been vested in the Controller General of Accounts, it is mandatory that Treasury Offices are converted into District Accounts Offices and placed under the direct administrative control of the respective Accountants General who in turn would be responsible to Controller General of Accounts. Thus, there is a need that in pursuance of Section 6(1) of the CGA's Ordinance 2001, the Provincial Government concerned notify transfer of the control of officers / staff of the treasuries / sub-treasuries to the Accountant General. While doing so, the relevant record, and the physical infra-structure available may also be transferred to the Accountant General.

It is requested that necessary notification for the above may kindly be arranged at the earliest possible under intimation to the Accountant General concerned as well as the Controller General of Accounts."

102.   The learned Advocate General, Punjab stated that the Government of the Punjab did not accede to the above request of the CGA and no notification requested to be issued by the CGA in terms of Section 6(1) of the CGA Ordinance, reproduced below, was issued by the Provincial Government:

"6. Certain offices to work under the control of the Controller General. –

(1)   The Controller General shall have such offices at the Federal, Provincial and district levels and such officers working in these offices as may be notified for this purpose by the Federal Government and the respective Provincial Government.

(2)   Until such time the offices of the Controller General specified in sub-section (1) are notified, the following accounting organizations shall work under the Controller General, namely: -

(a)   the Accountant General of Pakistan Revenues and its sub-offices;

(b)   the Military Accountant General and its sub-offices;

(c)   the Offices of the Provincial Accountants General of each Province and the offices subordinate to them;

(d)   the Chief Accounts Officers of the departmentalized accounting offices; and

(e)   any other departmentalized accounting organizations as well as their sub-offices.

(3)   The Controller General shall be the administrative head of all the offices subordinate to him with full authority for transfer and posting within his organization."

103.   The learned Attorney General for Pakistan asserted that a notification by the Provincial Government for transfer of control of officers / staff of the treasuries / sub-treasuries to the AG, Punjab under Section 6(1) of the CGA Ordinance was not necessary as the DAOs were already covered by Section 6(2)(c) of the CGA Ordinance in their capacity as offices subordinate to the Provincial Accountant General. This assertion was ferociously contested by the learned Advocate General, Punjab. He argued that The Treasuries / DAOs, Sub-treasuries and the Inspectorate of Treasuries and Accounts are subordinate offices of the plaintiff which performs the following functions in respect of these offices:

a) It has established these offices for performance of functions exclusively falling in provincial domain under Article 119 of the Constitution read with agreement of the plaintiff with the SBP;

b) It has provided office buildings for these offices and residential buildings for its employees working in these offices;

c) It bears the cost of running these offices;

d) It recruits persons to run these offices and pays them remuneration;

e) It determines and executes terms and conditions of service of its employees working in these offices e.g. posting / transfer, disciplinary action, promotions, ACRs, leave;

f) It determines the powers and functions of these offices and the employees working in these offices;

g) It has declared the treasuries its subordinate offices as these offices fall within the definition of "Subordinate Office" given in Note (b) below paragraph 1.2 of the Manual of Secretariat Instructions of the Government of the Punjab ('Subordinate Office' means an office of Government of the Punjab other than a Department, Attached Department or a Regional / Divisional Office');

h) It has assigned administration of these offices to the Finance Department under the Rules of Business framed in terms of Article 139 (3) of the Constitution. Similar provisions exist in the Rules of Business of all other Provincial Governments in Pakistan. On the other hand, Annex-B of the Auditor General's Manual of Standing Orders (Third Edition) printed and issued by the Research & Development Wing, Department of the Auditor General of Pakistan in December, 1992 details the accounts, audit and other offices under the control of the Auditor General. This exhaustive list does not include either the Federal Treasuries or the Provincial Treasuries / DAOs, implying that these offices are not subordinate to any Accountant General. Moreover, Rule 2 (xx) of the Rules of Business of the Federal Government defines "Subordinate Office" as a Federal Government office other than a Ministry, Division or an Attached Department". The subordinate offices of the Federal Finance Division are as follows:

1. Public Procurement Regulatory Agency

2. Office of DFA (I & C) & OSD Industry, Karachi.
3. Economic Minister & Financial Advisor, Washington
4. Pakistan Mint
5. Federal Treasury Office, Islamabad
6. Federal Treasury Office, Karachi
7. Monopoly Control Authority (SEC)
   (Source: Report of Higher Government Think Tank on Restructuring of the Federal Government, National Reconstruction Bureau, Prime Minister's Secretariat, Islamabad.)

The DAOs / Treasuries of the plaintiff are, therefore, not subordinate offices of the Federal Government or of the AG, Punjab.

i) It has framed the Punjab Treasury Rules Rule 4 (5) whereof states that no portion of the responsibility for the proper management and working of treasuries shall devolve upon the officers of the Pakistan Audit Department. Rule 1.1 of the Punjab Subsidiary Treasury Rules provides that the responsibility for the proper management and working of the treasuries rests entirely with the District Officers acting under the orders of the Government.

104.   To substantiate his assertion that Section 6(2)(c) of the CGA Ordinance is not applicable to the DAOs and the provincial employees working therein, the learned Advocate General, Punjab also relied upon the dictum of law down by the Hon'ble Supreme Court of Pakistan in a case reported as Mirza Muhammad Tufail Vs. District Returning Officer and others (P L D 2007 Supreme Court 16) in the following words:

> "There are five tests for such sub-ordination, namely, the power of the authority of the appointment to the office (ii) the power of removal or dismissal of the holder from the office (iii) the payment of remuneration (iv) the nature of functions of the holder of the office, he performs (v) the nature and strength of control and supervision of the authority. The decisive test is that of appointment and removal from service while the remuneration is neutral factor and not decisive. All the aforesaid tests need not be cumulated and not necessarily must co-exist and what has to be considered is the substance of the matter which must be determined by a consideration of all the factors present in a case ad whether stress will be laid on one factor or the other will depend on each particular case."

105.   We have given due consideration to the rival contentions with regard to Section 6(1) and (2) of the CGA Ordinance. It is admitted fact that a notification envisaged under Section 6(1) of the CGA Ordinance was requested to be issued and the request was turned down by the plaintiff. As regards the contention based upon Section 6(2)(c) of the CGA Ordinance, we asked the Attorney General for Pakistan to inform us that whether the Federation had allocated budget to finance operations of the DAOs in the Punjab and for remuneration of provincial employees working therein after coming into force of the CGA Ordinance treating these offices as offices subordinate to the Provincial Accountants General. He informed us that no budget was allocated by the Federation for the purpose and it was the Province which continued to bear the expenditure on running of these offices. Physical infrastructure of these offices is a property of the Province. We demanded the learned Attorney General for Pakistan to quote any Article of the Constitution under which the Federation can assume ownership or control of property of a Province through a federal law. He failed to quote any constitutional provision to this effect. He was also not able to refer to any Article of the Constitution under which administration of a Provincial Service (the Punjab Treasuries and Accounts Service in the instant case) can be snatched by the Federation from the Province through a Federal law. He, replying to our query, however, admitted that the posts being held by the members of the Punjab Treasuries and Accounts Service in the DAOs / Treasuries are posts in connection with affairs of the Province within the meaning of Article 240(b) of the Constitution and legislation under Article 169 or 240(a) of the Constitution in respect thereof would be in excess of the jurisdiction.

106.   After analysing the issue from all angles, we are convinced to hold that, in absence of a notification to be issued under Section 6 (1) of the CGA Ordinance, control of the DAOs / Treasuries in the Punjab does not vest in the CGA as these offices are not subordinate to the AG, Punjab within the meaning of Section 6(2) (c) of the CGA Ordinance. After 18th amendment in the Constitution, observance of the procedure prescribed for entrustment of provincial functions to the Federation under Article 147 of the Constitution must precede issuance of a notification under Section 6(1) of the Constitution. We further hold that neither control and ownership of provincial property can be assumed by the Federation through a federal law except in consequence of a proper agreement between the parties nor Services of the Province or posts in connection with affairs of a Province can be controlled or regulated by the Federation through a federal law made in terms of Article 169 or 240(a) of the Constitution.

107.   Our declarations made hereinabove now confront us to look into constitutionality of Section 5(b) of the CGA Ordinance. Before doing so, it would be appropriate to precisely determine what is meant by the expressions "pre-audit" and "treasury functions".

108.   The expression 'pre-audit' has not been defined in the CGA Ordinance. https://www.dictionary.com/browse/pre-audit defines 'pre-audit' as "an examination of vouchers, contracts, etc., in order to substantiate a transaction or a series of transactions before they are paid for and recorded." https://smallbusiness.chron.com/preaudit-30494.html clarifies the expression in these words:

> "A pre-audit is the first step in the process of an audit. During a pre-audit, a company or individual's financial documents are examined to ensure that all information is correct before the company or individual undergoes an official audit. The pre-audit process may be undertaken by employees of the company being pre-audited, or the company may hire an independent organization to examine its finances. Pre-auditing may be used to describe both a single instance of review directly preceding an official audit as well as the continuous process of monitoring finances throughout the year."

109.   https://internalaudit360.com/should-internal-audit-or-management-conduct-pre-audits/ defines 'pre-audit' in the following words:

> "Pre-audits are reviews of invoices, contracts, purchase orders, and other requests for funds to substantiate a transaction or series of transactions before they are executed and recorded."

110.   Audit Manual is a document which contains instructions issued by the Auditor General of Pakistan on the subject of audit. Paragraph 3 of the Audit Manual reads as follows:

> "As a rule, heads of offices and other Government servants who are called upon to make disbursements on behalf of Government draw money for the purpose from treasuries in accordance with the provisions of the Treasury Rules made under Article 38 of the Constitution and the audit conducted in respect of these transactions is post-audit in character. Pre-audit or audit before payment is exercised only in respect of such transactions which take place at the station where the Audit office is located and an arrangement has been made between the Government and the Auditor General that claims against Government at such stations shall be submitted to the Audit office. The necessary instructions for the audit and payment of such claims will be found in Chapter 16 (see also Article 213 of the Audit Code)."

111.   In the context of the Government of the Punjab, pre-audit was used to be conducted by the AG, Punjab in respect of payments entrusted to his office in terms of Rule 6 of the Punjab Treasury Rules. In this regard, definition of the Accountant General given in Rule 2 (f) of the Punjab Treasury Rules, reproduced below, is very meaningful:

> "Accountant-General" / "Director-General, Audit & Accounts (Works)" mean the head of the office of audit and accounts subordinate to the Auditor General of Pakistan, who keeps the accounts of the Province or of Federation and exercises audit functions in relation to those accounts on behalf of the Auditor-General of Pakistan;".

112.   The above definition of the expression "Accountant General" indicates that he is a subordinate to the Auditor General with dual responsibility of audit as well as maintenance of accounts. As all payments made by the Treasuries were required to be submitted to the AG, Punjab alongwith vouchers, the AG used to compile accounts and audit the payments. A prescribed part of functions of a Treasury Officer in Lahore was entrusted to the AG in terms

394

of Rule 6 of the Punjab Treasury Rules. Under directions of the Auditor General, he started audit of payments before issuance of cheques which was termed pre-audit and post-audit of these payments was not usually done by the AG, Punjab. Pre-audit results into either rejection of the pre-audited claim or issuance of pre-audit cheque. The office conducting pre-audit issues the pre-audit cheques. In this background, we may define pre-audit as examination of claims for payments before authorization of payments in order to ensure that only payments in accordance with law are made and to make payments if found in order. This examination has to be made by an authority which is vested by the power to operate bank account of the Province. It is a pre-payment process which constitutes due diligence in order to ensure compliance of the regulatory framework applicable to withdrawals from the Provincial Consolidated Fund and Public Account of the Province. This regulatory framework has been given in the rules framed or deemed to have been framed under Article 119 of the Constitution. Pre-audit is distinguishable from the audit to be conducted by the Auditor General which is audit after payment.

113.   With the separation of audit and accounts, office of the AG, Punjab has no jurisdiction to conduct audit. The separation of audit and accounts has also made the definition of the Accountant General given in Rule 2 (f) of the Punjab Treasury Rules redundant as the AG is now subordinate to the CGA and not to the Auditor General.

114   The learned Advocate General, Punjab has asserted that pre-audit being a pre-payment process does fall within treasury functions of the Province. He defines treasury functions of the Province as functions relating to regulation of receipts into and withdrawals from the Provincial Consolidated Fund and Public Account of the Province and matters related thereto. He states that banking business of the plaintiff stands statutorily assigned to the SBP in terms of Section 21 of the State Bank of Pakistan Act, 1956 read with the agreement between the SBP and the plaintiff paragraph 2 whereof reads as follows:

> "The general banking business of the Government of Punjab (hereinafter referred to as "the Government") including the payment, receipt, collection and remittance of money on behalf of the Government, shall be carried on and transacted by the Bank in accordance with and subject to the provisions of this agreement and of the Act and such orders and directions as may, from time to time, be given to the Bank by the Government through any Government officer or officers authorized by the Government in that behalf and at any of the offices, branches or agencies of the Bank for the time being in existence as may, from time to time, be so directed and for this purpose such accounts shall be kept in the books of the Bank and at such offices, branches or agencies of the Bank as shall be necessary or convenient or as the Government shall, from time to time, direct in the manner aforesaid."

115.   To illustrate his point, the learned Advocate General, Punjab presented before this Court the following definitions of the expressions "Treasury" and "Treasurer":

> **Treasury**
> A place or building in which stores of wealth are kept; esp., a place where public revenues are kept and from which money is disbursed to defray government expenses. (Black's Law Dictionary, Eighth Edition.)
>
> **Treasurer**
> An organization's chief financial officer. The treasurer's duties typically include prudently depositing (or, if authorized, investing) and safeguarding the organization's funds and otherwise managing its finances; monitoring compliance with any applicable law relating to such finances and filing any required report; disbursing money as

authorized; and reporting to the organization on the state of the treasury. (Black's Law Dictionary, Eighth Edition.)

Treasury

Arm of Government responsible for all financial decisions and regulation of the financial services sector. It is the responsibility of the Chancellor of the Exchequer and manages the collecting of taxes, government expenditure and national debt. Until 1997, the Treasury was responsible for the overall management of the economy. The Bank of England is now independent, and shares management of the economy with   the   Treasury. (http://www.lse.co.uk/financeglossary.asp?searchTerm=&iArticleID=24 9&definition=treasury)

Treasury

Place where public monies are kept; the office of treasurer. (Tomlin's Law Dictionary as quoted in K.L.R. Law Dictionary)

Treasurer

An officer to whom the treasure of another is committed to be kept and truly disposed of. One who is responsible for the funds of any public body, or corporation or association. [(S. 17 (2) (xa) Registration Act (16 of 1908)]; [Art. 31A (1) (d), Const.] (K.L.R. Law Dictionary)

Treasury

Treasury is defined as the funds of a group, institution or government, or to the department responsible for budgeting and spending. Noun (http://www.yourdictionary.com/treasury)

Treasury

A place in which private or public funds are received, kept, managed, and disbursed. The department of a government in charge of the collection, management, and expenditure of the public revenue. (The American Heritage® Dictionary of the English Language, Fourth Edition)

116.   We have seen with interest the definition of treasury functions made by the Chief Minister, Punjab in his letter No. NO.AS(IMPL.)/CMO/14/0T-4 dated 18.11.2014, according to which to operate bank accounts of the Government of the Punjab for the purpose of withdrawal of moneys therefrom is a treasury function with clear and loud claim that power of the Provincial Government to this effect under Article 119 of the Constitution is exclusive, inalienable and indivisible. It was claimed in that letter by the Chief Minister, Punjab that the Federal Government can neither assume treasury functions of the Provinces nor these powers of the Provinces can be subjected to any restraints except those specified in the regulatory framework enforced under Article 119 of the Constitution. We do not find any problem in adopting this definition of the treasury functions for the purpose of this judgment.

117.   Viewed in the above context, the learned Advocate General, Punjab has claimed that the treasury functions of the Federation including pre-audit of federal payments was not a function of the Auditor General of Pakistan under the Pakistan (Audit and Accounts) Order, 1973. To substantiate his argument, he referred to the following rules of the Federal Treasury Rules:

Rule 2 (o) of the Federal Treasury Rules

"Federal Treasury" means and includes any treasury or sub-treasury not being a treasury or sub-treasury under the control of a Province.

Rule 4.5 of the Federal Treasury Rules

Ordinarily no portion of the responsibility for the proper management and working of treasuries shall devolve upon the officers of the Pakistan Audit Department. The inspection of treasuries by officers of the

Pakistan Audit Department shall not relieve the Collector of his responsibilities for management and inspection.

Rule 38 of the Federal Treasury Rules

Subject to any general or special orders of the Government, the ultimate responsibility for the proper management and working of a Federal treasury shall rest entirely with the Head of the Local Administration.

Rule 6.2 of the Federal Treasury Rules

An Accountant General may, subject to such conditions and limitations, if any, as the Government may think fit to impose, perform all or any part of the duties of a Treasury Officer, in respect of claims against the Government that may fall due for disbursement and moneys that may be tendered for credit to the Federal Consolidated Fund or the Public Account of the Federation, as the case may be, at the office or within the jurisdiction of the said Accountant General; provided that where an Accountant General is subordinate to the Auditor General, the performance by the Accountant General of the duties aforesaid shall be subject to the consent of and such conditions as may be prescribed by the Auditor General."

118.   We have seen that Section 5(b) of the CGA Ordinance is the first law under which treasury functions of the Federal and Provincial Governments have been assigned to the CGA. It is interesting to note that whereas accounting functions of the Federal, Provincial and District Governments are purported to have been assigned to the CGA under Section 5(a) of the CGA Ordinance, treasury functions of only the Federal and Provincial Governments have been assigned to the CGA under Section 5(b) of the CGA Ordinance. The Law and Parliamentary Affairs Department of the Government of the Punjab rightly observed in its legal opinion bearing No. OP:15-55/2012/4482 dated 30.10.2012 that:

> "The words `district governments', although used in clause (a) of section (5) of CGA Ordinance, are conspicuously absent from clause (b) of the said section. The only inference is that the CGA Ordinance deliberately did not and could not assign the treasury functions of district governments to the CGA."

119.   It was further observed by the Law & Parliamentary Affairs Department in its aforesaid legal advice that:

> "Clauses (a) and (b) of section 5 of the CGA Ordinance separately deal with the functions of `preparation and maintenance of accounts' and `authorization of payments and withdrawals after pre-audited checks'. Clause (a) specifically empowers the CGA *inter alia* to prepare and maintain the accounts of district governments; however, in clause (b) he has not been empowered, and rightly so, to exercise any powers with respect to the treasury functions of district governments. A bare reading of the two provisions substantiates the view of the Finance Department that the `preparation and maintenance of accounts' in terms of clause (a) of section 5 of CGA Ordinance is clearly distinct from the `treasury functions' mentioned in clause (b). The same distinction has been maintained in subsection (2) of section 114 of the PLG Ordinance."

> "As the subject of `local governments' is not mentioned in the Federal Legislative List contained in Fourth Schedule of the Constitution, the legislative and executive authority in respect of all matters relating to

local governments fall within the exclusively ambit of the Provinces in terms of Article 142(c) of the Constitution; ----."

120. Learned counsel for the plaintiff also informed us that the Advocate General, Punjab, through a legal advice bearing No. 9406 / AG dated 12.05.2012, expressed his opinion that treasury functions of the District Governments have not been assigned to the CGA under the CGA Ordinance.

121. The learned Attorney General for Pakistan claimed that pre-audit is part of accounting and as accounting functions of the District Governments have been entrusted to the CGA under Section 5(a) of the CGA Ordinance, therefore, the CGA was competent to assume treasury functions of the District Governments.

122. With repeal of the Punjab Local Government Ordinance, 2001, District / City District Governments are not in existence in the Punjab. Their successor local governments are performing treasury functions in respect of their local funds without any involvement of the CGA. We required the learned Attorney General for Pakistan to inform us about the organizational capability of the CGA built for performance of treasury functions of the local governments in the Punjab. He admitted that no special capacity-building measures had been taken for the purpose and the CGA could not assume treasury functions of the local governments for want of capacity.

123. We required the learned Attorney General for Pakistan to present a copy of the pre-audit checks prescribed by the Auditor General with approval of the President of Pakistan in respect of federal, provincial and local governments. After seeking instructions, he informed us that no such prescription has so far been made by the Auditor General.

124. We find no reason to disagree with the logical conclusions drawn by the Law & Parliamentary Affairs Department and the learned Advocate General, Punjab to the effect that Section 5(b) of the CGA Ordinance does not assign treasury functions of the local governments to the CGA. It is, accordingly, held that the CGA has no role in the performance of treasury functions of the local governments.

125. As regards entrustment of treasury functions of the Federation to the CGA under Section 5(b) of the CGA Ordinance, the learned Advocate General, Punjab frankly admitted that the Federation can assign its treasury functions to any federal functionary through a federal law and there is no constitutional infirmity in Section 5(b) of the CGA Ordinance to the extent of entrustment of federal treasury functions to the CGA. In view of this admission, we do not, for the moment, deem it appropriate to further dilate upon the question of entrustment of treasury functions of the Federation to the CGA. We will, however, examine the arrangements made under Article 147 of the Constitution in respect of federal treasury functions in the Punjab at an appropriate place in this judgment.

126. In view of the above, only the question of entrustment of treasury functions of the Province to the CGA under Section 5(b) of the CGA Ordinance remains in the field requiring authoritative adjudication from this Court. Constitutionality of Section 5(b) of the CGA Ordinance, therefore, needs to be ascertained to this extent. We are conscious of the well-established rule that the question of constitutionality will not be decided unless it is necessary to the determination of the action. We quote with approval what was held by the Supreme Court of Indiana in Hoover vs. Wood, 9 Ind. 287 that:

> "While the courts cannot shun the discussion of constitutional questions when fairly presented, they will not go out of their way to find such topics. They will not seek to draw in such matters collaterally, nor on trivial occasions. It is both more proper and more respectful to a co-ordinate department, to discuss constitutional questions only when that is the very lis mota. Thus presented and determined, the decision carries a weight with it to which no extra-judicial question is entitled."

127. Power and duty of the judiciary to disregard an unconstitutional statute was explained in an argument approaching to the precision and certainty of a mathematical demonstration by Chief Justice John Marshall of the Supreme Court of United States of

America in the well-known case of Marbury vs. Madison {U.S. Reports: Marbury v. Madison, 5 U.S. (1 Cranch) 137 (1803)}, which was relied upon and approved in Saiyyid Abul A'la Maudoodi v. The Government of West Pakistan (PLD 1964 SC 673). Chief Justice John Marshall wrote in that case:

> "The question whether an act repugnant to the constitution can become the law of the land is a question deeply interesting to the United States; but happily not of an intricacy proportioned to its interest. It seems only necessary to recognize certain principles supposed to have been long and well established, to decide it.
>
> That the people have an original right to establish for their future government such principles as in their opinion shall most conduce to their own happiness, is the basis on which the whole American fabric has been erected. . . . This original and supreme will organizes the government and assigns to different departments their respective powers. . . . The powers of the legislature are defined and limited; and that those limits may not be mistaken or forgotten, the constitution is written. To what purpose are powers limited, and to what purpose is that limitation committed to writing, if those limits may at any time be passed by those intended to be restrained? . . . The constitution is either a superior, paramount law, unchangeable by ordinary means, or it is on a level with ordinary legislative acts, and like any other acts is alterable when the legislature shall please to alter it. If the former part of the alternative be true, then a legislative act contrary to the constitution is not law. If the latter part be true, then written constitutions are absurd attempts on the part of the people to limit a power in its own nature illimitable....
>
> If an act of the legislature repugnant to the constitution is void, does it, notwithstanding its invalidity, bind the courts and oblige them to give it effect? Or, in other words, though it be not law, does it constitute a rule as operative as though it was a law? This would be to overthrow in fact what was established in theory; and would seem at first view an absurdity too gross to be insisted upon. It shall, however, receive a more attentive consideration. It is emphatically the province and duty of the judicial department to say what the law is. Those who apply the rule to particular cases must of necessity expound and interpret that rule. If two laws conflict with each other, the courts must decide on the operation of each....
>
> This is the very essence of judicial duty. If, then, the courts are to regard the constitution, and the constitution is superior to any ordinary acts of the legislature, the constitution, and not such ordinary act, must govern the case to which they both apply. Those, then, who controvert the principle that the constitution is to be considered in court as a paramount law, are reduced to the necessity of maintaining that courts must close their eyes on the constitution and see only the law."

128.   When both the Constitution and an ordinary law deal with the same subject-matter but are in irreconcilable clash, the judiciary refuses to enforce the law to the extent it is found repugnant to the Constitution. By the refusal to recognize or to enforce a law, it is annulled, and this decision, by virtue of the doctrine of precedent, is generally followed in similar cases in future. It has been held in the legal encyclopedia, American Jurisprudence, that:

> "The general rule is that an unconstitutional statute, though having the form and the name of law, is in reality no law, but is wholly void and

ineffective for any purpose since unconstitutionality dates from the time of its enactment and not merely from the date of the decision so branding it; an unconstitutional law, in legal contemplation, is as inoperative as if it had never been passed ... An unconstitutional law is void." (16 Am. Jur. 2d, Sec. 178)

129.   Likewise, in the case of Fauji Foundation Vs. Shamimur Rehman (PLD 1983 SC 457), it is held that "-----------when a Court, which is a creature of the Constitution itself, examines the vires of an Act, its powers are limited to examine the legislative competence or such other limitations as are in the Constitution; and while declaring a legislative instrument as void, "it is not because the judicial power is superior in degree or dignity to the legislative power" but because it enforces the Constitution as a paramount law either where a legislative instrument is in conflict with the constitutional provision so as to give effect to it or where the Legislature fails to keep within its constitutional limits." It was observed by Chief Justice Cornelius in a case reported as Fazlul Ouader Chaudhry Vs. Mohammad Abdul Haq (PLD 1963 SC 486) that:

> "The administration of public justice is referred to the courts. To perform this duty, the first requisite is to ascertain the facts, and the next to determine the law applicable to such facts. The Constitution is the fundamental law of the State, in opposition to which any other law, or any direction or order, must be inoperative and void. If, therefore, such other law, direction, or order seems to be applicable to the facts but on comparison with the fundamental law the latter is found to be in conflict with it, the Court, in declaring what the law of the case is, must necessarily determine its invalidity, and thereby in effect annul it."

130.   The CGA Ordinance was promulgated on 17th of May, 2001. At that time, Constitution of 1973 was not in operation and legitimacy flew from the Proclamation of Emergency of 14th October, 1999 issued by the Chief of Army Staff and subsequently validated by the Hon'ble Supreme Court of Pakistan. Constitution of Pakistan was held in abeyance through the aforesaid Proclamation of Emergency. Article 2(1) of Provisional Constitution Order No. 1 of 1999 reads as follows:

> "Notwithstanding the abeyance of the provisions of the Constitution of the Islamic Republic of Pakistan, hereinafter referred to as the Constitution, Pakistan shall, subject to this order and any other order made by the Chief Executive, be governed, as nearly as may be, in accordance with the Constitution".

131.   Article 5 of the Provisional Constitution Order No. 1 of 1999 read with Article 2 of the Provisional Constitution Order No. 9 of 1999 reads as follows:

> "Notwithstanding the abeyance of the provisions of the Constitution, but subject to the orders of the Chief Executive, all laws, all ordinances, orders, rules, bye-laws, regulations, notifications and other legal instruments, other than the Constitution, in force in any part of Pakistan, whether made by the President or the Governor of a Province, shall continue in force until altered, amended or repealed by the Chief Executive or any authority designated by him".

132.   Article 2(1) of Provisional Constitution Order No.5 of 1999 provided as under:

> "Subject to the provisions of clause 2 of Article 3 of the Provisional Constitution Order No. 1 of 1999, the powers and functions of a Governor shall be the same as of a Governor under the Constitution of the Islamic Republic of Pakistan, including the functions and powers of a Chief Minister and such other powers and functions as may be conferred upon him by the Chief Executive"

133.	Article 11 of Provisional Constitution Order No. 7 of 1999 reads as follows:
	"The existing rules of the allocation and transaction of the business of the Federal Government shall remain in force subject to the Provisional Constitution Order NO. 1 of 1999 and any amendment, modification or alteration made therein by the Chief Executive from time to time".

134.	Article 11 of the Provisional Constitution Order No. 8 of 1999 reads as follows:
	"The existing rules for the allocation and transaction of the business of the Provincial Government shall remain in force subject to the Proclamation Order dated Fourteenth October, 1999 and Provisional Constitution Order No 1 of 1999 and any amendment, modification or alteration made therein by the Chief Executive from time to time or any order made by the Governor with the prior approval of the Chief Executive".

135.	The above is enough to indicate that notwithstanding the Constitution being held in abeyance:

(a) During the currency of the Proclamation of Emergency of 14th October, 1999, Pakistan was to be governed in accordance with the Constitution and a deviation from the Constitution was permissible only to the extent specified by the Chief Executive through a Provisional Constitution Order;

(b) Rules of Business of the Federal and the Provincial Governments remained effectively in the field during the aforesaid period;

(c) Powers of the Governor and effectiveness of the Punjab Treasury Rules remained intact during the period of emergency mentioned hereinabove;

(d) No Provisional Constitution Order amended the Punjab Treasury Rules or withdrew treasury functions of the Provinces and entrusted them to any federal functionary; and

(e) No Provisional Constitution Order authorized the Federation to assume ownership and control of provincial property or to legislate for Provincial Services or posts in connection with affairs of a Province.

136.	The CGA Ordinance has been given validity through Section 96 of the Constitution (Eighteenth Amendment) Act, 2010 which, inter alia, stated that:

"Except as provided in clause (1) and subject to the provisions of the Constitution (Eighteenth Amendment) Act, 2010, all laws including President's Orders, Acts, Ordinances, Chief Executive Orders, regulations, enactments, notifications, rules, orders or bye-laws made between the twelfth day of October, one thousand nine hundred and ninety-nine and the thirty-first day of October, two thousand and three (both days inclusive) and still in force shall, continue to be in force until altered, repealed or amended by the competent authority.

Explanation: - For the purposes of clause (2) and clause (6), "competent authority" means, -

(c) in respect of Presidents' Orders, Ordinances, Chief Executive's Orders and all other laws, the appropriate Legislature; and

(d) in respect of notifications, rules, orders and bye-laws, the authority in which the power to make, alter or amend the same vests under the law."

137.	This Court has noted in its judgment reported as Azhar Hussain and others Vs. Federation of Pakistan and others (IAH 2019 MOOT COURT JUDGMENTS 1) that:

"250. The question whether the validating provisions also have the effect of validating acts done coram non judice or without jurisdiction or mala fide has been addressed in a series of cases by the superior judiciary in Pakistan. In Federation of Pakistan Vs. Saeed Ahmad Khan (PLD 1974 SC 151), State Vs. Zia ur Rahman (PLD 1973 SC 49), Federation of Pakistan Vs. Ghulam Mustafa Khar (PLD 1989 SC 26), Muhammad Bachal Menton Vs. Government of Sind (PLD 1987 Kar 296), Rawalpindi Bar Association Vs. Federation (PLD 2015 SC 401), it has been held that purported validity granted and the ouster of jurisdiction of courts is not applicable to acts and orders without jurisdiction, coram non judice and mala fide."

138. We hold that a validating provision also validates statues if those are not without jurisdiction, coram non judice and mala fide. If we, for the purpose of arguments only, ignore the question of jurisdiction of promulgation of an Ordinance at the time of its promulgation, we find no lawful reason to avoid to test the Ordinance on the touchstone of the Constitution after restoration of the Constitution following cessation of operation of the Proclamation of Emergency of 14th October, 1999 and the Provisional Constitution Orders issued thereunder. An Ordinance deserves to be enforced only if it is not repugnant to the Constitution. If it is not repugnant to the Constitution in its entirety, it will be given effect to so far as it is not repugnant to the Constitution and shall be ignored to the extent of repugnancy.

139. As its preamble states, the CGA Ordinance has been promulgated to provide for separation of accounting functions and appointment of the CGA and for matters connected therewith or incidental thereto. In pith and substance, this law deals with the subject of accounts in terms of Article 169 of the Constitution read with entry appearing at serial number 58 of the Part-I of the Federal Legislative List in the Fourth Schedule of the Constitution ("Matters which under the Constitution are within the legislative competence of Majlis-e-Shoora (Parliament) or relate to the Federation"). There seems to be, however, no constitutional infirmity if the Federation, while legislating under Article 169 of the Constitution, assigns a function entrusted to the Federation under Article 79 of the Constitution, reproduced below, to a federal functionary (the CGA in the instant case):

> "79. Custody, etc., of Federal Consolidated Fund and Public Account.- The custody of the Federal Consolidated Fund, the payment of moneys into that Fund, the withdrawal of moneys therefrom, the custody of other moneys received by or on behalf of the Federal Government, their payment into, and withdrawal from, the Public Account of the Federation, and all matters connected with or ancillary to the matters aforesaid shall be regulated by Act of Majlis-e-Shoora (Parliament) or, until provision in that behalf is so made, by rules made by the President."

140. Legislative authority of the Federation extends to maintenance of federal accounts and performance of federal treasury functions. A federal law is, therefore, within jurisdiction when it creates a federal office for performance of federal accounting and treasury functions. Pre-audit of the Federal Government is a function which falls within four corners of Article 79 of the Constitution. The Federation may prescribe pre-audit checks in order to perform its treasury functions through the CGA and may seek help and advice from the Auditor General in formulation of these pre-audit checks. The Federation, however, lacks jurisdiction under Article 169 and 79 of the Constitution to assume to itself powers exclusively vested in the Provinces under Article 119 and 240(b) of the Constitution. There is no entry in the Fourth Schedule of the Constitution dealing with matters enumerated in Article 119 and 240(b) of the Constitution. Absence of such entry in the Federal Legislative List disables the Federation to legislate on any matter directly or indirectly forming subject-matter of Article 119 and 240(b) of the Constitution.

141. Article 119 of the Constitution gives exclusive jurisdiction to the Province in the matters enumerated therein. It is for the Province to determine, either through a provincial

law or through rules to be framed by the Governor, the parameters fulfilment of which must precede withdrawals from the Provincial Consolidated Fund and the Public Account of the Province. It is also for the Province to create machinery for execution of the legal dispensation prescribed under Article 119 of the Constitution. The Province is not required to seek approval of the Federation for regulating receipts into and withdrawals from the Provincial Consolidated Fund and Public Account of the Province. No Article of the Constitution, directly or by necessary implication, empowers the President of Pakistan or the Auditor General to determine checks to be exercised by the machinery created under Article 119 of the Constitution for performance of treasury functions of the Province. The very idea of permission of the federation for withdrawals from the Provincial Consolidated Fund and Public Account of the Province as a condition-precedent under the label of pre-audit is so offensive to the spirit of federalism and is impracticable to such an extent that it can reasonably be termed an absurdity. In accordance with the scheme of the Constitution, the Provincial Legislature has full powers, within its jurisdiction, to raise revenues for performance of functions assigned to the Province under the Constitution through levy of taxes, fees, fines etc.; only the Provincial Legislature can authorize expenditure from the revenues of the Province through budgetary allocations; only the Provincial Assembly has the jurisdiction to enact a law to regulate expenditure and receipts of the Province; the Provincial Legislature requires reports with regard to execution of the approved budget and it takes suitable corrective and remedial measures to plug avenues of wastefulness, embezzlement and misapplication of public funds. Nowhere in the whole process, the federation figures in. It is simply inconceivable in this constitutional scheme that the Federation denies a Province to perform its treasury functions through its own machinery. To say that payments from the Provincial Consolidated Fund and Public Account of the Province are permissible to be made through pre-audit cheques or other instruments to be issued by the CGA is to kill the theory of provincial autonomy and federalism.

142. The infrastructure built by the Province for performance of its treasury functions under Article 119 of the Constitution is a valuable asset or property of the Province. Nothing has been shown to us to legally substantiate federal claim to have control over or ownership of this provincial property.

143. The subject-matters of Article 169 and 119 of the Constitution are distinctly distinguishable from each other. A legislation under Article 169 of the Constitution would obviously be without jurisdiction to the extent it attempts to encroach upon the exclusive provincial sphere under Article 119 of the Constitution.

144. The Punjab Government Rules of Business assign the subject of administration of the Provincial Consolidated Fund and Public Account of the Province to the Finance Department. The Inspectorate of Treasuries & Accounts is an attached department of the Finance Department. The DAOs / Treasuries are subordinate offices of the Inspectorate. The Punjab Government Rules of Business have been framed under Article 139 of the Constitution. If administration and control of the DAOs / Treasuries is assumed by the Federation through the CGA, the same would amount to indirectly amend the Punjab Government Rules of Business and make the Inspectorate dysfunctional by divesting it of the control of its subordinate offices. It is well-established that what cannot be done directly is also not allowed to be done indirectly. As the Federation is without jurisdiction to frame or amend Rules of Business of the Provincial Government directly, therefore, it has no lawful authority to do indirectly.

145. Banking business of the Province is performed by the SBP under an agreement between the SBP and the plaintiff. This agreement specifies that the Bank shall provide banking services in accordance with directions of duly authorized officers of the plaintiff. The defendant or any of its functionaries is not a duly authorized officer of the plaintiff within the meaning of the agreement between the SBP and the plaintiff for the purpose of operation of the account of the plaintiff in the Bank and, therefore, no federal functionary including the

403

CGA has any authority of law to allow disbursements and withdrawals from the aforesaid bank account.

146. We have examined the argument of the defendant that pre-audit is part of accounting and is a service to assist the Province in its financial management. As the pre-audit includes issuance of pre-audit cheques or other payment instruments, it would be appropriate to hold that pre-audit is not a part of accounting and it is not a service of the Federation for the benefit of the Provinces. In plain words, claim of the Federation to conduct pre-audit of payments from the Provincial Consolidated Fund and Public Account of the Province is an assertion that the Province cannot draw moneys from these accounts without prior permission of the Federation. Further, the claim declares that it is for the Auditor General of Pakistan to prescribe and for the President of Pakistan to approve the conditions and procedures fulfilment and observance of which must precede payments from the Provincial Consolidated Fund and Public Account of the Province (labelled as pre-audit checks). The inseparable part of the federal claim is that the pre-audit checks are required to be applied exclusively by the CGA. If the federal claim is accepted, provincial autonomy is reduced to a mere nullity and the constitutional scheme enshrined in its Article 119 becomes nugatory and dysfunctional. We have seen earlier in this judgment that from enactment of the Government of India Act, 1935 till-date, there has been and is still today consistent constitutional scheme of exclusive entrustment of treasury functions of the Provinces to the respective Provinces. Exclusive provincial functions under Article 119 of the Constitution cannot be assumed by the Federation without, at least, appropriate amendments in the said Article 119.

147. We have also given due consideration to the argument advanced by the learned Attorney General for Pakistan that since bulk of receipts of the Provincial Consolidated Fund comes from the Federal Consolidated Fund as a share of the Province out of the divisible pool of taxes in accordance with the approved award of the National Finance Commission, therefore, federal oversight of expenditure of this money in the form of pre-audit through a federal functionary is justified. This argument is based upon ignorance of the constitutional provisions on the subject. Article 160(4) of the Constitution clearly specifies that share of the Provinces out of the divisible pool of taxes shall not form part of the Federal Consolidated Fund. Moreover, share of the Provinces out of the divisible pool of taxes is not a bounty but a right of the Provinces. As that share does not form part of the Federal Consolidated Fund, therefore, provisions of Article 78 and 79 of the Constitution are not applicable thereto. Since the share of the Provinces out of the divisible pool of taxes is compulsorily required to be credited to the Provincial Consolidated Fund, therefore, Article 118 and 119 of the Constitution are attracted. As the Federation has been assigned no role in the matters dealt with in Article 119 of the Constitution including oversight of expenditures from the Provincial Consolidated Fund and Public Account of the Province, therefore, the Federation enjoys no lawful authority to assume to itself treasury functions of the Province in the pretext of entrustment of pre-audit to the CGA.

148. Provincial Cabinet is collectively answerable to the Provincial Assembly. All executive entities of the Province are required to be subordinate to the Provincial Government within the meaning of this term as defined in the Mustafa Impex case (PLD 2016 SC 808). If treasury functions of the Province are entrusted to a federal organization to be run by federal employees, the accountability mechanism of the Provincial Assembly would be rendered impotent to the extent of that organization as the Public Accounts Committee of the Provincial Assembly would not be in a position to act against a federal organization and the federal employees acting on behalf of that organization. On the other hand, audit reports on the accounts of the Province are not laid before the National assembly. As a result, omissions and commissions of the CGA in respect of treasury functions of the Province would not be considered by Provincial as well as the National Assembly. This vacuum can encourage non-compliance and fraud with potential to go unnoticed,

undetected or at least not followed by requisite corrective and remedial actions. We hope that no one is going to defend such a state of affairs.

149. Section 11 and 12 of the CGA Ordinance, reproduced below, provide for making of the rules and regulations for carrying out the purposes of the CGA Ordinance:

> "11. Power to make rules. -The Federal Government may, by notification in the official Gazette make rules for carrying out the purposes of this Ordinance.
>
> 12. Power to make regulations. -The Controller General may with the previous approval of the Federal Government by notification in the official Gazette, make such regulations not inconsistent with the provisions of this Ordinance and the rules made thereunder, as he may consider necessary or expedient for carrying out the purpose of this Ordinance."

150. If it is accepted that entrustment of treasury function to the CGA under Section 5(b) of the CGA Ordinance is constitutional, then the rules and the regulations to be framed under the CGA Ordinance would, inter alia, definitely deal with the enforcement of the pre-audit checks in respect of withdrawals from the Provincial Consolidated Fund and Public Account of the Province. Thus, the rules and the regulations would encroach upon the exclusive provincial domain under Article 119 of the Constitution to the extent of treasury functions of the Province. In response to a query raised by us, the learned Attorney General for Pakistan has informed us that neither the rules nor the regulations have so far been made under the CGA Ordinance. No plausible reason has been submitted for failure to frame the rules and the regulations. This performance in the matter of making the rules and the regulations despite passage of a decade cannot be termed appreciable.

151. The argument that Article 170(2) of the Constitution empowers the Auditor General to determine the extent and nature of audit and the pre-audit is part of audit negates the very concept of audit and the separation of accounting and auditing functions. With separation of audit and accounts through the CGA Ordinance and the AG Ordinance, audit is a forbidden area for the CGA. If audit includes pre-audit, then the CGA lacks authority to conduct audit as audit is exclusive province of the Auditor General. Moreover, audit does not include power to authorize the Provinces to operate their bank accounts (the so called pre-audit). The AG Ordinance does not assign pre-audit or treasury functions of the Provinces to the Auditor General. In this view of the matter, the CGA as well as the Auditor General are not authorized to perform treasury functions of the Province in the pretext of pre-audit.

152. The CGA, in his letter No: 59 / 104 / Policy / CGA / 2001 dated 09.07.2001 addressed to the Chief Secretary, Punjab, also demanded issuance of a notification placing the Treasury Officers under the ultimate control of the CGA. What was meant by placing the Treasury Offices and the Treasury Officers under the administrative control of the CGA was to enable the CGA to exercise powers vested in the Provincial authorities over a Service of the Province and posts in connection with affairs of the Province under laws framed under Article 240(b) of the Constitution. The CGA intended to administer a Provincial Service and to perform treasury function of the Province with the help of members of this Service. This was and is not permissible without amendments in Article 240 of the Constitution.

153. It is inconceivable to perform treasury functions of the Province without keeping written records of moneys received and disbursed. The CGA, by no stretch of imagination and reasoning, can assume treasury functions of the Province by equating maintenance of written records of moneys received and disbursed in performance of treasury functions with the function of keeping and maintaining Appropriation Accounts and Finance Accounts of the Government as a whole.

154. Our attention was drawn towards Article 143 of the Constitution, reproduced below:

> "143. Inconsistency between Federal and Provincial law. - If any provision of an Act of a Provincial Assembly is repugnant to any provision of an Act of Majlis-e-Shoora (Parliament) which Majlis-e-

Shoora (Parliament) is competent to enact, then the Act of Majlis-e-Shoora (Parliament), whether passed before or after the Act of the Provincial Assembly, shall prevail and the Act of the Provincial Assembly shall, to the extent of the repugnancy, be void."

155. It was argued that the rules framed under Article 119 of the Constitution carry the status of provincial laws. The CGA Ordinance is a federal law. It was asserted that in case of clash between the CGA Ordinance and the rules framed under Article 119 of the Constitution, the CGA Ordinance must prevail and the rules framed under Article 119 must yield to the extent of clash. We are unable to understand that how a federal law made in absence of jurisdiction or in excess of jurisdiction can displace a competently made provincial law. Federal and provincial legislative jurisdictions are with reference to subjects. Each jurisdiction is exclusive. If the Federation enacts a law on a subject falling within exclusive provincial domain or on a subject assigned to the Federation but travels beyond the boundaries of its jurisdiction so as to encroach upon the provincial sphere, the enactment cannot be given effect to merely on the basis of the argument that federal law is superior to a provincial law. A federal law has to be within the legislative competence of the Parliament if it wants to avail enforceability on the strength of Article 143 of the Constitution. To say that a federal law has been enacted by the Parliament with lawful jurisdiction is to say that the Province lacks legislative competence on the same subject-matter. A provincial law made without or in excess of legislative jurisdiction is void to the extent of want of jurisdiction. Such a law is unenforceable even if it is not in clash with a federal law. The same is the case with a federal law made in absence of jurisdiction. We have observed that a lot of misunderstandings are caused by our inaccurate perception of the idea of concurrent legislative powers. We will dilate upon the subject in an appropriate case. For the moment, suffice is to say that the CGA Ordinance is not enforceable to the extent of want legislative jurisdiction of the Parliament merely by virtue of Article 143 of the Constitution. It is further clarified that matters enumerated in Article 119 and 240(b) of the Constitution do not fall within legislative competence of the Parliament.

156. We have also given our consideration to the true import of Article 148(1) of the Constitution which requires that the executive authority of every Province shall be so exercised as to secure compliance with Federal laws which apply in that Province. We hold that this Article is applicable in respect of laws on subjects falling within legislative competence of the Parliament and the laws enacted without or in excess of jurisdiction by the Parliament cannot be enforced by relying upon Article 148(1) of the Constitution.

157. For the aforesaid reasons, we find and declare Section 5(b) of the CGA Ordinance, to the extent it relates to the Provincial Consolidated Fund and Public Account of the Province, to be beyond legislative and validating power of the Parliament. The said Section 5(b) is hereby declared to have been promulgated and validated without jurisdiction and is of no legal effect to the stated extent. As a result, it is denied judicial enforceability to this extent for being repugnant to the Constitution and is annulled and struck down. For the purpose of clarity, it is held that the said Section 5(b) does not apply to the local funds of the provincial local bodies but the same is constitutionally valid to the extent of the Federal Consolidated Fund and Public Account of the Federation.

Question # 3

Whether accounting functions of the Provinces can be assigned to a federal functionary other than the Auditor General of Pakistan?

158. The Constitution speaks of functions of the Auditor General regarding audit and accounts. Audit is not an issue in these proceedings, therefore, we will focus on accounts only.

159. Two aspects of accounts of the Federation and of the Provinces have separately been dealt with by the Constitution. One is the function of prescribing and approving accounting policies and procedures and the other is maintaining accounts accordingly. As regards the

function of prescribing accounting policies and procedures, a survey of the applicable constitutional provisions from the Government of India Act till date, reproduced below, will make the matter clear:

Rules regarding Auditor General in India made by the Secretary of State in Council under Section 96 D (1) of the Government of India Act, 1915

18.   The Auditor General shall compile the Finance and Revenue Accounts of India in such form as may from time to time be prescribed by the Secretary of State in Council and shall send them to the Governor General in Council for transmission to the Secretary of State in Council. He may call upon any Government officer to furnish any information in such form as may be required for the completion of these accounts.

19.   The Auditor General shall have power to prescribe the forms in which accounts shall be kept in audit offices: provided that no change which will affect the form of the Finance and Revenue Accounts shall be made without the previous sanction of the Secretary of State in Council. Minor changes of detail, such as the opening of new minor heads, alterations affecting minor or detailed heads, and the like, are not changes "affecting the form of the Finance and Revenue Accounts" within the meaning of this rule.

Section 168 of the Government of India Act, 1935

The accounts of the Federation shall be kept in such form as the Auditor General of India may, with the approval of the Governor General, prescribe and, in so far as the Auditor General of India may, with the like approval, give any directions with regard to the methods or principles in accordance with which any accounts of the Provinces ought to be kept, it shall be duty of every Provincial Government to cause accounts to be kept accordingly.

Article 123 of the Constitution of Pakistan, 1956

The accounts of the Federation and of the Provinces shall be kept in such form as the Comptroller and Auditor-General may, with the approval of the President, prescribe.

Article 197 of the Constitution of Pakistan, 1962

The accounts of the Centre and of the Provinces shall be kept in

such form as the Comptroller and Auditor-General, with the

approval of the President, may determine.

Article 172 of the interim Constitution of Pakistan, 1972

The accounts of the Federation shall be kept in such form as the Auditor General of Pakistan may, with the approval of the President, prescribe and, in so far as the Auditor General may, with the like approval, give any directions with regard to the methods or principles in accordance with which any accounts of the Provinces ought to be kept, it shall be duty of every Provincial Government to cause accounts to be kept accordingly.

Article 170 (1) of the Constitution of Pakistan, 1973

The accounts of the Federation and of the Provinces shall be kept in such form and in accordance with such principles and methods as the Auditor-General may, with the approval of the President, prescribe.

160. Power of the Auditor General to prescribe accounting policies and procedures is exclusive and it cannot be withdrawn except through amendment in the Constitution. Accounts of all entities of the Federation as well as of the Provinces-executive, legislative and judicial-are compulsorily required to be maintained in accordance with the accounting policies and procedures prescribed by the Auditor General. These policies and procedures are applicable irrespective of the fact whether an agency is centralized accounting entity, self-accounting entity or exempt entity. Neither a federal law can withdraw the function of prescribing accounting policies and procedures from the Auditor General nor the Auditor General has power to abdicate or delegate this power to any other person or entity. We entertain no ambiguity that the transfer of accounting functions by the Auditor General to the CGA through Notification No. 114/DG (A)/9-2/97 dated 16.07.2001 does not include the transfer of function of prescribing accounting policies and procedures. The learned Attorney General for Pakistan and the Advocate General, Punjab are in agreement that the function of prescribing accounting policies and procedures is one of the constitutional mandates of the Auditor General and no sub-constitutional measure can deny the Auditor General to exercise his powers to this effect. We endorse this consensus and hold accordingly.

161. The accounting policies and procedures are required to the confined to answer the question that how and by following which principles and methods the accounts of the Federation and of the Provinces are to be maintained. It is beyond scope of Article 170(1) of the Constitution to prescribe that who will maintain these accounts or to substitute any arrangement for financial management or performance of treasury functions made under Article 118 to 126 of the Constitution or under any other relevant provision of the Constitution. Conversely speaking, no dispensation introduced under Article 118 to 126 of the Constitution or under any other relevant provision of the Constitution can prescribe accounting policies and procedures. The Constitution neither allows the Auditor General to deviate from the arrangements for financial management made by a Province in exercise of its constitutional authority nor a Province has been permitted to devise its own accounting policies and procedures and to disregard those prescribed by the Auditor General. We find ourselves in agreement with the principle laid down by the Government of the Punjab, Finance Department in its letter No. SO(TT)6-4/2012 pt.1 dated 10.10.2013 wherein it was stated that:

> "In case of clash between provisions of rules framed under Article 119 of the Constitution and those of the manuals issued under Article 170(1) of the Constitution, the provisions of rules shall prevail if the subject matter pertains to treasury functions and those of the manuals if the issues covered relate to accounting functions."

162. We have gone through the Account Code-Volume-I to IV word by word deemed to have been framed under Article 170 of the Constitution (Article 170 was made 170(1) through the 18th Amendment in the Constitution) and the rules issued or deemed to have been issued under Article 119 of the Constitution. We have noticed with appreciation that both the Account Code and the rules do not attempt to encroach upon the domain of each other.

163. The learned Attorney General for Pakistan informed us that the Auditor General prescribed the New Accounting Model (NAM), comprising the following, in December, 2000:

    i.   Chart of Accounts
    ii. Financial Reporting Manual
    iii. Accounting Policies and Procedures Manual (Book of Forms)
    iv. Handbook of Accounting Guidelines
    v.   Manual of Accounting Principles

vi. Accounting Code for Self-Accounting Entities

vii. Accounting Policies and Procedures Manual

164. A cursory glance of the NAM gives the impression that, prima facie, the jurisdictional boundaries of Article 170(1) of the Constitution have not strictly been observed with precision. Any dispute regarding encroachment of provincial domain in the name of prescription of accounting policies and procedures shall, therefore, be resolved, as and when it is raised, by observing the principle laid down in letter No. SO(TT)6-4/2012 pt.1 dated 10.10.2013 of the Government of the Punjab, Finance Department.

165. Before ascertaining constitutional position with regard to entrustment of function of keeping and maintaining accounts of the Federation and of the Provinces, it would not be out of place to glance through relevant paragraphs of the report of the Joint Committee on Indian Constitutional Reform (Session 1933-1934), reproduced below, in order to refresh our background knowledge:

THE EXISTING AUDIT SYSTEM

396. At present, audit in India, both Central and Provincial, is carried out by a staff under the Auditor–General. He is appointed by the Secretary of State in Council, who also frames rules defining his powers and duties. In India, accounts and audit are carried out by a combined staff, so that the Auditor-General has functions in relation to accounts as well as to audit. An experiment was tried in recent years in one province of separating accounts from audit but was abandoned on the ground of expense. There is at present no constitutional provision requiring the report of the Auditor-General to be laid before the Legislature in India, though in fact this is done. Audit of the accounts of the Secretary of State is carried out by the Auditor of Indian Home Accounts who, in accordance with Section 27 (1), Government of India Act, is appointed by the Crown by warrant countersigned by the Chancellor of the Exchequer. His report is, by statute, presented to Parliament. It has also been found convenient to use the services of the Home Auditor to audit expenditure by the High Commissioner.

The position and functions of the Auditor-General and the Home Auditor have been fully described by the Statutory Commission1.

FUTURE ARRANGEMENTS

397. When, under the future Constitution, the revenues of India are vested in the Federal and Provincial Governments, and no longer in the Secretary of State in Council as at present, it will clearly be necessary to provide that the Auditor-General in India shall report to those Governments and to the Legislatures in India, instead of to the Secretary of State in Council. It is desirable both, on grounds of economy and for other reasons, that the present centralized system of audit and accounts should be maintained, and it is to be hoped that the provinces will realize the advantages of such a course. Nevertheless, it would be difficult to withhold from an autonomous province the power of taking over its own audit and accounts if it desires to do so and we think that the Constitution must allow a province to take this step, subject to the following conditions. Long notice should be given of the change; a Provincial Chief Auditor should be appointed whose position would be no less independent of the Executive than that of the Auditor-General; a general form of accounts framed on the common basis for all the provinces should continue to be available for such purposes as the consideration by the Federal Government of applications for loans

---

1 Report, vol. I, para. 432.

from Provincial Governments or proposal for the assignment of revenues to Units of the kind mentioned in our earlier section on Federal Finance2.

AUDIT OF HOME ACCOUNTS

398.   As regards payments made by the Secretary of State in this county out of Indian revenues, these will in future be mainly on behalf of the Central Government, especially in relation to Defence. Constitutionally, they will not, in general, differ from those made by the High Commissioner, except that they will more often relate to Reserved Departments than will be the case with expenditure by the High Commissioner. It appears desirable that the audit of these payments should be made by a Home Auditor on behalf of the Auditor–General in India and that the report should go through the latter to the Indian Legislature.

399.   The White Paper contains no proposals relating to the Auditor-General or the Home Auditor, although it recognizes that the necessary provision would have to be made1. Our recommendations on this subject are as follows: -

AUDITOR GENERAL IN INDIA

(i)   The Auditor-General in India should be appointed by the Crown, and his tenure should be similar to that of a High Court Judge, that is, during good behaviour, subject to an age limit and he should be removable only by His Majesty in Council. He should not be eligible for further office under the Crown in India. His salary and general conditions of service should be prescribed by Order in Council, and his salary should not be votable.

(ii)   His duties and powers should be prescribed in the first instance by Order in Council, but the Federal Legislature should have power to amend and supplement these provisions, subject to the prior assent of the Governor-General in his discretion to the introduction of the legislation.

(iii)   The cadre of the Audit and Accounts Department should be fixed by the Federal Government. Salaries should be votable, except in cases where individual salaries are already non-votable under other provisions of the Act.

(iv)   Central audit and accounts should apply as at present to the Provinces for a period of at least five years; but provinces should be empowered to take over their own accounts, or audit as well as accounts, on giving three years' notice, the earliest date for such notice being two years after the establishment of provincial autonomy. The Constitution Act should provide that if a province elects to take over its own audit, the Chief Auditor of the Province shall be appointed by the Crown with tenure and conditions of service prescribed in the same way as those of the Auditor-General.

---

2 Supra, paras. 243-266.

1 White Paper, Introd., para 76.

(v)   The report of the Auditor-General on the federal accounts should be submitted to the Governor-General, who would be required to lay it before the Federal Legislature. His report on the provincial accounts (or the report of the Provincial Chief Auditor if the Province had taken over audit) should be submitted to the Governor who would be required to lay it before the Provincial Legislature.

(vi)   Whether a Province has taken over accounts or audit or not, it is essential **that there should be established a uniform general form of accounts for the Federation and for all British-India Provinces. Apart from this requirement, a province which had taken over accounts or audit should have the same powers, mutatis mutandis, as the Federal Government in relation to the duties and functions of the Auditor-General and his staff."**

166.   Accepting recommendations of the aforesaid Joint Parliamentary Committee, Provinces were allowed to appoint their own Auditor General vide Section 167 of the Government of India Act, 1935, reproduced below:

"167.   **PROVINCIAL AUDITOR GENERAL**

(1)   If a Provincial Legislature, after the expiration of two years from the commencement of Part-III of this Act passes an Act charging the salary of an Auditor General for that Province on the revenues of the Province, an Auditor General of the Province may be appointed by His Majesty to perform same duties and to exercise same powers in relation to the audit of the accounts of the Province as would be performed and exercised by the Auditor General of India, if an Auditor General of the Province had not been appointed:

Provided that no appointment of an Auditor General in a province shall be made until the expiration of at least three years from the date of the Act of the Provincial Legislature by which provision is made for an Auditor General of that Province.

(2)   The provisions of the last preceding section shall apply in relation to the Auditor General of a Province and his staff as they apply in relation to the Auditor General of India and his staff, subject to the following modifications, that is to say: -

a. a person who is or has been Auditor General of a Province shall be eligible for appointment as Auditor General of India;

b. in sub-section (3) of the said section, for the reference to Federal Legislature, there shall be substituted a reference to the Provincial Legislature, and for the reference to the Governor General, there shall be substituted a reference to the Governor; and

c. in sub-section (4) of the said section, for the reference to the revenues of the Federation, there shall be substituted a reference to the revenues of the Province:

Provided that nothing in this section shall derogate from the power of the Auditor General of India to give such directions in respect to the accounts of Provinces as are mentioned in the next succeeding section."

167.   Section 96(D)(1) of the Government of India Act read as follows:

411

"An Auditor-General in India shall be appointed by the Secretary of State in Council, and shall hold office during His Majesty's pleasure. The Secretary of State in Council shall, by rules, make provision for his pay, powers, duties and conditions of employment, or for the discharge of his duties in the case of temporary vacancy or absence from duty."

168. Rule 18 of the Rules regarding the Auditor General in India framed by the Secretary of State in Council under the aforesaid Section 96D (1) provided as under:

"The Auditor General shall compile the Finance and Revenue Accounts of India in such form as may from time to time be prescribed by the Secretary of State in Council and shall send them to the Governor General in Council for transmission to the Secretary of State in Council. He may call upon any Government officer to furnish any information in such form as may be required for the completion of these accounts."

169. Subsequent constitutional provisions on the subject are as follows:

Section 166 (3) of the Government of India Act, 1935

The Auditor General shall perform such duties and exercise such powers in relation to the accounts of the Federation and of the Provinces as may be prescribed by or by rules made under an Order of the Governor General or by any subsequent Act of the Federal Legislature varying or extending such an Order:

Provided that no Bill or amendment for the purpose aforesaid shall be introduced or moved without the previous sanction of the Governor General in his discretion.

Article 122 of the Constitution of 1956

The Comptroller and Auditor-General shall perform such duties and exercise such powers, in relation to the expenditure and accounts of the Federation and of the Provinces, as may be provided by act of Parliament.

Article 196 of the Constitution of 1962

The Comptroller and Auditor-General shall perform such functions and exercise such powers, and prepare such reports, in relation to the expenditure and accounts of the Centre and of the Provinces as may be provided or required by Act of the Central Legislature.

Article 170(4) of the interim Constitution of 1972

The Auditor-General shall perform such duties and exercise such powers in relation to the accounts of the Federation and of the Provinces as may be prescribed by, or by rules made under, an Order of the President or by any subsequent Act of the Federal Legislature varying or extending such Order:

Provided that no Bill or amendment for the purpose aforesaid shall be introduced or moved in the National Assembly without the previous sanction of the President.

Article 169 of the Constitution of 173

The Auditor-General shall, in relation to-

(a)   the accounts of the Federation and of the Provinces; and

(b)   the accounts of any authority or body established by the Federation or a Province,

perform such functions and exercise such powers as may be determined by or under Act of Majlis-e-Shoora (Parliament) and, until so determined, by Order of the President.

170.   Whereas the power to prescribe accounting policies and procedures is a constitutional power, the power to maintain accounts is statutory in nature. In this regard, analysis of the constitutionality of the CGA Ordinance made by the then learned Attorney General for Pakistan (Mr. Makhdoom Ali Khan) contained in letter No. F.1 (1) / 2002-AGP dated 6th of May, 2002 needs to be perused in some detail, relevant paragraphs whereof are as under:

"6.   The Constitution of Pakistan, 1973 has no provision corresponding to Section 167 of the Government of India Act, 1935. The Auditor General of Pakistan is responsible for the audit of accounts of both the Federation and of the Provinces. This deviation from the scheme of the Government of India Act, 1935 is inconsistent with the federal structure of the Constitution. It, however, clearly means that unless the Constitution is suitably amended, the audit of the accounts of the Provinces remains the responsibility of the Auditor General of Pakistan.

7.   Article 169 of the Constitution provides that the Auditor General shall, in relation to the accounts of the Federation and of the Provinces, perform such functions and exercise such powers as may be determined by an Act of Parliament and until so determined by Order of the President. The Pakistan (Audit and Accounts) Order, President's Order 21 of 1973 was issued on October 12, 1973 in exercise of the powers under Article 169 of the Constitution. It combined the functions of the preparation and keeping of the accounts of the Federation and of each Province and audit of such accounts in one person. Under Article 9, it was the Auditor General who was responsible for the keeping of the accounts of the Federation as well as for the Provinces. Under Article 11, it was also the Auditor General who was responsible for the audit of these accounts.

8.   The combination of the function of the preparation of the accounts with their audit in the same person compromised the independence of the auditor and made serious inroads into the freedom of the audit. One of the basic principles of audit is that the auditor must be independent of the persons preparing the accounts. The Order, 1973, ignored this rule. The Auditor General who was charged with the constitutional duty to scrutinize the financial transactions was also burdened with the preparation of the accounts. While there were advantages of uniformity and economy in creating and maintaining such a system, it ran counter to the principles of federalism as well as the independence of audit.

9.   On May 17, 2001, the President of Pakistan promulgated the Auditor General's (Functions, Powers and Terms and Conditions of Service) Ordinance, 2001 (Ordinance XXIII of 2001) and the Controller General of Accounts (Appointment, Functions and Powers) Ordinance 2001 (Ordinance XXIV of 2001). President's Order 21 of 1973 was repealed.

10.   Ordinance XXIII authorizes the Auditor General of Pakistan to audit the accounts of the Federation and the Provinces. It confers no power on him to keep or maintain accounts.

11.	Ordinance XXIV of 2001 created the office of the Controller General. Under Section 4, the accounting functions were transferred from the Auditor General to the Controller General. Section 5 made the Controller General responsible for preparing and maintaining the accounts of the Federation and of the Provinces.

12.	The accounts of the Federation and of the Provinces are, however, in view of Article 170 of the Constitution, to be kept in such form and in accordance with such methods and principles as the Auditor General may, with the approval of the President, prescribe from time to time.

13.	Section 4 of Ordinance XXIV of 2001 conforms to this constitutional command. The two Ordinances, insofar as they separate the authority responsible for keeping the accounts from the authority required to audit these, are a step in the right direction. The change in the law has created another issue, however. Whether the Controller General, appointed under Ordinance XXIV of 2001, a federal statute, has any constitutional authority to keep the accounts for a province? The following paragraphs contain my answer to the question.

14.	The Fourth Schedule to the Constitution does not list either audit or accounts as an item in the Federal Legislative List or the Concurrent Legislative List. A law in respect of any item which is not mentioned in either of the two lists can only be made by a Provincial Assembly. Article 142 (c) of the Constitution states this principle very clearly. It is apparent that a Provincial Assembly has and the Parliament has no power to make laws in respect of audit and accounts. This, however, is subject to Article 169 of the Constitution.

15.	Article 169, as stated above, provides that the powers and functions of the Auditor General in relation to the accounts of the Federation and of the Provinces are to be determined by an Act of Parliament or in the absence thereof by an Order of the President. The Federation can, therefore, either by an Act or by an Order confer on the Auditor General of Pakistan the function of keeping and maintaining the accounts of the Federation. The words, "in relation to the accounts" are wide enough to confer on the Parliament and the President, legislative authority to enable the Auditor General to keep as well as audit the accounts of the Federation and the Provinces.

16.	The Constitution has to be read harmoniously. The absence of an entry in the Fourth Schedule in respect of "audit and accounts" will not render the provisions of Article 169 nugatory. A harmonious reading of Article 142 (c), 169 and the Fourth Schedule to the Constitution leads to the conclusion that where a substantive provision of the Constitution has conferred a power on the federal legislature, the absence of an entry in the Fourth Schedule will not render the exercise of such power void. The functions of keeping, maintaining and auditing the accounts of the Federation and the Provinces could, therefore, be conferred on the Auditor General by federal law. P.O. 21 of 1973 was not ultra vires the Constitution.

17.	P.O. 21 of 1973 made the Auditor General responsible for the keeping of the accounts of the Federation and of each Province. Article 9(2) provided that as respect the accounts of the Federation, the President and in case of the Provinces, the Governor may make a provision after consultation with the Auditor General for relieving the Auditor General of the responsibility for keeping such accounts in certain cases. It was, therefore, recognized that keeping the accounts of the Provinces as well of the Federation by the Auditor General was not mandated by the Constitution. Had there been any such mandate, he could not have been relieved of such functions by a sub-constitutional measure.

18.   Article 170 of the Constitution commands that the accounts of both the Federation and the Provinces are to be kept in such form and in accordance with such principles and methods as the Auditor General may determine. One cannot, however, read into this constitutional requirement that the accounts must also be kept by the Auditor General.

19.   The Parliament or a President, who has the authority to direct the Auditor General to keep the accounts of the Federation and the Provinces, can also direct him not to keep such accounts. The authority to confer a power or a function includes the authority to take it away. The powers of the Auditor General to keep the accounts both for the Federation and the Provinces were statutory in nature and, therefore, could be curtailed or withdrawn by statute. On the other hand, the authority of the Auditor General to audit the accounts of the Federation and of the Provinces in view of the provisions of Article 170 and 171 of the Constitution are constitutional in nature and cannot be altered by statute.

20.   In view of the above, Ordinance XXIII which restricts the powers of the Auditor General to audit of the accounts of the Federation and Ordinance XXIV of 2001 which transfers the function of keeping the accounts of the Federation to the Controller General do not violate Article 169 of the Constitution.

21.   Article 169 confines the power of the Parliament and that of the President to "determine" the functions and powers of the Auditor General in relation to the accounts of the Provinces. Once the power to keep the accounts of a province has been taken away from the Auditor General through an Ordinance, that power could not have been conferred on any other authority or functionary by federal law. Article 169 does not authorize the conferment of such functions or powers on any authority except the Auditor General. The moment, therefore, these powers and functions are denied him, the authority to keep the provincial accounts vests in the Provinces under Article 142 (c) of the Constitution read with the Fourth Schedule thereto. The Federation has no power to legislate that any officer other than the Auditor General can keep accounts of the Provinces. Such legislation can only be made by a province.

22.   Section 5 of Ordinance XXIV of 2001 which provides that the functions of the Controller General shall include the preparation and maintenance of the accounts of the provinces and district governments is ultra vires Article 169 read with Article 142 (c) and the Fourth Schedule to the Constitution.

26.   The Constitution does not mandate that the Auditor General will keep the accounts. The Federation which assigned this function to the Auditor General could also abolish it in the absence of a constitutional impediment. There being no such clog, the function could have been and was abolished by Ordinances XXIII and XXIV of 2001. The Federation, however, had no authority to then confer the function of keeping the accounts of the Provinces on the Controller General under Article 169 or otherwise.

27. In view of the above discussion, my conclusions are as follows:

I. The audit of the accounts of the Federation and of the Provinces is the constitutional function of the Auditor General of Pakistan and it cannot be interfered with by the Federation or a Province in the exercise of any legislative or executive authority.

II. By an Act of the Parliament or by an Order of the President, the Auditor General can be authorized to perform such functions and exercise such powers in relation to the accounts of the Federation and of the Provinces as may be determined by such Act or Order. These functions and powers can include the keeping of accounts of the Federation or the Provinces by the Auditor General.

III. Since the function of the keeping of the accounts of the Federation or the Province is conferred on the Auditor General by an Act or an Order made in exercise of the powers under Article 169 of the Constitution, this function can also be taken away by such an Act or Order.

IV. Ordinance XXIII of 2001 which restricts the power of the Auditor General to the audit of accounts of the Federation and of the Provinces is constitutional.

V. Ordinance XXIV of 2001 which transfers the function of keeping the accounts of the Federation from the Auditor General to the Controller General is also constitutional.

VI. That by an Act of Parliament or by an Order of the President, while the Federation has the power to confer the function of keeping of accounts of a Province on the Auditor General, it has no power to confer this function on any other authority.

VII. That once the Federation denies the Auditor General the power to keep the accounts of the Provinces, then the authority in that respect vests in the provincial government. They alone can determine how these accounts are to be kept."

171. The above conclusions drawn by Mr. Makhdoom Ali Khan are logical and convincing. These are correct not only in the context of Article 169 of the Constitution of 1973 but are also valid when viewed in terms of the earlier constitutional provisions i.e. Rule 18 of the Rules regarding the Auditor General in India framed by the Secretary of State in Council, Section 166 (3) of the Government of India Act, 1935, Article 122 of the Constitution of 1956, Article 196 of the Constitution of 1962 and Article 170(4) of the interim Constitution of 1972. We are, therefore, convinced to hold that after withdrawal of the function of keeping and maintaining accounts of the Provinces from the Auditor General, the same became a residual subject and fell into exclusive provincial legislative jurisdiction. Once a subject becomes residual in facts and circumstances like those surrounding this plaint, what ensues is irreversible; transfer of a subject from federal to residual sphere is what a lighted match to a train of gunpowder.

172. We required the learned Attorney General for Pakistan to inform us about what precise function was withdrawn from the Auditor General and entrusted to the CGA under the CGA Ordinance in respect of keeping and maintenance of accounts of the Provinces? He explained that prior to promulgation of the CGA Ordinance, the Auditor General used to prepare Appropriation Accounts and Finance Accounts of the Province. It was not the function of the Auditor General to keep written records of financial transactions of individual

offices of the Provincial Government. It was also not his duty to maintain accounts of receipts and disbursements which was a necessary corollary of performance of the treasury functions of the Province by the DAOs / Treasuries.

173.   The learned Advocate General, Punjab, presented letter No. IT(FD)3-2/2003 dated 02.08.2012 of the Finance Department of the Government of the Punjab paragraph 5 whereof reads as follows:

> "Accounts means "appropriation accounts" and "finance accounts" as defined in Section 2 (a) and (d) of the CGA Ordinance and do not mean every written record of all financial transactions. If definition of accounts is stretched beyond "appropriation accounts" and "finance accounts", then lawfulness of keeping and maintaining accounts by entities of the federation and of the federating units and bodies established, managed or controlled by them through the staff other than the subordinates of the CGA would become questionable besides rendering the CGA Ordinance impracticable. Restriction of function of maintenance of   accounts to the extent of preparation of "appropriation accounts" and "finance accounts" of the Government as a whole and leaving departmental arrangements of maintenance of accounts of individual entities to the concerned departments is a fact of notable material significance."

174.   The view taken in the aforesaid letter is not the whole truth. Sections 7 and 8 of the CGA Ordinance, reproduced below, show that the CGA has to prepare appropriation accounts, finance accounts, annual Consolidated and General Financial Statement, summaries of monthly and quarterly accounts:

> "7. Reports.   - From the accounts directly kept or maintained by him or by accounts officers subordinate to him, and from the accounts kept and maintained by other entities, including self-accounting entities, the Controller General shall-
>
> (a)   prepare each year the appropriation and finance accounts and such other accounts as may be prescribed by rules for submission to the Auditor-General on such dates as may be specified by him;
>
> (b)   prepare and submit to the Auditor-General for each financial year a Consolidated and General Financial Statement incorporating the summary of the accounts of the Federation, all provinces and district authorities. The Auditor General, after authentication, shall forward the same to the Federal Government, Provincial Governments and district authorities;
>
> (c)   prepare and submit to the Federal, the respective Provincial Governments and the Auditor General, statements and summaries of monthly or quarterly accounts as on such formats, as may be prescribed by rules.
>
> 8. All accounting offices to assist and afford facilities. - All Accounting Offices shall afford all necessary facilities for efficient discharge and functioning of the office of Controller General."

175.   The periodic accounting reports required to be prepared by the CGA are reports of the Government as a whole and not of individual organizations of the Government. Individual organizations of even the Federal Government are not prohibited to maintain written accounts of moneys received or disbursed or assets acquired or disposed of or commitments made or discharged or debts raised or given etc. through their own internal arrangement. It is, however, their statutory duty to assist the CGA in discharge of his duties. As his duties pertain to preparation of accounting reports of the Government as a whole, therefore, such assistance takes the form of submission of such information as the

CGA may require in respect of an individual entity to enable him to perform his functions efficiently. The words "the accounts kept and maintained by other entities" used in Section 7 of the CGA Ordinance make it abundantly clear that the drawing and disbursing officers, controlling officers, principal accounting officers and the Federal Treasuries do not step out of their lawful jurisdiction when they maintain accounts of their financial transactions but they are statutorily bound to assist the CGA in performance of his duties through submission of information as he may require. Our declaration to this effect is for all entities of the Federation as well as of the Provinces with the clarification that the Provinces are constitutionally authorized to perform their own accounting functions as a residual subject. The responsibility of the Provincial Government is to the extent of provision of monthly, quarterly and annual accounting reports so that the CGA may prepare accounts depicting financial position of the country as a whole. In the Federal Government, however, all persons acting on its behalf are required to submit to the CGA such information as may reasonably be necessary to enable the CGA to efficiently perform his duties.

176.   In reply to a query raised by us, the learned Attorney General for Pakistan stated that organizational capability of the office of the CGA has not been built upon the assumption that this office has to keep and maintain individual accounts of all drawing and disbursing officers, controlling officers, principal accounting officers and the Federal Treasuries. He explained that, in practice and in law, such accounts are kept and maintained by the concerned federal entities through staff not subordinate to the CGA. Services of officers of the Pakistan Audit & Accounts Service are, however, requisitioned on deputation by federal organizations as and where need be but it is not necessary that internal accounting arrangements of individual entities be controlled by the CGA. He prayed that written defence of the defendant may be treated as modified to this extent.

177.   We asked the learned Advocate General, Punjab to submit a list of departmentalized accounting offices of the plaintiff. He submitted that the expression used for the departmentalized accounting offices in the NAM is the self-accounting entities. He referred to paragraph 1.2.3.5 of the Accounting Code for Self-Accounting Entities which defines a self-accounting entity in the following words:

> "1.2.3.5 A self-accounting entity is any accounting entity for whom the Principal Accounting Officer has primary responsibility for the accounting and reporting functions. Examples of these entities is given below:
> - National Savings Organisation
> - Pakistan Mint
> - Food Wing of the Food and Agriculture Division
> - Pakistan Public Works Department
> - Ministry of Foreign Affairs
> - Pakistan Post Office Department
> - Geological Survey of Pakistan
> - Pakistan Railways
> - Forest Department
> - Ministry of Defence"

178.   Referring to the above definition, the learned Advocate General, Punjab stated that after implementation of the PIFRA in the Punjab, accounts of public works departments and the forest department are being maintained on the SAP-system and the principal accounting officers of the aforesaid departments are no longer primarily responsible for maintenance of accounts of these departments. Even if it is accepted, he argued, that above-mentioned departments are departmentalized accounting offices, the CGA has no control or responsibility in respect of these offices as the CGA Ordinance is valid to the extent it relates to the Federation and is void so far as functions of keeping and maintenance of accounts of the Province is concerned.

179.   The question of entrustment of accounting functions of the district governments to the CGA under Section 5(a) of the CGA Ordinance is interesting one. The district governments were local governments in the Punjab established under the Punjab Local Government Ordinance, 2001. Since the said Ordinance has been repealed, therefore, the district governments are no more in existence. Accounts of the predecessor local governments of the district governments had never been maintained by any federal functionary nor there is any arrangement by the Federal Government to maintain accounts of the local governments that have succeeded the district governments. In view of admitted absence of organizational capability of the Federation to maintain accounts of the local governments in the Punjab and non-existence of the district governments, we do not deem it necessary to further dilate upon the question of maintenance of accounts of the district governments. When it is held that the CGA lacks constitutional mandate to keep and maintain accounts of the Provinces, accounts of the district governments and other local governments are automatically excluded from the purview of the CGA as the local governments in the Provinces is a subject which does not fall within federal legislative jurisdiction.

180.   To say that maintenance of accounts of the provincial and local governments by a federal institution is in interest of national unity and integration is not a legal argument. We do not feel ourselves obliged to find answer to such question as it would be a travel beyond our sphere of duty.

181.   In Writ Petition No.17856 of 2005 (Shamas-ud-Din and thirty other Assistant Accounts Officers Vs. Government of Pakistan and others) in the Lahore High Court, Lahore, it was argued that under Article 169 of the Constitution, only an Act of Parliament can deny the Auditor General of the responsibility to keep and maintain accounts of the Federation and of the Provinces. It was asserted that the AG Ordinance is not an Act of the Parliament and notwithstanding promulgation of this Ordinance, over-all control of the function of maintenance of accounts rests with the Auditor General. As the ultimate control of the Auditor General is intact in the matter of maintenance of accounts, therefore, it was argued, accounts of the Provinces are being maintained by the Auditor General through the CGA and it would not be correct to claim that the CGA Ordinance or the AG Ordinance have denied or can lawfully deny the Auditor General the responsibility of maintenance of accounts of the Provinces. We have examined this argument. Determination of functions and powers of the Auditor General through a Presidential Order under Article 169 of the Constitution or through an Ordinance issued by the President under Article 89 of the Constitution may be seen in the context of what was held in a case reported as 1990 MLD 1960 according to which an Ordinance "has to be deemed to be an Act of Parliament for all intents and purposes during the period of its enforcement." Upon validation by the Parliament, an Ordinance becomes an Act of Parliament, having perpetual enforceability, because validation by the Parliament does not mean rubber-stamping a law already made; it means fresh enactment as the Parliament has full competence to amend, reject or approve the Ordinance. Rejection or approval of an Ordinance, with or without amendments, is exercise of legislative power by the Parliament. The power of the Parliament to reject or approve an Ordinance is not inferior to or different from its power to enact new laws or repeal existing laws. With approval of the AG Ordinance by the Parliament, the requirements of Article 169 of the Constitution stand fulfilled. Since the Parliament has expressed its legislative intent to determine functions and responsibilities of the Auditor General in relation to accounts of the Federation and of the Provinces through approval of the AG Ordinance, therefore, it is for the Parliament to re-exercise its powers to amend or repeal the Ordinance. Till such time the Parliament exercises its revisional authority, the Ordinance shall be considered an Act of the Parliament as envisaged in Article 169 and as expressly stated in Article 89 of the Constitution. The exercise of revisional authority by the Parliament in respect of the AG Ordinance is obviously subject to Article 142(c) of the Constitution. For the moment, the

419

Auditor General lacks jurisdiction to directly or indirectly maintain accounts of the Federation and of the Provinces or their entities.

182.   For the reasons stated hereinabove, we are inclined to hold and do herby hold and declare that keeping and maintaining accounts of the Provincial and local governments is a residual subject in terms of Article 142 (c) of the Constitution. Section 5(a) of the CGA Ordinance, to the extent it purports to assign accounting functions of the Provinces and of the district governments to the CGA, is ultra vires Article 169 read with Article 142 (c) of the Constitution and, hence, void and of no legal effect.

Question # 4

Whether the Province is entitled to receive amount spent by it on performance of treasury functions of the Federation?

183.   Ever since enactment of the Government of India Act, 1935, all constitutions consistently contained provisions, reproduced below, allowing the Federation to entrust its functions to a Province in consideration of payment of extra cost to be incurred by the Province as a result of performance of these federal functions:

Section 124 of the Government of India Act, 1935

(1) Notwithstanding anything in this Act, the Governor-General may, with the consent of the Government of a Province or the Ruler of a Federated State, entrust either conditionally or unconditionally to that Government or Ruler, or to their respective officers, functions in relation to any matter to which the executive authority of the Federation extends.

(2) An Act of the Federal Legislature may, notwithstanding that it relates to a matter with respect to which a Provincial Legislature has no power to make laws, confer powers and impose duties upon a Province or officers and authorities thereof.

(3) An Act of the Federal Legislature which extends to a Federated State may confer powers and impose duties upon the State or officers and authorities thereof to be designated for the purpose by the Ruler.

(4) Where by virtue of this section powers and duties have been conferred or imposed upon a Province or Federated State or officers or authorities thereof, there shall be paid by the Federation to the Province or State such sum as may be agreed, or, in default of agreement, as may be determined by an arbitrator appointed by the Chief Justice of India, in respect of any extra costs of administration incurred by the Province or State in connection with the exercise of those powers and duties.

Article 127 of the Constitution of 1956

(1) Notwithstanding anything in the Constitution, the President may, with the consent of a Provincial Government, entrust either conditionally or unconditionally to that Government, or to any officer thereof, functions in relation to any matter to which the executive authority of the Federation extends.

(2) An Act of Parliament may, notwithstanding that it relates to a matter with respect to which a Provincial Legislature has not the power to make laws, confer powers and impose duties, or authorize the conferment of powers and the imposition of duties, upon a Province or officers or authorities thereof.

(3) Where by virtue of this Article powers and duties have been conferred or imposed upon a Province, or officers or authorities thereof, there shall be paid by the Federal Government to the Provincial Government such sums as may be agreed, or, in default of agreement, as may be determined in accordance with the procedure prescribed in Article 129,

in respect of any extra costs incurred by the Provincial Government in connection with the exercise of those powers and duties.

Article 143 of the Constitution of 1962

(1) Notwithstanding anything in this Constitution, the President may, with the consent of a Provincial Government, entrust either conditionally or unconditionally to that Government, or to any officer or authority of that Government, functions in relation to any matter to which the executive authority of the Republic extends.

(2) An Act of the Central Legislature may, notwithstanding that it relates to a matter with respect to which a Provincial Legislature has no power to make laws, confer powers and impose duties, or authorize the conferment of powers and the imposition of duties, upon a Provincial Government or officers or authorities of a Provincial Government.

(3) Where, by virtue of this Article, functions have been entrusted or powers and duties have been conferred or imposed upon, a Provincial Government or officers or authorities of a Provincial Government, there shall be paid by the Central Government to the Provincial Government such sums as may be agreed (or if there is no agreement, as may be determined by Act of the Central Legislature) in respect of any extra costs incurred by the Provincial Government in connection with the performance of those functions, the exercise of those powers or the discharge of those duties.

Article 147 of the Interim Constitution of 1972

(1) Notwithstanding anything contained in the Constitution, the Federal Government may, with the consent of the Government of a Province, entrust either conditionally or unconditionally to that Government, or to its officers, functions in relation to any matter to which the executive authority of the Federation extends.

(2) An Act of Federal Legislature may, notwithstanding that it relates to a matter with respect to which a Provincial Assembly has no power to make laws, confer powers and impose duties or authorize conferring of powers and the imposition of duties upon a Province or officers and authorities thereof.

(3) Where by virtue of this Article powers and duties have been conferred or imposed upon a Province or officers or authorities thereof, there shall be paid by the Federation to the Province such sum as may be agreed or, in default of agreement, as may be determined by an arbitrator appointed by the Chief Justice of Pakistan, in respect of any extra costs of administration incurred by the Province in connection with the exercise of those powers and duties.

Article 146 of the Constitution of 1973

(1) Notwithstanding anything contained in the Constitution, the Federal Government may, with the consent of the Government of a Province, entrust either conditionally or unconditionally to that Government, or to its officers, functions in relation to any matter to which the executive authority of the Federation extends.

(2) An Act of Majlis-e-Shoora (Parliament) may, notwithstanding that it relates to a matter with respect to which a Provincial Assembly has no power to make laws, confer powers and impose duties upon a Province or officers and authorities thereof.

(3) Where by virtue of this Article powers and duties have been conferred or imposed upon a Province or officers or authorities thereof, there

shall be paid by the Federation to the Province such sum as may be agreed or, in default of agreement, as may be determined by an arbitrator appointed by the Chief Justice of Pakistan, in respect of any extra costs of administration incurred by the Province in connection with the exercise of those powers or the discharge of those duties.

184.   No Act of Parliament has assigned treasury functions of the Federation in the Punjab to the Government of the Punjab. The fact of entrustment of treasury functions of the Federal Government in the Punjab to the Government of the Punjab, through arrangements made by the Governor General and the Governor of the Punjab, has, however, adequately been reflected in the Treasury Rules of the Federal Government as well as the Punjab Treasury Rules and the Subsidiary Treasury Rules, reproduced below:

Paragraph 4 of Preface to the First Edition of the Federal Treasury Rules

Under sub-section (1) of section 124 of the Government of India Act, 1935, as adopted by the Pakistan (Provisional Constitution) Order, 1947, the Governor General has been pleased to entrust officers in charge of Provincial treasuries and sub-treasuries with the functions of receiving and disbursing and authorizing the Bank to receive and disburse moneys of the Central Government with the stipulation that in respect of these transactions, the Treasury Officers and Sub-treasury Officers aforesaid shall act in accordance with these rules in so far as they are special to central transactions and do not refer to procedure already provided for in the rules of the Provincial Governments concerned.

Rule 34 of the Punjab Treasury Rules

Where such a course is authorized in consequence of a delegation of functions made under Paragraph (1) of Article 146 of the Constitution, the Treasury Officer may receive or authorize the Bank to receive moneys tendered on behalf of the Federation, and may make or authorize the Bank to make disbursements on behalf of the Federation in accordance with such procedure as may be specified in the rules made by or under the authority of the President. Such receipts and disbursements on behalf of the Federation shall be adjusted as far as practicable, directly against the balance of the Federation held by the Bank but where such transactions are temporarily taken into account against the balance of the Province, the Accountant-General/Director-General, Audit and Accounts (Works) will, on receipt of intimation from the Treasury, make the adjustments in respect of the aforesaid transactions through the Central Accounts Office of the State Bank of Pakistan against the balance of the Federation held by the Bank.

Rule 7.3 of the Punjab Subsidiary Treasury Rules

The Federal Government has entrusted officers in charge of the Treasuries and Sub-Treasuries in the Punjab with functions of receiving and disbursing, and authorizing the Bank to receive and disburse, moneys on their behalf. In dealing with such transactions, the Treasury / Sub-Treasury Officers act in accordance with the Treasury Rules of the Federal Government.

185.   After giving a patient hearing to the learned Attorney General for Pakistan and the learned Advocate General, Punjab, we observe that:

(a) The Federation has exclusive legislative and executive power in respect of its treasury functions;

(b) Treasury functions of the Federation in the Punjab are deemed to have been assigned by the President of Pakistan to the Governor of the Punjab;

(c) The Province has not earlier demanded and the Federation has not yet paid the extra cost incurred and being incurred by the Province in performance of the federal treasury functions;

(d) During pendency of these proceedings, the Province has demanded payment in terms of Article 146(3) of the Constitution but the parties are not in agreement on the amount to be paid;

(e) Both the parties have given their consent that the Hon'ble Chief Justice may appoint an arbitrator for determination of the amount to be paid by the Federation to the Province; and

(f) The Chief Justice has appointed Mr. Salman Siddique, a retired civil servant known for his hard work, intelligence, professional excellence, proven problem-solving abilities with rich experience of financial management and civil administration at federal and provincial level as a sole arbitrator for determination of the amount payable to the Province by the Federation under Article 146(3) of the Constitution with direction to conclude arbitration proceedings and announce his award not later than ninety days of his appointment as arbitrator.

186. The question of determination of the amount payable to the plaintiff in terms of Article 146(b) of the Constitution with respect to performance of treasury functions of the defendant stands settled for the moment in the aforesaid terms.

187. The plaintiff has asserted that despite promulgation of the CGA Ordinance and entrustment of treasury functions of the Federation to the CGA, the Federation has failed to establish its organizational capability for performance of its treasury functions in the Province. In this regard, we may observe that performance of treasury functions of the defendant by the plaintiff is a function which cannot be thrust upon the plaintiff without its consent. The plaintiff is at liberty to terminate arrangements deemed to have been made under Article 146 of the Constitution. We are, however, not convinced by the argument advanced by the learned Advocate General, Punjab that after promulgation of the CGA Ordinance, it is only the CGA who is statutorily authorized to perform treasury functions of the Federation as an enactment of the Parliament has to prevail over executive arrangements made under Article 146(1) of the Constitution. We find no inconsistency between clause (1) and (2) of Article 146 of the Constitution. Whereas the said clause (2) empowers the Parliament to statutorily assign a federal function to a Province, the clause (1) allows the Federation to assign a function statutorily assumed by it to itself to a Province through an executive arrangement. It is, therefore, possible for the Federation to assign its treasury functions to a Province despite promulgation of the CGA Ordinance. It is for the Federation and the Province to decide whether they want to continue the existing arrangements made under Article 146 of the Constitution or not. Any decision made by the parties in this respect shall be lawful if otherwise not in violation of any provision of the Constitution. The defendant also has the option to withdraw its workforce in the DAOs from provincial functions and deploy the same for performance of federal treasury functions.

188. Argument of the Federation that it incurs expenditure on performance of treasury functions of the Province entrusted to the AG, Punjab in terms of Rule 6 of the Punjab Treasury Rules and it has to repay the loan raised for the PIFRA (from which the Province has benefited in performance of its treasury functions) pales into insignificance after appointment of an arbitrator during pendency of these proceedings by the Hon'ble Chief Justice for determination of the amount payable by the Federation to the Province under Article 146(3) of the Constitution. It needs to be noticed that Rule 6 of the Punjab Treasury Rules was without support and backing of the Constitution as there was no legal provision

similar to Article 147 of the Constitution of 1973, reproduced below, in the Government of India Act, 1935 and the various Constitutions of Pakistan:

"147. Power of the Provinces to entrust functions to the Federation. - Notwithstanding anything contained in the Constitution, the Government of a Province may, with the consent of the Federal Government, entrust, either conditionally or unconditionally, to the Federal Government, or to its officers, functions in relation to any matter to which the executive authority of the Province extends:

Provided that the Provincial Government shall get the functions so entrusted ratified by the Provincial Assembly within sixty days."

189.   We are in agreement with the learned Advocate General, Punjab that Rule 6 of the Punjab Treasury Rules was void ab initio for want of constitutional sanction behind the arrangement introduced under this rule. Moreover, Article 147 of the Constitution of 1973 does not necessarily require payment of any amount by a Province in case a provincial function is entrusted to the Federation. Further, in absence of an agreement to the contrary, a Province is not liable to pay, partially or fully, loans raised by the Federation even if a part of the loan is spent on performance of provincial functions.

190.   In view of what has been stated hereinabove, we hold that the plaintiff is entitled to recover from the defendant the amount spent or to be spent by it in performance of federal treasury functions by it. We further declare that notwithstanding promulgation of the CGA Ordinance, the plaintiff and the defendant are at liberty either to continue or to terminate arrangements deemed to have been made under Article 147 of the Constitution with respect to performance of a prescribed part of the treasury functions of the defendant by the plaintiff.

Question # 5

Whether administration of the PA&AS as a joint audit and accounts service by the Auditor General is lawful after statutory separation of accounting and auditing functions?

191.   The learned Advocate General, Punjab has argued that prior to promulgation of the CGA Ordinance, the Auditor General used to simultaneously bear the following three caps:

1.   Prescribing accounting policies and procedures;
2.   Audit of the Federation and of the Provinces; and
3.   Maintenance of accounts of the Federation and of the Provinces.

192.   Giving an introduction of the PA&AS which comprised 832 career civil servants in September 2019, the learned Advocate General, Punjab invited our attention towards paragraph 63 of the Manual of Standing Orders (MSO), 4th edition issued by the Auditor General of Pakistan in February, 2017, reproduced below:

"63. In 1973 Accounts Group was formed vide O.M No. 1/2/74-ARC dated 23.01.1974 amended vide O.M. No.2/1/75-ARC dated 03-03-1976. It was later renamed as Pakistan Audit and Accounts Service vide O.M No. 1/17/92-CPII dated 10th December, 2002. The Pakistan Audit and Accounts Service (PAAS) comprises of all posts in:

(i)   The Pakistan Audit & Accounts Department, the Pakistan Military Accounts Department and the Railway Accounts Department;

(ii)   All Accounts posts under Ministries/Divisions and Departments of the Federal Government, other than the posts of Budget & Accounts Officers or Finance & Accounts Officers, in the Ministries/Divisions of the Federal Secretariat e.g. the office of the Chief Accounts Officer, Ministry of Foreign Affairs and its sub-offices, Pakistan Post Office (PPO) Department, Pakistan Public Works Department (PPWD) and other departments maintaining departmentalized Accounts.

The Service mainly comprises of two cadres namely Inter Departmental Cadre governed centrally by the Auditor General of Pakistan as an occupational group and departmental cadre administered by respective Head of Department of an Audit Office."

193. The learned law officer further stated that paragraph 26 of the Memorandum of Economic and Financial Policies (MEFP), attached with a letter jointly signed by the then Federal Minister of Finance and Economic Affairs and the Governor, State Bank of Pakistan on 18th of March 2001, addressed to the Managing Director of the International Monitory Fund, inter alia, provided that:

"Specific steps to improve public sector financial accountability over the coming months will include the promulgation before end-June 2001 of legislation separating the government audit and accounting functions into two separate departments, with effective application starting with the next budget."

194. The learned Advocate General, Punjab stated that according to an article published in the Daily Dawn on 18.06.2001, a spokesman of the Ministry of Finance justified the CGA Ordinance and the AG Ordinance by saying that:

"The separation of audit and accounting functions was one of the conditionalities of the IMF and the World Bank which we have implemented in the larger interests of the country...the IMF and the World Bank had been asking Pakistan for the last six years to separate the functions of audit and accounts but it could not be carried out."

195. The learned law officer of the plaintiff also referred to a news story released by the Associated Press of Pakistan (official news agency of the Government of Pakistan) on 17.05.2001, which, inter alia, stated that:

"While approving the draft laws on the subject, the Cabinet noted that the establishment of a separate office of Controller General of Accounts was in tune with the well-established principle that the authority which prepares the accounts should not be certifying those accounts as it creates a conflict of interest."

196. The learned Advocate General, Punjab also read out the following excerpts from "Proposals for Departmentalization of Accounts prepared under the directions of the Comptroller and Auditor General of Pakistan", published in 1962 by the Superintendent, Government Printing Press, West Pakistan, Lahore:

"21. The first step in this direction would be the separation of audit from accounts. This vexed question has been under consideration for a long time. Sir Fredrick Gauntle, the then Auditor-General of India, proposed it as early as 1922. It was tried in U.P. in 1924 but abandoned as too expensive in men and money. Various authorities and committees revived the question from time to time in India but so far it has not been possible to introduce it either in India or in Pakistan.

22. The arguments in favour of separations were fully stated in the dispatch of Government of India on this subject to the Secretary of State in 1925. ----. Audit, in theory, is a criticism of the completed work of others. The person performing it should be as detached and as independent as is possible. If, as happens in a combined office, he descends from his pedestal of independence, either by giving financial advice to the executive, by compiling or classifying accounts, by pre-auditing payments or by issuing pay authorities, his independence as a critic suffers.

49. Briefly the following changes are necessary for proper reorganization of accounts: -

(i)   Audit and Accounts should be separated. Maintenance of accounts should become the responsibility of the Central and Provincial Governments in their respective spheres.

(ii)   ------."

197.   The learned Advocate General, Punjab stated that Section 6 (3) of the CGA Ordinance made the CGA the administrative head of all the offices subordinate to him with full authority for transfer and posting within his organization. Quoting from https://www.yourdictionary.com/administration, he said that administration is defined as the act of managing duties, responsibilities, or rules with further explanation that the definition of administration refers to the group of individuals who are in charge of creating and enforcing rules and regulations, or those in leadership positions who complete important tasks. With reference to the separation of accounting functions and declaration of the CGA as administrative head of accounting organizations of the Federation, he stated that retention of the PA&AS as a combined audit and accounts service under administration of the Auditor General was not legally permissible after promulgation of the CGA Ordinance. The PA&AS could not survive as a combined service in view of Section 6(3) of the CGA Ordinance, he stated adding that the following arrangements became unenforceable because of their inconsistency with the CGA Ordinance:

(a) The Inter-Departmental Cadre will be administered by the Auditor General and the Departmental Cadres by the respective Heads of Department. The Auditor General will prepare and maintain a gradation list of all officers in Grade 17 and above in the Inter-Departmental Cadre while the Departmental Heads will maintain seniority lists of officers and staff in Grade 17 and below in the Departmental Cadres. (Estt. Division O.M.No.1/2/74-ARC, dated 23-1-1974).

(b) 67. -----. The matters relating to LFP/LHP, EOL, Medical Leave, Study Leave, Maternity Leave and Ex-Pakistan Leave in case of PA&AS/IDC and other Officers would be dealt by Auditor General of Pakistan being Cadre Administrator (except where delegated) as per rules in vogue. (Manual of Standing Orders of the Auditor General).

(c) 68. Postings and transfers from one office to another or outside department of all officers of Pakistan Audit & Accounts Service are made by the Auditor General being the Cadre Administrator. In cases of transfer to the organization of Controller General Accounts these are made in consultation with Controller General Accounts at appropriate levels as agreed. Controller General Accounts or other head of departments can order transfers within own departments. (Manual of Standing Orders of the Auditor General).

(d) The Auditor General is competent authority for the purpose of disciplinary action in respect of departmental and interdepartmental officers of the PA&AS in Basic Pay Scale 17 to 19 with power to place

(e) As per the entry appearing at serial number 1 of the table appearing below Rule 6(2) of the Civil Servants (Appointment, Promotion and Transfer) Rules, 1973, the Auditor General of Pakistan is the appointing authority for officers in BS. 17 to BS. 19 of the Pakistan Audit Department and Officers of Inter Departmental Cadre of Accounts Group (now called PA&AS). He has the power to place a BPS-20 and above officer of the PA&AS under suspension for such period as he may consider appropriate. (Establishment Division Notification SRO No.563(1)/2000, dated 15-8-2000).

198.   The learned Advocate General, Punjab stated that the plaintiff is adversely affected by non-bifurcation of the PA&AS into Audit Service and Accounts Service by the defendant despite clear requirement of the CGA Ordinance with respect to separation of accounting functions from auditing functions. He explained that conflict of interest of the auditors and non-availability of persons having specialized knowledge, skills and experience of audit are inescapable consequences of continued existence of the PA&AS as a combined audit and accounts service. In order to highlight the problems mainly caused by a joint service both for audit and accounts, the learned Advocate General, Punjab stated that addressing the thirtieth Annual International Financial Management Conference held on October 8-10, 1998 in Virginia, Mr. Antonio Sanchez de Lozada (former member, St. Anthony's College (Oxford), former Senator, Comptroller General and Finance Minister of Bolivia) remarked about the state of accounting and auditing in his country in the following words:

> "In Bolivia, we finally went to democracy in 1982. It is interesting to analyze the dysfunctional government inherited by the new democracy. There were no systems. Forget about management information systems. Forget about management systems. Budgeting was the biggest joke I have ever seen. When I entered the Controller General's Office, we were supposed to be carrying the accounts of government, but there was no way to do it. I entered the Controller General's Office at the end of 1982, and I think the first accounts I brought out were 1977 or 1978. They were not worth the paper they were printed on. At a meeting on this issue with at least 100 professional people, I said "The most important change we could make in the accounting report is not just accelerate it. We should publish it on paper that is absorbent and use ink that is non-irritable to human skin because that report might have some useful destiny for a society where there is such poverty and such a shortage of toilet paper.
>
> The tragedy is we go through the motions. I saw the auditing system, which we had in Bolivia. The auditing system was basically to do a review and find a noncompliance. And since there was such a hodgepodge, such an accumulation of regulations where each de facto government brought in new regulations, you could always find noncompliance. Noncompliance could then be carried to the criminal stage. At least they would be obligated to return the money.
>
> To compensate for this breakdown in public administration, they instituted a system of pre-controls. The Controller General's Office was given the power and duty to review and pre-authorize any payment order, any contract, and so on. We had a tremendous accumulation of volume there. Of the 1,100-odd people in the Controller General's Office, something like 750 were dedicated to this pre-review and preauthorization function. What ultimately happened is, of course, we just blocked government and we became one of the most talented, capable, extraordinary institutions in the technique of extortion. A signature of one of the Controller General's Officers was fundamental if you wanted to pay anything."

199.   The learned Advocate General, Punjab prayed that the legislative intent to separate accounting and auditing functions be given effect to through split of the PA&AS into separate Accounts Service to be administered by the CGA and the Audit Service to be administered by the Auditor General. He further prayed that this Court may declare that deputation / posting / transfer of auditors subordinate to the Auditor General on posts relating to accounts and other executive functions including financial management is against the statutory requirement of separation of audit from accounts.

427

200.   The learned Attorney General for Pakistan explained the arguments recorded by the defendant in its written reply and concluded that in view of constitutional powers of the Auditor General with respect to audit as well as accounts, it is incorrect to claim that separation of accounting and auditing functions must result into splitting of the PA&AS into separate Audit Service and Accounts Service and denying the Auditor General his role to administer the PA&AS. He said that institutional mechanism for gainful coordination between accounting and auditing organizations under the umbrella of the Auditor General is not in violation of the spirit of separation of audit and accounts. He further stated that postings / transfers of the PA&AS officers within accounting organizations are being ordered by the CGA and the Auditor General administers the PA&AS in consultation with the CGA in matters pertaining to accounting organizations.

201.   In order to properly understand the lis at hand, we required the learned Attorney General for Pakistan to submit the following in the Court:

       (a) A copy of the recruitment, composition and cadre rules of the PA&AS framed under Section 25(1) of the Civil Servants Act, 1973;

       (b) A copy of the rules and the regulations framed under the CGA Ordinance and the AG Ordinance;

       (c) A copy of the posting orders of the officers of the PA&AS presently holding the posts of Accountants General of all the four Provinces and the Accountant General, Pakistan Revenues, Islamabad; and

       (d) A list of measures taken for separation of accounting function after promulgation of the CGA Ordinance supported by copies of the relevant instruments.

202.   In response, the learned Attorney General for Pakistan informed us that no rules or regulations under the CGA and the AG Ordinances or rules required to be made under Section 25(1) of the Civil Servants Act, 1973 regarding recruitment, composition and cadre of the PA&AS have so far been framed. A perusal of the posting orders of the Accountants General of all the four provinces and the Accountant General, Pakistan Revenues, Islamabad, submitted by the learned Attorney General, reveals that all the orders have been issued by the Auditor General. As regards the measures taken for separation of accounting functions, Notification No. 114/DG (A)/9-2/97 dated 16.07.2001 of the Auditor General under which the function of preparing and maintaining accounts of the Federation and of the Provinces was transferred to be the CGA and Order No. F.No.7(2)-Policy-I/2002 dated 14.03.2013 of the Finance Division of the Federal Government, though which was reiterated what had already been written as Section 6(3) of the CGA Ordinance, were presented before this Court. We inquired about the status of a detailed exercise for separating the cadres of accounts and audit claimed to be undertaken by the Establishment Division, as was stated in the aforesaid Order No. F.No.7(2)-Policy-I/2002 dated 14.03.2013. The learned Attorney General for Pakistan stated that no action presentable to this Court had been taken by the Establishment Division with regard to splitting the PA&AS into separate cadres for accounts and audit.

203.   We have patiently heard the rival contentions. Our sole job is to discover the legislative intent as expressed in the statute on the issues under consideration and to apply that intent on the facts and circumstances of this case. We need first to ascertain whether separation of accounting and auditing functions is intended by the legislature or not.

204.   "The preamble of a statute is a prefatory statement at its beginning following the title and preceding the enacting clauses, explaining or declaring the reasons or motives for and the object sought to be accomplished by the enactment of the statute. It is the introductory part of the statute which states the reasons and intent of the law. It serves to portray intent of the framers and the mischief to be remedied." ((1954) 2 MLJ 737). Preamble of the CGA Ordinance, inter alia, states that:

       "WHEREAS it is expedient to provide for separation of accounting functions and appointment of Controller General of Accounts and for matters connected therewith or incidental thereto;".

205. When the above preamble is read with the decision of the Federal Cabinet dated 17.05.2001 and letter of the Federal Minister for Finance and Economic Affairs and the Governor of the State Bank of Pakistan dated 18.03.2001, it becomes abundantly clear that the CGA and the AG Ordinances are, inter alia, aimed at separation of accounting and auditing functions.

206. Section 6(3) of the CGA Ordinance makes the CGA administrative head of the accounting organizations subordinate to him. There is no dispute that accounting organizations of the Federation are subordinate to the CGA. The Hon'ble Lahore High Court, Lahore, in its judgment reported as Rana Fazal-e-Haq Vs. Director General of Accounts (PLD 2003 Lah 726) has declared that the CGA has exclusive administrative control and authority over all the departmentalized accounting organizations. With this judicial declaration, there remains no shadow of doubt about exclusive administrative control and authority of the CGA over accounting organizations of the Federation. This exclusive administrative control and authority is meaningless if the CGA is made an alien to matters concerning induction in the PA&AS, maintenance of seniority lists, sanction of leave, postings / transfers, discipline and powers of appointing authority up to a permissible limit etc. All aspects of personnel management do fall within sphere of administrative control and authority. A person who lacks a controlling or at least meaningful role in matters such as discipline, leave, posting / transfer, induction can be anything except the one having exclusive administrative control and authority over an organization. Till such time we are in our senses, it would not be possible for us to say that the CGA can actually be labelled an administrative head of the federal accounting organizations in absence of powers which are necessary ingredients of administrative control. We have seen with concern that despite Order No. F.No.7(2)-Policy-I/2002 dated 14.03.2013 of the Finance Division being lawfully in the field, none of the Provincial Accountants General has been posted by the CGA. We have not been able to understand that what is the substance in the claim of separation of accounting and auditing functions if a combined service of the Federation (PA&AS) continues to simultaneously deal with accounting as well as auditing functions under the umbrella of the Auditor General.

207. The argument of the plaintiff that existence of the PA&AS as a combined service for provision of accounting and auditing services promotes the conflict of interest seems to be reasonable. Our declaration earlier in this judgment to the effect that the function of keeping and maintaining accounts of the Province is a residual subject would surely cause this argument to disappear to the extent of accounts of the Province but the argument will continue to exist with full force in the matter of accounting and auditing functions of the Federation if the PA&AS is not split up into Accounts Service and Audit Service. Moreover, in this age of specialization, it would not be appropriate to put premium on jack of all trades but master of none. The Province is justified in apprehending that it would continue to be deprived of services of true auditing professionals if the PA&AS is kept intact as a combined service for audit as well as accounts. The concern of the plaintiff to this effect needs serious consideration even if the same does not constitute a legal cause of action as we have held earlier in this judgment that existence of a legal cause of action or being an aggrieved person is not a condition-precedent to initiate proceedings under Article 184(1) of the Constitution.

208. The Accounts Group was constituted vide O.M.No.1/2/74-ARC dated 23.01.1974 issued by the Establishment Division of the Federal Government. This office memorandum was issued after enactment of the Civil Servants Act, 1973. Section 25 of the Civil Servants Act, 1973 reads as follows:

> "(1)   The President or any person authorised by the President in this behalf, may make such rules as appear to him to be necessary or expedient for carrying out the purposes of this Act.

(2)   Any rules, orders or instructions in respect of any terms and conditions of service of civil servants duly made or issued by an authority competent to make them and in force immediately before the commencement of this Act shall, in so far as such rules, orders or instructions are not inconsistent with the provisions of this Act, be deemed to be rules made under this Act."

209.   Sub-section (1) of Section 25 of the Act ibid prescribes framing of rules to carry out the purposes of the Act. It is well-established that prescription of one is prohibition of another. Creation of services or cadres or functional units and providing for matters connected therewith or ancillary thereto falls within the purposes envisaged to be carried out through framing of rules under the said Section 25(1). What is statutorily required to be done through framing of the rules is not allowed to be done otherwise than through the rules. We have noticed that whereas sub-section (2) of the Act ibid protects rules, orders and instructions in respect of any terms and conditions of service of civil servants duly made or issued by an authority competent to make them and in force immediately before the commencement of the Act, the said Section 25(1) mentions only the instrument of rules to carry out the purposes of the Act. Admittedly, O.M.No.1/2/74-ARC dated 23.01.1974 does not constitute rules. Orders and instructions with respect to conditions of recruitment and of service of the federal civil servants can be lawful only if expressly provided for in the rules framed or to be framed under the said Section 25(1) and not in absence of such a delegation of powers. We are unable to accord sanctity and legal strength of the rules envisaged in the said Section 25(1) to the O.M.No.1/2/74-ARC dated 23.01.1974. This office memorandum is hereby declared to be void and of no legal effect being in violation of Section 25(1) of the Civil Servants Act, 1973 and Section 6(3) of the CGA Ordinance read with judgment of the Hon'ble Lahore High Court, Lahore reported as Rana Fazal-e-Haq Vs. Director General of Accounts (PLD 2003 Lah 726). For the purpose of clarity, it is held that the CGA shall exercise exclusive administrative control over accounting organizations of the Federation without any intervention of the Auditor General over the officers working therein. In order to fill the vacuum caused by our declaration made hereinabove regarding legality of the O.M.No.1/2/74-ARC dated 23.01.1974, the Federation may immediately frame separate rules under Section 25(1) of the Civil Servants Act, 1973 to provide for the Accounts Service of the Federation under exclusive administrative control of the CGA and the Audit Service of the Federation under the superintendence and control of the Auditor General.

Question # 6

Whether the Federation has lawful authority to post or depute federal employees on posts in connection with affairs of the Provinces?

210.   This Court has given a detailed judgment on the question of holding of posts in connection with affairs of a Province by federal employees through posting as well as deputation which has been reported as Azhar Hussain and others Vs. Federation of Pakistan and others (IAH 2019 MOOT COURT JUDGMENTS 1). Though that judgment mainly related to the All Pakistan Services and the PA&AS and the Divisional Accountants' Organization are not All Pakistan Services, yet the ratio decidendi of that judgment is attracted in the facts and circumstances of this case. Even then, for the purpose of clarity on the subject, we deem it our duty to legally analyse arguments of the learned Attorney General for Pakistan advanced to justify legality of the continued existence of the office of the Director General Accounts Works, Punjab (DGAW) with control over the Divisional Accounts Officers in the Punjab. It would serve no useful purpose to reproduce here the rival contentions already submitted in this case and summarized at the beginning of this judgment. We would, therefore, give our analysis and judgment on the contested questions of law involved in the matter under adjudication.

211.   We have earlier held in this judgment that performance of treasury functions of the Province has been an exclusive provincial domain ever since enactment of the Government of India Act, 1935 and the function of keeping and maintenance of accounts of the Province has become a residual subject with effect from coming into force of the CGA and the AG Ordinances. The inevitable and immediate effect of these declarations is that the office of the DGAW has lost authority to play any role in performance of accounting and treasury functions of the public works departments of the Province. The fact of redundancy of the office of the DGAW and a long series of illegalities in respect of existence and working of his office is also more than visible in view of, inter alia, the following:

a) Works accounts are maintained by the DAOs on the SAP-system and are consolidated by the office of the Accountant General, Punjab. The NAM does not require submission of works accounts by the DAOs to the DGAW. With implementation of the NAM under PIFRA through SAP, the DGAW has no role to play in keeping and consolidating works accounts of the Province;

b) The CGA Ordinance does not authorize the CGA or his subordinates including the DGAW to conduct audit of the works accounts. The Auditor General has exclusive jurisdiction on the subject of audit. With statutory separation of accounting and auditing functions, all rules, codes, manuals and instructions regarding entrustment of audit, post-audit, central audit or higher audit to accounting organizations have become obsolete and redundant;

c) Rule 14 (a) of the Punjab Departmental Financial Rules authorizes the DGAW to post a Divisional Accountant to assist the Divisional Officer in certain matters. This rule is not an existing law because of its inconsistency with the Constitution as there was no enabling provision in the Government of India Act, 1935, the Constitution of Pakistan, 1956 and 1962 allowing entrustment of provincial functions to the Federation. The said Rule is void and of no legal effect being not protected under Section 23 (2) of the Punjab Civil Servants Act, 1974 on account of its inconsistency with the Act ibid which assigns no role to the Federation in respect of services of a Province and posts in connection with affairs of a Province. Moreover, the said Section 23 (2) protects only those rules, orders and instructions which relate to terms and conditions of service of the civil servants. As per definition of the term 'civil servant' given in Section 2(1)(b)(i) of the Punjab Civil Servants Act, 1974, a person on deputation to the Province from the Federation is excluded from the definition of civil servant. There is no concept of posting of a civil servant of the defendant (other than member of an All Pakistan Service) to a post in connection with affairs of the plaintiff. A Divisional Accounts Officer is neither on deputation to the plaintiff nor a member of an All Pakistan Service. Rule 14 (a) of the Punjab Departmental Financial Rules is, therefore, held not to be protected by virtue of said Section 23 (2).

d) We are not in agreement with the argument that it is not necessary to regulate the Divisional Accounts Officers through rules to be framed under Section 25 (1) of the Civil Servants Act, 1973 as Chapter VII of the Manual of Standing Orders of the Auditor General is saved and protected under Section 25(2) of the Act ibid. The present Manual of Standing Orders of the Auditor General does not even mention the post of the Divisional Accountant or the Divisional Accounts Officer or the Divisional Accountants Organization. Absence of any legal cover to this organization makes it without lawful authority even in respect of posts in connection with affairs of the Federation.

e) A combined and harmonious reading of Article 119, 129, 137, 139, 147 and 240 of the Constitution and the laws / rules framed thereunder makes it clear that unless an arrangement duly made under Article 147 of the Constitution is validly in place, executive authority of the Province cannot be exercised by the Federation. Nothing has been placed on record to show existence of an arrangement under Article 147 of the Constitution with respect to the posting of the Divisional Accountant or the Divisional Accounts Officer except Rule 14 (a) of the Punjab Departmental Financial Rules. We have already declared this Rule void and of no legal effect hereinabove in this judgment.

f) The question of delegation of powers to the DGAW under Section 9 of the CGA Ordinance becomes meaningless after our declarations with respect to treasury and accounting functions of the Province.

g) The Federation lacks powers to abolish, create, re-designate or up-grade a post in connection with affairs of a Province. The post of the Divisional Accountant in works divisions of the Punjab is a post in connection with affairs of the Province. No federal functionary or institution has any authority of law to re-designate or up-grade this post. The DGAW issued an order on 5th of May, 2010 to the following effect:

> "In pursuance of Finance Division (Regulation Wing) O.M. No. F9(9)-R/2008-309 and the Controller General of Accounts, Notification No. 345/Estt-III/150-C/Court/Creation of Posts / 2008 dated 03.04.2010, the Director General Accounts Works, Lahore has approved up-gradation of following posts alongwith incumbents of this office w.e.f. 03.04.2010.

Name of post	Existing Scale	Up-Graded Scale
Divisional Accounts Officer	BS-16	BS-17
Senior Auditor working as Divisional Accounts Officer in Emergency cadre	BS-14/15	BS-16

The above order was made applicable to all posts of the Divisional Accounts Officers in the Punjab without any lawful authority. We declare that the Federation has no jurisdiction to create a charge on the Provincial Consolidated Fund or Local Fund of a provincial local body in the shape of up-gradation of a post remuneration of which is payable from the respective fund.

h) The Divisional Accounts Officers working under the DGAW filed a number of writ petitions in the Hon'ble Lahore High Court, Lahore to get a declaration that their prior written approval (pre-audit) is a condition-precedent to enable a Divisional Officer of works divisions of the Province to make payments. All these petitions were dismissed with no relief through intra-court appeals. The learned Advocate General, Punjab has placed on record certified copies of all the relevant documents the relevance and genuineness of which has not been called in question by the learned Attorney General for Pakistan.

i) It is obvious to us that the plaintiff is not dependent upon permission (pre-audit) of the defendant or any of its employees for release of budget and issuance of cheques. The orders of the plaintiff regarding opening of personal ledger accounts or special drawing accounts or release of funds in those accounts are not required to be ratified by the defendant for their validity. No decision of the plaintiff to this effect is subject to review, rejection or modification by the defendant.

212.   For the reasons recorded hereinabove, we declare that Rule 14 (a) of the Punjab Departmental Financial Rules is void ab initio. It is further held that it is not lawful for a federal employee to hold a post in connection with affairs of a Province either though posting under Section 10 of the Civil Servants Act, 1973 or on deputation under Rule 20A of the Civil Servants (Appointment, Promotion and Transfer) Rules, 1973.

213.   Before parting with the judgment, we place on record our grateful acknowledgement of the valuable assistance rendered by the learned law officers in this case.

214.   In the peculiar facts and circumstances of this case, we do not deem it essential to pass an order regarding imposition of costs on a party. Consequently, the parties are left to bear their own costs.

Sd/
Mr. Saleem Anwar Taya
Sd/
Mr. Jamal Mustafa Kundan
Sd/
Mr. Rasheed Ahmad

Announced in Open Court on 31st of December, 2019.

Sd/
Mr. M.B. Malik Taya

APPROVED FOR REPORTING

Chapter 5

In Aid of the Hon'ble

The Chapter finds that faithful obedience of Article 189 and 190 of the Constitution, reproduced below, is necessary for existence, strength, dignity and honour of the judicial organ of the state:

> "**189. Decisions of Supreme Court binding on other Courts.** Any decision of the Supreme Court shall, to the extent that it decides a question of law or is based upon or enunciates a principle of law, be binding on all other courts in Pakistan.
>
> **190. Action in aid of Supreme Court**. All executive and judicial authorities throughout Pakistan shall act in aid of the Supreme Court."

Two cases involving disregard of the judgments of the Hon'ble Supreme Court have been discussed in this Chapter. The nation has to act in aid of the Hon'ble Supreme Court if rule of law is intended to be ensured in letter and spirit.

IAH 2019 MOOT COURT JUDGMENTS 6

Present: Mr. Nasir Latif Darwesh
                  Mr. Jamal Mustafa Kundan
                  Mr. Saleem Anwar Taya
                  Mr. Syed Rizwan Ali Shah
                  Mr. Ahmad Nawaz Gondal
                  Mr. Abdul Aziz
                  Mr. Taseer Ahmad
                  Mr. Gulfam Mujtaba
                  Mr. Sarfraz Ahmad Bhatti

Constitution Petition No.1200000 of 2019

REGARDING CONVERSION OF INCREASES ALLOWED ON NET PENSION INTO INCREASES ON GROSS PENSION AT THE TIME OF RESTORATION OF COMMUTATED VALUE OF PENSION AND GRANT OF PENSION TO JUDGES OF THE HIGH COURT HAVING LESS THAN FIVE YEARS SERVICE AS JUDGE OF THE HON'BLE HIGH COURT

Mr. Zahoor Ahmad, Advocate General, Punjab for the Province of Punjab
Mr. Shahanshah Faisal Azeem, Attorney General for Pakistan for the Federation of Pakistan
Mr. Muhammad Asghar Yazdani, (applicant) in person
Ms. Faiza Akhtar, Muhammad Asif Ch., Israr Ahmad Mirza, Muhammad Arif Jan, Nazar Muhammad Chauhan, Qaiser Shah Gilani, Ashiq Hussain Dogar and Ameer Hussain, Advocates, Supreme Court of Pakistan for the private respondents
Dates of hearing: 04.11.2019, 18.11.2019, 19.11.2019, 20.11.2019, 21.11.2019,
                       22.11.2019

JUDGMENT

Mr. Nasir Latif Darwesh. – The Registrar of this Court submitted the following letter for information and orders of the Hon'ble Chief Justice:

Application of Mr. Muhammad Asghar Yazdani

"To

              The Hon'ble Chief Justice of Pakistan,
              Supreme Court of Pakistan,
              Constitution Avenue, Islamabad.

Subject: **NEED TO ENSURE IMPLEMENTATION OF THE DICTUM OF LAW LAID DOWN BY THE HON'BLE SUPREME COURT**

It is submitted with utmost humbleness and respect that rule of law and consequent existence of a civilized society is inconceivable without an effectively functional judiciary. hJudiciary cannot function effectively unless its judgments are implemented. Judgments of the Hon'ble Supreme Court are compulsorily required to be followed by all courts in Pakistan. In this regard, golden words of Mr. Justice Mian Saqib Nisar in a five-judge bench judgment of the Hon'ble Supreme Court of Pakistan reported as Constitution Petition No.127 of 2012 regarding pensionary benefits of the judges of superior courts from the date of their respective retirements, irrespective of their length of service as such judges (PLD 2013 Supreme Court 829) are worth quoting:

         "3.   ---the Supreme Court of Pakistan is the apex Court of the country. It is the final, the utmost and the ultimate Court, inter alia, in relation to, (a) resolving disputes inter se the parties before it, (b) securing and enforcing the fundamental rights of the citizen/person, when those (rights) are in issue before the Court, in any of its jurisdiction, either original or appellate or suo motu, (c) the interpretation and the enunciation of the law of the land, (d) examining and adjudging the legislative Acts and the executive order/actions of the State, in the exercise of its power of judicial review, (e) the exercise of original jurisdiction as per the mandate of Article 184 of the Constitution, (f) the advisory jurisdiction within the parameter of Article 186 of the Constitution, (g) the review of its decisions (judgments) (see Article 188) (h) a special jurisdiction conferred upon this Court by any law. And above all the power to do complete justice (see Article 187). In terms of Article 189 of the Constitution, "Any decision of the Supreme Court shall, to the extent that it decides question of law or is based upon or enunciates a principle of law, (emphasis supplied) be binding on all other courts in Pakistan". Moreover, according to Article 190 "All executive and judicial authorities throughout Pakistan shall act in aid of the Supreme Court".

4.   The aforestated legal position explains and highlights the true magnitude and the supremacy of this Court in regard to the dispensation of justice in the country and the enunciation and the declaration of the law by it. As the law laid down by the (apex) Court, and the order(s) passed by it, being the paramount and ultimate in nature, has to be imperatively and mandatorily followed, obeyed and adhered to by all the concerned. Reading Articles 189 and 190 conjointly, and while keeping in view the scheme of the constitution, the very purpose, the pivotal position and the status of this Court (prescribed above), it is expedient that correct law should be pronounced by the apex Court. And pursuant to the above object and due to the venerated position of this Court, the Court is cumbered with, inviolable responsibility, and a sacred duty, to interpret, declare and enunciate the law correctly, so that it should be followed, obeyed and adhered to purposively and in letter and spirit, by all the other organs of the State (including all other Courts in Pakistan) strictly in consonance with the true aim of the aforementioned Articles. It may be pertinent to mention here, that any invalid enunciation of law, shall contravene and impugn the very character, and attribute(s) of this Court and such bad/wrong law shall cause drastic adverse effects on the socio-economic, political, geographical, ethnic, cultural aspects and dynamics of the nation, the society, the people at large and the State in presentee or in futurio. In the above context, reference can also be made to Article 4 of the Constitution which enshrines (inter alia) an inalienable right of every citizen to be dealt with in accordance with the law, obviously this shall mean the law that is, correctly laid down by this Court. As it is a cardinal principle of justice, that the law should be worn by the Judge in his sleeves and justice should be imparted

according to the law, notwithstanding whether the parties in a lis before the Court are misdirected and misplaced in that regard. Therefore, if any law which has been invalidly pronounced and declared by this Court, which in particular is based upon ignorance of any provisions of the Constitution, and/or is founded on gross and grave misinterpretation thereof; the provisions of the relevant law have been ignored, misread and misapplied; the law already enunciated and settled by this Court on a specific subject, has not been taken into account, all this, inter alia, shall constitute a given judgment(s) as per incuriam; and inconsistent/conflicting decision of this Court shall also fall in that category. Such decision undoubtedly shall have grave consequences and repercussions, on the State, the persons/ citizens, the society and the public at large as stated above. Therefore, if a judgment or a decision of this Court which is found to be per incuriam (note: what is a judgment per incuriam has been dealt with by my brother), it shall be the duty of this Court to correct such wrong verdict and to set the law right. And the Court should not shun from such a duty (emphasis supplied). For the support of my above view, I may rely upon the law laid down in the dicta Lt. Col. Nawabzada Muhammad Amir Khan v. The Controller of Estate Duty, Government of Pakistan, Karachi and others (PLD 1962 SC 335 at page 340): --

> "Where, however, there is found to be something directed by the judgment of which review is sought which is in conflict with the Constitution or with a law of Pakistan, there it would be the duty of the Court, unhesitatingly to amend the error. It is a duty which is enjoined upon every Judge of the Court by the solemn oath which he takes when he enters upon his duties, viz., to "preserve, protect and defend the Constitution and laws of Pakistan" But the violation of a written law must be clear."

M. S. Ahlawat v. State of Haryana and another (AIR 2000 SC 1680): --

> "15. To perpetuate an error is no virtue but to correct it is a compulsion of judicial conscience."

2.   It is trite that when a bench of the Hon'ble Supreme Court lays down a law in terms of Article 189 of the Constitution, all courts in Pakistan including benches of the Hon'ble Supreme Court comprising equal or less judges are bound to follow that law.

3.   It pains me to observe that benches of the Hon'ble Supreme Court and the Hon'ble High Courts are disregarding ratio decidendi of judgments of larger benches of the Hon'ble Supreme Court. The tools used to defy judgments of the Hon'ble Supreme Court include directing officers to appear in person, passing strictures without necessity, verbally ordering transfers of or initiation of proceedings against officers, grating final relief through interim orders, forcing officers to implement interim orders granting final relief or face contempt of court

proceedings, entertaining proceedings without jurisdiction and getting orders issued in these proceedings implemented under threat of punishment on account of contempt of court and nullifying judgments of the Hon'ble Supreme Court in the name of implementation of those judgments.

4.   Disregard of the ratio decidendi of the Hon'ble Supreme Court is not justifiable on any ground. This tendency is breeding indiscipline and seriously denting prestige and honour of the Apex Court.

5.   Benevolence at public expense is sometimes preferred over adherence to the law laid down by the Hon'ble Supreme Court. The cost of such misconceived benevolent adventurism is thrust upon the public purse.

6.   Public exchequer is a sacred trust; it needs to be spent in accordance with the Constitution by those to whom this power has been given by the Constitution.

7.   The law laid down by the Hon'ble Supreme Court on the subject of pension of persons in the service of Pakistan was settled by a five-judge bench in a case reported as I.A. Sharwani case (PLD 1991 SCMR 1041) by declaring that pension is payable in accordance with the law / rules applicable on the date of retirement or death of a civil servant. The principle that pension is payable as prescribed through rules was followed and reiterated in a judgment delivered by a three-judge bench of the Hon'ble Supreme Court in a case reported as Secretary, Government of Punjab, Finance Department and 269 others versus M. Ismail Tayer and 269 others (2014 SCMR 1336). The question of competence of the Government to allow increase on net or gross pension was settled by the Hon'ble Supreme Court of Pakistan in a case reported as Akram ul Haq Alvi Vs. Joint Secretary (R-II), Government of Pakistan, Finance Department, Islamabad and others (2012 SCMR 106). Thus, the Hon'ble Supreme Court determined that pension is payable in accordance with the law / rules and increases in pension as may be allowed by the Government through executive orders. Both these principles were not accepted by an Hon'ble single bench of the Hon'ble Lahore High Court, Lahore despite written plea of the Government of the Punjab that the law laid down by the Hon'ble Supreme Court of Pakistan be allowed to be followed but that Government was forced, through different tactics, to implement judgments of the Hon'ble High Court which were not in lawful existence. The Hon'ble Supreme Court may, it is humbly requested, examine this case and set things right besides reconsidering its earlier decisions on pension and increases in pension and may make a declaration that except in case of pensions charged on the Provincial Consolidated Fund, determination of quantum of pension and sanctioning increases in pension are compulsorily required to be made through a Money Bill.

8.   Another case requiring judicial attention of the Hon'ble Supreme Court is violation of the ratio decidendi of the case reported as Constitution Petition No.127 of 2012 regarding pensionary benefits of the judges of superior courts from the date of their respective retirements, irrespective of their length of service as such judges (PLD 2013 Supreme Court 829) wherein it was categorically decided by the Hon'ble Supreme Court that a judge of a High Court having less than five years of service as such judge is not entitled to pension under

Article 205 read with Fifth Schedule of the Constitution and the High Court Judges (Leave, Pension and Privileges) Order, 1997 (President's Order No.3 of 1997). The Hon'ble Lahore High Court, Lahore disposed of writ petition No. 105298 of 2017 on 07.07.2018 in terms of written statement of the Federation allowing pension to judges of the Hon'ble High Court having less than 5 years' service. The Hon'ble Supreme Court of Pakistan granted leave to appeal and suspended operation of the High Court's aforesaid order through its order dated 29.09.2018. Later on, a three-judge bench of the Hon'ble Supreme Court finally disposed of the appeal through its order dated 27.03.2019 in terms of conceding statement of the Attorney General for Pakistan with the effect that the judges of the Hon'ble High Court were held entitled to pension even in absence of five years' service which was held mandatory by a five-judge bench of the Hon'ble Supreme Court in a case reported as PLD 2013 Supreme Court 829. This judgment (PLD 2013 Supreme Court 829) needs to be enforced with respect to minimum length of service for judges of the Hon'ble High Court to earn the right to pension. Moreover, this judgment held, by a majority of 3 in favour and a minority of 2 judges dissenting, that amounts drawn in good faith are not recoverable. To the extent that the aforesaid judgment prohibits recovery on the basis of absence of mala fides of the recipients and the likely hardship to be caused by the recovery, it seems to be per incuriam and merits to be revisited by the Hon'ble Supreme Court.

9. Every Hon'ble judge of the Hon'ble Supreme Court is under oath to preserve, protect and defend the Constitution from attacks and encroachments not only from the legislative over-reach or executive excesses but also from the judicial indiscipline.

10. Judicial action to arrest and laid to rest the judicial indiscipline is necessary for existence, strength, dignity and honour of the judiciary. Rule of law is the fountain from which flows the respect for the judicial organ of the state. On the other hand, judicial indiscipline is a sworn enemy of the rule of law.

11. An early and effective action is requested to be taken by the Hon'ble Supreme Court in public interest. It goes without saying that the public interest also envisions a judiciary which commands the confidence and respect of the nation for its effective role in ensuring rule of law.

Yours obediently

Sd/

(Muhammad Asghar Yazdani)

428-A, Allama Iqbal Town, Lahore"

2.   The Hon'ble Chief Justice was pleased to pass the following order on this application:

"The matter of alleged violations of the judgments of this Court, prima facie, represents a tendency which needs suitable action. Before proceeding further, it would, however, be appropriate to ascertain facts of the cases pointed out by the applicant. The Registrar is, therefore, directed to submit a resume of the facts of these cases, after consulting Mr. Muhammad Asghar Yazdani (the applicant) and perusing the relevant case files, within two weeks from today for my perusal and orders in the chambers."

3.   The Registrar did the needful and presented two sets of the facts. The first set pertained to the case reported as Secretary, Government of Punjab, Finance Department

and 269 others versus M. Ismail Tayer and 269 others (2014 SCMR 1336, hereinafter referred to as the Ismail Tayer case) whereas the second was in relation to the judgment reported as Constitution Petition No.127 of 2012 regarding pensionary benefits of the judges of superior courts from the date of their respective retirements, irrespective of their length of service as such judges (PLD 2013 Supreme Court 829, hereinafter referred to as the Third Judges' pension case). It is deemed advisable to have a look on the facts gleaned by the learned Registrar.

Facts regarding case relating to restoration of commuted value of pension of the retired civil servants

4.   The first set of facts is as follows:

"(a)   Article 260 of the Constitution defines 'remuneration' and 'pension, in the following words:

"remuneration" includes salary and pension;"

"Pension" means a pension, whether contributory or not, of any kind whatsoever payable to, or in respect of, any person and includes retired pay so payable, a gratuity so payable, and any sum or sums so payable by way of the return, with or without interest thereon or any addition thereto, of subscriptions to a provident fund;"

i.   Rule 1.6 (ii), (v) and (vi) of the Punjab Civil Services Pension Rules read as follows:

(ii)   Pension – Except when the term 'pension' is used in contradistinction to gratuity, pension includes gratuity.

(v)   Ordinary Pension – Ordinary pension means pensions other than extra – ordinary pension

(vi)   Full pension – Full pension means the amount of ordinary pension admissible including commuted portion of the pension, if any.

ii.   It has been held by a five-judge bench of the Honourable Supreme Court in I.A. Sherwani's case (1991 SCMR 1041) that:

"All forms of pensions, including the superannuation pension, payable by Government, are dependent upon statutory provisions. Under Article 240 of the Pakistan Constitution 1973 the terms and conditions of service of persons working with the Federal Government are determined by law passed by Majlis-e-Shoora (Parliament) and that of persons working with the Provincial Governments by law passed by the respective Provincial Assemblies. Section 19 of the Civil Servants Act, 1973, and similar provisions in the different Provincial Civil Servants Acts provide for payment of pensions to civil servants of the Federal and the Provincial Governments as may be prescribed, that is to say as prescribed by the rules. Likewise, under section 25(2) of the Civil Servants Act, 1973, and similar provisions in the different Provincial Civil Servants Acts, read with Article 241 of the Constitution, all rules, orders or instructions in force in respect of terms and conditions of civil servants competently made, are to be deemed to be rules made under the Act and as continuing in force. A host of rules deal with different types of pensions payable to different types of Government servants working at the

Federal level. Likewise, separate rules deal with different types of pensions payable to Government servants working at the Provincial level in the four provinces. A Government employee's claim to pay and allowances is regulated by the rules in force at the time in respect of which the pay and allowances are earned, whilst his claim to pension is regulated by the rules in force at the time when he retires, resigns, or is invalided out, or is compulsorily retired, or is discharged from service, or is injured, or killed whilst in service, depending upon the type of pension claimed. In respect of superannuation pension, the amount of pension payable is determined by the length of completed years of qualifying service put in by the Government servant, subject to the formula then in existence providing the mode of calculation of pension as prescribed by the rules."

iii. Commutation has been defined as

(i) "A substitution of lump-sum compensation for periodic payments. The lump sum is equal to the present value of the future periodic payments." (Black's Law Dictionary, 8th Edition)

(ii) "To commute periodic payments means to substitute a single payment for a number of payments, or to come to a "lump sum" settlement." (West's Encyclopedia of American Law, edition 2)

(iii) "conversion of the right to receive a variable or periodical payment into the right to receive a fixed or gross payment." (Jowett's Dictionary of English Law).

iv. Commutation of pension was regulated by Civil Pensions (Commutation) Rules, 1925. Rule 3 of the Rules ibid entitled the Government servants to commute a portion not exceeding one-half of the pension against a lump sum payment. Rule 6(2) of the said Rules prescribed that the commutation was final and absolute. Title of the Government servant to receive the commuted part ceased forever and only the un-commuted part remained receivable. This was also commonly known as selling half the pension for good.

v. Government of Pakistan, Finance Division introduced the concept of restoration of the commuted value of pension vide F.D.O.M. No.F.10(8)-Reg. (6)/845 dated 25-6-1985, reproduced below, which was adopted by the Government of the Punjab through its letter NO. FD.SR.III-4-54/83-C dated the 16th July 1985:

"The undersigned is directed to state that under the existing rules a pensioner on his option can get his pension commuted upto a maximum of 50 per cent. In such cases Government pays commuted value of such portion of pension for a number of years according to age next birthday after retirement as shown in the Commutation Table. The President has been pleased to decide that commuted portion of pension to the extent of 1/4th of gross pension shall be resorted w.e.f. 1st July, 1985 in the case of such civil pensioners including those paid from Defence Services Estimates who have already completed the number of years for which commuted value of pension was paid. The 1/4th Commuted portion of pension shall also be restored in the case of those retiring in future on completion, of the number of years for which commuted value is paid.

(2) In restoring the commuted portion of pension fraction of a year shown in the Commutation Table which is less than 6 months will be ignored and that of 6 months and more will count as one year.

(3) No arrears on account of restoration of commuted portion of pension will be payable in those cases in which the number of years paid for had been completed before 1st July, 1985."

vi.   The Government of the Punjab, through its letter No.FD.SR.III-4-58/86-D dated 10th August, 1986 directed as follows:

"I am directed to state that under the existing rules a civil pensioner is eligible to commute at his option 50% of his gross pension. He has also the option to draw 1/4th amount of gross pension as gratuity and 1/4th amount thereof as commutation. The Governor of the Punjab has been pleased to decide that w.e.f. 01.07.1986 gratuity shall be abolished altogether. Commutations up to 50% of gross pension shall, however, continue to be admissible at the option of a pensioner."

vii.   Rule 8.1 and 8.12 (a) of the Punjab Civil Services Pension Rules provided as follows:

"8.1   A competent authority may sanction the commutation for lump sum payment of a portion not exceeding one half of any pension which has been or is about to be granted under these rules.

8.12

(a)   The commuted portion of pension to the extent of 1/4th of full pension shall be restored to the pensioners on completion of the number of years for which commuted value is paid.

(b)   In restoring the commuted portion of pension under sub-rule (1), the fraction of a year mentioned in the Commutation Table which is less than six months shall be ignored and that of six months or more shall count as one year.

(c)   In the case of a pensioner who had surrendered 1/4th of his full pension for gratuity under the rules applicable to him at the time of his retirement, the amount surrendered for gratuity (i.e. 1/4th of full pension) shall be restored on completion of the period for which the gratuity was paid. The rate of gratuity shall be divided by 12 to arrive at the period for which gratuity was paid. For example, if a pensioner had received gratuity at the rate of Rs. 160 for each rupee surrendered, his period of gratuity would work out to 13.33 years.

(d)   A pensioner who had surrendered 1/4th of his full pension for commutation and 1/4th for gratuity, shall be entitled to the restoration of commuted portion of his pension only at the expiry of the period for which the commutation was allowed.

Note. The benefit of restoration of 1/4th of full pension surrendered for gratuity or commutation is not admissible in the case of family pension."

viii.   Government of the Punjab, Finance Department, through its letter bearing No. FD.SR.III-4-115/91 dated 30th September, 1991 issued the following instructions:

"I am directed to state that prior to 01.07.1986 a civil pensioner had the option to surrender 1/4th amount of gross pension for gratuity and get 1/4th there of commuted. Since then, payment of gratuity against surrender of 1/4th of pension has been discontinued and now a civil pensioner has the right, at his option, to get commuted value of up to 50% of his gross pension. At present, 1/4th of commuted pension and, if no commutation has been made, 1/4th amount of gross pension surrendered for gratuity by the civil pensioners is restored as and when the pensioner outlives the period for which the commutation/surrender for gratuity is made. Now the Governor of the Punjab is pleased to allow the restoration of remaining 1/4th of pension with effect from 01.07.1991 with the condition that no arrears shall be allowed for the period prior to 01.07.1991."

ix.   "The word "restore" relates to something having a previous existence, and is defined as meaning to bring back; to bring back or put back to a former position or condition; to bring back to a former and better state. It is also defined as meaning to heal. (Corpus Juris Secundum, Volume 77).

x.   Government of the Punjab, Finance Department, through a letter bearing No. FD. PC-2-1/2001 dated 22nd October, 2001, enforced a Scheme of the Basic Pay Scales, Allowances and Pension, 2001, for provincial employees and pensioners. The said Scheme, inter alia, provided as under:

(i)   The benefit of restoration of surrendered portion of pension in lieu of commutation/gratuity shall be withdrawn.

(ii)   In future the increase in pension to the pensioners shall be allowed on net pension instead of gross pension.

xi.   The Federal Government had introduced similar measures. Some pensioners of the Federal Government filed appeals in the Federal Service Tribunal, Islamabad, claiming that increases in pension can only be sanctioned on gross pension and not on net pension. Allowing the appeals, the Federal Service Tribunal, through a judgment dated 02.06.2003, held as under:

"18.   For the above reasons, we accept all the appeals to the extent only that increase in pension shall be allowed on gross pension which in fact is full pension-----."

xii.   The said judgments of the Federal Service Tribunal were appealed against by the Federal Government in the Hon'ble Supreme Court of Pakistan through Civil Appeals Nos. 1305 to 1327 of 2003. Accepting the appeals, the Hon'ble Supreme Court held that (this case hereinafter to be referred to as the first increases in pension case):

> "There is no provision in the Civil Servant Act, 1973 providing or the Rules specifically for increase in pension. However, section 19 of the Act provides that a civil servant shall be entitled to receive such pension as may be prescribed. This provision, therefore, empowers the Government to fix an amount of pension and also to increase the same from time to time. No formal rules have been framed for the purpose of increase in pension and the increase had been made from regularly through Office Memorandums. The documents relied upon by the respondents in support of their contention that previously the increase used to be on gross pension are in the form of Office Memorandums dated 29.6.1995, 23.7.1999, where it is stated that pension, for the purpose of increase, is the amount before commutation etc. However, in these Office Memorandums it has been expressly stated that the meaning given to the term 'pension' is relevant only for the purpose of interpreting pension as it appears in the Office Memorandums. Thus there is no general definition of pension for the purpose of calculating increase therein and it is to be given the meaning assigned to it in the instrument by which the pension is increased. In the Notification of 4.9.2001 it has been clearly laid down that the rate of increase in the pension is to be calculated on net pension. *For the sake of further clarity, Clause (f) of para 16 of the Notification declared that "in future the increase in pension to the pensioners shall be allowed on net pension instead of gross pension".* The Government undoubtedly is invested with the power to fix the amount of, or increase, pension, to lay down the method for its calculation, and to bring about changes therein. Reference may be made to Section 19 of the Civil Servant Act and Rule 4 of the C.S.R. In the absence of any statutory bar or restriction the Government is free to decide whether to grant enhancement in pension on gross or net pension. The Tribunal therefore erred in holding that the increase can only be on full and not net pension. Furthermore, the previous mode adopted by the Government cannot restrain it from changing it. Since the increase in pension is purely an executive act and is based on a policy, which takes into consideration various factors, including inflation and the Government financial constraints, the amount of increase given to the pensioner by the Notification in question must have been determined on the premise that the same would be payable on net and not gross pension. To accept the plea of the respondent would lead to creating an additional financial burden on the exchequer not envisaged by the Government at the time of issuing the

Notification in question. The Tribunal gave the impugned direction simply because of its misconception that pension can neither be 'net' nor 'gross' but simply "pension". As observed above such conclusion is untenable." (Emphasis supplied.)

xiii. The above conclusions were re-affirmed by the Hon'ble Supreme Court in a case reported as Akram ul Haq Alvi Vs. Joint Secretary (R-II), Government of Pakistan, Finance Department, Islamabad and others (2012 SCMR 106, hereinafter referred to as the second increases in pension case). In this case, a decision of the Federal Service Tribunal through which appeal of Mr. Akram Ul Haq Alvi challenging increase on net pension instead of gross pension was dismissed was assailed. The Hon'ble Supreme Court noted in paragraph 2 and 3 of the judgment:

"2. Appellant has argued his case himself and the main thrust of his submissions has been that in view of the judgments of this Court reported at Bashir Ahmed Solangi v. Chief Secretary, Government of Sindh (2004 SCMR 1864) and Government of Pakistan v. Village Development Organization (2005 SCMR 492) the Federal Government having allowed the increase on gross pension in terms of its earlier notification dated 23-7-1999 could not have withdrawn the said relief by a subsequent notification dated 4-9-2001 as appellant was retired in the year 2000 and was drawing benefit of the former notification of the year 1999 and the latter notification (of the year 2001) could not be used to deprive the benefit which had already accrued to him.

3. Learned Deputy Attorney-General, on the other hand, defended the impugned judgment mainly on the ground that the quantum of increase in pension is basically an executive function and the Government from time to time has got the power to review or modify the same keeping in view the host of factors including inflation, financial constraints and other factors tenable in law. He lastly relied on a judgment of this Court passed in Civil Appeals Nos. 1305 to 1327 of 2003 wherein this power of the Government was upheld."

After extensively reiterating the law as laid down by the Hon'ble Supreme Court in the first increases in pension case, it was held as under:

"5. Respectfully reiterating the earlier view taken by this court, to which reference has been made above, we do not find any merit in this appeal, which is dismissed."

xiv. The learned Federal Service Tribunal, Islamabad, in its judgment in Appeal No. 495(R) CS/2003 held as under:

"When considered in the backdrop of the generous dispensation in all the previous increases on gross pension, a reversal thereof in 2001 apparently looks odd. There was, however, a logical justification in allowing increase on net pension instead of gross pension as latter included the commuted portion which, in turn, had actually been bought over by the Government for a lump sum compensation and the Government decided not to pay increase on the portion the ownership of which had been transferred to it as it would have involved increases to be allowed in addition to the compensation paid already."

xv.   Mr. S.A.M. Wahidi retired as Solicitor, Ministry of Law, Justice and Human Rights, Government of Pakistan, on 13.12.1987. Commuted portion of his pension was restored on 14.12.2002. He made a representation to the Accountant General Pakistan Revenues, Islamabad, requesting therein that commuted portion of his pension should have been restored with effect from 14.12.2002 together with increases that had been allowed by the Government on the gross pension in the meanwhile and 15% dearness increase sanctioned with effect from 01.12.2001 should also be allowed on restored commuted portion of his pension. To get relief, he had to file an appeal (Appeal No. 495(R) CS/2003) in the learned Federal Service Tribunal, Islamabad, which ordered as follows:

> "In view of the foregoing, we allow the appeal to the extent that he is entitled to 15% increase on his pension inclusive of restored portion of commutation which in his case is net pension with effect from 14.12.2002 but his claim, even without arrears, to the increases allowed between the period of his commutation and its restoration is not justified as during the period, he drew increases on the gross pension as admissible. Such increases as earlier allowed on gross pension would, however, continue to be paid, if otherwise applicable as in his case the pension inclusive of the restored commuted portion is the net pension being drawn by him."

xvi.   Government of Pakistan, Finance Division (Regulations Wing), issued an office memorandum bearing No.F.13 (16)-Reg.6/ 2003 dated 29th February, 2008, to implement the judgment of the learned Federal Service Tribunal in Appeal No. 495(R) CS/2003 wherein it was stated as under:

> "The undersigned is directed to refer to Finance Division's O.M.No.F.5(2)-Reg.6/2002 dated 2nd July, 2002 on the above subject and to state that in pursuance of the Judgment dated 21-4-2007 passed by Federal Service Tribunal in civil petition No.495(R)/CS/2003, it has been decided that increase in pension admissible in the respective financial year be allowed on the restored commuted portion of pension to all those Government servants who retired on or before 30-6-2001 with effect from the date on which the commuted value of pension has been restored."

xvii.   On 22nd March, 2008, Government of the Punjab, Finance Department, issued a letter bearing No. FD.SR-III-4-41/2008 through which it was notified as under:

> "----it has been decided that increase in pension admissible in the respective financial year be allowed on the restored commuted portion of pension to all those Government servants who retired on or before 30.06.2001 with effect from the date on which the commuted value of pension has been restored."

It was subsequently clarified, vide Government of the Punjab, Finance Department's letter bearing No. FDSR-III/4-182/08 dated 4th of November, 2009, that if commuted portion of pension of a pensioner is restored in a particular financial year and no increase is sanctioned in that year, no increase will be given in that case.

xviii.   Mr. A.A. Zuberi, a pensioner of the Federal Government, filed Writ Petition No.2147 of 2009 in the Hon'ble Lahore High Court, Lahore. Relevant facts as mentioned in the judgment in this writ petition, reported as A.A. Zuberi Vs. Additional Accountant-General Pakistan Revenue, Lahore (2010 PLC (C.S.) 1211, hereinafter referred to as the first A.A. Zuberi case), are as under:

> "Facts leading to this writ petition are that the petitioner was retired as Member Income Tax Appellate Tribunal of Pakistan (BS-21) on 31.5.1993 and his pension was worked out at Rs. 11,176.83. Petitioner's half pension was commuted for the period of 15 years and a sum of Rs.8,87,128 was paid to him as lump sum, which was to be recovered from him in 15 years and thus the petitioner was paid a pension of Rs. 5,588 per month being half of the pension because the other half was to be adjusted towards the commuted pension paid to him in advance.
>
> 2.   Petitioner's 15 years' period was expired on 31.5.2008 and according to him the Government of Pakistan had not only recovered the entire amount recoverable from him but also recovered additional amount of Rs.3,26,689 over and above the recoverable amount.
>
> 3.   Learned counsel for the petitioner submits that during the period of 15 years Government gave increases in pension at percentages from 5% to 20% and this benefit of increase was restricted by the Government to the payable half of his pension, although the increase should have been on the entire pension and in this way the petitioner was deprived of the benefit of increase to the tune of Rs.3,26,689. After expiry of 15 years, the petitioner applied for restoration of his full pension and in response the pension is restored but the same is restricted to Rs.6,706 although after increase of pension from time to time the petitioner's one half receivable pension is Rs.17,428 and the restored one half pension should have been the same, meaning thereby that his pension should be double i.e. Rs.34,856 but the Government of Pakistan has refused to restore the

pension as requested, which otherwise amounts to exploitation which is against all canons of justice and violative of the specific provisions of Constitution of Pakistan."

Operative part of the judgment in the above-said writ petition is reproduced hereunder:

"For the reasons mentioned above, I see the impugned action by the authorities as highly indiscriminate and violative of the rights of the civil servants and, therefore, declare the same without lawful authority, having no legal effect, and direct the respondents to calculate the petitioner's revived pension amount reflecting the total increases from the date of expiry of period of 15 years i.e. with effect from 31-5-2008 and pay the arrears of the said period to the petitioner. However, the petitioner shall not be entitled for any increase prior to 31.5.2008 i.e. the period of 15 years' maturity."

xix.   Prior to 2001, increases in pension were used to be sanctioned on gross pension and not on net pension. Thus, Mr. A.A. Zuberi was allowed 10% increase in his gross pension with effect from 1st of July, 1993 and 20% increase in his gross pension with effect from 1st of July, 1999. Subsequent increases in pension were allowed to him on net pension till July, 2007, whereafter his commuted portion of pension was restored with effect from 31.05.2008 and amounts of gross and net pension became the same and, thus, all subsequent increases had been calculated on gross pension in his case.

xx.   The Federal Government filed an intra-court appeal in the Hon'ble Lahore High Court, Lahore, which was decided through a judgment reported as Additional Accountant-General Pakistan Revenue, Lahore Vs. A.A. Zuberi (2011 PLC (C.S.) 580, herein after referred as the second A.A. Zuberi case). The Hon'ble Division Bench found that the judgment of the learned Single Judge was not clear. The Hon'ble Division Bench noted that:

"6. Learned counsel for the appellant submitted that the word "Commutation" means "alteration change, substitution; the act of substituting one thing for another" and referred to Black's Law Dictionary, 5th Edition in this regard. He relied on the said meaning to submit that the respondent was not getting any pension during the period of commutation, therefore, the increments over the said period cannot accrue to the respondents."

It was also noted by the Honourable Division Bench that:

"10.   The contention of the respondents is that during the period of commutation increase in pension was granted ranging from 5% to 20% and therefore restoration of pension means the pension inclusive of increments granted over the last 15 years. Therefore, pension in the year 2008 should be double of the 50% pension received by the respondents per month. The counsel argued that the increase has been in the "pension" and, therefore, the respondents cannot be deprived of the said increments."

The Hon'ble Division Bench concluded as under:

"22.   We, therefore, hold that under Rule 3.29 of the Pension Rules (supra) the restoration of pension means the pension due to a retired civil servant in that year inclusive of all the increments till that time (i.e. accumulated over the last 15 years in this case). In other words, it would simply be double the amount of 50% pension the respondents are already drawing. These appeals are, therefore, dismissed. The order of the learned Single Judge is modified/clarified in the above terms."

xxi.   Petition for leave to appeal of the Federal Government against the second A.A. Zuberi case was dismissed by the Hon'ble Supreme Court of Pakistan vide order dated 10.12.2010 on ground of being time-barred.

xxii.   Relying upon the second A.A. Zuberi case, certain pensioners of the Federal Government succeeded in their appeals filed in the Federal Service Tribunal to the same effect against which leave to appeal was refused by a three-judge bench of the Hon'ble Supreme Court of Pakistan vide judgment reported as Federation of Pakistan Vs. Ghulam Mustafa and others (2012 SCMR 1914), reproduced below:

"**IFTIKHAR MUHAMMAD CHAUDHRY, C.J. -** The listed petitions have been filed against judgment dated 5.1.2012 passed by the Federal Service Tribunal, Islamabad, relevant paras therefrom are reproduced hereinbelow:

"2. The issue has been resolved in that judgment. However, the objection of the respondents is that in the said appeals Finance Division is not a party. Today, we have heard the Finance Division also. Two persons namely A.A. Zuberi and Syed Ibrar Hussain Naqvi had filed Writ Petition in the High Court and had succeeded in getting increases in commuted pension. Their appeals in the Hon'ble Supreme Court were dismissed as time barred. It means that the judgment of the High Court had attained finality. The two pensioners were granted increase on the commuted pension. Article 25 of the Constitution of Pakistan guarantees equal treatment to all. When two pensioners had been granted increase, it shall have to be granted to other pensioners also. Thus, the judgment of the Tribunal, mentioned above has relevance, when read in the light of judgment of the High Court. Relevant part of the judgment of the Tribunal is as under: -

"9. In the light of the Lahore High Court confirmed by the apex Court and the judgment of the Punjab Service Tribunal, we accept the appeals. The respondents are directed to determine the pension of the appellants from the date of restoration of their commuted pension at the rate at which they were drawing 50% remaining pension.

The arrears shall also be paid to them. It is also clarified that the appellants shall not be entitled to claim arrears for the period prior to restoration of their commuted pension."

3. in the above circumstances, we find that present cases are similar to the one decided by the Tribunal on the strength of the judgment of the High Court, confirmed by the Hon'ble Supreme Court. We accordingly hold that appellants are entitled to increases on their commuted pension in the same manner. Appeals are allowed."

2. When we have inquired from the learned counsel as to whether in view of the principles laid down by this Court under Article 25 of the Constitution as to why the respondents should not be treated at par with the employees named in the above para for the purposes of getting relief, he could not answer satisfactorily except saying that in another judgment announced by this Court in Akram ul Haq Alvi Vs. Joint Secretary (R-II), Government of Pakistan, Finance Department, Islamabad and others (Appeal No. 254-L of 2011)" it has been held that the petitioners shall not be given the increase on the commuted pension. We failed to understand the distinction which the learned counsel wanted to create in view of the judgment relied upon.

3. After hearing the learned counsel and having gone through the operative paras of the impugned judgment, we are of the opinion that as far as respondents are concerned, they have to be treated at par with the employees in whose favour decisions have been taken by the High Court as well as by this Court. Therefore, in absence of any reasonable classification, no exception can be taken to the impugned judgment.

4. Additionally, no question of law of public importance within the meaning of Article 212(3) of the Constitution of Islamic Republic of Pakistan, 1973 has been pointed out.

5. Accordingly, the listed petitions are dismissed and leave refused."

xxiii. A number of pensioners of the Government of the Punjab filed writ petitions in the Hon'ble Lahore High Court, praying for issuance of directions to the Government of the Punjab for doubling of their pensions relying on the second A.A. Zuberi case which were allowed by the Hon'ble Lahore High Court.

xxiv. Mr. Muhammad Ismail Tayer, a pensioner of the Government of the Punjab, reportedly sent a communication to various authorities in Government of the Punjab on 10.01.2009 stating therein that he retired on 18.01.1991 and commuted portion of his pension was restored with effect from 19.01.2006 but, as a result of misconstruction of Government of the Punjab, Finance Department's letter No. FD.SR-III-4-41/2008 dated 22.03.2008, he was not allowed increases sanctioned by the Government with effect from 01.12.2001, 01.07.2003 and 01.07.2004 on commuted portion of pension. He was aggrieved of provisions of a letter of the Finance Department bearing No. FD. PC-2-1/2001 dated 22nd October, 2001, to the extent of discontinuation of facility of restoration of commuted value of pension and increases on net pension instead of gross pension.

The aforesaid communication of Mr. Muhammad Ismail Tayer was allegedly not responded to; hence, he filed an appeal in the Punjab Service Tribunal, praying as under:

> "In view of the above submissions, it is respectfully prayed that the respondents may, kindly, be directed to allow the increases on 01.12.2001, 01.07.2003 and 01.07.2004 in addition to already allowed increase on 01.07.2005."

Relying on judgments reported as the first and the second A.A. Zuberi cases read with order of the Hon'ble Supreme Court of Pakistan dated 10.12.2010 referred to hereinabove, the learned Service Tribunal held as under:

> "The upshot of the above discussion is that this appeal is allowed and the competent authority is directed to determine the pension of appellant from the date of restoration of commuted portion at the rate at which the appellant was drawing 50% remaining pension and to pay him the arrears from the date of restoration of commuted pension, if any. However, the appellant would not be entitled to claim any arrears for the period prior to restoration of commuted pension."

xxv.   Government of the Punjab, Finance Department, filed civil petitions in the Hon'ble Supreme Court for grant of leave to appeal which were allowed in the following words:

> "After hearing learned Additional Advocate General Punjab, leave to appeal is granted inter alia to consider as to whether in view of the provisions of Article 212 of the Constitution of Islamic Republic of Pakistan and the judgment in the case titled Accountant General vs. Abdul Majeed Babar (1990 SCMR 790), a constitution petition under Article 199 before the High Court was maintainable? As a short point is involved, the office is directed to prepare appeals on the present record with liberty to the parties to file additional documents if so advised within a week. The appeals are to be listed for hearing after three weeks."

xxvi.   The Hon'ble Supreme Court heard the parties and announced its short order on 31.03.2014, which is reproduced hereunder:

> "For reasons to be recorded later in the detailed judgment, we are persuaded to hold that the interpretation being accorded to Rule 8.1 read with 8.12 of the Punjab Civil Services Pension Rules vide the office memorandum issued by the Government of Punjab dated 22.10.2001 is not only violative of those Rules but also of Article 25 of the Constitution of Islamic Republic of Pakistan. These appeals and petitions are, therefore, dismissed with no order as to costs."

xxvii.   On receipt of detailed judgment of the Ismail Tayer case, a four-member committee was constituted by the Government of the

Punjab, Finance Department, to devise the procedure to implement the above said judgment. The Committee found as follows:

"In view of above, we may construe judgment of the Honourable Supreme Court to mean that the Honourable Supreme Court has substituted operative parts of orders of the learned Service Tribunal and those of the Honourable High Court with its own order. Whereas the Service Tribunal and the High Court had given a formula for determination of amount of commuted value of pension at the time of its restoration and had not addressed the question of withdrawal of facility of restoration of commuted portion on expiry of the defined period, the Honourable Supreme Court of Pakistan has conclusively attended to the latter question and has declared the measure of withdrawal of facility of restoration of commuted portion violative of the relevant rules and Article 25 of the Constitution but it has not upheld the formula given by the Service Tribunal and the High Court for calculation of amount of commuted value of pension at the time of its restoration. This is obvious as increases on net pension have been validated by the Honourable Supreme Court of Pakistan."

The aforesaid Committee recommended as under:

"The order of the Honourable Supreme Court of Pakistan is recommended to be implemented through issuance of a letter deleting para 16 (e) of the Finance Department's letter bearing No. FD. PC-2-1/2001 dated 22nd October, 2001, with effect from the date of its issuance i.e. 22nd October, 2001."

xxviii.	The above recommendation of the Committee was accepted by the Government of the Punjab, Finance Department, and was implemented through issuance of a circular letter bearing No. FD-SR-III/4-41/2008 dated 22nd of July, 2014, wherein it was stated:

"I am directed to refer to the subject cited above and to state that in compliance of detailed judgment of the Honourable Supreme Court of Pakistan dated 31.03.2014 in the cases noted in the subject, para 16 (e) of this department's letter No. FD. PC-2-1/2001 dated 22.10.2001 is hereby omitted and shall be deemed to have been so omitted ab initio."

xxix.	The Finance Secretary, Government of the Punjab, after implementation of the said judgment in the aforesaid manner, constituted another Committee to explain legal principles leading the Committee to its findings and recommendations as contained in its report to serve as a guide to the Department in such cases in future. This Committee submitted a Supplementary Report which re-confirmed findings and recommendations of the earlier Report and opined that in view of implementation of the judgment of the Hon'ble Supreme Court in the Ismail Tayer case through circular letter bearing No. FD-SR-III/4-41/ 2008 dated 22nd of July, 2014, nothing more was required to be done. The Committee dispelled the impression that orders of the Hon'ble Supreme Court and those of the Hon'ble Lahore High Court as well as of the Punjab Service Tribunal are simultaneously in field because of dismissal of appeals and petitions of the Government of the Punjab. The Committee concluded that the only order lawfully in field is that of the Honourable Supreme Court.

xxx. Implementation of the said judgment of the Hon'ble Supreme Court in the manner aforesaid did not result into doubling of pension + increases in pension at the time of restoration of commuted value of pension as per wishes of the pensioners or conversion of increases in pension already allowed on net pension into increases on gross pension at the time of restoration of commuted value of pension. Aggrieved of this, certain pensioners filed contempt petitions in the Hon'ble High Court in order to get judgments of the Hon'ble High Court on the subject implemented.

xxxi. Hon'ble Lahore High Court, Lahore, in its order dated 13.11.2014, in the case of Crl. Org. NO. 1699-W/2014, was pleased to direct as under:

> "Be that as it may, considering the fact that the judgment of august Supreme Court of Pakistan dated 31.03.2014 is not being complied with by the Finance Department and no plausible explanation has been given why said judgment is not being complied with. *It appears that Finance Department is bluntly violating the judgments of the Supreme Court as well this Court*. It is also submitted that the benefit of this judgment has been extended to other pensioners but the present petitioners are being deprived of the same.
>
> In view of the above matter, let notice of contempt under the Contempt of Court Ordinance, 2003, be issued to the Secretary Finance, Government of the Punjab who will appear in person before this court on the next date of hearing to furnish his explanation why contempt proceedings should not be initiated against him unless, of course, the matter is resolved before the next date of hearing."

xxxii. In Crl. Org.NO. 1699-W/2014 and other cases, the Hon'ble High Court directed the Chief Secretary, and the Finance Secretary, Government of the Punjab, to appear in person in the Hon'ble Court on 5th of December, 2014. When they entered appearance, the Hon'ble Court desired submission of a payment plan in terms of the Ismail Tayer case. Accordingly, a payment plan was submitted in the Hon'ble High Court on 10.12.2014 by the Finance Secretary of the Government of the Punjab, which is reproduced hereinbelow:

> "SUBJECT: PAYMENT PLAN
>
> Government of the Punjab, Finance Department, will make payments to the eligible pensioners in accordance with judgment of the Honourable Supreme Court of Pakistan reported as Secretary, Government of Punjab, Finance Department and 269 others versus M. Ismail Tayer and 269

others (2014 SCMR 1336), following payment plan is being submitted before the Honorable Court:

Sr. #	Category of Pensioners	Instalment #	Payment Period
1	Who retired prior to 01.07.1991	1st	01.02.2015 to 28.02.2015
2	Who retired on or after 01.07.1991 to 30.06.1994	2nd	01.03.2015 to 31.03.2015
3	Who retired on or after 01.07.1994 to 30.11.2001	3rd	01.04.2015 to 31.05.2015
4	Who retired on or after 01.12.2001 to-date	4th	01.06.2015 to 30.06.2015

The said plan has been devised keeping in view the available financial resources as well as human resources required to depute and attend to the above mentioned categories of the pensioners in the offices of Accountant General Punjab, Lahore, all District Accounts Officers in the Punjab and Treasury Officers. A complaint cell is also being established to address the grievances of the pensioners."

xxxiii. The Hon'ble High Court passed the following order on 10.12.2014 in Crl. Org.NO. 1699-W/2014 and other cases:

"This consolidated order shall decide the instant petition, as well as, petitions mentioned in Schedule A to this order as common questions of law and facts arise in these cases.

2. Mr. Ashtar Ausaf, Advocate, has tendered appearance on behalf of Finance Secretary, Government of the Punjab and has placed on record "Payment Plan" dated 09.12.2014 which gives various categories of pensioners and the time frame when payments shall be made to them.

3. Learned counsel for the petitioners have also gone through the contents of the said "Payment Plan" and are satisfied with the same. The said "Payment Plan" has been placed on the record as "Mark-A". Therefore, the instant petition, as well as, petitions mentioned in Schedule A to this order are disposed of in the light of the above "Payment Plan".

4. In case any violation of the "Payment Plan" the petitioners are free to approach this Court for the redressal of their grievance after first exhausting their remedy before the Complaint Cell constituted under the aforesaid letter."

xxxiv. The Complaint Cell constituted in compliance of orders of the Hon'ble Court received complaints from the pensioners against orders of the Accountant General, Punjab, and of the District Accounts Officers through which applications of the pensioners for conversion of increases sanctioned on net pension into increases on gross pension and doubling of pension + increases already sanctioned at the time of restoration of commuted value of pension were rejected. The Complaint Cell disposed of complaints through a speaking order dated 28.02.2015 concluding paragraph whereof reads as under:

> "In view of, inter alia, what has been stated hereinabove, this Complaint Cell regrets its inability to agree to your demands regarding pension and increases in pension. Refusal of the office of the Accountant General, Punjab, to allow pension otherwise than in accordance with the applicable rules and increases in pension in violation of the orders of the Government of the Punjab, Finance Department, through which such increases were sanctioned, is hereby declared to be lawful."

It was declared by the Complaint Cell that under the doctrine of merger, the only judgment in the field was the Ismail Tayer case which stood implemented and that judgment did not require doubling of what is drawn by a pensioner on the date of restoration of the commuted value of pension.

xxxv. Aggrieved of the speaking order of the Complaint Cell, a number of pensioners filed petitions for initiation of contempt of court proceedings against the Finance Secretary, Accountant General, Punjab, and members of the Complaint Cell. The Finance Secretary and members of the Complaint Cell filed their written statements in the Hon'ble Court claiming therein that the judgment of the Hon'ble Supreme Court in the Ismail Tayer case had already been implemented. The Finance Secretary filed the following written statement:

1. That in compliance of orders of the Honourable Court, a Payment Plan was submitted on 10.12.2014 by the Government of the Punjab, Finance Department, to the effect that payments to the eligible pensioners will be made in accordance with judgment of the Honourable Supreme Court reported as Secretary, Government of Punjab, Finance Department and 269 others versus M. Ismail Tayer and 269 others (**2014 SCMR 1336**).

2. That, as per consolidated order dated 10.12.2014 in Crl. Org. NO.1699-W/2014, the Honourable Court was pleased to dispose of the petitions in view of satisfaction of counsels of the petitioners over the Payment Plan.

3. That a Complaint Cell was constituted in terms of para 4 of the said consolidated order dated 10.12.2014 with a clear mandate and duty to ensure payments, if any, to the pensioners in the light of the judgment reported as **2014 SCMR 1336**.

4. That no one has complained that the said Complaint Cell has failed to ensure payments to the eligible pensioners in accordance with the above-said judgment. Even otherwise, no complaint on behalf of a petitioner / pensioner is on record to the effect that he has been denied pension, including restoration of commuted portion thereof, as prescribed in the applicable rules or increases in pension

sanctioned, from time to time, by the Government have not been given to him.

5. That the Complaint Cell has intimated to the complainants detailed reasons (**_Annex-A_**) for its finding that the only judgment lawfully in the field is that of the Honourable Supreme Court reported as **2014 SCMR 1336** and the said judgment has held that pension is payable as prescribed in the applicable rules and increases in pension are to be calculated as directed by the Government in the order in which such increases are sanctioned.

6. That legality of reasons and conclusions recorded in the **_Annex-A_** can be challenged by an aggrieved person through appropriate proceedings in the prescribed manner before a forum having jurisdiction on the subject of pension.

7. That action will be taken in accordance with law if a competent forum finally declares that the reasons and conclusions given in the **_Annex-A_** are legally invalid.

8. That the Government of the Punjab, Finance Department, has always been, is and will remain committed to ensure payments to eligible pensions in accordance with the judgment of the Honourable Supreme Court.

9. That the Government of the Punjab, Finance Department, holds the Honourable Court in the highest esteem for being a symbol of justice in accordance with law and can never dare thinking of disobeying or disregarding any of its law lawful orders."

xxxvi. Thereafter, in compliance of orders of the Hon'ble Court, the Chief Secretary, Punjab, appeared in person in the Hon'ble Court on 27.03.2015 and filed the following written statement:

1. That in compliance of orders of the Honourable Court dated 20.03.2015 in the case cited above, the matter has been examined with respect to the Payment Plan dated 09.12.2014 whereby Government of the Punjab, Finance Department, had given an undertaking to make payments to the eligible pensioners in accordance with judgment of the Honourable Supreme Court reported as Secretary, Government of Punjab, Finance Department and 269 others versus M. Ismail Tayer and 269 others (**2014 SCMR 1336**).

2. That the said judgment of the Honourable Supreme Court holds as under:

   a. "Thus, under section 18 of the Act of 1974, a retired Civil Servant is entitled to receive pension as may be **_prescribed._**"

   b. "In case a portion of pension is commuted for a particular period of time, he surrenders his right to receive full pension in lieu of lump-sum payment received by him and on expiry of the commuted period, his right and entitlement to receive full pension, **_as prescribed_**, is restored and re-vested in him."

   c. "The dictum, as laid down is merely that a retired Civil Servant is entitled to the pension as may be

prescribed and a decision granting increase in pension has been interpreted by ***upholding the legal fiction of a net-pension created for the purpose of calculating the increase as granted by the decision under consideration."***

(Emphasis in a, b, c, hereinabove supplied).

    d. "----we are persuaded to hold that the interpretation being accorded to Rule 8.1 read with 8.12 of the Punjab Civil Services Pension Rules vide the office memorandum issued by the Government of Punjab dated 22.10.2001 is not only violative of those Rules but also of Article 25 of the Constitution of Islamic Republic of Pakistan."

("The office memorandum" referred to in 'd' hereinabove is Government of the Punjab, Finance Department's letter No. FD. PC-2-1/2001 dated 22nd October, 2001, and the interpretation accorded to Rule 8.1 read with 8.12 of the Punjab Civil Services Pension Rules is para 16(e) of the said letter which reads as follows:

    "The benefit of restoration of surrendered portion of pension in lieu of commutation / gratuity shall be withdrawn".

Para 16(f) of the said letter has been termed ***"decision under consideration"*** in para 17 of the judgment, reproduced below:

    "In future the increase in pension to the pensioners shall be allowed on net pension instead of gross pension."

3. That the above-said judgment of the Honourable Supreme Court has been implemented by the Government of the Punjab, Finance Department by restoring facility of restoration of commuted value of pension on expiry of the period of commutation vide circular letter No. FD-SR-III/4-41/2008 dated 22nd of July, 2014 (**Annex-A**).

4. That as a result of implementation of the judgment of the Honourable Supreme Court through the **Annex-A**, 163,306 retired civil servants of the Government of the Punjab have so far become entitled to restoration of commuted value of pension on expiry of the period of commutation with a one-time estimated cost of Rs. 945 million (Rs.6142.5 million estimated average per annum). Restoration of commuted value of pension of 21,877 retired civil servants has become due up to 31.03.2015 with a one-time expenditure of Rs.53.77 million (Rs.349.505 million estimated average per annum). Recurring cost of implementation of the judgment of the Honourable Supreme Court is not determinable at the moment because this will depend upon future decisions regarding increases in pension. Information provided by office of the Accountant General, Punjab, to this effect has been placed at **Annex-B.**

5. That financial impact of implementation of the judgment of the Honourable Supreme Court is much more than what has been stated at **Annex-B** because a number of entities

of the Government of the Punjab e.g. local and autonomous bodies follow policies of the Government regarding pay and pension which are applicable to employees who are or have been civil servants. The cost to be borne by such entities for implementation of the judgment of the Honourable Supreme Court is not included in the statements at **Annex-B**.

6. That no complaint of a pensioner is on record to the effect that he has been denied pension, including restoration of commuted portion thereof, as prescribed in the applicable rules or increases in pension sanctioned, from time to time, by the Government have not been given to him.

7. That since the matter stands resolved through implementation of the judgment of the Honourable Supreme Court in the manner afore-said, therefore, contempt petitions are liable to be dismissed."

xxxvii. Rejecting written statements of the Chief Secretary, Finance Secretary and members of the Complaint Cell, the Hon'ble High Court ordered as follows on 17.04.2015:

"Imran Iqbal, Accountant General, Punjab, M. Raza Ullah Khan, Deputy Accountant General, Punjab, Yusuf Khan, Secretary Finance and Khalid Mehmood Additional Finance Secretary, Government of the Punjab have tendered appearance and placed on the record a proposed Payment Plan for the payment of pension. They submitted that the said plan includes the current payment of pension, as well as, the arrears. It was noticed that at Sr. No.5 of the said Plan civil servants who retired on 01.07.1999 will be paid their full pension by 30.06.2020 which might be too late. The government in this view of the matter sought additional time to revise the said Payment Plan. They were additionally directed to keep the current payment separate from the arrears.

2. During the course of arguments it was felt that respondent government is still not clear regarding the import of the judgment in particular Secretary. Government of Punjab, Finance Department and 269 others V. M. Ismail Tayer and 269 others (2014 SCMR 1336). The import of the aforementioned judgment and the earlier judgments on the subject reported as Federation of Pakistan v. Ghulam Mustafa and others (2012 SCMR 1914) Akram ul Haq Alvi v. Joint Secretary CR-IJ) Government of Pakistan, Finance Division. Islamabad and others (2012 SCMR 106), Ghulam Yasin V. Accountant-General Punjab and others (2014 PLC (C.S.) 73) and Additional Accountant General Pakistan Revenue Lahore vs. A.A. Zuberi (2011 PLC (C.S) 580) is that the quantum of 50% pension when it becomes payable after the period of commutation should be equal to the drawn 50% pension at the time. This in simple words would mean that after the period of commutation 50% pension to be received by the civil servants would be exactly double of the 50% of the drawn pension.

3. Government is directed to rework the Payment Plan keeping in view the following parameters which are drawn from the above judgments: -

i.   After the period of commutation, the 50% pension payable will be double the amount of 50% of the drawn pension at the time and has to be paid to the petitioner immediately.

ii.   In case of arrears, accruing in this regard after the period of commutation, the may make Payment Plan and deal with this amount separately.

4. For the above exercise, I am willing to grant the respondent government time to work out the Payment Plan of the arrears only. Respondent government will ensure that as far as the current payment of pension is concerned, it will be regularized in the light of aforementioned judgments."

xxxviii. The Government of the Punjab, Finance Department issued a Notification bearing No. FD.SR-III/4-41/2008 dated 17.06.2015 stating therein:

"Increases in pension of pensioners of the Government of the Punjab who retired on or before 30-06-2001 and had opted for 50% commutation of their full pension will be re-fixed with effect from 1st of July, 2015 by converting increases allowed on net pension prior to restoration of commuted value of pension into increases on gross pension. No arrears resulting from such re-fixation of increases in pension pertaining to the period prior to the restoration of commuted value of pension would be admissible."

xxxix. The Hon'ble High Court observed about the aforesaid Notification in its order dated 16.06.2015 that:

"2. As the contents of notification are not clear, the Additional Finance Secretary was asked whether the said notification complies with the ratio settled in Secretary, Government of Punjab, Finance Department and 269 others versus M. Ismail Tayer and 269 others (2014 SCMR 1336) and are also in compliance with the order of this Court 17.04.2015 passed in this case, the Additional Finance Secretary as well as Deputy Accountant General, Punjab submitted that aforementioned judgment and order have been fully complied in the aforementioned Notification. This statement was made in open Court by the aforementioned officers."

xl. Government of the Punjab filed Civil Review Petitions No. 175 to 444 of 2015 which were dismissed by a three-judge bench of the Hon'ble Supreme Court through an order dated 11.08.2015 in these words:

"2. We have heard the learned counsel for the petitioners in all these review petitions at some length and have found that through these review petitions either want a reconsideration of the merits of the matter or they have tried to advance a case before the: Court which was never argued at the time of hearing of the main appeals /

petitions. We are afraid such attempts by the petitioners travel beyond the scope of review jurisdiction of this Court. These review petitions are, therefore, dismissed."

xli. When pensioners complained to the Hon'ble Lahore High Court that at the time of restoration, their pension was not being doubled but only the increases on net pension given prior to date of restoration of commuted value of pension were being converted into increase on gross pension, the Hon'ble High Court appointed A.F. Ferguson & Co. to ascertain accuracy of calculations being made in pursuance of Notification bearing No. FD.SR-III/4-41/2008 dated 17.06.2015. The formula being applied by the Finance Department was verified to be correct by the A.F. Ferguson & Co. whereafter the Hon'ble Court clarified that implementation of Notification bearing No. FD.SR-III/4-41/2008 dated 17.06.2015 is complete compliance of order of the Court regarding doubling of pension at the time of restoration of the commuted value of pension.

xlii. Members of the Complaint Cell initially stood by their written reply submitted in response to the contempt notice. They, however, later withdrew speaking order of the Complaint Cell and tendered unconditional apology after which proceedings against them were dropped.

Facts regarding case relating to pension of judges of the Hon'ble High Court having less than five years of service as such judges

5. The second set of facts presented by the learned Registrar is as under:

i. As recorded in PLD 2013 Supreme Court 829, Mr. Ahmed Ali U. Qureshi, a District and Sessions Judge was elevated as Additional Judge, High Court of Sindh in 1985. He retired on 25.10.1988 and was allowed pension at the rate of Rs. 4,200 per month with the benefit of commutation, gratuity and additional sum of Rs. 2,100 per month as cost of living allowance payable to a retired Judge of the High Court under paragraph 16-B of President's Order No.9 of 1970, as amended by P.O. No.5 of 1988. In pursuance of the Constitution (Twelfth Amendment) Act, 1991 (Act XIV of 1991), the pension of the respondent was revised and fixed as Rs.6300 per month and thereafter by virtue of P.O. No.2 of 1993, the pension of retired Judges of superior judiciary was again revised, wherein the pension of High Court Judges was fixed with minimum and maximum ratio of Rs.9,800 and Rs.10,902 per mensem but this increase in pension was declined to Mr. Ahmed Ali U. Qureshi on the basis of departmental interpretation of the President's Orders referred to above read with Fifth Schedule of the Constitution. Mr. Ahmed Ali U. Qureshi filed a writ petition in the Hon'ble Sindh High Court, with following prayers:

"(a) To declare the P.O. 9 of the 1970 so far its provision in Part III with regard to pension are repugnant to the Constitution of the Islamic Republic of Pakistan are void.

(b) To order the respondents to pay the petitioner maximum pension payable to a Judge of the High Court under P.O. 2 of 1993 along with arrears or in alternative.

(e) To order the respondents to fix the pension of the petitioner at Rs. 8,190/- per month admissible to him as

Civil Servant, add to it increments in pension allowed from time to time and pay all the arrears along with markup for the period this amount is illegally retained by respondent No .4."

ii.   The Hon'ble Sindh High Court was pleased to allow the writ petition and grant the relief prayed for by Mr. Ahmed Ali U. Qureshi (the First Judges' pension case) in the following words:

"11. In the result, the petition is allowed and the respondents are liable to fix the petitioner's pension at the maximum pension as allowed under President's Order No.2 of 1993. The parties are left to bear their own costs."

iii.   The Accountant General, Sindh filed a Civil Petition for Leave to Appeal (CPLA) in the Hon'ble Supreme Court which was granted in these words:

"2. So far the main petition is concerned, it is submitted by the learned Deputy Attorney General for the petitioner that respondent No.1 was a District and Session Judge and was elevated as Judge of the High Court in July, 1985 and retired after completing tenure of three years two months and twenty-seven days in that capacity, hence for the purpose of pension his case is covered by Article 15 of the High Court Judges (Leave, Pension and Privileges) Order, 1970, which is applicable to such judges of the High Court who retire before completion of five years' service in the High Court and are entitled to draw pension as having retired from the service they were taken from for elevation to the High Court.

3. Leave is granted to examine the following questions. Firstly, whether for claim of respondent No.1 for extra/maximum pension writ petition before the High Court was competent to and maintainable. Secondly, whether P.O.9/70 is to be read in conjunction with P.O.2/93, P.O.3/95 and Article 205 read with Fifth Schedule to the Constitution, if yes, what will be its effect on the claim of respondent. Thirdly, whether the President can only increase or decrease the amount of pension with altering the terms and conditions as contemplated under Article 205 read with the Fifth Schedule to the Constitution. Fourthly, whether respondent No.1 is entitled to the minimum and maximum amount of the pension as contemplated under P.O.2/93."

iv.   Pending disposal of the Appeal, a number of other retired Judges of the High Courts, who were not allowed pension on the ground that they having been not put minimum service of five years in terms of paragraph 3 of Fifth Schedule to the Constitution were not entitled to the grant of pension, moved a joint representation to the President of Pakistan, through the Ministry of Law, Justice and Human Rights, Government of Pakistan and having received no reply, filed direct petitions before the Hon'ble Supreme Court under Article 184(3) of the Constitution, whereas, some of the retired Judges filed miscellaneous applications to be impleaded as party in the proceedings before this Court.

v.   On 06.03.2008, the Civil Appeal No.1021 of 1995 and the connected constitution petitions involving common question of law and facts, were disposed of through the single judgment (PLD 2008 SC 522, hereinafter referred to as the Second Judges' pension case) by three-member Bench of the Hon'ble Supreme Court in the following terms:

> "34. In consequence to the above discussion, the Constitution Petitions Nos. 8/2000, 10/2001, 26/2003, 34/2003, 04/2004 and 26/2007, filed by the retired Judges of the High Courts are allowed and the petitioners/ applicants in these petitions and miscellaneous applications, along with all other retired Judges of the High Courts, who are not party in the present proceedings, are held entitled to get pension and pensionary benefits with other privileges admissible to them in terms of Article 205 of the Constitution read with P.O.No.8 of 2007 and Article 203-C of the Constitution read with paras 2 and 3 of Fifth Schedule and P.O. No.2 of 1993 and P.O.3 of 1997 from the date of their respective retirements, irrespective of their length of service as such Judges."

vi.   The Registrar of the Hon'ble Supreme Court submitted a written statement to the Hon'ble Chief Justice of Pakistan giving necessary details of the aforesaid case with the following proposal:

> "10. In view of the above, if approved, Suo Motu action may be taken in the matter for review of judgment dated 6-3-2008 passed in Civil Appeal No. 1021 of 1995 etc. and the matter may be fixed before a Larger Bench comprising minimum five members."

vii.   The Hon'ble Chief Justice of Pakistan was pleased to pass the following order on 23. 11.2012:

> "Perusal of above note prima facie makes out a case for examination of points raised therein. Therefore, instant note be registered as Suo Motu Misc. Petition and it may be fixed in Court in the week commencing from 3-12-2012. Notice to Hon'ble Retired Judges, who are beneficiaries of the judgment dated 6-3-2008 be issued. Office shall provide their addresses. Notice to Attorney General for Pakistan may also be issued.".

viii.   After a lengthy hearing, a five-judge bench of the Hon'ble Supreme Court announced the following short order on 11.04.2013:

> "We hereby, in exercise of all the enabling powers vested in this Court, hold and declare that the law enunciated in the case of Accountant General Sindh and others v. Ahmed Ali U. Qureshi and others (PLD 2008 SC 522) is per incuriam and consequently this judgment is set aside. The titled appeal is accepted and the judgment impugned therein is also set aside. Other miscellaneous applications

moved therein and in these proceedings are dismissed accordingly."

ix. Detailed reasons of the aforesaid short order were given in the order which, for the purpose of convenience, has been termed as the Third Judges' pension case reported as Constitution Petition No.127 of 2012 regarding pensionary benefits of the judges of superior courts from the date of their respective retirements, irrespective of their length of service as such judges (PLD 2013 Supreme Court 829). Writing the lead judgment, Hon'ble Justice Anwar Zaheer Jamali held that:

"71. A careful reading of above reproduced relevant constitutional provisions; Article 221 of the Government of India Act, 1935; Article 221 of the Constitution of India, 1949; Article 175 of the Constitution of Islamic Republic of Pakistan, 1956; Article 124 of the Constitution of Islamic Republic of Pakistan, 1962; and, Article 205 of the Constitution of Islamic Republic of Pakistan, 1973, read with relevant Schedules to the Constitution, reveals that they are "pari materia" to the extent of entitlement to privileges and allowances and to such rights in respect of leave of absence and pension, and in this context, from time to time, High Court Judges Order 1937, President's Order 9 of 1970 and President's Order 3 of 1997, were issued to determine the moot question as to their right to pension. Here a reference to some repealed provisions of the Constitution and the High Court Judges Order/ President's Orders has been made only to show that in the High Court Judges Order 1937, condition of minimum length of service for a High Court Judge for his entitlement/right to pension, in the normal course, was 12 years and on attaining the age of sixty years, it was seven years, so also in the cases where retirement was medically certified to be necessitated due to ill-health, while the President was further conferred with power that for special reasons, he may direct that any period not exceeding three months shall be added to a Judge's service for pension. The relevant provision of President's Order 9 of 1970, dated 17-6-1970, paragraph 23 whereof repealed the earlier High Court Judges Order 1937, was its paragraph 13, which provided one clear condition for entitlement of right to pension as minimum length of actual service of five years on attaining the retiring age in the normal course and in case of resignation not less than ten years' service. Further, paragraph 15 of this President's Order contained provision as regards the right to pension of other Judges, who were not covered by paragraph 13. In the President's Order 3 of 1997, introduced in the year 1997 and brought into force at once, except to the extent of its paragraph 15, which was made effective from 27-7-1991, in the definition clause, meaning of 'actual service', 'additional judge' and 'judge' were specifically provided, while section 14 dealt with the condition of admissibility of pension of the retired judges. A bare reading of President's Order 3 of 1997 clearly spells out that every Judge of the High Court, having completed not less than five years of actual service as such on attaining the retiring age, is entitled for pensionary benefits. This provision is further subject to paragraph 29 of the President's Order 3 of 1997, relating to the "subsidiary conditions of service". A close look at the Fifth Schedule to Article 205 of the Constitution of Islamic Republic of Pakistan, 1973, which is an important integral part of the constitutional mandate, applicable to the present case, further reveals that paragraphs-2 and 3 relating to High Court, are the two relevant provisions of the Constitution, which in unequivocal term provide that in terms of paragraph-2 "EVERY JUDGE" of a High Court shall be entitled to such "PRIVILEGES", "ALLOWANCES", and to such "RIGHTS" in respect of leave of absence and "PENSION" as may be determined by the President, and until so determined, with the privileges, allowances and rights, to which immediately before the commencing day, the judges of the High Court were entitled. From the language of paragraph-2, it is also clear that it only refers to one category of judges of the High Court i.e. "Every Judge". To put it in other words, there are no two categories of judges specified therein as many senior ASCs and retired judges of the High Court have argued before us while supporting their claim despite they having rendered less than five years' actual service as such. What is important to notice here is that firstly right to pension is to be determined by the President for every judge of the High Court and until such determination, the privileges, allowances and rights already in-force before the commencing day, are to be availed by all of them. Keeping in view this clear and unambiguous language of paragraph-2 (ibid), when we revert to the provisions of paragraph 13 of the President's Order 9 of 1970, relating to conditions of admissibility of pension, we find that till its repeal vide paragraph 30 of President's Order 3 of 1997, rights of every Judge of the High Court were already determined in the manner that unless they had completed not less than five years of service before retiring age, they were not eligible or entitled to any pensionary benefits. It was in this background that none of the retiring honourable judge of the High Court, having less than five years' service as such to his credit, ever ventured to agitate such claim. In the year 1997, when the President's Order 3 of 1997 was promulgated with immediate effect (except its section 15, which was made applicable retrospectively w.e.f. 7-7-1991), under paragraph 14, a similar condition of not less than five years' service before attaining the retiring age was engraved, and the position under paragraph 17 of the High Court Judges Order, 1937 (repealed on 17-6-1970) was also not much different, except that requirement of length of service to earn right to pension at that time was minimum 12 years' service in the normal course or in case of attaining the age of sixty years, not less than seven years.

72.   Reverting to the language of paragraph-3 of Fifth Schedule to Article 205 of the Constitution of 1973, we find that in its original text, paragraph-3 had different phraseology, but it was subsequently amended in the present form by 12th amendment Act of 1991. However, in both the situations, right to pension of a retired High Court Judge was made conditional to not less than five years' actual service, while a further table was provided for increase in the percentage of pension depending upon the length of his service as a Judge of the High Court upto the maximum of 80 percent of his salary. Thus, the two paragraphs 2 and 3 of Fifth Schedule to Article 205 of the Constitution either read separately/ conjunctively or disjunctively, do not alter/change in any manner the requirement of minimum five years' length of actual service for every Judge of the High Court as one of the basic condition to earn the right to pension. The arguments of learned ASCs based on the principle of reading down etc. are, thus, of no avail in this regard.

74.   ----This view of the matter gains further support from the fact that in case right to pension as regards honourable retired Judges of the High Court, having less than five years' actual service was yet to be determined, then why since the year 1937 uptil now, neither any such representation was made nor any legal remedy was followed by the honourable retired Judges allegedly qualifying for pension in that category. In this regard, we also confronted many learned Sr. ASCs to show us a single instance either of pre-partition days or thereafter wherein such interpretation of law was advanced or such grievance was ever agitated by any honourable retired Judge of the High Court falling in this category or earlier to judgment under challenge, any judge of the High Court was ever granted right to pension/ pensionary benefits on the basis of his length of service as such for a period of few months or few years, irrespective of minimum required length of actual service, as has been held through the judgment under challenge. In reply, they frankly conceded that they have not come across any such instance. All these facts taken together leave us in no doubt to hold that the judgment under challenge is outcome of improper assistance to the Court due to which number of relevant provisions of law necessary for a just and fair adjudication of this issue were entirely overlooked and the findings were built on entirely wrong premises."

x.   All the five judges were unanimous in holding that a judge of the High Court having less than five years' service as such judge was not eligible to get pension as judge of the High Court. Payment of pension to such judges and their families was stopped; however, three Hon'ble judges decided in favour of not effecting recoveries of amounts drawn by judges with less than five years of service or their families whereas two Hon'ble judges ordered to effect recovery of the amounts so drawn.

xi. The matter of grant of pension as judge of the Hon'ble High Court to judges having less than five years' service reemerged when a retired judge of the Lahore High Court (who had been elevated from the post of the District and Sessions Judge) filed a Constitution petition under Article 184(3) of the Constitution wherein amongst others he had prayed that fixation of his pension etc. by Accountant General Punjab being against P.O. III of 1997 as well as the Fifth Schedule of the Constitution be declared as unjustified, illegal, void, non-est and be set aside. The petition was not entertained by the office of the Hon'ble Supreme Court an appeal against which was also dismissed. The said judge and two other retired judges of the Hon'ble Lahore High Court (who were also elevated from the subordinate judiciary) filed writ petition No. 105298/2017 in the Lahore High Court, Lahore, with the following prayers:

(i) The impugned fixation of pensions of the petitioners by respondent No.1 being against P..0. III of 1997 as well as the Fifth Schedule of the Constitution and the settled law may graciously be declared illegal, void and non-est and set aside.

(ii) Respondents be directed to fix the, pension, etc. of the petitioners on pro rata basis as judges of the High Court in accord with their length of service as judges of the High Court with a further direction that service of six months or more be rounded off to one year in addition to the years of service rendered by each one of the petitioners and after such determination they should be paid their pension starting from their dates of respective superannuation.

(iii) Without prejudice to the above or conceding, in the alternative, the respondents may be directed to calculate and fix pension, etc. of the petitioners according to the last drawn emoluments of the petitioners in accordance with para 16 & 29 of P.O. III of 1997 Read with Regulation 474 B(b) and 486 of the CSR.

xii. A three-judge bench of the Hon'ble Lahore High Court, Lahore disposed of the aforesaid writ petition on 07.07.2018 through the following order (hereinafter referred to as the Fourth Judges' pension case):

"This writ petition and connected writ petitions (W.P. Nos. 105307 & 115014 of 2017), *inter alia,* seek a direction from this Court to the respondents to fix the pension of the petitioners, who are all retired judges of *this* Court, in accordance with length of their service.

2. The learned Deputy Attorney General has today placed on record a statement in writing by the Secretary Law and Justice, Government of Pakistan, giving details

of the pension package to the retired Judges of this Court. The relevant portions of the statement read as under:

> "3. The permanent judges under section 474(b) of CSR are entitled to receive proportionate pension at the rate of 17.5% per annum for each year of service and the period of service above 6 months is to be reckoned as 1 year of service of pension.
>
> 4. The retired Judges from the district judiciary, in addition to their pension as a judge of High Court shall also receive 2% extra pension for each completed year of service of Pakistan. The maximum pension not exceeding 70% of salary payable to a judge."

3. Learned counsel for the petitioners is satisfied with the pension package mentioned in the written statement and has no objection if the petitions are disposed of in view thereof.

4. Justice (R) Mian Saeed-ur-Rehman Farrukh was appointed on 29.08.1992 for a period of two years. He was then appointed again on l 0.1 0.1996 to 31.07.1998 with the total length of period of service coming to three years, nine months and twenty-one days, which period shall be reckoned for the purposes of pension.

S. The above mentioned pension package shall also enure to the benefit of all those retired judges of this Court who are not parties before this Court and to whom this package is applicable.

6. Disposed of in terms of the afore-mentioned statement in writing filed by the Secretary Law and Justice, Government of Pakistan."

xiii. Government of the Punjab filed CPLA in the Hon'ble Supreme Court against the aforesaid judgment of the larger bench of the Hon'ble Lahore High Court, Lahore. A two-judge bench of the Hon'ble Supreme Court granted leave to appeal vide its order dated 29.09.2018, reproduced below:

> "**MIAN SAQID NISAR, CJ.** The titled applications are allowed and the petitions are allowed to be numbered.
>
> 2. We have heard the learned Advocate General, Punjab who contends that pension is not a bounty and it has to be earned, as has been so held by this Court in Constitutional Petition No.127 of 2012 and Human Rights Case No. 40927-S of 2012 (Regarding Pensionary Benefits of the Judges of Superior Courts) (PLD 2013 SC 829). In the facts and circumstances of the case, when the President Order does not provide for the pension to the category of the respondent judges or it is not even mentioned in the Fifth Schedule of the Constitution, the pension could not be granted by the High Court. We, therefore, grant leave to appeal in this case to consider the same. The impugned order shall remain suspended till final disposal of the appeal."

xiv. On 27.03.2019, a three-judge bench of the Hon'ble Supreme Court of Pakistan disposed of the appeal of the Government of the Punjab through the following order (hereinafter referred to as the Fifth Judges' pension case):

> "**Sh. Azmat Saeed, J.-** The learned Attorney General for Pakistan, present in Court, states that the Federal Government stands by the statement made before the Lahore High Court.
>
> 2. The learned Advocate General, Punjab states that he has no objection or grievance against the order but states that immediate payment of arrears may be difficult. In these circumstances, it is suggested by the learned Attorney General for Pakistan that the arrears may be paid in the next three years. the respondents are not averse to this idea. These appeals are disposed of in the above terms with the consent of the parties."

xv. Subsequently, the Government of the Punjab advised the Accountant General, Punjab to meet the recurrent increased annual liability (estimated to be Rs. 310 million per annum) on pension of the retired judges of the High Court having less than five years of service as such judges and pay arears of difference of pension to them in three years @Rs. 500/ million each for 2019-20, 2020-21 and 2021-22.

6. The Hon'ble Chief Justice of the Court perused the aforesaid statements containing necessary facts in respect of cases pointed out by Mr. Yazdani in his application and observed as under:

> "Facts disclosed constitute a prima facie case which merits to be considered for taking up as a petition under Article 184(3) of the Constitution. In exercise of powers conferred vide Order XXXIII Rule 1 and 6 of the Supreme Court Rules, 1980, it is held that to grant relaxation from observance of procedural requirements for invoking jurisdiction of the Supreme Court under Article 184(3) of the Constitution is necessary for the ends of justice in the instant case and the requisite relaxation is hereby granted to the extent of this application. The application is converted into a petition under Article 184(3) of the Constitution. A nine-judge bench to be headed by Mr. Nasir Latif Darwesh and comprising Mr. Jamal Mustafa Kundan, Mr. Saleem Anwar Taya, Mr. Syed Rizwan Ali Shah, Mr. Ahmad Nawaz Gondal, Mr. Abdul Aziz, Mr. Taseer Ahmad, Mr. Gulfam Mujtaba and Mr. Sarfraz Ahmad Bhatti is constituted to start hearing of the case after two weeks. Notice to the Attorney General for Pakistan, Advocate General, Punjab, the applicant and beneficiaries of the disputed judgments and any other (s) deemed to be a proper and necessary party in these proceedings."

7. The case, thus, brought before us is entertainable only if we find it falling within our constitutional jurisdiction. Merits of the case will matter and will be considered after the application is found to have succeeded in crossing the bar of jurisdictional threshold prescribed in Article 184(3) of the Constitution.

Preliminary objections and decision on maintainability of the petition

8. Learned counsels for the private respondents have raised the following objections over the maintainability of the petition:

468

a) In the case relating to restoration of commuted value of pension of the retired civil servants, the remedies of appeal and review have been exhausted. Even if this petition is accepted to be maintainable under Article 184(3) of the Constitution, it would be futile to proceed in the matter as while exercising jurisdiction under Article 184(3) of the Constitution, the findings recorded by the Supreme Court in appeals cannot be set aside / modified nor any portion of it can be expunged or substituted. Reliance in this regard is placed upon a case reported as Dr. A. Basit Vs. Deputy Registrar (Judicial) (PLD 2001 SC 1028). It has also been held by the Hon'ble Supreme Court in the case reported as Syed Shabbar Raza Rizvi and Others Vs. Federation of Pakistan, Ministry of Law and Justice Division through Secretary, Islamabad and Others (2018 SCMR 514) that Article 184(3) cannot be invoked as a parallel review jurisdiction when decision has already been rendered in a review of a case.

b) It was held in a case reported as Qaim Hussain Vs. Anjuman Islamia (PLD 1974 Lah. 346) that the remedy of review could be availed of only by a person who initially was a party to the proceedings in which either a decree had been passed or an order had been made against him. Rule 9 of the Order XXVI of the Supreme Court Rules, 1980 prohibits second review. In the case relating to restoration of commuted value of pension, remedy of review has been availed; in the case of Hon'ble retired judges of the High Court, review has become time-barred. Even if delay is condoned, a stranger to an appeal is not allowed to file a review petition under Article 188 of the Constitution. Article 184(3) of the Constitution is being resorted to through these proceedings in order to get judgments issued in appellate or review jurisdiction modified by a stranger to the previous proceedings which is impermissible.

c) Before invoking original jurisdiction of the Hon'ble Supreme Court under Article 184(3) of the Constitution, the remedy provided by Article 199 of the Constitution must be exhausted.

d) The matter is neither of public importance nor it involves any question of enforcement of fundamental rights. Powers under Article 184(3) of the Constitution are exercisable only if these conditions are fulfilled.

e) Article 187 of the Constitution does not grant any jurisdiction to the Hon'ble Supreme Court; this Article is, therefore, not available to supplement the jurisdiction under Article 184(3) of the Constitution.

9.	Learned Advocate General, Punjab does not object to maintainability of the petition on the ground that the matter raised therein is of public importance as it relates to payment of pension to all present and future pensioners governed by the Punjab Civil Servants Act, 1973 and also the Hon'ble judges of the High Courts who on account of less than five years of service as such judges are to be treated as retired civil servants for the purpose of pension. He refers to the Third Judges' pension case and I.A. Sharwani case (PLD 1991 SCMR 1041) to contend that determination of questions relating to pension is necessary for the purpose of enforcement of fundamental rights of the retired civil servants. He further contends that pensions are payable from the Provincial Consolidated Fund. To ensure that pensions are paid only in the cases and to the extent as allowed by or under the Constitution is a question of public importance as well as of enforcement of the fundamental rights of those who have been in the Service of Pakistan, he argues. He is of the view that the matter falls within the purview of Article 184(3) of the Constitution as the conditions specified therein stand fulfilled in the instant case. He asserts that a person does not need to be an aggrieved person within the meaning of Article 199 of the Constitution to invoke jurisdiction under Article 184(3) of the Constitution. He refers to the case reported as General Secretary Vs. Director Industries (1994 SCMR 2061) in which it was held that:

> "It is well settled that in human rights cases/public interest litigation under Article 184(3), the procedural trappings and restrictions, preconditions of being an aggrieved person and other similar technical objections cannot bar the jurisdiction of the Court."

10. The learned law officer explains that the distinguishing feature of Article 184(3) of the Constitution has been summed up by the Hon'ble Supreme Court in a case reported as Benazir Bhutto Vs. Federation of Pakistan (PLD 1988 SC 416) in the following words:

> "The plain language of Article 184(3) shows that it is open ended. The Article does not say as to who shall have the right to move the Supreme Court nor does it say by what proceedings the Supreme Court may be so moved or whether it is confined to the enforcement of the Fundamental Rights of an individual which are infracted or extends to the enforcement of the rights of a group or a class of persons whose rights are violated."

11. Relying upon the case reported as Darshan Masih Vs. The State (PLD 1990 SC 513), the learned Advocate General, Punjab asserts that in a fit case of enforcement of fundamental rights, the Supreme Court has jurisdiction, power and competence to pass all proper and necessary orders as the facts justify. He further submits that application of the principle of locus standi on proceedings under Article 184(3) of the Constitution is destructive of the rule of law. He claims that strict observance of procedural formalities is not necessary in cases under Article 184(3) of the Constitution and cites the cases reported as Darshan Masih Vs. The State (PLD 1990 SC 513) and Shehla Zia Vs. WAPDA (PLD 1994 SC 693) in which the Supreme Court exercised its jurisdiction, under Article 184(3) of the Constitution, on a telegram and a letter respectively.

12. Relying upon the third Judges' pension case, the learned Advocate General avers that a combined reading of Article 188, 187 and 184(3) of the Constitution leaves no doubt that the Supreme Court has unlimited jurisdiction to reopen, revisit or review, and for such purpose examine any judgment earlier pronounced by it to set the law correct, to cure injustice, save it from becoming an abuse of the process of law and the judicial system and can pass any order to eliminate chances of perpetuating an illegality or to save an aggrieved party from being rendered remediless.

13. Attending to the objection that proceedings under Article 199 of the Constitution must precede action under Article 184(3) of the Constitution, he refers to I.A Sharwani case (1991 SCMR 1041) in which it was held that "this Court is competent to entertain a constitution petition if it considers that a question of public importance is involved with reference to the enforcement of any of the fundamental rights...notwithstanding that there might be an alternate remedy." He avers that it was held in Benazir Bhutto case (PLD 1988 SC 416) and reiterated in Wukala Mahaz case (PLD 1998 SC 1263) that Article 184(3) of the Constitution leaves the power of the High Courts under Article 199 intact and it is for the party to choose which of the two forums it wishes to invoke. He, however, frankly admits with reference to a case reported as Faroogh Ahmad Siddiqi Vs. Province of Sindh through Secretary, Excise and Taxation (1994 SCMR 2111) that when a petition under Article 199 is pending in the High Court, a petition under Article 184(3) of the Constitution on the same facts and for the same relief is not maintainable. He submits that as no petition under Article 199 of the Constitution is pending in a High Court on the facts and subject-matter of the instant petition, therefore, this petition cannot be objected to on this ground.

14. While admitting that second review petition is prohibited, he asserts that the Supreme Court has competence to overrule its earlier judgments which have attained finality after disposal of the review petition. He distinguishes between overruling a judgment earlier given and the second review petition by a party and submits that whereas latter is prohibited, the earlier is allowed to ensure complete justice in a pending proceeding. In this

regard, he refers to a judgment delivered by a five-judge bench reported as Akhtar Umar Hayat Lalayka and others Vs. Mushtaq Ahmad Sukhera and others (2018 SCMR 1218) wherein it has been held by the Hon'ble Supreme Court of Pakistan that:

"71. -----Second review is barred by law and no party can now approach this Court for a second review, however, this Court has absolute power to re-visit its earlier judgments/orders by invoking its Suo Motu Jurisdiction under Articles 184(3), 187 or 188 of the Constitution. This Power is not dependent upon an application of any party and it was so held in the case of Khalid Iqbal Vs. Mirza Khan (PLD 2015 SC 50), in the following words: -

"12. The question of maintainability of the 2nd Criminal Review Petition on the ground that this Court has to do complete justice by invoking Article 187(1) of the Constitution is also misconceived. The provisions of Article 187(1) cannot be attracted in the present case, as this Court has already recorded findings against the petitioner by the Judgment dated 28-2-2001, against which review was also dismissed and there was no 'lis' pending before this Court warranting exercise of its jurisdiction under Article 187(1) of the Constitution, besides Rule 9 of the Order XXVI of the Supreme Court Rules, bars 2nd Review Petition. There is a distinction between right of a party to approach the Court and jurisdiction of the Court to do complete justice on its own. Once this Court has finally determined the right of the petitioner in the judgment dated 28-2-2001, holding him guilty, the petitioner through 2nd Review Petition, cannot re-agitate it. If such a Review Petition is allowed to be entertained, it will land in a situation where findings of this Court against a party will never attain finality.

13. This, however, does not mean that the jurisdiction of this Court is barred by any restriction placed by the Constitution; there is no Article in the Constitution which imposes any restriction or bar on this Court to revisit its earlier decision or even to depart from them, nor the doctrine of stare decisis will come in its way so long as revisiting of the judgment is warranted, in view of the significant impact on the fundamental rights of citizens or in the interest of public good. ... ...

On perusal of the paragraphs referred to hereinabove, we can safely reach a conclusion that this Court has absolute powers to re-visit, to review and or to set aside its earlier judgments/orders by invoking its Suo Motu Jurisdiction under Articles 184(3), 187 or 188 of the Constitution. The Powers of this Court to exercise its inherent jurisdiction under the above referred Articles of the Constitution are not dependent upon an application of a party."

The same view has been reiterated in a recent judgment dated 5.1.2018 passed in the case of Syed Shabbar Raza Rizvi Vs. Federation of Pakistan (Const.P.No.1/2016)."

15.   As regards limitations of Article 187 of the Constitution, the learned Advocate General states that in a case reported as Lt. Col. Nawabzada Muhammad Amir Khan Vs. The Controller of Estate Duty, Government of Pakistan, Karachi and others (PLD 1962 SC 335), Chief Justice Cornelius held as under:

"For the present purpose, the emphasis should, in my opinion, be laid upon the consideration that, for the doing of "complete justice", the

Supreme Court is vested with full power, and I can see no reason why the exercise of that full power should be applicable only in respect of a matter coming up before the Supreme Court in the form of a decision by a High Court or some subordinate Court. I can see no reason why that purpose, in its full scope, should not also be applicable for the purpose of reviewing a judgment delivered by the Supreme Court itself: provided that thereby found a necessity within the meaning of the expression "complete justice" to exercise that power. It must, of course, be borne in mind that by assumption, every judgment pronounced by the Court is a considered and solemn decision on all points arising out of the case, and further that every reason compels towards the grant of finality in favour of such judgments delivered by a Court which sits at the apex of the judicial system. Again, the expression "complete justice" is clearly not to be understood in any abstract or academic sense. So much is clear from the provision in Article 163(3) that a written order is to be necessary for the purpose of carrying out the intention to dispense "complete justice". There must be a substantial or material effect to be produced upon the result of the case if, in the interests of "complete justice" the Supreme Court undertakes to exercise its extraordinary power of review of one of its own considered judgments. If there be found material irregularity, and yet there be no substantial injury consequent thereon, the exercise of the power of review to alter the judgment would not necessarily be required. The irregularity must be of such a nature as converts the process from being one in aid of justice to a process that brings about injustice. Where, however, there is found to be something directed by the judgment of which review is sought which is in conflict with the Constitution or with a law of Pakistan there it would be the duty of the Court unhesitatingly to amend the error. It is a duty which is enjoyed upon every Judge of the Court by the solemn oath which he takes when he enters upon his duties, viz., to "preserve, protect and defend the Constitution and law of Pakistan."

16.   He invites our attention to paragraph 10 of a case reported as Pir Sabir Shah Vs. Shad Muhammad (PLD 1995 SC 66) in which Justice Saleem Akhtar observed that:

"10. The Supreme Court is the apex Court. It is the highest and the ultimate Court under the Constitution. In my view the inherent and plenary power of this Court which is vested in it by virtue of being the ultimate Court, it has the power to do complete justice without in any manner infringing or violating any provision of law. While doing complete justice this Court would not cross the frontiers of the Constitution and law. The term "complete justice" is not capable of definition with exactitude. It is a term covering variety of cases and reliefs which this Court can mould and grant depending upon the facts and circumstances of the case. While doing complete justice formalities and technicalities should not fetter its power. It can grant ancillary relief, mould the relief within its jurisdiction depending on the facts and circumstances of the case, take additional evidence and in appropriate cases even subsequent events may be taken into consideration. Ronald Rotunda in his book "Treatise on Constitutional Law — Substance and Procedure" (Second Edition), Volume 2 at page 90 has stated that "The Supreme Court is in essence a continual Constitutional convention". The jurisdiction and the power conferred on the Supreme Court does empower it to do complete justice by

472

looking to the facts, circumstances and the law governing a particular case. Article 187 does not confer any jurisdiction. It recognises inherent power of an apex Court to do complete justice and issue orders and directions to achieve that end. Inherent jurisdiction is vested in the High Court and subordinate courts while dealing with civil and criminal cases by virtue of provisions of law. The inherent jurisdiction of this Court to do complete justice cannot be curtailed by law as it may adversely affect the independence of judiciary and the fundamental right of person to have free access to the Court for achieving complete justice. This enunciation may evoke a controversy that as Article 175(2) restricts Article 187 it will create conflict between the two. There is no conflict and both the Articles can be read together. The conflict in the provisions of the Constitution should not be assumed and if apparently there seems to be any, it has to be interpreted in a harmonious manner by which both the provisions may co-exist. One provision of the Constitution cannot be struck down being in conflict with the other provision of the Constitution. They have to live together, exist together and operate together. Therefore, while interpreting jurisdiction and power of the superior Courts one should look to the fundamental rights conferred and the duty cast upon them under the Constitution. A provision like Article 187 cannot be read in isolation but has to be interpreted and read harmoniously with other provisions of the Constitution. In my humble view this Court while hearing appeal under a statute has the jurisdiction and power to decide the question of vires of the statute under which the appeal has arisen and can even invoke Article 184 (3) in appropriate cases."

17.   The learned Advocate General further submits that it was held in a case reported as Baz Muhammad Kakar Vs. Federation of Pakistan (PLD 2012 SC 923) that Article 187 of the Constitution has itself enlarged the jurisdiction of the Supreme Court. He also refers to a case reported as Hitachi Ltd Vs. Federation of Pakistan (1998 SCMR 1618) wherein it was held that:

"This Court has been empowered to issue such directions, orders or decrees as may be necessary for doing complete justice in any case or matter pending before it, including an order for the purpose of securing the attendance of any person or the discovery or production of any document. It may be pointed out that the above provision is an enabling provision, which can be invoked in aid in a matter which is competently filed before this Court. While granting a relief the Court can dispense with the technicalities and may mould the relief according to the requirement, if the dictates of justice so demand."

18.   The learned Advocate General requests that in view of conflicting judgments regarding interpretation of Article 187, the Supreme Court may like to settle the controversy in this case.

19.   Mr. Yazdani states in very simple words that if the impugned judgments are not partly overruled, the beneficiaries thereof would continue to receive money from the Provincial Consolidated Fund in violation of the Constitution and law. He further submits that prohibiting recovery of amounts drawn in absence of lawful sanction or in excess of lawful sanction on the ground of want of fault on the part of the recipients or the potential hardship the recipients may face in case of recovery can destroy the entire fabric of any system based upon a written Constitution. He avers that these matters are of immense public importance and plugging the avenues of unlawful payments from the public purse is expected to make money available for provision of fundamental right to education, life and public safety. He states on oath that he was not a party to any of the impugned judgments

and is not a direct and immediate beneficiary in case the Supreme Court sets things right. He further assures that he is not a proxy of any interested party or meddlesome interloper.

20.   We have carefully examined the rival contentions. What we do in our judicial capacity is the exercise of judicial power of the state. The legislature legislates and the executive executes. When facts or laws are disputed, the parties to the dispute get the lis resolved through having resort to judiciary. Valid laws are given effect to in these disputes by the judiciary. If a law is competently made and is not inconsistent with the Constitution, it is valid and it has to be followed by the judiciary in provision of adjudicatory services to the society. Chief Justice John Marshall held in Osborn v. Bank of US (1824) 22 US (9 Wheat) 738, 866 that:

> "When they (the Judges) are said to exercise a discretion, it is a mere legal discretion, a discretion to be exercised in discovering the course prescribed by law; and when that is discovered, it is the duty of the court to follow it. Judicial power is never exercised for the purpose of giving effect to the will of the Judge; always for the purpose of giving effect to the will of the legislature, or in other words, to the will of the law."

21.   It was held by Lord Donaldson MR in (1990) 1 All ER 616111 that:

> "The constitutional position is clear. Parliament makes the law and it is the duty of the courts to enforce that law, whether or not they agree with it. Every citizen, every corporate body and every authority, whether national or local, is entitled to campaign to change the law, but until the law is changed it is their duty to obey it. That is what parliamentary democracy and the rule of law is all about. Each one of us surrenders a part of his personal freedom of action and choice and in return is protected by the law from the consequences of others seeking to exercise an unfettered freedom of action and choice."

22.   To do justice is to make judicial decisions strictly in accordance with law and to do complete justice means to doubly ensure that no deviation from the Constitution and the applicable law is made and if it has been made in a case the same is rectified without delay and is not tolerated or perpetuated under any pretext or because of any procedural hindrance. Law should be worn by a judge in his sleeves and justice should be imparted according to the law. To do complete justice is not the inherent or extraordinary or supra constitutional power or jurisdiction; it is the sole function of a court of law and the **raison d'être of the institution of judiciary.**

23.   When human beings do something, it is not possible to guarantee absolute absence of mistake or error. Same is true with respect to judges. It was observed by the Hon'ble Supreme Court of India in cases reported as K.P. Tiwari Vs. State of Madhya Pradesh (AIR 1994 SC 1031) and V.K. Jain Vs. High Court of Delhi and others [(2008)17 SCC 538] that a judge who has not committed an error is yet to be born. Justice Jackson of the USA rightly declared about judges that:

> "We are not final because we are infallible; we are infallible only because we are final."

24.   When a judge makes a mistake, parties to the case have remedies to get it corrected, inter alia, through appeal or review. It is possible that an erroneous judgment successfully crosses these in-built systemic barriers and attains finality inter se the parties. It is also possible that where more than one reasonable interpretations of a law are permissible, the one preferred by a court of law at a given point in time subsequently losses its reasonability and the changed atmosphere makes the competing reasonable interpretation more feasible. If a review is end of the game, then what is the constitutional mechanism to meaningfully respond to such situations?

25.   A court can exercise judicial power of the state only if it has jurisdiction in the matter. Article 175 (2) of the Constitution lays down the fundamental principle that no court

shall have any jurisdiction save as is or may be conferred on it by the Constitution or by or under any law. This Article lays to rest the idea of inherent powers. In these proceedings we are concerned with jurisdiction of the Supreme Court under the Constitution only. The Supreme Court has original jurisdiction (Article 184), appellate jurisdiction (Article 185, 203F and 212), advisory jurisdiction (Article 186) and review jurisdiction (Article 188). Article 191 of the Constitution provides that subject to the Constitution and law, the Supreme Court may make rules regulating the practice and procedure of the Court. The Supreme Court has framed the Supreme Court Rules, 1980 under Article 191 of the Constitution. The Supreme Court exercises its jurisdiction under these rules. Matters relating to appeals, reviews, advisory opinions and original jurisdiction are regulated in accordance with these rules.

26.   The Constitution does not grant a right to the litigants to appeal to the Supreme Court; it only permits submission of an application for grant of leave to appeal. The leave shall lie only if leave to appeal is granted and to the extent as specified in the leave granting order. Further, appellate and review jurisdictions are not available, except in case of quo warranto proceedings, to strangers to a case and can only be availed by a proper or necessary party.

27.   About review jurisdiction of the Hon'ble Supreme Court, we may refer to a case reported as Abdul Ghaffar Abdul Rehman Vs. Asghar Ali (PLD 1998 SC 363) wherein it was stated that:

> "14.   Article 188 of the Constitution confers power on this Court subject to the provisions of any Act of the Parliament and any rules made by the Supreme Court to review any judgment pronounced or any order made by it. Whereas Order XXVI, rule 1 of the Rules lays down that subject to the law and practice of the Court, the Court may review its judgment, order of any civil proceeding, on ground similar to those mentioned in Order XLVII, rule 1 of C.P.C. and any criminal proceeding on the ground of an error apparent on the face of the record.
>
> It may be observed that Order XLVII, rule 1 of C.P.C. gives a right to a party to apply for review if he is aggrieved by the orders or decrees, or decisions mentioned in sub-clauses (a), (b), (c) of rule 1 on the three grounds, namely, discovery of new and important matter or evidence which, after the exercise of due diligence, was not within his knowledge or could not be produced by him at the time when the decree was passed or order made, or on account of some mistake or error apparent on the face of the record, or for any other sufficient reason."

28.   A review is not a fresh hearing of arguments or appraisal of evidence to substitute a view earlier taken if that view was lawfully within the discretion of the court. If a law or precedent of the Supreme Court is considered and not applied to a case, it will not furnish a ground for review. In Sir Hari Shankar Pal and another Vs. Anath Nath Mitter and others [1949 FCR 36], a Five Judges Bench of the Federal Court of India while considering the question whether the Calcutta High Court was justified in not granting relief to non-appealing party, whose position was similar to that of the successful appellant, held:

> "That a decision is erroneous in law is certainly no ground for ordering review. If the Court has decided a point and decided it erroneously, the error could not be one apparent on the face of the record or even analogous to it. When, however, the court disposes of a case without adverting to or applying its mind to a provision of law which gives it jurisdiction to act in a particular way, that may amount to an error analogous to one apparent on the face of the record sufficient to bring

the case within the purview of Order XLVII, Rule 1, Civil Procedure Code."

29.   Not considering the law laid down by the Supreme Court amounts to an error apparent on face of record and is a ground for review as was held in a case reported as Commissioner of Sales Tax Vs. Hukumchand Mills [2004(2) MPLJ 492]. If miscarriage of justice is caused due to human fallibility of judges of the Apex Court, second review is not allowed to the concerned parties as a curative review and the parties have to suffer as an inevitable collateral damage of giving finality to the Apex Court consisting of human beings. If it is not possible to substitute fallible and imperfect human beings as judges of the court whose decisions are final with infallible and perfect persons, tolerating miscarriage of justice inter se the parties is a cost we have to pay till such time we develop a better system.

30.   Whereas a decision in review is final for the parties concerned, the society as a whole and all generations to come are not under an inescapable compulsion to learn to live with and perpetuate an illegality and face its consequences forever. The Supreme Court is also not a slave of what it once utters on a question of law. The Constitution has provided two corrective and remedial mechanisms. One is Article 184(3) and the other is Article 187 of the Constitution.

31.   Article 184(3) of the Constitution reads as follows:

> "Without prejudice to the provisions of Article 199, the Supreme Court shall, if it considers that a question of public importance with reference to the enforcement of any of the Fundamental Rights conferred by Chapter 1 of Part II is involved, have the power to make an order of the nature mentioned in the said Article."

32.   We do not find any express or implied provision in the Constitution according to which jurisdiction under Article 184(3) of the Constitution is not available if the subject-matter has been or can fall under appellate, review or advisory jurisdiction of the Supreme Court or it may legitimately be brought before a High Court under Article 199 of the Constitution even if the threshold requirements regarding question of public importance and enforcements of the fundamental rights specified in the said Article are fulfilled. Remedy of 184(3) of the Constitution is in addition to and not in substitution of the remedy provided under Article 199 of the Constitution. A party has option of appeal if he has availed remedy under Article 199 of the Constitution and not of a petition under Article 184(3) of the Constitution. We are in agreement with the proposition that Article 184(3) of the Constitution does not substitute appellate or review jurisdiction of the Hon'ble Supreme Court and does not provide a backdoor channel to the concerned parties to reopen and re-litigate their lost causes after exhausting appellate and review remedies but agreeing with this proposition does not automatically implies that all others are debarred to approach the Hon'ble Supreme Court if question of law intended to be agitated under Article 184(3) is exactly the same or materially identical to the one already settled by the Hon'ble Supreme Court in its appellate, review or original jurisdiction or is capable of being raised before a High Court under Article 199 of the Constitution or some aggrieved party has instituted proceedings in respect thereof in a High Court which are pending. It can also be unreasonable to assert that the Supreme Court, in proceedings under Article 184(3) of the Constitution, is not authorized to deviate from the law earlier laid down by it in its appellate, review, advisory or original jurisdiction. The Supreme Court can overrule its earlier judgments after examining them and giving reasons therefor provided the bench doing so comprises of the judges more than the bench the judgment of which is intended to be overruled. Thus, if a question of public importance with reference to the enforcement of any of the fundamental rights is raised by a person under Article 184(3) of the Constitution, and the Supreme Court is satisfied that the petitioner does not intend to bypass its appellate or review jurisdiction or intends to create additional opportunity to contest his lost case, the petition shall be maintainable even if adjudication of the questions raised may require overruling earlier judgments of the Supreme Court including those given in appellate or

review jurisdiction. Locus standi of a petitioner is irrelevant in proceedings under Article 184(3) of the Constitution and being an aggrieved person is neither a necessary qualification nor a disqualification for instituting proceedings under the said Article 184(3).

33.   Jurisdiction of the Hon'ble Supreme Court under Article 184(3) is judicial; it is nether legislative nor executive. It does not empower the Hon'ble Supreme Court to legislate or to exercise executive powers. It needs also to be clarified that a mere violation of the Constitution or a law does not provide a cause to invoke Article 184(3) if the necessary ingredients of a question of public importance and enforcement of fundamental rights are missing.

34.   In a case where question of public importance for enforcement of fundamental rights is not involved but violation of the Constitution or a law is alleged and appellate and review jurisdictions have either been exhausted or are not available, the parties who lost their cause have no remedy to avail jurisdiction of the Hon'ble Supreme Court under Article 184(3) of the Constitution. If the judgments given by the Supreme Court fall within the ambit of Article 189 of the Constitution and a party presents them to advance its cause or defeat that of its opponent, these are binding for all courts in Pakistan. The Supreme Court has two options in this respect; either to implement them or to overrule them if they are found to be per incuriam or otherwise it is found necessary to overrule them. The Supreme Court can do it on its own or on pleadings of a party to a pending case. If it finds that the law earlier laid down by it needs to be overruled, it will do so subject to the condition that a bench comprising judges more than that of the bench whose decision is to be overruled is empowered to do so through a speaking order. In other words, if complete justice is not possible because of a law laid down by the Hon'ble Supreme Court and without overruling the ratio decidendi of that case, then Article 187 of the Constitution will come into operation to clear the road to complete justice to the extent necessary to adjudicate upon the lis at hand and not more than what is necessarily required to do complete justice. In such a case, limitations as to time, parties, procedural requirements to approach the Hon'ble Supreme Court, summoning of records, enforcing attendance etc. shall not bar the Hon'ble Supreme Court to examine and overrule the ratio decidendi of a judgment. If the matter is between the private parties and no continuing wrong is involved, the overruling judgment may have prospective effect. In case the matter pertains to functioning of the Government involving payment of money from public purse, the overruling judgment shall have effect with effect from coming into force of the specific constitutional or statutory provision interpreted by the Hon'ble Supreme Court.

35.   Article 187 of the Constitution is restricted to a case or matter pending before the Hon'ble Supreme Court. Matters already decided do not fall within its purview. For a matter to be pending, it must be within jurisdiction of the Hon'ble Supreme Court in accordance with Article 175 of the Constitution. The law enunciated by the Supreme Court under Article 189 of the Constitution is to be corrected when in a subsequent case, that law is found to be per incuriam or otherwise liable to be overruled. Article 187 of the Constitution does not empower the Hon'ble Supreme Court to assume any jurisdiction. However, when jurisdiction is assumed under the Constitution and a matter becomes pending in the Hon'ble Supreme Court, then it has all procedural powers necessary and proper to do complete justice. As we have said earlier that complete justice means justice in accordance with law, therefore, the Supreme Court can cause presence of any person or production of any document through appropriate orders so that all concerned are heard before making a decision even if they are not parties to the pending case.

36.   Article 187 of the Constitution does not grant a new jurisdiction or enhances an existing one. This Article relates only to pending matters and aims at complete justice i.e. to discover the law applicable to the lis at hand and apply that law to the facts and circumstances of the case. It does not vest legislative or executive powers in the Hon'ble Supreme Court and in no way attempts to destroy or weaken the theory of trichotomy of powers. It provides all procedural powers proper and necessary to do justice and nothing

more. To read in this Article any constitutional intent to make the Hon'ble Supreme Court an entity not subservient to the Constitution and law would be too naïve an assertion to be attributable to a man in his senses. This Article does not substitute appellate, review, advisory or original jurisdiction of the Supreme Court and consequently wisdom or reasonability of legislative or executive actions cannot be judged or substituted under the pretext of complete justice. A power has to be exercised to achieve the intended results. Article 187 intends to ensure complete justice in a pending matter and nothing else. It does not include legislative or executive actions to ensure complete justice; it only relates to removal of procedural hindrances in the way of complete justice. By expressly limiting it to pending cases, it has properly been fenced against unfounded notions of unqualified powers of the judiciary. The Hon'ble Supreme Court of India held in a case reported as Prem Chand Vs. Excise Commissioner, (1963 A.I.R. S.C. 996) that "the wide powers which are given to this Court for doing complete justice between the parties can be used by this Court for instance, in adding parties to the proceeding pending before it, or in admitting additional evidence, or in remanding the case, or in allowing a new point to be taken up for the first time". It was held by the Hon'ble Supreme Court of India in A.R. Antulay Vs. R.S. Nayak (1988 A.I.R. S.C. 1531) about the power to do complete justice that "however wide and plenary the language of the article, the directions given by the Court should not be inconsistent with, repugnant to, or in violation of the specific provision of any statute". Article 187 of the Constitution does not make the Hon'ble Supreme Court a super legislature or bureaucracy in black robes with all powers and no responsibility.

37.   In the instant case, the prayer is also for partly over-ruling two judgments of the Hon'ble Supreme Court. No other court has jurisdiction to do so. The judgments sought to be partly over-ruled have not been relied upon or objected to in any pending proceedings before this Court. Article 187 of the Constitution shall be attracted only once the petition is held to be maintainable under Article 184(3) of the Constitution and same shall become a case or matter pending before the Hon'ble Supreme Court within the contemplation of Article 187 of the Constitution. The power to do complete justice in a pending case includes power to override earlier judgments of the Hon'ble Supreme Court. The third Judges' pension case makes it clear that under original jurisdiction of the Hon'ble Supreme Court, judgments of the Hon'ble High Court delivered under Article 199 of the Constitution and appellate or review orders of the Hon'ble Supreme Court can be modified or set-aside if the conditions specified in Article 184(3) of the Constitution are fulfilled.

38.   In view of the above discussion, we are persuaded to hold and do herby hold that the matter of pension of retired civil servants and civil servants retiring as judges of a High Court with less than five years of service as such judges is a question of public importance. As pension is payable from the Provincial Consolidated Fund and proceeds of this Fund are spent, inter alia, for provision and protection of fundamental rights, therefore, payment of pension in accordance with law has direct nexus with enforcement of fundamental rights. In this view of the matter, the instant petition presents questions of public importance with reference to enforcement of the fundamental rights; it is, therefore, maintainable under Article 184(3) of the Constitution.

39.   In the facts and circumstances of this petition, Mr. Yazdani has presented the following questions to be judicially determined by this court:

1. Whether a High Court has power in respect of matters falling within exclusive jurisdictions of the administrative tribunals created under Article 212 of the Constitution?
2. Whether principle of merger applies to the judgment of the learned Punjab Service Tribunal in appeal of Mr. Muhammad Ismail Tayer?
3. Whether the Ismail Tayer case holds that restoration of commuted value of pension means doubling of the amount being drawn as pension plus increases in pension on the date of restoration and whether determination of pension and increases in pension of the retired civil

servants of the Province other than through a money bill is constitutionally permissible?

4. Whether the Hon'ble High Court had valid constitutional powers to employ measures it employed to get the second A.A. Zuberi case implemented after judgment of the Hon'ble Supreme Court in the Ismail Tayer case?

5. Whether the ratio decidendi of the Third Judges' pension case stands overruled by the Fourth and Fifth Judges' pension cases and the position contained in the First and the Second Judges' pension case has revived? Whether the dictum of law laid down in the Third Judges' pension case to the extent of recovery of amounts drawn without lawful authority needs to be overruled?

40. Now we proceed to find answers to the above questions in the paragraphs that follow.

Question # 1

Whether a High Court has power in respect of matters falling within exclusive jurisdiction of a service tribunal created under Article 212 of the Constitution?

41. The learned Advocate General, Punjab contends that exercise of judicial power of the state by a court is dependent upon grant of jurisdiction to that court by the Constitution itself or through a statute. Referring to Article 175(2) of the Constitution, he argues that a judgment delivered without jurisdiction is void ab initio and binds no one. He avers that mere fact that a judgment delivered without jurisdiction attains finality when leave to appeal against that judgment is refused or review against that refusal is dismissed does not cure the jurisdictional want. He maintains that refusal by the Hon'ble Supreme Court to grant leave to appeal does not ipso facto endorses the judgment appealed against. Elaborating his argument, he further says that if a petition for leave to appeal or review petition against a leave refusing order is dismissed by the Hon'ble Supreme Court, it only signifies absence of grounds justifying exercise of appellate or review jurisdiction and not cannot be taken as confirmation of anything contained in the judgment impugned. He avers that dismissal of the petition of the Federation for leave to appeal against the judgment reported as the Second A.A. Zuberi case was on the ground of being time-barred. He submits that the Punjab Services Tribunal has exclusive jurisdiction in matters pertaining to terms and conditions of service of the serving as well as retired civil servants of the Province of the Punjab. He says that remuneration is one of the conditions of service and anything relating to remuneration is assailable by a civil servant only in the Service Tribunal. As the matter falls within the jurisdiction of the Service Tribunal, therefore, jurisdiction of the Hon'ble High Court stands ousted, he asserts adding that the Service Tribunal is bound to follow the law laid down by the Hon'ble Supreme Court in terms of Article 189 of the Constitution. As the Hon'ble High Court is without jurisdiction in respect of any matter entertainable by the Service Tribunal, therefore, any judgment delivered by the Hon'ble High Court on that matter would be a mere nullity for want of jurisdiction, he opines. He further submits that the Service Tribunal can place reliance on judgments of the Hon'ble Supreme Court and not on those of the High Court as jurisdictions of the Service Tribunal and of the High Court are exclusive and not concurrent. He advances his argument by stating that a judgment delivered without jurisdiction does not need to be appealed against and deserves to be ignored or, at best, be agitated in the court delivering the judgment. In this regard, he draws our attention towards Section 12(2) of the Code of the Civil Procedure, 1908 which, inter alia, says that challenge to a judgment without jurisdiction shall be through making an application to the court making the order. He says that it was held in a case reported as Secretary, Ministry of Religious Affairs and Minorities and 2 others Vs. Syed Abdul Majid (1993 SCMR 1171) that Section 12(2) of the Code of Civil Procedure, 1908 applies to orders made by the Hon'ble High Court under Article 199 of

the Constitution. He prays that this Court may declare that the appellate jurisdiction of the Hon'ble Supreme Court is invocable against orders allegedly made without jurisdiction only after exhausting the remedy provided by Section 12(2) of the Code of Civil Procedure, 1908 and Section 3(2) of the Law Reforms Ordinance, 1972 and leave to appeal shall be granted only if the judgment appealed against is prima facie found to be made with lawful jurisdiction. He argues that it would not be appropriate if other questions are attended to by the Hon'ble Supreme Court in appeals against judgments alleged to have been delivered without jurisdiction before first determining the question of jurisdiction. If the jurisdiction is found missing, the Hon'ble Supreme Court is required to declare so and refuse leave to appeal on that ground alone, without further dilating upon the matter, the learned Advocate General says. He avers that leave to appeal in the Ismail Tayer case was granted, inter alia, to consider as to whether in view of the provisions of Article 212 of the Constitution and the judgment in the case titled Accountant General vs. Abdul Majeed Babar (1990 SCMR 790), a constitution petition under Article 199 before the High Court was maintainable? He claims that by holding that Service Tribunal has jurisdiction in the matter of pension of the retired civil servants, jurisdiction of the Hon'ble High Court was held to be ousted by the Hon'ble Supreme Court in the Ismail Tayer case. By holding so, the judgments of the Hon'ble High Court appealed against were rendered a mere nullity in eyes of law, he submits. As the judgment of the Service Tribunal in the Ismail Tayer case was wholly dependent upon judgments of the Hon'ble High Court, therefore, with this declaration by the Hon'ble Supreme Court, the legs on which the judgment stood were chopped and the judgment of the Tribunal fell on ground as superstructures based upon a void order collapse with its destruction, he claims. He asserts that what lawfully remains in the field is the short order of the Hon'ble Supreme Court dated 31.03.2014 read with reasons penned down subsequently. This short order and the reasons given therefor do not require doubling of pension at the time of restoration of commuted value pf pension, he submits adding that the Hon'ble High Court got its void order in the Second A.A. Zuberi case implemented through initiating contempt of court proceedings. He cautions that knowingly and willfully doing violence against judgments of the Hon'ble Supreme Court by the Hon'ble High Court is destructive of the rule of law and the judicial discipline.

42.   Regarding case of the retired judges of the Hon'ble Lahore High Court with less than five years of service as such judges, he explains that such judges regain their status as civil servants or members of the subordinate judiciary for the purpose of their pension. In this regard, he refers to paragraph 16 of the High Court Judges (Leave, Pension and Privileges) Order, 1997 and claims that these judges have their remedy in any matter relating to their pension in the Punjab Subordinate Judiciary Service Tribunal created under the Punjab Subordinate Judiciary Service Tribunal Act, 1991. He avers that silence or consent of the parties cannot be construed as the Constitution or a law within the contemplation of Article 175(2) of the Constitution for the purpose of granting jurisdiction to a court of law. The learned Advocate General prays that this Court may make a declaration to this effect as a consequence of which the consent judgments in the matter of pension of the judges of the High Court with less than five years' service as such judges would become void and of no legal effect.

43.   Mr. Yazdani adopts the arguments advanced by the learned Advocate General, Punjab. He, however, adds that judgments delivered with jurisdiction and without jurisdiction must not be given similar sanctity and strength. He also asserts that judges knowingly and willfully crossing jurisdictional bar imposed by the Constitution violate their oath to preserve, protect and defend the Constitution. He further says that the Hon'ble Supreme Court has made scope of Article 212 of the Constitution crystal clear in numerous judgments and Article 189 of the Constitution makes it compulsory for a High Court to follow the law laid down by the Hon'ble Supreme Court. He claims that willful violation of an order of the Hon'ble Supreme Court constitutes misconduct within the meaning of Article 209 of the Constitution. In this regard, he refers to order passed by the Hon'ble Supreme Court of Pakistan on 3rd of November, 2007. He submits that because of violation of this

injunctive order of the Hon'ble Supreme Court, all permanent and additional judges of the respective High Courts who were appointed with consultation of Abdul Hameed Dogar were removed from their offices vide judgment reported as Sindh High Court Bar Association Vs. Federation of Pakistan (PLD 2009 SC 879). Some judges of the Hon'ble Supreme Court were also removed on the same ground, he adds. He further informs us that those judges who were already holding office on 3rd November, 2007 were declared to be liable to be dealt with under provisions of Article 209 of the Constitution. The point he wants to make is that willful disobedience of an order of the Hon'ble Supreme Court has been dealt with as misconduct for the purposes of Article 209 of the Constitution. He expresses his surprise that why the law laid down by the Hon'ble Supreme Court with respect to jurisdictional bar imposed by Article 212 of the Constitution is not being applied to the Hon'ble judges of the Hon'ble High Court and they have been licensed to do what they please to do in each case to which Article 212 applies. He wonders why thousands of cases of the serving and retired civil servants relating to the matters exclusively falling within jurisdiction of the tribunals established under Article 212 of the Constitution are pending in the Hon'ble High Courts. He ends his submissions on this aspect of the case by quoting Chief Justice John Marshal from Marbury v. Madison, 5 U.S. (1 Cranch) 137 (1803):

> "To what purpose are powers limited, and to what purpose is that limitation committed to writing, if those limits may, at any time, be passed by those intended to be restrained?"

44.   Learned counsels for the private respondents defend jurisdiction of the Hon'ble High Court and of the Hon'ble Supreme Court in the matter of pension of the retired civil servants, including the civil servants retiring as judges of the High Court but not having at least five years' service as such judges, on the following grounds:

a) Raising the question of jurisdiction at this belated stage is futile as the judgments objected to have been implemented and rights and obligations determined thereby have attained finality;

b) When the superior courts adjudicate upon cases and controversies through their judgments, the judgments have to be given full faith and credit and are to be accepted as made, unless proved otherwise, with lawful jurisdiction;

c) Even when a superior court delivers a judgment, without giving legal reasons therefor, in terms of settlement between the parties, it needs to be assumed that the court has satisfied itself about its jurisdiction in the matter and has consciously delivered the judgment after finding its jurisdiction under the Constitution or a law applicable to the subject-matter and parties to the consent judgment;

d) The Punjab Subordinate Judiciary Service Tribunal Act, 1991 is not applicable to the confirmed judges of the Hon'ble High Court even if they are not entitled to pension under the High Court Judges (Leave, Pension and Privileges) Order, 1997;

e) Application of the principle that a willful disobedience of an order of the Hon'ble Supreme Court is misconduct for proceedings under Article 209 of the Constitution, as held in Sindh High Court Bar Association Vs. Federation of Pakistan (PLD 2009 SC 879), would compromise independence of judiciary and result into indecisiveness in the High Courts; and

f) Jurisdiction of the Hon'ble Supreme Court in all matters falling within exclusive jurisdiction of the administrative tribunals created under Article 212 of the Constitution is admitted and undisputed. The Supreme Court is competent to adjudicate upon any such matter arising in any case even if ouster of jurisdiction of the court whose judgment is impugned is proven in the matter.

45.   Question of jurisdiction is of such primary importance that it is necessary to answer it in the context of the judgments impugned herein by Mr. Yazdani as we may not proceed further without resolving the question. We may, therefore, start our discussion from determining jurisdictional sanctity of the judgments under consideration.

46.   Before a court can claim to exercise judicial power, it must have jurisdiction positively vested in it by the Constitution or by or under any law (Article 175(2) of the Constitution) for jurisdiction is the authority of a court to hear a case and hence to exercise judicial power. {Fauji Foundation Vs. Shamim-ur-Rehman (PLD 1983 SC 457, 635)}.

47.   Powers of the Hon'ble High Court under Article 199 of the Constitution are not absolute but are subject to the Constitution. The phrase "subject to the Constitution", with which Article 199 of the Constitution begins, inter alia, means that jurisdiction under this Article is not available in matters excluded from jurisdiction of the Hon'ble High Court elsewhere in the Constitution. One such jurisdiction-ousting Article is Article 212 of the Constitution. This Article, inter alia, provides for establishment of administrative tribunals to exercise exclusive jurisdiction in respect of matters relating to the terms and conditions of persons who are or have been in the service of Pakistan, including disciplinary matters. The Legislature of the Punjab has enacted the Punjab Service Tribunals Act, 1974 for exclusive performance of functions enumerated in Article 212 of the Constitution read with the said Act. Section 4 of the Act ibid provides a right of appeal to a civil servant against any final order, whether original or appellate, made by a departmental authority in respect of any of the terms and conditions of his service. As per Section 2 (b) of the Punjab Service Tribunals Act, 1974, "civil servant" means a person who is or who has been a member of a civil service of the Province or holds or has held a civil post in connection with the affairs of the Province. Departmental Authority has been explained at the end of Section 4 of the Act ibid as any authority competent to make an order in respect of any of the terms and conditions of service of the civil servants. As held by a five-judge bench of the Hon'ble Supreme Court of Pakistan in a case reported as I.A. Sharwani case (PLD 1991 SCMR 1041), pension is one of conditions of service of the civil servants. Under section 18 of the Punjab Civil Servants Act, 1974, a retired civil servant is entitled to receive pension as may be prescribed. In accordance with Section 2 (1) (g) of the Punjab Civil Servants Act, 1974, "prescribed" means prescribed by rules. Rules mean rules framed under Section 23 (1) of the Act ibid or deemed to have been framed under Section 23 (2) of the Act ibid. Restoration of commuted value of pension is a subject which has been dealt with in the Punjab Civil Services Pension Rules, deemed to have been framed under Section 23 (2) of the Punjab Civil Servants Act, 1974 and having status of "existing laws" in terms of Article 268 of the Constitution and also protected by Article 241 of the Constitution. The Punjab Government Rules of Business, 2011 have been framed under Article 139 of the Constitution. Allocation of business among several departments has been made in the Second Schedule under Rule 3 (3) of the Rules ibid. According to serial # A (1) (h) under title "Finance Department" in the Second Schedule of the Punjab Government Rules of Business, 2011, formulation of laws, rules, policies and instructions relating to pay, allowances, pension, provident fund, leave etc. and interpretations thereof is the function of the Finance Department. The Punjab Civil Services Pension Rules, therefore, have the status of a final order made by a competent departmental authority regarding restoration of commuted portion of pension and any appeal against the said order shall lie with the Punjab Service Tribunal. No other departmental authority has any lawful competence to pass final orders in respect of pay, allowances, pension, provident fund, leave etc. and interpretations thereof in respect of the civil servants as defined in the Punjab Service Tribunals Act, 1974. If vires of statutory rules is challenged as affecting the terms and conditions of service, the bar in Article 212 of the Constitution applies; in such a case, the statutory rule or notification will be treated as an order appealable under the Service Tribunal Act. In this regard, reliance is placed on the

dictum of law laid down by the superior courts in their judgments reported as Iqan Ahmed Khurram Vs. Government (PLD 1980 SC 153) and Muhammad Hashim Khan Vs. Province of Balochistan (PLD 1976 Quetta 59). A civil servant cannot bypass the jurisdiction of the Service Tribunal by adding a ground of violation of the Fundamental Rights. "The Service Tribunal will have jurisdiction in a case which is founded on the terms and conditions of the service even if it involves the question of violation of the Fundamental Rights." (I.A. Sharwani case-PLD 1991 SCMR 1041). It has further been held that the Tribunal established under Article 212 can also examine the question whether an order of the departmental authority is with or without jurisdiction. (Muhammad Aslam Bajwa Vs. Federation of Pakistan ----PLD 1974 Lah. 545). Moreover, even if the challenge is on ground of mala fides, the jurisdiction of the Service Tribunal is exclusive. (Mazhar Hussain v. Secretary 1998 SCMR 1948). It has been held in judgments reported as Muhammad Anis Vs. Abdul Haseeb (PLD 1994 SC 539), Asadullah Rashid Vs. Muhammad Muneer (1998 SCMR 2129) and Khalid Mahmood Watto Vs. Govt. of Punjab (1998 SCMR 2280) that an administrative tribunal established under Article 212 of the Constitution is possessed with exclusive jurisdiction to consider, examine and thereby rule on the vires of a notification that is germane to the terms and conditions of service of civil servants. All questions relating to pension of those who have been civil servants, therefore, fall within exclusive jurisdiction of the Punjab Service Tribunal under Article 212 of the Constitution and the Hon'ble High Court completely lacks jurisdiction in this regard. The subject-matter of pension of retired civil servants is outside the jurisdictional competence of the Hon'ble High Court under Article 199 of the Constitution.

48.   First and the Second A.A. Zuberi cases are silent on the question of jurisdiction. All other judgments of the Hon'ble High Court and of the learned Service Tribunal are primarily based upon the above said judgments. Petitions for leave to appeal of the Government of the Punjab were allowed by the Hon'ble Supreme Court in the following words:

> "After hearing learned Additional Advocate General Punjab, leave to appeal is granted inter alia to consider as to whether in view of the provisions of Article 212 of the Constitution of Islamic Republic of Pakistan and the judgment in the case titled Accountant General vs. Abdul Majeed Babar (1990 SCMR 790), a constitution petition under Article 199 before the High Court was maintainable? As a short point is involved, the office is directed to prepare appeals on the present record with liberty to the parties to file additional documents if so advised within a week. The appeals are to be listed for hearing after three weeks."

49.   The question of jurisdiction was determined by the Hon'ble Supreme Court in the Ismail Tayer case. The Hon'ble Supreme Court has not held in the Ismail Tayer case that the Hon'ble High Court has jurisdiction concerning any matter enumerated in Article 212 of the Constitution and entrusted to the Punjab Service Tribunal. The Hon'ble Supreme Court in para 7 of the Ismail Tayer case has referred to a judgment reported as Government of Punjab, through Secretary Education, Civil Secretariat, Lahore and others Vs. Sameena Parveen and others (2009 SCMR 1) wherein it has been held that a decision of the Tribunal or of the Supreme Court in respect of service matters is binding. By holding so, the inescapable consequence is that no entity, including the Hon'ble High Court, other than the Tribunal or the Supreme Court is competent to adjudicate upon matters enumerated in Article 212 of the Constitution. This is obvious for more than one reasons. Firstly, prescription of one is prohibition of another; and secondly, jurisdictions conferred vide Article 199 and 212 of the Constitution are exclusive and are not concurrent. If pension of retired civil servants is a subject-matter falling within exclusive jurisdiction of the learned Service Tribunal, then, no stretch of imagination or reasoning can drag it under purview of the Hon'ble High Court. Judgments of the Hon'ble High Court on the question of pension of the retired civil servants are, therefore, without jurisdiction, hence, void and of no legal effect.

50.   If a Service Tribunal is in existence under Article 212 of the Constitution and a civil servant files a petition under Article 199 of the Constitution in respect of any of his conditions of service and of appointment, the Hon'ble High Court has to invoke its constitutional jurisdiction only if

    (1) The Service Tribunal lacks jurisdiction in that particular matter;
    (2) No other adequate and efficacious remedy is available to the petitioner;
    (3) The civil servant is an aggrieved person;
    (4) Disputed questions of facts are not involved;
    (5) Territorial jurisdiction of the High Court extends to the parties involved; and
    (6) The respondents fall within the definition of person as given in Article 199 of the Constitution

51.   Finding answers to the above threshold questions as a condition-precedent to invoke jurisdiction is certain to ensure that the Hon'ble High Court takes up a matter relating to conditions of appointment and of service brought before it by a civil servant only if that matter does not fall within jurisdiction of the Service Tribunal and other conditions enabling the Hon'ble High Court to exercise its constitutional jurisdiction are fulfilled. This criterion is obvious and free from ambiguity. It cannot be said that insistence on the desirability to follow it would have adverse impact on the independence of judiciary as the idea of independence of judiciary does not include impunity for the Hon'ble judges to cross jurisdictional barriers erected by the Constitution. Independence of judiciary is necessary to do justice in accordance with law in cases falling within jurisdiction of the court taking cognizance of the matter. It does not require a licence to do violence to the Constitution and the laws competently framed thereunder to perform the duty of provision of adjudicatory services. If a person claims that he needs IQ level of Einstein to ascertain whether a matter agitated by a civil servant with respect to his conditions of appointment and of service falls within jurisdiction of a High Court or not, then he needs to be quarantined one thousand miles away from the building of the Hon'ble High Court and must not be allowed to see the building of a High Court even on Google maps. And if that person succeeds to outwit the gatekeepers, Article 209 of the Constitution must come forward to nip the misconduct in the bud.

52.   We are not in agreement with the proposition that the Hon'ble Supreme Court can deal with matters covered by or under Article 212 of the Constitution through invoking its jurisdiction under Article 185 of the Constitution. The Hon'ble Supreme Court can deal with such matters under Article 212(3) and 184(3) of the Constitution provided the conditions specified therein are fulfilled. Article 184(3) grants original jurisdiction to the Hon'ble Supreme Court if the matter involves a question of public importance with reference to the enforcement of any of the fundamental rights and Article 212(3) provides that an appeal to the Supreme Court from a judgment, decree, order or sentence of an Administrative Court or Tribunal shall lie only if the Supreme Court, being satisfied that the case involves a substantial question of law of public importance, grants leave to appeal. Whereas Article 184(3) of the Constitution is invocable if the conditions of question of public importance and enforcement of fundamental rights, Article 212(3) can be invoked only if the case involves a substantial question of law of public importance. Article 185 of the Constitution, reproduced below, does not prescribe any such condition-precedent for invoking appellate jurisdiction of the Hon'ble Supreme Court:

    "185. Appellate jurisdiction of Supreme Court. __
    (1)   Subject to this Article, the Supreme Court shall have jurisdiction to hear and determine appeals from judgements, decrees, final orders or sentences of a High Court.
    (2)   An appeal shall lie to the Supreme Court from any judgement, decree, final order or sentence of a High Court—

(a) if the High Court has on appeal reversed an order of acquittal of an accused person and sentenced him to death or to transportation for life or imprisonment for life; or, on revision, has enhanced a sentence to a sentence as aforesaid; or

(b) if the High Court has withdrawn for trial before itself any case from any court subordinate to it and has in such trial convicted the accused person and sentenced him as aforesaid; or

(c) if the High Court has imposed any punishment on any person for contempt of the High Court; or

(d) if the amount or value of the subject-matter of the dispute in the court of first instance was, and also in dispute in appeal is, not less than fifty thousand rupees or such other sum as may be specified in that behalf by Act of [Majlis-e-Shoora (Parliament)] and the judgment, decree or final order appealed from has varied or set aside the judgment, decree or final order of the court immediately below; or

(e) if the judgment, decree or final order involves directly or indirectly some claim or question respecting property of the like amount or value and the judgment, decree or final order appealed from has varied or set aside the judgment, decree or final order of the court immediately below; or

(f) if the High Court certifies that the case involves a substantial question of law as to the interpretation of the Constitution.

(3) An appeal to the Supreme Court from a judgment, decree, order or sentence of a High Court in a case to which clause (2) does not apply shall lie only if the Supreme Court grants leave to appeal."

53. Constitution is the fundamental and supreme law of the land. Each and every word of the Constitution has to be given full effect. The Constitution has envisaged indulgence of the Hon'ble Supreme Court in the matters entrusted exclusively to the administrative tribunals created under its Article 212 in original jurisdiction only if the two conditions spelled out in Article 184(3) are fulfilled and in appellate jurisdiction if requirements of Article 212 (3) of the Constitution are satisfied. Prescription of one is prohibition of another. The appellate jurisdiction under Article 185 of the Constitution is, therefore, not available in respect of judgments of the Hon'ble High Court under Article 199 of the Constitution dealing with conditions of appointment and of service of the civil servants exclusively entrusted to the Service Tribunal. If an Hon'ble High Court travels beyond its jurisdiction under Article 199 of the Constitution and encroaches upon the territory exclusively reserved for the Service Tribunal, the aggrieved party has the remedy of filing an application under Section 12(2) of the Code of the Civil Procedure, 1908 to the same court explaining lack of jurisdiction of the court in the matter. If that application is dismissed, Section 3(2) of the Law Reforms Ordinance, 1972 provides the remedy of intra-court appeal. If the intra-court appeal is dismissed, the aggrieved party may knock the door of the Hon'ble Supreme Court under Article 185 of the Constitution. The Hon'ble Supreme Court may refuse leave to appeal on the ground that it deals with service issues of the civil servants in an appeal against a judgment of the learned Service Tribunal in matters falling within exclusive jurisdiction of the Service Tribunal and that too only if it raises a substantial question of law of public importance and not through entertaining an appeal against a judgment of the Hon'ble High

Court. This declaration of the Hon'ble Supreme Court will make the judgment of the Hon'ble High Court void and of no legal effect. The Hon'ble Supreme Court is not required to deal with any matter under Article 185 of the Constitution in case it finds a matter exclusively entrusted to the Service Tribunal and consequently the jurisdiction of the Hon'ble High Court ousted in that matter after making a declaration regarding absence of jurisdiction of the Hon'ble High Court. If the Hon'ble Supreme Court arrives at the conclusion that the Hon'ble High Court has invoked its jurisdiction under Article 199 of the Constitution on an application of a civil servant on a matter which does not fall within jurisdiction of the learned Service Tribunal, then the Hon'ble Supreme Court can competently exercise its appellate jurisdiction under Article 185 of the Constitution by allowing leave to appeal to consider the questions allowed to be considered in the leave granting order. Moreover, the principle of merger shall apply to a judgment given by an appellate court if the appellate court has jurisdiction in the matter and not otherwise.

54.   The scope of appeal under Article 212(3) of the Constitution has authoritatively been determined by the Hon'ble Supreme Court in a case reported as Secretary, Revenue Division, Islamabad Vs. Iftikhar Ahmad Tabassam (2019 PLD 563 Supreme Court) in these words:

> "11. ----The remedy under Article 212(3) is, therefore, not an appeal in the ordinary sense of the word but is a unique constitutional jurisdiction that is to be exercised if the question of law raised before the Court impinges on the rights of the public or a segment of public or a community of civil servants. Thus any question of law (i) that involves interpretation of the law, rules, instructions, notifications or governmental policy; (ii) that has not been finally settled by the Supreme Court or is not free from difficulty or ambiguity or calls for discussion of alternative views1 (iii) that highlights a state of uncertainty in the law, arising from a contradictory precedent or (iv) that points out blatant abuse of due process, may pass for a substantial question of law of public importance. On the other hand, a mere factual inter-party dispute, devoid of the nature of questions of law, mentioned above, will not attract the jurisdiction of this Court under article 212(3) of the Constitution.
>
> 12. The framers of our Constitution by giving exclusivity to the constitutional jurisdiction under Article 212(3) also underlined that the Tribunal is the final forum of fact and the law (other than
> a substantial question of law of public importance, as discussed above). As a matter of background it is useful to remember that a civil servant has a remedial structure of in-house appeal or representation before the concerned authority and then the facility of appeal before the Service Tribunal. This adjudicatory or dispute resolution process reaches finality at the Tribunal unless the aggrieved party can invoke the constitutional jurisdiction under Article 212(3) by raising substantial question of public importance." 2

55.   Thus, the threshold requirements under Article 212(3) and 185(3) of the Constitution are not identical. In matters enumerated under Article 185(2), an appeal to the Supreme Court shall lie. In other matters, appeal is not a right but only filing of a petition for leave to appeal is a right and appeal lies only if the leave to appeal is granted. Granting leave to appeal is, generally, restricted to the questions framed in the leave granting order. What

1 see AIR 1962 SC 1314 or Sarkar on Civil Procedure Code, vol 1, 11th edition. p.665.
(Footnote herein was footnote 2 in the PLD as well website of the Hon'ble Supreme Court)
2 Serial number in paragraph 11 corrected as serial number (iii) was missing therein which has been assumed a clerical or typographical mistake.

cannot be done directly is also not allowed to be done indirectly. Requirements of Article 212(3) of the Constitution cannot be bypassed through taking up matters exclusively reserved for the machinery and subject to the conditions specified in Article 212 of the Constitution by dealing with the same matters under Article 185(3) of the Constitution where conditions of Article 212(3) are not applicable. It is, therefore, not admissible to allow a party to invoke the appellate jurisdiction of the Hon'ble Supreme Court under Article 185(3) of the Constitution in a matter exclusively entrusted to a Service Tribunal and assailable in appellate jurisdiction of the Hon'ble Supreme Court under Article 212(3) of the Constitution.

56.   The judicial organ of the state starts losing its effectiveness and the consequent respect if it delivers judgments which are not legally enforceable for want of jurisdiction. Process of the court does not produce intended results if it is too late, gives judgments which are incapable of execution and frequently need contempt of court proceedings for implementation of the judgments. It is an acknowledged principle that the dignity of a judge and courts must rest more on the conduct of Hon'ble judges, the soundness and speaking nature of their verdicts more than resort to the contempt of court law. Dignity of courts that rests merely on resort to contempt law is said to be resting on fragile foundations. And in case of judgments delivered without jurisdiction, resort to the contempt of court proceedings is futile as the jurisdictional want is a valid defence in contempt of court proceedings. We may elaborate this point in some detail.

57.   Jurisdictions to hear cases and initiate contempt proceedings are co-extensive. Where there is no jurisdiction to hear a case, there is no jurisdiction to initiate contempt proceedings. A person may be proceeded against on the charges of contempt of court if he disobeys an order of the court he is legally bound to obey. No one is legally bound to obey a void order made in absence of jurisdiction. Holding otherwise would mean that in matters outside jurisdiction of a court, the court can deliver judgments and can get those judgments implemented through initiating proceedings on the charges of contempt of court if the judgments are not complied with. This conclusion could grant non-compliance of a judgment made without jurisdiction the status of the Constitution or the law which are the only sources of jurisdiction under Article 175(2) of the Constitution. This militancy against law, reason and logic is simply intolerable for a man who is not a certified lunatic.

58.   Justice (R) Fazal Karim, an Hon'ble retired Judge, Supreme Court of Pakistan, at pages 386-387 of Volume-1 of his book "Judicial Review of Public Actions" (First Edition) has explained the principle that a party may ignore an order without jurisdiction in the following words:

> "A party against whom an order without jurisdiction has been made may ignore it in the sense that it may not have it formally set aside in appeal or revision under the statute under which it was purportedly made and this fact will not disentitle him from challenging it in collateral proceedings,3 e.g. by means of a petition under Article 199 of the Constitution, nor would the fact that the appeal or revision had been filed after the prescribed period of limitation and had been rejected on that ground by itself be a ground for refusing the relief in appropriate proceedings that the order was without jurisdiction.4 Or, the party may ignore the order till the same is enforced against him or his rights are otherwise affected by it, as in Ali Abbas v, Vishan Singh,5 where the permanent allottees of

---

3   Ch. Altaf Hussain v. Chief Settlement Commissioner PLD 1965 SC 68, also see Ali Muhammad v. Hussain Baksh PLD 1976 SC 37.

4   Ali Muhammad v. Hussain Baksh PLD 1976 SC 37.

land did not move in the matter until proceedings were commenced for their ejectment; or if the judgment, order or decree which is relevant under Article 54, 55 or 56 of Qanun-e-Shahadat, 1984, has been proved by the adverse party to a suit or proceeding, the party concerned may show that the same was delivered by a court not competent to deliver it6. It is in this sense that the proposition that an act or order which is a nullity has simply to be ignored and proceedings need not be initiated to get it annulled7 or that if an order is without jurisdiction and void, then it need not be formally set aside8, is to be understood. The reason behind this principle is that if an order is a nullity, there is nothing to appeal against; and it is not, therefore, incumbent upon the party concerned to file an appeal or revision against it, for its omission to do such a step "could not convert an order made without jurisdiction into an order passed by court of competent jurisdiction."9 Thus in Yusoff Ali v. The King10, a case decided under Section 403 Cr. P.C., it was held that if the orders were a nullity, there was nothing to appeal against. The Government, if embarrassed by the order of acquittal might have appealed, but the omission to take such a step, which was not incumbent, could not convert an order made without jurisdiction into an order passed by a court of competent jurisdiction."

59.   As regards contempt of an order without jurisdiction, Hon'ble Justice (R) Fazal Karim, at page 387 of Volume-1 of his book "Judicial Review of Public Actions" (First Edition), has opined as under:

"Under a written Constitution, the Courts have only such jurisdiction as is conferred upon them by the Constitution or laws made under it.

It seems to be well-settled in America11 as well as in Pakistan12 that disobedience or disregard of a court's order which is without

---

5   PLD 1967 SC 294

6   Article 58 of Qanun-e-Shahadat, 1984.

7   Mahmud Alam v. Mehdi Hussain PLD 1970 Lah. 6 at 26

8   Ali Muhammad v. Hussain Baksh PLD 1976 SC 37 at 39.

9   Yusoff Ali v. The King PLD1949 PC 108, relied upon in Khuda Baksh v. Khushi Mohammad PLD 1976 SC 208.

10   PLD 1949 PC 108 relied upon in Khuda Baksh v. Khushi Mohammad PLD 1976 SC 208.

11   17 Corpus Juris Secondum, Section 14: "Disobedience of or resistance to a void mandate, order, judgment or decree or one issued by a court without jurisdiction of the subject matter and parties litigant is not contempt-----."

12   Sultan Ali v. Noor Hussain (PLD 1949 Lah. 301 in which a High Court Judge had, in a revision from an order of a Civil Judge in a civil suit, stayed the proceedings of an election petition before the Election Commission. The Election Commission in disobedience to the High Court's order continued the proceedings and the question was whether this was contempt. Held by majority that the order of the High Court judge was without jurisdiction and

jurisdiction is not contempt of court. This will be so despite the fact that the order without jurisdiction has attained finality.13

60.   In Indian jurisdiction, in a judgment reported as Vivekanand Atmaram Chitale Vs. Vidyavardhini Sabha (1984 Mah LJ 520), it has been held as follows:

"22. It is well settled that an order without jurisdiction is a nullity, which can be ignored with impunity. This is the ratio of the decision of this Court in Abdullamiyan Abdulrehaman v. Government of Bombay 44 Bom LR 577: (AIR 1942 Bom 257) (FB). In that case, relying on the decisions (1) in Surannanna v. Secretary of State (1900) 2 Bom LR 261, (2) Malke Jappa v. Secretary of State Rasulkhan Hamadkhan v. Secretary of State 17 Bom LR 513 : (AIR 1915 Bom 72), (4) Dhanji v. Secretary of State 23 Bom LR 279 : (AIR 1921 Bom 381), (5) Padaya v. Secretary of State 25 Bom LR 1160 : (AIR 1924 Bom 273), (6) Suleman v. Secretary of State 30 Bom LR 431 : (AIR 1928 Bom 180), (7) Menibhai v. Nadiad City Municipality (29 BLR 1963) (Sic) AIR 1927 Bom 53, the learned Judges held that where an authority which purports to pass an order is acting without jurisdiction, the purported order is a nullity and it is not necessary for a party, who objects to that order, to apply to set it aside. He can rely on its invalidity when it is set up against him although he has not taken steps to set it aside.

23. Another decision, which is pressed into service by Shri Mahendra Shah in support of the above mentioned proposition is Sultan Ali v. Nur Hussain AIR 1949 Lah 131: (1949-50 Cri LJ 598) (FB). In that case Election Petition Commission was sought to be indicted for contempt of Court for disregarding the order of stay passed by a single Judge of the Lahore High Court. It was found that the order was without jurisdiction and the Full Bench by majority held that the order was void and bound nobody and disobedience of that order not amount to contempt of Court.

24. Reliance was also placed on behalf of the contemnors on the decision of the Supreme Court in Kiran Singh v. Chaman Paswan. In that case their Lordships held that it is the fundamental principle that a decree passed by a Court without jurisdiction is a nullity and that its invalidity can be set up whenever and wherever it is sought to be enforced or relied upon even at the stage of execution and even in collateral proceedings. It was further held that a defect of jurisdiction, whether it is pecuniary or territorial, or whether it is in respect of the subject-matter of the action, strikes at the very authority of the Court

the Commission's disobedience did not amount to contempt of court. In Province of Punjab v. Muhammad Zafar Bukhari (PLD 1997 SC 351), the High Court made an order, which, by Article 212 of the Constitution, it was not empowered to make. The order was not implemented and it was held that as the order was without jurisdiction, no contempt of court was committed.

13   In Muhammad Zafar Bukhari case (PLD 1997 SC 351), the order of the High Court was without jurisdiction; against it leave to appeal was refused by the Supreme Court on ground of limitation. Thus, it attained finality; yet when the question of contempt arose, it was held that the High Court's order being without jurisdiction and void, no question of obeying it arose, and no contempt was committed.

to pass any decree and such a defect cannot be cured even by consent of parties. It would be worthwhile to observe that this decision was ignored by the Madras High Court while deciding Nalla Senapathi v. Sri. Ambal Mills. The same proposition was reiterated by their Lordships of the Supreme Court in Amrit Bhikaji Kale v. Kashinath Janardhan Trade .

25. In Dwarkadas Mulji v. Shantilal Laxmidas 1980 Mah LJ 404 Sawant J. elaborately considered the question whether the breach of an undertaking given by a party in a proceeding, which is ab initio void for lack of jurisdiction, amounts to contempt. While answering the question in the negative, the learned Judge rightly distinguished the decision of the Allahabad High Court in State of U.P. v. Ratan Shukla and placed reliance upon the decision of the Punjab High Court in Narayan Singh v. S. Hardayal Singh. He also quoted American Law on the subject as found in Corpus Juris Secondum Vol. XVII para 19. The relevant quotation is as follows: -

> "Disobedience of, or resistance to, a void mandate, order, judgment or decree or one issued by a Court without jurisdiction of the subject matter and parties litigant, is not contempt, and where the Court has no jurisdiction to make the order, no waiver can cut off the rights of the party to attack its validity".

In support of the proposition, which the learned Judge laid down, he also placed reliance on the decisions of the Supreme Court of the United States in Ex Parte Rowland (1881) 26 Law ed. 861, Ex Parte Fisk (1884) 28 Law ed. 117, Ex Parte Sawyer (1887) 31 Law ed. 402 United States of America v. United Mine Workers of America (1946) 91 Law ed. 884 and Joseph F. Maggio v. Raymond Zeitz (1947) 92 Law ed. 476, in which unanimous view was taken that there is no contempt when breach is of the order passed in the proceedings, which are ab initio void for lack of jurisdiction from their very inception."

61.   Hon'ble Supreme Court of India has observed in a case reported as Chirangilal Shrilal Goenka (deceased) through LRs. Vs. Jasjit Singh (at p. 1448 of AIR SCW):

> "18. It is settled that a decree passed by a Court without jurisdiction on the subject-matter or on the grounds on which the decree made which goes to the root of its jurisdiction or lacks inherent jurisdiction is a coram non judice. A decree passed by such a Court is a nullity and is non-est. Its invalidity can be set up whenever it is sought to be enforced or is acted upon as a foundation for a right, even at the stage of execution or in collateral proceedings. The defect of jurisdiction strikes at the very authority of the Court to pass decree which cannot be cured by consent or waiver of the party."

62.   In a case reported in 1980 Maharashtra Law Journal page 404, it has been held that breach of an undertaking given in a proceeding which is void ab initio does not amount to contempt of Court. It has been held in a case reported as AIR 1978 Cal 37 that:

> "It is well settled that if the Court passes any order without jurisdiction the order is a nullity and is void."

63.   It has been held in a case reported as PLD 1958 SC 104 that:

> "And if on the basis of a void order subsequent orders have been passed either by the same authority or by other authorities, the whole

series of such orders, together with the superstructure of rights and obligations built upon them, must, unless some statute or principle of law recognizing as legal the changed position, of the parties is in operation, fall to the ground because such orders have as little legal foundation as the void order on which they are founded."

64.   Are judicial verdicts meant to be ignored or to resolve controversies and thus provide relief, maintain order and ensure certainty? Certainly not to be ignored. If judgments are delivered which can be defied and ignored with impunity and which are incapable of neither binding the party against which these are given nor giving any relief to the aggrieved litigant simply because of want of jurisdiction, then delivering such judgments amounts to lowering the dignity and respect of the institution of judiciary. We cannot put premium on the tendency to indulge in any matter if lawful jurisdiction is missing. Allowing courts to assume jurisdiction in matters not brought within their jurisdiction would result into causing contempt and disrespect for the courts.

65.   For the above reasons, it is necessary to ascertain whether the Hon'ble High Court had jurisdiction in the matter of any question relating to restoration of commuted value of pension of the retired civil servants. The question can be settled very easily by asking the question that whether this matter falls within jurisdiction of the leaned Service Tribunal. The subject of pension of the civil servants has been dealt with in the Punjab Civil Servants Act, 1974. It is one of conditions of service of a civil servant. It is deferred part of remuneration earned by a civil servant after putting in satisfactory service for prescribed minimum period of time. It is payable after retirement in accordance with law. Any grievance of a civil servant in respect of his pension is assailable before the Punjab Service Tribunal through an appeal. The reason given in the case reported as Ghulam Yasin Vs. Accountant-General Punjab and others (2014 PLC (C.S.) 73) that absence of an adverse final order of a departmental authority keeps jurisdiction of the Hon'ble High Court intact is transparently fallacious. If nothing adversely affecting a civil servant is in the field, then the civil servant is not an aggrieved person so as to be able to invoke jurisdiction of the Hon'ble High Court under Article 199 of the Constitution as being an aggrieved person is a condition-precedent except in case of writ of quo warrant or of habeas corpus. In Ismail Tayer case, the Hon'ble Supreme Court invoked its appellate jurisdiction under Article 212 (3) of the Constitution. Leave to appeal in the Ismail Tayer case was granted to examine jurisdiction of the Hon'ble High Court in the matter. It is not appropriate to assume that the judgment in the Ismail Tayer case did not answer the question framed in the leave granting order. The Hon'ble Court has decided the issue in favour of jurisdiction of the learned Service Tribunal. With this settlement, all judgments of the Hon'ble High Court on the question of restoration of commuted value of pension of the retired civil servants are rendered void and of no legal effect being rendered without jurisdiction. These judgments of the Hon'ble Lahore High Court were not implementable after having been declared to have been delivered without jurisdiction. The judgment of the learned Punjab Service Tribunal was totally based upon the judgments of the Hon'ble High Court and no additional legal reason was recorded by the learned Service Tribunal while giving relief to Mr. Ismail Tayer. Thus, the only judgment lawfully implementable was the judgment of the Hon'ble Supreme Court known as Ismail Tayer case. We, therefore, conclude and hold that all judgments of the Hon'ble Lahore High Court on the question of restoration of commuted value of pension of the civil servants are without jurisdiction and hence, nullity in eyes of law and absolutely without any legal effect.

66.   Now we see the case of the Hon'ble judges who were elevated from the subordinate judiciary but retired before completion of five years' service as judges of the Hon'ble High Court and who were refused pension as retired judges of the High Court.

67.   Judges of the subordinate judiciary are governed by the Punjab Civil Servants Act, 1973. They are civil servants, but on their elevation as judge of the High Court, Article 205 read with Fifth Schedule of the Constitution and the High Court Judges (Leave, Pension and Privileges) Order, 1997 (President's Order No.3 of 1997) becomes applicable in the matter

of their remuneration. As per definition of the term 'remuneration' given in Article 260 of the Constitution, remuneration includes salary and pension. So long they continue to serve as judges of the High Court, they remain entitled to salary as specified in the High Court Judges (Leave, Pension and Privileges) Order, 1997. They do fall within the definition of persons in the Service of Pakistan and are public servants within the meaning of the Pakistan Penal Code but in the matters covered by the High Court Judges (Leave, Pension and Privileges) Order, 1997, they do not remain governable under the Punjab Civil Servants Act or other legal instruments applicable to the civil servants. Their disciplinary matters come under the purview of Article 209 of the Constitution and the Punjab Employees Efficiency, Discipline and Accountability Act, 2006 (Act XII of 2006) ceases to be applicable to them.

68.   If a confirmed judge of the Hon'ble High Court elevated from the subordinate judiciary retires from service as such judge, there are two options in respect of his pension which are as follows:

(a) Grant of pension as judge of the High Court under paragraph 14 read with paragraph 15 of the President's Order No.3 of 1997 if minimum length of service as judge of the High Court is five years or more; and

(b) Grant of pension as civil servant under paragraph 16 of the President's Order No.3 of 1997, reproduced below, if minimum length of service as judge of the High Court is less than five years:

"A Judge who immediately before his appointment as such was a member of a civil service in Pakistan or was holding a post in connection with the affairs of the Federation or of a Province and who does not fulfill the conditions laid down in paragraph 14 shall, on retirement, be entitled to such pension as would have been admissible to him in his service or post, had he not been appointed a Judge, his service as a Judge being treated as service for the purpose of calculating that pension."

69.   After providing the dispensation of adding service as judge of the High Court to service in the Service of Pakistan of a judge with less than five years of service through its paragraph 16, the High Court Judges (Leave, Pension and Privileges) Order, 1997 loses its relevance and applicability to the retired civil servants.

70.   Prior to elevation from the subordinate judiciary, the Punjab Judicial Service Rules, framed under Section 23(1) of the Punjab Civil Servants Act, 1974 are applicable to the District and Sessions Judges. The Punjab Subordinate Judiciary Service Tribunal created under the Punjab Subordinate Judiciary Service Tribunal Act, 1991 (Pb. Act XII of 1991) has been entrusted with the exclusive jurisdiction in respect of matters relating to the terms and conditions of service of the members of subordinate judiciary including disciplinary matters. Pension of the members of the service of the subordinate judiciary is dealt with by and under the Punjab Civil Servants Act. If, on account of less than five years of service as judge of the Hon'ble High Court, the civil servants elevated from the subordinate judiciary are held not entitled to receive pension as such judge, all laws and rules applicable to them as civil servants are once again attracted except the length of service as judge of the High Court which is added to the service as civil servant for the purpose of determining years of qualifying service reckonable towards pension. Section 2(e) of the Punjab Subordinate Judiciary Service Tribunal Act   defines "Member of subordinate judiciary" as meaning and including all Judicial Officers who are or have been under the administrative control of the Lahore High Court. Any matter relating to pension of a retired civil servant falling within the definition of member of subordinate judiciary falls within exclusive jurisdiction of the Punjab Subordinate Judiciary Service Tribunal.

71.   We asked the learned Advocate General, Punjab and the learned counsels for the retired judges to quote any example, prior to the Fifth Judges' pension case, of a confirmed judge of the Hon'ble High Court with less than five years of service as such judge whose

pension was not finalized under the Punjab Civil Servants Act or the rules framed thereunder. They could cite no example. Departmental interpretation on the subject offered by the learned Advocate General, Punjab and consistent practice of more than a century lead but to one conclusion: when constitutional provisions with regard to remuneration of Hon'ble judges of the Hon'ble High Court become inapplicable because of less than required minimum length of service, the pension of judges elevated from the subordinate judiciary is determined in accordance with the legal dispensation which would have been applicable to them had they not been elevated with the sole difference that the service rendered as judge of the High Court is added to the length of their service as member of the subordinate judiciary for the purpose of calculating service qualifying for pension.

72.   It is relevant to note that in the Third judges' pension case, it was held that the judges of the High Court with less than five years' service as such judges are not entitled to pension as retired judges of the High Court. It was not held in that case that the judges elevated from the subordinate judiciary having requisite service qualifying them for pension as civil servants are not entitled to pension as civil servants. The leaned Attorney General for Pakistan has confirmed before us that pension of the such judges belonging to the subordinate judiciary was discontinued as retired judges of the High Court as a result of the Third judges' pension case but they started to get their pension as retired civil servants and the service as judge of the High Court was added to their service qualifying for pension. What is deducible from this is that it has been consistent practice that whenever a dispensation governing remuneration of a judge of a High Court ceases to be effective, the dispensation applicable to him as civil servant revives and becomes applicable. When we say that the Punjab Subordinate Judiciary Service Tribunal provides the remedy in respect of pension of the members of the subordinate judiciary who cease to be governed by the High Court Judges (Leave, Pension and Privileges) Order, 1997 in the matter of their remuneration, jurisdiction of the Hon'ble High Court under Article 199 of the Constitution is ousted as a necessary implication. Existence of an administrative tribunal under Article 212 of the Constitution blocks operation of Article 199 of the Constitution to the extent of matters falling within exclusive jurisdiction of the administrative tribunal. Since in the instant case, the administrative tribunal is in existence and has jurisdiction in the matter of pension of members of the subordinate judiciary, therefore, the Hon'ble High Court lacks jurisdiction in the matter.

73.   As observed earlier in this judgment, the Hon'ble Supreme Court has appellate jurisdiction under Article 212(3) of the Constitution in respect of matters exclusively falling within jurisdiction of a Service Tribunal; this appellate jurisdiction is not available under Article 185 of the Constitution if the matter is within exclusive jurisdiction of a Service Tribunal. If a matter falling within exclusive jurisdiction of the Service Tribunal is brought before the Hon'ble Supreme Court in the form of an appeal against a judgment of the Hon'ble High Court made in its constitutional jurisdiction under Article 199 of the Constitution, the Hon'ble Supreme Court has to make a declaration of absence of jurisdiction of the Hon'ble High Court in its leave refusing order and that is the end of the case. Appellate jurisdiction under Article 185 is invoked only if a judgment made with jurisdiction is appealed against and the Supreme Court finds the questions involved worthy of consideration in its appellate jurisdiction.

74.   In view of the above, we do hereby hold and declare that the Fourth Judges' pension case was heard by the Hon'ble Lahore High Court, Lahore without jurisdiction and hence, the consent judgment delivered therein is void and of no legal effect. Further, the consent judgment given by the Hon'ble Supreme Court in the Fifth Judges' pension case was without fulfilling conditions-precedent specified in Article 212 of the Constitution. The Hon'ble Supreme Court lacks appellate jurisdiction under Article 185 of the Constitution in respect of a judgment of the Hon'ble High Court in matters falling within exclusive jurisdiction of a Service Tribunal. Whenever jurisdiction of the Hon'ble Supreme Court is invoked in such a matter under Article 185 of the Constitution, the Hon'ble Supreme Court has to decline

leave to appeal confirming want of jurisdiction of the Hon'ble High Court in the matter. Thus, the consent order in the Fifth Judges' pension case is without jurisdiction and is incapable of confirming rights and obligations of the parties.

75. Just to make the matter crystal clear, the objections raised by the counsels of the retired civil servants are answered hereinbelow, seriatim:

    a) Question of want of jurisdiction can be raised at any time and at any stage;

    b) Full faith and credit is available only to the judgments made with lawful jurisdiction;

    c) A party alleging want of jurisdiction has to prove it;

    d) The Punjab Subordinate Judiciary Service Tribunal Act, 1991 is applicable to the confirmed judges of the Hon'ble High Court if they are not entitled to pension under the High Court Judges (Leave, Pension and Privileges) Order, 1997;

    e) Article 209 is attracted if willful violation of an order of the Hon'ble Supreme Court is involved; and

    f) The Hon'ble Supreme Court lacks appellate jurisdiction under Article 185 in matters exclusively entrusted to the Service Tribunals under Article 212 of the Constitution.

76. After our declarations in the paragraphs hereinabove, we still feel need to proceed further in the matter in order to ascertain true import of the Ismail Tayer case and the Fifth Judges' pension case and matters inseparably connected therewith or ancillary thereto in order to bring clarity on the subject and to obviate, to the extent possible, chances of future litigation on the same issues.

Question # 2

Whether principle of merger applies to the judgment of the learned Punjab Service Tribunal in appeal of Mr. Muhammad Ismail Tayer?

77. The learned Advocate General, Punjab addresses us in detail on the applicability of the principle of merger in the context of the judgments relating to restoration of commuted value of pension. He submits that principle of merger applies to the first A.A. Zuberi case in view of the second A.A. Zuberi case but refusal of the Hon'ble Supreme Court to grant leave to appeal against the second A.A. Zuberi case on the ground of being time-barred does not attract principle of merger. He wants to make the point that what has been held in the second A.A. Zuberi case has not been declared valid by the Hon'ble Supreme Court. Dismissal of petition for leave to appeal by the Hon'ble Supreme Court vide order dated 10.12.2010 made the impugned judgment final only in the sense that no second petition for leave to appeal could lie, he explains adding that this finality cannot be extended to reasons and conclusions of the judgment against which leave to appeal was sought. He further argues that the second A.A. Zuberi case is void and of no legal effect so far as matter of restoration of commuted value of pension of the retired civil servants of the Government of the Punjab is concerned because of the reasons that the judgment has been delivered without jurisdiction, it relates to retired civil servants of the Federation and is based upon mistaken assumptions of fact. He argues that dismissal of appeals and petitions for leave to appeal of the Government of the Punjab in the Ismail Tayer case does not mean that the ratio decidendi of the second A.A. Zuberi case has been upheld by the Hon'ble Supreme Court. The short order and the reasons therefor in the Ismail Tayer case are in the context of the judgment of the learned Punjab Service Tribunal on the appeal of Mr. Muhammad Ismail Tayer and the judgment of the Hon'ble Supreme Court in this case attracts principle of merger, he submits. He claims that the principle of merger prescribes that there cannot be, at one and the same time, more than one operative order governing the same subject-matter and the judgment of the inferior court stands substituted with the judgment of the superior court irrespective of the fact whether order of the lower court is affirmed, reversed

or modified. He asserts that the legal tragedy in the instant matter is this that the second A.A. Zuberi case was got implemented by the Hon'ble Lahore High Court through contempt proceedings despite the fact that it was not in lawful existence in the matter of restoration of commuted value of pension of the civil servants of the Government of the Punjab and was in irreconcilable clash with the Ismail Tayer case. He opines that the lis at hand cannot satisfactorily be resolved if legality of the second A.A. Zuberi case is not ascertained with reference to its applicability on the civil servants of the Government of the Punjab.

78.   Mr. Yazdani submits that it is a text-book example of indiscipline to ignore valid judgment of the Hon'ble Supreme Court by the Hon'ble High Court despite written submissions of the highest-ranking officers of the Provincial Government (Chief Secretary and Finance Secretary) to the effect that the judgment of the Hon'ble Supreme Court in the Ismail Tayer case had duly been implemented and the second A.A. Zuberi case was void and non-existent in eyes of law. He wonders that the Hon'ble High Court simply ignored written statements of the Chief Secretary, Finance Secretary and members of the Complaint Cell though these written statements were relevant and contained legal arguments. He prays that the principle of merger be explained so that chances of miscarriage of justice in future are obviated.

79.   Learned counsels of the private respondents plead that the petition for grant of leave to appeal of the Federation against the second A.A. Zuberi case was refused by the Hon'ble Supreme Court for being time-barred. They contend that petition for leave to appeal against a judgment delivered by the learned Federal Service Tribunal, which was based upon the second A.A. Zuberi case, was dismissed by the Hon'ble Supreme Court of Pakistan vide its leave refusing order reported as Federation of Pakistan Vs. Ghulam Mustafa and others (2012 SCMR 1914). They argue that after dismissal of petitions for leave to appeal under Article 185(3) as well as Article 212(3) of the Constitution by the Hon'ble Supreme Court, the ratio decidendi of the second A.A. Zuberi case stands affirmed, authenticated and sanctified by the Hon'ble Supreme Court and any legal hair-splitting in the matter finally determined by the Hon'ble Supreme Court is uncalled for. They submit that implementation of the second A.A. Zuberi case by the Hon'ble High Court through contempt proceedings was necessary as the Government of the Punjab was not willing to comply with judicial orders given in the second A.A. Zuberi case. They are of the view that the Ismail Tayer case is complete endorsement of the ratio decidendi of the second A.A. Zuberi case. In this view of the matter, they plead that there is no need to reopen and re-litigate matters conclusively settled by the Hon'ble Supreme Court in the Ismail Tayer case.

80.   Adjudication of the rival contentions require correct exposition of the principle of merger. The Hon'ble Supreme Court of India extensively dealt with the principle of merger in its judgment reported as Kunhayammed & Ors Vs. State of Kerala & Anr (AIR 2000 SC 2587) in which it was held that:

> "The logic underlying the doctrine of merger is that there cannot be more than one decree or operative orders governing the same subject-matter at a given point of time. When a decree or order passed by inferior court, tribunal or authority was subjected to a remedy available under the law before a superior forum then, though the decree or order under challenge continues to be effective and binding, nevertheless its finality is put in jeopardy. Once the superior court has disposed of the lis before it either way - whether the decree or order under appeal is set aside or modified or simply confirmed, it is the decree or order of the superior court, tribunal or authority which is the final, binding and operative decree or order wherein merges the decree or order passed by the court, tribunal or the authority below. However, the doctrine is not of universal or unlimited application. The nature of jurisdiction exercised by the superior forum and the content

or subject-matter of challenge laid or which could have been laid shall have to be kept in view.

Stage of SLP and post-leave stage

The appellate jurisdiction exercised by the Supreme Court is conferred by Articles 132 to 136 of the Constitution. Articles 132, 133 and 134 provide when an appeal thereunder would lie and when not. Article 136 of the Constitution is a special jurisdiction conferred on the Supreme Court which is sweeping in its nature. It is a residuary power in the sense that it confers an appellate jurisdiction on the Supreme Court subject to the special leave being granted in such matters as may not be covered by the preceding articles. It is an overriding provision conferring a special jurisdiction providing for invoking of the appellate jurisdiction of Supreme Court not fettered by the sweep of preceding articles. Article 136 opens with a non-obstante clause and conveys a message that even in the field covered by the preceding articles, jurisdiction conferred by Article 136 is available to be exercised in an appropriate case. It is an untrammeled reservoir of power incapable of being confined to definitional bounds; the discretion conferred on the Supreme Court being subjected to only one limitation, that is, the wisdom and good sense or sense of justice of the Judges. No right of appeal is conferred upon any party; only a discretion is vested in Supreme Court to interfere by granting leave to an applicant to enter in its appellate jurisdiction not open otherwise and as of right. The exercise of jurisdiction conferred on this Court by Article 136 of the Constitution consists of two steps: (i) granting special leave to appeal; and (ii) hearing the appeal. This distinction is clearly demonstrated by the provisions of Order XVI of the Supreme Court Rules framed in exercise of the power conferred by Article 145 of the Constitution. Under Rule 4, the petition seeking special leave to appeal filed before the Supreme Court under Article 136 of the Constitution shall be in form No.28. No separate application for interim relief need be filed, which can be incorporated in the petition itself. If notice is ordered on the special leave petition, the petitioner should take steps to serve the notice on the respondent. The petition shall be accompanied by a certified copy of the judgment or order appealed from and an affidavit in support of the statement of facts contained in the petition. Under Rule 10, the petition for grant of special leave shall be put up for hearing ex-parte unless there be a caveat. The court, if it thinks fit, may direct issue of notice to the respondent and adjourn the hearing of the petition. Under Rule 13, the respondent to whom a notice in special leave petition is issued or who had filed a caveat, shall be entitled to oppose the grant of leave or interim orders without filing any written objections. He shall also be at liberty to file his objections only by setting out the grounds in opposition to the questions of law or grounds set out in the S.L.P. On hearing, the Court may refuse the leave and dismiss the petition for seeking special leave to appeal either ex-parte or after issuing notice to the opposite party. Under Rule 11, on the grant of special leave, the petition for special leave shall, subject to the payment of additional court fee, if any, be treated as the petition of appeal and it shall be registered and numbered as such. The appeal shall then be set down for hearing in accordance with the procedure laid down thereafter. Thus, a petition seeking grant of special leave to appeal and the appeal itself, though both dealt with by Article 136 of the Constitution, are two clearly distinct stages. In our opinion, the legal position which emerges is as under: -

1.   While hearing the petition for special leave to appeal, the Court is called upon to see whether the petitioner should be granted such leave or not. While hearing such petition, the Court is not exercising its appellate jurisdiction; it is merely exercising its discretionary jurisdiction to grant or not to grant leave to appeal. The petitioner is still outside the gate of entry though aspiring to enter the appellate arena of Supreme Court. Whether he enters or not would depend on the fate of his petition for special leave;

2.   If the petition seeking grant of leave to appeal is dismissed, it is an expression of opinion by the Court that a case for invoking appellate jurisdiction of the Court was not made out;

3.   If leave to appeal is granted the appellate jurisdiction of the Court stands invoked; the gate for entry in appellate arena is opened. The petitioner is in and the respondent may also be called upon to face him, though in an appropriate case, in spite of having granted leave to appeal, the court may dismiss the appeal without noticing the respondent;

4.   In spite of a petition for special leave to appeal having been filed, the judgment, decree or order against which leave to appeal has been sought for, continues to be final, effective and binding as between the parties. Once leave to appeal has been granted, the finality of the judgment, decree or order appealed against is put in jeopardy though it continues to be binding and effective between the parties unless it is a nullity or unless the Court may pass a specific order staying or suspending the operation or execution of the judgment, decree or order under challenge.

Dismissal at stage of special leave - without reasons - no res judicata, no merger

Having so analysed and defined the two stages of the jurisdiction conferred by Article 136, now we proceed to deal with a number of decisions cited at the Bar during the course of hearing and dealing with the legal tenor of an order of Supreme Court dismissing a special leave petition. In Workmen of Cochin Port Trust Vs. Board of Trustees of the Cochin Port Trust and Another 1978 (3) SCC 119, a Three-Judges Bench of this Court has held that dismissal of special leave petition by the Supreme Court by a non-speaking order of dismissal where no reasons were given does not constitute res judicata. All that can be said to have been decided by the Court is that it was not a fit case where special leave should be granted. That may be due to various reasons. During the course of the judgement, their Lordships have observed that dismissal of a special leave petition under Article

136 against the order of a Tribunal did not necessarily bar the entertainment of a writ petition under Article 226 against the order of the Tribunal. The decision of Madras High Court in The Management of W. India Match Co. Ltd. Vs. Industrial Tribunal, AIR 1958 Mad 398, 403 was cited before their Lordships. The High Court had taken the view that the right to apply for leave to appeal to Supreme Court under Article 136, if it could be called a right at all, cannot be equated to a right to appeal and that a High Court could not refuse to entertain an application under Article 226 of the Constitution on the ground that the aggrieved party could move Supreme Court under Article 136 of the Constitution. Their Lordships observed that such a broad statement of law is not quite accurate, although substantially it is correct.

Dismissal of SLP by speaking or reasoned order - no merger but Rule of discipline and Article 141 attracted.

The efficacy of an order disposing of a special leave petition under Article 136 of the Constitution came up for the consideration of Constitution Bench in Penu Balakrishna Iyer and Ors. Vs. Ariya M. Ramaswami Iyer and Ors. - AIR 1965 SC 165 in the context of revocation of a special leave once granted. This Court held that in a given case if the respondent brings to the notice of the Supreme Court facts which would justify the Court in revoking the leave earlier granted by it, the Supreme Court would in the interest of justice not hesitate to adopt that course. It was therefore held that no general rules could be laid down governing the exercise of wide powers conferred on this Court under Article 136; whether the jurisdiction of this Court under Article 136 should be exercised or not and if used, on what terms and conditions, is a matter depending on the facts of each case. If at the stage when special leave is granted the respondent-caveator appears and resists the grant of special leave and the ground urged in support of resisting the grant of special leave is rejected on merits resulting in grant of special leave, then it would not be open to the respondent to raise the same point over again at the time of the final hearing of the appeal. However, if the respondent/caveator does not appear, or having appeared, does not raise a point, or even if he raised a point and the Court does not decide it before grant of special leave, the same point can be raised at the time of final hearing. There would be no technical bar of res judicata. The Constitution Bench thus makes it clear that the order disposing of a special leave petition has finality of a limited nature extending only to the points expressly decided by it.

Leave granted - dismissal without reasons - merger results

It may be that in spite of having granted leave to appeal, the Court may dismiss the appeal on such grounds as may have provided foundation for refusing the grant at the earlier stage. But that will be a dismissal of appeal. The decision of this Court would result in superseding the decision under appeal attracting doctrine of merger. But if the same reasons had prevailed with this Court for refusing leave to appeal, the order would not have been an appellate order but only an order refusing to grant leave to appeal.

Once a special leave petition has been granted, the doors for the exercise of appellate jurisdiction of this Court have been let open. The order impugned before the Supreme Court becomes an order appealed against. Any order passed thereafter would be an appellate order and would attract the applicability of doctrine of merger. It would not make a difference whether the order is one of reversal or of modification or of dismissal affirming the order appealed against. It would also not make any difference if the order is a speaking or non- speaking one. Whenever this Court has felt inclined to apply its mind to the merits of the order put in issue before it though it may be inclined to affirm the same, it is customary with this Court to grant leave to appeal and thereafter dismiss the appeal itself (and not merely the petition for special leave) though at times the orders granting leave to appeal and dismissing the appeal are contained in the same order and at times the orders are quite brief. Nevertheless, the order shows the exercise of appellate jurisdiction and therein the merits of the order impugned having been subjected to judicial scrutiny of this Court."

81. The aforesaid judgment sums up conclusions of the Hon'ble Supreme Court of India in the following words:

> "(i)   Where an appeal or revision is provided against an order passed by a court, tribunal or any other authority before superior forum and such superior forum modifies, reverses or affirms the decision put in issue before it, the decision by the subordinate forum merges in the decision by the superior forum and it is the latter which subsists, remains operative and is capable of enforcement in the eye of law.
>
> (ii)   The jurisdiction conferred by Article 136 of the Constitution is divisible into two stages. First stage is upto the disposal of prayer for special leave to file an appeal. The second stage commences if and when the leave to appeal is granted and special leave petition is converted into an appeal.
>
> (iii)   Doctrine of merger is not a doctrine of universal or unlimited application. It will depend on the nature of jurisdiction exercised by the superior forum and the content or subject-matter of challenge laid or capable of being laid shall be determinative of the applicability of merger. The superior jurisdiction should be capable of reversing, modifying or affirming the order put in issue before it. Under Article 136 of the Constitution the Supreme Court may reverse, modify or affirm the judgment-decree or order appealed against while exercising its appellate jurisdiction and not while exercising the discretionary jurisdiction disposing of petition for special leave to appeal. The doctrine of merger can therefore be applied to the former and not to the latter.
>
> (iv)   An order refusing special leave to appeal may be a non-speaking order or a speaking one. In either case it does not attract the doctrine of merger. An order refusing special leave

to appeal does not stand substituted in place of the order under challenge. All that it means is that the Court was not inclined to exercise its discretion so as to allow the appeal being filed.

(v)   If the order refusing leave to appeal is a speaking order, i.e. gives reasons for refusing the grant of leave, then the order has two implications. Firstly, the statement of law contained in the order is a declaration of law by the Supreme Court within the meaning of Article 141 of the Constitution. Secondly, other than the declaration of law, whatever is stated in the order are the findings recorded by the Supreme Court which would bind the parties thereto and also the court, tribunal or authority in any proceedings subsequent thereto by way of judicial discipline, the Supreme Court being the apex court of the country. But, this does not amount to saying that the order of the court, tribunal or authority below has stood merged in the order of the Supreme Court rejecting special leave petition or that the order of the Supreme Court is the only order binding as res judicata in subsequent proceedings between the parties.

(vi)   Once leave to appeal has been granted and appellate jurisdiction of Supreme Court has been invoked the order passed in appeal would attract the doctrine of merger; the order may be of reversal, modification or merely affirmation.

(vii)   On an appeal having been preferred or a petition seeking leave to appeal having been converted into an appeal before Supreme Court the jurisdiction of High Court to entertain a review petition is lost thereafter as provided by sub-rule (1) of Rule (1) of Order 47 of the C.P.C."

82. It was held by the Hon'ble Supreme Court of India in a case reported as Commissioner of Income-tax Bombay Vs. M/s. Amritlal Bhogilal & Co.([1959] S.C.R. 713) that:

"There can be no doubt that, if an appeal is provided against an order passed by a tribunal, the decision of the appellate authority is the operative decision in law. If the appellate authority modifies or reverses the decision of the tribunal, it is obvious that it is the appellate decision that is effective and can be enforced. In law the position would be just the same even if the appellate decision merely confirms the decision of the tribunal. As a result of the confirmation or affirmance of the decision of the tribunal by the appellate authority the original decision merges in the appellate decision and it is the appellate decision alone which subsists and is operative and capable of enforcement."

83.   When the principle of merger is applied to the facts and circumstances of this case, there remains no problem which poses difficulty in its resolution. The first A.A. Zuberi case merged into the second A.A. Zuberi case. There is no appellate order of the Hon'ble Supreme Court in respect of the second A.A. Zuberi case. There is also no appellate order in respect of judgements of the learned Federal Service Tribunal in the matter of restoration of commuted value of pension. The case reported as Federation of Pakistan Vs. Ghulam Mustafa and others (2012 SCMR 1914) is a leave refusing order; it is not an appellate order. In this view of the matter, there exists no decision of the Hon'ble Supreme Court on the subject of restoration of commuted value of pension of the federal retired civil servants

which may be termed binding decision on a question of law or principle of law or an enunciation of a principle of law within the contemplation of Article 189 of the Constitution. We reject the view that the ratio decidendi of the second A.A. Zuberi case has been confirmed by the Hon'ble Supreme Court by refusing to allow leave to appeal against that case. The second A.A. Zuberi case, we have found earlier in this judgment, is a judgment on a subject-matter which falls within exclusive jurisdiction of the learned Federal Service Tribunal and the same is void and of no legal effect for being rendered without jurisdiction.

84.   The Ismail Tayer case dismissed petitions for leave to appeal against judgments of the Hon'ble High Court and entertained appeal of the Government of the Punjab against judgment of the learned Service Tribunal on the appeal of Mr. Muhammad Ismail Tayer. To the extent of the judgment of the learned Service Tribunal on the appeal of Mr. Muhammad Ismail Tayer, the principle of merger applies as the Ismail Tayer case is an appellate order of the Hon'ble Supreme Court in the case of Mr. Muhammad Ismail Tayer and a leave refusing order in respect of judgments of the Hon'ble Lahore High Court against which leave to appeal was sought. As the question of jurisdiction on the subject-matter of pension of retired civil servants has been settled by the Hon'ble Supreme Court in the Ismail Tayer case accepting jurisdiction of the learned Service Tribunal in the matter and consequently ruling out jurisdiction of the Hon'ble High Court on the subject, the judgments of the Hon'ble Lahore High Court are void and nullity in eyes of law being rendered without jurisdiction. Thus, the only judgment on the subject of restoration of the commuted value of pension is the Ismail Tayer case which is binding on all courts throughout Pakistan. In presence of this judgment, there was absolutely no justification to insist on implementation of the second A.A. Zuberi case or the case reported as Ghulam Yasin Vs. Accountant-General Punjab and others (2014 PLC (C.S.) 73). Moreover, the second A.A. Zuberi case is void so far as the matter of restoration of commuted value of pension of the retired civil servants of the Government of the Punjab is concerned, inter alia, for the following reasons:

a) The judgment has been rendered without jurisdiction and, hence, is void and of no legal effect. It has been held in Thompson v Tolmie, 2 Pet. 157, 7 L. Ed. 381; and Griffith v. Frazier, 8 Cr. 9, 3 L. Ed. 471 that "where there is absence of proof of jurisdiction, all administrative and judicial proceedings are a nullity, and confer no right, offer no protection, and afford no justification, and may be rejected upon direct collateral attack."

b) It has been rendered in case of federal pensioners who are governed by laws made under Article 240 (a) of the Constitution; hence, it cannot be made applicable to provincial pensioners who are governed by laws made under Article 240 (b) of the Constitution;

c) It is per incuriam because it has been delivered without considering judgments of the Hon'ble Supreme Court of Pakistan in the first and the second increases in pension cases. The Hon'ble Supreme Court has held in these cases that decision of the Government to allow increase on net pension instead of gross pension is valid;

d) The Ismail Tayer case and the second A.A. Zuberi case are in irreconcilable clash and are incapable of giving simultaneous effect. The concepts of restoration of commuted value of pension as contained in second A.A. Zuberi case and the Ismail Tayer case cannot co-exist. In such case, the judgment of the Hon'ble Supreme Court merits to be given effect in letter and spirit;

e) The second A.A, Zuberi case also militates against the law laid down by a five-judge bench of the Hon'ble Supreme Court in the I.A. Sherwani's case (1991 SCMR 1041) in which it was held that pension is payable in accordance with legal dispensation applicable on the date of retirement etc. There was no express or implied legal dispensation applicable on the date of retirement of Mr. A.A, Zuberi which necessitated doubling of pension plus increases in pension on the date of restoration of the commuted value of pension. By ordering doubling of the amount being drawn at the time of restoration of the commuted value of pension, the Hon'ble High Court exercised powers vested in the legislature by Article 240(b) and 115 of the Constitution. In Government of Pakistan Vs. Begum Justice Soofi (PLD 1959 SC (Pak.) 237), it was held by the Hon'ble Supreme Court that "any encroachment by the High Court in the field reserved for the Executive would amount to a judicial invasion and excess, and would be contrary to the spirit of the Constitution". The same is true when the Hon'ble High Court invades the territory exclusively reserved for the legislature in the instant matter;

f) The second A.A. Zuberi case is based upon mistaken assumption of fact. Paragraph 19 of the second A.A. Zuberi case, reproduced below, is a mistaken assumption of fact:

> "Respondents commuted their 50% pension for a period of 15 years, which means that a lump sum payment of 50% of the pension on the basis of the pension as it stood in the year 1993 was worked out over a future period of 15 years and handed over to the respondents. Therefore, during these 15 years benefit of increase in pension was enjoyed by the respondents only to the extent of 50% i.e., the pension received by them monthly."

The above assumption is mistaken. Mr. A.A. Zuberi was allowed 10% increase on his gross pension with effect from 1st of July, 1993 and 20% increase on his gross pension with effect from 1st of July, 1999. Subsequent increases in pension were allowed to him on net pension till July, 2007, whereafter his commuted portion of pension was restored with effect from 31.05.2008 and amounts of gross and net pension became the same and, thus, all subsequent increases were sanctioned on gross pension in his case. It is incorrect to assume that pensioners who opted for commutation of a prescribed part of their pension were deprived increases in pension before restoration of the commuted part of pension. They were given increases in pension in accordance with the formula of calculation of such increases. In no case, they were denied increases in pension. Thus mistaken assumption of fact has rendered the judgment non-implementable as it results into undue enrichment for M. A.A. Zuberi and unjust burden and deprivation for the public purse.

85. In view of the above, we are persuaded to hold and do hereby hold that the appellate order of the Hon'ble Supreme Court of Pakistan in the Ismail Tayer case attracts principle of merger and deserves the sanctity of Article 189 and status of Article 190 of the Constitution to the extent of restoration of commuted value of pension of the retired civil servants of the Government of the Punjab.

Question # 3

Whether the Ismail Tayer case holds that restoration of commuted value of pension means doubling of the amount being drawn as pension plus increases in pension on the date of restoration or conversion of increases sanctioned on net pension into increases on gross pension and whether determination of pension and increases in pension of the

retired civil servants of the Province other than through a money bill is valid?

86.   The learned Advocate General, Punjab submits that right to pension is earned by a civil servant after putting in satisfactory service for a prescribed minimum period and a right so earned is property so as to attract Articles 23 and 24(1) of the Constitution. He argues that power of the purse is legislative power and the doctrine of trichotomy of powers does not allow any other organ of the Province to exercise this power. It is the legislature which is competent to create a charge on the Provincial Consolidated Fund and appropriate moneys to liquidate that charge, he asserts. He further submits that pension payable from the Provincial Consolidated Fund has been a subject falling within the Provincial Legislative List under the Government of India Act, 1935 and this is a residual subject under the Constitution of 1973. He is of the view that Article 240(b) of the Constitution prescribes that conditions of appointment and of service of the members of the Services of a Province and persons holding posts in connection with affairs of a Province can be determined by or under an Act of the Provincial Assembly. He says that Article 240 of the Constitution is subject to the Constitution and, therefore, Article 115(2)(d) of the Constitution has to be followed in case a charge in the form of a legal claim to pension from the Provincial Consolidated Fund is created. He argues that the I.A. Sharwani case (PLD 1991 SCMR 1041), the Ismail Tayer case and the first and second increases in pension cases have held that pension is payable as prescribed in the rules. He avers that whereas all aspects of appointments and conditions of service can be dealt with, subject to the legislative intent expressed in the statute, through rules but matters regarding creation of a charge on the Provincial Consolidated Fund can only be determined through a money bill. He says that power to dispose of public property lying in or forming part of the Provincial Consolidated Fund is essentially a legislative power and the executive has to act in this regard in the manner and to the extent as legislatively determined through a money bill. He opines that the subject of pension and increases in pension of the retired civil servants of the Province is compulsorily required to be legislatively settled through a money bill. He avers that absence of a Pension Act comprehensively dealing with pension and increases in pension of the civil servants is a major cause of litigation on the subject and until the constitutional requirement in this respect is fulfilled, things are not expected to improve. He suggests that past payments of pension as prescribed in the rules and increases in pension as sanctioned through executive orders may be accepted as quantum meruit and the legislature may express itself on the subject through a money bill so as to settle things in the way desired by the Constitution.

87.   The learned Advocate General, Punjab submits that the Ismail Tayer case determined three things:

(a) Pension is payable as a right in accordance with the rules;

(b) Legal fiction of net pension is valid for the purpose of increases in pension; and

(c) If a portion of pension is commuted for a defined period, the right to receive full pension stands restored on completion of that period.

88.   The learned Advocate General states that the aforesaid conclusions drawn by the Hon'ble Supreme Court in the Ismail Tayer case are correct but the Hon'ble Lahore High Court did not accept this judgment and got the second A.A. Zuberi case implemented by employing various tactics. He prays that this Court may set things right in the instant case.

89.   Mr. Yazdani, though in broad agreement with the conclusions drawn in the Ismail Tayer case, has two submissions:

(a) The Ismail Tayer case is based upon mistaken assumptions of fact. In this regard, he refers to the following statements of the judgment which are alleged to be factually incorrect:

i.   On 22-3-2008, the Finance Department, Government of the Punjab issued a letter, in light of an Office Memorandum

No.F.13(6)-Reg-6/2003, dated 29-2-2008, issued by the Government of Pakistan, Finance Division (Regulation Wing), as a consequence whereof the increase in pension granted during the commuted period was deducted from the pension paid to the respondents.

ii. The said Office Memorandum of the Federal Government was called into question before the learned Lahore High Court. The Office Memorandum was struck down by a learned Single Judge of the said High Court in the case reported as A.A. Zuberi v. Additional Accountant General Pakistan Revenue, Lahore [2010 PLC (C.S.) 1211]. The said judgment of the learned Single Judge was challenged in appeal through an Intra Court Appeal, which was dismissed by a learned Division Bench of the said High Court vide judgment dated 16-6-2010, reported as Additional Accountant-General Pakistan Revenue, Lahore v. A. A. Zuberi [2011 PLC (C.S.) 580].

iii. Thus, the very decision of the Federal Government in the light whereof the Office Memorandum dated 22-3-2008 had been issued is no longer in force having been struck down through a judicial decision, which has been implemented.

iv. Such right in terms of section 18 of the Act of 1974 would obviously mean the pension, as prescribed by the Rules payable on the date of restoration and would obviously include any increase in pension granted by the Government during the intervening period of commutation, as such, increase is envisaged by the Rules.

(b) A departure from the hithertofore acceptance of prescription of pension through rules and determination of increases in pension through executive orders is essential in order to fully implement the doctrine of trichotomy of powers and to safeguard the legislative power of the purse from executive encroachment and judicial outreach.

90. Mr. Yazdani submits that the fact that a judgment delivered by the Hon'ble Supreme Court is rendered nugatory and a contrary judgment of the Hon'ble High Court is implemented be given due consideration so that rising trend of indiscipline is arrested and rule of law is assured.

91. Leaned counsels of the beneficiaries of the second A.A. Zuberi case argue that dismissal of appeals and petitions for leave to appeal filed by the Government of the Punjab in the Ismail Tayer case and dismissal of review petition in this regard is a conclusive determination by the Hon'ble Supreme Court that restoration of commuted value of pension means doubling of the amount drawn by a pensioner as pension plus increases in pension on the date of restoration of the commuted value of pension. They contend that the Hon'ble Lahore High Court correctly interpreted the Ismail Tayer case and there exists no legal ground to call in question what has been done by the Hon'ble Lahore High Court in the matter of enforcement of the second A.A. Zuberi case by the Government of the Punjab.

92. Before ascertaining constitutional validity of pension rules and determination of increases in pension through executive orders, we deem it appropriate to understand the true import of the short order in the Ismail Tayer case and the detailed reasons later given therefor.

93. In consideration of rendering service in the Service of Pakistan, a civil servant is entitled to remuneration. He receives this remuneration in the form of salary during service and in the form of pension after retirement, subject, obviously, to eligibility in accordance

with the applicable rules. Once admissibility of pension is determined, the Punjab Civil Services Pension Rules provide him an option to sell some part of the pension to the Government in exchange for advance payment for a prescribed period. This payment is not returnable if the pensioner dies before expiry of the period for which lump sum advance payment (commutation) is received. This commutation used to render the pensioner ineligible to get the commuted portion added to his pension after expiry of the commutation period. In 1985, this policy was changed and the commuted portion was declared to be restorable on expiry of the commutation period. In 2001, the pre-1985 policy was revived through Government of the Punjab, Finance Department's letter No. FD. PC-2-1/2001 dated 22.10.2001, and it was held that the commuted portion of pension shall not be restored. The Ismail Tayer case held that a pensioner is entitled to get full pension in accordance with rules and if he gets a part of pension commuted he is ineligible to get that part alongwith his monthly pension till the expiry of the commutation period whereafter he becomes entitled to get the commuted portion of the pension restored in accordance with the Punjab Civil Services Pension Rules. This judgment of the Hon'ble Supreme Court was implemented by the Government of the Punjab through its letter No. FD-SR-III/4-41/2008 dated 22nd of July, 2014 by omitting the provision introduced in 2001 regarding prohibition of restoration of the commuted portion of pension (para 16 (e) of this department's letter No. FD. PC-2-1/2001 dated 22.10.2001). All the relevant documents have very intelligently been arranged by the learned Registrar of this Court in the first set of facts an examination whereof leaves no measure of doubt in arriving at the conclusion hereinabove recorded by us.

94.   It was held by the Hon'ble Supreme Court in the first increases in pension case, reiterated in the second increases in pension case, that no law or rules exist to regulate increases in pension. These increases in pension are allowed through executive orders and it was held by the Hon'ble Supreme Court that the Government is free to decide whether to grant enhancement in pension on gross or net pension. Challenge to competence of the Government to sanction increase on net pension and not on gross pension was repelled by the Hon'ble Supreme Court. As a matter of historical fact, there is no dispute that the increases in pension sanctioned prior to 2001 were on the amount of pension before commutation plus increases sanctioned on pension from time to time. This benevolence was exceptional on the ground that a pensioner, for the purpose of increases in pension, who had not opted for commutation was being treated at par with a pensioner who opted for commutation. When a pensioner opts for commutation, he receives a part of pension commuted for a prescribed period and the Government transfers him public property in the form of money which he is free to invest or spend and the Government has no right to reclaim this property if the pensioner dies before expiry of the commutation period. There was logic and wisdom in the policy in force prior to 1985 whereunder commutation was for good and there was no concept of its restoration. With discontinuation of this policy, it was not logical to sanction increase on that part of the pension which was not in possession of the Government. We endorse the following comments of the learned Federal Service Tribunal recorded in its judgment in Appeal No. 495(R) CS/2003:

> "When considered in the backdrop of the generous dispensation in all the previous increases on gross pension, a reversal thereof in 2001 apparently looks odd. There was, however, a logical justification in allowing increase on net pension instead of gross pension as latter included the commuted portion which, in turn, had actually been bought over by the Government for a lump sum compensation and the Government decided not to pay increase on the portion the ownership of which had been transferred to it as it would have involved increases to be allowed in addition to the compensation paid already."

95.   It would not be out of context to illustrate the above comments of the learned Federal Service Tribunal through an example based upon facts. A civil servant (Mr. A) in BS. 17 retires on 14.07.1995. His pension is calculated in accordance with applicable rules. His full pension comes to Rs. 5108.18. He does not opt for commutation. He receives increases in pension as sanctioned from time to time and his take-home on account of pension + increases in pension, on expiry of a period of fifteen years i.e. on 15.07.2010, totals to Rs. 20968.79 per month.

96.   Mr. B, having identical particulars, opts for commutation of 50% of his pension and receives Rs. 473985/ as commuted value of pension. He receives increases in pension as sanctioned from time to time by the Government and becomes entitled to receive Rs. 15296.27 per month on 15.07.2010 i.e. after restoration of commuted value of pension.

97.   Mr. B had invested Rs. Rs. 473985/ received as commuted value of pension in Defence Savings Certificates which becomes Rs. 3,100,850/ on expiry of fifteen years. (Rates of interest actual). After 15 years, Mr. B invests Rs. 3,100,850/ in Monthly Income Scheme of the National Savings Centre and starts receiving Rs. 28,424/ per month as profit. Thus, besides having an asset of Rs. 3,100,850/, he is in receipt of Rs. 15296.27 + Rs. 28,424= Rs. 43,720.27 per month. Before expiry of period of fifteen years, Mr. A received Rs. 1,045,191/ more than Mr. B as pension + increases in pension. On expiry of fifteen years, net assets of Mr. B are Rs. 3,100,850/ and per month yield of pension + increases in pension + monthly return on assets created out of commuted value of pension is Rs. 43,720.27 per month.

98.   If Mr. B is compared with Mr. A in terms of pension + increases in pension on expiry of fifteen years, Mr. B is in receipt of Rs. 15296.27 + Rs. 28,424= Rs. 43,720.27 per month whereas Mr. A is receiving Rs. 20968.79 per month. Thus, Mr. B is in receipt of more than double of what is received by Mr. A. If pension + increases in pension of Mr. B are doubled on the date of restoration of commuted value of pension, then Mr. B would be in receipt of Rs. 28,424 + Rs. 24,462.74=Rs. 52, 887 per month.

100.   There are two conditions precedent to justify doubling of pension + increases in pension on the date of restoration of commuted value of pension, which are as follows:

    i.   No increase in pension would have been allowed on commuted portion of pension from date of commencement of pension till date of restoration; and

    ii.   It is legally established that the Government is not competent to sanction increases on net pension and increases in pension are compulsorily required to be on gross pension.

101.   It is an admitted fact that all increases in pension sanctioned up to the year 1999 were on gross pension and not on net pension. Prior to the year 2001 (last increase on gross pension was sanctioned in the year 1999; there was no increase in pension in the year 2000; and first increase on net pension was sanctioned in the year 2001), for the purpose of admissibility of increase in pension, the term 'pension' used to be defined as "pension means gross pension (i.e. pension before commutation and / or surrender of 1/4th thereof) plus dearness / ad hoc increases in pension sanctioned from time to time, where admissible." Thus, up to the year 1999, for the purpose of calculation of increases in pension, commuted portion of pension was also used to be taken into consideration. As an unavoidable consequence of this finding of fact, a pensioner, who has been given increase on gross pension even once, cannot demand doubling of his pension + increases in pension at the time of restoration of commuted value of pension as such a demand would amount to more than double benefit to a pensioner. Since gross pension includes commuted portion of pension, therefore, increases on commuted portion had already been allowed up to the year 1999. Doubling of pension + increases in pension at the time of restoration of commuted value of pension would multiply this benefit and would perpetuate such multiplication for all times to come.

102. Mr. A.A. Zuberi was allowed 10% increase in his gross pension with effect from 1st of July, 1993 and 20% increase in his gross pension with effect from 1st of July, 1999. Subsequent increases in pension were allowed to him on net pension till July, 2007, whereafter his commuted portion of pension was restored with effect from 31.05.2008 and amounts of gross and net pension became the same and, thus, all subsequent increases were admissible on gross pension in his case.

103. The policy of 2001 whereunder increases on pension were restricted on net pension only was erroneously interpreted by the treasuries to mean that even after restoration of commuted portion of pension, the increase in pension shall be allowed after subtracting the restored portion of the pension. This caused another round of litigation which finalized in 2008 and it was held that increases in pension allowed in the year of restoration would be admissible also on the commuted portion of pension. However, the prohibition on restoration of commuted value of pension remained intact. The competence of the Government to allow increases on net pension and not on gross pension was judicially endorsed by the Hon'ble Supreme Court in the first and the second increases in pension cases. Ever since 2001, increases in pension are being allowed on net pension by the Federal and Provincial Governments in Pakistan without any judicial challenge. Paragraph 17 of the Ismail Tayer case also upheld increases on net pension in these words:

> "--The dictum, as laid down is merely that a retired Civil Servant
> is entitled to the pension as may be prescribed and a decision
> granting increase in pension has been interpreted by upholding
> the legal fiction of a net-pension created for the purpose of
> calculating the increase as granted by the decision under
> consideration."

104. As per Black's Law Dictionary, 804 (5th ed. 1979), a 'legal fiction' is a fact assumed or created by courts which is then used in order to apply a legal rule which was not necessarily designed to be used in that way. It is a presumption of fact assumed by a court for convenience, consistency, or to achieve justice.

105. The term "net pension" has been used in the Finance Department's letter No. FD. PC-2-1/2001 dated 22nd October, 2001, therefore, para 17 of the Ismail Tayer case refers to the above said letter only. As a logical consequence, "the decision under consideration" as referred to in para 17 of the judgment is the decision as declared in para 16 (f) of the Finance Department's letter No. FD. PC-2-1/2001 dated 22nd October, 2001, (*In future, the increase in pension to the pensioners shall be allowed on net pension instead of gross pension.*) and not anything else. Since legality of the said para 16 (f) is well-established, therefore, the Federal Government and all the Provincial Governments in Pakistan have been sanctioning, since 2001, increases in net pension and not on gross pension. No court of law in Pakistan has held that the Government is not lawfully competent to sanction increases in pension in accordance with the formula of calculation of amount of such increases determined by the Government. It is not understandable that if a decision of the Government regarding calculation of an increase in pension on net pension exclusive of commuted portion thereof is lawful at all times, then how increases in pension so allowed can be converted into increases on gross pension at the time of restoration of commuted value of pension.

106. The discrimination in payment of full pension after expiry of period of commutation, introduced through para 16 (e) of Finance Department's letter No. FD. PC-2-1/2001 dated 22nd October, 2001, (*The benefit of restoration of surrendered portion of pension in lieu of commutation/gratuity shall be withdrawn*) stands discontinued through circular letter No. FD-SR-III/ 4-41/2008 dated 22nd of July, 2014, issued by the Government of the Punjab, Finance Department. Thus, the discrimination pointed out in para 16 of the Ismail Tayer case read with para 19 thereof was removed. The said para 16 reads as follows:

> "Thus, under section 18 of the Act of 1974, a retired Civil Servant is
> entitled to receive pension as may be prescribed. In case a portion of

pension is commuted for a particular period of time, he surrenders his right to receive full pension in lieu of lump-sum payment received by him and on expiry of the commuted period, his right and entitlement to receive full pension, as prescribed, is restored and re-vested in him. The restoration of the right to receive pension in terms of Rule 8.12 of the Rules of 1963, is without any rider and upon re-vesting of such right, the status of such retired Civil Servant in law is brought at par with the other retired Civil Servants, who had not exercised their option by seeking commutation of their pension. Such is the obvious effect of the term "restoration" as used in the Rules in question. In the circumstances, a retired Civil Servant, on expiry of the period of commutation, cannot be discriminated against by being paid less pension, than his colleagues, who had not sought commutation, as there was no valid classification available in law between the two. If the Government were to adopt such a course of action as has been attempted to be done, it would offend against Article 25 of the Constitution of the Islamic Republic of Pakistan, 1973. Such right in terms of section 18 of the Act of 1974 would obviously mean the pension, as prescribed by the Rules, payable on the date of restoration and would obviously include any increase in pension granted by the Government during the intervening period of commutation, as such increase is envisaged by the Rules."

107. Here a few words to precisely identify the discrimination. A retired civil servant is entitled to full pension for life. In case, he opts for commutation of a part of his pension for a defined period, he receives pension of the commuted portion in advance for that period. A retired civil servant who does not opt for commutation continues to receive full pension for life. If the civil servant opting for commutation is denied the right of restoration of commuted value of pension after expiry of the defined period, it would imply that he has been given full pension for the period of commutation only and not thereafter. Such creation of two classes of pensioners---one getting full pension for life and the other getting full pension for a defined period only- is without lawful justification. After expiry of the defined period, the civil servant opting for commutation would be in receipt of less amount as pension (here pension means 'full pension' and does not include increases in pension) than the one who did not opt for commutation in case right of restoration of commuted value of pension is denied to him.

108. Though Mr. Yazdani has correctly pointed out mistaken assumptions of fact, yet the short order in the Ismail Tayer case has not been materially affected by these assumptions as it relates only to the commutation and its restoration in accordance with the rules. However, in order to dispel mistaken assumptions of fact, the factual position is clarified hereunder:

i. Government of the Punjab, Finance Department's letter No. FD.SR-III-4-41/2008 dated 22.03.2008 does not order deduction of increases allowed on pension during the commutation period. Rather, it allowed increase on commuted portion of pension also if sanctioned in the year of restoration.

ii. Government of Pakistan, Finance Division's office memorandum No.F.13 (16)-Reg.6/ 2003 dated 29.02.2008 was not struck down in the first or the second A.A. Zuberi case.

iii. Letters of the Federal Government dated 29.02.2008 and of the Government of the Punjab dated 22.03.2008 are validly in the field and are being implemented even today.

iv. There is not even a single occasion when pensioners opting for commutation were denied increases in pension in accordance with the formula prescribed by the Government for calculation of increases in pension i.e. on gross pension when sanctioned and otherwise on net pension.

109.   We are in agreement with the recommendation of the committee constituted by the Finance Department of the Government of the Punjab which was implemented through circular letter No. FD-SR-III/ 4-41/2008 dated 22.07.2014. Through this letter, the facility of restoration of the commuted value of pension was revived. We are of the opinion that the aforesaid circular letter was the complete and full implementation of the ratio decidendi of the Ismail Tayer case. The Hon'ble Supreme Court does not hold in the Ismail Tayer case that restoration of commuted portion of pension means doubling of pension and increases in pension being drawn at the time of restoration. It also does not order that the increases allowed on net pension be converted on the increases on gross pension at the time of restoration of the commuted value of pension. The judgment is in line with the I.A. Sharwani case, the third Judges' pension case, the first and the second increases in pension case and other judgments of the Hon'ble Supreme Court of Pakistan. On the other hand, the second A.A. Zuberi case was got implemented by the Hon'ble Lahore High Court firstly by multiplying by two the pension plus increases in pension on the date of restoration of commuted value of pension and subsequently, when the report of M/S. A.R. Ferguson held that doubling of pension and increases in pension was not possible, as conversion of increases allowed on net pension into increases on gross pension. By doing so, the Hon'ble single bench of the Hon'ble High Court not only modified judgment of a two-judge bench but also reviewed judgments of the Hon'ble Supreme Court for which it had no authority of law. We have not been able to find any acceptable justification which may convince us that what Mr. Shubhankar, Dean of the National University of Judicial Sciences, India, in his comments (2005 Public Law 239) observed, reproduced below, about the case reported as Vineet Narain Vs. Union of India (AIR 1998 SC 889) may be utterly irrelevant to what the Hon'ble Lahore High Court did for implementation of the second A.A. Zuberi case:

> "Vineet Narain exemplifies the Indian Supreme Court's contempt for limitations, constitutional or otherwise, in fulfilling what it sees as the rightful task of the judiciary. The 'creative' activism of the Supreme Court in the 1980s has now evolved into a form of judicial arrogance------. By choosing 'justice' over 'law' in the quest for legitimacy as a people's institution, judges have driven the final nail in the coffin of the very Constitution they are under oath to uphold, preserve and protect….."

110. It pains us to observe that what the Hon'ble High Court did in the aforesaid case was not only without jurisdiction but was also exercise of legislative and executive authority of the state. It goes without saying that the Hon'ble High Court is not at liberty to decide cases brought before it under Article 199 of the Constitution in accordance with what appears to it to be just and equitable and not according to existing applicable law and by ignoring ratio decidendi of judgments rendered by the Hon'ble Supreme Court of Pakistan. We have also not been able to find justification for disregard of the principle of 'departmental construction' which, as held by the Hon'ble Supreme Court in a case reported as Haider Automobile Vs. Pakistan (PLD 1971 SC 623) "applies only in those cases where a rule made by a department is interpreted by it in a particular way, upon the ground that those who have framed the rules are likely to know its intention better than others." In Muhammad Ali Khan's case (PLD 1958 (WP) Lah. 1), it was held:

> "It is also clear that if a particular interpretation has been placed on the rules in the past by authorities who had to apply them to cases as they arose, the court should be reluctant to place a different interpretation unless it came to the conclusion that the interpretation placed by Government for a long time was so palpably wrong that by upholding it the court would be

countenancing the perpetuation of an injustice ----- paving the way for similar injustice in the future."

111.   It has been held by the Hon'ble Supreme Court of India in a case reported as CIT Vs. Taj Mahal Hotel ((1971) 3 SCC 550) that:

> "It is well settled that where the definition of a word has not been given, it must be construed in its popular sense if it is a word of everyday use. Popular sense means that sense which people conversant with the subject-matter with which the statute is dealing, would attribute to it."

112.   After dealing with the question of doubling of pension and increases in pension on the date of restoration of commuted value of pension, we now proceed to examine the prayer of Mr. Yazdani regarding over-ruling of ratio of I.A. Shairwani case, first and second increases in pension cases and the Ismail Tayer case to the extent of determination of pension and increases in pension of the retired civil servants of the Province only through a money bill.

113.   It is by now well-established that power of the purse is a legislative power. The executive executes the budget as approved by the legislature. Receipts and disbursements of the Provincial Consolidated Fund are regulated in accordance with the legal dispensation as envisaged in Article 119 read with Article 115 and other relevant constitutional provisions. A civil servant earns right to remuneration from the Provincial Consolidated Fund in consideration of rendering services as a person in the Service of Pakistan. A legal claim to receive money from the Provincial Consolidated Fund is a charge within the meaning of Article 115 of the Constitution, reproduced below:

> **"115. Provincial Government's consent required for financial measures. -**
>
> (1)   A Money Bill, or a Bill or amendment which if enacted and brought into operation would involve expenditure from the Provincial Consolidated Fund or withdrawal from the Public Account of the Province shall not be introduced or moved in the Provincial Assembly except by or with the consent of the Provincial Government.
>
> (2)   For the purposes of this Article, a Bill or amendment shall be deemed to be a Money Bill if it contains provisions dealing with all or any of the following matters, namely:
>
> (a)   the imposition, abolition, remission, alteration or regulation of any tax;
>
> (b)   the borrowing of money, or the giving of any guarantee, by the Provincial Government or the amendment of the law relating to the financial obligations of that Government;
>
> (c)   the custody of the Provincial Consolidated Fund, the payment of moneys into, or issue of moneys from, that fund;
>
> (d)   the imposition of a charge upon the Provincial Consolidated Fund, or the abolition or alteration of any such charge;
>
> (e)   the receipt of moneys on account of the Public Account of the Province, the custody or issue of such moneys; and
>
> (f)   any matter incidental to any of the matters specified in the preceding paragraphs.
>
> (3)   A Bill shall not be deemed to be a Money Bill by reason only that it provides—

(a)   for the imposition or alteration of any fine or other pecuniary penalty or for the demand or payment of a licence fee or a fee or charge for any service rendered; or

(b)   for the imposition, abolition, remission, alteration or regulation of any tax by any local authority or body for local purposes.

(4)   If any question arises whether a Bill is a Money Bill or not, the decision of the Speaker of the Provincial Assembly thereon shall be final.

(5)   Every Money Bill presented to the Governor for assent shall bear a certificate under the hand of the Speaker of the Provincial Assembly that it is a Money Bill and such certificate shall be conclusive for all purposes and shall not be called in question."

114.   Determination of remuneration payable from the Provincial Consolidated Fund entitles a person in the Service of Pakistan to receive that money on fulfillment of conditions-precedent therefor. As per Corpus Juris Secundum. Vol. 67, a pension system is intended to promote efficient, continued and faithful service to the employer and economic security to the employees and their dependents, by an arrangement under which, by fulfilment of specified eligibility requirements, pensions become property of the individual as a matter of right upon the termination of public service. The Hon'ble Supreme Court of Pakistan has made it clear in a case reported as Government of NWFP Vs. Muhammad Said Khan (PLD 1973 SC 514) that it must now be taken as well-settled that a person who enters Government service has also something to look forward after his retirement, to what are called retirement benefits, grant of pension being the most valuable of such benefits. A five-judge bench of the Hon'ble Supreme Court of Pakistan held in I.A. Sharwani case (PLD 1991 SCMR 1041) that the right to receive pension by a Government servant is property so as to attract Articles 23 and 24(1) of the Constitution. In Indian jurisdiction, it was held by the Hon'ble Supreme Court of India in a case reported as Deokinandan Prasad Vs. State of Bihar (1971 AIR 1409, 1971 SCR 634) that:

"The question whether the pension granted to a public servant is property attracting Art. 31(1) came up for consideration before the Punjab High Court in Bhagwant Singh v. Union of India (AIR 1962 Punj 503). It was held that such a right constitutes "property" and any interference will be a breach of Art. 3 1 (1) of the Constitution. It was further held that the State cannot by an executive order curtail or abolish altogether the right of the public servant to receive pension. This decision was given by a learned Single Judge. This decision was taken up in Letters Patent Appeal by the Union of India. The Letters Patent Bench in its decision in Union of India v. Bhagwant Singh (ILR (1965) 2 Punj 1) approved the decision of the learned Single Judge. The Letters Patent Bench held that the pension granted to a public servant on his retirement is "property" within the meaning of Art. 3 1 (1) of the Constitution and he could be deprived of the same only by an authority of law and that pension does not cease to be property on the mere denial or cancellation of it. It was further held that the character of pension as "property" cannot possibly undergo such mutation at the whim of a particular person or authority.

The matter again came up before a Full Bench of the Punjab and Haryana High Court in K. R. Erry v. The State of Punjab (AIR 1967 Punj 279). The High Court had to consider the nature of the right of an officer to get pension. The majority quoted with approval the principles

511

laid down in the two earlier decisions of the same High Court, referred to above, and held that the pension is not to be treated as a bounty payable on the sweet will and pleasure of the Government and that the right to superannuation pension including its amount is a valuable right vesting in a Government servant.

This Court in State of Madhya Pradesh v. Ranojirao Shinde and another ([1968] 3 S. C. R. 489) had to consider the question whether a "cash grant" is "property" within the meaning of that expression in Arts. 19(1)(f) and 31(1) of the Constitution. This Court held that it was property, observing "it is obvious that a right to sum of money is property".

115.   Pension is not a bounty but a property in terms of Article 23 and 24 of the Constitution. Thus, right to acquire and hold this property is a fundamental right and a person cannot be deprived of this property except in accordance with law. Now, the question is: whether a law made under Article 240(b) of the Constitution is sufficient for the purpose or a money bill under Article 115 of the Constitution is required for determination of pension?

116.   Article 240 is subject to the Constitution. It means that if the Constitution has specifically dealt with any matter relating to conditions of appointments and of service of members of Services of the Province or persons holding posts in connection with affairs of the Province, that specific dispensation would not be disturbed by an arrangement under Article 240 of the Constitution. Determination of pension of the retired civil servants is a matter which directly affects the Provincial Consolidated Fund. Such determination gives legal right to persons in the Service of Pakistan as members of the Services of the Province or holders of posts in connection with affairs of the Province to claim, as a right, the pension earned by them in consideration of their services in accordance with their employment contract. A legal claim on the Provincial Consolidated Fund can only be created through a money bill. What follows from this line of reasoning is this that pension payable from the Provincial Consolidated Fund is necessarily required to be determined through a money bill.

117.   There may arise occasions necessitating withholding of payment of pension from the Provincial Consolidated Fund. As right to remuneration is a fundamental right, therefore, the pension earned can neither be denied nor withheld except in accordance with law. This is the plain meaning and obvious interpretation of Article 23 and 24 of the Constitution. This law has to be a money bill as envisaged in Article 115 of the Constitution.

118.   As per entry appearing at serial number 7 of the Provincial Legislative List of the Government of India Act, 1935, Provincial pensions, that is to say, pensions payable by the Province or out of Provincial revenues was a provincial subject to be regulated through a provincial law. Further, according to the entry at serial number 61 of the Provincial List in the Fifth Schedule of the Constitution of Pakistan, 1956 the subject of Provincial Pensions exclusively fell in the provincial legislative domain. The Constitutions of 1962 and 1973 do not contain Provincial Legislative Lists. The subject of provincial pensions, is, thus, a residual subject under the prevailing constitutional dispensation. The Provincial Assembly has, therefore, to legislatively deal with this subject through enactment of a money bill (which may be labeled a Pension Act), inter alia, to:

(a) determine conditions-precedent to earn right to pension;
(b) provide legislative policy or formula for determination of amount of pension;
(c) specify conditions under which right to pension can be curtailed or withheld; and
(d) give legislative policy to regulate increases in pension or allow increases through money bill only.

119.   The Punjab Civil Servants Act, 1974 does not provide comprehensive legislative policy on the above issues. Everything under the sun relating to pension has been left to be

determined through rules to be framed by the Chief Minister or deemed to have been framed under the Punjab Civil Servants Act. Even the rules are silent on the issue of grant of increases in pension. There is no dispute between the parties that increases in pension have always been and are still being sanctioned through executive orders. The learned counsels appearing on behalf of the beneficiaries of the second A.A. Zuberi case have offered no plausible legal justification that why Article 115 of the Constitution is not applicable to matters relating to pension which directly affect the Provincial Consolidated Fund.

120. In view of, inter alia, what has been stated hereinabove, we are convinced to hold and do hereby hold that any matter relating to pension, which directly or indirectly affects the Provincial Consolidated Fund, is determinable only through a money bill. Matters of procedure and detail may be left for subordinate legislation subject to legislative policy contained in the applicable money bill. We also hold that provincial executive is not authorized to order increases in pension through executive orders without backing and support of such a money bill. The I.A. Sharwani case (PLD 1991 SCMR 1041), the first and the second increases in pension case and the Ismail Tayer case are accordingly overruled to the above extent.

121. Determination of pension through rules and increases in pension through executive orders in the past is held to be quantum meruit. The Provincial Assembly may consider desirability of statutorily validating, with or without amendments, past payments of pension made in accordance with the Punjab Civil Services Pension Rules and of increases in pension as per executive orders sanctioning such increases. It may also legislatively determine the matter of payments made on account of pension and increases in pension in excess of entitlement and may specifically deal with the matter of wrongful restoration of commuted value of pension in the way directed in the second A.A. Zuberi case or as was directed by the Hon'ble single-bench of the Hon'ble Lahore High Court, Lahore after getting report from the M/S. A.F. Ferguson & Co. It is expected that the needful shall be done at the earliest. In case, wrong payments of pension and increases in pension are not statutorily condoned and the recoveries thereof waived off, the recoveries shall be effected in accordance with law without delay.

Question # 4

> **Whether the Hon'ble High Court had valid constitutional powers to employ measures it employed to get the second A.A. Zuberi case implemented after judgment of the Hon'ble Supreme Court in the Ismail Tayer case?**

122. The learned Advocate General, Punjab submits that the Hon'ble single bench of the Hon'ble Lahore High Court took the following measures to get the A.A. Zuberi case implemented:

(a) ordering senior officers to appear in person:
(b) publically passing strictures regarding civil servants;
(c) initiating contempt of court proceedings;
(d) threatening the civil servants with transfers, loss of job etc.;
(e) giving final relief through interim orders; and
(f) reviewing the second A.A. Zuberi case on the report of the A.F. Ferguson & Co.

123. The learned Advocate General, Punjab argues that the Hon'ble High Court has been given judicial power of the state, inter alia, through Article 199 of the Constitution for the purposes specified in that Article. Power granted by Article 199 of the Constitution is a judicial power and by no stretch of imagination or reasoning executive and legislative powers of the state can be assumed to have been vested in the Hon'ble High Court under that Article, he submits. He avers that judicial process is to ensure ascertainment of legal rights and obligations of the litigants and their enforcement. He is of the view that power to adjudicate is power to adjudicate in accordance with law and this power does not entitle a

513

court to call a litigant in person if he is not required by law to appear in person. Judicial process is not for appraisal of conduct and performance of a litigant, he submits adding that uncalled for strictures regarding civil servants serve no purpose as adjudication of the lis does not necessarily depend upon or demand such strictures. He argues that the Hon'ble High Court has no power or duty to initiate proceedings on the charges of contempt of the Hon'ble Supreme Court. He emphatically asserts that public threats by the Hon'ble High Court to the civil servants that they shall be sent behind the bars and will be kicked out from the Service of Pakistan if they refuse to surrender to the wishes of the Hon'ble judges do not earn respect for the esteemed institution of judiciary. He says that frequent resort to grant of final relief through interim orders, modifying Division Bench's judgments by a Single Bench and simply ignoring all written as well as oral arguments of the civil servants by the Hon'ble High Court reflects a mindset which is feared to cause institutionalized erosion of the institution of judiciary. He prays that this Court may lay down law on these issues so that prestige and strength of the judicial organ of the state is preserved and enhanced.

124.   Mr. Yazdani submits that recruitments in the Hon'ble superior judiciary must be made on merit to be determined through open competitive process. He is of the view that in the institution of the law officers of the state, spoils system is the order of the day. He submits that it is extremely essential for the continued existence and material strength of the institution of judiciary that this Court may keep all within their allotted areas and anything done without or in excess of lawful authority is corrected in a deterrent way. He submits that the two cases relating to pension have cost more than fifty billion rupees which were not due in accordance with law. He avers that honest errors of judgment and willful disobedience of the Constitution and law need not be equated and given same treatment so far as Article 209 of the Constitution is concerned. He submits that the instant case may comprehensively address all problems so that confidence of the nation in the institution of judiciary is retained and enhanced.

125.   Learned counsels of the private respondents dismiss the arguments of the learned Advocate General, Punjab and of Mr. Yazdani terming them devoid of merit. They maintain that the Hon'ble High Court has unqualified powers to order personal appearance of the civil servants and to reprimand them if facts and circumstances of a case so require. They argue that civil contempt proceedings are initiated to get orders of the court implemented. If an officer refuses to obey orders of a court, he has to face punishment and loss of job as without such measures, judicial process will lose its sanctity, they argue. They further contend that sometimes it becomes essential to grant final relief through interim orders and it is for the Hon'ble judge to exercise his judicial discretion in the matter. As regards modification of the second A.A. Zuberi case after receipt of the report of the A.F. Ferguson & Co. by a Single Bench of the Hon'ble Lahore High Court, the learned counsels submit that to change the order of doubling of pension on the date of restoration of commuted value of pension into conversion of increases allowed on net pension into increases on gross pension on the date of restoration of commuted value of pension is a minor judicial action taken in interest of justice which needs to be ignored in public interest and to safeguard independence of judiciary. They argue that worthless written and oral submissions of the civil servants deserve to be ignored and the Hon'ble High Court is under no legal obligation to attend to every written word or utterance of the civil servants and to waste its precious time.

126.   We have given a patient hearing to the arguments of the parties. The issues raised before us need due consideration and proper adjudication. A society claiming to be governed by a written Constitution and publically taking pride in its adherence to the rule of law cannot ignore these questions of law.

127.   The Province is a person within the definition of this term in Article 199 of the Constitution. The Hon'ble Supreme Court of Pakistan has held in a case reported as Province of Punjab Vs. Muhammad Hussain (PLD 1993 SC 147) that:

"Section 79 of the C.P.C. requires, and so does Article 174 of the Constitution, that all suits against the Central Government have to be filed in the name of Pakistan and against a Provincial Government in the name of Province."

128. Article 174 of the Constitution and Section 79 of the Civil Procedure Code are mandatory non-compliance whereof makes a suit or writ non-maintainable. Reliance in this regard can safely be placed on the dictum of law laid down in the judgments reported as Government of Balochistan, CWPP&H Department and others Vs. Nawabzada Mir Tariq Hussain Khan Magsi and others (2010 SCMR 115) and Province of Punjab Vs. Muhammad Hussain (PLD 1993 SC 147). A writ petition can be filed against the Province through the concerned administrative Secretary.

129. Under Article 140(2) of the Constitution, it shall be the duty of the Advocate-General to give advice to the Provincial Government upon such legal matters, and to perform such other duties of a legal character, as may be referred or assigned to him by the Provincial Government. Paragraph 1.6 (c) of the Law Department Manual provides that the Advocate General will appear or arrange for the appearance of Law Officer/State Counsel, in the following civil cases:

   (i)   Cases in the High Court and Supreme Court to which the Punjab Government is a party or cases relating to the affairs of the Punjab Government to which the Federal Government is a party.

   (ii)   Cases in the High Court and Supreme Court to which officers serving under the Punjab Government are parties and which the Punjab Government has decided to conduct on behalf of such officers.

   (iii) Cases in the High Court and Supreme Court in which either the Punjab Government or such officers are directly interested but in which Government considers itself to be sufficiently interested to render it advisable to conduct the case on behalf of some third person.

   (iv)   Appeals from the cases referred to above.

130. Proceedings in the Hon'ble High Court are civil proceedings and it has been held by the Hon'ble Supreme Court of Pakistan in a case reported as Secretary, Ministry of Religious Affairs and Minorities and 2 others Vs. Syed Abdul Majid (1993 SCMR 1171) that the Code of Civil Procedure, 1908 applies to orders made by the Hon'ble High Court under Article 199 of the Constitution.

131. It is, thus, clear that if a writ petition under Article 199 of the Constitution is filed against the Province through the concerned Secretary, the Advocate General or a law officer deputed by him will represent the Province. He will plead the case and defend the cause of the Province in accordance with instructions to be given by the concerned Secretary to the Government of the Punjab. It is well-established that jurisdiction under Article 199 of the Constitution is not generally meant to decide disputed questions of fact. What the Hon'ble High Court, inter alia, does in proceedings under Article 199 of the Constitution is to direct a person to do what he is legally bound to do or declare something done or omitted to have been done as done or omitted to have been done without lawful authority. These are questions of law which are determined by the Hon'ble High Court under Article 199 of the Constitution. The writ petition and the report and para-wise comments are filed in writing in proceedings under Article 199 of the Constitution. No law requires personal appearance of the petitioner or the respondent in civil proceedings under Article 199 of the Constitution if they are represented through their counsels. Article 4 of the Constitution makes it crystal clear that no person shall be compelled to do that which the law does not require him to do. Thus, if the Province has filed written report and para-wise comments in a writ petition and is duly represented through a counsel, the Hon'ble High Court has to adjudicate upon the questions of law after perusing the case file and hearing the rival counsels without insisting upon personal appearance of the public servants. If adjudication of a lis requires professional assistance of a public servant, he may be required to render such assistance

515

but making it a routine to order personal appearance of senior officers without just and compelling reasons needs to be avoided.

132.   The Hon'ble Supreme Court of India in a case reported as State of Uttar Pradesh & Ors. Vs. Jasvir Singh & Ors. (2011) 4 SCC 288) has held that summoning of senior officers of the Government should be when absolutely necessary. In this regard, pertinent observations are as under: -

"7. It is a matter of concern that there is a growing trend among a few Judges of the High Court to routinely and frequently require the presence, in court, of senior officers of the government and local and other authorities, including officers of the level of Secretaries, for perceived non-compliance with its suggestions or to seek insignificant clarifications. The power of the High Court under Article 226 is no doubt very wide. It can issue to any person or authority or government, directions, orders, writs for enforcement of fundamental rights or for any other purpose. The High Court has the power to summon or require the personal presence of any officer, to assist the court to render justice or arrive at a proper decision. But there are well settled norms and procedures for exercise of such power.

8. This court has repeatedly noticed that the real power of courts is not in passing decrees and orders, nor in punishing offenders and contemnors, nor in summoning the presence of senior officers, but in the trust, faith and confidence of the common man in the judiciary. Such trust and confidence should not be frittered away by unnecessary and unwarranted show or exercise of power. Greater the power, greater should be the responsibility in exercising such power. The normal procedure in writ petitions is to hear the parties through their counsel who are instructed in the matter, and decide them by examining the pleadings/affidavit/evidence/documents/material. Where the court seeks any information about the compliance with any of its directions, it is furnished by affidavits or reports supported by relevant documents. Requiring the presence of the senior officers of the government in court should be as a last resort, in rare and exceptional cases, where such presence is absolutely necessary, as for example, where it is necessary to seek assistance in explaining complex policy or technical issues, which the counsel is not able to explain properly. The court may also require personal attendance of the officers, where it finds that any officer is deliberately or with ulterior motives withholding any specific information required by the court which he is legally bound to provide or has misrepresented or suppressed the correct position.

9. Where the State has a definite policy or taken a specific stand and that has been clearly explained by way of affidavit, the court should not attempt to impose a contrary view by way of suggestions or proposals for settlement. A court can of course express its views and issue directions through its reasoned orders, subject to limitations in regard to interference in matters of policy. But it should not, and in fact, it cannot attempt to impose its views by asking an unwilling party to settle on the terms suggested by it. At all events the courts should avoid directing the senior officers to be present in court to settle the grievances of individual litigants for whom the court may have sympathy. The court should realize that the state has its own priorities, policies and compulsions which may result in a particular stand. Merely because the court does not like such a stand, it cannot

summon or call the senior officers time and again to court or issue threatening show cause notices. The senior officers of the government are in-charge of the administration of the State, have their own busy schedules. The court should desist from calling them for all and sundry matters, as that would amount to abuse of judicial power. Courts should guard against such transgressions in the exercise of power. Our above observations do not of course apply to summoning of contemnors in contempt jurisdiction."

133.   The Hon'ble Supreme Court of India held State of Gujarat Vs. Turabali Gulamhussain Hirani (2007 (14) SCC 94) that:

"A large number of cases have come up before this Court where we find that learned Judges of various High Courts have been summoning the Chief Secretary, Secretaries to the Government (Central and state), Directors General of Police, Director, CBI or BSF or other senior officials of the Government. There is no doubt that the High Court has power to summon these officials, but in our opinion that should be done in very rare and exceptional cases when there are compelling circumstances to do so. Such summoning orders should not be passed lightly or as a routine or at the top of a hat. Judges should have modesty and humility. They should realize that summoning a senior official, except in some very rare and exceptional situation, and that too for compelling reasons, is counterproductive and may also involve heavy expenses and valuable time of the official concerned. The judiciary must have respect for the executive and the legislature. Judges should realize that officials like the Chief Secretary, Secretary to Government, Commissioners, District Magistrates, senior police officials, etc. are extremely busy persons who are often working from morning till night.

10. Hence, frequent, casual and lackadaisical summoning of high officials by the Court cannot be appreciated. We are constrained to make these observations because we are coming across a large number of cases where such orders summoning of high officials are being passed by the High Courts and often it is nothing but for the ego satisfaction of the learned Judge."

134.   We have examined the file relating to the contempt proceedings initiated for implementation of the ratio of the second A.A. Zuberi case. We have found that detailed written defence of the Province is available in the file. There was no specific point required to be clarified by the civil servants. Senior officers like the Chief Secretary, the Finance Secretary and others were ordered to appear in person many times. Mr. Yazdani has informed us that the Hon'ble High Court threatened to call in person the Chief Minister, Punjab for implementation of the second A.A. Zuberi case. We are not in agreement with the assumption that the constitutional office of the Advocate General is not competent enough to the assist the Hon'ble High Court in any matter because of spoils system on which it is based. Even if that be correct, the Province has to pay the price of its preference of spoils system over a merit system. This argument does not justify summoning of senior officers in the courts, especially keeping in view the fact that thousands and thousands of cases are pending against departments of the Government of the Punjab and it is a human impossibility for a Secretary to appear in person even in a fraction of these cases. We hold that no public servant shall be summoned in proceedings under Article 199 of the Constitution if written response of the Province is on record and the Province is represented through a qualified counsel and no extremely intricate and technical issue requiring expert opinion and professional advice of a public servant is involved.

135.	The matter of summoning senior officers of the Government gets more serious when they are subjected to strictures. We have not been able to find a reason that why executive officers are not entitled to the treatment to which judicial officers have been held entitled to by the Hon'ble Supreme Court of Pakistan in Miss Nusrat Yasmin Vs. The Registrar, Peshawar High Court, Peshawar & others (Criminal Appeal No.03-P of 2017) in these words:

> "Therefore, it is desirable that the High Court, while performing its judicial function, avoids passing strictures regarding the ability, competence, integrity, and behaviour of the judge whose judgment is under scrutiny before it.
>
> Passing strictures and publically rebuking, condemning and reproaching a judge does not sit well with the judicial character of the High Court. It is equally inappropriate to summon a judge of the District Judiciary to court for a public reprimand, during the hearing of the case against his judgment, in open Court. The character of judicial determination by the High Court does not allow the court to go beyond and assess, evaluate and appraise the competence, diligence, conduct, integrity or temperament of a judge of the District Judiciary, other than judicial bias or malice if it is borne out from the record of the case and is essential for the determination of the lis."

136.	The following observation by Sulaiman, J. in Panchanan Banerji Vs. Upendra Nath Bhattacharji (AIR [1927] All 193) was cited with approval by the Hon'ble Supreme Court of India in a case reported as Niranjan Patnaik v. Sashibhusan Kar and Anr. (1986 2 SCR 569)

> "It is, therefore, settled law that harsh or disparaging remarks are not to be made against persons and authorities whose conduct comes into consideration before Court of law unless it is really necessary for the decision of the case, as an integral part thereof to animadvert on that conduct."

137.	It was held by the Hon'ble Supreme Court of India in a case reported as 'K', A Judicial Officer, In re (AIR 2001 SC 972) that:

> "Though the power to make remarks or observations is there but on being questioned, the exercise of power must withstand judicial scrutiny on the touchstone of following tests:- (a) whether the party whose conduct is in question is before the Court or has an opportunity of explaining or defending himself; (b) whether there is evidence on record bearing on that conduct justifying the remarks; and (c) whether it is necessary for the decision of the case, as an integral part thereof, to animadvert on that conduct. The overall test is that the criticism or observation must be judicial in nature and should not formally depart from sobriety, moderation and reserve [see Mohmmad Naim (supra)]."

138.	In A.M. Mathur Vs. Pramod Kumar Gupta ([1990] 2 SCC 533), the Supreme Court of India sounded a note of caution emphasizing a general principle of highest importance to the proper administration of justice that derogatory remarks ought not to be make against persons or authorities whose conduct comes into consideration unless it is absolutely necessary for the decision of the case to animadvert on their conduct and said:

> "Judicial restraint and discipline are as necessary to the orderly administration of justice as they are to the effectiveness of the army. The duty of restraint, this humility of function should be constant theme of our judges. This quality in decision making is as much necessary for judges to command respect as to protect the independence of the judiciary. Judicial restraint in this regard might better be called judicial respect, that is, respect by the judiciary. Respect to those who come before the court as well to other co-ordinate branches of the State, the executive, and legislature. There

must be mutual respect. When these qualities fail of when litigants and public believe that the judge has failed in these qualities, it will be neither good for the judge nor for the judicial process."

139.   The duty to act justly, reasonably and fairly is not only the duty of everyone in executive or legislative branch of the Government but all those who exercise judicial power of the state are also expected to refrain from acting unjustly, unreasonably and unfairly. A judge is required to be cautious, restrained, respectful, and deferential with regard to the executive as well as the legislature. One-way traffic is likely to cause accidents, injury and pain. The legislature and the political executive comprises of elected representatives of the people. The civil and military bureaucracy obtains employment in the Service of Pakistan on merit determined through open competitive process. Neither of them is a product of nomination system--- a system inherited from the East India Company under which employment in military, civil or judicial service of the Company was not based on merit. "Success was ultimately dependent upon connection and influence rather than the possession of any skills and aptitude for the post," writes Huw Bowen in his book "Business of Empire". Of late, the Company substituted the system of nomination by the Directors of the Company and the Board of Control with a system based upon merit of the candidates determined through open competition at the time of entry into service in respect of its civil and military bureaucracy. Macaulay Committee Report recommended that an appointment to the civil service of the Company will not be a matter of favour but a matter of right. He who obtains such an appointment will owe it solely to his own abilities and industry, the report said. We do not deem it essential to further dilate upon the issue.

140.   When passing a stricture is unnecessary and is not based upon the evidence available in the case file, then it is obviously necessary to refrain from doing so. We have found in the instant case that it was absolutely unnecessary to comment upon conduct and competence of the executive officers summoned to appear in person before the Hon'ble High Court. We direct all concerned that strictures shall not be passed by a court of law unless the tests specified by the Hon'ble Supreme Court of India in a case reported as 'K', A Judicial Officer, In re (AIR 2001 SC 972) are fulfilled. Moreover, whereas a judge cannot be prohibited to raise interrogatories with inquisitorial spirit in order to correctly understand facts of a case and the law applicable thereto, it is his detailed judgment, short orders or written interim orders which can be allowed to be reported in print, electronic or social media. Article V of the Code of Conduct for Judges of the Supreme Court and High Courts framed by the Supreme Judicial Council says that functioning as he does in full view of the public, a Judge gets thereby all the publicity that is good for him. He should not seek more. We, therefore, order that the print, electronic and social media shall not report any utterances of a judge during proceedings of a case except what is written in his signed judicial order. For the purpose to ensure access to information, it is directed that all orders of the superior judiciary shall be displayed on the website of the concerned court on the date an order is signed by the judge. We have to ensure that only judgments speak, not the judges.

141.   As regards initiation of contempt of court proceedings for implementation of judgements of the Hon'ble Lahore High Court based upon the second A.A. Zuberi case, we have observed that:

> (a) The judgments of the Hon'ble Lahore High Court regarding doubling of pension plus increases in pension on the date of restoration of the commuted portion of pension of the retired civil servants of the Government of the Punjab were based upon the second A.A. Zuberi case, a judgment dealing with federal pensioners;
>
> (b) The judgments in respect of the provincial pensioners were without jurisdiction and, hence, void and of no legal effect. The Hon'ble Supreme Court decided the question of jurisdiction in the Ismail Tayer case;

(c) With implementation of the principle of merger, these judgments were not in lawful existence after the Ismail Tayer case which was the only judgment lawfully in the field on the subject. There is no law or reason to get a judgment implemented which is not in lawful existence;

(d) The matter of civil contempt is between the alleged contemnor and the court orders of which have not been complied with. In this regard, reliance can be placed on the dictum of law laid down by the Hon'ble Supreme Court in a case reported as West Pakistan Water and Power Development Authority Vs. Chairman National Industrial Relations Commission (PLD 1979 SC 912). The Hon'ble Supreme Court is competent in terms of Article 204 of the Constitution, the Contempt of Court Ordinance, 2003 and the Supreme Court Rules, 1980 to punish anyone found guilty of its contempt. Under Section 4 of the Contempt of Court Ordinance, 2003, the High Court can take action on charges of its own contempt and also a contempt in relation to any court subordinate to it. The Hon'ble High Court has no power to punish a person on charges of contempt of the Hon'ble Supreme Court. An Hon'ble High Court cannot accept or reject apology tendered by a person accused of civil contempt of the Hon'ble Supreme Court;

(e) Powers under Article 204 of the Constitution and the Contempt of Court Ordinance, 2003 are to punish the contemnors and not for enforcement of a judgment of any court. Reliance in this regard can be placed on Mehdi Hassan, Additional Secretary, Food and Forests Department, Government of West Pakistan and another Vs. Zulfiqar Ali, Conservator of Forests, Development Circle, Lahore [PLD 1960 (W.P.) Lahore 751] and Mrs. Razia Yaqub Vs. Malik Muhammad Ashiq and 2 others [PLD 2003 Lahore 486];

(f) The Hon'ble High Court is not meant, in proceedings under Article 199 of the Constitution, to be an executing court for the learned Service Tribunal. It has been held by the Hon'ble Balochistan High Court in a case reported as Niaz Muhammad Khoso Vs. Government of Balochistan through Chief Secretary, Quetta (2012 PLC (C.S) 106) that:

> "The above provision of law leads us to conclude that since the Balochistan Service Tribunal is a civil court for the purpose of deciding any appeal regarding the terms and conditions of a civil servant, therefore, it has all the powers of a civil court including those required to implement its judgments as provided under the provisions of the Code of Civil Procedure, 1908."

(g) The contempt proceedings were initiated on the basis of a protected statement in terms of Section 16(ii) of the Contempt of Court Ordinance, 2003 without any charge of willful disobedience; and

(h) The written defence of the contemnors was not analysed and held invalid and no charges were framed against the alleged contemnors despite a number of hearings fixed for the purpose. Even the defence of impossibility of compliance, which was neither self-created nor post-litigation, was not taken into consideration and was simply ignored.

142. In the celebrated judgment reported as Attorney General v. Times Newspaper Ltd.; 1974 AC 273: (1973) 3 All ER 54: (1973) 3 WLR 298; Lord Diplock stated:

> "There is an element of public policy in punishing civil contempt, since the administration of justice would be undermined if the order of any court of law could be disregarded with impunity."

143. Article 204 of the Constitution and the contempt of court law are meant to ensure that the judicial process does not degenerate into a mere formality, incapable of effectively determining and enforcing legal rights and obligations of the litigants.

144. As representation by state counsel in contempt proceedings is not permissible {Abdul Majeed Vs. Government of Sindh through Secretary, Food Department, Karachi and 2 others (PLD 2000 Karachi 310)}, therefore, initiation of contempt proceedings is equal to fiscally burdening a public servant in the form of imposing upon him expenses on hiring a private counsel to defend an action performed in discharge of official duty.

145. An analysis of the facts on file indicates that contempt of the Hon'ble Supreme Court of Pakistan was caused through nullification of the judgment of the Hon'ble Supreme Court in the Ismail Tayer case. This was done despite the fact that the Chief Secretary, Finance Secretary and the members of the Complaint Cell gave detailed written justifications for their interpretation of the Ismail Tayer case. Due diligence on the part of the Government of the Punjab in faithful implementation of the Ismail Tayer case is floating on the surface of the record. We are at loss of words when Mr. Yazdani labels what was done as judicial indiscipline.

146. We are convinced to hold and do hereby hold that:

a) The Hon'ble High Court cannot initiate proceedings on the charges of civil contempt of the Hon'ble Supreme Court;

b) When want of jurisdiction of the Court or impossibility of compliance by the alleged contemnor are taken as defence or a written defence is submitted by an alleged contemnor, the court shall not proceed further without adjudicating upon the questions of jurisdiction and impossibility defence and holding the written defence legally invalid;

c) When a civil contempt is alleged in an adversarial proceeding, it shall not be unlawful for the Province to defend its officers through the office of the Advocate General, Punjab or other arrangements at state expense if the charge relates to performance of official duties of the alleged contemnor; and

d) If the Hon'ble Supreme Court holds, in its appellate jurisdiction, that the proceedings on the charge of civil contempt were without jurisdiction or the impossibility defence was not taken into consideration or proceedings were continued and finalized without first declaring the written defence submitted in consequence of a show cause notice legally invalid, it shall be treated a misconduct in terms of Article 209 of the Constitution on the part of the Hon'ble High Court.

147. The learned Advocate General, Punjab submits that threats of transfers, initiation of disciplinary or criminal proceedings and loss of employment as a result of punishment on the charges of civil contempt of court are frequently used when courts observe that the public servants are not toeing the line thought just, fair and reasonable by the court. He avers that there is a general misperception that whatever is said by an Hon'ble judge is his judicial capacity is binding for all irrespective of the fact whether the order amounts to exercise of a power exclusively vested in the executive. He argues that it is necessary to make it clear that a court of law is subject to and not beyond the Constitution and law. He submits that when executive officers feel threatened that sticking to a stand or argument distasteful to a court of law may cause personal problems for them, they generally do not burn the midnight oil to vehemently plead the case or to assist the court. What generally ensues is miscarriage of justice or perpetuation of injustice, generally against the Government, he argues. In this regard, he refers to thousands of appointments made or regularized on courts' orders which he terms litigious appointments. He also prays that this

Court may clarify that whether conviction on the charges of civil contempt of court renders the convicted person ineligible to serve or continue to serve in the Service of Pakistan?

148. Mr. Yazdani opines that a system can function efficiently if its sub-systems confine themselves to their assigned jobs and no sub-system crosses its boundaries and meddles in the working of another sub-system. He claims that entrustment of executive, judicial and legislative powers to different organs of state is the fundamental way our Constitution balances power so that one part of the government doesn't overpower another. He argues that power to appoint, post/transfer and take disciplinary action in respect of persons in the Service of Pakistan working in the executive branch is an executive power. He submits that exercise of this power by a court violates the principle of trichotomy of powers and is patently a travel beyond judicial territory. He is of the view that pious intentions of an Hon'ble judge cannot compensate absence of lawful authority to assume to himself executive functions of the Government. He prays that this Court may dispel misconceptions in this regard and issue appropriate orders so that the principle of trichotomy of powers is effectively implemented and deviations therefrom are meaningfully checked.

149. The learned counsels for the private respondents contend that a court will be rendered toothless if it is prohibited to order appointments, transfers, postings and initiation of disciplinary and criminal proceedings against public servants in appropriate cases and for just causes. They submit that sometimes it becomes necessary to remove a public servant from his post to disable him to impede process of the court. They also claim that glaring violations of law observed during proceedings of a case compel the Hon'ble judges for initiation of action against the offenders. They submit that judges without sticks are not likely to ensure complete justice. It is better to have no courts if the Hon'ble judges are reduced to the status of slaves of written law, they aver. As regards the litigious appointments and regularizations of employees, the learned counsels contend that the courts are created to provide relief which includes ordering appointments and regularizations where need be. They argue that no one should expected clerical mentality from the Hon'ble judges of the superior judiciary. They prayer that all submissions and arguments offered by the learned Advocate General, Punjab and Mr. Yazdani deserve to be laid to rest in the dustbin of the Court.

150. We have analysed the rival contentions. We find it unnecessary to dilate upon the question of litigious appointments as the lis at hand can be adjudicated upon without doing so. So far as the question of posting / transfer of the public servants is concerned, there is no dispute that Article 240(b) of the Constitution authorizes the Provincial Assembly to regulate appointments to and terms and conditions of service of the members of the Services of the Province and posts in connection with affairs of the Province. Powers to appoint, post / transfer, appraise performance and take disciplinary action in respect of the public servants are vested in various authorities specified either in the Act of the Provincial Assembly or the rules framed thereunder. These designated authorities apply their mind to facts and circumstances of a case and take decisions based upon their judgment. Their decisions are challengeable on grounds of legality and not of reasonability or wisdom. A court of law has no power to substitute, modify or undo an administrative decision taken by an officer as per his discretion if the decision does not suffer from a fatal illegality. The matters relating to postings / transfers / disciplinary actions of the civil servants are beyond the jurisdiction of a High Court. Even if a court of law has jurisdiction in the matter, it may review an executive decision on legal grounds and not on the touchstone of policy or reasonability. If an authority has lawful power to transfer an employee, it is that authority alone which can order the transfer. The court is not authorized to issue his transfer orders or to direct the competent authority to order the transfer. If the question of lawful authority of a person to hold a public office in quo warranto proceedings under Article 199 of the Constitution is under adjudication, the Hon'ble High Court can declare that the holder of a public office lacks lawful authority to hold that office and can declare the office so held vacant and direct that the vacancy be filled in accordance with law. But in no case, the

Hon'ble High Court can order transfer / posting of a particular civil servant from or against a specific post. If an Hon'ble High Court does so, it would be usurping lawful powers of an executive officer.

151. Performance appraisal of the civil servants and making decisions to initiate departmental or criminal action against them are legal powers vested in executive officers. A court of law has no power to assume to itself these powers. What cannot be done directly is also not allowed to be done indirectly. As the court cannot exercise these powers through issuance of its own orders, it also lacks powers to direct executive officers to issue such orders. The court will intervene only when a justiciable case is presented before it and legality of an act or omission requires determination. The court can exercise judicial power of the state duly vested in it on points of law and not of policy. Policy is a province prohibited for the judiciary. If a judgment speaks of inefficiency, misconduct or corruption of a civil servant, it is for the competent authority to examine material on the subject and proceed in accordance with law. A court is debarred to dictate an executive officer to suspend his reason and mechanically follow what is said by an Hon'ble court. Mr. Yazdani has pointed out in a lighter vein that if the executive and the legislature have never tried to usurp powers of the Hon'ble Chief Justice to constitute benches of the court and to assign any case to any bench, then why an Hon'ble judge can be allowed to say that a particular civil post be held or not held by a particular civil servant.

152. We have learnt a number of times that the civil servants are threatened that they shall lose their job if they are convicted on the charges of civil contempt of court. Reference in this regard is made to Article 63(1)(g) of the Constitution, reproduced below:

> "63. Disqualifications for membership of Majlis-e-Shoora (Parliament).
>
> -(1) A person shall be disqualified from being elected or chosen as, and from being, a member of the Majlis-e-Shoora (Parliament), if—
>
> (g) he has been convicted by a court of competent jurisdiction for propagating any opinion, or acting in any manner, prejudicial to the ideology of Pakistan, or the sovereignty, integrity or security of Pakistan, or the integrity, or independence of the judiciary of Pakistan, or which defames or brings into ridicule he judiciary or the Armed Forces of Pakistan, unless a period of five years has lapsed since his release; or"

153. A bare perusal of Article 63(1)(g) of the Constitution reveals that it pertains to disqualification for membership of the Parliament and not to gain or retain employment in the Service of Pakistan. Even for the purpose of disqualification from the membership of the Parliament, what is relevant in the context of conviction with respect to judiciary is conviction for propagating any opinion, or acting in any manner, prejudicial to the integrity, or independence of the judiciary of Pakistan, or which defames or brings into ridicule he judiciary. On the other hand, civil contempt is disobedience or disregard of any order, direction or process of a Court, which a person is legally bound to obey. Thus, conviction on the charges of civil disobedience does not furnish a ground envisaged in Article 63(1)(g) of the Constitution. Moreover, the Punjab Civil Servants Act, 1974 and the Punjab Employees Efficiency, Discipline and Accountability Act 2006 and the rules framed thereunder do not provide that conviction on the charges of civil contempt of a court disqualify a person to obtain or retain employment in the Service of Pakistan. Article 4 of the Constitution, inter alia, provides that no person shall be prevented from or be hindered in doing that which is not prohibited by law. Further, the fundamental right to trade and profession includes the right to compete for and get employment in the Service of Pakistan and to retain that employment in accordance with law. We have found no legal basis to hold that conviction on the charges of civil contempt of a court may render the contemner ineligible to gain or

retain employment in the service of Pakistan. We hope that this declaration is enough to dispel misconceptions on the subject.

154.   The learned Advocate General, Punjab states that the Hon'ble High Court not only converted contempt proceedings into proceedings for execution of a judgment but also granted final relief through interim orders. He submits that the practice of granting the main relief through interim order amounts to grant of final relief without adjudication on the point in controversy on which the grant of that relief depends is in violation of the law laid down by the Hon'ble superior courts. He further avers that grant of main relief through interim order denies respondents the opportunity of intra-court appeal and burdens them with the duty to either approach the Apex Court for obtaining stay order or face contempt of court proceedings at an interim stage. He argues that grant of main relief through interim orders is offensive to the concept of fair trial and due process, guaranteed by Article 10-A of the Constitution. He is of the view that grant of final relief through interim orders which interfere with laws, rules, regulations or disturb working of Government departments is not legally permissible.

155.   Mr. Yazdani submits that the Province is also entitled to due process and fair trial under Article 10A of the Constitution. When final relief is granted in the form of interim orders or injunctions, the party benefiting from such order becomes interested in employing delaying tactics, he states. He prays that this court may make an appropriate declaration to ensure plugging the avenues of misuse of interim orders against the Governments. He is of the view that interim orders are the main cause of civil contempt of the court in a number of cases. He refers to a case relating to an election dispute which remained pending in the Hon'ble High Court for a long time while a party to the dispute took refuge behind an injunctive order and ultimately the Hon'ble High Court dismissed the proceedings for want of jurisdiction.

156.   The learned counsels for the private respondents claim that issuance of interim orders has been, is and shall continue to be an inseparable part of judicial process. Dispensation of justice is not possible in some cases without resort to the issuance of interim or injunctive orders, they argue admitting that continuance of these orders for indefinite or unreasonable time is, however, not defendable. They also submit that there is no prohibition in granting main relief through interim orders if justice so demands. They further state that injunctive orders can also be issued in respect of laws, rules, regulations or executive instructions even if the result is disruption in normal functioning of department of the Government. They pray that punitive costs may be imposed on Mr. Yazdani for raising meaningless questions just to gain publicity.

157.   We have considered the conflicting views of the parties. We may begin our discussion by referring to a case reported as Province of East Pakistan Vs. Md. Mehdi Ali Khan (PLD 1959 SC 387) in which the Hon'ble Supreme Court of Pakistan held that:

> "The essential steps of a judicial process are the ascertainment of facts, determination of the law applicable to the facts found or admitted, an inference as to the existence or otherwise of a right or obligation from the determination of the law and a decision as to the final order to be made in respect of such right or obligation. Since the ultimate object of such process is the enforcement of a right or obligation, every step of the process has a necessary reference to and is limited by that object."

158.   Final or main relief depends upon the adjudication of the point in controversy. It is not permissible to be granted without adhering to the due process. Granting main relief through interim orders is against the dictum of law laid down by the Hon'ble superior courts in cases reported as Sardar Muhammad Abdullah Khan Tahir Vs. Sahibzada Muhammad Usman Khan Abbasi (1998 CLC 612), United Bank Limited and others Vs. Ahsan Akhtar and others (1998 SCMR 68) and Islamic Republic of Pakistan through Secretary, Establishment Division, Islamabad and others Vs. Muhammad Zaman Khan and others (1997 SCMR 1508).

The Hon'ble Supreme Court of India has consistently been emphasizing that the Court while dealing with the case at an interim stage cannot grant a relief which amounts to final relief. In this regard the cases reported as (1) Titaghur Paper Mills Co. Ltd. Vs. State of Orissa (AIR 1983 SC 603), (2) Siliguri Municipality Vs. Amalendu Das (AIR 1984 SC 653), (3) Union of India Vs. Oswal Woolen Mills Ltd. (AIR 1984 SC 1264), (4) Assistant Collector, Central Excise Vs. Dunlop India Ltd. (AIR 1985 SC 330), (5) Samarias Trading Company Pvt. Ltd. Vs. S. Samuel (AIR 1985 SC 61), (6) State of Rqjasthan Vs. Swaika Properties (AIR 1985 SC 1289), (7) State of West Bengal and Ors. Vs. Calcutta Hardware Stores and Ors. (AIR 1986 SC 614), (8) State of Jammu and Kashmir Vs. Mohammad Yakoob Khan and Ors. {(1992) 4 SCC 167}, (9) U. P. Junior Doctors' Action Committee and Ors. Vs. Dr. B. Sheetal Nandwani (AIR 1992 SC 671), (10) Guru Nanak Dev University Vs. Parminder Kumar Bansal and Anr. (AIR 1993 SC 2412), (11) St. John's Teachers Training Institute (for Women) and Ors. Vs. State of Tamil Nadu and Ors., {(1993) 3 SCC 595} (12) Dr. B.S. Kshirsagar Vs. Abdul Khalik Mohd. Musa, (1995 Suppl (2) SCC 593), (13) Bank of Maharashtra Vs. Race Shipping and Transport Company (P.) Ltd. (AIR 1995 SC 1368), (14) Commissioner/Secretary, Government Health and Medical Education Department Vs. Dr. Ashok Kumar Kohli (1995 Suppl (4) SCC 214), (15) Visakhapatnam Dock Labour Board Vs. E. Atchanna and Ors., {(1996) 2 SCC 484}, (16) Union of India Vs. Shree Ganesh Steel Rolling Mills Ltd. {(1996) 8 SCC 347}, (17) State of Madhya Pradesh Vs. M. V. Vyavsaya & Co. {AIR 1997 SC 993), (18) Council for Indian School Certificate Examination Vs. Isha Mittal and Anr.{(2000) 7 SCC 521} and (19) Union of India Vs. Modi (Luft) Ltd. {(2003) 6 SCC 65)} can be relied upon.

159.   It has been held by the Hon'ble Supreme Court of Pakistan in a case reported as Marghub Siddiqui Vs. Hamid Ahmad Khan (1974 SCMR 519) that although ad interim injunctions are granted under Order XXXIX rule 1 CPC, the principles which govern the grant of perpetual injunctions, as contained in the Specific Relief Act, 1877, have also to be kept in view. By section 56, clause (d) of the Specific Relief Act, no injunction can be granted which interferes with the public duties of any department of the Federal or Provincial Government. Business of the Government is run in accordance with the law, rules, regulations and executive instructions. Issuance of an injunctive order to a department of the Government amounts to refrain it from transacting its business in accordance with the law or, in other words, to suspend operation of laws, rules, regulations and executive instructions governing the operation. It has been held by a 12-judge bench of the Hon'ble Supreme Court of Pakistan in a case reported as Federation of Pakistan Vs. Aitzaz Ahsan and another (PLD 1989 SC 61) that until a law is finally held to be ultra vires for any reason, it should have its normal operation. In this view of the matter, the practice of suspending the operation of laws, rules, regulations and executive instructions having the force of law before declaring them ultra vires or otherwise legally invalid cannot be construed a judicious exercise of judicial power of the state. A court of competent jurisdiction may, if it finds a matter requiring urgent adjudication, proceed on day-to—day basis and then deliver a judgment on the legality of anything. As in most cases, the parties can be compensated through imposition of costs, therefore, we do not find it appreciable to have resort to injunctive orders concerning business of a Government unless human life is under threat. We think that any matter concerning property does not need to be adjudicated upon through issuance of injunctive orders against the Government. Right to life is a fundamental right for protection of which an Hon'ble High Court may, however, in very special and compelling circumstances, issue an injunctive order for a period not exceeding the period prescribed by law.

160.   In view of the above discussion, we hold, declare and direct that main relief shall not be granted through interim orders and the Hon'ble High Court or the Hon'ble Supreme Court shall not issue injunctive orders against laws, rules, regulations or executive instructions having the force of law except for protection of human life. In case an urgent action is deemed essential in a case, the case shall be concluded through day-to-day hearing and the

legal validity of laws, rules, regulations or executive instructions having the force of law shall expeditiously be determined only through final orders.

161. The learned Advocate General, Punjab has seriously questioned the lawfulness of review of judgment delivered by a Division Bench of the Hon'ble Lahore High Court by an Hon'ble Single Bench of the same court. He says that in addition to objections raised on the proceedings initiated by the Hon'ble Single Bench, it needs to be noted very seriously that an Hon'ble Single Bench modified judgment delivered by a Division Bench. Learned counsels of the private respondents are silent on the issue. On the other hand, Mr. Yazdani terms it a text-book example of judicial indiscipline.

162. There is no doubt that direct or indirect modification in or review of a judgment delivered by a Division-Bench does not fall within the competence of a Single Bench. No stretch of imagination or reasoning can empower an Hon'ble Single Bench to play with judgment of a Division or a Full Bench of the Hon'ble High Court under the pretext of implementation of that judgment or on any other ground. We deem it wastage of our precious public-paid time to quote authorities to support this proposition; it is as clear and certain as death. We declare that what was done by the Hon'ble Single Bench in the name of implementation of the second A.A. Zuberi case was not only without jurisdiction and void but was also against all norms of judicial discipline. This is in addition to our earlier declarations hereinabove in this judgment regarding the second A.A. Zuberi case.

Question # 5

Whether the ratio decidendi of the Third Judges' pension case stands overruled by the Fourth and Fifth Judges' pension cases and the position contained in the First and the Second Judges' pension case has revived? Whether the dictum of law laid down in the Third Judges' pension case to the extent of recovery of amounts drawn without lawful authority needs to be overruled?

163. The learned Advocate General, Punjab submits that it is of no use to argue that a judge of a High Court with less than five years of service as such judge is entitled to pension as a retired judge of the High Court or not? He cites the dictum of law laid down by a five-judge bench of the Hon'ble Supreme Court of Pakistan in the Third Judges' pension case in his favour and argues that until that judgment is overruled, it has to be given the sanctity of Article 189 and enforceability of Article 190 of the Constitution. He avers that it is within jurisdiction of the Hon'ble Supreme Court to overrule its earlier judgments but after fulfilling the following three conditions:

   a) the Bench of the Hon'ble Supreme Court comprises the judges greater in number than that of the Bench the judgment of which is intended to be overruled;
   b) the judgment intended to be overruled is considered and discussed and reasons for overruling it are given; and
   c) procedural formalities e.g. notice to the affected parties are observed.

164. The learned Advocate General, Punjab argues that Article 189 of the Constitution binds the Hon'ble High Courts to follow a decision of the Hon'ble Supreme Court to the extent it decides a question of law or is based upon or enunciates a principle of law. He submits that the Hon'ble High Court utterly lacks jurisdiction to modify, substitute or set aside the ratio decidendi of a judgment of the Hon'ble Supreme Court or to refuse to follow it while adjudicating upon the cases under Article 199 of the Constitution. He further avers that the Third Judges' pension case was cited in its defence, in writing as well as orally, by the Government of the Punjab before the Hon'ble Lahore High Court in the Fourth Judges' pension case but the Hon'ble High Court did not like to consider or discuss this case. He states that the leave to appeal granting order of the Hon'ble Supreme Court dated 29.09.2018 specifically mentioned the Third Judges' pension case but it was not considered

or discussed by the Three-Judge Bench of the Hon'ble Supreme which disposed of the appeal through its order dated 27.03.2019. He is of the view that the Fourth and the Fifth judges' pension cases practically overruled the ratio decidendi of the Third Judges' pension case. He thinks that neither the Hon'ble Lahore High Court nor a three-judge bench of the Hon'ble Supreme Court have any power to directly or indirectly overrule the Third Judges' pension case. He argues that the Fourth and the Fifth Judges' pension cases are against the dictum of law laid down in the Third Judges' pension case. He avers that whereas an Hon'ble judge enjoys complete impunity when he acts judicially in exercise of powers given to him by or under the Constitution and honest human errors of judgment cannot furnish a ground for proceedings under Article 209 of the Constitution, any willful non-compliance of the dictum of law of the nature mentioned in Article 189 of the Constitution is a valid reason to invoke Article 209 of the Constitution. All executive and judicial authorities are under a constitutional duty to act in aid of the Supreme Court so much so that "if a judgment is not implemented, the person at fault commits contempt of the Court and is punishable." {Al-Jehad Trust Vs. Federation (PLD 1997 SC 84) and Dr. Mobashir Hassan Vs. Federation (PLD 2010 SC 265)}. He states that the Hon'ble Supreme Court passed a restraining order on 3rd of November, 2007, directing: --

a) Government of Pakistan i.e. the President and Prime Minister to restrain from undertaking any such action, which was contrary to the independence of the judiciary;

b) Chief of the Army Staff (then President of Pakistan also), all Corps Commanders, General Staff Officers and all other concerned military and civil authorities to restrain from acting on the Proclamation of Emergency, P.C.O. No. 1 of 2007 etc.; and

c) The President and the Governors not to administer fresh oath to Judges of the Superior Judiciary under PCO No. I of 2007 and Judges' Oath Order No. 1 of 2007. Judges of the superior judiciary were also directed not to make oath under the above mentioned two Orders.

165. He says that violation of the restraining order of the Hon'ble Supreme Court dated 03.11.2007 cost dozens of judges of the Hon'ble superior judiciary their jobs. He submits that the Hon'ble Supreme Court through a case reported as Sindh High Court Bar Association Vs. Federation of Pakistan (PLD 2009 SC 879) itself removed all permanent and additional judges appointed in consultation with the then Chief Justice of Pakistan (Mr. Abdul Hameed Dogar). He states that the aforesaid judgment held the judges who took oath in violation of the restraining order of 03.11.2007 liable to be proceeded against under Article 209 of the Constitution. The view that willful non-compliance of an order of the Hon'ble Supreme Court is actionable under Article 209 of the Constitution was reiterated by a 14-judge bench of the Hon'ble Supreme Court in a case reported as **Justice Khurshid Anwar Bhinder Vs. Federation of Pakistan (2010 PLD 483).** The Hon'ble Supreme Court followed the same principle in its 4-member bench's judgment reported as Justice Hasnat Ahmed Khan Vs. Federation of Pakistan (PLD 2011 SC 680). He expresses the fear that if the Fifth Judges' pension case is not held void and of no legal effect, the Hon'ble judges shown the way out by the Hon'ble Supreme Court of Pakistan in cases cited by him would also claim pensionary benefits despite less than five years of service as judge of the High Court.

166. The learned Advocate General, Punjab submits that an Hon'ble judge has to apply his judicial mind if parties to a pending case present a consensus settlement on the dispute. The learned law officer opines that in such case an Hon'ble judge is not required to substitute the consensus settlement of the parties if the arrangement is legal and the court has valid jurisdiction in the matter. But the Hon'ble Court shall never accept a consensus settlement if it is illegal or the court lacks jurisdiction, he adds. He expresses the view that judicial power of the state is for the purpose of adjudication of justiciable controversies in

accordance with law. The majesty of a court lies in strengthening the rule of law and not in perpetuating illegalities in the pretext of approving consensus settlements, he says.

167.   The learned Advocate General, Punjab also questions competence of the Secretary, Ministry of Law and Justice, Government of Pakistan to concede to any claim payable from the Provincial Consolidated Fund terming him a perfect stranger for the purpose of giving any statement in this regard.

168.   The learned Advocate General further argues that a civil servant elevated as judge of a High Court who retires without serving as such judge for a minimum period of five years once again becomes, on his retirement, amenable to the Punjab Civil Servants Act, 1974 and the rules framed thereunder. He is of the view that pension of such judge is governed neither under the High Court Judges (Leave, Pension and Privileges) Order, 1997 (President's Order No.3 of 1997) nor under any rules applicable to the federal civil servants. The only rules attracted in such cases are the rules framed under the Punjab Civil Servants Act, 1974 with the sole difference that the service as judge of the Hon'ble High Court is added to the service qualifying for pension of the retired civil servants, he submits.

169.   The learned Advocate General prays that the consent orders in the Fourth and the Fifth Judges' pension cases be declared void, inter alia, for the aforesaid reasons. He further prays that the Third Judges pension case merits to be overruled to the extent of waiving of recoveries of amounts drawn from the Provincial Consolidated Fund without or in excess of lawful authority.

170.   Mr. Yazdani argues that consent of the parties does not grant valid jurisdiction on a subject which is otherwise missing. He submits that order of a court that a pending case is disposed of in terms of a consensus settlement of the parties does not cure or permit illegalities and if a consensus settlement is in violation of the Constitution or a law, it remains invalid and can confer no rights or impose no obligations. He avers that A Court may dispose of a matter before it in terms of settlement between the parties only if it has jurisdiction on the subject-matter and the parties and the settlement does not violate the Constitution, law, rules or instructions having the force of law. To illustrate his argument, he presents the following case scenarios:

a) Mr. A files a write petition in the Hon'ble High Court praying for his appointment as a judge of the High Court against a vacancy saying that he has all the qualifications for the post and suffers from no disqualification. The Federation and the Province have been assailed as the respondents. The petitioner and the Secretary, Law & Parliamentary Affairs Department submit a consensus settlement in the Hon'ble High Court that the petitioner shall be appointed as a District & Sessions Judge instead of a judge of the High Court. The Hon'ble High Court disposed of the writ petition in terms of the consensus settlement and the petitioner is appointed as a District & Sessions Judge.

b) Mr. A is working as Additional Secretary in the office of the Chief Minister and is in receipt of a monthly remuneration of Rs. 2,63,000/. He files a petition in the Hon'ble High Court praying for raising of his remuneration to Rs. 6.00,000/ per month as he merits this remuneration on account of his academic qualification, experience and professional expertise. The Principal Secretary to the Chief Minister is the respondent. The petitioner and the respondent reach a compromise and submit a consensus agreement to enhance monthly remuneration to Rs. 4,00,000/. The Hon'ble High Court disposes of the writ petition in terms of the settlement between the parties.

c) The Lahore Development Authority leases out a petrol pump to Mr. A for one year on a lease money of Rs. 15,000/ per month. After expiry of one year, Mr. A does not vacate the petrol pump. He illegally continues to operate the petrol pump for four years. The real lease value of the petrol pump in the open market is Rs. 45,00,000/ per month. The Lahore Development Authority decides to auction out the lease rights through open competitive process. Mr. A files a writ petition in the Hon'ble High Court and succeeds in getting interim relief of staying of the auction proceedings. The case remains pending for two and half years. The parties then arrive at the agreement that Mr. A will continue to enjoy lease rights for an indefinite period on payment of lease money of Rs. 50,000/ per month. When a written agreement to this effect is presented in the Hon'ble Court, the Court disposed of the writ petition in terms of the agreement between the parties.

d) Mr. A was employed by the Lahore Waste Management Company on contract basis for a period of three years on a project post. Upon completion of the project, his services were dispensed with. He challenges termination of his services on completion of the prescribed period through an appeal in the Punjab Services Tribunal. The case lingers on for three years. Fatigued by pendency of the case, the Lahore Waste Management Company agrees to rehire services of the appellant without observing the open competitive selection process. The learned Services Tribunal disposes of the appeal in terms of the agreement between the parties.

e) The auditors appointed by the Auditor General of Pakistan point out that Mr. A has drawn Rs. 19,00,000/ in excess of his lawful remuneration and recommend recovery of the amount overdrawn. Mr. A approaches the Hon'ble High Court by filing a writ petition under Article 199 of the Constitution praying for setting aside demand of recovery on the ground that though he was not entitled to receive the excess amount pointed out by the auditors, yet since the amount was drawn in good faith, hence, recovery was illegal. The petition undergoes the standard judicial drill for some years during which recovery stands stopped. In the end, the petitioner and the respondent agree to effect recovery of Rs. 7,00,000/ instead of Rs. 19,00,000/. The Hon'ble High Court pleases to dispose of the writ petition in terms of the agreement between the parties.

171. Mr. Yazdani argues that he is not competent enough to distinguish the consent orders given in the Fourth and the Fifth Judges' pension cases from the aforesaid illustrations. He prays that though consent judgments need not be disallowed but these must be subject to jurisdiction of the law and absence of violation of the applicable legal dispensation.

172. Mr. Yazdani wonders that when the matter of recovery from the Hon'ble judges arises, the judiciary intervenes to waive off the recovery but when a claim of an Hon'ble judge is held to be valid retrospectively, arrears are ensured to be paid. He submits that the Province may not be unjustly burdened and the Hon'ble judges unjustly enriched in absence of a legal reason justifying the same. He prays that the question of recovery of amounts drawn illegally from the public purse may authoritatively be determined by this court to make things clear for all times to come.

173. The learned counsels appearing on behalf of the beneficiaries of the Fourth and the Fifth Judges' pension cases argue that the relief granted to the judges with less than five years of service as judges of the Hon'ble High Court was not caused by coercion or undue

influence and was a voluntary benevolence of the Federation and the Province. They submit that the relief granted has been enjoyed and the principles of res judicata and the locus poenitentiae do not allow withdrawal thereof. They state that the benefits flowing from the Fifth Judges' pension case have been enjoyed by the respondents in good faith and without any fault on their part and an order of recovery of the amounts alleged to be overdrawn is definite to cause extreme hardship and misery for the Hon'ble retired judges and their families. They aver that the Hon'ble justices have gotten justice and it would be grave injustice to allow Mr. Yazdani to unjustly challenge the same. They state that even if the respondents are denied pension as retired judges of the Hon'ble High Court, the respondents shall remain entitled to the benefit of treating the last pay drawn as judge of the High Court for the purpose of calculation of their pension. They argue that taking last pay drawn as judge of the High Court for calculation of pension is the only benefit they can draw as adding service as judge of the Hon'ble High Court to the qualifying service as civil servant is inconsequential in most of the cases for the reason that their service as civil servant normally exceeds thirty years and no benefit of having service in excess of thirty years is permissible under the instructions of the Government. As regards conceding statement of the Secretary, Law and Justice Division and disposal of the Fourth and the Fifth Judges' pension cases in terms thereof, the learned counsels contend that it is universally accepted that cases can be disposed of in terms of an agreement reached between the parties during pendency of a case in a court of law. The learned counsels argue that there exists no lawful ground or compelling need to overrule the Third Judges' pension case in the matter of recovery of amounts drawn by the Hon'ble judges or their families. They contend that the consent of the Government of the Punjab conveyed through the learned Advocate General, Punjab in the Fifth Judges' pension case is equal to an undertaking submitted during pendency of a case and any deviation therefrom would constitute a civil contempt of the Hon'ble Supreme Court. It is prayed that the petition of Mr. Yazdani may be dismissed being devoid of merit.

174.   The learned Attorney General for Pakistan defends the written statement of the Secretary, Law and Justice, Government of Pakistan submitted in the Fourth Judges' pension case and argues that in the matter of remuneration of the judges of the Hon'ble High Court, the President is the competent authority under Article 205 read with Fifth Schedule to the Constitution. He opines that the statement given by the Secretary, Law and Justice is valid one even in absence of any consultation with and concurrence of the Province whose Consolidated Fund has to bear the burden of expenditure caused by such a statement. He submits that the Secretary, Law and Justice Division is legally competent to interpret the High Court Judges (Leave, Pension and Privileges) Order, 1997. He is of the view that the statement given by the said Secretary in the Fourth Judges' pension case does not create any new right or liability but only states the rights and liabilities already in lawful existence. He submits that the Hon'ble High Court and the Hon'ble Supreme Court committed no wrong by disposing of the pending cases in the light of the said statement and the conceding statements of the law officers of the Federation and of the Punjab Province. He does not support the idea of overruling the Third Judges' pension case in the matter of recovery from the retired judges.

175.   We have heard all on the subject with patience and have refreshed our minds with respect to facts of the case and the law applicable thereto.

176.   Article 175(2) of the Constitution leaves no room for ambiguity on the subject of sources of grant of jurisdiction. The only sources of jurisdiction of a court of law including the Hon'ble Supreme Court and the Hon'ble High Court are the Constitution itself and the statues competently enacted thereunder read with Article 189 and 201 of the Constitution. Consent of the parties to a case is not a source of grant of jurisdiction to a court.

177.   The Hon'ble Supreme Court and the Hon'ble High Courts perform their judicial functions through the benches constituted by the respective Chief Justices. These benches dispense justice in accordance with law. The Constitution is the supreme law. Any provision

of the Constitution and a law validly enacted by a legislature has the meaning assigned to it by the Hon'ble Supreme Court in terms of Article 189 of the Constitution. If in a matter pending before an Hon'ble High Court, a decision of a question of law or an enunciation of a principle of law made by the Hon'ble Supreme Court is presented which applies to the facts and circumstances of the case in hand, the Hon'ble bench of the Hon'ble High Court, even if comprising all judges of the Hon'ble High Court, is under compulsion in terms of Article 189 of the Constitution to follow the decision of or enunciation made by the Hon'ble Supreme Court. There is no prohibition for the Hon'ble Supreme Court to overrule its earlier decisions. But jurisdiction to do so vests in a bench of the Hon'ble Supreme Court comprising judges more than that bench decision of which is sought to be overruled. In this regard, enough is to reproduce hereinbelow a headnote of the case reported as All Pakistan Newspapers Society Vs. Federation of Pakistan (PLD 2004 Supreme Court 600):

> "Issue raised in subsequent case before Bench of Supreme Court comprising of three Judges stood earlier resolved by a Bench of Supreme Court comprising of five Judges. Effect. Bench comprising of three Judges could not take different view qua judgment passed by a Bench comprising of five Judges, which had binding effect upon such issues.
>
> Province of East Pakistan v. Azizul Islam PLD 1963 SC 296; Province of East Pakistan v. Sirajul Haq Patwari PLD 1966 SC 854, Pir Baksh v. Chairman, Allotment Committee PLD 1987 SC 145; Multiline Associates v. Ardeshir Cowasjee PLD 1995 SC 423; Muhammad Saleem v. Fazal Ahmed 1997 SCMR 314; Babar Shehzad v. Said Akbar 1999 SCMR 2518; Ardeshir Cowasjee v. Karachi Building Control Authority 1999 SCMR 2883; Zulfiqar Mehdi v. Pakistan International Airlines Corporation 1998 SCMR 793 and Watan Party v. Chief Executive PLD 2003 SC 74 fol."

178.   No party before us has disputed the fact that the question of entitlement of judges of the Hon'ble High Court with less than five years of service as such judges was decided by the Hon'ble Sindh High Court in the First Judges' pension case by holding that such judges are entitled to pension as retired judge of the Hon'ble High Court irrespective of their length of service. A three-judge bench of the Hon'ble Supreme Court confirmed this view in the Second Judges' pension case but a five-judge bench of the Hon'ble Supreme Court declared the Second Judges' pension case per incuriam and held that a judge of a High Court with less than five years of service as such judge is not entitled to pension as judge of the High Court. This position of law was on record in the Fourth and the Fifth Judges' pension case. The Hon'ble High Court was under constitutional compulsion to follow the dictum of law laid down by the Hon'ble Supreme Court in the Third Judges' pension case. On the other hand, petition for leave to appeal against the Fourth Judges' pension case was liable to be dismissed with a declaration that Fourth Judges' case was void for being without jurisdiction and matters coming within the purview of Article 212 cannot be allowed to be raised under Article 185 of the Constitution. After grant of leave to appeal, a three-judge bench of the Hon'ble Supreme Court in the Fifth Judges' pension case had option either to follow the ratio decidendi of the Third Judges' pension case or to refer the case to the Hon'ble Chief Justice for constitution of a bench comprising more than five judges. The matter of implied overruling of the ratio decidendi of the Third Judges' pension case in the Fifth Judges' pension case is not only a cause of concern for not being in line with the noble traditions of judicial discipline but it also raises a question of jurisdiction. Jurisdiction to hear a case and jurisdiction to overrule a judgment earlier rendered by the same court are two different jurisdictions. Whereas a bench constituted by the Hon'ble Chief Justice of the Hon'ble Supreme Court, comprising any number of judges, is competent to exercise jurisdiction of the Hon'ble Supreme Court in any matter falling within jurisdiction of the Hon'ble Supreme Court, the jurisdiction to overrule a judgment earlier delivered by the Hon'ble Supreme

Court in vested only in a bench comprising judges greater in number than that the judges who delivered the judgment intended to be overruled.

179. The Fourth and the Fifth Judges' pension cases have simply overruled the ratio decidendi of the Third Judges' pension case. We are pained to declare that the Hon'ble High Court and a three-judge bench of the Hon'ble Supreme Court had no jurisdiction to overrule the ratio decidendi of the Third Judges' pension case. Both the consent orders are without jurisdiction and, hence, void, nullity in eyes of law and of no legal effect. After arriving at this conclusion, there remains no need to analyse reasons recorded in the Third Judges' pension case as no counter-narrative is available in the Fourth and the Fifth Judges' pension cases. We are convinced that the ratio decidendi of the Third Judges' pension case to the extent that a judge of a High Court having less than five years' service as such judge is not entitled to pension as retired judge of the High Court suffers from no legal infirmity and we do hereby endorse and approve the same.

180. The question of applicability of the Punjab Civil Servants Act, 1974 and the Punjab Subordinate Judiciary Service Tribunal Act, 1991 to the retired civil servants elevated as judges of the Hon'ble High Court who are not entitled to pension as judges of the High Court because of less than five years' service as such judges has already been determined by us earlier in this judgment. With our declarations on this subject, the applicability of the High Court Judges (Leave, Pension and Privileges) Order, 1997 or the Civil Service Regulations (CSR) of the Federal Government on such judges stands automatically ruled out. In this view of the matter, the written statement of the Secretary, Law and Justice Division of the Federal Government is a statement by a person who is not legally authorized to interpret the Punjab Civil Servants Act, 1974 and the Punjab Subordinate Judiciary Service Tribunal Act, 1991 or to burden the Provincial Consolidated Fund through such interpretation or undertaking. We are, therefore, convinced to hold that undertaking given by an incompetent person does not bind a competent authority. Moreover, undertakings given in void proceedings are also void and their violation does not constitute a civil contempt of the court to which such undertaking is furnished.

181. Pension of civil servants who retired as confirmed judges of the Hon'ble High Court does not constitute a charged expenditure if they, due to service being less than five years, are retired as such judges but are allowed pension as civil servants. If pension of a judge of the Hon'ble High Court is governed by the Punjab Civil Servants Act, 1974, it would be violative of Article 121 (2) (a) of the Constitution to sanction his pension as an expenditure charged upon the Provincial Consolidated Fund.

182. When a court passes a consent order or decree or disposes of a case in terms of a consensus settlement between the parties, it exercises judicial power of the state. This power is vested in the institution of judiciary for dispensation of justice in accordance with law. Consent of the parties does not create rights not legally vested in the parties or impose obligations not legally binding for a party. What implies is very simple: a consensus settlement between the parties has to be perfectly in accordance with law in order to be capable of judicially determining rights and obligations of the parties. A consensus settlement between the parties saves time of the court but does not allow it to rubber stamp a consensus settlement without satisfying itself that it has jurisdiction in the matter and the settlement does not contain any illegality. Whereas parties enjoy discretion to agree to any settlement but this discretion is only a legal discretion: discretion to select one option if many options are permissible under the law governing the matter. In this regard, the illustrations offered by Mr. Yazdani are suitable. We are in agreement with the statement that, in pith and substance, there is no substantial difference between those illustrations and the two consent orders impugned herein. We do not want to undervalue the utility of consensus settlements but crossing jurisdictional bar and affixation of judicial stamp on illegal agreements is too

high a price and we cannot afford to pay it. The argument of saving of a court's time is important. A typical judgment contains the following elements:

- ✓ A statement of the facts of the case, and lower court rulings;
- ✓ Identification of the legal issues involved in the case;
- ✓ Arguments raised and cases cited by the parties;
- ✓ The legal reasoning that is relevant to resolve those issues;
- ✓ The ruling of the court on questions of law; and
- ✓ The result of the case: the court's order.

183.   In order to retain benefits of consensus settlements and to safeguard against misuse of the same, we direct that though a detailed conventional judgment would not be necessary in case of a consensus settlement between the parties, yet no court shall dispose of a case in terms of the consensus between the parties without recoding the certificate that the court has lawful jurisdiction in the matter and the consensus settlement does not suffer from any legal infirmity.

184.   In view of our declarations hereinabove in this judgment, it is not legally necessary to adjudicate upon the question that whether last pay drawn as judge of the Hon'ble High Court by a civil servant is required to be treated as the last pay drawn for the purpose of calculation of pension under the Punjab Civil Servants Act, 1974 and the rules framed or deemed to have been framed thereunder. However, we deem it in public interest to briefly clarify the law on the subject.

185.   The Hon'ble High Court has jurisdiction under Article 199 of the Constitution, inter alia, to order a person to refrain from doing anything he is not permitted by law to do, or to do anything he is required by law to do or to declare something done to have been done without lawful authority or to give a direction for enforcement of the fundamental rights. The law includes the law laid down by the Hon'ble Supreme Court in terms of Article 189 of the Constitution. The Third Judges' pension case is a valid determination of the question of law of the right of pension of the judges of the Hon'ble High Court with less than five years' service as such judge. Thus, any order, declaration or direction of the Hon'ble High Court under Article 199 of the Constitution on that question of law could not violate the dictum of law laid down in the Third Judges' pension case as no one could be refrained to follow that case or to act thereagainst or to do anything in the name of enforcement of the fundamental rights which violates the ratio decidendi of the said case. For the purpose of Article 199 of the Constitution, the law does not include a law laid down by a foreign court. It is for the Hon'ble Supreme Court to benefit from persuasive value of foreign judgments but till such time a valid determination of a question of law or enunciation of a principle of law made by the Hon'ble Supreme Court is in the field, a High Court is bound to follow that as Article 189 of the Constitution does not grant any exemption in this regard. No doubt, right to pension is a fundamental right but Article 23 allows reasonable restrictions on right to property. The dictum of law laid down by the Hon'ble Supreme Court in the Third Judges' pension case is a reasonable restriction on the right to pension of a civil servant having less than five years' service as judge of a High Court. The High Court Judges (Leave, Pension and Privileges) Order, 1997 does not empower the President of Pakistan to relax the minimum length of five years' service for becoming eligible to pension as a judge of the High Court. The Third Judges' case is overruled on the question of relaxation of deficiency in the minimum length of service for being eligible to draw pension as a judge of a High Court. A power not given by the Constitution and the law cannot be given by a court of law, irrespective of the desirability to show sympathy to hardship of a judge of the Hon'ble High Court. The Punjab Civil Servants Act, 1974 and the rules framed or deemed to have been framed thereunder do not provide that if a civil servant retires as judge of the High Court and is entitled to pension as a civil servant, the last pay drawn as civil servant shall not be taken as the last pay drawn for the purpose of calculation of his pension as a civil servant. We do not find any legal problem with this interpretation of the last pay drawn for the purpose of calculation of pension of the civil servants who retire as judges of the High Court

but are not entitled to pension as such judges. Not treating the last pay drawn as judge of the Hon'ble High Court for the purpose of calculation of pension if he lacks less than five years' service as such judge is in accord with the departmental construction of the applicable rules, is being followed from times immemorial and sounds logical and reasonable. We do hereby declare so.

186.   There is, of course, no doubt that service rendered as judge of the High Court shall be added to the service qualifying for pension. It has been stated before us that the civil servants who rendered less than five years' service as judge of the High Court have service of more than thirty years as civil servant. It has been stated that no benefit beyond the maximum of thirty years of service qualifying for pension is allowed for the purpose of calculation of pension. In this regard, we have seen Rule 4.4(3) of the Punjab Civil Services Pension Rules which reads as follows:

> "In case the qualifying service of a Government servant is more than 30 years, a benefit, to the extent of 2% of his full pension for each completed extra year of service beyond 30 years, shall be allowed subject to a maximum of 10% of the full pension."

187.   It was declared by a five-judge bench of the Hon'ble Supreme Court of Pakistan in the I.A. Sharwani case (PLD 1991 SCMR 1041) that:

> "33. We would, therefore, allow the above petitions to the extent of declaring that denial of additional benefit of 2% of pension for each year of service exceeding 30 years' subject to a maximum of 10% of pension sanctioned referred to hereinabove in para. 19 (a)(xvii) to the pensioners who retired prior to 1.7.1986, and denial to the petitioner in C.P. No.5R of 1990 of the benefit under P.O. No.5 of 1988 referred to hereinabove in para 19(b)(vi) on the ground that he retired prior to 1.7.1987 founded on above eligibility criteria as to the date of retirement, being discriminatory and violative of Article 25, and, they are entitled to the same (if not already granted) so long other pensioners are paid."

188.   When we required the learned Advocate General, Punjab whether the benefit mentioned in Rule 4.4(3) of the Punjab Civil Services Pension Rules and paragraph 33 of the I.A. Sharwani case (PLD 1991 SCMR 1041) was being extended to the civil servants retiring as judge of the High Court but entitled to get pension under the Punjab Civil Services Pension Rules, he replied in the negative and cited paragraph 16 (c) of the No. FD. PC-2-1/2001 dated 22.10.2001 of the Finance Department of the Government of the Punjab which provided as follows:

> "The additional benefit of 2% - 10% for extra years of service after completion of 30 years of qualifying service in respect of Civil Pensioners shall be discontinued."

189.   We required the learned Advocate General, Punjab to provide us a copy of the notification through which Rule 4.4(3) of the Punjab Civil Services Pension Rules was amended and the law laid down by the Hon'ble Supreme Court in the I.A. Sharwani case (PLD 1991 SCMR 1041) was displaced. It was surprising for us that Rule 4.4(3) of the Punjab Civil Services Pension Rules is still intact and has not been amended or omitted through an amendment in the Punjab Civil Services Pension Rules. We are not able to understand that how statutory rules can be amended or made ineffective through executive orders. An attempt was made to withdraw the benefit of restoration of commuted value of pension through paragraph 16 (e) of the No. FD. PC-2-1/2001 dated 22.10.2001 of the Finance Department of the Government of the Punjab. The Hon'ble Supreme Court did not approve the same in the Ismail Tayer case. As a result, the Government of the Punjab had to omit the said paragraph 16 (e) vide its letter No. FD-SR-III/4-41/2008 dated 22nd of July, 2014. No legal justification has been offered for impliedly amending a statutory rule through executive orders. We hold that a statutory rule cannot be amended or made ineffective

through executive orders. Without prejudice to our declaration regarding creation of a charge on the Provincial Consolidated Fund through a money bill, we do hereby hold and declare that Rule 4.4(3) of the Punjab Civil Services Pension Rules and the I.A. Sharwani case (PLD 1991 SCMR 1041) cannot be amended or suspended through an executive order as has attempted to be done through paragraph 16 (c) of the letter No. FD. PC-2-1/2001 dated 22.10.2001. The said paragraph 16 (c) is, therefore, held to be ultra vires Rule 4.4(3) of the Punjab Civil Services Pension Rules and, hence, void and of no legal effect. It is accordingly declared that all civil servants including the civil servants retiring as judges of the Hon'ble High Court are entitled to the benefits granted by Rule 4.4(3) of the Punjab Civil Services Pension Rules read with the I.A. Sharwani case (PLD 1991 SCMR 1041). They are also entitled to draw arrears, if any. This, however, does not preclude the right of the competent authority to introduce any dispensation through a suitable legal instrument in the prescribed manner. It is hereby held for the purpose of clarity that what was attempted to be done through paragraph 16 (c) of the letter No. FD. PC-2-1/2001 dated 22.10.2001 is legally doable through a money bill.

190.   If an amount lawfully due is withheld without authority of law, it has to be paid from the date when it became due. On the other hand, an amount drawn from the public purse without authority of law is recoverable when lack of authority is established and the recovery of the entire amount is necessary. In this regard, we may refer to a judgment of this court reported as Ali Waqar and others Vs. Province of the Punjab and others (IAH 2019 MOOT COURT JUDGMENTS 2) in which it was held that:

> "378.   Federal Consolidated Fund and the Provincial Consolidated Fund and their receivables are property of the Federation and a Province respectively. Appropriation of this property is a legislative function. This legislative function not only determines lawful entitlements to receive moneys from the funds (creation of charge on the fund) but also provides appropriations for liquidation of those lawful entitlements or claims. We have held earlier in this judgment that determination of remuneration is creation of a charge on the consolidated fund. Save a few constitutional exceptions, anything required to be paid from the consolidated fund as remuneration necessarily needs to be perfectly in accordance with the Money Bill in which the remuneration was fixed. Any amount drawn in excess of the amount fixed as remuneration in the applicable Money Bill is without lawful authority and is of no legal effect. When we say "of no legal effect", we mean to say that recipient of money, however innocent, is not legally entitled to retain that money or enjoy its fruits. The Government is under duty to recover the amount paid in absence of lawful authority and the recipient is bound to return such amount. It has been held in United States v. Wurts, 303 U.S. 414, 415 (1938) that:
>
>> "The Government by appropriate action can recover funds which its agents have wrongfully, erroneously, or illegally paid."
>
> 379.   It has further been held in Aetna Casualty & Surety Co., 526 F.2d at 1130 that:
>
>> "In exercising its right to recover amounts illegally or erroneously paid, the government cannot be estopped by the mistakes of its officers or agents."
>
> 380.   It was also declared by the Supreme Court of America in *United States v. Wurts*, 303 U.S. 414, 416, 58 S. Ct. 637, 82 L. Ed. 932 (1938) that:
>
>> "Ordinarily, recovery of Government funds, paid by mistake to one having no just right to keep the funds, is not barred by the passage of time."

381. The Court of Claims of the United States of America has declared in a case reported as Fansteel Metallurgical Corp., 172 F. Supp. at 270 that:

> "As a matter of fact, when a payment is erroneously or illegally made it is in direct violation of article IV, section 3, clause 2, of the Constitution. [Citation omitted.] Under these circumstances it is not only lawful but the duty of the Government to sue for a refund thereof, and no statute is necessary to authorize the United States to sue in such a case."

382. It was held in Pacific Hardware & Steel Co. v. United States, 49 Ct. Cl. 327, 335 (1914) that:

> "It follows that, without a clear statutory basis, an agency has no authority to forgive indebtedness or to waive recovery."

383. The Supreme Court of the United States of America in Royal Indemnity Co. v. United States, 313 U.S. 289, 294 (1941) has laid down the following dictum of law:

> "Power to release or otherwise dispose of the rights and property of the United States is lodged in the Congress by the Constitution. Art. IV, § 3, Cl. 2. Subordinate officers of the United States are without that power, save only as it has been conferred upon them by Act of Congress or is to be implied from other powers so granted.".

384. If public money is paid in absence or in excess of lawful authority, it means that the money was spent without legislative sanction. This situation can fairly be equated with loss of money in which case the tax-payer ends up paying twice for the same thing or paying for nothing. In view of the above, it is neither executive nor judicial function to forgive recovery of illegally drawn amounts. Once an amount is declared to be drawn without lawful authority and such drawl is consequently held to be of no legal effect, the only action required to be taken is recovery of the amount in question. Recovery of amounts drawn illegally is not a matter of discretion; it is a matter of compulsion. Discretion is exercised when more than one lawful options are available; it is not available when a sole option is there and no deviation therefrom is permissible.

385. When it is concluded that pay and allowances were paid in excess of lawful entitlement, then the Court is left with no discretion and it has to do nothing except to order recovery of the excess amounts unlawfully paid. Here this Court lacks competence to determine a threshold and exempt persons receiving unlawful salaries below that threshold from refunding the excess amounts or to offer them any preferential treatment. Of course, sympathy is not a legal ground in proceedings before this Court. If hardship is caused to persons who received money in excess of their entitlement, the remedy lies in legislative organ of the state and not in this Court. The Court is not empowered by the Constitution or any law to usurp legislative or executive powers of the state in its desire to do, what some say, "complete justice", in a case. All said and done, complete justice is nothing more than adjudication of cases and controversies in accordance with law. We are under oath to preserve, protect and defend the Constitution; we have to adjudicate cases and resolve controversies in accordance with applicable law and, unless the applicable law is found to be in violation of the Constitution, remain

within four corners of the law. Even if some statutory provision is held to in irreconcilable clash with the Constitution, our jurisdiction ends after making a declaration to this effect."

191.   With respect to the argument of good faith, it was held by this court in the aforesaid judgement that:

"97.   The arguments of good faith and public interest cannot be advanced to justify violations of a law. Intent or lack of good faith do not affect the basic determination of whether a violation of a law has occurred. In one of his decisions (A-86742, June 17, 1937), the Comptroller General of the United States of America laid down the following principle in respect of good faith argument:

"Where a payment is prohibited by law, the utmost good faith on the part of the officer, either in ignorance of the facts or in disregard of the facts, in purporting to authorize the incurring of an obligation the payment of which is so prohibited, cannot take the case out of the statute, otherwise the purported good faith of an officer could be used to nullify the law."

98.   There is no hard and fast rule for judicial determination of presence or absence of good faith in facts and circumstances of a case. It was held in Sanders v. United States, 594 F.2d 804, 813 (Ct. Cl. 1979) that there is a "strong, but rebuttable, presumption that government officials discharge their duties correctly, lawfully, and in good faith." But if a patent illegality is detected in an act or omission of an executive person or authority, good faith alone cannot legitimize or legalize the illegality. Same is the fate of argument of public interest. To protect public interest is the job of the legislature. The judiciary has to decide cases in accordance with the Constitution and, subject to the Constitution, the laws. The judiciary has no power to issue license for violations of the Constitution and the laws on the plea of public interest. When we say that state functionaries are compulsorily required to act in accordance with law, the underlying assumption is that the public interest can be best served by obeying a law and not by violating it. Holding otherwise would be putting premium on anarchy which propagates the theory that every person should be his own law, state and religion. Good faith and public interest are, therefore, not materially relevant in judicial determination of legality of an act or omission."

192.   On the question of likely hardship as a result of order of recovery, it was held in the aforesaid judgment of this court that:

"322.   ---. The likely hardship to the respondents in case of an adverse declaration of this Court is also immaterial to the question of determination of legality of their appointments and remunerations. This Court cannot refuse to lay down dictum of law on a question of law under an apprehension of a hardship likely to be caused thereby. If someone has unduly enriched himself, without constitutional and valid statutory sanction, and has, thus, caused loss to public exchequer, we have to set things right and preserve, protect and defend the Constitution. We will discharge our judicial duties and will not be prevented to be true to our oath merely because of likely hardship to a party in a case as a consequence of declaration of law by this Court. After all, sympathy is not a ground to determine legality of actions or omissions in a country governed by the written Constitution."

193. It is not possible for us to digest the theory that since a judgment normally has prospective effect, therefore, benefits declared illegal under a judgment are to be disallowed prospectively and the benefits already drawn are protected. Once legality of drawl of an amount is determined, the consequences flowing therefrom are inescapable and automatic. Recovery, arrear or no action if the drawl is found lawful are the only three options. The argument of locus poenitentiae is irrelevant to legality of an action. (Locus poenitentiae is a Latin phrase associated with contractual law which means opportunity to withdraw from a contract or obligation before it is completed or to decide not to commit an intended crime. This signifies repentance in the context of criminal law and provides an opportunity of withdrawing from a projected contract, before the parties are finally bound or of abandoning the intention of committing a crime.) Similarly, the principle of res judicata does not prohibit the Hon'ble Supreme Court to overrule its earlier judgments. Both these principles cannot be used to justify the proposition that amounts illegally drawn from the public purse are not recoverable. We dismiss these principles as these are totally irrelevant to the question under consideration.

194. Now, we proceed to see split opinions on the question of recovery in the Third Judges' pension case. Two Hon'ble judges were in favour of effecting recovery and three Hon'ble judges did not allow recovery for various reasons. Hon'ble Mr. Justice Anwar Zaheer Jamali was of the view that:

> "111. Considering the question of indulgence or sympathetic consideration of the case of the honourable retired Judges of the High Court, having been already benefited from the judgment under challenge, we cannot lose sight of the fact that the heavy sums paid to them, as partly reflected in the above reproduced chart, were made from public exchequer, which is a sacred trust. Thus all care and caution is required to see whether a mistake or illegality committed by the Court could make them entitled for payment of more than Rs. 1,647,130,156/- and further liability of payment of Rs. 32,604,359/- towards monthly pension. In view of our discussion in this context made in the foregoing paragraphs, we have no option but to hold that all the sums paid to each of the honourable retired judges, who were made entitled for pensionary benefits in terms of the judgment under challenge, are liable to be recovered from them.
>
> 112. It is necessary to mention here so as to make the things more clear that admittedly before his retirement as a Judge of the High Court on 19-10-1994, retired Justice Ahmed Ali U. Qureshi had served as such for a period of 3 years and 4 months (approximately) and since by this judgment the Constitutional Petition No.D-2308 of 1994 filed by retired Justice Ahmed Ali U. Qureshi before the High Court of Sindh has also been dismissed, therefore, all the benefits, except as per his entitlement as a retired District Judge qua paragraph 15 of President's Order 9 of 1970, availed under the said judgment of the Sindh High Court and the judgment under challenge are to be recovered from the legal heirs of the deceased to the extent of their liability in this regard, but in accordance with law.
>
> 116. As regards the issue of recovery of pensionary benefits availed by some honourable retired judges of the High Court in terms of judgment under challenge, when we look at the recent pragmatic approach employed by this Court to safeguard public interest qua securing public exchequer, we find that in the case of Syed Mehmood Akhtar Naqvi v. Federation of Pakistan (PLD 2012 SC 1054) and Syed Mehmood Akhtar Naqvi v. Federation of Pakistan (PLD 2012 SC 1089), wherein declaration was issued against number of elected

MNAs, MPAs and Senators for their disqualification from being Members of Majlis-e-Shoora (Parliament), Provincial Assemblies and the Senate, because of holding dual nationalities and consequent disqualification under Article 63(1)(c) of the Constitution, despite they having served their respective Institution (Parliament) during the intervening period, Court ordered that all these Members of the Parliament and Provincial Assemblies etc. being declared disqualified are also directed to refund all monetary benefits drawn by them for the period during which they kept the public office and have drawn their emoluments etc. from the public exchequer, including the remuneration, T.A./D.A., facilities for accommodation along with other perks which shall be calculated in terms of the money by the Secretaries of the National Assembly, Senate and Provincial Assemblies accordingly.

117. In another case of similar nature titled Muhammad Yasin v. Federation of Pakistan (PLD 2012 SC 132), relating to appointment of Chairman, OGRA, which was declared illegal and void ab inito, it was further ordered that all salaries, value of perquisites and benefits availed from the date of his appointment till the date of the judgment shall be recovered by the Government from the beneficiary Chairman at the earliest. In contrast the facts of these two cases, the beneficiaries of judgment under challenge (the honourable retired judges of the High Court) during the intervening period have not worked or undertaken any assignment so as to make their cases worth consideration for some concession or relief on this ground.

118. The above discussed recent trend adopted by this Court to safeguard public exchequer from being misused has persuaded us to follow a similar course in the present case. More so, as this principle cannot be deviated merely for the reason that this time the affectees of this judgment are some honourable retired judges of the High Court, who are very respectable citizens of the Country. Rather, adoption of this course in the present proceedings is all the more necessary to strengthen the inbuilt process of self-accountability, which is necessary to earn public confidence in our judicial system."

195. Hon'ble Mr. Justice Ejaz Afzal Khan ordered recovery in the following words:
"But when asked how the Judges who have put in less than five years' service, could retain the benefits they have received or continue to receive if the judgment furnishing basis for grant of such benefits is set at naught and thus rendered nonexistent, no satisfactory reply was given by any of the counsel representing them. Granted that a subsequent precedent overruling a previous one being prospective in operation cannot be applied retrospectively but this principle will not apply when the judgment furnishing a basis for a right or entitlement stands annulled on having been reviewed. Therefore, a judgment reversing or declaring a judgment per incuriam in review cannot be treated at par with a judgment overruling or declaring a precedent in another case as per incuriam. As for example, a pre-emptor, succeeding to get a decree from a Court, in a pre-emption case without having a superior right of pre-emption and without making demands which are sine qua non for the enforcement of such right, cannot claim any right or benefit much less vested on the basis of such decree when it is annulled by the Court granting it in the exercise of its review jurisdiction. Retention of a benefit or right thus acquired cannot

be justified under any cannons of law, justice and propriety. It cannot be justified on the plea of bona fide either. What is illegal would remain illegal. It cannot be changed into legal by pleading bonafide.

7.   I have also been deliberating since the commencement of hearing of their case till the writing of this note to find some justification for the retention of the benefits received by the learned Judges but could not find any. In case I create or contrive one in this behalf, I cannot find any reason to deny the same relief to the others whose case is either in the pipeline or who have yet to retire. I also could not find any intelligible differentia for a classification amongst the Judges who have received the benefits and those who have yet to receive notwithstanding they are similarly placed. Even otherwise, a benefit extended in derogation of the law cannot be justified to be retained simply because it has been received as such."

196.   Three Hon'ble judges of the Hon'ble Supreme Court (Mr. Justice Mian Saqib Nisar, Mr. Justice Muhammad Ather Saeed and Mr. Justice Iqbal Hameedur Rahman) did not order recovery, expressing themselves on the issue in the following words:

Mr. Justice Mian Saqib Nisar

" It is nobody's case that they have practiced and played any fraud or committed some foul in gaining and procuring the pension, so as to disentitle them to retain such gain, on the known principle, that no one should be allowed to hold the premium of his wrong/fraud and/or retain ill-gotten gains.

If a wrong and an error has been committed in the declaration of law (PLD 2008 SC 522), the responsibility rests on this Court and it is fundamental rule of law and justice, that the act of the Court shall prejudice none; in my view this principle tilts in favour of the Judges, rather the State. Because on account of the lapse of considerable time, most of the Judges might have spent and consumed the amount received by them, as they are expected to have decent living after their retirement; the amount so received might have expended on the education and marriages of their children; the possibility that they might have acquired an abode to spend rest of their life to avoid dependency on their scion cannot be ruled out. This amount might have been utilized on their daily expense and sustenance and in the discharge of their other social and financial obligations. And if now the amount is ordered to be recovered from them they might have to sell their assets (shelter) and belongings. Those who have no assets or saving might be compelled and constrained to entreat others or borrow which would definitely not behoove with their status and position as the retired Judges; baring few, most of them are of old age and I am not sure they have the ability and capacity, at such an advance age to generate the requisite amount for the refund. Enforcing the refund of the amount upon them may cause innumerable predicament for them and may lead to a very pathetic and a ludicrous situation for them. And all those who have once graced the superior judiciary, might in this scenario be rendered destitute and precarious and deprived of even a modest life and living in future. But for the commission of no wrong, fraud, foul and fault on their part. Rather as stated earlier an error and mistake perpetrated by this Court. Therefore, I am of the considered view that the present judgment be given prospective effect.

Therefore, following the above dictum, I hold that the amount so far received by the Judges should not be recovered, from them, as it shall be oppressive and more prejudicial to the Judges, as against the respondent of the case i.e. (of PLD 2008 SC 522) and the State, which (State) even never ever filed any review against "the judgment", even after the success of the movement for the restoration of real judiciary. And even now the recovery has not been pressed for before us by the State. However, as now the judicial verdict (PLD 2008 SC 522) under which the Judges had and have been receiving the pension, is declared per incuriam and is set aside, obviously their right to receive the pension has ceased and come to an end, rather they are disentitled to receive pension in future. And as mentioned earlier, such right for the future receipt of pension is not protected under any principle, rule and on jurisprudential plain.

Mr. Justice Muhammad Ather Saeed

9.   I am, therefore, of the considered view that our judgment declaring earlier judgment per incuriam should be given prospective effect and the pensionary benefits being paid to these Judges should be stopped forthwith but no direction should be given to them for returning the pensionary benefits they had acquired till the passing of this judgment.

Mr. Justice Iqbal Hameedur Rahman

3.   I, therefore, consider the judgment Accountant-General, Sindh (supra) to be per incuriam, which should be given prospective effect and the pensionary benefits being paid to the Judges should be discontinued with effect from passing of the judgment and order by this Court, but no direction for the recovery of pensionary benefits and emoluments already availed by them can be given, as the same are undoubtedly not obtained by them on account of any commission of wrong, fraud or fault on their part rather the same have been availed on account of a mistaken judgment by this Court. As such, the instant judgment and order cannot be given retrospective effect."

197.   We have tried our best to find a legal reason to agree to the conclusion that an amount drawn illegally from the public purse should not be recovered if the payment has not proximately been caused by a contributing fault or bad faith of the recipient or the likely recovery would cause hardship for the recipient or if the recipient is an Hon'ble retired judge of an Hon'ble High Court or his family. None of these is a legal ground to refrain the state from performing its duty to protect tax-payer's money and not to recover money drawn without authority of law.

198.   In view of the above, we accept the prayer of Mr. Yazdani and overrule the Third Judges' pension case to the extent of recovery of amounts drawn from the public purse without authority of law and do hereby hold that the concerned public functionaries are under duty to recover any amount disbursed from the Provincial Consolidated Fund without or in excess of authority of law. It is further held that only the legislature is competent to waive of such recovery. Recovery of amounts disbursed illegally cannot be withheld or waived of on grounds such as mistakes of public functionaries, passage of time, innocence of recipients or the likely hardship to the recipients. We further hold that the judiciary has no jurisdiction to stop or forgive recovery on any ground other than a legal ground properly falling within its adjudicative jurisdiction.

199.   We appreciate the valuable assistance rendered by the learned counsels of the parties in this case. Mr. Muhammad Asghar Yazdani deserves a pat on his back for his hard word, devotion, consistency and clear headedness.

200.   The Federation shall pay a punitive cost of Rs. Five million (Rs. 50,00,000)/ to Mr. Yazdani not later than fifty working days, reckonable from the date of announcement of this judgment.

Sd/
Mr. Nasir Latif Darwesh
Sd/
Mr. Saleem Anwar Taya
Sd/
Mr. Jamal Mustafa Kundan
Sd/
Mr. Syed Rizwan Ali Shah
Sd/
Mr. Ahmad Nawaz Gondal
Sd/
Mr. Abdul Aziz
Sd/
Mr. Taseer Ahmad
Sd/
Mr. Gulfam Mujtaba
Sd/
Mr. Sarfraz Ahmad Bhatti

Sd/
Mr. Nasir Latif Darwesh

Announced in Open Court on 28th of November, 2019.

APPROVED FOR REPORTING

About the Author

In his career spanning over twenty-four years, Mr. Muhammad Akhtar has gained experience in preparation and execution of budget, performance of treasury functions, pay and pension roll management, maintenance of accounts, audit of public entities, internal audit and controls, inter-governmental fiscal relations, public expenditure policy formulation and cash management etc.

Mr. Akhtar graduated from the Government College, Lahore, earning Roll of Honour in co-curricular activities and Certificate of Merit besides serving as Editor of the Government College Gazette and member of the Seniors Club, an elite club of the College. He was also honoured with the Quaid-e-Azam Scout Badge, highest honour for a boy scout in Pakistan. He joined the civil service as District Accounts Officer in 1995. He has served as District Accounts Officer in four districts, Treasury Officer, Lahore, District Officer (Finance & Budget), Assistant Director Audit, Section Officer in the Finance Department, Director Finance, Lahore Ring Road Authority, Director Financial Services, Chief Minister's Office, Additional Director Budget, Finance Department, Inspector of Treasuries & Accounts, Financial Advisor, Benevolent Fund Board, Punjab and Director Finance, Lahore Development Authority.

He was engaged by the Asian Development Bank as a Consultant to prepare a plan for provincialisation of accounts in the Punjab. He worked for the Adam Smith International and undertook studies, drafted laws e.g. the Khyber Pakhtunkhwa Education Monitoring Authority Bill, the Khyber Pakhtunkhwa Boards of Elementary & Secondary Education Bill, the Khyber Pakhtunkhwa Textbook Board Bill, rules e.g. the Khyber Pakhtunkhwa Right to Education Rules, the Khyber Pakhtunkhwa Time-scale Promotion Rules for Teachers' Rules, the Khyber Pakhtunkhwa Private Schools Regularity Authority Rules, the Khyber Pakhtunkhwa Financial Autonomy to Higher Secondary Schools Rules, and executive instructions for the Elementary and Secondary Education Department of the Government of Khyber Pakhtunkhwa. He also assisted in resolution of day-to-day problems faced in budget execution and introduced school-based budgeting and got the School Education Plan costed.

He specializes in regulatory framework for personnel and financial management in the public sector. He has a deep insight of laws / rules / regulations / executive policies on audit, accounts, budgeting, personnel management, internal controls and treasury functions and offers practicable solutions synchronized with computerized and paper-less environment.

Made in the USA
Columbia, SC
27 September 2020